P9-EER-895

Selling the Right Way!

Brooke Quigg
Bern Wisner

Prentice Hall
Upper Saddle River, New Jersey 07458

Library of Congress Cataloging-in-Publication Data
Quigg, Brooke.
   Selling the right way! / Brooke Quigg, Bern Wisner
      p.   cm.
   Includes index.
   ISBN 0-13-613654-0
   1. Selling.   I. Wisner, Bern.   II. Title.
HF5438.25.Q55   1998
658.85--dc21   98-2510
                                      CIP

Production Supervision and Electronic Paging: *Kathryn Pavelec*
Managing Editor: *Mary Carnis*
Director of Production and Manufacturing: *Bruce Johnson*
Manufacturing Manager: *Marc Bove*
Acquisitions Editor: *Elizabeth Sugg*
Editorial Assistant: *Emily Jones*
Marketing Manager: *Frank Mortimer, Jr.*
Proofreading: *Julie Boddorf*
Cover Design: *Miguel Ortiz*
Interior Illustrations: *Newsom & Associates*

©1998 by **Prentice-Hall, Inc.**
A Pearson Education Company
Upper Saddle River, New Jersey 07458

*All rights reserved. No part of this book may be reproduced,
in any form or by any means,
without permission in writing from the publisher.*

Printed in the United States of America

10 9 8 7 6 5 4

ISBN 0-13-613654-0

Prentice-Hall International (UK) Limited,London
Prentice-Hall of Australia Pty. Limited, Sydney
Prentice-Hall Canada Inc., Toronto
Prentice-Hall Hispanoamericana, S.A., Mexico
Prentice-Hall of India Private Limited, New Delhi
Prentice-Hall of Japan, Inc., Tokyo
Pearson Education Asia Pte. Ltd., Singapore
Editora Prentice-Hall do Brasil, Ltda., Rio de Janeiro

Brief Contents

Contents

Chapter Two ESTABLISHING MEANINGFUL COMMUNICATION

Preface

It is not often, in any discipline, that a truly new textbook comes along. *Selling the Right Way!* is just such a venture. This is the first text that truly "says it like it is." The authors approach selling and the selling profession in a very open, straightforward manner, offering real-world applications and scenarios to spice up the delivery. Your students will love the learning experience.

Selling the Right Way! takes a skills-based approach to the field of professional selling. The way that it presents a practical, hands-on learning experience is different from other texts. By devoting entire chapters to the skills needed for success in sales, this book becomes more of a training manual than just another academic review.

The chapter on Creating the Professional Image is like no other found in selling textbooks. Generated from information provided by image consultants, this section really brings home the importance of impression. In addition, this area points out the importance of motivation in creating the selling image necessary for achievement.

The process of establishing communication and locating prospects receives prime attention, and the coverage of buying behavior is thorough. Considerable space is given to the development of prospect profiles and determining decision-making status. The selling process is spelled out in detail, and unique attention is paid to establishing believability. Sales resistance and how to handle it is covered in detail, and closing is presented in an unusual, helpful format.

In *Selling the Right Way!*, the importance of attitude in professional selling receives deserved attention, as does time management. Proper coverage is given to specific needs in the retail and industrial arenas. Technology in professional selling is covered in depth. Topics include the use of e-mail, the Internet, and cellular phones as tools for prospecting and presentation.

The text is full of practical exercises and helpful hints. Along with dialogue-style cases, each chapter contains the basis for role playing exercises and experience sharing exercises. Personal profiles of former students now working in professional selling highlight most chapters. Ethical considerations appear throughout the text as You Decide! inserts, and the end-of-chapter materials really get students involved in handling real selling issues.

Selling the Right Way! really shines, when compared with other texts, in its easy-to-read, practical approach to the field of professional selling. Students love this text, and so do those who teach in this field. For all of those in the classroom who have contributed ideas and thoughts to the creation of this text, we are most appreciative. Special thanks are given by the authors to the following dedicated individuals:

David Hammarich
George McNally
Kal Robinson
Dr. Robert Smiley
Marion Martin
Al Gaudio
Michael Kuba

Dr. Letty Fisher
William Baker
Barbara Curtin
Jackie Smith
Brian Brockway
Eugene Finnegan
Harry Dower, Esq.

Donald Kaufman
Thomas Hora, Esq.
George Lindenmouth
Nga Thach
Anita Ortiz

BROOKE QUIGG
BERN WISNER

About the Authors

BROOKE QUIGG

Brooke Quigg has been teaching marketing and sales since 1974. He began his teaching career at the Pennsylvania State University, and is presently a professor of marketing at Peirce College in Philadelphia, Pennsylvania. He has performed marketing research consulting and sales training, and has developed a comprehensive sales training workbook for practicing sales professionals. He is an active member of the Association of Marketing Educators, where he has served as President, Vice President, and Secretary. Professor Quigg teaches marketing, sales, consumer behavior, and organizational behavior.

BERN WISNER

Bern Wisner is a marketing professor at Central Oregon Community College. He received his B.A. in Economics from Duke University and an M.B.A. from California State University. He has held field sales positions with two *Fortune 500* corporations and has served as National Sales Manager for a medium-sized manufacturing firm, in charge of establishing an international sales organization. He was the owner/manager of a manufacturers' representative agency and marketing consulting firm for twelve years prior to entering the field of education. Professor Wisner teaches marketing, sales, advertising, and international business, and is the author of *Applied Marketing*, published by Prentice Hall.

Chapter 1

The Nature of Selling

THE JOB TO BE DONE . . .

Everyone sells something, sometime. Whether trying to convince a friend to join you for lunch, persuade a professor that you know the subject, or induce a company to hire you, selling is involved. Chapter 1 enables you to:

...examine the role of personal selling in the economy.

...appreciate the importance of the salesperson.

...understand the role of personal selling in the marketing process.

...discover the fundamentals of success in personal selling.

...be aware of recent and present changes in selling.

...dispel the myths of salespeople and selling.

...learn what a sales job might entail.

...survey the variety of selling careers available.

...appreciate the reasons for studying selling.

THE ROLE OF PERSONAL SELLING IN THE ECONOMY . . .

Personal selling plays a significant role in the American economy. Through personal selling, $1 trillion worth of goods and services are moved annually, and salespeople are responsible for producing more revenue than any other category of worker. About one of every four American workers is involved in some form of selling. Contributing to this total are small proprietorships, which form the bulk of the nation's businesses and whose owners function as company salespeople.

According to the U.S. Department of Labor's Bureau of Labor Statistics, people working in sales number close to 15 million, or about 14 percent of the total workforce in the United States. The expected growth rate for selling jobs until the year 2000 is 19.6 percent, which is greater than the projected growth rate for jobs in general. Sales positions in the services sector are expected to grow at a much greater rate. For example, securities and financial services sales positions are expected to increase a whopping 55 percent.

Personal selling is most important in the sale of major commercial and industrial products and **consumer durables**. These goods are usually expensive and often require training to use. Personal selling is also crucial in industries that are on the cutting edge of technology, like telecommunications and computers.

Women in Selling . . .

Almost half of the selling jobs in the United States are occupied by women. Although men hold down the majority of industrial sales positions, females dominate the retail arena, outnumbering men by more than two to one. Women make up more than 40 percent of the financial and business services sector, and more than half of the real estate industry.

The number of women employed in all areas of selling is expected to increase. Although some industries already hire a significant percentage of female salespeople, others, such as chemicals and fabricated metals, lag behind. As women in increasing numbers graduate with technical degrees, this imbalance will begin to disappear.

The Importance of the Salesperson . . .

A salesperson's most important goals are (1) satisfied customers, (2) long-term customer relationships, (3) favorable referrals to new prospects from present customers.

Personal selling is frequently the most important part of a firm's promotional program, especially in high-technology industries. Even firms that produce mass-marketed consumer products rely heavily on personal selling efforts. Procter & Gamble, one of the world's largest advertisers, also has a huge sales force. This giant consumer goods house requires all its marketing employees to spend time in the field with salespeople.

Many firms depend on salespeople to carry out promotional activities that go beyond advertising. Salespeople analyze customer needs, answer the questions of prospective buyers, finalize sales transactions, provide training, check inventories, and resolve product complaints. In addition, they staff booths at trade shows and sometimes install products or handle warranty service. Salespeople have different duties and responsibilities depending on the company or industry, but their basic function is always the same—to serve the customer using the firm's resources.

Salespeople don't just sell, they educate. They inform customers of their firm's latest products and their most innovative use. In a specialized and ever-changing marketplace, customers rely on salespeople to keep them up to date. Without salespeople, business and technical knowledge would not spread as quickly or accurately. The role as an educator is one of the most important parts the salesperson plays.

By providing information and assisting customers in purchasing goods and services, salespeople improve personal and socioeconomic well-being. Technicians in all industries rely upon salespeople to keep them abreast of the latest developments. In addition, salespeople increase the value of products by giving them **time**, **place**, and **possession utility**, that is, by making them available to buyers at the time and place needed.

Salespeople not only share information with consumers, they gather it for their firm's management. Usually, sellers are in a better position than anyone else in the firm to analyze customer needs. Salespeople report to management concerning customer complaints and potential new product possibilities. Modifications to existing products or new goods and services are often created from suggestions of salespeople.

Salespeople also provide management with the data required to make accurate sales forecasts, including competitive intelligence. Having direct customer contact, salespeople can easily find information on the activities of competing companies. Quite often, the only way company management learns of new competitive activity in a certain sales territory is through the reports filed by the salesperson. For example, if a competitor is conducting a test market for a new product, the salesperson will usually learn of it when he or she visits prospective buyers.

Through everyday activities, salespeople can gauge the economic environment in their territory and learn customers' opinions of their firm's advertising and the salability of company products. They are also the first to learn of market resistance to a new product.

Salespeople are responsible for pinpointing customer needs that can be satisfied by their firm. The information they gather should travel to the sales manager, then on to top management, and finally back to the sales force in the form of new product offerings or marketing strategies. The firm can use a sales force survey to estimate potential sales volume at various prices.

In gathering information from present and potential customers (marketing research), a salesperson has four important advantages over the traditional market researcher:

1. Collecting data is less expensive because the salesperson is already meeting with customers.

2. The salesperson can get the data back to the firm with a minimum of effort.

3. A salesperson's relationship with customers means a stronger awareness of customer needs.

4. Customers may look to the salesperson for a solution to their problem, so they may be more likely to reveal their needs to a salesperson than to a market researcher.

On the other hand, leaving market research solely up to the sales force is not without its problems. Companies have discovered that information gathered by salespeople may be distorted, returned late, or not returned at all. Worse, spending time on market research takes away from the primary task of selling.

THE ROLE OF SELLING IN THE MARKETING PROCESS . . .

Personal selling is the dominant strategy in the marketing of **industrial goods** and consumer durables, whereas media advertising is dominant in the marketing of nondurable consumer goods. This makes sense. Orders for industrial goods and consumer durables involve larger sums of money, justifying the high cost per contact of personal selling. Typically, these products require detailed explanations that cannot be done through advertising. Additionally, the total markets for industrial goods are usually smaller, making mass promotion impractical.

Large companies often employ staffs of salespeople who specialize in certain customers or aspects of technology. The deregulation of many industries has led to the creation of sales positions that never existed before. For example, banks and telephone companies have had to develop highly competitive sales forces to regain segments of their once-captive markets. Even established products are new to customers entering a market for the first time, so personal selling is an ever-important force in marketing. And when products are improved, personal selling is needed to inform the public.

The Marketing Concept and the Marketing Mix . . .

The **marketing concept** is a companywide business philosophy that states that a firm exists for the satisfaction of its customers. The focus of firms that have adopted the marketing concept is not on the goods or services they sell, but rather on the satisfaction of needs and desires. Products are updated or replaced as better ways of satisfying are discovered. A list of goods and services, along with the needs they satisfy, follows. The marketing concept calls for producers of these products to be constantly seeking better ways to satisfy their customers.

Product	**Need or Desire**
Skin care products	Beauty
Motorcycle	Fun, excitement
Vitamins	Good health
Movie	Entertainment
Life insurance	Family security
Accounting service	Improved profits
Office equipment	Greater productivity
Encyclopedia	Information, knowledge

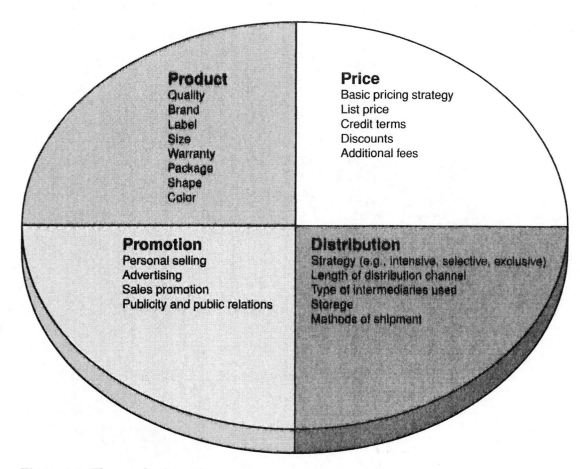

Figure 1-1 The marketing mix.

When a firm adopts the marketing concept, everyone in the company works to satisfy the customer. The business may establish a specific group or department to coordinate the four elements of its marketing program, or the **marketing mix**. Some smaller firms seek help from outside the company.

The marketing mix (see Figure 1-1) is the firm's combination of product, price, distribution, and promotion. To support the firm's marketing program, these four elements must work together. For example, fine leather shoes would be offered at premium prices, carried at exclusive stores, and advertised in fashion magazines. The marketing mix would be at odds with itself if the shoe-maker tried to sell this shoe at discount department stores.

The Promotional Mix . . .

Personal selling falls under the promotion element of the marketing mix. It is part of the **promotional mix**, which is a combination of personal selling, advertising, sales promotion, and publicity (see Figure 1-2, next page). Promotion is also referred to as marketing communication.

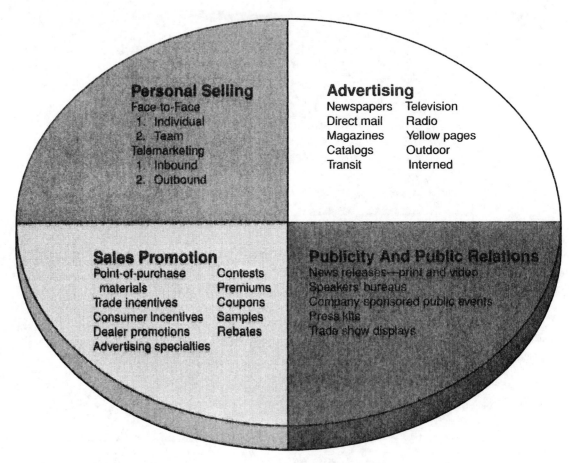

Figure 1-2 The promotion mix.

Advertising is nonpersonal communication through the media, such as TV, radio, magazines, newspapers, direct mail, and outdoor, which includes billboards and transit signage. **Publicity**, the main tool in **public relations** efforts, often promotes the firm rather than its products. Efforts in this category include press releases, open houses, speakers' bureaus, and other events involving the firms many publics. **Sales promotion** efforts are activities or items that support the promotional effort, such as product samples, contests, gifts, coupons, specialty items, combination offers, and dealer promotions, including point-of-purchase displays and banners.

Personal Selling and Advertising Compared . . .

Advertising is promotion to mass audiences through purchased time or space in the media. Personal selling usually calls for a one-on-one relationship between the sender and receiver, with the communication tailored for that customer. Even in instances where the salesperson presents to a buying committee, each individual usually receives a personal, unique message.

Opportunity is what you make of it. Many years ago a large American shoe company sent two sales reps to the wilds of Australia to sell shoes to the aborigines. Both salespeople noticed that none of the natives wore shoes. The first wired home saying, "Returning on next plane. No business here. Natives do not wear shoes." The other rep also sent a wire, which read, "Quick, send millions of shoes, all sizes. Everybody here needs a pair."

Michael Iapoce

Personal selling tends to be more important in a firm's promotional program when customers are relatively few in number and concentrated geographically. Personal selling is also ideal when the product is expensive, technically complex, custom-made, and requires special handling, or when the sale involves a trade-in. Further, products with relatively high prices or short channels of distribution typically call for personal selling. Advertising, on the other hand, tends to be more important when customers are many in number and geographically dispersed. This form of promotion is also preferred when the product is inexpensive, simple to understand or standardized, or travels through long channels of distribution.

Personal selling offers several advantages over advertising:

1. Personal selling can be custom-tailored to the individual prospect; advertising must be more general to appeal to the many people in its audience.
2. Personal selling allows for two-way communication between the prospect and the seller; advertising is a unilateral message from the seller.
3. Personal selling appeals to all five physical senses; advertising reaches two senses at most. Only with sophisticated and expensive techniques (sound chips, "scratch and sniff," and so on) can an advertiser create greater stimulation.
4. A personal selling effort, with the ability to answer questions and overcome resistance, can lead to an immediate sale; most advertising only suggests that prospects purchase at some time.

Personal Selling and Advertising as Complements . . .

Advertising and personal selling complement each other. An increase in media promotion often results in a greater need for salespeople or may improve a salesperson's productivity. Advertising by a firm that markets consumer goods gives a boost to retailers that carry such products. **Retailers** are marketing intermediaries that sell directly to consumers. The store's salespeople can point to this promotion when meeting prospective buyers. Advertising is also used to introduce a little-known firm to the public so that the sales force can greet prospects as a known entity rather than as total strangers. Both forms of marketing communication should and do work together, each enhancing and reinforcing the other.

Promotional Strategies . . .

Any firm may promote itself with a push strategy, a pull strategy, or a combination of the two. These promotional tactics are distinguished by the audience that is targeted and the types of promotion used.

A **push strategy** targets marketing wholesalers and retailers. **Wholesalers** are marketing intermediaries that sell to other businesses, contrasted with retailers who sell to consumers. Push strategy places heavy emphasis and a large portion of the promotional budget on personal selling. Marketers use this push strategy to distinguish themselves in the minds of their dealers. Intermediaries who stock the products will then generate demand at the retail level to "push" the products through the channels of distribution. Promotion targeting wholesalers or retailers includes advertising and sales promotion, but personal selling often dominates the effort.

Pull strategies target the end user, primarily through advertising. Such promotion creates demand among the ultimate customers, drawing them either to the marketer or to retailers. In this manner, the products are "pulled" through the distribution channel. When intermediaries are involved, consumer requests for a firm's product will encourage the dealer to stock it. Although personal selling may be used at the retail level, most of the promotional effort is advertising and sales promotion.

A combination **push–pull** strategy uses all the elements of the promotional mix. This tactic may use advertising, sales promotion, and personal selling to create interest among intermediaries, while promoting heavily to end users or consumers. This means that wholesalers and retailers receive the push, while the ultimate buyers get the pull. Most large consumer goods marketers use this combination strategy.

The Product Life Cycle . . .

All goods and services go through a **product life cycle** consisting of four stages, as illustrated in Figure 1-3. First there is the introduction, when the product itself (not a specific brand of it) is new to the market. During this period, a marketer's objective is to create an awareness of the product that leads to the desire to buy it. Sales promotion is used heavily during this phase, and advertising tends to be rather generic.

Once the good or service catches on, it enters the growth stage, during which sales climb sharply. Advertising increases in this phase, as the marketer struggles to develop brand loyalty against the introduction of competition. Sales promotion often tapers off in this adolescent period.

During the product's maturity stage, sales begin to level off as competitors saturate the market. National brands often stress their unique features, as store brands offer lower prices. Profit percentages drop as competition increases, driving some firms or products out of the market. Many products remain in the maturity stage indefinitely, but others decline quickly in the face of innovative replacements or changing consumer tastes. In the decline stage, products experience sharp drops in sales. Typically, firms will either try an updated marketing strategy to give the product a lift or quietly withdraw it from the market to concentrate on newer introductions.

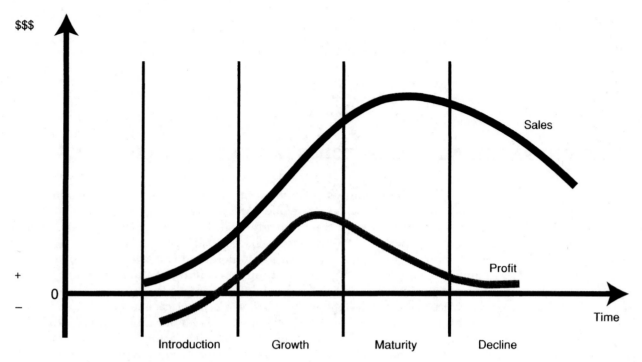

Figure 1-3 The product life cycle.

The role of the salesperson, and the emphasis of the sales presentation, will change with each stage of a product's life cycle. For instance, during the introduction stage, salespeople must open channels of distribution. The emphasis of the sales presentation at this time is on creating basic demand and overcoming objections based on a perceived lack of need. When the product receives acceptance and enters the growth stage, the emphasis changes to concentrate on distinctive features. Salespeople must now convince prospective purchasers that their brands are better than the competitions'. In the maturity phase, selling effort attempts to maintain loyalty for the marketer and the marketer's brands.

Selling as Distribution . . .

Although personal selling is clearly a promotional activity, it is closely related to distribution. A firm gets its product to end users or consumers through its channels of distribution. One such channel is the sales force. In recent years, some marketers have set up different kinds of channels of distribution to serve different customers. Some customers buy directly from the factory with the help of a field sales force. Others might be served through retail outlets, with the emphasis on advertising. Business machine manufacturers, for example, have experienced price competition that makes field selling less profitable than before. Some firms, like IBM, are selling through retailers, such as Sears, to reach smaller business customers and ultimate consumers while maintaining their traditional sales force to call on large clients.

> He who has a thing to sell and goes and whispers in a well, is not so apt to get the dollars as he who climbs a tree and hollers.
>
> Anonymous

THE FUNDAMENTALS FOR SUCCESS IN PERSONAL SELLING . . .

Success in selling requires a combination of many qualities, none of which are secrets. A professional image, solid product knowledge, persuasiveness, an optimistic attitude, good communication skills, a strong visual presence, and an outgoing personality are assets for any salesperson. In addition, sellers need organization skills, the desire to understand the customer, the ability to manage their time, and a thorough understanding of their company, market and competitors.

Success in selling depends on hard work, practice, observation, and study, as well as on an understanding of customer behavior and selling techniques. Selling ability isn't something one is born with, something that you either have or don't have. Granted, some people are more gifted at selling than others, but no one is created with all the knowledge and skill needed for achievement. Successful selling is as much a product of education and training as it is instinct. A new salesperson must develop his or her budding talent by selling and failing to sell, by learning from mistakes and building on experience.

Fortunately, every skill or quality needed for success in selling can be learned and developed. If this were not true, companies would not spend the money they do to send their salespeople to training schools. In fact, some firms prefer to hire people who have had no selling experience at all. These marketers want to train employees from the very beginning in the ways of professional selling rather than work with more experienced salespeople who might have already developed poor selling practices.

People Skills . . .

One of the most important requirements for a salesperson is good **people skills**, or soft skills. Prospects (potential buyers) must instinctively like you and consider you capable of helping them. You must be able to take command of a selling situation, handle the dynamics of your relationship with the prospect, and bring the transaction to a successful conclusion. You must also be reliable. A salesperson who is forthright and honest will gain the prospect's respect and build the prospect's trust, two crucial factors in personal selling.

Although the ability to develop effective interpersonal relationships isn't the only thing needed for success in selling, the inability to relate with others often means certain failure. More customers switch suppliers because of poor relationships with the salespeople than for any other reason. The inability to get along with others is the number-one reason that not only salespeople but all workers lose their jobs.

Communication Skills . . .

A salesperson must be an effective persuader and skilled communicator. In this respect, your first successful sales call occurs when you sell yourself to the firm that hires you. You will always need strong **communication skills** to deal effectively with the many people you meet as a salesperson. Communication skills help you in getting to know your prospects. The better you know potential buyers, the better you'll be at identifying their needs.

Because of the independent nature of many selling positions, you must be self-motivated to succeed in sales. You must derive a great deal of personal satisfaction from making a sale and be able to adjust to the frustrations of those unsuccessful attempts as well. Success in this field requires the determination to succeed that comes with a positive attitude.

Successful Salespeople . . .

Successful salespeople have a number of traits and behaviors in common. Typically, professional sellers exhibit a clear sense of image and reputation, and a strong work ethic. Success driven, these people are motivated by financial rewards and the gratification of helping customers. Salespeople are skilled at analyzing the prospect's buying motives and decision-making processes. Their ability to uncover customer needs and discover creative solutions earns them reknown as excellent sources of information and help.

Successful salespeople like and respect their prospects and customers, enjoy their company, treat them fairly, and invest time in building long-term relationships. These sellers place greater emphasis on customer relationships than on product knowledge, knowing that poor people skills can ruin any selling effort. Those who sell to businesses think of their prospects as people, not organizations.

Sales superstars rarely follow a planned selling formula. They don't hesitate to skip a step in the selling process if the customer seems ready to purchase. They know how to match the customer's personality, and will alter their own style to make the prospect comfortable and build his or her trust.

Successful salespeople enjoy what they sell. Real estate agents frequently say they find it easier to sell a house if they've fallen in love with it than if they haven't. You will find it less difficult to sell a product that relates to your personal interests because you have more motivation to learn about it.

Professional salespeople are **consultative** rather than hard-sell. Consultative, or customer-oriented sellers strive to form a partnership with their customers. They listen carefully, encourage a potential buyer's involvement, and focus efforts on solving problems. **Hard-sell** types, on the other hand, dominate the sales interview, are poor listeners, have no interest in learning the prospect's viewpoint, attempt to force an immediate buying decision, and ask repeatedly for the order.

Sales jobs can be physically and psychologically demanding. Forty-hour work weeks are more the exception than the rule. Yet when successful salespeople are asked to explain why they enjoy selling, most mention the same basic reasons. They like the challenge of the work, the freedom to set their own schedules, and the financial rewards.

The smaller the firm, the less likely it is to offer formal **sales training**. In fact, less than a quarter of all businesses formally train their salespeople. According to some estimates, as many as three of every four salespeople begin selling without specific education or preparation.

Many marketing-oriented firms are becoming increasingly aware of the need to train the field sales force. More and more companies are offering in-house training programs. Others enroll their new salespeople in courses designed by firms that specialize in such training, such as Wilson Learning Corporation, Zig Ziglar Training, Tom Hopkins International, and Learning International.

Depending on your industry or firm, the time you spend in sales training may be from several days to more than a year. If you begin your selling career with a large company, some of your time will be spent in one of the employer's district or regional sales offices. Here, you will be introduced to the firm's selling strategy and be provided with the basics of product knowledge. You may then be assigned to work with an experienced salesperson for several weeks, gaining firsthand observation of various selling situations. Even after you are assigned to a sales territory, you may still spend the first month or so making sales calls with your sales manager or sales training officer.

Sometimes a sales trainee starts selling under the supervision of a company trainer. Many firms rely on the sales manager to handle all aspects of the training effort. Others use **mentoring**, a formal interpretation of the "buddy system." Here, trainees make calls with experienced salespeople who serve as career guides. Usually, the firm's top salespeople are selected as mentors. The advantages of having a trainee observe a seasoned performer in action must be balanced against the risk that the mentor may not be an effective teacher.

Expert Modeling and Interactive Training Methods . . .

A concept known as **expert modeling** is growing in popularity as a nontheoretical approach to sales training. In this model, sales trainees pattern themselves after the firm's senior salespeople so as to improve their performance. Sales superstars within the company are videotaped several times a year, and inexperienced sellers learn by observing them in action.

Sales training programs may employ the use of computer simulations, videotapes, lectures, seminars, one-on-one instruction, and role playing. Slides, films, games and simulations, case studies, videoconferencing, self-tests, home assignments, and other aids are also common. Your training may include exposure to all phases of your company's production and distribution process.

Interactive sales training is growing in popularity as firms discover that active participation in the learning process improves learning and retention. Face-to-face role playing, the traditional form of proactive learning, is now supplemented with interactive videodisks. Using this model, the

Elizabeth Newkirk

Some people just naturally gravitate toward a career in selling. Elizabeth Newkirk fits that description. After completing her education through Genesee Community College and Syracuse University, Elizabeth found her niche with PAYCHEX, Inc. She attributes some of her interest in selling to courses that she took, including Sales Techniques, Marketing Principles, and Public Speaking and Advertising. Other campus activities, such as student government, the Rochester Professional Sales Association, the Rochester Advertising Federation, and Sales and Marketing Executives added to her interest and broadened her education. Elizabeth is still pursuing her education, taking courses toward an MBA at Rochester Institute of Technology.

This active young woman climbed the corporate ladder through sales positions to become the National Sales Support Trainer for the corporation. In this position, Elizabeth is in charge of training all sales support representatives for PAYCHEX. She created the training manual, makes joint calls with and coaches salespeople, represents the company at career fairs and college interviews, and conducts seminars and other presentations to a variety of organizations. Elizabeth is one busy woman.

Elizabeth believes that to be successful in sales you must believe in what you are selling. Knowledge about your product, your industry, and your competition are the foundation for building confidence. She also believes in creating a personal development plan to keep on top of your profession, which includes reading pertinent materials, networking through community organizations, such as the Chamber of Commerce, and attending seminars and presentations pertaining to your career and industry. Most importantly, Elizabeth believes you should have fun in your profession!

sales trainee uses a keyboard to respond to questions and objections posed by a customer projected on a video screen. This system can be augmented with audio, where the new salesperson actually converses with the person on screen, thereby refining his or her verbal communication skills.

At the vanguard of sales training methods is **business television**, or BTV. Here, company trainers transmit sessions live from a television studio to locations throughout the country. The television signal is sent to a satellite, which in turn sends it back to a specific site equipped with a satellite dish. Trainees who participate in these teleconferences can ask questions and share ideas with the on-camera presenters. Many firms have found it less expensive to train salespeople with BTV than to send them to distant locations. Thanks to declines in the cost of satellite technology, firms that don't have their own network can rent the required airtime and equipment to create their own BTV training programs.

CHANGES IN SELLING . . .

Selling skills will have to be sharper than ever in the coming decade as salespeople learn to adapt to an ever-changing environment. Major changes in the marketing process for many products have already occurred. Whereas industrial salespeople traditionally went out on their own to negotiate with one purchasing agent, today's buying-and-selling process often involves many people, with negotiations spanning several layers of the organization. Upper managers, including presidents and chief executive officers, are constantly performing selling functions.

Like their counterparts in industry, top buying personnel at large retail organizations prefer to do business with their equals in the selling organization. Retailers are increasingly basing their purchase decisions on computerized calculations of sales, turnover, and profits. Salespeople have an especially challenging task when working amid computers that supposedly contain every bit of knowledge a retail buyer needs.

International selling has also increased in importance, and this trend will continue as trade with Eastern Europe and other locations increases. Salespeople who sell in the global marketplace should acquaint themselves with the **International Sales Code**, a document adhered to by the United States, the European Union, and Japan, which covers legal aspects of international commercial transactions.

The Use of Personal Computers by Salespeople . . .

Salespeople will definitely need to understand and work with computers. Many salespeople's duties are becoming more technical as methods of prospecting, marketing, and selling change. In their growing capacity as an information source for both customer and employer, salespeople will have to become technologically proficient, or at least computer literate.

Personal computers are a standard piece of equipment for many salespeople. PCs are used to enter and track orders, write sales reports, correspond with customers, make sales forecasts, and compose bid or quote proposals. They help salespeople design and deliver sales presentations, track leads, keep informed of current inventory levels, conduct mass mailings, manage time, make travel plans, and schedule sales calls.

The salesperson's personal computer can help in the management of a customer's inventory and in the monitoring of competition as well. Client management software allows salespeople easy storage of and access to customer databases. Other, more sophisticated programs even help the salesperson analyze the prospect's personality or determine which selling technique would be most effective for a particular potential buyer.

> Knowledge is of two kinds. We know a subject ourselves, or we know where we can find information upon it.
>
> Samuel Johnson

Portable Computers . . .

Salespeople who travel often carry portable personal computers in their cars and onboard airplanes. Some are being equipped with telephone modems that connect them to the company computer and enable them to enter customer orders and receive messages. The traveling salesperson can obtain information on competing products from a public telephone or from their hotel room or automobile.

The lightest personal computers are called pocket computers, or palmtops, which weigh about 1 pound. Next come notebooks. They weigh 7 pounds or less and operate on rechargeable batteries. One size up from the notebook is the laptop, which, at 15 pounds or less, is smaller than the standard desktop personal computer. Laptops use rechargeable batteries and can be operated from the cigarette lighter in the salesperson's car. Some have built-in cellular telephone modems. Another new development in the subcompact computer market is the pen-based computer, a portable unit that functions without a keyboard.

Electronic (Text) Mail and Voice Mail . . .

Electronic mail enables the salesperson to send messages between computers that are connected either directly by wire or by telephone modem. This model frees salespeople to move about with a portable computer yet access the company computer's mainframe or networking system from a hotel room or customer's office. The salesperson can send a message to several terminals all at once through e-mail, avoiding the inconvenience of telephone calls. Electronic mail also permits electronic conferencing for group discussions. You can even use an outside service to e-mail a message to a prospect who doesn't have a computer.

Voice mail requires only a telephone call to a receiving computer. This electronic method integrates voice and digital technology into a single system that allows for one-way communication when a two-way conversation is not needed. Salespeople can call their office or company headquarters and leave messages via voice mail with little or no chance of loss or error. They can also call their office to check for other messages. Voice mail has been around for some time, but only in recent years has it become popular as system costs have declined.

The Internet . . .

Not enough can be said regarding the use of the Internet as a selling tool. Although relatively new to the field of sales, the "Web" has become an integral part of the selling process. Many innovative firms, especially smaller ones, are using the Internet to handle the complete selling process. With the creation of a Web page, such firms can reach millions of prospects worldwide, provide complete product information—often with pictures—and arrange for direct ordering using order forms and credit card processing data.

In addition to actually selling over the Internet, many firms use this medium as a sales aid. Tremendous amounts of data can be processed using this computer technology, allowing businesses to provide product information, pricing and ordering details, and potentially, demonstrations. Sales brochures in full detail can be displayed more economically on the Internet than in printed form.

The Internet is also an excellent tool for generating new customers. Some companies use the Internet as a back-up salesperson, collecting prospect information and determining needs first via the Web, thereby better arming the seller when she or he makes the actual call. Prospecting through this medium is quick, inexpensive, and accurate. There can be no question about the usefulness and potential growth of the Internet as a selling tool.

FACSIMILE (FAX), CELLULAR PHONES, AND PAGERS . . .

More and more, salespeople are using all manner of technology in their selling efforts. Facsimile machines can send printed messages to clients and employers from office, automobile, public telephone, or personal computer. Equipped with VCRs, these devices can show videocassette presentations produced by their firms. Teleconferencing can be used for group discussions with people in several locations at once.

Cars with mobile telephones or battery-operated cellular units are gaining popularity. Pocket telephones, which use radio frequency transmission, are the rage. This digital technology may eventually replace telephones that rely on the cell system.

Salespeople use pagers whose variable tones identify their callers. Some even have voice mail capability. Digital diaries with calculator and calendar functions, along with memo storage capabilities, allow interaction with personal computers. Voice-activated dictaphones with digital displays show the salesperson what has been recorded.

While driving, salespeople might even use a computer-generated navigation system. Using this recent development, the driver signals his or her position to a satellite, which in turn conveys the message to a computer center. This "earth station" then sends a map of the area to the screen on the driver's dashboard. This system is expensive and is not yet widely available as a factory option on automobiles.

Increased Productivity . . .

Technology is increasing the salesperson's productivity. Salespeople are being freed from many of the mundane tasks traditionally associated with selling. Paperwork, often referred to as the bane of professional selling, can now be handled "on the go." Sellers now can devote more of their precious time to the development of personal skills and analysis of customer needs.

Order taking is the area of professional selling that will be most affected by advances in technology. Although many small wholesalers continue to use salespeople for ordering purposes, the use of computers has eliminated many of these low-paying positions. Customers are now directly online with their suppliers, using their own input devices to place orders without involving personal contact.

THE MYTHS OF SALESPEOPLE AND SELLING . . .

Selling is a prestigious, rewarding career. Unfortunately, an outdated image of salespeople still lingers. Many prospects and potential salespeople continue to be influenced by a picture of salespeople as fast-talking glad-handers who are greedy and crooked. People think of Professor Harold Hill, the gaudy-suited trombone salesman in Meredith Wilson's *The Music Man*, or they are haunted by the image of Willy Loman, the tragic figure in Arthur Miller's *Death of a Salesman*. Such images carry the power of stereotype, but new and experienced salespeople alike must overcome that influence. Remember that Hill and Loman were individual characters, not typical salespeople. Success will not come to the salesperson who believes in or fears the negative images associated with selling.

According to some, salespeople are smooth talkers who are willing and able to charm unsuspecting prospects out of their money. Caring only about their own profit, these myths use hard-sell techniques to pressure customers into bad deals. All they need is a firm handshake, a shoeshine, and of course, a garish plaid suit. Ironically, many of us may even have met a couple of salespeople who fit the stereotype pretty closely. But if we insist on believing in old stereotypes, we miss the reality of present-day professional selling.

Today's Salespeople . . .

Today's salespeople, new or experienced, are ambitious, well trained, and ready to offer a worthwhile commodity or service. They don't see the customer as someone to be sold, but as an individual who needs assistance in a buying decision. They are experts in their field, often with specialized backgrounds. Through their education, training, and contact with specialists in buying companies, modern salespeople gain knowledge of disciplines related to their work, such as engineering, marketing, and production.

Today's salespeople often have two-year, four-year, and even postgraduate degrees from reputable colleges. Some, such as automobile, real estate, and securities salespeople, earn licenses to practice their profession only after passing rigorous state or national examinations. After successful completion of a standardized exam, professional certification (developed by the National Automotive Dealers Association) is now available for automobile salespeople. Others gain certification from their specific industries.

As representatives of America's largest and most successful companies, salespeople enjoy some of the most attractive jobs. Research reveals that today's college students consider sales positions rewarding and challenging, and often look upon selling as a desirable career.

Customers don't care how much you know, until they know how much you care.

Mary Lou Dobbs

THE NATURE OF SELLING . . .

Because the essence of selling is communication and persuasion, we all sell. Life has trained us in the techniques of persuasion. Whether convincing your parents to buy you a bicycle or, more recently, talking a professor into giving a makeup exam, most of us spend our lives practicing to sell. Selling is both a science and an art. It is a science in that it relies on clearly defined techniques that have been tested and proven effective. Selling is an art in that it requires creativity to meet the individual challenges of each situation.

Salespeople perform the following functions on a daily basis:

1. **Prospecting**—actively seeking out those who may have the need and ability to purchase the product to be sold, and determining if they do.

2. Gathering **preapproach data**—deciding the objectives of sales calls and obtaining background information on the prospect in question so as to prepare and deliver a customized presentation.

3. Delivering **sales presentations**—approaching prospects, presenting the product or service to them, answering their questions, overcoming their objections to buying, and closing the sale.

4. Providing **after-the-sale follow-up** and service—making sure the customer is happy with the product, that he or she is using it correctly, and that it is maintained in working order.

5. Completing **sales reports**—keeping management abreast of customers and conditions within a salesperson's territory.

Not all companies require all salespeople to fill out sales reports, but the following paragraphs provide a sampling of the types of reports most often submitted.

Call report. The **call report** gives specific, detailed information on every call the salesperson makes. The salesperson reports the date, time, length, and results of a sales call, as well as the identity and classification of the customer. The contact method (personal or telephone) is described, as is the follow-up planned and the current status of the account. Call reports reveal how often the firm's high-volume customers, known as key accounts, are being visited, and if the true decision makers in these firms are being seen.

Expense report. The **expense report** gives a breakdown of a salesperson's expenses for a certain task or period. Salespeople are typically required to list all expenses relating to their job, including tolls, taxi fares, gasoline, meals, lodging, and incidentals. This report allows for the reimbursement of sales-related expenses and lets management evaluate sales performance by comparing costs to volume. The Internal Revenue Service requires all outside salespeople to keep track of expenses for tax purposes.

Customer complaint report. The **customer complaint report** details the subject, nature, method, and status of a customer's complaint, including when and how a settled complaint was resolved.

Lost order/lost account report. The **lost order/lost account report** is filled out whenever the firm loses an order or account to the competition. The salesperson notes the customer's name, the competitor's name, and why the sale was lost.

Qualifying report. A **qualifying report** provides all relevant information on a new prospect. If the prospect is a business, the salesperson describes the type of industry, the products purchased, the prospect's present suppliers, the name of buying personnel and key decision makers, and the best time of the day or week to call.

Competitive activity report. The **competitive activity report** provides information on competitors' pricing and promotional strategies, as well as new product entries into the market or the salesperson's territory. The salesperson may also submit profiles that break down sales in his or her territory by competitor.

Itinerary. An **itinerary** is a daily or weekly travel plan. It tells management where and how to reach the salesperson and provides evidence of careful call planning. Although some salespeople feel that following an itinerary is restrictive, differences in planned and actual activities are brought to light when management compares itineraries with earlier selling plans.

The Reality of Selling . . .

Selling positions vary quite a bit in terms of nonselling responsibilities. Some salespeople are provided with technical or clerical help by their employers, whereas others may have to perform these tasks on their own or hire someone at their own expense. One company might have a field service department, whereas others might ask salespeople to handle these tasks. A salesperson may have to collect bills, set up displays in a dealer's facility, or even attend intermediaries' sales meetings. A salesperson with a large territory might have to travel frequently. The McGraw-Hill Laboratory for Advertising Performance says that the typical industrial salesperson spends less than half of his or her time actually selling.

The sale of expensive industrial goods can require an especially large investment of the salesperson's time. Tasks may include making presentations to a **buying center**, a group of people in the prospect's organization, or separate calls to each decision maker. **Multiple buying influences** may mean talking to someone from engineering, research, production, marketing, or even the company president. Countless visits to the prospect's facility may be needed. Success may also call for **team selling**, with specialists from the salesperson's company forming a team to deliver a sales presentation, usually to their counterparts in the prospect's company. The lead salesperson is usually responsible for coordinating the team's effort and planning its strategy.

Not only do transactions involving sales teams and multiple buying influences often take months or years to complete, the signing of the contract may be only the beginning of the salesperson's job. The sale could be followed by many months of **customer service**. Salespeople often oversee delivery and installation, train the buying firm's employees to use the product, and attend to periodic maintenance and service.

If you sell to a wholesaler or retailer, an important part of your job will be helping these **intermediaries** resell your product to their customers. You may even accompany your wholesaler customers on their sales calls to retailers. You may have to train retailers in the techniques of selling your product and persuade them to participate with you in cooperative advertising. In this arrangement, the store and the manufacturer share the cost of advertising a product.

JOBS IN SELLING . . .

Selling occupations are broken into several categories. The retail field is growing in importance as more stores place greater emphasis on customer service through personal selling. Increased training for salespeople entering the retail field offers greater potential for advancement in this arena. Consumer services, such as insurance, financial services, and travel agencies provide excellent opportunities for those interested in a selling career. Industrial selling relates to business-to-business transactions in production goods, equipment, accessories, and supplies. Trade selling refers to transactions between manufacturers and marketing intermediaries, such as wholesalers and retailers.

Retail salespeople sell to the ultimate consumer. Most retail salespeople work in stores where customers call on them. Although retail selling pays less than other forms, such work has its distinct advantages. For example, the retail salesperson has a controlled physical selling environment, so the presentation setting is predictable and comfortable. The retailer typically has a wider variety of merchandise to show as well as the support of point-of-purchase promotions. In addition, the store's permanent location allows sellers to be available when customers are ready to purchase or need service.

Industrial Selling . . .

Manufacturers' salespeople typically do the calling on prospects and customers. These sellers may be directly in the employ of the producer or may operate as independent agents. The latter are called **manufacturer's representatives**. Sellers whose prospects are manufacturers are typically known as **industrial salespeople**. They commonly sell raw materials, component parts, production equipment, and operating supplies. Industrial salespeople are often better paid than retail salespeople because of the technical nature and educational requirements of their work.

Salespeople in the service industries work for banks, transportation companies, utilities, stockbrokers, consulting firms, and insurance companies. These individuals may sell to businesses, to consumers, or to both. **Telemarketing** is a growth area in the sale of both consumer and industrial goods. This is a method in which all or a part of the selling process takes place over the telephone.

Sales engineers, or **technical specialists**, are highly trained salespeople who usually have engineering degrees. These sellers typically handle technical goods and services, including products that require installation, such as capital equipment. They help their clients solve complex problems and work with customers on their production processes. Typically, technical specialists work with well-established accounts and develop close working relationships with these customers.

Trade Selling . . .

Companies that sell a line of consumer products to wholesalers or retailers practice **trade selling**. Customers include marketing intermediaries, such as wholesalers or retailers, professional or service organizations, or in rare cases, the ultimate consumer. Most consumer goods and services are purchased directly from retailers and providers. In this field, the seller has an established base of customers, and the product is often presold to ultimate consumers through advertising. Intermediaries don't need a lot of convincing to carry the line. However, trade selling requires more than the routine taking of orders and reorders. A survey conducted by the A.C. Nielson company showed that supermarket managers can be quite demanding. Store managers said they expect trade sales reps to advise them of deals and allowances, pick up old or damaged goods, introduce new products, advise them on coupon activity and advertising plans, check prices, stock shelves, and make price changes.

Other duties of **trade salespeople** may include handling the retailer's customer complaints, staging in-store demonstrations, arranging displays and promotions, and checking stock levels. A major challenge in trade selling comes when the salesperson must convince a retailer to stock an untried product. In this respect, trade salespeople are called upon to do creative selling.

In-Home and Party-Plan Selling . . .

In-home selling concentrates on building a solid foundation of repeat customers, eliminating the need for the salesperson to spend a great deal of time generating new prospects. Avon Products has a 500,000-member sales force to sell cosmetics and home products. Amway, another home-products marketer, is also a giant in this field. Coventry, Jafra, and other consumer goods firms market exclusively using this method.

Party-plan selling is set in customers' homes, too, but calls for a larger gathering of prospects at one home. Mary Kay Cosmetics conducts in-home "skin care classes," which take about two hours and are attended by three to six guests. Tupperware, a direct distributor of home products, is famous for its selling parties, complete with games.

A cynic is a man who, when he smells flowers, looks around for a coffin.

H. L. Mencken

Missionary Selling . . .

Missionary selling is a special support technique often used by manufacturers. Missionary salespeople work to generate interest in a product rather than to make an immediate sale. For example, drug manufacturers hire **pharmaceutical representatives** called detailers to visit doctors, give them information on new products and side effects, and encourage the doctors to prescribe the drug.

Missionary salespeople are also common in the construction industry. Representing firms in the building products field, these sellers call on architects and engineers. Similar to those in the pharmaceutical industry, these salespeople typically do not work to receive orders, but rather strive for specifications.

Special Selling Positions . . .

Different salespeople within a firm might have different selling duties. A company with a broad product mix might divide its sales positions according to customer or product category. For example, a business that manufactures photocopiers might assign some salespeople to sell only to large corporate customers, whereas others are assigned to serve smaller prospects. Similarly, a clothing retailer might put one salesperson in charge of better dresses, another in women's shoes.

The extra attention required for important customers has driven many firms to establish **key-account sales forces**. These salespeople exist expressly to service high-volume customers. IBM handles its key accounts through sellers who are expert in their customers' businesses. This type of salesperson may have only one very large and important customer, and his or her livelihood can virtually depend on that firm's business. Key accounts or the most profitable territories may be handled by the sales manager or by the firm's top sales representatives, who are sometimes called senior salespeople or seniors. When the firm enters a new territory, seniors and sales managers might also perform missionary tasks.

Businesses use many names to describe their salespeople. You may be called an account executive, account manager, marketing support representative, sales rep, or customer representative. Sales consultant, sales engineer, territory manager, account representative, sales specialist, marketing consultant, account director, sales associate, and sales agent are other frequently used titles.

> Life is like a dogsled team. If you ain't the lead dog, the scenery never changes.
>
> Lewis Grizzard

SALES MANAGERS . . .

The **sales manager** leads the sales force by planning, organizing, and controlling the sales force. Specific duties might include evaluating market potentials, developing budgets and sales forecasts, analyzing selling expenses, assigning sales quotas or territories, and designing compensation plans. Recruiting, selecting, training, motivating, and evaluating salespeople are additional tasks of sales management. Other assignments will vary depending upon the scope of the firm's operations and the experience of the individual.

Many sales managers make a practice of spending several days each month or quarter in the field with their sales representatives. This way they can hold curbstone conferences immediately after calls to advise sellers on ways to improve their techniques. Regular field work also keeps management attune with the pulse of the market.

Interestingly, the best salespeople are not necessarily the best sales managers. In fact, many do not jump at the opportunity to move into management positions. Effective salespeople enjoy the people contact, the potential for unlimited earnings, and the freedom of their flexible work schedule. These job features are not commonly available to managers.

WHAT ABOUT INCOME? . . .

A beginning salesperson should expect to earn about as much as anyone else in an entry-level position requiring a similar educational background. But once off and running, the similarity between jobs ends. A successful salesperson's income will increase at a greater rate than the incomes of nonselling employees with the same tenure and background. Top salespeople often make more than company managers, including the chief executive officer. Sales managers usually earn more than other company officers at the same level in their organization. In addition to the income flexibility that accompanies commissions and fast promotions, salespeople might enjoy indirect financial benefits like company cars and liberal expense accounts.

Salespeople as a group earn more than the national average for all workers. Those with technical training or graduate degrees can easily earn more than $40,000 their first year. The Bureau of Labor Statistics reports that more people working in sales have annual compensation of over $500,000 than people in any other occupation. A salesperson's income potential is limited only by his or her skills and level of motivation.

Methods of Compensation . . .

The **straight salary plan** offers sellers maximum security and earnings stability. Straight salary is often used for new salespeople when opening new territories that need development time, or in industries where lengthy negotiation is needed. Under this compensation plan, salespeople are more apt to consider their prospect's best interests rather than personal gain. Since this method lacks incentives, the burden of motivating rests more heavily on sales management.

It is common practice for people in the selling profession to receive **incentive** pay. This can be in the form of **commission** or **bonus**, often paid on top of a salary. A commission is compensation based on the dollar volume of sales. A bonus is additional compensation that may be awarded for exceeding an assigned sales goal.

Straight commission arrangements sometimes include guaranteed or nonguaranteed drawing accounts. A draw against commissions enables the salesperson to maintain a steady and predictable level of income. A **nonguaranteed draw** against commissions, also known as a recoverable draw, is an advance from the company to the salesperson that can be thought of as a loan. The portion of it that is not paid back with commissions earned must be returned by the salesperson or is carried forward as a deficit into the next pay period. A **guaranteed draw**, or nonrecoverable draw, need not be returned and is not carried forward if commissions earned don't equal it. Some firms offer guaranteed draws only to trainees. Companies usually limit the total draw they will pay out before a salesperson is required to produce.

Many firms are replacing the drawing account with a base-salary plus commission plan, in which salespeople receive a percentage of the dollar volume sold in addition to a normal salary. Although the idea of depending on commission earnings scares some people, the fact is that skilled professionals who switch from straight salary to some incentive arrangement invariably increase their income. Commissions account for most of the income of today's highest-paid salespeople.

Bonuses might be based either on individual performance or on the firm's overall accomplishments for the year. This type of incentive pay could be linked to the results of team competition or to a salesperson's ranking compared to other sellers. Bonuses could also be calculated using subjective evaluations, such as the amount of effort the salesperson seems to devote to the job. When the selling process is known to be long and drawn out, the typical compensation arrangement is a salary throughout the process, coupled with a bonus when the sale becomes final.

Other Incentives . . .

Salespeople also work for incentives in the form of merchandise or prizes awarded for exceeding specified goals. They may also compete with other salespeople in their company in selling contests. These competitions may be linked to special promotions or introductory products, or they may be a continuing method of compensation.

Nonmonetary aspects of a salesperson's compensation plan, commonly called perks (for **perquisites**), might include use of a company car, extra time off, company stock, supplemental life insurance, or tax preparation assistance. Car phones, club memberships, company resort facilities, telephone credit cards, discounts on merchandise, or universal credit cards are other common perks offered to professional salespeople.

You Decide!

Dave is a sales trainer for a medium-sized electronics manufacturer in New England. After spending almost thirty years in the field in this industry, two years ago he was assigned to his present job. The firm hires an average of twelve new recruits each summer. Although he is not involved in the hiring process, Dave generally has been pleased with the quality of the trainees. His training program lasts six months. It includes extensive education in the company and its products, as well as specific exercises to develop selling skills. The first two classes that Dave passed on to the Sales Manager have performed well in the field.

This year's class is typical of new hires. Of the thirteen trainees, all have degrees from reputable institutions, many in technical areas, and three have MBAs. On the first day of class, Dave notes that one of the men with an MBA wears his hair long, but neatly pulled back in a pony tail. One of the female recruits is impeccably groomed, but her fingernails, an obvious source of pride, are quite long and gaudily decorated. A third trainee has shaved his head and wears a subdued earring. Dave knows that times have changed since he first entered sales; yet he is concerned about the impression that these new salespeople might make—his company operates in a rather sophisticated industry.

Should Dave discuss the impact that physical appearance might have on potential customers? If so, how should he approach the subject? Might he consider discussing his dilemma with the Sales Manager? Or perhaps his best solution is to ignore his feelings and get on with the training. **You decide!**

WHY STUDY SELLING? . . .

Sales careers are the ultimate challenge for dynamic, success-driven individuals. Learning to sell for a living is the foremost reason for studying selling, but it isn't the only benefit. Learning to sell can help you get and keep the job of your choice, regardless of the field. You will find that many of the qualities found in salespeople are required of personnel in other jobs as well. Image, attitude, personality, and the ability to communicate—all typical salesperson qualities—are commonly cited as prime reasons why certain people are hired or promoted. Almost every occupation requires selling ability of some kind. The skills you gain in selling are easily transferred from one job or selling environment to the next.

The benefits of learning how to sell are both immediate and long term. First, you learn techniques that can readily be converted into income. You are tested with every sales call, and your success is measured with every sale.

Selling gives a clear and concrete measure of job performance, unlike many nonselling jobs. A salesperson's rewards are directly based on results, not on seniority or the subjective evaluation of managers. You don't need a lot of experience to achieve success quickly in selling although increased knowledge enhances your chances for prolonged success.

Freedom and Communications Skills . . .

In many sales jobs, you work independently, free from direct supervision. No two days are the same because you set your own schedule. Selling is probably the most autonomous job around that still provides the benefits of working for an organization. Outside selling provides variety and freedom for the person who dislikes desk or office work.

Communicative and persuasive ability are two of the fundamentals of leadership. All great leaders are good at communicating and persuading others. Because management requires leadership qualities, selling is an excellent training ground for managerial jobs of all types. Managers in a firm's marketing division usually have had sales experience. Most firms believe that someone who is successful at selling has the personal ability and experience to be good advancement material. Selling has also proved to be the entry-level position for many senior management positions. In fact, a sales background is one of the fastest routes to the top. Studies indicate that top company officers are more likely to have a marketing and sales background than any other. Former salespeople now hold key managerial positions in many of the *Fortune 500* companies.

Finally, because developing meaningful interpersonal relationships is at the heart of selling, the skills learned can be carried over into your personal life. The techniques of selling are the techniques of friendship; as a good salesperson, you will become more aware of others' feelings, you'll make friends more easily, you'll understand how to communicate your true feelings, and you'll learn how to persuade without antagonizing.

Summing It Up . . .

This chapter provided an introduction to the nature and importance of personal selling in the American economy, and offered insight into the many benefits of a sales career. Selling's role in the marketing process was examined. The services rendered by knowledgeable, professional salespeople were explored, as were the requirements for success in selling and the characteristics of successful salespeople. Innovative methods of sales training were examined, and the use of computers and other technology by salespeople was surveyed. We reviewed the spectrum of available sales positions, and the variety of compensation arrangements available to people in sales. Chapter 2 focuses on the role of communication in the selling process. Chapters 3 through 13 concern themselves with the stages in the selling process.

Key Concepts and Terms . . .

advertising
after-the-sale follow-up
bonus
business television
buying center
call report
commission
communication skills
competitive activity report
consultative selling
consumer durable
customer complaint report
customer service
detailer
electronic mail
expense report
expert modeling
guaranteed draw
hard-sell selling
incentive
industrial good
industrial salesperson
in-home selling
interactive sales training
intermediary
International Sales Code
itinerary
key-account sales force
lost order report
manufacturer's representative
marketing concept
marketing mix
mentoring
missionary selling

multiple buying influences
nonguaranteed draw
party-plan selling
people skills
perquisites
personal selling
place utility
possession utility
preapproach data
product life cycle
promotional mix
prospecting
public relations
publicity
pull strategy
push strategy
qualifying report
retailer
retail salespeople
sales engineer
sales manager
sales presentation
sales promotion
sales report
sales training
team selling
technical specialist
telemarketing
time utility
trade salespeople
trade selling
voice mail
wholesaler

Building Skills . . .

1. Describe the ways that salespeople help lower prices.
2. Explain the ways that personal selling becomes more justifiable in industrial than in consumer markets.

3. Briefly explain the role of salespeople as educators.

4. Assess the advantages of gathering market data through a salesperson rather than through a market researcher.

5. Describe the marketing concept, the elements of the marketing mix, and the elements of the promotional mix.

6. Verify that advertising and personal selling complement each other.

7. Examine the most important skills and characteristics needed for success in selling.

8. Reply to the following comment: "Salespeople are born, not made. You either have selling ability or you don't."

9. Evaluate the more common methods of training inexperienced salespeople.

10. Describe some of the ways that computers will change the work of salespeople.

11. Explore some of the myths about salespeople, offering methods that a salesperson can use to overcome the influence of the old stereotypes.

12. Describe selling as both an art and a science.

13. Outline some of the daily activities of selling.

14. Describe multiple buying influences, centering on the need for team selling.

15. Discuss the tasks of missionary salespeople.

16. Explain trade selling, focusing on the major challenge for the trade salesperson.

17. Explain the various compensation plans.

18. Examine how selling skills can enhance your personal life.

19. Define the ways that selling gives a clear and concrete indication of your talent and success.

20. Analyze why sales is considered an excellent training ground for management.

Making Decisions 1-1:

Paul Price, a college senior majoring in marketing, recently attended his college's job fair, where he met with several employers. One memorable interview was with a recruiter from Polk Industries, a national manufacturer of fiberglass and plastic tanks.

Paul:	Do you have any openings for management trainees?
Recruiter:	We're here to recruit *sales* trainees. Will you be graduating soon?
Paul:	Yes.
Recruiter:	What's your major?
Paul:	Marketing.
Recruiter:	Let me give you some information on our firm's sales training program. As you'll see, it's quite extensive. It lasts eight months and covers all aspects of sales and marketing.
Paul:	I'm really not interested in sales.

Recruiter:	You might be interested to know that many of our managers started out in sales. Sales is an excellent training ground for management, and our sales trainees start at a higher salary than any other trainee we hire.
Paul:	No, I'm really not interested.
Recruiter:	Well, if you change your mind, feel free to send me a résumé. I'll be happy to talk with you about this excellent career opportunity.

Later, Paul recounts the conversation to his roommate, Lee Malick.

Paul:	The recruiter seemed very impressed with me.
Lee:	Of course he did. They probably can't get anyone for the job.
Paul:	Well, how about the fact that many of Polk's managers started out in sales?
Lee:	That's just his own selling tool. He'd say that to anyone.

Comment on Lee's remarks and perception of selling. Explore ways that Paul could have better handled his interview with the recruiter. Should he follow up?

Making Decisions 1-2:

Anita Ortiz is a recent college graduate looking for a job. One day she overhears a friend of the family, Shawn Davids, telling her mother about the phenomenal growth taking place at her firm, Sheridan Drafting Equipment. Shawn mentions Sheridan's need for more salespeople, and Anita enters the room to join the conversation.

Anita:	I've always been interested in selling.
Shawn:	Are you sure you'd be interested in something like this, Anita?
Anita:	Why not? I had several part-time sales jobs in college. I won a number of sales contests, and once I was voted salesperson of the month.
Shawn:	You'd be the only woman on the sales force.
Anita:	That doesn't bother me.
Shawn:	All of our buyers are men. Would you feel comfortable going into an office or shop with mostly men?
Anita:	Sure I would. I can do the job.
Shawn:	Well, okay, but I just wanted to warn you before you apply.

Explain why Anita should or should not consider selling for Sheridan. Describe the challenges she is likely to encounter if she is hired.

Making Decisions 1-3:

Interview three successful salespeople. Each should have a minimum of three years of full-time selling experience, each should sell a different product or service, and no more than one should sell in a retail store. Learn why each pursues a sales career, the qualities they consider most important for success in selling, and their personal characteristics.

Comment on the characteristics that the three people you chose have in common.

Making Decisions 1-4:

Describe the personal qualities you possess that you feel would be of value to you as a salesperson. Describe the qualities you feel would hamper you.

Making Decisions 1-5:

Select any product as a subject, and do an Internet search for that item. List all of the contacts available for that product, noting how firms or individuals are promoting the sale of their products.

Practice Makes Perfect 1-1:

Play the part of an employee and attempt to convince your supervisor that you need a cellular telephone for your car.

Establishing Meaningful Communication

THE JOB TO BE DONE . . .

Communication is the essence of selling. The sales process cannot progress without meaningful communication. Chapter 2 helps you:

...appreciate the role of communication in selling.

...recognize the verbal and nonverbal channels of communication.

...develop the ability to encode and decode messages.

...appreciate and use the dual roles played by the salesperson and the prospect.

...know how to interpret mixed messages and overcome interference.

...appreciate the predominance of listening in communication.

...know how one's personal conduct communicates.

...recognize the need for receiver-oriented communication.

...understand how the prospect's perception, selective attention, and selective retention affect communication.

COMMUNICATION SKILLS IN PERSONAL SELLING . . .

Good **communication skills** are the essence of selling. Your ability to communicate well with prospects (potential buyers), current customers, and colleagues will be a bigger determinant of your success in selling than any other knowledge or skill. The focus of this chapter is on channels of communication.

Because communication is the essence of selling, the subject is covered before the steps in the selling process.

In all of your selling efforts, your objective is to be sure that prospects understand you and that you understand prospects. Mutual comprehension is what communication is all about. Generally, professionals estimate that only about 10 percent of our communication is in writing, compared to over one-third in speaking. Yet the most significant finding is that to gain mutual comprehension, we must spend a majority of our communicating effort on listening and reading. For salespeople, communication channels include face-to-face meetings, written memos or letters, FAX and voice mail transmissions, and using the Internet.

As a salesperson, you are your firm's most important communicator. Your strengths and weaknesses in this area will reflect upon your employer. If you communicate well, your prospects will think well of your firm.

The Channels of Communication . . .

All people communicate using both verbal and nonverbal **channels of communication**. Verbal communication is an exchange of messages that involves the use of words. Only about 7 percent of our total interaction is verbal, as shown in Figure 2-1. Nonverbal communication is an exchange of messages that involves the use of signals other than words. Most personal interchange is not direct, but coded in a complex language made up of verbal and nonverbal signals. Communication is the process of encoding and decoding these messages.

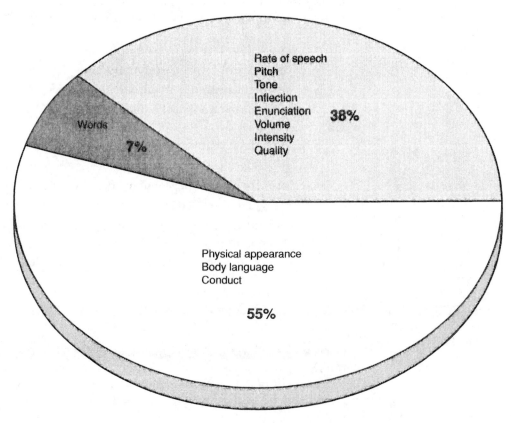

Figure 2-1

The salesperson and the prospect play dual roles when communicating. They are both senders and receivers of messages. Both parties encode and decode messages. The sender encodes a statement by assembling its verbal and nonverbal elements into a single message. The receiver decodes the sender's message by breaking it down into its verbal and nonverbal elements.

Effective communicators are good senders and receivers of coded messages; that is, they excel at both encoding and decoding. No matter how skillful a communicator you become, you will always find room for improvement. Each prospect or contact presents a new challenge, with a whole additional set of verbal and nonverbal signals to understand.

The Communication Process . . .

Of course, messages sent in isolation usually do not produce true communication. Interaction is effective only when the parties are responding to each other. Each provides a message that answers the previous message and moves the conversation forward. Remember that the sender is also a receiver, just as the receiver is a sender. When the receiver decodes a message, a response should be encoded. This response, known as **feedback**, is a necessary part of the four-part communication process:

The communication process flows like this:

1. The first party encodes a message and sends it.
2. The second party receives the message and decodes it.
3. The second party encodes a response (feedback) and sends it.
4. The first party receives the feedback and decodes it.

The codes of feedback may be verbal or nonverbal, voluntary or involuntary. If potential buyers ask questions or make comments in response to your communication, view these signals as forms of feedback. Voluntary feedback is a deliberate attempt to be understood; whereas a response that is reflexive and not controlled by the communicator is involuntary.

If the prospect gives no voluntary feedback, when there is no response or you don't understand the response, you will need to request it. The prospect's contribution will tell you if your messages are understood, your examples are relevant, and the buying motives you appeal to are of interest. This interchange will help you determine whether your pace, content, and style are appropriate. In short, feedback is an indispensable part of effective communication.

VERBAL COMMUNICATION: LANGUAGE . . .

Even though **verbal communication** is only a small percentage of the total package, it has tremendous influence over your selling success. Strong verbal skills enable you to communicate with ease, thus enhancing your selling effort. Any improvement in these skills will have a positive effect on your success as a salesperson.

One way to improve your verbal skills is to expand your vocabulary. The broader your wording, the greater your ability to speak precisely and persuasively. Through the use of verbal communication, you can make exactly the points you wish to make and learn exactly what you need to learn from your prospects. Although there is nothing wrong with adding "a word a day" to your vocabulary, people who are skillful with words have one main thing in common: They are well read. New words introduced in context are easier to understand than isolated words looked up in a dictionary.

Remember that the reason for using verbal language is to communicate, not to intimidate. A good vocabulary is best used in a manner that will be comfortable for your prospects. Use familiar, conversational words rather than unusual, uncommon ones. Choose short, specific words rather than long, vague words.

As you broaden your vocabulary, you will notice more and more words that can have different meanings to different people. If you suspect that a potential buyer's meaning of a word is different from your own, check it out. Even if your definition is the more correct or accepted one, be diplomatic and go along with your prospect's understanding. If you introduce a new word into the conversation, be sure to explain your meaning from the start, eliminating the chance for misunderstanding.

Figurative Language . . .

The skillful use of figurative language can be very effective in selling. **Figurative language** is symbolic; it takes the form of simile, metaphor, proverb, or analogy. A **simile** is a direct comparison that uses the word *like* or *as*, for example, "Skin that is as smooth as silk." A **metaphor** is an implied comparison that assigns the characteristics of one thing to another; to illustrate, "Wouldn't you like to live here in the autumn of your years?" A **proverb** is a short saying that expresses a well-known truth; in this case, "He who hesitates is lost." An **analogy** is a comparison that emphasizes similar functions in dissimilar things; for instance, "Think of this annuity as a small stream. There may not be much water in it, but it flows steadily."

Of course, figurative language has its pitfalls. Since it lends itself to cliché, it can be boring. If you mix metaphors or misquote common sayings, you might succeed only in looking foolish. In addition, figurative language loses its effect entirely if the prospect doesn't "get" it. Simile, metaphor, proverb, and analogy should be used only if they come naturally to you and truly enhance communication with your prospects.

Nonverbal Communication . . .

Nonverbal communication, or paralinguistics, is the exchange of "wordless" messages. It takes place through paralanguage, body language, conduct, and physical appearance. We cover the first three components of nonverbal communication here physical appearance we discuss in detail in Chapter 15.

> His thoughts were slow, his words were few, and never made to glisten.
> But he was a joy, wherever he went. You should have heard him listen.
>
> Anonymous

Paralanguage . . .

Paralanguage, or intonation, is vocal or sonic language, the sound that characterizes our spoken communication. It consists of eight elements:

1. Rate
2. Pitch
3. Tone
4. Inflection
5. Enunciation
6. Volume
7. Intensity
8. Quality

The elements of paralanguage are often referred to as **vocal cues** because they signal meaning. Paralanguage is a very powerful communication tool. These vocal cues can convey meanings that completely contradict the words used in speech. For example, "It's good to see you" can mean "Go away" if spoken in the wrong tone.

Rate. The rate or speed at which we speak relates much about our state of mind, personality, degree of respect for the listener, and attitude toward the subject. Fast talk can be the mark of nervousness, dishonesty, or rudeness, but it can also suggest a sense of excitement and enthusiasm. Slow talk can be the mark of boredom or laziness, but it can also suggest sincerity and thoughtfulness, or the desire to be understood.

Pitch. Pitch is frequency, which we hear as the highness or lowness of a voice. Our pitch can go up or down depending on our mood. When we are calm, we tend to speak at a lower pitch. As our excitement or stress level rises, we speak at a higher pitch. The next time you call your friends on the telephone, notice what their pitch tells you about how they are feeling.

Tone. Tone is the sound or manner of expression that conveys attitude or emotion. Tone can communicate anger, happiness, formality, humor, caring, or sarcasm, completely independent of the words actually spoken. If used effectively, it can also reinforce the words spoken instead of weakening them.

Inflection. Inflection is a change in pitch or tone, which we often think of as expression. A voice without inflection is described as expressionless; it communicates lack of emotion or depressed emotions. We use inflection to emphasize meaningful words in speech. Consider this eight-word sentence: "I didn't say my assistant stole my coat." Now say it eight times, putting emphasis on a different word each time. Notice how the meaning of the sentence changes each time you change emphasis.

Enunciation. Enunciation is the pronunciation and articulation of words. It includes not only accuracy but clarity. If we mispronounce, slur, or mumble our words, we fail to communicate as well as we could. Poor enunciation suggests ignorance, laziness, and lack of consideration for listeners. Word pairs are often slurred to the point where they sound like one word, such as "kinda," "gimme," and "wanna."

Volume. Volume, or loudness, communicates many meanings. We raise our voices when we are surprised, excited, or angry. We lower our voices when we are speaking of serious matters or want to say something confidential.

Intensity. Intensity is the force or concentration of energy behind our voice. It conveys the degree of feeling we have about what we are saying. The more intensity you invest in your statements, the more feeling you project. Again consider that sentence, "I didn't say my assistant stole my coat." Say it mildly, then forcefully. Notice how the feeling you communicate seems to coincide with the degree of intensity behind the statement.

Quality. Quality encompasses the overall attributes of sound. When you listen to music on the radio, you might notice that the sound quality is tinny or flat, or that it is full and resonant. A human voice of poor quality is one that is nasal, harsh, whiny, raspy, or too mellow.

Fillers and Pauses

Most people habitually use **fillers**, words or sounds that fill out a sentence, such as "well," "you know," "uh," and "mmm." These are sometimes called idlers or "tics." They can be a problem when used excessively. Try to avoid using fillers, but remember that an occasional filler is to be expected in normal conversation.

Pauses are more acceptable than fillers, and in fact, should be used for effect. For example, pause momentarily after making key points. This ensures that your comments have their full impact and also allows the prospect some time to absorb your meaning. You should also pause briefly after the prospect speaks. This shows that you are listening and thinking about the prospect's comments.

BODY LANGUAGE . . .

Body language is physical communication. The statement we make with our facial expressions, our handshake, our posture and carriage, our movements, and our response to space and distance all have impact. People read signs of character and attitude in our body language. A sincere smile and firm handshake can indicate friendliness, whereas an avoidance of eye contact can be seen as a sign of insecurity, low self-esteem, or dishonesty.

Unlike its verbal counterpart, nonverbal communication through body language tends to be involuntary. We are usually unaware of the signals we send through our body movements or positioning. Speech is more easily controlled because it is intellectual and conscious, whereas body language is reflexive and unconscious. Properly used, it can be a very effective tool of communication. As a salesperson, you should learn both to interpret your prospect's body language and to control your own. The more you know about this fascinating subject, the better you will communicate with prospects and colleagues alike.

To improve upon your own body language, start by observing yourself. Watch yourself in a mirror or, better yet, on videotape. Ask a friend to film you entering a room for a presentation, greeting a prospect, and shaking the prospect's hand. Take note of your posture, facial expressions, and gestures. You might be surprised to discover aspects of your own body language that you have viewed as undesirable in others.

The Face

The face is the body's most subtle and complex instrument for conveying nonverbal communication. Everything we feel registers on the face. Although most of us can control extreme facial expressions, few of us can control every tiny sign of emotion. Only great actors and accomplished card players can maintain a "poker face" all the time.

The most communicative aspects of the face are the eyes and mouth. The reflexive action of our eyes speaks powerfully, revealing our true sentiments despite our best efforts, both verbal and nonverbal. You can "put on a happy face" and enter a room calling out a cheery greeting, only to have a friend look into your eyes and ask, "What's wrong?" Scientists have discovered that excitement and fond feelings make our pupils dilate; this subtle difference in the appearance of our eyes may be what people see when they "can tell" we're in love or happy about something. Research indicates that strong emotions, such as happiness, sadness, anger, fear, or surprise appear more intensely on the left side of the face.

Eye Contact

Not only do the eyes reveal our feelings, but **eye contact** is the subject of much discussion among body language experts. Making eye contact may indicate interest, affection, or honesty, and avoiding it may indicate boredom, dislike, or discomfort.

Watch a conversation between two people who work together. Even if you don't know them, you will know which person is the superior and which is the subordinate by their relative use of eye contact. The person in the power position will use less eye contact, whereas the subordinate will be concerned with communicating respect and attentiveness.

Psychologists tell us that too much eye contact is aggressive. But for salespeople, too little eye contact can be just as dangerous as too much. Not only does eye contact communicate sincerity, it also shows respect for the person speaking. It conveys the message that you are interested in the prospect's ideas. It reassures the prospect that you are friendly and honest, and that you like the prospect. The most important message you can convey with your eyes is that your prospect is important to you. Maintain eye contact both when you are talking and when you are listening.

Try not to become a man of success, but rather become a man of value.
Albert Einstein

The Mouth

As an instrument of nonverbal communication, the mouth is considered by many to equal the eyes. A prospect with tight or pursed lips indicates dissatisfaction or disagreement. Open lips indicate that the prospect is relaxed, comfortable, or content.

Expressions of the mouth send a host of messages that may enhance or contradict all other messages sent. This is why the **smile** is so powerful and so necessary in selling. The smile is a universal communicator of goodwill. The salesperson who smiles freely is far ahead of the one who is afraid to or who doles them out as if they were priceless commodities.

A sincere smile speaks volumes. Studies indicate that the best facial expressions are the ones that say the person is relaxed, happy, sociable, and sensitive. A smile helps convey all these feelings. With your smile, you show that you are glad to see your prospect and that you are cooperative and agreeable. You convey a positive outlook and general happiness. A warm smile is inviting and open to the world.

As a salesperson, you should make the smile a constant part of your body language. Watch smiling people for inspiration; usually they smile at everyone, their face brightens up the room, their spirits are contagious, and people compliment them for their cheerfulness. Like them, you can learn to smile by consciously practicing until it comes naturally to you. Remind yourself to smile at times you're not accustomed to smiling, such as when passing other employees in the hallway or when encountering someone you greeted earlier in the day. Before long, your smile will be a part of you.

The Handshake

The handshake is the most common and acceptable form of physical contact in our society. In American business, it is the most important aspect of the greeting ritual. As a safe and friendly form of touch, the handshake paves the way for the conversation to come. A proper handshake gets your presentation off to a good start by setting a cordial tone. It communicates confidence, goodwill, and respect for protocol. In contrast, a poor handshake of any kind communicates negative messages. A weak or passive handshake says you are only observing a ritual that means little to you. An extremely firm handshake is just as bad as a fishy one. The salesperson who crushes a prospect's hand until rings puncture the flesh is not being friendly at all. At the very least, this aggressive handshake suggests insensitivity or extreme tension. At worst, it communicates hostility.

Be the first to offer your hand to prospects. Making this initial move is acceptable for women as well as for men in sales. By waiting for the prospect to initiate a handshake, you leave too much in your prospect's control. You should also learn to read your prospect's behavior with regard to handshakes. To refuse or ignore an extended hand is a definite slight.

To improve your handshake, try practicing it with friends, asking them to give their impressions. Here are some general guidelines for the business handshake:

1. Stand facing the prospect and lean slightly forward.
2. Use the right hand. To ensure a full handshake, interlock palms as well as fingertips.

3. Hold the prospect's hand gently but firmly, and shake up and down without "pumping."

4. Maintain eye contact for the duration of the handshake, about three seconds.

If you have a problem with cold or sweaty hands, take measures to correct it before meeting prospects. Arrive for your presentation early enough to visit the restroom and run hot water over cold hands until they are warm. Dry your hands thoroughly and rub them discreetly to keep them warm until you meet the prospect. If your palms sweat, carry a handkerchief or napkin and pat your hands dry before seeing the prospect.

Carry your briefcase in your left hand so that you will be ready to shake hands without a clumsy switch. If the prospect is seated and will not or cannot stand, don't offer your hand. Further, wait until the prospect is close to you before extending your hand so that you won't find yourself standing waving an empty hand in the air while she or he approaches you. Ending your sales call with a handshake is just as important as beginning with one. Not only does a final handshake remind the prospect that you are happy to have paid your visit, it also concludes the meeting with a comfortable ritual.

Aside from the handshake, most other forms of physical contact are inappropriate in business. Back slapping, playful punching, and arm grabbing are unprofessional even among businesspeople who know each other well. Putting an arm around someone's shoulder is much too personal and can suggest sexual harassment among other things.

Posture and Carriage

Posture or **carriage**, the way you hold or carry yourself, is a very revealing form of body language. It communicates attitude, mood, even self-esteem. Alert posture suggests attentiveness, respect, and energy, whereas a slouch suggests boredom, disrespect, and tiredness. A person who stands erect exudes self-confidence, whereas one who slumps emits insecurity and unhappiness. An open posture is a **softener**. It builds rapport between you and your prospect.

Good posture does not have to be stiff. Correct standing posture simply means holding your back and legs straight but relaxed, your feet slightly apart, your head up, shoulders back, and stomach in. Your hands should be down at your sides. If you carry a briefcase, hold it with one hand at your side, never in front of you with both hands.

Good sitting posture should also be relaxed but alert. An overrelaxed posture may indicate a lack of enthusiasm or indifference in what the prospect is saying. Both feet should be on the floor. If you cross your legs, cross them at the knees, and keep the knees bent. You can rest your elbows on the arm of your chair, or rest your hands in your lap or on the table or desk in front of you.

Hands and Arms

When you are not using your hands to help convey a message, you should keep them still, and away from your mouth and chin. One way to keep nervous hands under control is to fold them with all fingers loosely woven. Another idea is to rest one hand, palm up, in your lap and rest the other hand in it. You might also try holding a pencil or piece of paper, as long as you don't fidget with them. If you're standing, you can put one hand in the side pocket of your skirt or pants. Avoid placing your hands on your hips, which can indicate impatience, anger, or aggressiveness.

Although some people feel comfortable with their arms folded, most body language experts read negative meaning in the position. Folded arms might represent a closed attitude, a "wall" designed to block out unwelcome people and ideas. This is certainly not the message you want to communicate in selling. To be on the safe side, avoid folding your arms in front of prospects. Learn to interpret your prospect's folded arms. Is the prospect skeptical, close-minded, or just comfortable? Watch for signs that you are doing a good job in creating interest, such as when the prospect opens his arms, moves closer, or nods.

Motion

Scholars of communication study **kinetics** (motion) and **proxemics** (the human use of distance and space) to gain insights into body language. Our use of motion speaks volumes about our feelings and personality. The fact that we choose to raise a hand to express an idea says something, and the way that we raise it says even more. A smooth, methodical walk suggests calmness, whereas a quick, jerky walk usually indicates tension. Sometimes we use a gesture purposely to achieve a certain effect, and other times we develop habits of motion that may or may not communicate favorable messages. Not all of our movements are voluntary or conscious. The more conscious we are of our own bodies, the more we can learn to control them and use them as we see fit.

Gestures and mannerisms are two categories of motion that prevail in selling-related communication. A **gesture** is a conscious motion used to emphasize or express a point. Gestures help reinforce your words and provide an outlet for nervous energy as well. Many people use hand gestures to punctuate their verbal statements or to act out nonverbal messages.

Head nodding is commonly used as a gesture to say yes or indicate agreement, but it actually can say much more. As a complement to the smile and good eye contact, a nod tells your prospects you are listening to their comments. It shows that you understand the prospect, and it does so without necessitating a verbal interruption. An occasional nod of the head encourages the prospect to keep talking.

Not only should you develop effective use of your own gestures, you should also learn to read those of your prospects. If you are addressing a group of potential buyers, you will probably notice the one who nods. When you see this, you know you have made a connection. Answer this person's nod by making eye contact and nodding in return.

A **mannerism** is a distinctive behavioral trait or habit. Unlike a gesture, it is usually unconscious and tends to communicate negative messages. Mannerisms are typically seen as odd and annoying, and can be distracting to others. Although you might want to learn the effective use of gestures, you should take care to avoid developing mannerisms.

Fingernail biting, lip licking, hair twisting, foot tapping, and pen clicking are just a few of the mannerisms to avoid. If you have any of these habits, break them. You may notice others with annoying mannerisms too. Throat clearing, hand rubbing, leg jiggling, pen chewing, pencil drumming, toe tapping, knuckle cracking, coin-and-key jingling are a few other disruptive habits. Most people have mannerisms, but as a salesperson you should be especially careful to recognize yours and control them. Even seemingly innocent mannerisms can annoy prospects enough to interfere with your selling effort. Mannerisms communicate nervousness, impatience, and insecurity.

Space

Have you ever noticed how people space themselves at approximately equal distances in an elevator? And then when another person boards the elevator, everyone shifts around to equalize the space again?

No matter where we are, we instinctively lay claim to a certain amount of space between ourselves and others. The more immediate the space, the more personal it is. We feel uncomfortable sharing our personal or intimate space with strangers and casual acquaintances. Business executives use their large desks to keep visitors out of their personal space. Psychologists divide this personal space into so-called proxemic zones, as shown in Figure 2-2.

Many sales presentations take place in the **social zone**, with 4 to 12 feet between the prospect and salesperson. This is standard in American business encounters. It is a comfortable distance for people who don't know each other well, and conversation can remain comfortably formal. Other selling encounters, particularly those in which both parties are standing, may occur in the **personal zone**, with the salesperson and prospect as little as 2 feet apart.

Occupying someone else's personal space conveys all kinds of messages. When we see two people standing very close to each other, we assume they are intimates. If we know they are not, we think something must be wrong. Perhaps one person is offending the other by getting too close.

As a salesperson, you must respect your prospect's personal space, whatever its depth. Stay one or two arm's lengths away from prospects until you know for sure how close is comfortable for them.

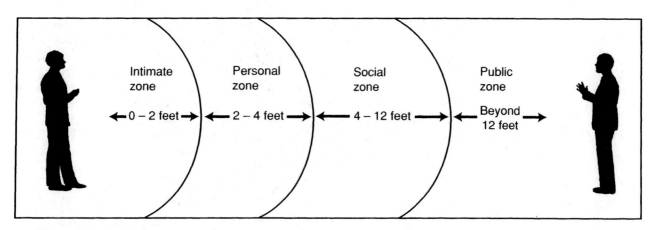

Figure 2-2 Proxemic zones.

Mixed Messages

Body language is extremely powerful. Not only can it reinforce or take the place of our words, it can betray us when we try to disguise or hide our feelings. It does this by contradicting our words. When a prospect says, "I'm very interested in what you have to say," and then gazes at the ceiling while you speak, a mixed message is sent. A **mixed message** is the communication conveyed when two or more conflicting signals are sent by the same person. In this case, the prospect's nonverbal message says he or she is very *bored* with what you have to say.

Jeff Adams

Jeff Adams developed an interest in the medical field while serving as a medical corpsman in the military. After his stint serving Uncle Sam, he returned to his Minnesota roots and worked towards an Associate of Applied Science degree in Sales and Marketing. It was at Inver Hills Community College that Jeff received initial recognition, earning citations for Outstanding Achievement—Sales and Marketing, Motivational and Leadership Award, and Outstanding Student Award. There was little doubt in Jeff's mind that after college he would pursue a career in sales in the medical industry.

He began his career with Zimmer Inc., and soon began to display the same success that he enjoyed at Inver Hills, being selected as "Success Story of 1987" from a field of over 400 salespeople. Jeff was wooed to Biomet, Inc./R. H. Medical, Inc. in 1989, where he remains today as Senior Sales Associate. Biomet is the world's leading manufacturer of reconstructive orthopedic inserts such as hip, shoulder, and knee replacement parts. The firm markets its products through local distributors and sales associates in over one hundred countries worldwide.

Orthopedic devices have gone through a significant change over the past decade, as has the medical profession itself. When one thinks of an implant that the patient will never see again, unless additional surgery is required, the very essence of selling becomes rather intimate. Not only have materials changed, with the inclusion of more exotic metals and plastics, but the industry itself has undergone mergers and buyouts. This field has become highly technical and competitive. Jeff finds that his drive and ambition have helped him achieve recognition within his firm and the trade, as well as financial rewards. Just seeing patients walking or throwing and knowing that his firm's products were instrumental in the results provides him with all of the personal gratification anyone needs. Jeff's is a satisfying and interesting career.

Chances are, you already know how to interpret many mixed messages. When the conflict is between verbal and nonverbal elements, you can usually rely on the saying "Actions speak louder than words." Body language tends to outweigh verbal interaction as a true indicator of the speaker's feelings. This fact of life is no secret. Your prospects will undoubtedly use it to interpret your messages just as you use it to translate theirs.

However, not all mixed messages are so easy to figure out. What if your prospect says how good it is to see you, and then glances at the clock several times during the conversation? Perhaps your future customer is simply pressed for time. And what if two conflicting signals are *both* nonverbal, as when the prospect shakes your hand while looking away from you? Mixed messages are a reality in all communication, and certainly in the selling scenario. It is because of mixed messages that we need to develop sophisticated encoding and decoding skills.

INTERFERENCE . . .

There is a saying, "We cannot not communicate." True, everything we say and do communicates something, but sometimes, accurate interaction is impossible because of interference. **Interference** occurs when the signals we exchange are blocked or distorted. The two main types of interference are barriers and noise.

Signals are blocked by **barriers**, which may be described as active or passive. An **active barrier** blocks communication by way of the action of one party in the effort. For example, a prospect who monopolizes the conversation is creating an active barrier. A **passive barrier** blocks communication by way of a party's inaction or failure to play an active role in the communication process. In this case, a prospect who does not respond to your questions or cues is creating a passive barrier.

Signals can also be distorted by a factor called noise. **Noise** is anything that obscures a signal and can include interferences that have nothing to do with sound. Poor lighting or an uncomfortable temperature can be called "noise" just as easily as the sound of voices in the next room. If an interference makes a signal unclear, it can be called noise.

HOW YOUR CONDUCT COMMUNICATES . . .

Conduct is behavior, the way we act. As a communication tool, the salesperson's conduct should send signals of courtesy and poise. By behaving in a poised and courteous manner, you make the prospect comfortable with you and show respect for the prospect's feelings.

Courtesy is simply politeness based on consideration for the comfort of others. If you are not sure what the prospect needs from you, you can ask the prospect directly. Most prospects will be flattered and pleased with your thoughtfulness.

> Your words are not the message—you are.
>
> Paul LeRoux

Poise, defined literally, is balance. In communication, poise means the ability to maintain composure and manage one's emotions. A poised person does not display extremes of surprise, embarrassment, impatience, anger, or even happiness. Excessive emotion of any kind tends to reflect poorly on the person who displays such feelings in a business setting. By remaining cool-headed and organized when unexpected events happen, you tell your prospect that you are secure no matter what your situation. This puts the potential buyer at ease and builds confidence in you.

Poise and courtesy should be the basis of your overall business conduct. They can help you through many unfamiliar situations. Some situations, however, will come up again and again. Since you will meet people every day, you should know how to handle a business handshake. Furthermore, you should know how to treat others' possessions, and what smoking and gum-chewing communicate.

Personal Possessions . . .

Touching or handling someone else's belongings can be as much an invasion as standing in their personal space. It can even be as offensive as touching the person. Philadelphia attorney John Curtin shares this story:

> One afternoon a salesperson visited me, and before I had a chance to prepare my office for the presentation, the salesperson moved my armchair from the corner of the room to the side of my desk! I was insulted. *I* arrange the furniture in my office, and *I* want to be the one who rearranges it.

The salesperson "took possession" of the attorney's chair, and in fact invaded the prospect's territory as well, by making himself too much at home in it. As a salesperson, you must be sensitive to your prospect's sense of possession, with regard to both belongings and territory. Never spread your papers out on a prospect's desk as if it is your own, or borrow a pen of your choice. These are the prospect's things to give or lend.

Smoking and Gum Chewing . . .

Smoking is offensive to most nonsmokers. If you smoke, light up only when you are away from prospects. If you see no ashtrays around, don't ask the prospect if you can smoke. It is not advisable to smoke even if the prospect does. Pipe smoking has problems of its own even though some nonsmokers consider pipe smoke less offensive than cigarette and cigar smoke. The routine of filling, lighting, and cleaning a pipe detracts from the salesperson's ability to move freely and convey an energetic image.

Gum chewing, like smoking, should be avoided in front of prospects. If you chew gum during the day to freshen your breath, be sure to dispose of it before meeting with potential buyers. The jaw motion and noises associated with gum chewing are distracting and annoying to many people. Besides, this custom is often seen as an immature habit.

TELEPHONE COMMUNICATION . . .

Salespeople spend a great deal of time talking on the telephone. Qualifying leads, confirming appointments, and providing after-the-sale follow-up are just a few of the selling activities handled over the phone. In telemarketing (see Chapter 19), the telephone is the vehicle for part of or even the entire selling process. Telemarketers are defined by their telephone voice. But even if you are not in telemarketing, your telephone voice and general telephone behavior will say a lot about you.

When you are on the telephone, your prospect's sense of hearing works alone, neither aided nor distracted by the other senses. Just as a portrait photograph captures every blemish on the subject's face, the telephone captures every imperfection in the speaker's voice. What seems acceptable in a live voice may be inappropriate over the telephone.

If you would like to improve your telephone voice, start by taping a telephone conversation and playing it back to study it. Your voice should be clear and businesslike, yet pleasant and personal. You will want to correct nasal sounds and any unpleasant habits such as talking too fast, too slow, or too loud. Believe it or not, a smile can be "heard" over the telephone. So, if you want to sound more pleasant, smile when you talk. Standing and gesturing add dimension to your voice as well.

Like your telephone voice, your telephone behavior communicates, too. Never eat or chew gum on the telephone, or call out to someone while talking to your prospect. When answering the telephone, say "hello," not "Jones" or "Yes," both of which sound curt. When calling, identify yourself and your company first, then the reason for your call. Never refuse to identify yourself after asking for the prospect.

If you have an important telephone sales call to make, practice your words once or twice ahead of time. Don't make telephone calls when you are rushed for time or in an improper frame of mind.

> I keep six honest working men (they taught me all I knew). Their names are What and Why and When, and How and Where and Who.
>
> Rudyard Kipling

WRITTEN COMMUNICATION . . .

Although the word *verbal* is often used to indicate "oral" as opposed to "written" communication, it actually refers to anything using words, including written words. As a salesperson, you will have many occasions to communicate in writing with your prospects and business colleagues. Written communication may take the form of letters, memos, e-mail, fax, and promotional literature such as signs and flyers. This aspect of verbal communication should not be ignored.

In all written communication, the care you take with spelling, punctuation, and grammar will communicate as much as the basic message you are trying to convey. If you misspell someone's name, pluralize a word by using the possessive apostrophe, or fail to notice a typo, your mistake will "stick out" and your message will be lost.

All of your correspondence should have a personal touch. Rather than end a letter by saying, "The Crousewell Company welcomes your business," say, "We welcome you as a customer!"

COMMUNICATING WITH THE PROSPECT . . .

Communicating with prospects will be more successful if you remember to keep your communication receiver oriented. In other words, focus completely on the prospect. Place the potential buyer's needs and interests first, and keep the discussion relevant. The more relevant your message, the more receptive your prospect will be. To stay relevant, make sure your examples are about people in similar situations, such as people in the same age group, economic status, education level, and location.

Phrase your sentences with "you" and "yours" instead of "I," "me," and "mine." Don't say, "If I were you, I'd buy my family the large model." Say instead, "Since your family is growing, you might want to consider the large model."

Try to match your prospect's style and manner as closely and comfortably as possible. Be prepared to meet the potential buyer's energy level and modulate your rate of delivery. Practice "body echo" by adjusting your body language to match the future customer's style. Consider your prospect's age, education, and experiences, and know how to speak his or her "language."

You may need to become familiar with industry **jargon**. Salespeople are expected to know the prospect's business as well as their own, and any ignorance of specialized language will be noticed. You may also need to set aside your own jargon to communicate with consumers who are not in your industry. For example, if you are demonstrating a stereo system to a customer who is unfamiliar with such equipment, you may have to explain many of the terms. Audiophiles will not need such an explanation.

Before you can achieve receiver-oriented communication, you need to know a few things about the way prospects obtain your signals. Comprehension is influenced by perception, selective attention, and selective retention.

**Figure 2-3 How many squares do you see? You're right!
Perception is an individual phenomenon. We all see
things differently. Some of us see 16 squares, whereas
others only see one, and still others see one of many possible configurations of the 16 small squares, perhaps
arriving at a number that totals as high as 22. The question isn't how many squares exist, it's how many do you
see. Your task as a salesperson is to determine how the
prospect perceives your product in terms of benefits,
value, and purpose.**

Perception . . .

Perception is the meaning we attach to a given stimulus based on our personal insight. Our perceptions of products, events, and people are influenced
by lessons learned through experience. If you perceive a new acquaintance as
warm and friendly, your insight is based on similar encounters with other people who turned out to be warm and friendly. A prospect who perceives your
product as dangerous, useless, or full of problems does so on the basis of personal experience or that of a trusted source.

As Figure 2-3 points out, perception is highly individual. No two people
perceive things in the same way. Because of this fact, communication with
prospects can break down. As a salesperson, you must take care to know your
prospect's perception and correct any wrong impressions.

Selective Attention . . .

People view the world through a psychological filter. They take notice of information that meets their needs and interests, and they ignore or fail to notice
everything else; that is, attention is selective. For example, we may notice
pushy salespeople because they irritate us, yet fail to be aware of those that
are non-assertive and polite.

If your prospect is not shopping for your product, the filter of **selective
attention** will be in place. A prospect's selective attention filter not only
screens out salespeople and their messages, it places a limit on the prospect's
attention span. You will have a very short time to convince potential buyers
that they should consider your message. Some salespeople believe that attention is at its height during the beginning and ending of a presentation, and
they convey their most important messages at those times.

> We can't all be heroes, because somebody has to sit on the curb and clap as they go by.
>
> Will Rogers

Selective Retention . . .

Like attention, retention is also selective. We remember information that meets our needs and interests, and we block out or forget everything else. We consciously or unconsciously evaluate new information all the time. If we don't think the information is worth remembering, we fail to "register" it. We retain or ignore information on the basis of how relevant it seems to us and how well it coincides with our beliefs.

As a salesperson, you will have to know how to convey messages that seem important, relevant, and agreeable to the prospect in order to penetrate the **selective retention** barrier. If the potential buyer's decision does not come immediately, repeated communications over time may help gradually wear down the barrier.

LISTENING: THE KEY TO EFFECTIVE COMMUNICATION . . .

Listening well is more important than speaking well. This truth about communication is doubly certain in selling, where good listening is vital to success. Listening should make up at least 80 percent of your communication with prospects, especially early in sales interviews, when you need to determine needs. Figure 2-4 offers listening guidelines and provides a list of poor listening habits.

Difficulties in listening arise because thought is faster than speech. We can take in about 800 words per minute, but we can speak only about 125. Because our mind processes spoken information faster than the speaker sends it, we think ahead. We know the end of the speaker's sentence, so our mind wanders off, and we miss the beginning of the speaker's next spoken thought. Practiced listeners are able to overcome this discrepancy. They use the extra time to interpret the speaker's nonverbal signals. Instead of allowing your mind to wander, you keep it firmly on the speaker's whole message, the message the speaker transmits through all communication channels.

Since communication is both verbal and nonverbal, listening means taking in more than audible signals. Part of listening will include observation of your prospect's symbolic communication, for example. **Symbolic communication** is the self-revealing statement a prospect makes through nonverbal behaviors that are meant to be noticed. Potential buyers communicate symbolically through the cars they drive, the houses they choose to live in, the way they dress, and the way they decorate their offices.

> You win some, you lose some, and some get rained out, but you gotta suit up for them all.
>
> J. Askenberg

A Word About Projection . . .

Projection is a psychological term for the unconscious attribution of our own needs and feelings to others. Projection is an easy behavior to fall into. A feeling that you understand your prospect thoroughly is only one step away from an assumption that the potential buyer has the same needs and priorities as you. Because it dispenses with questions, projection destroys communication.

Avoid projecting your feelings onto your prospects. The things that are interesting and important to you may not be at all the same to the prospect. Resist the urge to emphasize product features that fascinate you before you have found out whether they will have a similar effect on the prospect. No matter how much you think you have in common with future customers, remember that the person with whom you are communicating is an individual with highly personal tastes and desires. If we were all alike, there would be no need for marketing research to determine consumer needs. Indeed, there would be no need for salespeople.

You Decide!

As part of her sales training for a cosmetics house, Sabrina is told of the importance of body language. The trainer explains that enthusiastic expressions of surprise and excitement do wonders in selling the products, especially when working with older customers. Four ways of using body language are demonstrated: 1) raising both arms in the air with palms extended upward; 2) placing the palm of your right hand firmly against the upper right side of your head, while slowly nodding affirmatively; 3) placing the tips of your left finders lightly on your left cheek, making little clucking noises while smiling; and, 4) saying very slowly, while smiling, "you look simply wonderful."

On her first assignment to a major department store, Sabrina is anxious to practice all that she has learned. Her first afternoon goes quite well, but towards the end of her shift a particularly homely woman asks for help. While applying a sample, Sabrina remembers her training, but questions whether she should use body language and flattery on a person with whom it might not be appropriate. She is even concerned that this customer might take offense. **You decide!**

Chapter 2 • Establishing Meaningful Communication

Good Listening Guidelines

1. Anticipate the customer's listening problems, such as ambient noise or interruptions.

2. Summarize what the customer is saying.

3. Analyze what is not being said or what is implied.

4. Encourage feedback to clarify both what is said and what is not said.

5. Listen for voice patterns to disclose attitudes and emotions.

6. Scan for conflicts in body language.

Poor Listening Habits

1. Preoccupation with hearing yourself talk.

2. Predicting what the customer will say and formulating a response in advance.

3. Letting bias or stereotyping influence translation of message.

4. Tuning out because information is too simple or too difficult.

5. Giving in to distractions, including daydreaming.

6. Assigning improper emphasis based on the customer's status.

Figure 2-4

Your Dual Role in Communication . . .

As a salesperson, you are responsible for effective communication with your prospects. Your responsibility spans all four parts of the communication process. In your dual role as both sender and receiver, you must decode as well as encode messages, and you must give as well as seek out and interpret feedback.

Take responsibility for any potential communication failure. When you need feedback from the prospect, say, "Just to make sure I've explained things correctly, would you give me your interpretation?" This technique can also be used when you are the receiver and wish to give feedback: "I'm not sure I understand you. Could you explain it again?"

Rather than waiting until the end to summarize your presentation, review each section as you conclude it, and solicit feedback along the way. Remember, too, that your prospect may need input. Potential buyers will want to know that you understand their needs. Answer their questions, paraphrase their remarks, and confirm your agreement when they come to conclusions.

Never take it for granted that the prospect is decoding your message correctly. Even when you are in the encoding position, take an active role in helping the prospect decode your message. Rephrase your sentences, use examples, and ask for the prospect's interpretation of your message. When you are in the decoding position, paraphrase the prospect's sentences and ask plenty of questions.

Summing It Up . . .

Salespeople need good communication skills. This chapter focused on the role of communication in selling and the aspects of the communication process. The ability to communicate clearly and effectively is as important for success in selling as any other skill or quality you can possess. Strong communication skills enable you to deliver messages your prospects understand and interpret their messages for what they really mean. The communication process involves encoding, decoding, noise, and feedback, and you must be active in each part of the process.

Verbal and nonverbal channels of communication include words, paralanguage, body language, and conduct. The messages we send through our tone of voice, rate of speech, eyes, lips, handshake, and posture and carriage combine to form our nonverbal communication, and when these messages contradict our words, the receiver attaches greater importance to them than to what we say. Skilled salespeople are good listeners, send receiver-oriented messages, realize that a potential buyer's attention and retention are selective, and avoid projecting personal feelings onto their prospects.

Key Concepts and Terms . . .

active barriers
analogy
barriers
body language
carriage
channels of communication
communication skills
conduct
courtesy
decoding
encoding
enunciation
eye contact
feedback
figurative language
fillers
gesture
inflection
intensity
interference
jargon
kinetics
mannerism
metaphor
mixed message
noise

nonverbal communication
paralanguage
passive barriers
pauses
perception
personal zone
pitch
poise
posture
projection
proverb
proxemics
quality
rate
selective attention
selective retention
simile
smile
social zone
softener
symbolic communication
tone
verbal communication
vocal cue
volume

Building Skills . . .

1. Explain the differences between verbal and nonverbal communication.
2. Describe the four-part communication process.
3. Contrast language and paralanguage.
4. Define body language, and explain why it is harder to control than verbal language.
5. Analyze the communication roles of the face, eye contact or failure to make eye contact, posture, and common gestures.
6. Describe mannerisms and why they should be avoided.
7. Explain proxemics, or personal space, and the effect of occupying another person's space.
8. Describe mixed messages.
9. Contrast the two main types of interference.
10. Critique the communication presented by personal conduct.
11. Describe perception and the ways we develop our perceptions.
12. Contrast selective attention and selective retention, including the ways that they act as barriers to communication.
13. Compare the salesperson's dual roles in communication, describing how you might simultaneously encode and decode a message for prospects.
14. Define symbolic communication by citing some examples.
15. Explain the concept of receiver-oriented communication.

Making Decisions 2-1:

Stanley Schweitzer recently started selling for Carisona Automated Products, a marketer of remote-control garage door openers. Early one morning as he leaves for work, Stanley sees his neighbor, Irene Feeney, getting out of her car to shut her garage door by hand. What an opportunity! Stanley immediately decides to pull into Irene's driveway and tell her about the Carisona garage door opener.

Stanley:	Hello Irene. How are you?
Irene:	Fine, Stan, and you?
Stanley:	Very good. I switched jobs recently. I'm now a salesperson for Carisona.
Irene:	That's great. (Irene glances at her two children approaching the car.)
Stanley:	As a matter of fact, that's why I stopped. When I saw you getting out of your car to shut the garage door, I thought I'd stop and tell you about the safety and convenience offered by the Carisona automatic garage door opener.
Irene:	(Taking a backward step) No thanks. With my luck it would break and my car would be stuck inside the garage!
Stanley:	These openers are very dependable, Irene. Besides, you could still open the door by hand.

Irene:	(Hesitating, then opening the rear passenger door of her car) No, I don't think so, Stan. (To the children) In you go, kids.
Stanley:	Okay, but let me get some literature out of my car. You can read it and I'll stop by again.
Irene:	(Hurrying around to the driver's side of the car) No need to. But thanks for stopping. It's always good seeing you.

Evaluate what Irene was attempting to "tell" Stanley. Describe Irene's nonverbal communication.

Making Decisions 2-2:

In your next five face-to-face conversations, make note of the physical distance between you and the other party. Examine the ways that this distance varied between the types of people you were talking with and the subject matter. Develop a model that correlates proxemics with the communication and the communicators.

Making Decisions 2-3:

The next time you have a face-to-face conversation with someone who is talking about something that doesn't interest you, devise a way to improve your listening ability. Afterwards, ask yourself if it worked. Analyze whether your effort made the conversation more enjoyable or more trouble.

Making Decisions 2-4:

List several products you intend to buy in the near future. Have you noticed or paid attention to commercial messages for them that you didn't notice or pay attention to before you were shopping for them? Describe several of the commercials, including when and where you last saw them.

Practice Makes Perfect 2-1:

Give three different meanings to the exact same sentence by varying the intensity of emphasis in each.

Practice Makes Perfect 2-2:

Use body language to convey impatience, anxiety, relief, anger, surprise, fear, boredom, disrespect, tiredness, and happiness.

Locating and Identifying Prospects

THE JOB TO BE DONE . . .

Selling involves turning prospects into customers. One of the primary tasks of salespeople, then, is to develop a substantial stable of potential buyers. Chapter 3 teaches you to:

...understand the basics of qualifying a prospect.

...appreciate the need for continuous prospecting.

...see how prospecting fits into the overall selling process.

...learn how to plan and organize your prospecting efforts.

...explore the specifics of various prospecting systems.

...identify and concentrate on the high-volume and high-probability prospect.

...recognize past and present customers as possible sources of future sales.

PROSPECTING . . .

Welcome to prospecting, the first of the seven steps in the personal selling process as illustrated in Figure 3-1. **Prospecting** is the process of seeking and finding persons who qualify as potential buyers of the product or service being sold. Successful prospecting entails spreading your sales net over as many potential buyers as possible.

Unless you have a prospect to call, your persuasive and communicative abilities won't mean much. Nor will your visual presence, or any of the techniques associated with discovering what motivates a person to buy, making

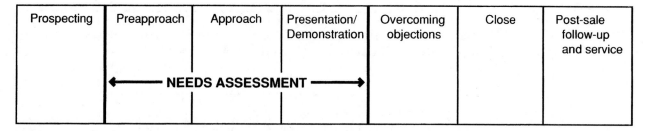

Prospecting	Preapproach	Approach	Presentation/ Demonstration	Overcoming objections	Close	Post-sale follow-up and service
	← NEEDS ASSESSMENT →					

Figure 3-1

sales presentations, overcoming resistance to buying, or closing the sale. "You can't be a successful salesperson without good prospects," says Pennsylvania car salesperson Bob Sugg. And you can't hope to have good prospects unless you know how to locate them.

You will recall from Chapter 1 that a salesperson engages in many activities aside from personal selling. Much of your schedule will go into traveling, attending meetings, and waiting in reception rooms, yet the only activity that directly contributes to your income is selling. To make the most of this situation, you need to prospect as economically as possible; you can't afford to invest your limited selling time and financial resources in just anyone. An estimated two-thirds of all industrial sales calls are made to the wrong person. One purpose of this chapter is to help you learn to call on the *right* person, by explaining how to determine which people you want to see and how to find them. In this chapter, we cover all the major methods of prospecting, along with some basic rules of prospecting to keep in mind.

Qualifying the Lead . . .

The first and most crucial step in prospecting is **qualifying**, which is the process of classifying a lead as a prospect or nonprospect. Although the terms *lead* and *prospect* are often used interchangeably, they are not the same. A **lead** (or contact) can be almost anyone: someone who visits your store or showroom, a person whose name is given to you by a friend, or an individual who calls you on a recommendation. Leads are also individuals at companies who have responded to an advertisement. A **prospect**, on the other hand, is someone who qualifies as a potential buyer. Since your personal selling time is scarce, you need to ferret out the true prospects: those who should be the target of your sales efforts because they have the greatest probability of buying.

Qualifying is determining whether a lead meets the three criteria required of a prospect: need, ability, and authority to buy. In some selling situations, almost everyone you meet will be a prospect; in others, very few will be. But all legitimate prospects have these three qualities in common:

1. Prospects have a current need that your product or service can satisfy.
2. Prospects have the ability, that is, the financial resources, to buy your product or service.
3. Prospects have the authority to make the purchase or place the order.

> As you wander through life, brother, whatever be your goal, keep your eye upon the donut and not upon the hole.
>
> Anonymous

Only when a lead has been properly qualified should you attempt a sales presentation. You should never try to persuade a person to buy a product that isn't needed or is unaffordable. One interesting aspect of prospecting is that sometimes you come across people who qualify but don't believe they do, and vice versa. Some people might think they have both the need and the ability to buy your product, when you believe they have neither; others might think they have neither the need nor the ability, when you believe they have both.

Avoiding Stereotyping . . .

First meetings don't always provide a complete picture of your leads, so it's best not to qualify a lead until you have investigated further. The salesperson who qualifies by stereotype makes a big mistake. Even if experience tempts you to indulge in stereotyping, avoid the impulse. Never assume, for instance, that women can't handle heavy or mechanical products, or that young people can't afford luxuries. These kinds of assumptions prevent you from selling to true prospects who don't happen to fit a certain mold. Before you know it, you will be approaching all sales encounters with a closed mind and will defeat yourself with your own assumptions.

Past circumstances, like stereotypes, can be misleading. People you once qualified as nonprospects may have become prospects since you last saw them, so it's a good idea to stay informed. Perhaps their income has increased and they can afford products that were previously beyond their means. When people move into a higher income bracket, they usually like to "trade up" to merchandise that comes at a higher price and offers better quality. You might find that a former nonprospect is ready at last to buy one of the luxury condos you sell.

Uncovering Need . . .

One way to discover a business lead's need for your materials and components is to determine what kinds of products the company makes or sells. You can do this by learning the firm's four-digit Standard Industrial Classification (SIC) number. The Standard Industrial Classification system, developed by the U.S. government to facilitate the collection and dissemination of business and industrial information, classifies each business according to the major industry group into which it falls and the products it manufactures. The SIC number of a firm that manufactures inorganic pigments is 2816. The first two digits denote the industry group (chemicals). The third number indicates a subcategory of the chemicals industry (industrial inorganic chemicals), and the fourth number specifies the products manufactured (inorganic pigments).

If you gather basic information on a business at the outset, you can avoid the wasted effort of approaching a lead whose finished products don't match your materials in quality, or who doesn't even manufacture or sell products that require your components. Why try to sell nail care supplies to a beauty salon that doesn't offer manicures? If you sell a product that is to be resold by a retailer, you will need to learn something about the merchandise carried by your retailer leads. Retailers usually offer product lines that are similar in cost and quality. You can simply browse through a clothing store, for example, to see if your line of suits would fit in. You should also observe the store's clientele, sales staff, and general atmosphere.

Qualifying Individuals . . .

Qualifying individual customers requires careful listening and observation. Shoppers at your car dealership may give verbal or nonverbal clues to how much they are willing or able to spend. They may state their spending limit in no uncertain terms or just look away in disappointment after reading a sticker price. You can save yourself time and trouble by getting a picture of a lead's financial ability and spending limits as early as possible.

Just because a customer seems focused on a particular car, don't assume you can begin your presentation without knowing the shopper's budget. A flashy red $40,000 sports coupe is a natural attention-getter, but most people who admire it are "lookers," not "buyers." You would be very frustrated indeed if you attempted to make a serious presentation to everyone whose eyes widen at the sight of leather bucket seats. Give yourself a break and find out a shopper's financial intentions first, then direct the person to a model in an appropriate price range.

If you sell financial services such as investments or insurance, you need to know a lead's financial ability early in order to offer a package that best suits the person's needs. Rather than asking directly for yearly income and savings figures, you would be better off asking your lead to complete a questionnaire that asks for this sensitive information.

Occasionally, you may feel comfortable asking customers how much they can spend. But aside from situations like the ones described, such a direct question is usually inadvisable because the answer might reveal something about their budget that they do not wish to reveal. Direct questioning is also not recommended when the product's price is negotiable. It works best when you are comfortable with the prospect, your product comes in different and clearly stated price lines, and the purchase is obviously a minor part of the customer's budget.

Direct or indirect questioning is best done early in the interview. This will allow you not only to qualify your lead in short order but also to get an honest answer more easily. If you leave the financial question unanswered until the end of a presentation, your customer will be more likely to use "no money" as an objection to buying.

> Don't worry what's ahead. Go as far as you can see. From there you can see farther.
>
> B. T. Gaigus

The True Prospect Profile . . .

A great way to increase your accuracy in qualifying leads is to create a **true prospect profile** and use it as a guide. The true prospect profile is a composite picture of the ideal prospect, complete with all the characteristics that a "perfect" buyer might have.

To compose such a profile, you would describe in detail the geographic, demographic, and psychographic traits of the ultimate prospect. The **geographic** profile would tell you what part of the country this person or business calls home (the Midwest, the Southeast, the farmbelt, the Rocky Mountains, and so on), as well as the environment and population (rural, 5,000; urban, 1 million plus; suburban, 10,000). **Demographics** would tell you the prospect's age, sex, income, occupation, level of education, ethnic background, and household life-cycle position (dependent, single, married with dependent children, or married with grown children). **Psychographics** would tell you a prospect's lifestyle, interests, and activities, as well as opinions, self-image, and reference (social) group memberships (student organizations, sports teams, professional societies).

Once you have assembled these ideal characteristics, you will have a profile of your dream prospect. The more closely your leads match this profile, the better your chances of helping them buy.

Remember: If true need and ability do not exist, the lead is not a prospect. It's better not to make a sale than to sell to a nonprospect because the overall outcome of such a sale will be negative. Salespeople who sell to nonprospects not only harm their own reputation and damage their chances for long-run success but also discredit their profession.

PROSPECT CATEGORIES . . .

Contacts or leads can be placed into three categories for qualifying purposes: (1) nonprospects, (2) prospects who have not yet purchased, (3) current users (the active current market). Here are some points to keep in mind when qualifying.

Nonprospects may be the largest for your product or service. Nonprospects are not the target of your selling efforts. They don't meet the criteria of prospects. Either they have no need for the product or they can't afford it. This category includes not only leads who don't qualify as prospects but also past purchasers who will never need to purchase again.

You may encounter leads who have no need or ability to buy your product, but who don't realize it. You should not try to sell to these people even if they give you the impression that they could be persuaded to buy. If you sell to them, they will inevitably discover the purchase was a mistake and will dislike you for having sold it to them. Furthermore, you will have perpetuated the unfortunate image of salespeople as unconcerned about the people to whom they sell.

Prospects who have not yet purchased are those who meet the need and ability criteria, but are not currently buying from you or the competition. A "not yet" prospect sees no need to purchase your product or service, or continually defers the buying decision. Your task is to generate **primary demand**, that is, to create a desire for the type of product, not a particular brand. The most common objection to buying raised by prospects in this category is "no need." They feel the product would serve no useful purpose. More often than not, the lack of perceived need is all that keeps these true prospects from enjoying the benefits of your product.

Current users, or buyers in the active current market, are those who repeatedly buy the product or service you sell. They have purchased either your brand or that of a competitor, and they intend to purchase again. Since primary demand is already established, your task is to generate **selective demand**, which is the desire to own your brand rather than a competitor's brand. Your efforts will include attempts to attract customers away from the competition as well as the ongoing attempt to keep current customers loyal.

The High-Volume Customer . . .

There is a well-known axiom in marketing called the **80-20 principle**. It states that 20 percent of your customers account for 80 percent of your business, and 80 percent of your customers account for 20 percent of your business. The percentages may vary somewhat from one situation to the next, but the basic principle always holds.

About 20 percent of your customers will generally fall into the "heavy user" category. They are repeat customers or **high-volume purchasers**, and they provide you with about 80 percent of your income. If you sell for a landscaping service, you might find that a handful of construction firms account for most of your employer's business; if you sell power tools, you might find that a long list of small businesses and consumers accounts for only a thin slice of your sales revenue.

High-volume customers may very well be keeping you or your firm in business. It's only natural that you pay extra attention to them. Although in principle all customers should be treated equally, in practice the high-volume customer is given special treatment. The wise salesperson will keep that customer's business by offering custom payment or delivery schedules, special service arrangements, and plenty of personal attention.

We mentioned in Chapter 1 that a single account can produce such a large volume of revenue that you or your firm can virtually make a living from that one source of income. However, nothing is forever. Companies go out of business, are merged with other firms, and even take their business to competing sellers. Remember, too, that key decision makers in a client firm go through changes that are equally threatening to your livelihood. They are promoted out of buying capacity, accept positions with other firms, even retire. Regardless of how lucrative your present accounts might be, you should always be trying to open more accounts, especially high-volume ones.

> In putting off what one has to do, one runs the risk of never being able to do it.
>
> Charles Baudelaire

Call on Your Best Prospects First . . .

In an effective prospecting system, new prospects will materialize even as you call on current prospects. How do you make the most of this happy coincidence? The best way to use your ever-evolving prospect list is to establish priorities based upon their likelihood of buying. One way to do this is to classify potential buyers as either "loose leads" or "tight leads." **Loose leads** are not likely to buy in the near future. Don't focus your efforts on them. **Tight leads** intend to purchase the product soon. Prioritize them, call on the most promising ones first, and work down the list.

You should call on prospects in order of their probability of purchasing for several reasons:

1. You need income, and earning it will be easier and faster if you call on your best prospects first.

2. If your prospecting system is effective, you might never have to call on prospects that show only a slim chance of buying. You will be constantly providing yourself with a fresh list of high-probability contacts, and pushing marginal prospects to the bottom of the list.

3. Your attitude and self-confidence will remain strong. Because your sales revenue is directly connected to the quality of prospects on whom you call, you can keep your morale and motivation high by calling only on prospects who can contribute to your healthy sales volume.

4. Time, or the scarcity of it, dictates that you plan your schedule economically. Because your work is divided among many nonselling activities, your limited selling time must be devoted to your best prospects.

Of course, when you call on prospects, logistics and practicality should play a part in your plans. For example, if you visit a high-probability prospect in an out-of-the-way neighborhood and another prospect is located next door to him or her, you should call on that prospect too, even if this person is low on your probability list. You might handle a sales trip to a distant city similarly, calling on all prospects in the area regardless of their probability of buying. If, in fact, the higher-probability prospects are found elsewhere, this may be your most practical course if you don't plan to return to the area for quite some time.

DEVELOPING AN EFFECTIVE PROSPECTING SYSTEM . . .

The development of an effective prospecting system is a wise investment of your time and money. No matter what process you choose, any routine that constantly provides a fresh list of high-probability prospects is a good one and will pay for itself many times over.

The following list shows various prospecting methods:

1. The cold canvass
2. The endless chain

3. The center of influence
4. The personal observation
5. The news
6. Bird dogs
7. Direct mail and telephone prospecting
8. Past and present customers
9. Local organizations and events
10. Seminars
11. Miscellaneous sources
12. Networking

None of these prospecting methods is mutually exclusive. Each works well in combination with others and, in fact, are put to best use in this manner. One method alone cannot be expected to generate a sufficient number of prospects. As a new salesperson, you should try each method described in this section to see which works best for you. Perhaps one method deserves more of your time, money, and attention because it is more fruitful than the others.

The Cold Canvass . . .

The **cold canvass** method of prospecting, sometimes referred to as random calling or cold calling, is used commonly in both industrial and consumer selling. Cold canvassing means calling on leads without the benefit of pregathered information that would help qualify them as prospects. You may have read a newspaper article about the person you're visiting or received a tip from another salesperson, but you have not conducted a fact-finding campaign. In cold canvassing, you know little or nothing about a lead beyond the minimum needed to justify your visit.

Cold canvassing also means calling on leads without an invitation or appointment. "Dropping in cold" has been called the scourge of selling, and not without reason. Some salespeople dislike cold canvassing because it makes them feel like intruders. Others find that prospects won't make time for unannounced sales visits. Still others think the method is only for beginners who have not yet refined better methods. Unannounced visits do sound risky, yet most salespeople recognize the need to make them, and many claim cold canvassing is their single best source of prospects. Fans of cold canvassing say that the most important thing they can do is get their names in front of as many people as possible, and this method does just that. The cold canvass can be made in person, by mail, and on the telephone. (Direct mail and telephone prospecting, discussed later in the chapter, can be variations of the cold canvass.)

Cold Canvassing and the Law of Large Numbers

As chancy and time consuming as it sounds, the cold canvass method of prospecting is supported by sound theory, the law of large numbers. Under this statistical theorem, the probability of a particular outcome in a future event can be predicted from the outcomes seen in a large number of past events.

Consider **market saturation** as calculated by students of introductory marketing. If the total number of potential users of a product is 20 million, and the total number of actual users is 10 million, then the market is 50 percent saturated. The remaining 50 percent of the people are prospects. If 30 percent of all homeowners in the United States own a certain appliance, and anyone who owns a home qualifies as a prospect for this appliance, then 70 percent of America's homeowners are prospects.

Of course, market saturation statistics are beyond the realm of the individual salesperson, but the law of large numbers is at work nonetheless. The principle can be used to predict the salesperson's rate of success from cold canvassing. In the homeowner example, a salesperson who sells the appliance in question can assume that about 70 percent of the leads contacted will be true prospects. Similarly, if statistics show that three of five small businesses intend to computerize their operations within the next two years, a microcomputer salesperson should find a receptive audience in a majority of the small firms that are visited "cold."

For some products or services, one of every two people will be a prospect; for others, it will be one of every two thousand. If only one in a hundred families will use your product, cold canvassing door to door would be a waste of time. By using the law of large numbers, you can determine whether cold canvassing will be worth your time. The greater the chances of any one person being a prospect, the greater your chances of success with this method.

Applications of the Cold Canvass

Although cold canvassing alone will probably not generate the number of prospects you need for success, it can be applied to your benefit in other ways. You should never feel guilt or embarrassment if the person or firm you cold canvass turns out not to be a prospect.

Cold canvassing, thanks to its often unpredictable nature, frequently yields unexpected rewards. You might use cold calls to fill in the gaps that invariably exist in your schedule, knowing you have little to lose and surprisingly much to gain. For example, if you are a salesperson for building supplies on your way back from a construction site, and you notice another house under construction, you should stop. You might discover that the builder has yet to purchase the materials you sell, and through your impromptu visit and short presentation you make a sale. Or suppose you have just completed an appointment in another city. It's 3 p.m., and your train doesn't leave until 5:30. Your appointment was with a firm located in the middle of an industrial park with dozens of companies in related businesses. All of them are prospects. This is a prime opportunity for some cold canvassing. Make unannounced visits to several of the larger, more successful appearing firms in the park. Even if you meet with only limited success, you will have made wise use of your extra time. Besides, one successful call can easily compensate for six that were unsuccessful. For many salespeople, a high percentage of new accounts comes from cold calling.

When using the cold canvass method, you can save yourself a lot of time and energy by recognizing that demographics and geographics often go hand in hand. For example, the people who reside in an upper-class suburb of a large city are far more likely to have the income needed to purchase an expensive luxury than are those who reside in or near economically depressed areas. Incomes, occupations, and levels of education all have a way of being correlated with geographic area.

Weaknesses of the Cold Canvass

The cold canvass method of prospecting has several weaknesses, not the least of which is the salesperson's unfamiliarity with the prospect. Chapter 4 discusses the importance of knowing as much in advance about your prospect as possible, and cold canvassing breaks that rule. Cold leads may feel slighted when it becomes obvious that you have spent little or no time learning about them or their business. If the prospect's firm has recently made headline news for the introduction of a new product and you enter the office unaware of this, the prospect may well feel insulted or think you are not very smart. (Imagine what a big-league baseball player must think while signing an autograph book and the celebrity hound of a fan looks up and says, "What position do you play, anyway?")

Cold leads might also be offended if you mispronounce their name or the name of their company. Even the most pleasant people can react badly to this offense if they're caught on a bad day.

Probably the worst thing a salesperson can say on a cold call is, "I just happened to be in the area, so I thought I'd drop by." Prospects are almost sure to recoil at such an opening remark. This seemingly casual comment says between the lines that you attach very little importance to your prospects and their business. The prospect wasn't important enough to go out of your way for, and if you didn't have some free time to fill in you wouldn't be here now. If you make the mistake of saying this, don't be surprised to hear that the contact is too busy to talk to you. If you do nothing to learn about your prospects and show no consideration for their schedule, why should they bother to talk to you? The challenge of cold canvassing is in showing potential buyers how important their business is and proving your call was worth a special effort.

Many salespeople resist calling on unfamiliar prospects when they can just as easily concentrate on old, familiar ones. This resistance can be described as an inertia not to prospect, and no prospecting method will suffer more from it than the cold canvass.

> Why not go out on a limb? Isn't that where all of the fruit is?
>
> Frank Sculley

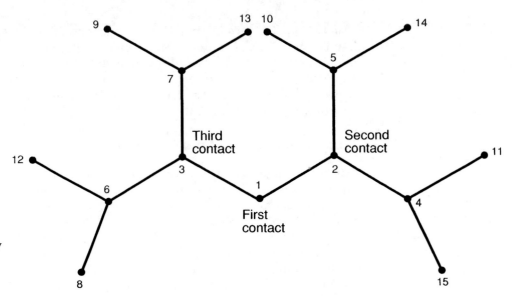

Figure 3-2 The endless chain. This diagram shows how one contact can lead to additional prospects.

The Endless Chain . . .

The **endless chain** is one of the most commonly used prospecting methods and involves the least amount of effort. All it requires is asking your present prospects for referrals. As can be seen from the diagram in Figure 3-2, the endless chain develops like a tree. Your list of referrals grows geometrically, as do the branches of a tree. First there is one referral, then two grow from that, then two from each of those, and so on. Each time you make a call, you can add to your endless chain simply by asking your prospect to name two or three other people who might need your product or service.

The endless chain method can be used successfully even if you have not managed to sell to your present lead. You may call on leads who turn out not to be prospects because they recently purchased your product elsewhere, or because they don't meet the criteria required to be a prospect. Nevertheless, you should seize the opportunity to ask for the names of other possible prospects.

Whether or not your leads turn out to be prospects or even buyers, you will need to convince them that you have something to offer the people you are asking them to name. They will not give you the names of friends or business associates unless they consider you reputable and capable of satisfying their needs. Most people realize that friends and acquaintances are not fond of having salespeople referred to them unless they truly need and can afford what the salesperson is selling.

Since your best referrals come from satisfied customers, your endless chain will work better if you put more effort into obtaining leads from people to whom you have sold than from people to whom you have not sold. Buyers are far more likely to give you a few names if they are pleased with what you have done for them. They may even feel that they are doing their friends and colleagues a favor. And if they are enjoying the benefits of your product, why shouldn't they want others to enjoy the same? When you receive leads from current customers and are told, "Be sure and mention my name," you can be certain that these customers are happy to supply the names, and see themselves as performing a service.

Narrow the Prospect's Thinking

For a more effective endless chain, you should try to narrow the prospect's thinking when you ask for referrals. In other words, give your present prospects a few clues to help them focus on the more promising leads. If you were to ask a life insurance customer to recommend someone else, most won't. They aren't privy to the personal or financial affairs of their friends and neighbors, know very little about the range of services you offer, and have limited awareness of the many situations that call for different types of insurance. If you want good leads, or any leads at all, you must narrow their thinking by asking for names of people in specific circumstances. People who are recently married, or who have purchased a house, had a baby, or bought a vacation home are good illustrations. This focusing technique will direct the customer's thoughts toward prospects that offer some real potential.

When you get a few names, try to qualify them immediately with help from your source, instead of simply accepting the names and saying thank you. Ask a number of "qualifying questions," such as the referred person's age, level of education, and family size. Avoid personal or private information such as the person's income or financial situation. By qualifying the referral on the spot, you will be less likely to call on someone who is not a prospect. In fact, your present sales call might be an opportunity to qualify anyone you plan to call, even mutual acquaintances not referred to you by the person you're visiting. For example, if you are visiting someone you went to high school with and you plan to call on other schoolmates, use the opportunity to qualify or disqualify these other contacts if your present contact has information about them.

The endless chain method has its limitations. Not only will many nonbuyers be resistant to make referrals, but buyers, too, will sometimes be unwilling. Regardless of how happy they may be with your product, they may not want to be a part of anything that their friends or associates might see as an intrusion. Present contacts who say "Just don't say where you got the name" are expressing doubt over their decision to mention the name, and perhaps doubt over your product's merits as well.

The Center of Influence . . .

In the **center of influence** method, the salesperson asks an influential person to pass the salesperson's name along to others who will benefit from the product. This method is different from the other methods in that it has prospects calling on the salesperson rather than the other way around.

A center of influence is, in general terms, anyone who is respected by others. People may seek someone's advice because the person is an expert in a given field, or they simply admire her or his accomplishments. If you need to know whether you should invest in a deferred-income retirement plan, your tax accountant may be a center of influence for you. Famous athletes act in the same role when they promote breakfast cereals, as do models when they advertise certain brands of shampoo or makeup.

We are all centers of influence in one way or another. A teenager can be a center of influence at school by being a trend-setter, or at home because of the admiration of a younger brother or sister. Such influential people need not be rich or famous. All that is required is that others are impressed with this person's accomplishments or expertise in areas that concern them. A banker, a lawyer, a doctor, a service garage owner, a high school guidance counselor, and a college professor are all centers of influence in the eyes of people who ask for their specialized advice.

A center of influence may not be important in all regards or to all people. We may admire certain prominent local citizens for their work as preservationists, but we don't ask them what toothpaste to use, what car to buy, or what electives to take during our senior year in college. We ask our dentist the first question, our mechanic the second, and a successful graduate in our field of study the third. We ask the preservationist how to get a Victorian home registered as a historical building.

Qualifying Centers of Influence

Depending on what you are selling, only certain people will qualify as centers of influence. If you sell for a residential construction firm, then a banker and a lawyer are important centers. If you sell new cars, remember that the owner of a busy service garage is respected by the garage's customers and may be a center of influence. If you head the admissions office at a local college, the high school guidance counselors in your area are centers of influence since students seek their advice when selecting a college.

A bank manager can be an important center of influence in many ways. Suppose a young couple visit the bank one afternoon to ask the manager what would be involved in taking out a mortgage to build a new house. The manager describes the mortgage application procedure, and then asks what other aspects of the home-building process they have examined. They say none, and wonder what the bank manager would recommend. At this point, the banker could recommend a real estate agent, a builder, an attorney, a surveyor, a general insurance agent, even a title insurance company. Obviously, if you sell in any of those capacities, this bank manager is a major center of influence, one you should get to know.

The more important a center of influence is in the eyes of others, the more important it is for you to establish a good relationship with him or her. People like to be associated with well-known, successful people. They enjoy doing business with them and are eager to follow their recommendations. They also hope that some of the center's success will rub off on them. Finding a good center of influence can often be more rewarding than finding a high-probability prospect. You should work to establish lasting contact with influential members of your community; they will, over time, refer many people to you.

Center of Influence Process

The center of influence method is a four-step process:

1. Identify a center of influence.
2. Seek this person out.

3. Convince the center of the merits of your product or service.

4. Maintain periodic contact with the center.

In the ideal situation, the center of influence buys your product or service. Then, others can learn of the center's personal experience with it. However, the center may already own the product, or simply not qualify as a prospect. If several of your centers of influence are middle-aged individuals who have long since purchased life insurance, they simply aren't prospects, even for more. But they can still direct younger people in their insurance purchases. Perhaps a center is not a prospect because occupation is a qualifying criterion. Small business consultants, for example, will not be targets for a fleet of trucks. This does not mean that those who seek their opinion will not be prospects.

A significant advantage of the center of influence method is that it brings about an "arranged encounter" that eliminates some of the awkwardness of first meetings. Prospects will have obtained information on you and your product before they call you. And since they were referred to you by someone they trust, they feel somewhat comfortable with you. They do not feel as though they are meeting a total stranger.

Kevin Burckhard

Kevin Burckhard started in the insurance business while he was still in college at Minot State University. While working toward his Associate of Arts degree, he was an intern for Northwestern Mutual Life. He has been with "the Quiet Company" ever since. Kevin attributes much of his present success to the strong background in sales and marketing classes that he received at the North Dakota campus. Role-playing exercises in the selling classes contributed to his ability to "jump start" his professional career in the insurance industry.

In his present position as Special Agent and College Unit Director, he is responsible for promoting the company's internship program at MSU. He strongly feels that the job of an insurance salesperson is to protect the standard of living of the policy holder and family in case of disability or death, as well as to save for the future. He gives his clients the same advice that he follows personally. En route to this goal, Kevin has been awarded his company's National Quality Award twice along with being the recipient of the National Sales Achievement Award.

Kevin feels that there always will be a need for personal sellers. At times, in our hi-tech world of Internet, FAX machines, cell phones, and the like, it is easy to lose sight of the role that people play in business. He believes that no matter how technologically advanced the world becomes, there always will be a shortage of people who can stand face-to-face, with a listening ear, to build the kind of trust that customers and clients need and appreciate.

Using the Center of Influence Method

People who know that their opinion is sought and their advice respected are proud of their reputation. Before you can expect these people to refer others to you, they will want to know a lot about you. They must believe in you and your product or service, and will not refer someone they feel cannot benefit from purchasing what you sell. Tell your centers of influence everything they want to know. Mention the names of others you have helped, especially people they know or have heard of.

Most centers of influence are busy people. Unless they are personal friends, your contact with them should only be periodic. This means a phone call or visit every several months, not daily or weekly lunch dates. Don't rely on any one center of influence too heavily. If you give these people the impression that you are counting on them for leads, they'll wonder why you can't seem to generate prospects in other ways. They will also feel they are being used.

Too little contact with a center of influence can be as bad as too much contact. Make no mistake about it, these folk can forget about you. You can prevent this by taking them out to lunch every six months and remembering them at holidays with a card or perhaps a small gift. The best way to keep in touch with your centers is to thank them for each referral. To do this, you will need to ask everyone who contacts you who referred him or her to you. Then, even if you don't make a sale, let the center know that you heard from so-and-so and you appreciate the referral. Another way of maintaining contact with your centers of influence is to provide them with any information you come across that might be of importance to them or their business. For example, you might occasionally send them magazine clippings or notes mentioning research projects you've recently heard about.

There is no better way of building a healthy relationship with centers of influence than to return the favor by referring prospects to them. Whenever you recommend a center's product or service to your contacts, tell them to mention your name. Most people will oblige because they expect more favorable treatment from a friendly source. A center who hears of your referral is more likely to remember you pleasantly and reciprocate.

Rewarding Centers of Influence

Under no circumstances should you ever attempt to pay your centers of influence for their referrals. They might be insulted and sever your relationship. Centers of influence don't refer people to you for money; they do it for the benefit of their friends, customers, and business associates. The rewards they derive from making referrals are strictly nonmonetary.

The center of influence prospecting method is a slow one. Weeks, months, even years may pass before you hear from a lead who was referred to you. Typical centers of influence are willing to send people to you, but by no means do they go out of their way to do it. Usually, one of their customers or associates will mention something that focuses their thoughts on you or your business. Perhaps this person is a tax accountant and a client requests the name of a good IRA program. Only then does the center remember that you happen to offer an excellent financial package. Centers of influence are not only confident in their ability to judge a good deal, they are also flattered when people ask their advice and happy to help out.

The center of influence method of prospecting differs from other methods in several ways. Because leads call you instead of the other way around, you will not have the advantage of qualifying them before your first contact. Further, referrals come in at uneven and unpredictable intervals over which you have no control, so they cannot be the basis of your income. Finally, centers of influence see themselves as doing a favor for their referrals, not for you. They are more concerned with making their own customers happy than with increasing your business. Of course, happy customers and increased business go hand in hand. Satisfying the people referred to you is a surefire way of receiving more referrals.

The Personal Observation . . .

If you enjoy selling and believe in your product or service, you will have no trouble using the **personal observation** method of prospecting. Using this method simply means keeping a constant lookout for leads, recognizing potential prospects whenever and wherever they appear. Although your selling activities might be confined to the normal business day, prospecting never stops. With the personal observation method, looking for new potential buyers is a part of your lifestyle. You are always wearing your selling hat.

On the surface, the personal observation method may sound obsessive, but it isn't. We all require time away from our work if only to relax, but a sales job should not be something you need to escape from. If you cannot or will not think about selling during off hours, you have a problem that is hampering your sales potential. Perhaps something about the job or the product you sell has become unappealing to you, or maybe your attitude about work isn't compatible with the selling profession. The reality of selling is that prospects come along at any time, not just from 9 to 5, Monday through Friday. If you are to be successful as a salesperson, you must always be ready to take unscheduled business.

Because prospects appear anytime, anywhere, your off hours may provide many opportunities to meet and qualify them. This is not to say that you should be questioning people at wedding receptions or handing out business cards at class reunions, but social occasions often do yield leads. If you sell hot tubs, and while attending a garden party you overhear the host express a desire for one, you have a prospect. Similarly, you may be able to qualify someone as a prospect during a casual conversation over dinner Saturday night. Remember, however, that to many prospects off hours will always be off limits. Your restaurant companion is not interested in hearing about your product over dinner, and a garden party is not the proper setting for a sales presentation. Make a note of the leads or prospects you discover during leisure time, and save your selling efforts for Monday morning.

> The average person who has been burned tells nine to ten colleagues, and 13% of dissatisfied customers will spread the bad news to more than twenty people.
>
> Frank Sonnenberg

The personal observation method is almost effortless when the need for your product or service is noticeable to the general public. The most common activities can, for you, be prospecting opportunities. For example, if you sell refrigeration equipment and you notice that your neighborhood service station is adding a minimarket, you have located a possible prospect. If you represent a vending machine service, and while grocery shopping you overhear the store owners complaining about problems with their present machines, you have a potential sale.

The Best Opportunities for Personal Observation

The personal observation method works better in some fields than in others. Salespeople whose products are in general use or who sell to ultimate consumers will find personal observation much more useful than will salespeople whose products are in limited use or whose sales are to businesses. A seller of pianos, landscaping, or skin care products will be more likely to discover prospects through this method than will someone selling pharmaceuticals, college textbooks, or rail freight delivery.

The personal observation method of prospecting differs from other processes in that prospects come incidentally rather than as a result of deliberate effort. Because of this, it is considered a secondary method, and is used mostly as a backup to more conscious methods such as the cold canvass or the endless chain. Your success with the personal observation method will depend on the amount of time you are willing to devote to prospecting. If you prefer not to qualify a prospect because it's Saturday night and you're at a football game, you will not generate as many potential buyers as those salespeople who are willing to seek out prospects regardless of where they are or what they are doing.

The News . . .

Keeping up with the news is a very good application of the personal observation method. Television, radio, newspapers, trade journals, and industry publications are all excellent sources of prospects for the salesperson who knows how to use them. The weekly business paper may run an article about a shopping mall opening up in the area, or a local TV news program might be investigating the crime problems in a certain neighborhood. Perhaps a national trade or industry journal features a story on a local entrepreneur. All these have the potential of revealing prospects and, if you follow through immediately, can be very timely.

The Internet provides some of the most up-to-the-minute information available through today's news media. On-line services are available from all of the major broadcast networks, as well as from private sources. Cable news networks are also good sources for the latest information on the day's happenings, both in business and in the world. The daily newspaper is full of information significant to many salespeople, whether it be property transfers, weddings, births, promotions, graduations, or death notices. Every day, the salesperson has the opportunity of discovering prospects over breakfast.

> The greater the difficulty, the more glory in surmounting it.
>
> Jean Baptiste Moliere

Bird Dogs . . .

A **bird dog** is a selling term for someone who is commissioned by the salesperson to come up with prospects. A bird dog's work naturally puts this person in contact with potential prospects, and a referral can go in either direction: Either the prospect calls the salesperson or the salesperson calls the prospect. The bird dog makes referrals with the expectation of receiving a fee if a sale is made.

Your best bird dogs will have the following characteristics:

1. They are people you can talk to easily.
2. They are motivated by the thought of making money.
3. They have interest in and knowledge of the product you sell.
4. They have many contacts.
5. They can quickly spot high-probability prospects.
6. Their decision to refer their own customers to you is always in the customer's best interest, thus avoiding ethical and legal dilemmas that may result from a referral plan.

The bird dog method can be used very effectively in the sale of products that need occasional service, in which case the provider could be the bird dog. If you sell appliances, for example, you might consider a service technician a good bird dog. The repair person may be called in to service someone's refrigerator only to discover the old one is beyond fixing. Because the technician must inform the customer of the need for a new refrigerator, this person is in a prime position to recommend an appliance dealer. The bird dog in this case advises the prospect to contact you. If you were to initiate the call, the customer might believe the technician was participating in a high-pressure sales scheme, and would never call the repair person again for service.

If you sell automobiles, you might consider a bird dog relationship with someone who works at a garage or body shop. A mechanic constantly meets people whose vehicles need extensive repairs or have been wrecked and sometimes must tell unlucky drivers that their car is beyond hope or its market value doesn't justify the cost of repairs. If the customer hasn't already considered shopping for a car, the dealer mentioned by the mechanic may be the first one visited.

Bird dogs are, in an informal sense, employed by the salesperson in that they are compensated for their referrals. But they are not employed by the salesperson's firm. The relationship between a bird dog and a salesperson is usually a private one. Each salesperson in the firm will have a separate list of bird dogs.

Bird-Dogging Made Easy

Establishing a network of bird dogs is not easy. Although you might think that most people are motivated by the commission you offer, the fact is that people operating their own businesses are often unwilling to become bird dogs for others. Especially if their business is successful, they will not be attracted to the extra income. If anything, the manager of an auto body shop would rather be seen as a center of influence than a bird dog. He or she might be willing to recommend a car or dealer if the customer were to ask, but reluctant to give the customer's name to the salesperson.

The bird dog method may seem similar to the center of influence method, but it is different in several important regards:

1. Centers of influence are those whose opinions are sought out and respected. A bird dog's opinion may or may not be either.
2. Bird dogs expect compensation for their referrals. A center of influence would be insulted by an offer to pay.
3. Centers of influence value their image, and so must be convinced of the merits of your product. A bird dog is less concerned with these things.
4. Bird dogs seek out prospects, and make referrals without prompting. The center of influence makes referrals only when potential prospects ask for advice.
5. Centers of influence seek to help those who solicit their advice. A bird dog's objective is to help the salesperson.
6. Centers of influence tell the prospect to contact the salesperson, and leave it at that. A bird dog gets more involved in the contact process, usually telling the salesperson a prospect's name or suggesting that the prospect call the salesperson, mentioning the referral.

Just as a center of influence is selective in making referrals, you should be selective in choosing bird dogs. A bird dog must be able to recognize a true prospect. Otherwise, you will waste your time making fruitless calls to people who are not going to buy.

Direct Mail and Telephone Prospecting . . .

Salespeople use **direct mail** and **telephone prospecting** in a variety of ways: They generate prospects at random, qualify leads, set up appointments, even make sales. Our focus here is on using direct mail and the telephone as prospecting devices. We address the use of the telephone as a sales tool in Chapter 18, which covers telemarketing.

When used to make random contact, direct mail and telephone prospecting are variations of the cold canvass method. Letters and phone calls provide inexpensive channels through which the salesperson can qualify leads. Prospecting by telephone or direct mail is mostly recommended when leads are geographically dispersed or the probability of any one person being a prospect is small. It is also handy when time and budget limitations do not allow for many personal visits.

Direct mail or telephone contact is advisable not only for leads who are unlikely to become prospects, but also for prospects who are unlikely to buy. In one of these situations, you can use a mail or telephone campaign inexpensively as a screening device. Then if a lead proves to be a prospect, or if a prospect proves to be more promising than you thought originally, you can schedule a personal call and presentation with reasonable hope of success.

Even though its response rate is often low, direct mail remains an economical method because it allows you to reach large numbers of people you could never call on individually. A mailer is an excellent qualifying tool. All you have to do is ask the recipients of your mailer to answer several questions on a response card and return it. Not only may the answer prove them to be prospects, but the very act of responding indicates that they are somewhat interested in the product or service you are selling.

A series of telephone calls can be equally helpful in your prospecting efforts. Through one phone call to a business, you can learn if your lead or prospect still works there, and if not, you can learn the name of the new person. You can also find out whether this is the person you need to reach, and if not, who is. You might even find out the former employee's new employer. If you attempt to call the home number of someone who has moved, a prerecorded message may provide you with the person's new telephone number.

Direct mail and telephone prospecting both have advantages and disadvantages, as the following table shows:

Direct Mail

Advantages
1. It does not intrude on the recipient at an unsuitable time.
2. The recipient can choose when to read and respond to it.
3. Since a mail questionnaire can be completed at the person's leisure, a large amount of information can be requested.
4. A mass mailing is less costly than individual telephone calls.
5. A response indicates interest.

Disadvantages
1. Since there is no personal request to respond, the response rate is low.
2. Some recipients will immediately discard a mailer if it appears to be too long or complicated.
3. There is no flexibility, such as the ability to respond to unique situations or ask additional questions of a very interested prospect.
4. The process is very slow.

Telephone Prospecting

Advantages
1. A lead can be immediately qualified.
2. The response rate is higher than with direct mail.
3. A telephone conversation allows for flexibility; questions and comments can be adjusted for the prospect.
4. It is more timely than direct mail (for example, you can call prospects for your snow-plowing service the day after a snowstorm).
5. A sale might actually be made over the telephone.

Disadvantages
1. Telephone prospecting is more time consuming than direct mail.
2. Some prospects consider it high-pressure selling.
3. A phone call may intrude on people at unsuitable times, when they are unwilling or unable to respond.
4. Because a telephone call is unexpected, the method is not useful for obtaining a great deal of detailed information.

Obtaining a Mailing List

There are many ways to obtain mailing lists appropriate to your prospecting and selling needs. Salespeople often use in-house lists, such as a roster of their employer's credit card customers. They might purchase lists from mail-order houses and stores that mail merchandise to distant customers. Local government records, such as property transfer listings many also provide leads, and a prospector might purchase subscriber lists from magazines or trade journals. Mailing list brokers are also available for a fee.

A mailing **list broker**, or compiler, is a firm that assembles specialized mailing lists and rents them for one-time use. A broker knows what kinds of lists are available and will either rent out an existing list or assemble a new one tailored to your specifications. Large mailing list brokers own thousands of lists. Brokers are located throughout the country; some are regional firms, whereas others, like Dun's Marketing Services or R.L. Polk & Co., are national. They are found in the business-to-business yellow pages under "Mailing Lists," or in the classified sections of mail-order trade magazines. The Direct Marketing Association can also refer you to a mailing list broker.

Renting a mailing list with fewer than 5,000 names is probably a bad investment. Only when a large list is purchased for an entire sales force is this a cost-efficient method of prospecting.

Prospecting on the Internet

One of the most popular and convenient methods of looking for new prospects is using the Internet. Searching the Web using a specific topic will bring you loads of leads of people and businesses interested in that subject. You could then qualify those leads by communicating directly through Internet. For example, suppose you are selling keychain emblems for sports cars. Surfing the Web under Corvette, Porsche, and Ferrari will produce a list of individuals and firms interested in those cars. You can then respond to those leads, promoting your product.

For more sophisticated prospecting on the Internet, create your own web page. Using an attractive, full color presentation on the Internet is relatively inexpensive, outside of the original developmental cost. You then have created an avenue where interested parties can contact you. You can even use this device for preliminary qualifying by asking respondents to provide credit information and specific needs descriptions. Depending upon your product, you can even take orders directly over this medium.

Past and Present Customers . . .

Keeping in touch with past and present customers is good business for many reasons, not the least of which is the dual role they play in your prospecting efforts. Someone who purchased from you once before or who regularly purchases from you now is an excellent lead or prospect for future sales. Satisfied past or present customers are also a great source of new prospects; they will refer others to you and you to them.

Selling to your past and present customers is the sensible thing to do: A great deal of effort goes into gaining a new customer, and somewhat less to keep an established one. It is usually easier to sell to an existing customer than to a stranger because buyers already know you, your product, and your company.

Products, Industries, and Individual Needs Change Constantly

Don't make the mistake of assuming that a customer who has bought from you will never need your product again or will never need to be sold again. Past customers don't always keep up with the latest news on the products they purchase. You may be able to help your long-ago buyers by letting them know your product or industry has changed a great deal since they last made a purchase.

Not only will the product be changed by your employer, but the model your customer bought may be wearing out with age. You may come across customers in your firm's service department from time to time who tell you that their present product has received so much use, this is the third time they have had it in for service. They are excellent prospects. They need a new one!

You should make personal contact with past customers periodically, even if it means taking time away from your other prospecting efforts. Remember that while you are calling on new prospects, competing salespeople are calling on your past or present purchasers. Although a telephone call may lack the warmth of a personal visit, occasional calls help keep you aware of your customers' present needs, and also keep them from forgetting you or thinking you have forgotten them. If past or present purchasers begin to feel neglected, they may take their business to a firm that makes them feel more important.

Contact with former purchasers usually requires only a minimum of effort. If you sell automobiles, each time a past purchaser brings the car in for service, you should ask how many miles it has. If the customer says 48,000 you should mention that the trade-in value decreases dramatically once a car has 50,000 on the odometer. Perhaps this person is in a position to buy a new car, and the information you share will help prompt the customer to act.

Record Keeping

Regardless of what you sell, you should keep detailed records on your customers. Note when a customer makes a purchase, what model or item is purchased, and the customer's intended use of it. You might also ask at the time of purchase how frequently the customer usually buys the product or how long it has been since this person's last purchase. This information helps you predict when present customers might be ready to buy again, and therefore when you should contact them.

Here are several important reasons for maintaining periodic customer contact:

1. Past purchasers won't forget you.
2. You are able to serve a customer's needs as they arise.
3. You can inform your customers of changes or replacements in the product or service and update them on industry innovations.
4. Past purchasers won't get the impression that the only time they were important to you was when they purchased.

If your business attracts regular customers, you might find that present clients are your best source of increased sales. Suppose you are a hair stylist, and most people who visit you get one trim a month, or twelve trims a year. Suppose that several customers get their hair trimmed a little more often. They visit without fail every third Friday. You know they consider the appearance of their hair important, and you also know that the ideal interval for a trim is every two weeks. You mention this to your third-Friday clients, and they decide to get their hair trimmed every two weeks. On their old schedule, they were getting about seventeen trims a year. Now they are going to get twenty-six trims a year. By informing them of an essential fact of good grooming, you gain nine trims a year per customer, 75 percent of the volume you would gain by adding another once-a-month customer to your clientele.

Local Organizations and Events . . .

Membership in local organizations and participation in local events can be rewarding, not only personally but also professionally. Community involvement puts you in contact with people you might never meet otherwise, so it can be used indirectly as a prospecting method. Your dedication to a cause others believe in will draw them to you and provide a positive basis for future dealings.

Consider volunteering for activities that interest you, and chances are they will relate to the product or service you sell. Fund-raisers, youth organizations, social events, and philanthropic clubs are all good candidates. Join the Kiwanis, Rotary, or Lions club, or work for the Special Olympics or March of Dimes. Whatever moves you to serve others will undoubtedly return to you in positive ways. Your activities may reap indirect rewards, such as a mention in the local newspaper or listing in a membership directory. Little by little, you will spread your sphere of influence throughout the community.

Seminars . . .

Seminars have become a popular method of prospecting, particularly among firms that sell financial services. These companies offer seminars to generate new business and keep present customers informed of their most recent product offerings. Whether the seminar lasts all day or is a breakfast session, it is a cost-effective way of discovering and educating potential customers. The very act of attending a seminar indicates that the attendee is at least somewhat interested in the product or service being discussed. This guarantees presenters an attentive audience.

Whether or not you charge admission to your seminar, you should focus it on a single topic, and keep commercial content to a minimum. There should be constant interaction between the presenters and the audience, question-and-answer sessions, and periodic refresher breaks. Above all else, remember that your purpose is to educate your attendees, not sell to them. A educational seminar is not the place to try to close a sale. At the conclusion of the seminar, ask attendees to complete a short evaluation form, and request that they specify how the product or service discussed might benefit them. After you review this information, contact those attendees who qualify as prospects.

Planning, organizing, and conducting a seminar is often a companywide effort. The cost and time involved puts seminar scheduling beyond the realm of the individual salesperson.

Miscellaneous Sources . . .

Prospects can be found almost everywhere you look. Many of the following sources can be incorporated into the prospecting methods described:

1. Home shows and trade shows
2. **Bingo cards** in magazines (also known as reader service information cards, see Figure 3-3)

IW Free Information Request Form

READER'S RESPOND TODAY

1	31	61	91	121	151	181
2	32	62	92	122	152	182
3	33	63	93	123	153	183
4	34	64	94	124	154	184
5	35	65	95	125	155	185
6	36	66	96	126	156	186
7	37	67	97	127	157	187
8	38	68	98	128	158	188
9	39	69	99	129	159	189
10	40	70	100	130	160	190
11	41	71	101	131	161	191
12	42	72	102	132	162	192
13	43	73	103	133	163	193
14	44	74	104	134	164	194
15	45	75	105	135	165	195
16	46	76	106	136	166	196
17	47	77	107	137	167	197
18	48	78	108	138	168	198
19	49	79	109	139	169	199
20	50	80	110	140	170	200
21	51	81	111	141	171	201
22	52	82	112	142	172	202
23	53	83	113	143	173	203
24	54	84	114	144	174	204
25	55	85	115	145	175	205
26	56	86	116	146	176	206
27	57	87	117	147	177	207
28	58	88	118	148	178	208
29	59	89	119	149	179	209
30	60	90	120	150	180	210

☐ Mr. ☐ Ms. Name _____

Title _____

Company _____

Division _____

Address/P.O. Box _____ Mail Stop _____

City _____ State _____ ZIP _____

Phone (_____) _____ Fax (_____) _____

What is the primary end product manufactured or service performed at this location?

_____

ANY QUESTIONS??? CALL PAUL AT IW CUSTOMER SERVICE (800) 326-4146 x 4039

Figure 3-3 **Bingo cards (reader service cards) enable magazine advertisers to contact readers who have expressed an interest in learning more about the advertiser's product. The reader circles the number on the card that corresonds with the advertisement and returns it to the publisher.**

3. Party-plan selling
4. Company workshops, open houses, in-store demonstrations, and so on
5. **Direct-response advertising**
6. The yellow pages (business-to-business yellow pages also)
7. The local chamber of commerce
8. Professional societies
9. **Trade directories** or **industrial buying guides**
10. Libraries
11. A card file of those who have visited your store or showroom
12. Your present prospect's competitors
13. The new employer of a client firm's former employee
14. Your firm's nonselling employees
15. Noncompeting salespeople (network groups, lead clubs)
16. A geographic or historical approach to name recall
17. Computerized data base
18. On-line services
19. Specialized business publications
20. Present suppliers

If you or your company has a booth at a home show or trade show, you can ask visitors to fill out a name and address card, perhaps for a prize drawing. These are leads worth following up on in the near future. You might consider party-plan selling depending on your product or service. Under the party plan, you make arrangements with someone to hold a gathering of friends and neighbors at the other person's home, where you can demonstrate your product to everyone at once. Your company's newspaper or trade advertisement could include a **response coupon** for interested parties to fill out and mail.

Your city or multicounty chamber of commerce membership directory contains listings of leads both alphabetically and by business classification. You may be able to purchase such a directory or even a set of preprinted mailing labels from the chamber. Joining the chamber is a less expensive way to obtain the directory, however, and membership gives you opportunities to meet potential prospects in a nonselling environment. You should also join and be active in your industry's professional societies, which are often national in scope.

Figure 3-4 lists published sources of information on business prospects. Trade directories and buying guides are excellent sources of prospects. The *Thomas Register of Manufacturers* may be helpful if you work in industrial sales. Most libraries carry trade directories such as *Moody's Industrial Manual* or *Dun and Bradstreet's Million Dollar Directory*.

Regional industrial buying guides are published by the Thomas Regional Directory Company. You may also wish to purchase a state directory of manufacturers from Manufacturers' News. These directories, which are released by various state chambers of commerce and publishers such as McRae's, Manufacturers' News, and the Commerce Register, are available for every state but Alaska and Hawaii, plus Puerto Rico and several Canadian provinces.

Published Sources of Information on Business Prospects

Published Sources of Information on Business Prospects

Standard and Poor's Industry Surveys, Corporate Record, Compustat Services

Poor's Register of Executives and Directors

Dun and Bradstreet Reference Book of Corporate Management

Dun and Bradstreet Marketwatch (CD/Rom database)

Encyclopedia of Business Information Sources

Wall Street Transcript

Funk & Scott Index of Corporations and Industries

Government publications (e.g., U.S. Dept. of Commerce)

State Manufacturers Directories

Figure 3-4

The Commerce Register's *New York Metro* and *New York Upstate* directories contain alphabetical, geographic, and product breakdowns of more than 15,000 manufacturers. To learn the product lines of major area manufacturers, you can consult your local library, or you can call the companies directly and ask them to send you information on their products.

Another good prospect source is a card file with the names of people who have visited your office or showroom and appeared interested in your product. By keeping such a file and reviewing it periodically, you will not only find prospects to contact, but also make visitors happy when you remember their name or other information they gave you in the past.

Whenever you call on a business prospect, learn who the firm's competitors are. They use the same products and services, so they are prospects too. Further, if you call on a company and discover the person who was in charge of purchasing is no longer there, ask the receptionist where this person went. You will want to make contact with the new employer as well as with the new purchaser of the old employer.

Your firm's other salespeople are prospect sources not to be overlooked. Industrial salespeople frequently find their most important sources are within their own company's sales force. Nonselling colleagues can also be a gold mine.

Networking . . .

Network groups and lead clubs, such as those sponsored by the National Association of Sales Professionals, are growing in popularity as a prospecting tool. Club members are noncompeting salespeople, usually from related industries. These groups meet regularly to exchange the names of sales leads and other business information. Fellow network club members not only provide you with the names of leads or prospects, they share news about prospects, the status of a prospect's business or industry, or bits of information that will help qualify your leads.

Networking does not require membership in an organization. It takes place whenever salespeople exchange leads. It's common for noncompeting salespeople to meet and exchange information. If you run into a fellow salesperson in a plant you are calling on, why not suggest lunch? Perhaps this noncompetitor recently visited a buyer who is looking for aluminum forgings, which is your line. This coincidence will certainly come out during your conversation. Repay the salesperson for the lead by offering several leads or some helpful information in return.

Be sure to remember your friends and acquaintances when you prospect. You might be able to discover prospects among your past and present acquaintances by thinking about them in a geographic or historical context. With the geographic approach, you study a map of the surrounding area, reading the names of all the streets, housing developments, and apartment complexes. This exercise will help remind you of people you otherwise might miss. With the historical approach, remember what activities you were involved in over the past few years. Browsing through yearbooks, family scrapbooks, and engagement calendars will jog your memory. By recalling members of your old softball team, the community band you played with, or the organizers of your Girl Scout troop, you can rediscover people who might otherwise be lost and forgotten forever.

Not only should you be searching for those who are prospects now, you should also be making note of those who will become prospects in several months or years. Perhaps because of a change in age, income, or family status, these old leads can be revitalized. Furthermore, make time your ally. In other words, do your prospecting at a time when conditions influence your leads to consider your product or service. If you sell roofing materials, the best time to call homeowners is soon after they've experienced a hard rain. In dry season, memories of water damage will be faint.

You Decide!

After years of working for other janitorial service companies, Bob has just opened his own domestic cleaning business. Although competition is heavy, he is convinced that he can make his niche in this market. He has advertised during the local television newscast, and is offering special discounts for seniors, yet things have been pretty slow. Bob's funds are dwindling, and he is seriously considering closing down his business.

While discussing his problems with Rachel, a woman acquaintance who works in a nursing home, Bob learns that she has access to the names, addresses, and phone numbers of all new admissions. It dawns on him that if an older person is admitted to the facility that the house is either being kept by an elderly partner or not maintained at all. He knows that Rachel is fond of him, and wonders if he should ask her to supply him with the information about these new patients so that he could try to sell his service. On the other hand, Bob knows that this is privileged information, and although Rachel would probably do anything he asks, she could easily lose her job if she did as he asked. **You decide!**

Summing It Up . . .

Prospecting is the first stage in selling—the stage where you seek those individuals or organizations that have a need for your product, the ability to pay for it, and the authority to buy it. The chapter explored various methods of locating potential purchasers. You should compare each lead to your true prospect profile, contact qualified leads according to their probability of buying, and concentrate your efforts on your high-volume prospects.

Keep your prospecting methods up to date, and evaluate each by determining the number of successful sales that result from it in relation to the time and expense you invest in it. Many sales managers require their salespeople to submit weekly reports on their prospecting efforts so as to be sure that constant and effective prospecting is taking place. Although prospecting may sound like a tedious routine, sales results come in direct proportion to prospecting efforts. And you must make a deliberate attempt to follow through on the names your prospecting methods generate. As a publishing services salesperson once told the author, you are guaranteed to regret the sales *calls* you don't make far more than the *sales* you don't make.

Key Concepts and Terms . . .

bingo card	networking
bird dog	nonprospect
center of influence	personal observation
cold canvass	primary demand
demographics	prospect
direct mail	prospecting
direct-response advertising	psychographics
80-20 principle	qualifying
endless chain	response coupon
geographics	selective demand
high-volume purchaser	seminars
industrial buying guide	telephone prospecting
lead	tight leads
list broker	trade directory
loose leads	true prospect profile
market saturation	

Building Skills . . .

1. Explain the difference between a lead and a prospect.
2. Describe the criteria needed to qualify a lead as a prospect.
3. Using three goods or services of your choice, explain how qualifying your prospects requires nothing more than observation.

4. Define a true prospect profile.

5. Explore the differences between primary and selective demand.

6. Define the 80-20 principle and its relationship to prospecting.

7. Assume you represent the continuing education division of your college. Identify the high-volume prospects.

8. List the reasons you should call on your prospects in the order of their probability of buying.

9. Describe the important marketing principle that is the basis for cold calling.

10. Analyze the endless chain method of prospecting as it relates to a prospect who has purchased your product.

11. Explore the benefits of putting forth a greater effort to secure the names of new prospects from those who have purchased your product versus those who haven't.

12. Compare the advantages and disadvantages of center of influence prospecting.

13. Suppose you operate a florist service. Describe the prospects you might find in the following sections of your daily newspaper: Business, Home Entertainment, Real Estate, Sports.

14. The bird dog plays an active role in locating prospects for you, whereas the center of influence plays a passive one. Explain.

15. Evaluate the difficulties faced in trying to establish a strong network of bird dogs.

16. Compare the contacts and situations that are most recommended for the direct mail and telephone methods.

17. List the advantages of telephone prospecting over direct mail.

18. Explore the advantages of prospecting on the Internet.

19. Investigate the benefits in maintaining detailed records on past and present customers.

20. Suppose you sell expensive ski equipment. List the reasons that non-prospects might become prospects in the future.

21. Suppose you are the New York State sales representative for a time-sharing condominium in Florida. Describe the phrase "make time your ally" in your prospecting efforts.

Making Decisions 3-1:

Charlie Shaner has just become a marketing representative for Gramcourt Distributors, a dealer in facsimile equipment. A small amount of Charlie's business comes from occasional showroom visitors, and a handful of leads result from direct-response cards. But Charlie also has a territory, a five-county area measuring about 90 square miles, and he is responsible for prospecting.

Acting on the assumption that only a small percentage of the businesses in his territory are already using facsimile equipment, Charlie decides to map out a targeted travel plan: He will visit all businesses classified in the regional business directory as having yearly sales of $1 million or more. Much to his surprise, Charlie discovers that his list of leads amounts to more than 1,600 firms. Charlie is required to spend Wednesdays in the Gramcourt showroom, plus two afternoons a week in sales meetings. Even on his free days, Charlie couldn't realistically visit more than five firms a day. Given his schedule limitations, it would take him more than three years to visit everyone on the list. Charlie thought he had developed a good prospecting method, but now he has no idea how to pursue so many leads.

Develop a prospecting plan for Charlie.

Making Decisions 3-2:

Todd Tomascello is the owner of Old Mill Gallery, a fine-arts dealer specializing in works by regional painters. One morning a man named Jake Preston visits the gallery. He expresses an interest in buying a painting by local watercolor artist Mildred Bond.

Todd: Thanks for stopping by, Mr. Preston, but I don't have a Bond painting in stock right now.

Jake: Do you know where I can get one?

Todd: Well, she's very popular, and her paintings rarely come on the market...but let me make some calls. Give me your telephone number, and I'll call you if something turns up.

Jake: (Writes his name and number) Thanks.

Several days later, Todd locates someone who owns a Bond painting. After lengthy negotiations, he and the owner agree on a selling price. Todd telephones Jake that evening.

Todd: Mr. Preston, I've got some good news for you.

Jake: Oh?

Todd: I've located *The White Church*. The price is $3,500, not counting my $100 finder's fee.

Jake: Thirty-five hundred! You've got to be kidding. That's way too much.

Todd: Do you mean it's more than you wanted to pay, or that it's not worth the price?

Jake: Both! I knew her paintings were expensive, but $3,500 is out of the question. Call me back when you find something that's sensibly priced.

Describe how Todd failed to qualify.

Making Decisions 3-3:

You sell a $5,000 snowmobile. Construct a true prospect profile containing six characteristics.

Making Decisions 3-4

You are a sales representative for a firm that leases call pagers and signaling equipment. List the characteristics of your high-volume customers.

Making Decisions 3-5

Describe how you would design a web page to prospect on the Internet for a new design of sunglasses that you will be selling to resorts, sporting goods stores, drugs stores, and so on.

Practice Makes Perfect 3-1:

Carry on a mock conversation with another student who you met in a shopping mall. Secure as many leads as possible for your lawn care service in a three-minute time span.

Practice Makes Perfect 3-2:

Assume you are making a cold call on a busy prospect. Count how many *wrong* things that you can say to turn this person off.

Understanding Prospects

THE JOB TO BE DONE . . .

Gaining a list of potential buyers is not sufficient. Professional sellers must perform a number of functions and gather significant information before progressing into the sales call. In Chapter 4, you will:

...learn to appreciate the value of a thorough preapproach effort.

...understand the scope of preapproach activities.

...explore ways of gathering preapproach data,

...understand what is necessary to learn about the business prospect.

...see the importance of learning the prospect's present state of decision.

PREAPPROACH DEFINED . . .

The **preapproach** is the stage of the selling process in which the salesperson gathers background information on which to base a sales presentation. This phase of the selling process is similar to prospecting in that it involves gathering facts, but the nature of the information at this stage serves a different purpose. Whereas prospecting is used to determine whether a lead is a potential buyer, preapproach data is used to learn how best to appeal to an already qualified prospect. If a lead is not yet qualified, we still should gather preapproach information on the chance that qualification will happen. In short, we use this method to obtain the kind of knowledge that will help us map out a sales plan unique to the prospect.

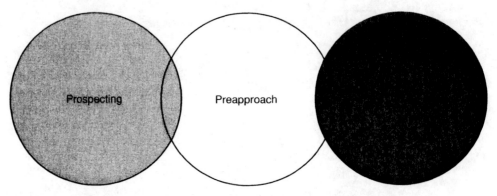

Figure 4-1 Although the preapproach is a distinct stage in the selling process, it begins during prospecting and continues into the sales presentation.

Gathering preapproach data can take place at any time or in any setting. You can collect it in advance of the sales call or during the sales call, from people other than the prospect or directly from the potential buyer.

As shown in Figure 4-1, there are no clearly defined points at which one stage of the selling process ends and the next begins. Prospecting and the preapproach often overlap, just as the preapproach and the sales presentation may coincide. Gathering background information usually begins during normal prospecting and often continues well into the sales presentation.

You may discover that a person with whom you're casually talking is a potential prospect. If you're as quick-thinking as you are alert, you might ask a few well-directed questions, by way of making conversation, that help you not only to qualify this person but also to plan a future presentation. Small talk doesn't have to be meaningless talk. Here are some preapproach questions that can be asked in any normal conversation with a new business acquaintance:

1. What business are you in?
2. Where is your main office?
3. What means of shipping do you use?
4. Do you use the Internet?
5. How many people do you employ?

Perhaps a certain answer to one or more of these questions will qualify this person as a prospect, and the response to the others may provide you with important preapproach information.

To plan and deliver a customized presentation, you will need specific details peculiar to your prospect. Each potential buyer has personal characteristics, financial circumstances, and buying motives that are unique and deserving of special attention. Wants, needs, purchasing ability, and buying behavior will vary among people who differ in age, family background, personality, and place of residence. If you represent a travel agency, for example, you know that the interests of young, single travelers are different from those of older couples. Before you can begin to suggest a good vacation package to your prospects, you will have to know their age and marital status at the very least.

Chapter 4 • Understanding Prospects

The Importance of the Preapproach . . .

The preapproach is essential to the sales effort because it helps you prepare for all the circumstances that will affect your success. Preapproach information is gathered so that you may plan:

1. The focus of your sales presentation
2. Responses to likely questions and objections
3. Your personal conduct
4. The timing of your visit

A good salesperson understands the importance of preparing for the sales presentation. Just as the recent graduate gathers facts on a potential employer before a job interview, and the college football coach examines scouting reports on upcoming opponents, so the salesperson gains any information that will help her or him better understand and persuade the prospect. The motto "Be prepared" is just as meaningful to salespeople as it is to Boy Scouts.

Preapproach work should be done as far in advance as possible. That way you will have time to study and think calmly about what you've learned, and devise a presentation that takes the prospect's special circumstances into consideration. If you don't have enough information, or if you must get some important fact at the last minute, your lack of preparation can only hurt your presentation. The absence of some essential item can cause you to completely misdirect your sales effort.

Not the least important reason for conducting your preapproach in advance is the self-confidence that comes with preparation. We cannot expect a prospect to be convinced in us or our claims if we seem to lack confidence in ourselves. A thorough preapproach translates into self-confidence; the lack of it brings about anxiety.

Consider, for example, a group of students about to take an exam. With hardly a thought you can guess which ones have come prepared and which ones have not. Those who are nervously paging through their notes and textbooks exude a lack of preparation, whereas those who sit relaxed as they await the test radiate preparation and confidence. As you enter a prospect's office, your own preparation or lack of preparation will be just as obvious, and your success in sales will correspond with your preparation.

THE QUALIFIED PROSPECT . . .

Your preapproach effort will be an extension of the research you conducted to qualify your prospect. The difference being that at this stage it will be much more comprehensive and personal because you want to custom-tailor a presentation to a unique customer. In Chapter 3, we discussed creating a true prospect profile using demographic, geographic, and psychographic ideals. These categories will be used again in the preapproach, this time to focus on the particulars about an actual prospect.

Demographic information includes the prospect's age, income, ethnic background, and occupation. For preapproach purposes, you will need to know whether your prospect is an auto executive or an assembly line worker, not just that the prospect's employer manufacturers automobiles. Geographic information includes the prospect's place of residence, perhaps defined by state, county, or zip code, and the specific type of living environment, such as urban, suburban, or rural. You may also want to know how long your prospect has lived in the same place.

Psychographic information includes the prospect's personality traits, values, beliefs, hobbies, habits, and tastes. It also includes frame of reference—the combination of forces that have shaped the prospect's behavior—such as physical surroundings, family, friends, and accumulated experiences. You might need to know your prospect's political affiliation, house-pet preference, or charitable giving habits.

Whereas the true prospect profile provides a model against which to compare leads for qualification purposes, the information you gather now is much more relevant and detailed. It is meant to help you form a comprehensive portrait of the qualified prospect, with the purpose of increasing your chances of making a sale. Any information is relevant if it somehow plays a part in shaping the prospect's reasons for buying or in determining the prospect's purchase behavior.

Overlook no aspect of prospect information during your preapproach activities. Even the ability to correctly pronounce a prospect's name is evidence of your desire to sell. Particularly among prospects who know that their name is often misspelled, your ability to spell it correctly indicates the importance you attach to their business. Prospects who expect salespeople to mispronounce their name will appreciate the one who says it correctly.

Demographics . . .

Learning the prospect's level of education or work background will be extremely important if your presentation includes technical information. For instance, if your prospect's secretary tells you the boss worked eleven years as an electrical engineer before coming to this firm, you may feel comfortable skipping over certain elementary engineering aspects because you can safely assume the prospect understands them. It might also be in your interest to learn your prospects' household life-cycle position, that is, their stage in the family development process. Household life-cycle stages include (1) single; (2) married, with no children; (3) married, with dependent children; (4) divorced; (5) married, with children grown and on their own.

Household life-cycle position is an important determinant of discretionary income, the money spent on luxuries rather than necessities. Single adults, for example, are likely to spend a greater percentage of their money on luxuries than married adults. Household life-cycle position may even determine

> A good conversationalist is not one who remembers what was said but says what someone wants to remember.
>
> John Mason Brown

the degree to which a person is a prospect. The father of several young children may be a better prospect for a camper than a professional couple with no children. The family's discretionary income may be lower, but their desire for the product is greater. Spousal roles in the purchase decision vary.

Avoid assumptions about demographic relationships. A relationship between two demographic factors may be common, but this doesn't mean it is absolute. For example, you might be mistaken if you assume that because a couple has children they are married to each other, or that because your prospects are nurses they are all women. Assumptions like this will not only make you look foolish but also lower your chances of success. Also, spousal rules in the purchase decision vary depending on the product or service being purchased.

Psychographics . . .

Psychographic information can be useful in many ways. You should learn whatever you can about the prospect's activities, interests, and opinions, commonly referred to as AIOs. You should also learn about the prospect's personality. Find out if the prospect is adventurous, independent, critical, skeptical, or emotional.

Psychographics include the prospect's leisure time activities. Suppose you learn through the preapproach that your prospect is a classical music buff. If you took a music appreciation course in college, you may want to find your old notes and review them. Then when you call on the prospect and notice a collection of classical CDs, you can start a conversation on the subject. Although you are not the collector your prospect is, you can at least show some knowledge of classical music. By asking questions, you show your prospects that you view them as experts in certain subjects. People enjoy talking about their favorite subjects, especially when their knowledge is recognized and they are placed in the role of informing an interested listener.

Psychographic research can be applied to businesses as well as to individuals. If you sell to businesses, you might want to find out various psychographic traits of a prospect firm's management, such as:

1. The importance they place on their image in the market
2. Their openness to new ideas and methods
3. Their attitudes toward suppliers, employees, and customers
4. The relative importance they place on quality of product and volume of sales

Demographics and psychographics often go hand in hand. Psychographics such as a prospect's leisure-time activities can indicate a link to certain demographics such as occupation, level of education, and financial situation. Does your prospect shoot darts in a league, or play golf every Saturday? Information like this can provide important clues to a prospect's overall profile.

The connection between demographics and psychographics can be apparent in the reverse as well. When you encounter prospects who work in department stores or factories, you can explore the likelihood that as hard-working members of the middle class they are value-conscious and unwilling to part easily with their money. Again, you run the risk of making false assumptions; demographics and psychographics are best used as a guideline that directs your research rather than as a guarantee.

THE FOCUS OF THE PRESENTATION . . .

Information gathered during preapproach lays the foundation for the presentation. The more specific this data, the better you can tailor the presentation to couple the prospect's needs with your product's benefits. In addition to needs, the state of the decision process and buying capability can be uncovered in this preliminary step. Here are some of the aspects of a presentation that can be planned with the help of preapproach information:

1. The motive or motives you will appeal to
2. The product features or options you will demonstrate and the sequence in which you will cover them
3. The product or products out of the variety offered that you will select for your presentation
4. The prospect's state of decision
5. The rate of delivery and the amount of influence to use

Defined in its simplest terms, the sales presentation is the explanation and proof of how your product or service will meet the prospect's needs. Your goal is to plan your presentations so that you show potential buyers how your product or service can solve their problems. The preapproach, then, should be used first to determine what exactly the prospect's needs are. Needs will translate into dominant **buying motives**, and when you know the prospect's buying motives, you can decide what features to concentrate on, the sequence in which you will cover them, even which products to present.

If your preapproach is inadequate, you might discover too late that you are making the wrong appeal to your prospect. A good preapproach will reveal the buying motive, which will determine the direction of your presentation. It may also reveal that your prospect has more than one buying motive. Moreover, different customers may have different buying motives for the same product because the product offers more than one benefit and satisfies more than one need.

Suppose you are selling a kitchen workstation, and your showroom has numerous visitors every day. Your first task with each new prospect is to determine the prospect's dominant reason for wanting the workstation. Is it economy, space usage, or versatility? Your kitchen workstation carries a modest price and provides a variety of functions within a limited amount of space. But until you know which motive dominates the prospect's thinking, you cannot plan a presentation around the features that will be most important to this person. The preapproach will help you determine not only which qualities to concentrate on but also when to cover them.

Generally speaking, the features that are most important to the prospect should be presented first. Some features may be so minor that you decide to skip them entirely. Motivation research is an important part of the preapproach. Chapter 5 is devoted to the subject of buying behavior.

The preapproach will also help you determine which products to present. If you sell a line of cosmetics, you will need to know your prospect's skin type, coloring, and chemical sensitivities, as well as personal preferences. Learning these details in the preapproach allows you to plan a presentation involving only the appropriate products and eliminate those that have no chance of being sold.

The Prospect's State of Decision . . .

Prospects goes through six stages of thought before deciding to buy. These buying stages may occur in any order and take any amount of time, but few people buy before going through all six of them. As you can see in Figure 4-2, different prospects may have passed through different stages in the buying process by the time you meet them. To plan a successful sales presentation, you will need to learn the prospect's present **state of decision**, that is, the prospect's nearness to buying as defined by which stages the prospect has passed through. The stages are:

1. The prospect recognizes a need and wants to satisfy it.
2. The prospect recognizes your product as the best way to satisfy the need.
3. The prospect recognizes an ability to afford the product, and considers its utility (want-satisfying power) at least equal to that of other products in the same price range.
4. The prospect feels comfortable doing business with you and considers you qualified and capable of providing need satisfaction.
5. The prospect has confidence in your firm and believes it is prepared to stand behind its product.
6. The prospect thinks now is the time to buy.

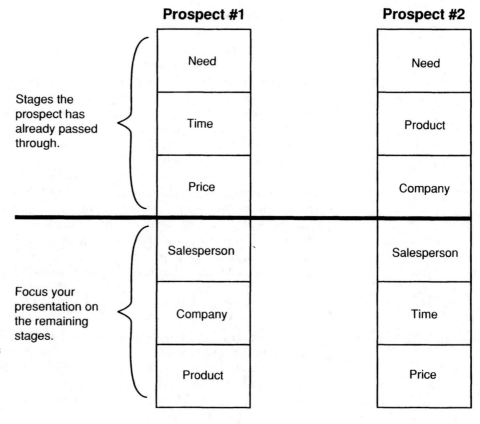

Figure 4-2 You cannot plan your presentation effectively without knowing the prospect's present state of decision. Different prospects will have passed through different stages in the buying process by the time you meet them.

Some prospects may take years to decide that they need your product, whereas others may pass through all six buying stages in the time it takes you to introduce the product and make your presentation. The sequence of buying stages, too, will vary from one potential buyer to the next. Perhaps Susan sees the need for your product but does not have complete confidence in you or your firm. Sharon, on the other hand, might have confidence in you and your firm, but fails to recognize the need for your product. Through the preapproach, you learn which stages your prospect has passed through and tailor your presentation to address those remaining.

Only by knowing the prospect's present state of decision can you truly customize your presentation. For the potential buyer who has gone through all stages but one, a customized presentation focuses on the one remaining stage. This customer is certainly closer to buying than one who has progressed through only two stages, and the proper focus of your presentation should be obvious to you. Suppose you are selling to a repeat customer who already knows that you and your company are reliable. In fact, this prospect has passed through every phase of buying except the time stage, which is to defer the purchase until next year. Knowing this, you can prepare your presentation to focus on the advantages of buying immediately and the disadvantages of waiting until later. Don't waste time explaining how reliable your company is. Covering unnecessary information will only bore the prospect. Once the prospect has passed through all six stages, remember this saying: "If the customer is ready to buy, you should be ready to sell."

The Rate of Delivery . . .

The information you gather during the preapproach should help you determine your **rate of delivery**, which is the time you will take to make your presentation. Your rate of delivery should correspond with the prospect's ability to comprehend. If a potential buyer owns a construction company, there will be no need to explain the relative qualities of the common building materials you sell. You can plan on covering that information briefly and spending more time on details of the sales agreement.

If your preapproach reveals that a certain prospect is completely unfamiliar with the type of product you sell, plan to spend some time explaining basic information before moving on to the traits that distinguish your brand from others. You may discover during preapproach that the potential buyer has difficulty making decisions when confronted with too many new choices. Instead of bringing out all fifteen varieties of your product, select the four or five that seem most appropriate. Begin a narrowing process from there. Too many choices may leave the prospect confused and indecisive, and the sale may never be closed.

Of course, too few choices may be a problem if your prospect is familiar with the product and determined to make decisions without your help. This, too, is the type of information you should look for during the preapproach. With prospects who insist on arriving at their own decision, you must make a presentation that is very subtle. Never seem manipulative or try to pressure the prospect into making a certain choice.

> Individual commitment to a group effort—-that is what makes a team work, a company work, a society work, a civilization work.
>
> Vince Lombardi

Preparing for Questions and Objections . . .

An effective preapproach should enable you to anticipate and plan for a prospect's most likely questions and objections. You may be able to predict a customer's comments on the basis of background information. This is because prospects who share demographic, geographic, and psychographic traits seem to raise similar questions and objections. If you have called on numerous potential buyers who share a similar set of characteristics and circumstances, all of whom have asked the same questions or raised the same objections, you can be almost certain that a new prospect displaying similar traits will do likewise.

With experience, you can actually categorize prospects according to what they are likely to ask and what they will or will not like about your product. This can be very useful in planning your presentation. For example, suppose you sell personal computers, and family-oriented prospects all seem to be concerned with a child's ability to use a PC. Other prospects, the ones with experience on a competing model, seem to consider yours too expensive. With adequate preapproach data, you will know which of your prospects are parents of young children and which ones have worked on a competing PC. Then you can prepare for their most typical questions and objections by incorporating your answers into custom-tailored presentations. Using the preapproach in this way, you have the advantage of overcoming objections before they are ever raised.

Planning Your Personal Conduct . . .

Knowing how to conduct yourself with a given prospect is another important reason for gathering preapproach information. Of course a professional salesperson should be aware of the basic rules of behavior to be observed with all prospects. For instance, you should address a new prospect by title and last name, such as Ms. Smith or Dr. Jones, unless the prospect expresses a desire to be called otherwise. You shouldn't smoke in the presence of a nonsmoker. You should avoid joking with unfamiliar prospects, and avoid discussing controversial topics.

Basic rules of behavior, however, are not what you are trying to learn during preapproach. For a new prospect, you will want to know about circumstances that suggest special consideration in your conduct. Potential buyers are people, and their personalities vary tremendously. You need to accommodate each prospect's personality in your conduct. Behave in a way that every potential buyer will deem appropriate and will make them most comfortable.

For example, you might learn that one prospect enjoys small talk and always uses it to begin conversation, whereas another prefers to get right down to business without such pleasantries. Knowing these things during the preapproach, you can plan to chat about the weather or a ball game with the first prospect, and give the second a straightforward presentation.

You may learn that your prospect has a serious temperament. No matter how well you get to know this person, it would never be wise to make even the most innocent jokes. Or a potential buyer might be self-centered, which means your presentation should focus on the prospect's needs and exclude those of others who might benefit from the purchase.

The Timing of Your Call . . .

Your preapproach can also indicate the best time to make your sales call. Prospects can vary quite a bit in their time preferences. You may learn that one potential buyer has very busy afternoons and will take visitors only in the mornings. Another prospect may be tired and grumpy in the morning, meaning you must schedule your calls after lunch. The preapproach is the best time to learn whether your prospect is a "morning person" or has a limited schedule for callers.

HOW TO GATHER PREAPPROACH INFORMATION . . .

Gathering preapproach information does not have to be a very complicated process. There are two basic ways to learn what you need to know to prepare your presentation: (1) asking questions and (2) using observation.

Asking Questions . . .

The most widely used and probably the easiest way to gather preapproach information is to ask for it. You can obtain plenty of useful information directly from prospects by asking well-directed questions early in the sales interview. Potential buyers not only help you with their response, they also open up to general conversation with you. It is usually a good idea to tell the prospect your purpose in asking certain questions. For example, as you ask the questions you can complete a questionnaire. You might also consider having your prospects themselves complete the questionnaire. Some may see this as a bothe, since the process is less personal. On the other hand, they may also feel more comfortable choosing not to answer certain questions.

Using Observation . . .

Another important method of gathering preapproach data is by observation. We explained in Chapter 3 how a salesperson might observe product lines, clientele, and sales staff to qualify a retailer as a prospect. Observation can be equally important as a preapproach tool with qualified prospects. As a manufacturer's representative, you can discover not only if a retailer you observe is a prospect but also how best to approach the store's manager or buyer. And you can do this without ever saying a word. You might even shop at the store to observe the quality of customer service.

As a practiced observer, you will discover scientifically; that is, you will know what details are important to notice, both before and during your sales call. You must constantly be on the lookout for clues that provide an indication of the prospect's self-image, outlook, and buying motives.

Observation of prospects' residences or offices can give you valuable insights into their interests, activities, and priorities, which in turn may suggest the most likely buying motives. Vacation snapshots, family portraits, trophies, and other souvenirs can, to the keen observer, say something about the prospect's travel interests, domestic orientation, or fondness of sports. Style of dress tells the sharp observer much more than a potential buyer's personal tastes or company standards. People dress the way they do for many emotional reasons: They may desire prestige and status, might like to make a fashion statement, or simply want to be comfortable or fit in with their peers.

Although observation can be very informative, there is a danger in sizing up prospects too quickly, or misjudging their need and ability to purchase. For this reason, a comprehensive preapproach, one involving many questions as well as more than a little observation, is advised. Looks, speech, and mannerisms are helpful but also deceiving, so it's best not to rush into a presentation without confirming your assumptions. A shopper who enters your expensive clothing store wearing old jeans may be just as likely to purchase a silk shirt as a stylishly dressed customer. Don't make the mistake of assuming the customer in jeans is just looking. A few well-thought-out questions will quickly reveal whether shoppers are prospects and what merchandise to direct them to.

SOURCES OF PREAPPROACH INFORMATION . . .

Whether you are asking questions or using observation, you can look to many sources for preapproach information. Consider the following:

1. The prospect
2. Personal friends or acquaintances of the prospect, especially mutual friends or acquaintances
3. The prospect's business associates, co-workers, subordinates, suppliers, or customers
4. The source of the lead
5. Noncompeting salespeople who also call on the prospect
6. Salespeople in your firm who have done business with the prospect
7. Salespeople in the prospect's firm
8. Printed matter, such as reading material on the prospect or the prospect's company

> The best time to make a decision is before you have to make one.
>
> J. Pierpont Morgan

The Prospect . . .

Prospects themselves may be your best and most important source of preapproach information. Your primary and perhaps sole purpose during your initial call may be to get information, not to give it. This is because a lot of important data will not be available in advance of the sales interview. Some can be gathered only during your conversation with the prospect. Perhaps you have no other source of information or don't know who else might have it, or the information is too personal to discuss with anyone but the potential buyer. Further, the prospect is almost certain to give you information that you have not gathered elsewhere.

If you are using a cold canvass method of prospecting and have had no opportunity to gather advance information, you must be prepared to steer your presentation in the proper direction with the knowledge that you gain directly from the prospect. You may also learn something while talking to the prospect that forces you to change your initial sales strategy.

Friends, Associates, and Contacts . . .

Although the prospect is usually a necessary source during the preapproach, you should learn as much as you possibly can before the sales call. This means talking to friends and acquaintances, business associates, and the source of the referral. Finding acquaintances and associates should not be a problem. Noncompeting salespeople, for example, are excellent sources of preapproach data and are usually willing to share information, assuming you will return the favor.

Confidential or personal information is a different story. You cannot expect others to share such details with you. Further, if you do receive confidential information, keep it to yourself. Otherwise, your sources will vanish as soon as they discover you cannot keep a confidence. In fact, you should consider any information that someone has been kind enough to share with you as being classified.

Printed Matter . . .

Many printed sources of preapproach information are likely to be available to you. The firm's annual report is an excellent source, as are sales and product brochures and biographies and background stories of company personnel. If you got a potential buyer's name from a printed source, such as the business-to-business yellow pages, a manufacturer's directory, a newspaper article, or a magazine, that source may also provide you with valuable preapproach data. Major printed sources for industrial salespeople are the publications that pertain to their product or industry. Trade directories and industry journals are valuable for these reasons:

1. They allow you to accumulate the names of prospects.
2. They provide preapproach data on prospects.
3. They keep you abreast of the latest happenings in the industry.

Gathering Information While You Wait . . .

The company receptionist is an excellent source of preapproach information. This person is usually very courteous, friendly, outgoing, and easy to talk to. Receptionists expect salespeople to ask questions, and usually willingly share nonconfidential data. Like administrative assistants, these employees can also provide information on company expansion plans or product line diversification.

If you arrive fifteen minutes before your appointment, you can learn enough to make minor adjustments in your presentation or incorporate new information into it. Of course, we are referring to knowledge that is not required in planning your presentation and can be gathered in several minutes. Some of the typical information gathered on the spot would include the prospect's official title or the proper way to pronounce his or her name. The person you question might be a shop foreman in the prospect's organization or a co-worker who is present. The office secretary, like the receptionist, is an excellent source of information on the prospect and the company.

Ask to see reading material on the company, and be sure to scan the guest register. Most firms require their visitors to sign in for security and insurance purposes. Because you are required to sign your name, the name of your company, the time and purpose of your call, and the person you are there to see, it is not unusual for the receptionist to refuse to answer any questions until you have done so. The register enables someone from your firm to call and find out or confirm that you are on the company's premises.

Usually, this register is open for all to see, and in the time you spend waiting for your appointment, you should check it to see who has visited the firm in recent days. Look for the names of other salespeople, be they competing or noncompeting. This will give you some indication of who your competition is, and perhaps you will recognize the name of another source nonconfidential information about the prospect.

> You look at any giant corporation, and I mean the biggies, and they all started with a guy with an idea, doing it well.
>
> Irvine Robbins

THE PREAPPROACH FOR A BUSINESS PROSPECT . . .

The preapproach for a business prospect may be quite different from that for a consumer. Certain information on a business prospect is basic and must be learned in all instances:

1. The person or persons you want to see
2. The quality level of the firm's finished product
3. The firm's track record, such as its years in business and rate of growth
4. The firm's present sales volume
5. The firm's **market share** (its yearly sales as a percentage of the total yearly sales of all firms in the market)
6. Whether the firm practices reciprocity
7. The firm's present customers
8. The firm's financial state of affairs
9. The firm's receptivity to change
10. The firm's **philosophy of business**
11. The age and condition of the firm's present equipment
12. The present supplier of the item or items you sell
13. Background information on the firm's board of directors and high-ranking company officers
14. The compatibility of your product with the prospect's present equipment
15. The firm's purchasing structure and purchasing guidelines
16. The prospect's feelings or philosophy about changing suppliers
17. The firm's purchase priorities
18. The priority of your product in the firm's purchasing plans
19. The **sales cycle** (estimated time that will elapse before the transaction is finalized)
20. The extent to which you should refer to a person's personal interests or leisure-time activities
21. The unique aspects of the prospect's needs
22. The firm's standards of ethical conduct

If you discover that the company's product quality level is different from the quality level of the raw material or component part you sell, you were incorrect in qualifying the company as a prospect. If you sell several quality levels, you will know which one to focus on during your presentation. If the prospect produces a medium-quality product, it will not need or be willing to pay for a top-quality raw material. Nor is a low-quality raw material suitable for use in producing a premium-quality finished product. You will improve your chances of making the sale by learning the importance the prospect attaches to the factors listed in Figure 4-3.

During your preapproach, learn the importance the prospect attaches to:

1. The reputation of the supplier
2. The price and terms of sale
3. A supplier's ability to adjust the terms of sale
4. The supplier's experience with this type of customer
5. The supplier's technical expertise
6. The convenience of the purchase
7. The supplier's product's reputation and it's length of time on the market
8. The salesperson's experience and expertise
9. The type and extent of training offered by the supplier
10. The type and extent of after-the-sale folllow-up and service offered by the supplier

This information will help you to plan your presentation, focus on your strong points, and successfully remove likely objections.

Figure 4-3 Prospect characteristics.

The Person to See . . .

Knowing exactly which person or persons to see when you call on a business firm is not always as easy as it seems. The mechanics of organizational buying are often complex, with different people at different levels involved to various extents. This means that during the preapproach, you must make a point of learning who has the final authority to purchase your product. It also means learning who are the influencers, gatekeepers, and roadblocks. An **influencer** is someone to whom the purchaser usually turns for advice. A **gatekeeper** is someone you must get past in order to reach the true **decision maker**. This person has the ability and authority to keep you from the key decision maker. A **roadblock** is someone who opposes the purchase from the outset.

If a company has a purchasing department, anything that is bought falls under its authority. However, the **purchasing agent** is not necessarily the buyer of your product. If the firm has many buyers, the purchasing agent may be the one who oversees the entire department. You will have to determine whether you want to see the purchasing agent or a specific buyer. A buyer might have budgetary control over the department in which your product will be used, or be restricted to purchasing only certain types of products. One buyer might be responsible for heavy equipment, another stationery, and yet another office furniture.

In smaller firms, a supervisor will likely purchase capital equipment out of the department's budget. The role played by the purchasing agent is to locate possible vendors and set up interviews. The salespeople who visit the company meet with people from the using department. The purchasing agent is not directly involved in the interviewing process.

Suppose you discover that a firm's design engineer has complete authority to decide what components will be used in a product being designed. This individual, then, would be your prime prospect if you sell industrial components. You hope the parts you sell will go into the product being created for manufacture. But there's a catch. Even though the engineer is your prospect, you must first make contact with the company's purchasing department. This group must be included because of budgetary concerns. Besides that, the purchasing personnel may not take kindly to your bypassing them since they expect to be included in the buying process.

So make contact first with purchasing, and then find someone who can introduce you to the engineer. When you meet with this person, ask him or her what kinds of materials are needed in order to build a better product. Once you have a good idea of the requirements, you can submit information on the parts you sell. If you are successful, the design engineer will choose your company or brand name and include it on the specifications for the new product. The purchasing department, not being the final authority in this decision, does not have the option of shopping around for the component.

If the buying decision is made by a committee or group, try to learn which members of the team are in favor of purchasing your product and which ones are opposed to it. You will need a plan for dealing with both types of prospects as well as with anyone who has special influence over committee members. Call on the conflicting prospects separately, and build your presentation to the "opposition" around their objections to buying. When calling on influential parties or members in favor of your proposition, subtly request their help in convincing the others.

Your goal in determining which person or persons to see is to make your presentation only to people who have the power to make a buying decision. By approaching only those with buying authority, you'll never find yourself taking no for an answer from someone who proves not to have any business refusing you. Figure 4-4 summarizes the various roles in the business buying process.

The Prospect's Name . . .

Nothing is a greater sign of poor preparation than not knowing the name of the person you are calling on. Granted, many businesspeople are accustomed to salespeople entering their firm and asking for their name, but this does not mean they consider it the most professional practice. You should use preapproach research to gather as much information in advance of the sales call as you possibly can, and that certainly includes your prospect's name and job title. If you know only the title of the person you want to see, call in advance and ask for the name of the research director, public relations manager, or computer center coordinator. Once you have the name, more thorough preapproach work can start immediately.

When you make your sales call, you should ask for the person by name instead of by title or function. A salesperson should never need to ask, "Who's in charge of shipping here?" or "Who on your faculty teaches the business

Roles in the Business Buying Process

Initiator– submits the purchase request or discovers a presently unfulfilled need.

User– exerts influence over the buying process by specifying needed product requirements, but has no say in the buying decision. May initiate the purchase request. Usually operating and service personnel.

Influencer– assembles purchase criteria and evaluates alternative solutions. Has direct impact on the purchase decision because of strong product knowledge or an understanding of the firm's needs. Typically technicians and operating personnel.

Gatekeeper– regulates the interaction and flow of information between salespeople and those involved in the buying process. Determines which salespeople communicate with influencers, deciders, and users, protecting them from unwanted or unscheduled telephone calls and visits. Typically receptionists and purchasing personnel.

Decider– selects the product and supplier to be used, but may lack the authority to place the order.

Buyer– schedules sales presentations, handles purchase details, and places the order. Serves as decider in the purchase of routine items. Usually a purchasing department employee.

Roadblock– objects to the purchase or the salesperson's brand. Sees no need for the product. Prefers another brand, or thinks the timing isn't right.

Figure 4-4

courses?" This not only reveals lack of preapproach, but also makes the prospect feel unimportant. If you use the name, on the other hand, the prospect is much more likely to find time for you, knowing you have made some effort at personal attention.

The Prospect's Business . . .

Many aspects of a prospect's business should be researched during the preapproach. To plan an effective presentation for a business prospect, you will need to know certain basic facts, such as the company's sales volume and market share, its use of reciprocity, and its current financial status.

The prospect's sales volume and market share can give you an indication of your potential for selling a certain volume, as well as an appropriate pricing structure. The concept of derived demand also comes into play here. By **derived demand**, we mean a demand that arises as a result of another demand. The demand for components or materials is derived from the demand for the end products into which they go. So if you know your prospect company's sales volume and market share, you know the extent to which they will need the materials you sell and the price range they will consider.

Your preapproach should also reveal whether the prospect firm practices **reciprocity**, an arrangement in which companies buy from each other. If a prospect firm produces something your firm could buy, relay this information to your purchasing department. Including your prospect on the "Approved Suppliers" list will create the potential for reciprocity, a step in the right direction in your sales efforts. One word of caution: Many firms dislike reciprocal buying situations, and their buyers work very hard to avoid them. You should learn your prospect's attitude toward reciprocity before suggesting that your company place an order with the prospect firm.

Aspects of your prospect firm's financial status are especially important if they tell you whether the firm is in a phase of growth, cost cutting, or trouble. You will also want to learn how your prospect sees you compared to your competition. Is the prospect a loyal customer of one of your competitors, or does it appear to be completely open-minded when it comes to deciding where to buy? If you are selling a product that the potential buyer will soon purchase, what are the priorities? Is a purchase decision urgent, or is it one that might be deferred?

The Business Prospect's Personal Interests . . .

You may discover some of your prospect's personal interests during the preapproach. If so, you will need to determine whether the individual would welcome discussion of nonbusiness topics. With some prospects, the best bet is to play it safe, that is, stick to business when opening a conversation. Although discussing personal interests can be perfectly acceptable with a known prospect, it can be detrimental with an unfamiliar one. Wait until you get to know the person before getting too personal.

If you know your prospect will accept casual conversation, feel free to bring up bits of personal information you have learned during the preapproach. For example, you might mention that you attended the same college, and chat briefly about certain professors or courses you both had. Bringing up a subject of personal interest or importance to the prospect can capture attention, build conversation, and break down any initial resistance. After breaking the ice, you can comfortably shift to the purpose of your call.

Smart salespeople take special interest in their clients' companies. This means keeping up with nonbusiness news that is of personal interest to the company. Follow the firm's softball team, for instance, and you will impress the customer with the importance you attach to their entire operation. You will also never be at a loss for casual conversation while on company premises.

Although background information may help you plan your presentation, it is sometimes too sensitive to discuss directly with prospects. You may have heard about a recent divorce or withdrawal from college before graduation, or about the lawsuit pending against the firm, and any of these facts may influence your approach. But this doesn't mean you should reveal exactly what you know. The prospect may feel that you have pried too deeply into personal matters or that certain things are just none of your business. Even if the information you learn is more pleasant, like the prospect's fondness of baseball, you might discover it's best to steer clear of the subject. Perhaps the prospect won't talk about baseball with anyone but personal friends or is tired of talking about it. If conversations about the World Series have been circulating among salespeople who call on the firm, it will be obvious why you're bringing it up, and the prospect will know where the information came from.

Sally Omran

Diablo Valley College in the San Francisco Bay area has reason to be proud of Sally Omran. Twice honoring her as "outstanding business student of the year," DVC can point to a long string of successes by this dynamic, energetic woman. Some of her many accomplishments while in college include sitting on the Business Advisory Board, serving as a member of the board of directors of the Contra County Ballet Foundation, organizing the first Bay Area Economic Summit, and assisting with the Kennedy King Scholarship Committee. She also managed internships with Beverages and More! and KGO-TV.

Before coming to Diablo Valley College, Sally owned and operated two small businesses. The most successful of these ventures was a gourmet wine and food market located on Nob Hill in San Francisco. This eatery was featured on several occasions by noted columnist Herb Caen, writing in the San Francisco Chronicle. Although she achieved financial success in her business ventures, Sally felt strongly that education was the ultimate goal, and returned to college to continue her marketing studies. She handled her reentry much as she directs most of her efforts, by creating a personal marketing plan. With the help from several key mentors on the college faculty and staff, Sally polished her writing skills and developed her confidence. She still feels that sales and marketing "...affects every aspect of my personal and professional life."

It was with KGO-TV that Sally was really able to let her native bent for marketing flourish. While working at this ABC affiliate, she produced segments for MARKETPLACE, a program with local emphasis on women in business. Her work with Beverages and More! included the development of a marketing plan for this local distributor. She designed, created, and executed the media coverage for a fashion show at the Nordstrom outlet in Walnut Creek, California and handled the public relations for the Contra Costa Ballet Foundation. She is now employed in the marketing department at Chas. Schwaub, the investment brokerage, where she continues her work with marketing and promotion.

> In the end, all business operations can be reduced to three words: people, product, and profits. People come first.
>
> Lee Iacoca

Preapproaching Regular Customers . . .

The preapproach is not only important for your first-time prospects. You will need to gather information in advance of your calls to repeat customers as well. It is important to keep up to date on these buyers. Fortunately, gathering information on current customers will probably not require as much effort as gathering information on new customers.

In selling situations where the salesperson calls on the prospect only once or twice a year, significant changes may take place between visits. Things of interest to you are constantly happening to your regular customers, so each time you call you should ask them what the future appears to hold. If a client tells you the firm is planning to upgrade its quality standards, you may have to change the focus of your next presentation. If a client tells you the company will merge next month with another company and everyone's job is in danger, you will have to keep your eye out for changes in everything, including the company's purchasing policies and buying personnel.

In the cases of mergers or buyouts, you will want an updated copy of purchasing guidelines before making your next sales call. Further, you will want to gain a feel for what the new organization is like, such as how its operating procedures have changed or the characteristics of those now in command. The merger may call for a major change in your selling strategy.

KEEPING CUSTOMER FILES . . .

We mentioned in Chapter 3 the importance of maintaining detailed records on past, present, and future purchasers. Keeping **customer files** is a must in selling. A constantly maintained customer file is the best way to keep up to date on your customers and their needs. There should be a separate file for each customer or prospect, and it should contain all the information you gathered during and between previous visits, including data received from sources other than the customer. Be sure to review this information before each personal call. Each time you come across news about customers or of interest to them, put it in the customer's file.

If a purchasing agent informs you of the firm's expansion plans, make a note of it in that company's file and follow up on it before your next visit. Record personal information as well. If it serves no other purpose, it often provides an excellent conversation opener. For example, you may be able to say,

"Bill, the last time I visited, you were planning a fishing trip to Canada. How was it?" This encourages conversation, and the prospect is sure to be impressed by the fact that you remembered something you were told so long ago. It is also a good idea to include notes of the examples and suggestions you made on your last call so that you are sure not to use the same ones again.

With many regular buyers, it may well be impossible for you to remember all the information you accumulate. The customer file will do for you what your memory will not. Many client management software programs are available that enable you to store information on your prospects. A more traditional way of managing prospect information is the tickler file. Tickler files are covered in Chapter 17.

Another, though less suitable, way to keep information on customers is on a daily calendar. In this method, you would mark the key points of your last visit on the calendar page that corresponds with your next anticipated visit. For example, if you intend to call on the customer again in six months, skip ahead to that date on the calendar and jot down your notes. When the time for your next visit comes, you will see the information. You could also consider recording information from your last visit on tape and playing it back as you drive to the prospect's home or office for your next visit. This is most appropriate when calls are close together and the information need not be studied in advance.

You Decide!

Harry, a salesperson for a large manufacturer of storage shelving, is working with another seller and their Sales Manager on putting together a presentation for a major aerospace firm. This would be a significant purchase, and the proposal must be handled well. The prospective customer was recently rocked with a sexual harassment scandal that was widely publicized in the local papers, and Harry's boss wants to learn if any members of the buying team might have been involved.

The Sales Manager corners Harry and asks him to have lunch with an acquaintance in the aerospace company with whom Harry golfs. The object is to learn who is on the buying team, if anyone was involved in the harassment case, and what leverage this knowledge might create. Harry's boss even suggests that he ply his golfing buddy with a few drinks to loosen his tongue. Harry is a bit concerned that he is treading on thin ice and his questioning might be construed as prying, but on the other hand, he is anxious for the bonus that would come with the large sale, should his company get the business. Should he or shouldn't he try to get information from his friend? **You decide!**

Summing It Up . . .

It is important that you carefully plan your sales effort. This requires gathering as much information on your prospect in advance of your sales call as you can. Your goal is to form a complete profile of the prospect, which might include geographic, demographic, and psychographic characteristics. Further, by learning the prospect's present state of decision, you prepare yourself to address the most likely questions and objections.

The preapproach is integrally related to the sales presentation and crucial to successful selling. There are many advantages to forming a complete and accurate image of the prospect. Potential buyers are happy to meet salespeople who can solve a problem for them at a price they are willing to pay. When you gather preapproach data your most important goal is to find out your prospect's problems or needs, even if they are not recognized. From there, you can determine the most appropriate solution, which will suggest the focus of your presentation.

Key Concepts and Terms . . .

buying motive	philosophy of doing business
customer file	preapproach
decision maker	purchasing agent
derived demand	rate of delivery
household life-cycle position	reciprocity
gatekeeper	roadblock
influencer	sales cycle
market share	state of decision

Building Skills . . .

1. Contrast the prospecting and preapproach stages of the sales process.
2. Explain the benefits derived from having conducted a thorough preapproach.
3. Define the profile of the prospect.
4. Define what is meant by the prospect's psychographic characteristics along with the concept of psychographics as it applies to business firms.
5. Explain the confidence-building effect of preapproach for both the salesperson and the prospect.
6. Explain how the aspects of the salesperson's personal behavior are likely to vary from prospect to prospect.
7. Explore the reasons that noncompeting salespeople usually are very willing to share prospect information with you.

8. Examine the means of gathering preapproach data while you await your sales interview.

9. Explain the concept of derived demand.

10. Describe reciprocity and the importance of determining if your prospect practices it.

11. Explore the reasons that personal conversation topics are not recommended when the prospect is a businessperson you do not know well.

12. Describe the dangers of an inadequate preapproach.

13. You discover that the prospect has a difficult time making a decision. Describe the impact of this knowledge on your preparation for the sales presentation.

14. Define the prospect's "present state of decision" and its impact on the design of a custom-made sales presentation.

Making Decisions 4-1:

Tom Bilger is a sales associate for North Shore Equipment, the area's exclusive dealer of Great Bear kerosene heaters. One day he is visited by Marilyn DiRocco, who lives two miles south of town in Meadows Township. Marilyn wants to buy a kerosene heater for her second-floor apartment.

Tom:	Have you ever used a kerosene heater?
Marilyn:	No.
Tom:	That shouldn't be a problem. How big is your apartment?
Marilyn:	Well, I've never measured it…but it has one bedroom, a large bathroom, a small kitchen, and a good-sized living room.
Tom:	Where do you intend to use the heater?
Marilyn:	In the living room, I guess. My landlady just had the old heating system torn out and replaced with separate gas heaters for each apartment. So now the tenants have to foot the heating bill. I'm trying to cut expenses.
Tom:	(Directing Marilyn to a heater on display) This is the model I recommend. (Tom spends ten minutes showing Marilyn how to use it.)
Marilyn:	Are you sure kerosene heaters are legal in my township? I've heard they're illegal in apartments here.
Tom:	Yes, they are. As far as your township is concerned, I really don't know.
Marilyn:	I'd better call my landlady and ask her.
Tom:	You should also call your fire department. They're probably legal, though. I've sold many of these to people from Meadows Township.

Describe how Tom could have been better prepared for Marilyn's visit. Explore any reason for his lack of preparation and his fundamental mistakes.

Making Decisions 4-2:

Emi Hamamoto is a salesperson for Gypsy Rose Furniture. One afternoon she meets Bill Raneri, an elementary school teacher who tells Emi he has just moved with his wife and two children into a large Tudor-style house in an exclusive community near Emi's store.

Emi:	Congratulations. You'll love it there.
Bill:	Thank you, I'm sure we will. But I need one more thing to make the house complete.
Emi:	What's that?
Bill:	I've always wanted an oak rolltop desk, but I've never had room for one.
Emi:	Let me show you the one we have in stock. (Emi leads Bill to the rear of the showroom.)
Bill:	(Checking the price tag) Do you recommend this one?
Emi:	Yes, I do.
Bill:	(Opening a drawer) Why?
Emi:	Its colonial style is time-tested, and this wood goes with just about any decor. At $1,000, it's very reasonably priced.
Bill:	(Opening the desk top) Do you have anything else in stock?
Emi:	Not in stock, but we have others in our catalog. Would you like a catalog? (Emi reaches for a catalog.)
Bill:	Yes. Thank you. I'll go through this tonight and stop back if I see something I like.

Describe Emi's assessment of Bill's needs, including any background information that she should have gathered.

Making Decisions 4-3:

You represent a firm that provides automated payroll services for small to medium-sized companies. What preapproach data would you want to gather on prospects prior to your visit?

Making Decisions 4-4:

You sell waterbeds. List six questions a prospect might ask.

Practice Makes Perfect 4-1:

Place yourself in the role of a real estate broker in a resort/retirement area (such as Tucson, Arizona) who has a web page on the Internet. What types of preapproach information would you request from people responding to your listing?

Understanding Buying Behavior

THE JOB TO BE DONE . . .

In order to sell, you have to understand why people buy. This chapter primarily explores individual buying behavior, but you should keep in mind that it is people who buy for businesses and organizations. Some of the things you will discover in Chapter 5 are to:

...appreciate the role of motivation research in selling.

...recognize the variety of buying motives at play in selling.

...understand the importance of appealing to the right buying motive.

...realize the difference between rational and emotional buying motives.

...understand the nature of hidden buying motives.

...develop the ability to identify buying motives.

...discover the prospect's strongest buying motive.

...examine the relationship between product features and buying motives.

...recognize the influence of self-concept over buying behavior.

...know how frame of reference affects buying behavior.

...appreciate the role of reference groups in buying behavior.

BUYING BEHAVIOR . . .

Why do people buy products and services? For what reasons might they buy your product or service? **Motivation research** is the subject of this chapter. We will examine the reasons people buy what they buy, and determine the buying motive or motives to which you should appeal. Motivation research is used to determine the underlying causes of buying behavior, the wants that drive prospects to purchase. It is an extension of the preapproach and an integral part of selling. Because of its direct relationship to selling success, motivation research is a responsibility of all salespeople.

THE SATISFACTION OF NEEDS AND WANTS . . .

What do people really buy when they buy your product? They buy satisfaction. The purchase of clothing or food satisfies a basic need. The sports-car enthusiast purchases not just a sports car but excitement, status, and self-esteem. The satisfaction of these needs or wants produce those good feelings prospects hope to gain through product ownership.

The drive to satisfy needs or wants is the basis of all purchases. The more your product satisfies and the more apparent its satisfaction potential is, the better it will sell. Your prospects will judge both you and your product on the ability to satisfy their needs or wants. In approaching selling from a problem-solving perspective, as we will do in Chapter 7, when a person has an unsatisfied need or want, there is a "problem" to be solved. Your product or service must provide the solution to that problem.

The needs or wants that can be satisfied by products may be on any level. Some goods satisfy immediate biological needs like hunger and thirst. Others gratify higher concerns like the desire for personal achievement. Some prospects buy products that please both immediate wants and long-term objectives. For example, a customer might choose a certain computer program because it meets both an immediate need for simplicity of operation and an ongoing desire to spend more time at home with the family.

The most direct path to making the sale is the satisfying route. You must know what prospect needs your product can satisfy. Some are universal, whereas others are specific to the individual. Once you determine a given prospect's needs, including how this person wants to feel, you can sell satisfaction of those feelings. Rather than supply a wordprocessing system, you can sell convenience and portability. Rather than sell a house, you provide comfort, pride, and homelife.

> Winning doesn't mean getting ahead of others. Winning means getting ahead of yourself. Winning means breaking your own records. It means outstripping your yesterdays by outselling yourself today.
>
> Roger Staubach

Motivation Research in Selling . . .

All behavior, including buying behavior, is motivated. Motivation is the drive to behave in a way that will satisfy a perceived need. The greater the need, the more rewarding the satisfaction. The greater the rewards of acting a certain way, the stronger the drive or motivation. As a student, you may be motivated to do well in school by the possibility of good grades. But you may be even more driven by the possibility of obtaining a better job after completing your classes successfully. We are motivated to buy some products more than others, and our motivation to buy certain things changes over time.

A buying motive is a reason for buying, a reason for wanting a given product. A prospect's buying motives are usually apparent in his or her behavior. These desires determine whether a person is a prospect. If one does not have a motive that relates to your product, he or she is not a prospect. If your product is known for its status appeal, you must approach people who are motivated by such symbols. Don't approach people who have no desire for status.

Through motivation research, you can understand seemingly illogical buying behavior and improve your chances of success in selling. For example, some people insist on paying high prices for certain products that can be bought at lower prices. A look at these buyers' motivations may reveal that they associate quality with price. One dentist found it all but impossible to sell a set of dentures for $500, but managed to sell the same product for $1,000 to quality-conscious patients.

You may be able to determine your prospects' most likely buying motives on the basis of their personal characteristics. For example, you might find that younger potential buyers want excitement, whereas your business-oriented clients want to save money. If you sell life insurance, you will find that single people in their twenties are more motivated by career advancement, independence, and fun than by financial security and family protection. You will not be surprised to discover, then, that they don't want to buy life insurance. Knowing their motivations, you can prepare to increase the importance of financial security in their minds by discussing the family they might have in a few short years.

THE VARIETY OF BUYING MOTIVES . . .

Different people often have different motives for buying the same product. One person might play golf to relax, another prefers the camaraderie of friends, and still another thrives to compete. Yet they all buy golf clubs. A teenager joins a health club to build his muscles, whereas a middle-aged adult is motivated to stay in shape and live longer. Each is interested in different features the club has to offer: The teenager uses the weight room, the adult uses the cardiovascular exercise equipment.

Pet-care product marketers might have to appeal to three different target prospects with three different sets of motives. Pet shop proprietors may be motivated by profits, veterinarians might be more concerned with health in pets, and pet owners are interested in products that keep their pets looking and feeling good. As a seller of pet-care products, you would need to identify

> Remember, a dead fish can float downstream, but it takes a live one to swim upstream.
>
> W. C. Fields

these various buying motives and learn to appeal to each prospect's most important drive.

Most products appeal to more than one buying motive. This is especially true of major or multiple-use items. A homeowner who installs an in-ground swimming pool might be concerned with health, recreation, and family enjoyment. This same potential buyer might also be motivated by an increase in the property value. Although the basic motive for purchasing an automobile is transportation, buyers will likely have multiple interests. One might place importance on safety, economy, and quality, whereas another looks for performance, comfort, and status.

Usually, products will satisfy some buying motives more than others. A luxury car might appeal to the comfort motive more than to performance. A sports car might do just the opposite. Consumers are generally suspicious of products that claim to offer seemingly conflicting benefits, such as an apartment that is supposed to be both economical and luxurious.

Brand-Related Motives . . .

If brand awareness in your industry is strong, as it is in the fashion industry, then **brand-related motives** come into play. Once you determine your prospect's most likely reason for purchasing your product, you should also consider those associated specifically with your brand.

If brand awareness is not very strong, you might be able to build brand-related motives into your sales approach. Suppose you are selling that swimming-pool contract. Not only should you know that your prospect wants recreation and increased property value, but that there is also a desire to have a pool that is constructed by a reputable contractor.

Rational and Emotional Buying Motives . . .

Buying motives can be classified as either rational or emotional. **Rational motives** relate to factors that are thought of logically and objectively, such as long-term cost, performance, and productivity. **Emotional motives** are subjective and based on feelings rather than intellect. People might have emotional responses to factors such as safety, comfort, and self-esteem. Rational purchases are easy to explain, but emotional purchases are not. An emotional acquisition is one that cannot be described in reasonable terms. Rational motives might be said to come from the head, and emotional motives from the heart.

Low-unit-value purchases are often, but not always, rational. If you purchase a soda on the way home from school to quench your thirst, your motive is rational. It satisfies an immediate physical need. However, if you purchase a certain brand of soda because it is what your friends drink, emotion has entered the picture. Your desire to fit in with the crowd satisfies an emotional need.

If a business purchase decision is made by a buying team, each team member may have separate motives and concerns. For example, the member from engineering may consider a short design lead time to be of utmost importance, whereas the person from manufacturing may be most concerned with quality control and avoiding frequent retooling. The representative from finance is likely to be preoccupied with the budgetary aspects of the transaction, and the team member from purchasing is sure to be concerned with order size and purchase frequency.

Business purchases are often considered purely rational, but the assumption of pure rationality is false. Business purchases do tend to be more rational than those made by consumers, but emotion remains a factor. An executive may decide to purchase a certain computer system partly because another successful company owns the same brand. Such a motive is emotional. Emotion might also enter the picture through your own behavior. Even if you handle the finest product on the market, you might fail to sell a certain buyer simply because you repeatedly mispronounce his or her name.

The majority of purchase decisions are based upon both rational and emotional motives. For example, your rational reason for buying a new coat is to replace an old one. In strictly rational terms, any warm coat will do. But you choose a full-length wool coat because you are going to wear it to work and social events, where you must project a certain image. You might feel uncomfortable going to parties in a more casual coat. Your choice of coats is both rational and emotional.

Opportunity Cost . . .

Psychologists tell us that the higher a product's price, the greater the degree of emotional involvement in its purchase. This increase is partly due to the opportunity costs associated with major purchases. **Opportunity cost** is a loss of purchasing options. When we make a purchase, we sacrifice the option to spend our limited funds in another way. The more expensive the product is, the greater the sacrifice, so the greater our emotional investment.

Have an absolute and total belief that what you're selling is worth more than the price you ask for it. Your belief in your product should be so great that you ought to be using it.

Zig Ziglar

When we buy a glass of lemonade to quench our thirst, we give up very little. But when we buy a motor home, we sacrifice a great deal. For most people, buying a house is the most important and expensive purchase they will make. Their emotional involvement is high because they are spending so much of their money on it and will be committed to it for many years. They want their house to provide them with safety, comfort, and happiness, as well as with financial security. No wonder selling a house requires so much effort.

Most people can't afford to buy costly items for purely emotional reasons. Because we work with limited budgets, we must restrict our purely emotional purchases to an affordable few. Prospects in comfortable circumstances have met their basic wants and are more inclined to purchase for complicated emotional reasons. This is not to say, however, that purely emotional purchases are associated only with the wealthy. People in lower economic brackets buy products out of pure emotion, too.

Rationalizing an Emotional Purchase . . .

Buyers often feel the need to rationalize their purchases both to themselves and to others. This is especially true if they fear they are making an insensible purchase. For example, family-oriented individuals may want to justify a $400 gym membership because they know the fitness program will take them away from home three nights a week. Their rationalization? Their improved physical condition will ensure them a longer life to share with their family.

You might find it necessary to help your prospects rationalize their purchases. If you can provide them with sensible reasons for their decisions, you will help them feel good about purchases that they fear are frivolous.

Hidden Buying Motives . . .

People often have buying motives that they aren't willing to disclose. If you have covered all the motives that you thought were important and you still have not stimulated your prospect's interest, chances are the prospect has a **hidden buying motive**.

The most likely motives to be kept hidden are emotional ones. Because higher-priced items carry more emotional weight, prospects for these items are more likely to have hidden motives. This is why personal selling plays a bigger role in the purchase of "big-ticket" items than it does in inexpensive products.

Determining hidden buying motives is not easy. People keep their feelings hidden from friends and strangers alike. You cannot assume that prospects will share their secrets with you because they know you or don't know you. People with hidden buying motives will not respond with full candor to your questions. You will have to question them very discreetly and piece together the information they disclose. Try to determine what the prospect's past buying behavior was like. Previous purchases say a lot about a prospect's present behavior.

After you have been selling your product for some time, you will know the hidden motives associated with it and can quickly assess those of each given prospect. If you think you know the prospect's buying motive, don't reveal your knowledge. Tactfully steer your presentation to a different appeal or even to a different product. For instance, if you realize your prospect is put off by the price of your product, suggest a comparison with another, less expensive product in your line. You need not embarrass the prospect by asking, "Is price the problem?"

Using Syllogism to Determine the Prospect's Motive . . .

One way to determine a prospect's hidden buying motive is through the use of syllogism. **Syllogism** is a form of deductive logic that allows you to reason from the general to the specific. It takes the form of a major premise, a minor premise, and a conclusion. Here is an example of a simple syllogism:

Major premise: All men are foolish.

Minor premise: Smith is a man.

Conclusion: Therefore, Smith is foolish.

In a valid syllogism, both premises must be accepted as truths. Only if it is based on true premises can your conclusion be valid. Now, suppose you are selling a seemingly expensive product to an elderly couple, and they are not responding favorably to you. Here is how you might use syllogism to determine their hidden motive:

Major premise: Most people over sixty-five are living on fixed incomes.

Minor premise: This man and woman are over sixty-five.

Conclusion: Therefore, this man and woman are living on a fixed income.

From this bit of reasoning, you know that your prospects are not responding because they feel your product is more costly than they can afford. Although syllogism can be a handy tool when you don't know why your prospects are resisting your selling efforts, it should be used with care. Never assume too much about your prospects.

> The main purpose of a salesperson is not to make sales, but to create customers.
>
> Gerhard Gschwandtner

A Closer Look at Buying Motives . . .

The variety of common buying motives, both rational and emotional, is so great that a complete list would be impossible. Here is a closer look at some of the motives:

Attention: The need to be noticed, as when we buy flashy clothing.

Self-esteem: The need to feel better about ourselves, as when we buy grooming products.

Belongingness: The need to be accepted by our peer group, as when we buy certain brands of products. Children and teenagers often are strongly motivated by the need to belong; they have to wear a certain sneaker or drink a certain soft drink because all of their friends are doing it. Even adults need to belong and will buy certain kinds of houses and cars to fit in with the right social groups.

Creativity: The need to make something original, expressive, and imaginative. A retired executive might be motivated by creativity to buy a drawing board and a set of paints.

Fear: The desire to avoid bad consequences. Fear motivates people to buy insurance, preventive maintenance contracts, and all kinds of safety equipment.

Immortality: The desire to "live" forever by having a lasting effect. The desire for immortality may be just as strong a motivator as fear for buying life insurance. Heads of families who buy life insurance gain immortality by protecting the family even after their death. Wealthy college alumni "buy" immortality when they donate to their alma maters and have campus buildings named after them.

Convenience: The desire for ease of use and savings of time. Convenience motivates people to buy processed foods or to buy non-food items while they are in the grocery store. Convenience may very well be the most important buying motive today. Retailers are especially sensitive to this motivation. They advertise store location, offer extended hours, provide large parking facilities, and design special floorplans, all with one thing in mind: customer convenience.

Self-gratification: The desire to please oneself and take pride in one's accomplishments. You might throw yourself a party to celebrate the completion of a major project. Or you might take up gardening, which has become one of America's favorite outdoor pastimes.

Privacy: The need for quiet and solitude. The privacy motivation can come from our present environment or the background in which we grew up. Prospective renters may seek a private apartment because they were always surrounded by noisy siblings or, being an only child, they are accustomed to peace and quiet.

Security: The need to feel safe from harm or disadvantage. Security is often a hidden motive. A prospect who grew up in poverty might claim to be buying a large freezer for the sake of convenience, but the buyer's real reason may be to keep food on hand because it was once too scarce.

Status: The desire to enhance one's image. People sometimes buy luxurious cars because of the status the cars provide.

Quality: The desire for complete satisfaction with the finest product. Status and quality often go hand in hand. Many manufacturers and sellers gain status because of their reputation for producing the highest-quality products.

Sexual reassurance and gender identity: Strong motives in the face of sex-role changes at work, school, and home. Women and men alike need gender-specific products that reassure them of their sexual identity and their place in society. Perfume and cigar sales have increased dramatically in recent years, and body building has become very popular.

Work ethic: The belief in productivity, efficiency, and honest work. A strong work ethic will motivate buyers to purchase products that help them increase the quality and quantity of their work and make them feel good about work.

Charity: The desire to give to others less fortunate. The charity motive explains the success of ticket sales for circuses, ice shows, rodeos, and Christmas shows. People buy tickets to events they have no intention of attending, strictly because their purchase contributes to a worthy cause.

Nostalgia: A longing for what is past or absent. Nostalgia motivates many to purchase collectibles, antiques, classic movie memorabilia, and so on.

Love: An extremely important buying motive. Love motivates the purchase of everything from greeting cards to extravagant gifts to appliances to insurance.

Conspicuous Consumption . . .

Much of our buying is done to impress others, often referred to as **conspicuous consumption**. We buy to show who we are or to prove that we are successful. We take comfort knowing that others get a certain message about us based on our purchases. Such image-conscious purchase behavior is especially common among people who desire recognition or who want to be seen as members of a higher social class. Interestingly, people who historically have high social and economic standing (the so-called old rich) often do the opposite. They downplay their status. They see no need to demonstrate their place in society and might even take pains to purchase products that convey a less wealthy image.

> Luck sometimes visits a fool, but never sits down with him.
> Old German proverb

THE PROSPECT'S STRONGEST BUYING MOTIVE...

Determining the prospect's strongest buying motive is an important objective of your preapproach. Making an immediate appeal to this primary desire is often the most effective way of opening a presentation. At any rate, you should approach these reasons to buy in order of their significance to the prospect, starting with the most important one and working down. Starting at the top is necessary to stimulate interest in your presentation. This is why you should present your most important selling points first. It is the prospect's strongest buying motive that determines what are your strongest selling points.

Making the Right Appeal...

The objective of motivation research in selling is to discover what moves a prospect to purchase. You use motivation research to help you target the right buying motive, to make the right appeal. Your product's primary appeal is the central element of your sales presentation.

The terms *want, benefit, buying motive,* and *appeal* refer to different aspects of the same concept. A **want** can be defined as a desire or need your product satisfies. **Benefits** are the positive qualities your product offers. **Buying motives** are the inner drives that compel the prospect to purchase your product. An **appeal** is the idea you build your presentation around. But whatever qualifies as a want also qualifies as a benefit, a buying motive, and an appeal. For example, prospects might want economy, so economy is the buying motive that compels them to consider your product. Economy is also one of the benefits your product offers and is the appeal around which you center your presentation.

Making the right appeal is easier if your prospects tell you what they hope your product can accomplish or what goals it can help them reach. Because products usually satisfy several buying motives, you will have to decide what appeal to use. Ask yourself what is the quickest way to arouse the prospect's desire for your product.

If you are unsure of your product's appeals, ask yourself, "Why would someone want to buy my product?" The reasons you list are the benefits your product offers, and these benefits produce your appeals. If your product is compact and easy to use, you list convenience as the benefit, and it becomes the focus of your appeal. Also ask your current customers why they like your product. The reasons they give are your product's major appeals, although the customers may not describe them as such. For example, your customers might say they buy your product because their friends buy it and wouldn't like a lesser product. To you, this means social approval is an appeal. You can indirectly refer to the social-approval benefit in your next presentations. Figure 5-1 provides an answer to the question "What is **benefit selling**?"

What is Benefit Selling?

Benefit Selling is a sales approach that focuses on your customer's needs rather than specific features of products or services. *Features* are impersonal characteristics of the product that exist independent of the uses. For instance, the apples you see in this illustration have these features: roundness, colorfulness, firmness, and juiciness with a crisp texture. *Benefits* include all the types of satisfactions that different customers can personally derive from the product or service. In the case of apples, they're thirst-quenching, good-tasting, nutritious, versatile as a cooking ingredient, great for still-life painting, and can even serve as a "natural" toothbrush. Benefits are the "connections" between products and your customer's needs. So you must first help the customer to determine what are his or her real needs. Then, the products or services can be recommended which fit those needs. The result is that your customer has the best of all reasons to buy...he or she gets a real or perceived *benefit* from the product or service.

Hypochondriac:

"I need something to keep the doctor away."

Mother:

"I need to get my kids off junk food."

Health Type:

"I need a way to brush my teeth after lunch. Without brushing."

Homemaker:

"I need to make a pie that everyone will love."

Figure 5-1

Relating Product Features to Buying Motives . . .

A sales presentation is a way of communicating a collection of product features that relate to a buying motive. In a well-designed sales presentation, the product features discussed are those that will satisfy the prospect's primary buying motive. There are as many sales presentations available as there are buying motives to satisfy. When you design your presentation, start by listing the motives a person might have for buying your product, and then list under each one the product features that help satisfy that motive. Product features, or talking points, are meaningful only if they relate to buying motives.

Here are some product features that might be on your list:

Price

Ingredients

Color

Warranty

Size

Terms of sale

Design

Form

Packaging

Service

Quality

Shape

Suppose you have an apartment to rent, and you want to know how to relate your product features to renters' buying motives. You would begin your selling effort by asking and answering two questions:

1. What do renters look for in an apartment? (Your answer will be a list of buying motives, such as comfort, convenience, economy.)
2. What are the appealing traits of this apartment? (Your answer will be a list of talking points or product features, such as quiet location, fireplace, wall-to-wall carpeting.)

As you begin to answer the first question, you might realize that your apartment doesn't satisfy every buying motive renters might have. For example, some renters want luxury in an apartment, yet you cannot honestly list luxury as a motive for wanting your apartment. Here are some buying motives you might list:

Convenience

Economy

Safety

Privacy

Comfort

There is no need to list every single buying motive that applies to your apartment; just the major appeals. Next, answer the second question by listing your apartment's features, or talking points, under the related buying motives. Some talking points will belong under two or more motives, and you might have more talking points listed under some motives than under others.

This is what your list might look like:

Convenience

1. Two blocks from supermarket; several churches nearby
2. Bus stops at door (important to senior citizens)
3. Plenty of free parking
4. Washer and dryer in basement
5. Extra-large kitchen
6. Built-in trash compactor and disposal
7. Walking distance to center of town

Safety

1. Deadbolt locks on all doors; front door locked at all times
2. Metal door with peephole
3. Hallway light has automatic timer
4. Second-floor location (no chance of break-in through window)
5. First-floor tenants are retired and are home most of the time
6. Good neighborhood; well-lit corner location

Comfort

1. Air conditioning
2. Extra-large kitchen and bathroom
3. Enclosed yard area for tenant use only
4. Wall-to-wall carpeting
5. Extra cabinets and closets; private storage area
6. Soundproof doors and walls
7. Zoned heating

Economy

1. Fireplace
2. Walking distance to shopping
3. Free parking
4. Low rent compared to similar apartments
5. Discounted rent for singles and senior citizens
6. Wintertime rent reductions for heat savings

Privacy

1. Soundproof doors and walls
2. Only two other units in building
3. Quiet neighborhood
4. Front door locked at all times
5. No neighboring residences in back of building or on the side

Turning Product Features into Benefits . . .

You've listed the benefits your apartment offers and the talking points that relate to them, so you are ready to show the apartment. Before you meet your prospect, or as soon as you do, determine the prospect's most important buying motive. Then build your presentation around it.

As we mentioned before, you can make as many presentations as you have buying motives for your product. In this apartment example are the structures for five possible sales presentations. The presentation focusing on safety is not the one you deliver to someone concerned with convenience. If your prospect tells you that two things are important, privacy and convenience, try to determine which is more important, and appeal to that buying motive first. And start with the most important talking points under that motive. If low rent is the most important feature you list under economy, talk about it before free parking.

Of course, the order of importance you assign to talking points will vary from prospect to prospect. So even if two potential customers share the same buying motive, they may hear different presentations because they are interested in different aspects. Suppose two prospects say they are concerned with convenience. If one is a senior citizen, the bus stop at the door may be the most important talking point. When the other is a mother of young children, proximity to schools may be the most important.

You can often determine the prospect's most important motive by noticing which product features seem to be of greatest interest—those that seem to attract the prospect or those that are constantly looked at or even touched. If the prospect pays careful attention to the door locks, safety is probably important. Questioning must often accompany your observation. If the prospect admires the extra-large kitchen, you aren't sure if the dominant buying motive is comfort or convenience, so you must ask.

When prospects are unable to identify their most important motive, ask them why they want to move. The potential renter might say, "I'm not young anymore and I want a place that's easier to clean," or "The person in the apartment next to mine watches TV too loud at night and it keeps me awake," or "My present apartment has been broken into three times in the past year and I'm scared to stay there."

If you determine while making your presentation that you have misread the prospect's motive, shift your focus to another one and its accompanying set of talking points. Usually, your presentation will include two or more features anyway because people rarely rent for just one motive.

HOW BUYING BEHAVIOR IS SHAPED . . .

Buying behavior is influenced by our recent activities, our current environment, and our future plans. External and internal forces all affect purchasing decisions. Some factors that play a significant role in shaping our buying behavior are:

Physiological and psychological needs	Personal values
Goals and objectives	Frame of reference
Self-concept	Reference groups

Physiological and Psychological Needs . . .

According to noted psychologist Abraham Maslow in **Maslow's hierarchy of needs**, human needs are categorized as physiological needs, safety needs, social needs, esteem needs, and self-actualization needs (see Figure 5-2). **Physiological needs** include the need for food, sleep, shelter, sex, warmth, and muscular activity. **Safety needs** comprise the need for physical and economic security. **Social needs** are the need for love and a sense of belongingness. **Esteem needs** incorporate the need for respect from others, recognition of our achievements, and a feeling of self-worth. **Self-actualization**, which Maslow says is the highest human need, refers to our need to grow as a person, to become whatever we are capable of becoming.

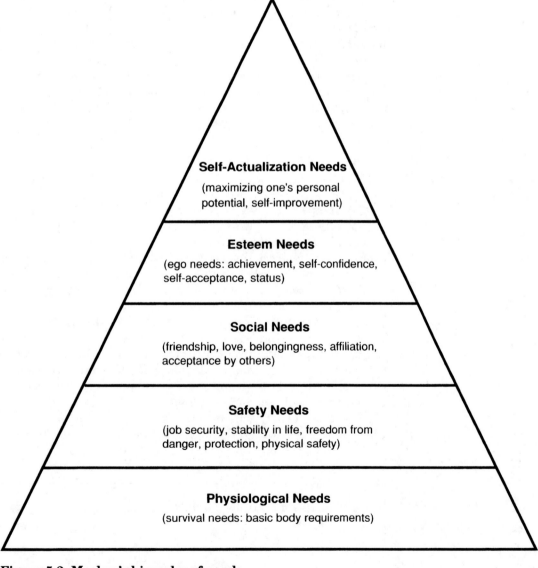

Self-Actualization Needs
(maximizing one's personal potential, self-improvement)

Esteem Needs
(ego needs: achievement, self-confidence, self-acceptance, status)

Social Needs
(friendship, love, belongingness, affiliation, acceptance by others)

Safety Needs
(job security, stability in life, freedom from danger, protection, physical safety)

Physiological Needs
(survival needs: basic body requirements)

Figure 5-2 Maslow's hierarhy of needs.

How Buying Behavior is Shaped

Products are purchased for the satisfaction of all five levels of needs. Often, products purchased for the satisfaction of physiological needs, such as food, drink, and clothing, also contribute to the satisfaction of higher needs. However, purchasing decisions cannot satisfy higher needs if those lower have not been met. A person in need of food or adequate housing must fill those basic requirements before buying to develop esteem or self-actualization.

Goals and Objectives . . .

Products are purchased for the attainment of either short-term or long-term goals and objectives. Goals and objectives are referred to interchangeably, but can be defined somewhat differently. A goal is an ideal, whereas an objective is a measurable step toward the goal. For instance, your goal might be to lose weight, whereas your objective to that end would be to lose 20 pounds within three months. A businessperson might say, "Our goal is to overtake the cosmetics market. Our objective is to command 50 percent of the region's cosmetics market in five years."

The more specific and heartfelt a prospect's goals and objectives are, the more predictable his or her buying behavior will be. The prospect who is determined to make an A in chemistry is more likely to hire a tutor than is the prospect who is happy just to pass chemistry.

Self-Concept . . .

Self-concept is the way one sees oneself. Each of us has this characteristic. It is also known as self-image or self-perception. The way we see ourselves is for the most part the way others see us, too. This is because we form our self-concept partly on the basis of feedback we receive from others over time. If people frequently tell you how witty you are, you will think of yourself as witty. If you receive compliments about your athletic abilities, you will see yourself as a good athlete.

Social behavior tends to be consistent with our self-concept. Our actions reinforce others' impressions of the image we have of ourselves. Because we project this perception in all that we do, our self-concept is apparent in our interpersonal relationships. If you consider yourself friendly, you make an extra effort to talk to people. Others then assume you see yourself as friendly, and they, too, see you as friendly.

For most of us, self-concept becomes clearer with maturity. We get to know ourselves better through experience, and we become more realistic

I am an optimist. It does not seem too much use to be anything else.
Winston Churchill

about the expectations we have for ourselves. The baseball player who once dreamed of the big leagues may eventually be happy to play for fun on a local softball team. The fact that our self-concept becomes clearer and perhaps more accurate with age is apparent in our buying decisions. An adult who wants to play simple songs for fun will choose a portable electronic keyboard rather than invest in a grand piano. Such a person entertains no unrealistic fantasies about becoming a concert pianist. This is not to say that all people past adolescence know themselves. A prospect who is going through a midlife crisis may have a temporarily distorted self-concept.

Self-concept can be viewed as a complex of four parts: the real self, the ideal self, the real other, and the ideal other. All these aspects of the self-concept influence our buying behavior. As you can see in Figure 5-3, the "real" categories make up a larger portion than do the "ideal" categories. We think more about our current image than the one we hope to attain.

The **real self** is our current self-perception. In addition to our good qualities, it includes all of our faults and any other traits that we would like to change. We buy some products to reinforce the positive aspects of our real self and others to improve upon the negative aspects.

The **ideal self** is the person we would like to become, the self we dream of. It is the person we would be upon total goal achievement, a long-term goal. Although we will never become the ideal self, we can move closer to the dream through self-improvement. The desire for betterment is behind many of our purchase decisions. As a salesperson, you are in a position to help your prospects move toward their ideal selves. The U.S. Army, when it says, "Be all that you can be," is claiming it can help move young recruits closer to their ideal self.

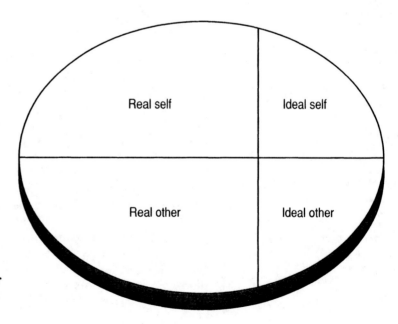

Figure 5-3 Your self-concept. The real self and real other account for a larger part of the self concept that the ideal self and ideal other.

The **real other** is the image of ourselves that we think others have. We are not always right about what people think of us. You might think no one wants to hear your opinion at student government meetings. At the same time, you might think your fellow classmates consider you intelligent because they are always asking you to fill them in on lectures they missed. Like the real self, the real other is someone with faults as well as favorable qualities. Sometimes we buy products to enhance our real other without enhancing our real self.

The **ideal other** is the way we would like others to see us. Because self-image and social image are different, we may desire an ideal other that is unlike ideal self. For example, a businessperson might want to be *seen* as community minded, even though this might be an insignificant part of the self he would like to *be*. People who are concerned about their ideal social image will buy products that enhance that image.

Even though the self-concept may have four distinct parts, it is one complete, multifaceted picture. You might be pleased with some of yourself but not all of it. Perhaps you consider yourself too dull to throw a successful party, but you also consider yourself financially astute and trustworthy. You can accept your own shortcomings because you know that no one is perfect.

As a salesperson, you need not understand all parts of the prospect's self-concept, just those that relate to your product. If you are selling life insurance, the fact that ruggedness is part of your prospect's image will not be important to you. More meaningful is her or his self-concept as a family-oriented person. If you represent an investment service, you will want to appeal to prospects who consider themselves astute investors. Always appeal to the aspect of self-concept that relates to the buying motives for your particular product.

You Decide!

Marsha has been hired by a company that markets a combination flashlight/mace gun. This is a well manufactured product that has been getting national publicity. She has been assigned a territory that includes the inner-city where the crime rate is high and mugging is common. Although she sells to a variety of retail outlets, part of her assignment is to talk to women's groups regarding the effectiveness of this deterrent.

Marsha feels that calling on battery and rape alliances would be a good way to get the message of her product out to prospective buyers. Obviously, those who have experienced abuse know full well the need to protect oneself. She feels that by putting on demonstrations at such groups she can raise interest and demand for her product, and can recommend where it can be purchased. On the other hand, she is concerned that asking others to recall painful and traumatic experiences might be disturbing for them. Should she hold meetings with these audiences or take another tack? **You decide!**

Self-Concept and Buying Behavior . . .

Buying behavior is a direct reflection of our self-concept. People buy products that improve the positive aspects of their image and correct the negative aspects. Enhancement of our self-concept is our most basic buying motive.

As a salesperson, you should build features into your product that your prospects associate with themselves. These characteristics may already be apparent in the brand name. Consider magazines such as *Iron Man* and *New Woman*. Like other products, periodicals are named to reflect the real and ideal selves of the people who buy them. If your product is strongly identified with one gender, build on the positive aspects of that identity. A cleansing lotion appeals to some women because it promises beauty and youthfulness as well as cleanliness. A bracing aftershave appeals to some men because it reinforces masculine attractiveness in addition to toning the skin.

Prospects don't always know whether your product reflects or enhances their self-concept. In fact, they aren't always thinking about their own image. Your responsibility is to uncover each prospect's self-concept and find ways to enhance and preserve it. If you meet prospects who tell you they want to change jobs so that they can spend more time with their family, they are projecting their self-concept as a devoted family member. If they say their firm has an image to keep up, they are telling you that they are proud of their firm's reputation and will do nothing to harm it.

One of the strongest and most common self-concepts is that of the caring parent. Anything you say that reinforces this concept will help you in your selling effort, and anything that implies your prospect is not a good parent means trouble. Many modern products for the home have had to overcome strongly ingrained family ideals to succeed in the marketplace. For instance, ready-made cake mixes and other convenience foods can be seen as an insult to those who take pride in baking cakes from scratch and spending hours preparing dinner. Marketers have dealt with this dilemma by showing how the use of these products frees the homemaker to spend more time with the family, thus preserving homemakers' self-concept instead of injuring it.

Personal Values . . .

A **personal value** is a principle, standard, or quality considered worthwhile. It can also be described as an idea that leads to judgment prior to action. Although values are internal, they are strongly influenced by external factors such as family, friends, religion, school, economics, heroes, role models, mass media, and business. We begin developing our values early in life.

Unconsciously, we rank our values in a kind of hierarchy that becomes our value system. You might include honesty, family, money, and good health among your values. Perhaps you think they are all equally important, but if something forced you to choose, you might eliminate one value for the sake of another. For example, you might choose to take a cut in pay rather than work at a job that makes you feel dishonest. Thus you discover that money isn't as important to you as honesty is.

We all have values. Values are not restricted to those individuals with strict moral standards or strong religious convictions. How we spend our time and money, and the importance we place on certain activities, reflects our values. You might say that your family is important to you, but if you always have something better to do than be with them, you don't value your family life as much as you claim. With respect to values, your mission as a salesperson is to convince your prospects that your product is consistent with their values.

Frame of Reference . . .

A **frame of reference** (FOR) is a system of ideas against which we measure and assign meaning to new experiences. Past and current experience, including upbringing, family life, our living and working environment, and events such as war, illness, and economic circumstances, all combine to form our FOR. Our frame of reference makes us conservative, liberal, skeptical, religious, trusting, or cautious.

We understand new ideas and events by putting them in the context of our frame of reference. One person might be fascinated with snakes, and another is terrified of all reptiles. Suppose this is because the first person lived near a reptile zoo, whereas the second was bitten by a snake as a child. The difference in frame of reference dictates the behavior of the individuals.

Buying behavior is influenced by frame of reference in much the same way. Each prospect's perception of your product will be shaped by FOR. You may meet prospects who never drink tea for pleasure because they grew up taking tea only as cold remedy and still associate tea with sickness. Prospects who don't trust salespeople feel that way because their FOR includes experience with dishonest salespeople.

Age can have a lot to do with frame of reference. Many people who were young during the Great Depression will be scarred for the rest of their lives. Never forgetting the financial uncertainty of the early 1930s, they are likely to be very risk-conscious, and generally wary of volatile investments. Many Depression-era survivors continue to avoid buying stocks or real estate because they or others were ruined by such investments long ago. Like the Depression, the Vietnam war era and times of heavy racial tension have influenced people's frames of reference.

A word of caution about age and FOR: Never assume older prospects have greater frames of reference. Specific experiences have meaning only for certain age groups. For example, the peace movement of the 1960s will be a more significant factor to prospects who were in their twenties at the time than it will be for those in their forties. Just as some people may have been too young to have certain historical events incorporated into their frame of reference, so may others have been too old.

Geographic location is also an important factor in our frames of reference. A rural resident might be very comfortable leaving doors unlocked at night, whereas the urban dweller might be the perfect prospect for a home security system.

Once something becomes incorporated in our frame of reference, it may be there to stay. Beliefs formed by experience are difficult to change. If a prospect has believed for many years that the products sold at a well-known chain store are low quality, such a belief is ingrained. It may take years to change that prospect's mind in spite of the store's constant improvements in merchandise.

By learning as much as possible about a person's frame of reference, you can use stories and examples that fit that prospect's experiences, becoming an ally instead of opponent. For instance, inflation is an ally of most salespeople because most people feel that prices only go up, never down. By making the point that your product is sure to increase in value, or is likely to cost more next year, prospects are inclined to believe you because rising prices are consistent with their FOR.

Reference Groups . . .

A **reference group** is any collection of people with a common bond, such as an interest, activity, or goal. Some of these are small and well-defined, whereas others are very large and so widespread that members don't know one another. Most reference groups are **informal groups** (as opposed to clubs and societies), such as college students or young urban professionals. Group members share the same value system. Identification and interaction with a reference group shapes the behavior and attitudes of its members.

Reference groups exert three basic types of influence over their members. One is **normative** influence, where the expectations of the group and membership requirements determine what members buy or do not buy. **Identification** influence occurs when a member's purchases indicate belonging to that party. When individual members are used as sources for what to buy or where to buy, the group is exerting **informational** influence.

Most of us need to feel we belong to certain reference groups, and we will sacrifice other objectives to that end. Because these associations have a common bond, our reward for being a member is identity. We want to be recognized not only by the other members but also by nonmembers who attach status to belonging. Conformity to group standards is the price we pay for membership.

Reference groups can be classified as membership groups, aspirational groups, or dissociative groups. **Membership groups** are the groups we belong to, whereas **aspirational groups** are those we wish to join. **Dissociative groups** are the ones we don't want to be associated with in any way. All three reference groups influence buying behavior. We make purchases to keep our good standing in membership groups, to move us closer to joining aspirational groups, and to move us farther away from dissociative groups. Figure 5-4, next page, describes reference groups.

Clothing is a visible symbol for any reference group. It designates your membership and gives you the identity that you seek. College students of the 1960s wore bell-bottomed jeans and tie-dyed shirts, and men and women both wore their hair long and unstyled. You might not think that today's student can be as easily identified, but even off campus you can sense when you are among your peers. Figure 5-5, next page, offers some insight on the influence that reference groups exert over certain consumer purchases.

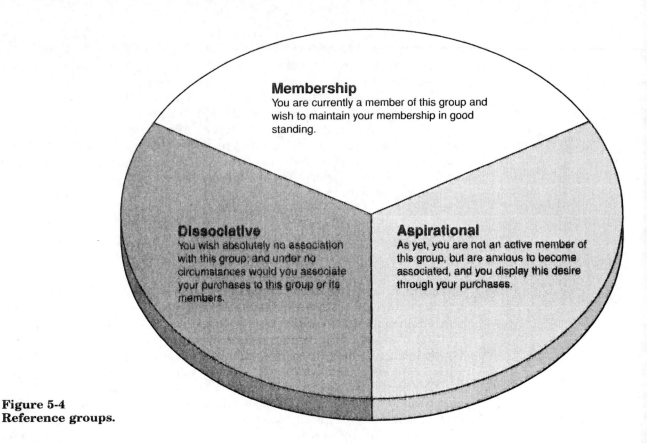

Figure 5-4
Reference groups.

Public necessities	Public luxuries
Weak influence on generic product	Strong influence on generic product
Strong influence on brand	Strong influence on brand
automobile	wine
clothing	golf clubs
food items	vacation trips
Private necessities	**Private luxuries**
Weak influence on generic product	Strong influence on generic product
Weak influence on brand	Weak influence on brand
mattress	videogame
refrigerator	hot tub
tires	lingerie

Figure 5-5 The influence of
reference group membership
on consumer purchases.

Summing It Up . . .

Need-satisfaction is the reason for all purchases. In this chapter, we examined various buying motives in order to gain a better understanding of purchase behavior. Although some buying motives are product related, others are influenced by brand. Some purchases are made primarily for logical reasons, but others are largely motivated by emotion. Although business purchases are primarily rational, emotion enters the picture nevertheless. Sometimes prospects hide their true buying motive, and you are on your own to uncover it. One way of doing this is to use syllogistic reasoning. Selling is further complicated when different prospects have different reasons for wanting the same product.

Six factors that shape buying behavior are physiological and psychological needs, goals and objectives, self-concept, values, frame of reference, and reference groups. We purchase products to enhance the positive aspects of our self-concept and improve upon the negative aspects. Our goal is to become our ideal self. Our buying behavior also considers the reference groups to which we belong, aspire to belong, or with which we do not want to associate.

Key Concepts and Terms . . .

appeal	membership group
aspirational group	motivation research
benefit	opportunity cost
benefit selling	physiological needs
brand-related motive	rational motive
buying motive	real other
conspicuous consumption	real self
dissociative group	reference group
emotional motive	safety needs
esteem needs	self-actualization
frame of reference	self-concept
hidden buying motive	social needs
ideal other	syllogism
ideal self	values
informal group	wants
Maslow's hierarchy of needs	

Building Skills . . .

1. State the fundamental purpose of motivation research.
2. Explain the distinction between an objective and a goal.
3. Define an appeal.
4. Describe the difference between rational buying motive and emotional buying motive.

5. Describe situations in which the need for a product is rational, but the need for a specific brand is emotional.

6. Examine the kinds of buying motives that are most often hidden and the reasons prospects conceal them.

7. Define syllogistic reasoning, explaining its use in determining buying motives.

8. Define conspicuous consumption.

9. Explain how to design a sales presentation by arranging talking points according to buying motives.

10. Explore the factors that determine the number of sales presentations you can deliver on your product.

11. Examine two questions you would you ask yourself to determine buying motives and talking points giving the answers. Give an example.

12. Explain the role of self-concept in shaping buying behavior.

13. Some products have had to overcome strongly ingrained ideals and values to become market successes. Give some examples. Explain how marketers deal with this dilemma.

14. Examine the role that the prospect's value system plays in shaping purchase behavior.

15. Explain frame of reference. Give several examples of how a prospect's frame of reference influences buying behavior.

16. Explore the roles played by reference groups in shaping purchase behavior.

Making Decisions 5-1:

Toby Toth works at the Summit Ski Shop. One day a customer named Walt Sweeney enters, walks straight up to the main ski rack, and begins examining a $660 pair of skis. Toby approaches him.

Toby:	Hello. What may I show you this morning?
Walt:	This is exactly the ski I'm looking for, but the price is out of sight.
Toby:	This is our finest ski. It's hand-made and designed for top performance.
Walt:	I know. That's why I want it. My kids have started to ski, and I want to get out there with them.
Toby:	Do you ski a lot?
Walt:	Not in the past seven years, but I used to *live* on the slopes. In fact, I was a ski instructor in college. I can't wait to get back into it with Billy and Lisa.
Toby:	Well, you certainly picked the right ski.
Walt:	Yeah, but not at this price. Every time I turn around, I have another bill to pay. I just can't justify spending this much money on frills.
Toby:	Well, we have another fine ski over here. It's $150 less.

Walt:	(Zipping his jacket) No, if I'm going to buy, it's got to be the best. I think the best thing for me to do is rent a pair at the slope. Maybe I'll see you next year.

Describe Walt's true buying motive. Explore how Toby might have helped Walt rationalize the purchase.

Making Decisions 5-2:

Betty Markle is a customer representative at Main Line Stereo. One afternoon a customer approaches Betty in the store and says she wants to buy a video-cassette recorder.

Betty:	What features are you looking for in a VCR?
Shopper:	I'm not sure I know what you mean.
Betty:	Well, do you have a particular type of VCR in mind?
Shopper:	All I know is, I don't want anything too complicated. I'm not good with mechanical devices. I just want something that will record one show while I watch another.
Betty:	(Pointing to a VCR on the shelf) This is our best-selling model. It does anything you'd want a VCR to do.
Shopper:	Can you show me how to use it?
Betty:	Sure (turning it on and inserting a tape). To record, you press the Play and Rec buttons simultaneously, like this. Then when you're done recording, you press the Stop button, like this. To watch what you've recorded, you set your TV to channel 3 and press the Play button, like this. Fast forwarding and rewinding the tape are just as simple. (Betty demonstrates fast forwarding and rewinding.) See?
Shopper:	It seems easy enough. How about hooking it up?
Betty:	If you're not too good at mechanics, I suggest you get a friend to do it. It can get a little tricky.
Shopper:	Well, it sounds pretty good....
Betty:	The best thing about a VCR is your ability to watch shows that you ordinarily would miss. For instance, suppose you're going to be out of town for a week and you want to tape your favorite soap opera every day at 2:30. All you have to do is follow this eight-step procedure (points out a page in a thick user's manual), and you won't miss a thing!
Shopper:	That seems complicated.
Betty:	Not at all. Once you get the hang of it, it's really quite simple.
Shopper:	(Pointing at the timer, clock, and counter buttons) Maybe so, but all these buttons scare me. I'll have to think it over.

Evaluate what Betty did right and did wrong. Explain whether Betty appealed to the shopper's strongest buying motive.

Making Decisions 5-3:

You are selling a 30-inch strand of genuine pearls that is listed at $1,300. Describe four appeals you could make.

Practice Makes Perfect 5-1:

You sell real estate and have just listed a single-family house with the features listed here. Next to each feature name one or more relevant buying motives. Then list the motives in columns across the top of a separate page, and underneath each motive the corresponding features. Some features may be listed under more than one motive.

Living room fireplace

Dome skylight in kitchen

Elevated hardwood deck

Wet bar

Trash compactor

Intercom system

Central cleaning system

Fully equipped laundry room

Bedroom skylight

Plaster walls

Wired security system

Living room ceiling fan

Self-cleaning oven

200-amp electrical service

Island cabinet in kitchen

Dishwasher

Laundry chute

Marble bath fixtures

Wall-to-wall carpeting

Two-car garage

Secluded location

Hardwood floors

Ductless air conditioning units built into the walls

Professional sodding and landscaping

Located within two miles of large shopping complex

Basement can be finished into a den, office, or family room

Opening Your Sales Presentation

THE JOB TO BE DONE . . .

All sales activities have a starting point. How you approach a prospect will have much to do with what follows. All aspects of the sales call affect the final objective of getting an order and gaining a customer. Chapter 6 covers the approach, helping you:

...understand the basics of a good approach.

...appreciate the importance of a good opening.

...understand the importance and proper use of your business card.

...realize the need and requirements for creating a comfortable sales setting.

...appreciate the need to build an immediate dialogue with the prospect.

...examine the various methods of approaching a prospect.

THE APPROACH . . .

The **approach** is the official opening of your sales presentation. In the approach, you greet the prospect, introduce yourself, and explain the reason for your visit, usually by making reference to your company and its product or service. Some salespeople call this the "meet and greet." As we mentioned in Chapter 4, there are no clearly defined breaking points between parts of the selling process, and at times both prospecting and the preapproach take place in the prospect's presence. The approach is the first step in the selling process that *always* takes place in the prospect's presence.

BEFORE THE SALES CALL . . .

Before making a sales call, it is usually a good idea to send the prospect some information, such as product literature and material on your company. This will enhance your approach in several ways:

1. The prospect will be expecting you.
2. The prospect will likely be more receptive to seeing you and listening to your presentation.
3. The prospect will have had the opportunity to check the materials you provided.
4. The prospect will have no reason to raise the common objection, "I haven't heard of you, your product, or your firm."

If your prospect knows about your company's track record, years in business, position in the market, and philosophy of business, your introduction will be that much easier. Much of this information is contained in your firm's annual report. If one is available, send it to the prospect along with a brief fact sheet on yourself. In this way, many of the questions about you and your firm will be answered in advance of your visit.

Even if detailed information isn't available, it's often a good idea to send a letter stating your intention to visit. Whether or not to announce your pending visit will depend upon individual circumstances. Certainly in the cases of selling personal services, such as insurance or stocks, paving the way with a new prospect is advisable. In many industrial selling scenarios, you may not need to or want to send information in advance of the sales call. In those instances where specific customer need has not been determined, sending data ahead of time may be confusing or redundant to the person you wish to see.

The Letter of Introduction . . .

Another way to prepare the prospect for your sales call is to send a **letter of introduction** written by a mutual acquaintance. This is neither a letter of recommendation nor a suggestion that the prospect purchase your product. Your purpose in sending a letter of introduction is merely to break down the barrier of unfamiliarity that exists when you call on the prospect as a total stranger. In the case of a referral, the awareness that you and the prospect have a mutual acquaintance should make the prospect more receptive to you. The prospect will assume a friend or associate wouldn't have recommended you if there were doubts about your product.

There is the possibility that the prospect may look down on a letter of introduction, seeing it as trading on a friendship. To avoid this problem, you should ask your mutual associate how the prospect would view such a letter. In many cases, the referring party would much rather that you simply use her or his name rather than having to sit down and write a formal introduction. You may want to write the letter of introduction yourself, for the referral's signature.

Meeting the Receptionist or Secretary . . .

When you call on a buyer in business or industry, the first person you are likely to meet will be a receptionist, secretary, or assistant. This "screen" is often the one who determines who does and who does not get to see the boss. You will need to impress this person and convey the importance of your visit. Even if the assistant doesn't actually screen salespeople, news of a person's lack of manners travels fast. Secretaries who have been treated rudely by visitors have ways of quickly informing their bosses. If you have been unpleasant to the person who receives you, the boss is likely to know it by the time you introduce yourself.

Here are several guidelines to follow when you are in the presence of a secretary or receptionist:

1. While you are waiting, make conversation with the secretary if conditions permit. Be open and friendly. Although you can use the conversation to gather information on the prospect, you should also share in small talk.

2. Answer all the secretary's questions. Take time to explain the reason for your visit so that the secretary will be able to relay an accurate explanation to the buyer. The more the secretary knows, the better are your chances of seeing the buyer.

3. Emphasize the importance of your call, but pleasantly: Don't demand to see the buyer. If you do, you may find the buyer unreceptive, or you may not get an audience at all.

4. Don't become impatient if you must wait. Waiting time is an excellent time to review your presentation, scan preapproach data on prospects you will see later in the day, or read a trade magazine. As we mentioned in Chapter 4, some reading material on the prospect's company is likely to be available. You should ask to see it, and use your waiting time to read it.

   Waiting times can be long. Set a limit on the time you can wait, and leave if you haven't seen the buyer by the time you've waited your limit. Try to make an appointment, or say you will call again at another time and leave your business card. This conveys the message that your time is valuable. Further, the next time you call, the buyer is more likely to make a special effort to see you, knowing that the two of you didn't meet the first time you called.

The time to repair the roof is when the sun is shining.

John F. Kennedy

YOUR BUSINESS CARD . . .

Your business card should be presented to anyone appropriate: centers of influence, leads, prospects, purchasers, secretaries, and receptionists. A well-designed business card serves several important purposes:

1. It suggests that you are established and important, here to stay.
2. It clarifies the relationship between you and your company.
3. It is a source of future reference.
4. It informs the holder of your official title.
5. It enables the holder to call you by your name without needing to ask for it.

One of a business card's greatest benefits is its function as a confidence-builder. Prospects are far less likely to assume you are "here today, gone tomorrow" if you have a business card. So much the better if you represent an established organization because the name of your firm is usually in the largest print on the card. If it is a prestigious firm, prospects will immediately attach the prestige of the firm to you. They will be more receptive to your visit if you represent a company they know and respect. Figure 6-1 offers tips for the design and use of a business card.

Your business card is also a source of relevant information on you. It contains your business address and telephone number. Some sellers have their home address and phone number printed on the card although having this information on the card might interrupt your personal life. Your official title may be both impressive and enlightening. It might give the prospect some idea of your official duties and responsibilities.

When to Present Your Card . . .

In most cases, the best time to present your business card is at the time of introduction. Early presentation will allow your card to serve all its purposes, especially that of allowing your prospect to call you by name. Prospects who aren't expecting you may not catch your name the first time you say it. This is because their mind is on other matters, and you do not yet have their full attention when you introduce yourself. Most people don't remember names given at introduction, especially when they aren't sure they want to meet the person they're meeting.

If you hand the prospect your card as soon as you introduce yourself, you can focus on your sales presentation instead of on repeating your name. When the prospect wants to call you by name, he or she can simply glance at the card. The prospect need not say, "Excuse me, but what did you say your name was?" In this way, a business card serves the same purpose as a name tag at a business conference or class reunion. The prospect is saved some embarrassment when he or she can discreetly read your name, and the sales call can focus on the presentation rather than on repeated introductions.

Figure 6-1

> ## Business Cards
>
> A business card is a basic business accessory. The card you carry and the way you use it say a lot about your professionalism and your attitudes toward yourself.
>
> - Keep it simple: Your name, address, title, and phone number. Logos are fine. Honors like the Million Dollar Round Table are great. Irrelevant titles, degrees other than a doctorate, and cutesy pictures are out.
>
> - Stick to standard sizes and colors. Ivory card stock with a slight texture is very respectable. Navy and black ink are solid. Stick to standard sizes that fit in card files.
>
> - The higher the quality the better. A tacky business card says, "I'm not worth much."
>
> - Keep your cards handy. Don't fumble. Plan ahead: slip a few in your pocket before making calls.
>
> - Don't be shy. Offer your card with "Here's my card," not "Would you like my card?"
>
> - The only thing you should ever write on your card is a short note, "Sorry I missed you." Never use old cards with phone or address corrections. Get new cards.
>
> - Cards are to give out, not save. How many can you give away? Give everyone two cards so they can keep one and pass one on to a possible prospect. Slip them in with your letters. Clip them to your sales literature. Cards are like photographs. People are afraid to throw them away. If you get enough cards in people's hands, they'll pay off in business.

Of course, there are exceptions to every rule. In many selling situations, the time to present the card is at the *end* of the sales interview. How would you feel if an automobile salesperson approached you in the showroom and immediately handed you a business card? Most likely you would feel awkward. In this situation, the time for salespeople to present their card would be at the end of the discussion for future reference.

GREETINGS . . .

When you meet the prospect, you greet the prospect. If you are seated, rise when the prospect arrives. Introduce yourself immediately, and be the first to extend your hand. Let your prospects see that you are happy to see them.

Figure 6-2

> **"You've gotta have a cup of coffee."**
>
> For whatever the reason, there are prospects who are extremely difficult to see. Perhaps they are frequently out of the office, or their co-workers and subordinates "shield" them from salespeople. Business-person Eugene Finnegan recalls a time when he was too busy to see uninvited salespeople.
>
> > A certain salesperson tried on four occasions to see me. Unsuccessful again on the fourth try, he asked the front desk receptionist these five questions.
> >
> > > "What time does your lobby open?
> > >
> > > What time does Mr. Finnegan arrive at work?
> > >
> > > What kind of car does he drive?
> > >
> > > How will I know him when I see him?
> > >
> > > Does he drink coffee?"
> >
> > The receptionist told him that the lobby opens at 7:00 A.M., I usually arrive at 7:45 A.M., I drive a brown stationwagon, he'll know me because my necktie will be untied around my neck, and yes, I do drink coffee. One morning, as I entered the building at a quarter to eight, there he was, seated in the lobby. He said, "Gene?" I said, "Yes." He said, "Gene, you've gotta have a cup of coffee. Why not have it with me?" Over the course of the next year I did $500,000 worth of business with him. It was the most unique way ever used by a salesperson to see me, and it worked!

Smile, tell them that it's a pleasure to meet them, and address them by name. Figure 6-2, entitled "You've gotta have a cup of coffee," tells the story of one salesperson's greeting that proved to be quite effective.

Creating a Comfortable Setting . . .

During your first minute or so with the prospect, you will need to create a comfortable setting for your sales presentation. By the setting, we mean both the physical and emotional atmosphere. The furnishings of a prospect's office are not usually under your control, but there are a number of factors you can modify to set the appropriate mood.

Here are some rules to follow in creating a comfortable setting for your presentation:

1. Make your presentations as convenient for your prospects as possible. Don't burden them with the need to make you comfortable. Try to leave all items unnecessary to the presentation outside the prospect's

office. When you arrive, ask the receptionist if there is a place for you to leave your coat and other personal effects.

2. If the prospect doesn't offer you a seat, ask if you may sit down, or try to arrange a setting that allows for both of you to be seated. It will be awkward and uncomfortable if one of you is sitting and the other is standing. Any difference in height between you and the prospect quickly disappears when both of you are seated, and the presentation will feel more relaxed. A standing delivery appears to be done "on the run."

3. Determine the degree of formality your prospects wish to use, and behave accordingly. Prospects who want a formal tone will probably set it themselves. If they greet you as Ms. or Mr., they probably prefer that you address them by title too. If they call you by your first name, they probably prefer to be less formal and should be called by their first name. If they give no indication of the degree of formality they prefer, ask them if you may call them by their first name, especially if they are the same age as you or younger. A possible exception to the first-name preference would be a meeting with a prospect who is a great deal older than you or in a position of high authority. Regardless of age or position, there will always be some prospects who seem to command formality. Follow your instincts and address these people by their titles until they tell you to do otherwise.

Building an Immediate Dialogue . . .

Just as you use the first minute with your prospect to create a comfortable setting, it is also the time to build an immediate dialogue. If you have seen the prospect before, you can open with the subject you talked about the last time you were together. If you have developed a close relationship, you might ask about the family, the golf game, or other points of interest. If this is your first meeting, perhaps you can chat about an interesting item decorating the desk or room, or the renovation work that is going on down the hall.

The first few moments of your visit with a prospect who enjoys casual conversation should be small talk. Many potential buyers expect it although there are salespeople and prospects alike who prefer to defer casual conversation until the end of the visit. Small talk helps to break the ice between prospect and buyer, and allows you to gain some insight of a personal nature about this potential buyer. Savvy salespeople always make note of these casual conversations and use them to initiate the dialogue at future meetings. If the prospect mentions a bad round of golf or a teenager preparing for college, you can use these topics in casual conversation on your next visit.

Avoiding the Early Dismissal . . .

The primary purpose of building an immediate dialogue with your prospect is to avoid "the early dismissal." This is when the prospect succeeds in getting rid of the salesperson without ever having to listen to a presentation. You should expect your prospects to attempt early dismissals because they are frequently close-minded to both you and your proposal when you first call.

Some prospects are experts at effecting an early dismissal. Here is an example:

> A salesperson approaches a prospect, says hello, and explains the reason for the visit. The prospect replies, "Isn't this a coincidence! We were just talking about you people the other day. We know your product, we know your company, and you have a great reputation and a great price. As a matter of fact, we will be making a purchase decision in a few days, and there's an excellent chance your product will be the one we buy. Why don't you leave me your business card, or call me in a week or so? I may have some good news for you then." The salesperson leaves the office feeling elated, believing the sale has been made without even the need for a formal presentation. In reality, the salesperson has fallen for a perfectly executed early dismissal. The prospect had no intention of buying and dismissed the salesperson with a minimum of effort.

Be wary of prospects who sound over-eager, who are too sure they will get back to you later. Do some subtle investigating, and turn an early dismissal into an opportunity. Say, "That's great. I'm glad you're selecting us. Let me give you some additional information I have in my briefcase." Ask to see the information the prospect has on your product, just to be certain it's complete and up to date. If the prospect says that it is at home or in another office, say that you have some additional data that has just come out, which is more recent. By requesting the opportunity to update the prospect on your product, you could transform an immediate dismissal into a discussion.

THE THREE OBJECTIVES OF THE APPROACH . . .

There are many methods of approach, but only three objectives. Regardless of the method you use, your approach should be judged according to its ability to (1) capture the prospect's attention, (2) stimulate the prospect's interest, (3) lead into your sales presentation.

Capturing the Prospect's Attention . . .

Capturing the prospect's attention is the first objective of the approach. Don't even bother to make your presentation until you have the prospect's undivided attention.

Prospects often fool salespeople with body language that would seem to indicate that they are listening when in fact they are not. Constant head nodding and steady eye contact can easily be construed as signs of careful listening, when in reality they merely conceal a lack of attention. Some salespeople contend that giving prospects a brochure or something to hold in their hand helps keep their attention. A better way is to make immediate reference to your ability to meet the prospect's needs.

A prospect's undivided attention is both difficult to gain and easy to lose. Even if the two of you are meeting face to face, the prospect's thoughts may be elsewhere. Such a preoccupation with other matters can prevent the prospect from fully comprehending your message. Your task is to break through this "preoccupation barrier." To do so, you will need to make a powerful appeal at the outset of your presentation. Unless your prospects quickly decide that you and your product are more important than the task they are performing or the matter on their mind when you arrive, you won't get their attention. And if you do manage to get their attention, as soon as they conclude that your product is not for them, you will lose it.

Attention-Getting Techniques . . .

To make a powerful appeal at the outset of your meeting, you will need to develop a number of effective, attention-getting techniques. Perhaps your product itself is an attention-getter. If it's portable, take it with you, and immediately focus the conversation on it. You can also get your prospects' concentration by making quick reference to the benefits they would like to receive. To arouse their curiosity, ask them a question that requires a well thought-out reply, present them with a token of your appreciation for seeing you, or give them a sincere compliment. All these attention-getting techniques are methods of approach, which we will discuss in detail later in the chapter. Whatever means you use, remember that you need to capture your prospects' lasting attention, not their temporary focus.

Stimulating the Prospect's Interest . . .

Stimulating your prospects' interest means giving them a reason to continue listening after you have gotten their attention. Paying attention to a sales presentation does not mean the prospect is truly interested; that is, it doesn't indicate a desire to own the product. Some prospects will pay attention to your entire presentation without ever becoming interested in owning your product. Most prospects decide during the opening minutes of your presentation whether there is any benefit to ownership of your product. If they decide that there is, they are likely to play an active role in the presentation.

> Selling and showmanship have one element in common that is so vital for success: First, you have to have their attention. No matter whether your audience consists of a single person or one hundred thousand people, before you can sell or show them anything, you have to have their focus on you.
>
> Ed McMahon

Keeping the Prospect's Interest . . .

Arousing the prospect's initial interest is not enough. You must stimulate interest to the point where the prospect sees the possibility of benefits that are definitely worth obtaining. Once you do, you have the remainder of the presentation to confirm that these benefits exist.

As with attention, interest is something that you have a short time to capture, and once it is lost it will probably not be regained. If the prospect's initial interest disappears, the remainder of your presentation will be an uphill and probably a losing battle. As soon as a prospect decides the answer is no, his or her attention and interest both quickly fade. A potential buyer may decide, out of politeness, not to end the presentation, remaining uncomfortably and inattentively in your presence even though the possibility of a purchase has been ruled out.

If you detect that the prospect's interest in your proposition is fading, abandon your present course of action and attempt another avenue. You may be able to rekindle interest by creating a more active role for the potential buyer in the presentation. Ask for his or her feelings concerning the product, or request a further clarification of needs or the problem. Perhaps your product was initially seen as capable of satisfying a need, but the customer's opinion has changed. Find out why. You may need to redirect your presentation with an appeal to a different buying motive.

Leading into Your Sales Presentation . . .

We mentioned earlier that the approach is the official opening of your sales presentation. Although it is considered a distinct stage in the selling process, the approach doesn't just end at some clearly marked place to make way for the presentation. As a lead-in, the approach moves to the presentation invisibly.

A well-executed approach provides for a natural flow into the body of your sales presentation. It gets the delivery off to a good start by instilling in the prospect a desire to hear and see more. Judge your approach on its ability to open your presentation as much as on its ability to capture attention and stimulate interest. Once the presentation has begun, the prospect should be fully involved.

> If you want to sell something, you would do well to put yourself in the shoes of the prospective buyer. From that perspective, you're better able to determine what will induce or influence the buyer to purchase whatever it is you are selling. I think that reversing roles would make it easier.
>
> Cliff Robertson

METHODS OF APPROACH . . .

There are at least ten common methods of approach, each having its own strengths. These techniques should be judged on their ability to meet the objectives of approach. You will notice that some techniques meet only one of the three. Ideally, you would want to combine methods to meet all three objectives most effectively. We discuss the following methods of approach in this chapter:

> Introductory approach
> Product approach
> Benefit approach
> Curiosity approach
> Question approach
> Statement approach
> Premium approach
> Survey approach
> Compliment approach
> Shock approach

In Chapter 18, we will discuss three additional approaches that relate specifically to retail selling.

Introductory Approach . . .

The most common method of approach is the **introductory approach**. This is where you state your name, the name of your company, and the reason for your visit: "Hello, Ms. Cooper, I'm Mickey Dale from Marshall and Thomas Corporation. How are you today?" A friendly introduction creates a warm and pleasant tone for the presentation.

Opening the sales interview with nothing more than an introduction, however, is not recommended. Unless you are well known to your prospects or represent a prestigious firm, you cannot expect a mere introduction to capture their attention and stimulate their interest. An introductory approach, unsupported, does not meet any of the three approach objectives. You will need to quickly give the prospect a good reason for listening further.

We mentioned earlier that unless the prospect is expecting you, your name will be quickly forgotten. In fact, it may never have registered in the first place. This is because, at the outset of an unannounced visit, your product is unimportant to the prospect and so is your name. If you succeed in generating interest in your product, the prospect will need to look at your business card or ask you again for your name. This is why some salespeople argue that introductions at the beginning of the presentation are useless. They contend that until you have captured the prospect's attention, your name will not be memorable.

However, starting your presentation without an introduction can be a distraction. Prospects will hardly pay attention if they're wondering who you are and why you haven't introduced yourself. In some selling situations, such as trade shows and conventions, it is advisable to wear a name badge. When shaking hands, the line of sight naturally travels toward the other person's hand and arm, hence, name badges should always be displayed on the right side where they are more easily seen and read.

Even though the introductory approach does little toward your three objectives, it is an essential element of your first meeting. Observe the formality of an introduction, but combine your introduction with a more attention-getting, interest-building approach. The product method is one such approach.

Product Approach . . .

Using the **product approach**, the salesperson engages the prospect in trying or examining the product at the outset of the presentation. You introduce the product when you introduce yourself. The product approach is based on the fundamental principle that the product is often its own best sales representative.

The product approach can work in countless settings. It is especially common in retailing. For example, a well-dressed shopper enters a boutique and begins to examine an expensive coat, which is attached to a rack with a locked chain. A salesperson greets the shopper, unlocks the chain, and suggests a try-on. What's the shopper to say? A try-on will be fine. In an instant, the salesperson and shopper are in front of a three-way mirror, the salesperson turning the shopper gently so that the coat can be viewed from every angle. This is the product approach in action. The salesperson knows that a coat on a locked chain won't sell itself, and that unless shoppers see how good they look in the coat, they have no indication of its benefits to them. The salesperson also knows that very few shoppers turn down a try-on.

People like to handle and examine products, and this technique capitalizes on this urge. If you have ever had kittens to give away, you know that your task will be made easier if you let inquiring children hold and pet them. Forget displaying them in a cardboard box.

The product approach is most effective with goods that appeal to one of our five physical senses: sight, hearing, taste, smell, and touch. If you are not sure your product lends itself to this method, ask yourself:

Does it look good?

Does it sound good?

Does it taste good?

Does it smell good?

Does it feel good?

If you answer yes to any of those questions, the product approach is recommended. As you might imagine, this method is very effective with stereo speakers, perfume, foods, clothing, fabrics, and jewelry.

> Give everyone a chance to buy. Take it for granted that everybody can buy, rather than determining without an interview that some people will not buy.
>
> John Henry Patterson

In fact, if the good has profound sensory appeal, the product approach may be your only logical choice. How can you expect a candy retailer to stock your line of sweets if you don't offer the merchant a taste? If you are selling cologne, offer to place a small amount on the shopper's arm. The point is simple. If the product can sell itself, let it. The only requirement is that the sensory appeal of the product is strong enough to gain your prospects' attention and stimulate their interest.

The product approach is not limited to small items or just to situations where the salesperson is visiting the prospect. This approach works well with many larger products, including furniture and boats. If you are selling a plush sofa, invite the prospect to "sink down" in it. Even luxury cars are suitable for the product approach. Prospects may soon become buyers if they enjoy the smell and feel of the leather upholstery, the purr of the engine, and the glimmer of the paint job.

The product approach is especially effective when you are presenting to experienced buyers or to prospects who have clear ideas about what they want. These types of customers place their own expertise above yours, and may want little or no guidance from you. A college professor may cut short your presentation on a certain textbook to say, "Thank you for your summary, but the book and its supplements are all I really need to see." Here, the product approach means getting the textbook and supplements into the prospect's hands as quickly as possible.

The superiority of the product approach over most others is that there is no need to negotiate a transition between the approach and the presentation; they are one and the same. As soon as your prospects take possession of the product, which they do at the outset, the presentation is under way. With this technique, the prospect immediately becomes involved. Of course, this method is suitable only for certain tangible goods, not intangibles or services.

You can help your own cause when you use the product approach by asking the prospect to affirm your opinion of it. For example, as you take the gold bracelet out of its case, say to the prospect, "It's beautiful, isn't it?" Getting this affirmation will start the prospect thinking the same way. If the prospect already has a similar product, a subtle comparison between the two is an excellent technique. This is especially so when your objective is to get the prospect to trade up to a nicer, more expensive model. You goal, however, is not to find faults with the present product. You want to focus on the qualities or features of your product that are important to the prospect.

There are certain requirements and limits to the product approach. For example, if you are visiting the prospect, the product must be portable and cannot be too fragile. If the product is mechanical, you may have to show the potential buyer how to operate it or assemble it. However, you can also use your instructions as a way to get the item back in your own hands so that you will not have to compete for the prospect's attention as you attempt to explain an important point of the sale.

America St. Thomas

Some people have an innate, burning desire to be in business for themselves. The entrepreneurial spirit burns bright and shines as a lure for many, in spite of the promise of long hours of hard work and the risk of failure. America St. Thomas felt this draw while she was still in college, where she was the first student to graduate from the entrepreneurial program at Kapiolani Community College in Hawaii. As the recipient of the Vocational Education Award from the state of Hawaii, she is continuing her marketing education while managing her growing business.

As Chief Executive Officer of America's Family Furniture Inc., this energetic woman oversees all aspects of the business, yet follows her love of sales and marketing. The primary product of the company is a line of furniture that was ten years in the making, which America designed and has patented. She describes the eight-piece set as being industrial strength, yet lightweight and comfortable. Ideal for small living spaces, the pieces can be aranged to create everything from a crib to a king-size bed. The furniture conforms to the body, producing restful slumber minus the tossing and turning. In addition, it is virtually childproof, with rounded corners and a stain-resistant plastic frame.

America is a dedicated entrepreneur. While working with major distributors to expand sales, she busies herself selling stock in the venture and meeting with clients. Having sacrificed much to make her dream come true, she now donates her efforts to a variety of local causes. She works diligently at convincing the state of Hawaii to provide increasing opportunities for entrepreneurs, which she feels are the future of her island home. Thanks in no small part to America St. Thomas, the American dream is alive and well.

Benefit Approach . . .

In the **benefit approach**, the salesperson opens the sales interview by referring to a benefit the prospect would realize by purchasing the product. Along with the product approach, this method is one of the two most highly recommended. The benefit approach may be even more useful than the product approach if your product's features are its most significant attention-getting factors. It is certainly the most appropriate method in the sale of intangibles (services), or of products that lack sensory appeal. In fact, if a benefit is particularly strong, you may prefer this method even though the product is physically appealing as well.

The benefit approach immediately focuses the prospect's thoughts on *relevant* advantages. This opening technique is then followed by confirmation of these benefits during the sales presentation.

Effectively using the benefit approach requires:

1. Knowing all possible benefits that can be derived from your product.
2. Deciding which of your product's benefits are most important to your prospect.
3. Incorporating or making reference to these benefits in your opening remarks.

Any time you open with a reference to a product benefit, you are using this method. When a representative of an industrial cleaning service says to an office manager, "An experienced, efficient cleaning service takes less time to clean your offices and cuts your overhead," two benefits are being referred to at the same time: saving time and lowering costs. Salespeople for specialized financial services might begin by saying, "Last year our clients realized an average portfolio gain of 10 percent, which is 2 percent above the industry average." If financial growth and family security are important benefits of their service, they can also open by saying, "The goals of financial growth and family security are prime reasons why 2,000 people just like you used our services last year."

A benefit and a buying motive are one and the same, and their list is endless. Some of the benefits (buying motives) that are common to many products and important to many people are:

Security	Health
Safety	Financial growth
Fun	Status
Beauty	Comfort
Luxury	Economy
Relaxation	Convenience

You might think the more benefits you can incorporate into your approach, the better, but this is not necessarily so. Here are some reasons to be selective:

1. Some of the benefits you offer may not be relevant to the prospect.
2. The prospect may be overwhelmed by the sheer range of benefits, and thus unable to concentrate on any one.
3. Your product is likely to sound "too good to be true."
4. Your benefits may seem to contradict one another as would be the case if you mentioned both economy and status.

Key to the benefit approach is the use of relevant benefits, that is, benefits that are important to the individual prospect. Important benefits to someone renting an apartment might be privacy, economy, convenience, or comfort. If you know which of these are important to your prospect, and if you can offer it, incorporate it into your opening remarks. You might say, "As you can see, this unit has a private setting," or "Here is the perfect combination of comfort and carefree living."

If you are a sales representative for a travel agency in charge of signing people up for a midwinter Florida vacation, remember the benefits of such a trip to busy Midwesterners. Open your presentation by referring to the relaxation, change of pace, and break from winter awaiting the vacationer.

If you represent a certified public accountant, your benefit approach might take this form: "Mrs. Lucas, there are no benefits in using a CPA service if your profits do not increase. Am I correct?" This is an excellent opening statement. You have mentioned one of the most powerful words in the business vocabulary, "profits." Even though this method is posed in the form of a question, it is not to be confused with the question approach, which has a different purpose. Regardless of how the reference is made, a benefit reference means a benefit approach.

Problem Solving as a Benefit

Product benefits can be seen as solutions to customer problems. By customer problems, we mean needs. The easiest way to show what benefits your product offers is to show what problems it solves or what needs it meets. The salesperson who takes the problem-solving approach is not there merely to sell, but to make life easier for the prospect. This does not mean that prospects or their business are in a bad state of affairs, only that you as a salesperson can be of valuable service to them.

To use a problem-solving focus in the benefit approach, you simply direct the potential buyers' attention to a problem or need they know they have. Sometimes you make them aware that such a problem or need exists. You capture their attention with this problem and stimulate their interest by showing how your product can solve it.

In the financial services example, the salesperson first focuses the prospect on the problem, and then immediately refers to the solution. The problem is the prospect's inability to maximize the return on investments, and the solution is to buy the salesperson's securities.

The benefit approach has many applications. Any product that offers benefits, and all do, is suitable for this method. If your product offers more than one benefit, and most do, you can base your opening remarks on the most relevant one, the benefit that you have learned, through your preapproach, is most important to your prospect. For example, if your product offers the benefits of economy, convenience, and comfort, you will refer to economy in your approach to the budget-conscious prospect, convenience in your approach to the busy prospect, and comfort in your approach to the luxury-loving prospect.

Curiosity Approach . . .

The **curiosity approach** involves opening the sales interview with a question or statement intended to arouse the prospect's curiosity. Its purpose is simply to get the prospect's complete and undivided attention. The best way of doing this is to make compelling reference to something that is of primary importance to the prospect.

Here is an example of the curiosity approach. As a salesperson for an investment consulting firm, you say to your prospects: "What do you intend to do with the large tax savings that Uncle Sam has made available to you?" They will say, "What tax savings? I don't know of any tax savings!" Their attention is captured. You can then go on to explain that recent, little-known changes in tax law have made huge tax savings possible for them.

Even prospects who will not admit that their curiosity is aroused will probably allow you to continue talking just so they can find out what you are getting at. For this reason, you should make best use of the curiosity approach by not telling prospects immediately what you mean by your opening remarks. As long as specialty retailers don't know exactly why you think they lost 250 customers last month, they remain curious enough to pay attention. Use the time you've bought to introduce your product and explain its benefits, and then satisfy their curiosity: "Each month," you tell them, "300,000 consumers across the country buy this product, and it averages out to 250 customers a store."

The curiosity approach may sound like only a temporary attention-getter, but if it is done in good taste and is well planned, it serves another important purpose. Once you gain attention by engaging the prospect's curiosity, you set the stage for a free-flowing conversation. The prospect's active participation will continue as you steer the conversation to the product or service you are selling.

Question Approach . . .

In the **question approach**, the salesperson opens the sales interview by asking a question with the purpose of getting a brief reply that will lead into the presentation. Remember that a question referring to benefits is a benefit approach, which is different. In the question approach, you might ask, "Mrs. Yox, when was the last time you reviewed your heating bills?" or "Ted, have you seen our new Model 360?" Or you might make a brief statement and follow with a question such as, "I noticed that your office receives many telephone calls. Do you own a fax machine?" or "Thank you for stopping by. What prompted your interest in our diet program?" By posing your questions this way, you are initiating and taking part immediately in a conversation with the customer. Retail salespeople use the question approach when they greet customers and ask, "What can I show you today?" This question is known in retail selling as the service approach.

Your strategy with the question approach is to get prospects talking and to use their answers as a lead-in. In other words, the prospect's answer should open the door for your explanation of benefits. If you are the sales representative for a New England ski lodge calling on the activities director of a company that is planning an employee ski trip, your approach might be, "Miss Fischer, what do you look for when you select a ski lodge?" Not only will you immediately get the prospect talking, but also you will learn what features to focus on during your presentation.

> Every accomplishment starts with the decision to try.
>
> Anonymous

The question approach is most effective when you already know the prospect's answer to your question. Suppose you say, "Mr. Deegan, if you save as much money in the next five years as you did in the last five, will you be satisfied?" Suppose also that you have planned your presentation around the assumption that Mr. Deegan will say no. Be prepared for your prospect's reply, and pose your questions so as to leave no possibility of being caught by surprise.

The question approach requires careful planning, not only to avoid surprise answers but also to create the right impression. The question, "How would you like to earn $45,000 next year?" sounds like a come-on for a "get-rich-quick" scheme. Similarly, a poor question can betray an inadequate preapproach. Suppose you said to an excavating contractor, "Have you considered the benefits of owning a 17,000-pound dump truck?" and the contractor happens to own several. You would look pretty foolish. Probably the worst question a salesperson can open with is a request for time: "May I have fifteen minutes of your time?" By requesting your prospects' time, you are inviting them to say no. Besides, the question implies that you are asking them for a favor.

Statement Approach . . .

In the **statement approach**, you open the sales interview with a short but effective statement. The following remark seems simple, but is actually quite strong: "Sue, I've been looking forward to showing you these beautiful designer wall silks." The reason this statement works is it indicates your interest in both the prospect and your product. An antiques dealer will often have the opportunity to use the statement approach: "This lamp dates back to 1855." Such a statement is powerful because it impresses prospects and encourages them to admire the lamp or ask questions about it.

The salesperson selling a line of pet supplies may open a conversation with this statement: "Our products are made especially for people who really love their pets." A remark like this can quickly break down whatever resistance or preoccupation barrier exists in the prospect's mind.

Premium Approach . . .

The **premium approach** involves beginning the sales interview by presenting the prospect with a small gift known as a premium. To be effective, the premium must be (1) valuable, yet not elaborate or expensive, (2) useful, (3) seen as a token of appreciation, not as a bribe or otherwise obligatory.

A premium given to the prospect at the outset of the interview sets a friendly tone for the presentation to come. You are offering prospects a small thank you for the time they are taking to see you. The idea of presenting the prospect with a gift so soon may sound awkward, but it need not be. In fact, it must be done if the approach is to be effective or, for that matter, to be an approach at all. You can gracefully incorporate the premium into your approach simply by mentioning that you want to give it to the prospect "before you forget" or "before you go any further."

The premium approach capitalizes on the concept of receiving something for nothing. The salesperson's goal is to build the prospect's receptivity by creating a sense of obligation to listen to the sales presentation. This is why the premium must be of value. If your prospects see no value, they will feel no obligation to listen to your sales presentation. Prospects can quickly assess the value of the premiums they are given, and will have no time for a salesperson who gives them a piece of junk.

Here are some guidelines to follow when selecting the premium or premiums you will use:

1. A good premium reminds the prospect of you, your product, or your company, for example, a coffee mug with the company's name on it. If you sell lighting equipment, a flashlight containing your firm's logo would be an excellent premium. Since both your product and the premium deliver light, the association between them will make you more memorable.

2. A good premium is something the prospect never has enough of. Perhaps an office manager can always use another solar calculator or a salesperson would appreciate an extra umbrella to leave in the car or office.

3. A good premium is anything the prospect would probably not go out and buy, yet is happy to receive, for example, a stopwatch. Have you ever noticed how public TV stations, in their fund-raisers, offer unique items that encourage people to donate?

4. A good premium relates to the product you sell or the industry you serve. A cosmetics salesperson presents the prospect with a small cosmetics kit or an eyeglass manufacturer offers sunglasses as a premium.

5. A good premium parallels the value of the product you sell. The more upscale the item you sell, the more expensive your premium should be.

6. Different prospects can be given different premiums. If you sell athletic supplies, give a golfer a set of golf balls, a resistance trainer a pair of weight-lifting gloves.

A timely use of the premium approach is particularly advantageous. At the end of the year, give customers a calendar or appointment book for the upcoming year. If yours is the first datebook your prospects receive, they are likely to use it for the next full year. They will be constantly reminded of your company, whose name appears on the book. Further, if you make periodic visits to the same prospect and offer premiums each time, you should have different ones. If you offer prospects the same thing call after call, they will start to value their time more than the premium, and be too busy to see you.

A few words of caution: Some prospects will not accept gifts of any kind. In fact, many firms expressly prohibit their employees from giving or receiving gifts. Potential buyers who do accept your gift should see it as a token of your appreciation for their allowing your visit, not a bribe. Further, you must be certain that the people you give premiums to are true prospects. Since a good premium has value, it will cost you or your firm a certain amount of money to make or buy. Not only will you need to make the investment a wise one, you will also need to convey the message that you consider the privilege of the interview worth more than the cost of the premium.

You Decide!

After receiving an associate's degree from a community college, Leslie hired on as a salesperson for a Ford dealership. Although she had to put up with ribbing from some of her classmates, she really had the desire to sell, and the car business offered some good commissions. She was a quick learner, and had a pleasant, easygoing attitude that prospects seemed to appreciate. Her low-key approach to selling automobiles seemed to work, and she quickly became a pretty successful seller.

Leslie's sales manager, however, was not overly impressed with her methods or results. He constantly pressured her to be more aggressive and push harder. During its annual fall sale, the dealership began to run low of inventory, and many of the advertised models were no longer available. The sales manager cornered Leslie and pressured her to divert buyers from the advertised specials to some other model that was in stock. Leslie recalled something from her college marketing class regarding such tactics, but still was anxious to move cars. Should she use this ploy? **You decide!**

Survey Approach . . .

In the **survey approach**, you open the sales interview with a request that the prospect allow you to perform an information-gathering survey. Your study might require observation at the prospect's facility or an interview recorded on a written questionnaire. Naturally, there is always a relationship between the survey and the product you are selling. If you are selling heating-pipe insulation, your survey approach might be, "May I briefly visit your boiler room to determine if our pipe insulation would save you money?" or "May I walk through your building to see if that expensive heat you're producing is being properly distributed?"

You can also combine the survey approach with another method, such as the benefit approach. For example, if you sell specialized computer equipment, you might say, "Mrs. Erb, may I examine the operation of your automated data processing equipment? Our new Model 1420 is saving $500 a month in operating expenses in offices where its use is suitable."

In some instances, your survey may require the prospect's active participation. Perhaps you ask the prospect questions from a printed questionnaire, and as the prospect answers, you complete the form. This type of survey should be short, and you should inform the prospect at the outset that the questionnaire will not take long to complete. If the survey is suitably brief and the questions are not confidential, the prospect will probably have no objection to answering them.

There are three important advantages to opening your presentation with a request for information through the survey approach:

1. Prospects appreciate specialized attention and are more likely to heed recommendations that are obviously the result of painstaking analysis.
2. By responding to your questions or guiding you in your observation, the prospect will be actively participating in the sales process.
3. The survey approach shows prospects that you recognize their uniqueness and wish to appeal to their individual needs. Prospects know their situation is unique and want you to know it, too. If you say to them, "May I observe your office employees at work so that I can best determine your particular needs?" they will surely appreciate your respect.

When you use the survey approach, always assure your prospects that your observation or questionnaire will involve no inconvenience to them. If they believe you will disrupt their schedule or their operation or take too much time, they will probably deny your request for a survey. Furthermore, don't make it seem as if you are on a secret mission. Explain at the outset your reasons for the survey; make sure the prospect immediately knows your product and your purpose. Point out how your past studies have always resulted in some benefit to the customer and that you are not there to sell something the prospect doesn't need.

Many prospects will agree to your request for a survey because they know their situation is not perfect. Some prospects may feel they have a problem, but don't know how to solve it, and they welcome your observation or survey. Other prospects may not be so certain they have a problem, but are willing to use your analysis to determine any need for improvement. Many prospects know they have complicated situations requiring the observation of a trained professional. They know, too, that if they disagree with your analysis, all they need to do is say no.

Before you use the survey approach, be certain that the person or company you are visiting is a prospect. Surveys take valuable time and considerable thought as well as some expense. You don't want to put too much into a survey only to discover that the person or firm is not a prospect.

Finally, there are instances in which the survey approach is not appropriate. If the office or company is unusually busy, as would be an income tax preparation service right before the filing deadline, there is probably no time for a salesperson to conduct a study. And of course, if the prospect's operation is considered confidential, you should not request permission to observe it.

Compliment Approach . . .

A sincere, heartfelt compliment is an excellent way to open a sales interview. It boosts the prospect's ego, and if it focuses on a favorite topic, it excites the desire to talk. This is why it's a good idea to "think compliment" as soon as you

> Eagles don't flock—you have to find them one at a time.
>
> H. Ross Perot

meet the prospect. If you use your powers of observation effectively, you may quickly find several reasons to compliment your prospect.

We all enjoy recognition for our efforts and talents. Any compliment that focuses on our achievements is good because it reinforces our sense of pride and accomplishment. When you visit prospects who have founded their own company, and you have a chance to tour the offices, you can open the sales interview by saying, "This the ultimate state-of-the-art facility!" Your compliment works in several ways. As an honest expression of your attitude, based on observation of something your prospects know to be true, the compliment immediately puts you on good terms with them. They know you respect them and are receptive to their story. They will happily begin telling you how they built their firm from humble beginnings, and they will be that much more receptive to your message as well. Regardless of how many times prospects have received this compliment before, they still enjoy hearing another one, so you have brought them pleasure. A **compliment approach** is highly recommended in any situation in which the prospect is accomplished in some way.

Major achievements are not the only traits deserving of compliments. When you visit busy managers, compliment them on their ability to run a productive office. Make the point that each time you visit them, their office is buzzing, and you are impressed that their staff can do all that they do. If you visit prospects at their home, any number of things decorating the living room may stimulate a compliment. Perhaps you notice a collection of antique spoons or a distinctively modern taste in art and furniture. A display of prized possessions invites comment and conversation. Compliment your prospect freely. If you happen to notice something no one has ever noticed before, your compliment will be that much more appreciated.

Since one purpose of the compliment approach is to create and contribute to a conversation, you should try to stay within your realm of knowledge. By choosing a subject you are familiar with, you can follow up on your compliment with intelligent comments or questions. If you find the prospect in the garden when you arrive, your impulse might be to say, "This is a beautiful garden." However, if you know nothing about flowers or plants, your compliment will die on the vine. On the other hand, if you can identify certain flowers by name, and mention your own attempts to grow them, your compliment will blossom into a full conversation.

Your ability to converse on the subject of your compliment may also provide you with an excellent lead-in to your sales presentation. If you are selling clothing and you compliment prospects on their eye for fashion or their taste in apparel, your compliment affirms your ability to recognize quality. Don't just say, "That's a nice suit." Anyone can say that. Show that you recognize its designer and admire the details of workmanship that put it in a class of its own.

A compliment should not be artificial or mechanical. Your prospect may want to discuss the subject after you have brought it up, and you should be happy to participate. Your compliment will seem insincere if you quickly change the subject or fail to elaborate. Don't just say, "What an interesting chair." Show a sincere interest in the prospect's antique chair. Go on to ask what period it was made in, who refinished it, and how long it has been in the family. You should also use selective judgment in making compliments. Prospects know that not everything they touch is worthy of a compliment.

A compliment need not always be direct. In fact, some of the most effective compliments are subtle statements. If you are selling pet supplies to a veterinarian, you might start off by saying, "Many people come to you because they want the best for their pets." Although you are not saying, "You're a great vet," you are implying it.

If your compliment concerns itself with a subject unrelated to the reason for your visit, the time will come when you will need to change the subject. This should not be a difficult or awkward thing to do; the prospect expects you to do it. Even as a separate subject, a good compliment serves an important purpose. It makes the prospect want to talk to you, creates a feeling of friendship and mutual interest, and sets a pleasant mood for your sales presentation.

The compliment approach should be used in sincerity or not at all. There are countless ways in which we can compliment prospects without resorting to phony flattery. Indeed, if you can't give the prospect a sincere compliment, then the compliment approach is not appropriate.

Shock Approach . . .

The **shock approach** is not a pleasant approach, nor is it ever intended to be. Its purpose is to bring home a certain reality to the prospect by playing upon the emotions. A fire insurance salesperson uses the shock approach by showing a prospect pictures of burned-out buildings. The shock approach reminds prospects that such a catastrophe could happen to them, and their insurance coverage isn't adequate.

The shock approach is especially useful in the sale of insurance or other protective services, which people often avoid thinking about. Young heads of households are often shocked to learn that their present life insurance coverage would not support their family for even a year if they were to die suddenly. Prospects for an automobile alarm system are shocked to see how quickly the salesperson can open a locked car door with a slimjim.

If you sell safety glasses and other such industrial supplies, you might find the shock approach effective with both management and labor. They need to be brought to the reality that accidents can and do happen, and the consequences are not attractive. Factory management may begin requiring its workers to wear safety glasses when it hears of the staggering fines and lawsuits levied against firms that have neglected safety issues. The workers themselves may voluntarily start wearing safety glasses when they hear about the permanent eyesight impairment that even a minor accident can cause.

Although the shock approach is meant to touch the prospect's emotions, it should not take the form of an emotional outburst. If possible, it should be subtly integrated into casual conversation. The salesperson for steel safety doors calling on a plant security manager might say, "Harry, have you read about the lawsuit over in Berks County? Three kids opened the door of a factory that was left unlocked. Inside, one of them fell down a flight of stairs. The parents sued for $50,000 and won! It just makes you wonder who's right and who's wrong today." Handled this way, the shock approach remains as tactful as possible without losing its effect. Owners of old buildings probably know that their doors are worn and easy to open. If they don't, the salesperson can go on to point this out to them. One thing is certain. The thought of such a tragic event scares the owner.

Many salespeople feel uncomfortable using the shock approach because it focuses the prospect's thoughts on unpleasant situations and circumstances. Salespeople know that prospects don't want to think of such things ever happening to them and may resent being forced to think of them. Yet more than one salesperson has been thanked by a customer who was shaken into action by the shock approach.

RETHINKING THE SELLING PROCESS . . .

After studying prospecting, the preapproach, and the approach, it is appropriate to take another look at the selling process. As important as it is to realize the flow of activities defining personal selling, it is equally significant to understand that there is no rigidity to this process. Many of the steps are not clearly defined, and specific objectives are often addressed in more than one area.

For example, much of the information gathered in the preapproach might be garnered during prospecting. Similarly, needs assessment may actually be a continuing process all the way through post-sale activities. Figure 6-3 reflects this continually changing aspect of the selling process.

Figure 6-3

Prospecting	Preapproach	Approach	Presentation	Handling objections	Close	After-the-sale follow-up and service

1. Prospecting and the preapproach often take place simultaneously.

2. The preapproach almost always continues into the presentation.

3. The approach is the official opening of the sales presentation.

4. Objections are raised and removed throughout the course of the presentation.

5. A trial close takes place as part of the sales presentation, and a successful close concludes the presentation.

6. Customer service and after-the-sale follow-up take place after purchase.

Summing It Up . . .

A successful approach gets your sales presentation off to a good start. The proper opening for your sales interview breaks down the prospect's initial resistance to you and your product, and it stimulates the prospect's interest in listening to and participating in your sales presentation. Your approach should not be aggressive. Behavioral scientists tell us that people are generally opposed to accepting ideas presented by salespeople. If you use an aggressive approach, perhaps one that immediately suggests a purchase, you may never have the opportunity to present your product or determine if a true interest in buying exists.

Various types of approach were discussed in the chapter. The two most recommended methods are the product approach and the benefit approach. When you select your approach, consider the product or service you are selling and the prospect's characteristics. Whichever method you use, you will increase your chances of making the sale by sending prospects information on you, your product, and your firm before you visit them. Creating a comfortable setting for your presentation and presenting your business card early in the interview are additional suggestions.

Key Concepts and Terms . . .

approach	premium approach
benefit approach	product approach
compliment approach	question approach
curiosity approach	shock approach
introductory approach	statement approach
letter of introduction	survey approach

Building Skills . . .

1. Name and explain three reasons sending information in advance of the sales call is a good idea.
2. Describe the guidelines you should use when you ask someone to write a letter of introduction for you.
3. Describe your behavior when you are in the presence of the company receptionist or the prospect's secretary.
4. Explore the reasons for handing the prospect your business card at the beginning of your sales call.
5. Explain how to create a comfortable setting for your presentation.
6. Discuss the importance of building an immediate dialogue with your prospect.
7. Explain briefly the three objectives of the approach.

8. Explain the introductory approach, including its fundamental weakness.

9. Explain the product approach, including its limitations.

10. Explain the benefit approach, including the types of goods or services that complement this method.

11. Explore how you would incorporate a problem-solving focus into the benefit approach.

12. Explain the curiosity approach.

13. Explain the question approach, including any cautions that should be exercised.

14. Explain the premium approach, including the characteristics of good premiums.

15. Explain the survey approach.

16. Explain the compliment approach, and the importance of choosing a subject on which you are knowledgeable.

17. Explain the shock approach, including its dangers.

Making Decisions 6-1:

Jeff Tierney is a representative for Woodside Advertising Specialties. One day he calls on Stacie Gordon, the general manager of Lebaris Modeling School, to present a new line of cosmetic specialties.

Jeff:	Good morning, Ms. Gordon, I'm Jeff Tierney from Woodside Advertising Specialties.
Stacie:	Hello.
Jeff:	I stopped by today to show you our new line of advertising specialties. Would you like to see them?
Stacie:	Well, I don't see why not.
Jeff:	Great. They're designed especially for a school like yours. (Jeff hands Stacie a comb, then a makeup kit, then a compact mirror.)
Stacie:	Where would you put our name?
Jeff:	It would go right here. (He points to a spot on the makeup kit.)
Stacie:	How much do these items cost?
Jeff:	Here's a cost breakdown sheet. It gives the cost per dozen, per hundred, and per thousand.
Stacie:	(Examining the sheet) The cost seems reasonable, but we really don't need any advertising specialties. (Stacie hands the rate sheet and the samples back to Jeff.)
Jeff:	(Returning the items to his briefcase) Well, thanks for your time. Here's my business card. Call me if you change your mind.

Describe the approach used by Jeff. What other approaches may have been more effective?

Making Decisions 6-2:

Marc Weiss is a regional sales engineer for Venske Air and Gas Compressors. He has been trying for the past three months to get an appointment with Ivan Souder, owner of Newhall Equipment. Souder, who founded Newhall more than forty years ago, before Marc was born, has been out of the office because of failing health. Recovering from his second major operation, Souder is keeping a light schedule since he plans to retire. When Marc arrives for his appointment, several minutes pass before Souder appears at the door to greet him.

Ivan:	How can I help you, Mr. Weiss?
Marc:	(Walking toward Ivan and extending his hand) The question, Ivan, is how can I help you?
Ivan:	(Hesitantly extending his hand) What do you mean?
Marc:	I've waited a long time to tell you about our revolutionary new product. I think you'll find the next sixty minutes very enlightening. (Marc pulls product literature out of his briefcase.)
Ivan:	(Frowning at the product literature) I don't have sixty minutes, Mr. Weiss. Leave your literature with my secretary. I'll review it when I get a chance.
Marc:	But, Ivan…
Ivan:	(Turning away from Marc) As I said, I'll read it later. Good-bye now.

Evaluate Marc's approach, suggesting your own method.

Making Decisions 6-3:

You work in a bridal shop. Write three benefit approaches.

Practice Makes Perfect 6-1:

You sell exercise equipment. Describe a product approach for a $2,200 computerized stair-climbing machine.

Practice Makes Perfect 6-2:

You sell life insurance. Respond to a prospect who tries to give you an early dismissal.

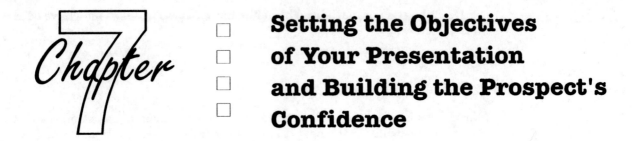

Chapter 7

Setting the Objectives of Your Presentation and Building the Prospect's Confidence

THE JOB TO BE DONE . . .

One of the most important steps in selling is planning. Good presentations rarely just happen. Learning how to properly set the stage for making the sales call and creating prospect confidence is important for success, and Chapter 7 shows you how to:

...examine selling from a problem-solving perspective.

...understand the two basic objectives of a sales presentation.

...identify the prospect's progress toward the buying decision.

...know what it means to control and to lose control of the sales presentation.

...recognize the importance of establishing the prospect's confidence in you, your product, and your company.

...examine specific ways of gaining the prospect's confidence.

...understand how the prospect's confidence can be lost.

...appreciate the importance of your reputation as a salesperson.

THE SALES PRESENTATION . . .

The sales process revolves around one central issue, the prospect's "problem," or need for the product. As you can see in Figure 7-1, buying can be viewed as a problem-solving process, but this insert is presented from the

---
The Purchase Process from a Problem-Solving Perspective

1. The prospect recognizes a problem.

2. Alternative solutions to the problem are sought out.

3. Information on these alternatives is gathered.

4. The alternatives are evaluated.

5. One alternative is selected, including:

    a. which product, brand, or model to buy
    b. where to buy it
    c. from whom to buy it

6. The time of purchase is determined.

Figure 7-1

buyer's perspective rather than the salesperson's. When salespeople view personal selling as a problem-solving process, their overall tasks are:

1. Identify the need or the problem. This process qualifies leads as prospects.
2. Make the prospect aware of the problem by bringing needs out into the open and confirming that the prospects recognize the problem.
3. Help the prospect satisfy the need or solve the problem using the purchase of the salesperson's product or service.
4. Follow up to make certain the need has been satisfied or the problem solved with the use of the product or service.

As the center of the selling process, the presentation focuses on the second and third steps of these tasks. It is through your presentations that your prospects' needs are brought out and satisfied or their problems are revealed and solved. Your presentation thus has two basic objectives:

1. Need awareness or **problem recognition**. Your first objective is to make prospects aware that they have a situation that can and should be improved or a problem that needs correcting.
2. Need fulfillment or **problem solving**. Your second objective is to make prospects recognize that your product is the best solution for need fulfilling or problem solving.

ALL PRODUCTS ARE PROBLEM SOLVERS . . .

As we mentioned in Chapter 6, the word *problem* is loosely used. It need not, and usually does not, refer to misfortune or unhappiness. To say that all prospects have a problem is only to say that some aspect, be it personal or business, could be made better. Those shopping for a pair of water skis probably don't think they are trying to solve a problem, but that is how the ski salesperson should see it. Simply put, shoppers buy water skis because they want to improve the quality of their leisure time. This desire for improvement is the need or problem in question.

Any product or service that improves life, increases profits, or makes work easier is providing the same kind of benefit as a product or service that solves a problem in the traditional sense of the word. A microwave oven solves a problem when it saves time for the homemaker or expands the weekly menu. An office security system, an orthopedic shoe, and a weight-reduction program all solve problems. If the prospect's immediate or long-run situation is improved, a problem is solved. The problem that is relevant to one buyer may be totally irrelevant to another.

Problem Recognition: The First Objective . . .

The first objective of the sales presentation, making prospects aware that they have a need or a problem, is often more difficult than the second objective, satisfying the need or solving the problem with your product. Unfortunately, many salespeople rush into the second objective, concentrating on the features and benefits of their product before ensuring that the prospect is aware of the need or problem they are trying to solve. If prospects don't make this recognition, they will see no value in discussing a solution.

When you call on prospects, you should assume they don't realize a need or recognize a problem. If they did, they would have called on you in search of a solution. You must create the desire to discuss your product by introducing your prospects to a feeling of dissatisfaction with their present lot. To plant the seed of dissatisfaction, you will need to make prospects realize the disadvantages of being in their current situation or of continuing to use their present product. Analyze the prospect's circumstances, and expose any relevant shortcomings that the prospect may not notice.

For example, if you call on a toy manufacturer, you begin by assuming the company doesn't think it has a problem with the equipment on their assembly lines. You tour the plants and discover the firm is using outdated equipment that cannot be repaired or replaced when it breaks down. Perhaps the machinery is inefficient or unsafe. These are the kinds of things you will need to point out in order to create dissatisfaction with the prospect's present situation. Only after you have done so will the potential customer be interested in hearing your solution.

Problem Solving: The Second Objective . . .

After you have helped the prospect recognize the problem, you can proceed to the second objective of your sales presentation, proposing your product as the solution. You do this by presenting your product's relevant benefits. For example, suppose you have persuaded an office manager that the firm's manual bookkeeping operation is inefficient and costly. Your next step would be to show how your computerized bookkeeping system will save office employees many hours of time and the firm a small fortune in paper. Similarly, once you have convinced homeowners that their heating bill is too high, you must then prove that your solar heating system will cut their energy costs in half.

Sometimes prospects recognize their problem independently and will come to you in search of solutions. If this is the case, you need not devote time to the first presentation objective. The homeowner with a leaky roof is aware of the need for a new one. It's just a matter of deciding what type to install and which contractor to hire for the job. As the sales representative for a roofing contractor, you can go to work immediately on the solution to this homeowner's acknowledged problem. Your entire presentation can focus on the second objective, problem solving.

Overcoming Inertia . . .

Inertia, or the tendency to resist change, is a powerful influence on all of us. As a salesperson, you must recognize that in persuading prospects to buy your product you must overcome this resistance to change. Buying your product calls for a change of habit or lifestyle, and the prospect's inertia competes strongly with the need for improvement.

Helping prospects overcome inertia is a delicate task. Rather than pushing for a quick decision, you will have to give each time to adjust to the thought of making a change. Suppose you are an agent for a truck leasing company and you call on prospects who own their own fleet of trucks. Your proposal that they start leasing trucks requires a major change in the way they do business. Being accustomed to ownership, they may be very uncomfortable with such a new concept. You must respect their need to get used to the idea. Using the **problem-solving approach**, bring up tactfully some of the common problems of fleet ownership. Then explain how leasing your trucks can make life easier in the short and long term. Any attempt to get an immediate contract from prospects who have not had ample time to compare their present situation to your proposal will probably fail.

The Prospect's State of Decision . . .

You will recall from Chapter 4, that potential buyers must pass through six stages of decision making before purchasing your product:

1. Recognize a need
2. Consider your product the best way of satisfying the need
3. Be able to afford the product, know they can afford it, and consider its utility at least equal to that of other, similarly priced products
4. Feel comfortable doing business with you and have confidence in your abilities
5. Have confidence in your firm
6. Believe that now is the time to buy

Although there is no set sequence in which prospects pass through the later stages of decision, need recognition is usually first. If your prospect displays no primary demand, the need for the product itself, you will have to generate it before developing selective demand, or the desire for a specific brand. Prospects who have not passed through the need stage will have no reason to continue on through the other phases. However, this does not mean that the need stage cannot occur later in the selling process. If you call on established customers to introduce a new product, for instance, they may certainly feel comfortable doing business with you and your firm before they see a need for new items.

Sometimes a prospect makes a purchase without having satisfactorily passed through each of the decision stages. For example, an executive who must relocate quickly to an unfamiliar city may hastily buy a house that proves to be too small for his family. Another prospect might buy a particular product that is not totally satisfactory because of an unawareness that better brands exist. Customers who buy without having passed through all six buying stages are likely to experience **postpurchase dissonance**. They will question the value or satisfaction of their purchase and wonder if they did the right thing. To avoid postpurchase dissonance, buyers must feel without any doubt that their purchase decision was the right one.

Designing Your Presentation . . .

The prospect's state of decision will govern the design of your presentation. As Figure 7-2 indicates, the buying phases on which you focus your presentation depend on the stages through which the prospect has already passed. You must determine the length, emphasis, order, and content of the presentation based on your knowledge of which buying stages remain. You should also consider how much difficulty the prospect experiences in reaching any single point in the buying process. The length of your presentation is determined by the distance that remains on the prospect's road to decision making. If a normal presentation takes forty-five minutes, don't be distressed when one takes two hours. Remember the ones that took you only twenty minutes.

Suppose an aspiring athlete with ambitions of cycling stardom sets out to find the right racing bike. This prospect has carefully studied the bicycles used by most professional racers, and one day visits the largest athletic distributor in the area to inspect several models. The need stage has already been passed through, and the prospect is well on the way to going through the product and company stages. As the sporting goods salesperson, you have to recognize this and focus your presentation accordingly. Since you are dealing with a prospect who is well informed about the product, your main objective is to build confidence in you and your firm. A presentation to this prospect may take only moments compared to the presentation you would make to someone who is just beginning to consider a racing bike.

Be careful not to cover buying stages prospects have already passed through. If you do, they might cut you short before you reach the part of your presentation that would be important to them. For instance, you needn't spend time convincing the ambitious cyclist of the need for a sleek, light-

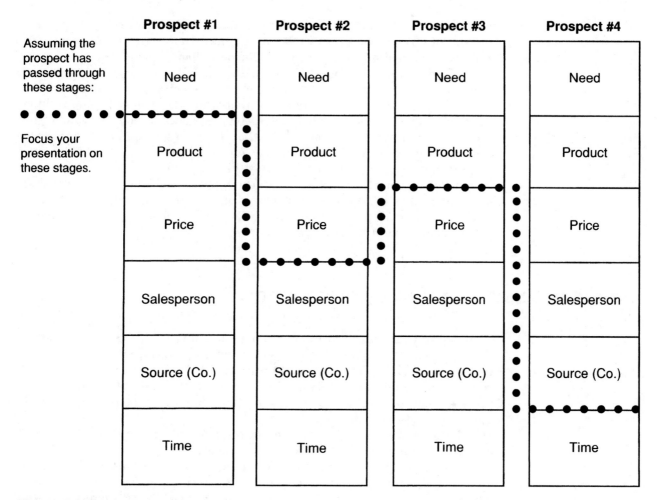

Figure 7-2 Buying stages.

weight bike. This prospect already understands that and also knows which racing bikes are the best for her or his needs. What this person might not know is that your firm supports the sale of its bikes with a unique service-replacement warranty.

Governing the Timing of Your Presentation . . .

You should structure your presentation according to the number and logical sequence of buying stages remaining for the prospect. If you have to lead your prospect through four stages, your presentation should have four components, each focusing on the stage that is most appropriate to the situation. For example, if your prospect must pass through the product, price, and time stages, deal with them in that order. There would be no sense in promoting your attractive price if the prospect is still not convinced that your product is the best choice. And there would be even less sense in saying that now is the time to buy if the prospect is unconvinced that your price is right. You will need to question the potential buyer periodically to determine your success in progressing through the various stages. Be sure you handle one stage completely before you shift the focus of your presentation to the next.

After you have made many sales presentations, you will come to know which buying stages are likely to be the biggest challenges in the sale of your product. For example, you may notice that most prospects like your product's price, but are concerned about the newness of your firm. This knowledge might tempt you to develop a standard presentation in which you immediately focus on your firm's expertise. Although we will discuss in a later chapter the benefits of limited standardization in personal selling, you should remember that all prospects are not alike. Differences in prospects require customizing of your sales presentations.

CONTROLLING THE SALES PRESENTATION . . .

Controlling the sales presentation means keeping the presentation focused on the product, keeping the prospect interested, and guiding the prospect toward ownership of the product. Control is not domination, nor does it imply rigidity. You maintain control of the presentation not by outtalking the prospect but by keeping the conversation moving smoothly through the stages of the buying decision.

Think of your sales presentation as an automobile trip through a stretch of scenic countryside. The point where you begin your journey depends on what sights your prospects are interested in seeing and what sights they have already seen. Your prospects belong in the driver's seat. They are more comfortable there. With them driving the car, they can better determine what speed they want to travel and what they want to see along the way. Your role is to navigate. You maintain control of the journey from the passenger's seat with a road map. You choose the general direction that will allow for the most enjoyable and informative trip. Through your navigation, you keep the car on the right road, avoiding exits, detours, and unnecessary stops and side trips. Figure 7-3 presents possible off-ramps along the road to buying.

A salesperson who insists on taking the driver's seat by dominating a presentation often does so out of fear or insecurity. Insecure salespeople feel safe as long as they are talking. They think talking keeps them in control. They believe that prospects shouldn't have the chance to talk. Such sellers fear that they will be thrown off track or that potential buyers might prove the seller or the seller's product unworthy.

> I don't deserve this, but then, I have arthritis and I don't deserve that either.
>
> Jack Benny

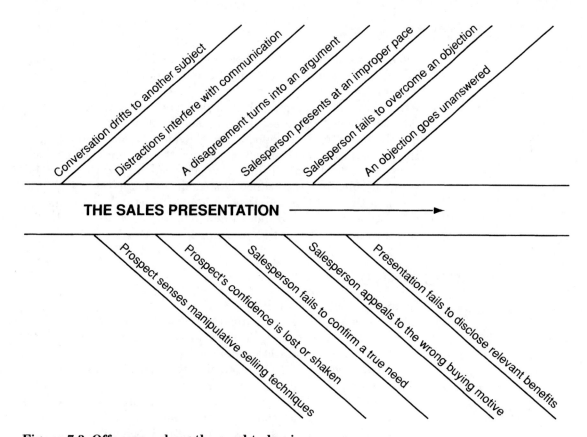

Figure 7-3 Off-ramps along the road to buying.

Some people refuse to buy from salespople who talk too much. They feel pressured, pushed, and even left out. Prospects want their thoughts to be heard, respected, and responded to. Interested parties want to be actively involved in the presentation and to feel that you are sensitive to their presence.

Overcoming Fear . . .

A confident salesperson does not fear the prospect's comments. Just as experienced teachers welcome questions from their students, skilled salespeople do not fear inquiries from potential buyers. Sellers should be prepared for queries and objections, knowing that only by handling the prospect's questions and addressing concerns will the sale be made.

You must have a positive attitude toward the input of prospects, be open to their ideas, and accept them without judgmental response. You need to create an atmosphere in which prospects feel free to comment. The conversation must be two-sided, with you asking frequent questions and giving every opportunity for potential buyers to contribute comments, questions, and objections.

Think of the prospect's questions and objections as the grounds on which to reformulate plans that were improperly made. You learn by listening, not by talking. When you listen to prospects, you compliment them, earn their friendship, and assure them that their feelings are important to you.

Staying on Track . . .

Keeping a sales presentation on track is more an art than a science. If the conversation drifts to another subject, you cannot abruptly stop and say, "Now, if we could get back to my product...." You must find a smoother, more tactful way of getting back on track. One way is to allow the conversation to reach a low point, when the prospect is presently at a loss for something to say, and use the opportunity to refocus the conversation on the problem or product. If the presentation has completely changed to another subject, you have, at least temporarily, lost control. It is time for you to turn the conversation back to your intended purpose, which is to help the prospect satisfy a need or solve a problem through the purchase of your product. When the discussion changes to another subject, you must know when enough is enough. Often you must resist your own temptation to change the subject.

Losing Control . . .

Losing control of the sales presentation means saying or doing something that causes prospects to decide against purchasing your product. It can cause the loss of their confidence or their desire to do business with you. Allowing a conversation to drift off the subject is one way to lose control; but it is not the only way.

Perhaps you perform a product test and something goes wrong. The product fails. You could take the product apart and not be able to reassemble it, or you could make claims or promises that your prospects believe are impossible to fulfill. If you are not completely truthful with potential customers and they know it, you will definitely lose control. A personality clash, a thoughtless word, or an aimless conversation can cause you to lose control, and that ultimately means losing the sale.

Weighing the Pros and Cons . . .

Generally, prospects make their purchase decision after comparing the pros and cons of the purchase. Some prospects might decide that a high price is offset by a prestigious brand name. Others might decide that their unfamiliarity with the salesperson is offset by a pressing need for the product. Your knowledge that prospects will balance the "good" against the "bad" compels you to make sure that the points in favor of purchasing your product outweigh those against it. In ideal circumstances, there would be no negative aspects, but realistically there are always pros and cons. The prospect's weighing process can never be entirely eliminated.

The sharper your selling and human relations skills, the fewer negative aspects potential buyers will identify. For example, prospects may be so impressed with the quality of your product that they will not consider its price too high. Your expertise and ability to get along well with others means that prospects will consider dealing with you to be a positive experience.

Not only will the pros and cons be different for each prospect, but each prospect will place individual weight on his or her needs or problems. For example, one buyer may have a concern over the newness and small size of your company, whereas another may consider it a minor fault. Some potential customers may even consider it an asset.

ESTABLISHING THE PROSPECT'S CONFIDENCE...

One fundamental purpose of the sales presentation is to establish the prospect's confidence. To be receptive to your message, potential buyers must have confidence in you, your product, and your firm. Words spoken by someone we trust have more value. Only through trust will the prospect receive your message favorably. This need to establish confidence is especially important in major purchases. Some examples of sales situations in which building customer confidence is essential include:

1. The purchase involves a large sum of money.
2. Extensive after-the-sale maintenance or service is required.
3. The product affects the safety or well-being of prospects, their families, or companies.
4. There is an element of risk involved with the purchase.

Rick Gerkhe

Different people gain different insights and rewards during their educational years. For Rick Gerkhe, it wasn't so much the course work but the mindset of the instructors that helped him develop confidence. Having left Plattsburgh State University in New York, just two terms shy of a dual degree in biology and environmental science, Rick moved West and enrolled in business classes at Linn-Benton Community College. This experience triggered a career switch from production to sales. He also credits his life-long love of athletics in helping him create the competitive spirit and time management skills needed for success in selling.

Presently, Rick is employed as a realtor and sales associate with ERA in Albany, Oregon. He sells and leases both residential and commercial real estate, and, after being named "Rookie of the Year for ERA nationwide" in 1994, has been the top producer in a 25-person office for four straight years. In addition, he was awarded "Realtor of the Year" in 1995 by the Albany Board. He feels that a good deal of his success is attributable to being honest and straightforward with his clients.

Rick is truly in love with the field of sales. He says that is doesn't take much to separate yourself from the pack, as long as you refuse to settle for mediocrity. By constantly striving to improve yourself, both professionally and personally, nothing is out of reach. He also is a strong believer in physical fitness as a benefit in improving the stamina and appearance of well-being that is important in any position. Rick stresses that people want to work with people who exude confidence, so advises that you should never be afraid to ask for the order.

Suppose you represent an excavating firm and are visiting a family who has a flooded yard caused by faulty drainage. You are in a situation in which confidence building is essential. Perhaps these homeowners have no idea what the proper solution to their problem is. They may not even be sure that they have called the right person for help. Perhaps they wonder if they should have called a landscape architect, or a building contractor, or a plumber. Given their state of insecurity, this prospect needs immediate reassurance that the right person has been contacted.

BUILDING THE PROSPECT'S CONFIDENCE IN YOU . . .

From the outset of the presentation, you should begin to plant confidence builders in the prospect's mind. Once you prove yourself worthy, potential buyers will respect you as someone to whom they can turn for the correct answers. Here are some things you might do to build your prospect's confidence in you:

1. Refer to your education and experience.
2. Demonstrate your product knowledge.
3. Subtly refer to your success as a salesperson.
4. Prove whatever you claim.
5. Mention others your prospects know whom you have helped, or give your prospects a letter of recommendation or a testimonial letter written by a satisfied customer.
6. Refer to your long standing in the community.
7. Refer to your membership in professional societies and trade associations.
8. Establish a common bond with your prospects.
9. Confirm that you have properly qualified your prospects. Prove to them that they can afford the product and benefit from it.
10. Make it clear to your prospects that you are concerned about them and what is best for them.
11. Always tell the truth. Admit when you don't know the answer to a prospect's question.
12. Make claims that are realistic and relevant.
13. Dress professionally.

Confidence is a seed of slow growth. Usually, prospects need to have considerable experience with a salesperson before they readily accept her or his honesty. Although gaining a potential buyer's confidence takes time, it also takes root. Once confidence is established, it can withstand powerful challenges. For example, if prospects know that you have always been truthful with them in the past, they will be inclined to trust you when you say something they may find hard to believe.

Referring to Your Education and Experience . . .

Even if your prospects assume from the beginning that you sincerely wish to serve their interests, they may think you lack the education and experience to do so. You must gain this trust by actively establishing your expertise. Referencing your background in the early stages of your sales presentation is one way to do this.

You should immediately find ways to inform the prospect of your education history and your years of selling, servicing, or even building the product you sell. Phrases such as "What I have learned" or "My experience has been" are good because they help you make passing mention of these confidence-building details.

Establishing credibility is an especially challenging task for the new salesperson. Few prospects are anxious to do business with a novice. But before you sell yourself short, approach the subject of experience from every angle. Often, new salespeople don't realize how much they have learned until they think about it in creative ways. Experience is a broad, general term that should refer not just to job titles but to activities on and off the job that contribute to knowledge and competence.

Suppose you are establishing your own contracting company and your first prospect is hoping to build a $300,000 house. They are not likely to entrust the job to a bidder who has never constructed a residence before. They may assume you have limited experience because your name is not familiar. However, if you have worked in all phases of house construction, building homes under someone else's name, you have plenty of experience. The only thing new about you is your contracting firm. You need only prove to the prospect that you know what you are doing.

Looking at Your Entire Background . . .

As a new salesperson, you need to look at your entire background to find experiences that translate into a selling context. Perhaps you have spent time training with senior salespeople and have witnessed them in action. Maybe you had hands-on experience during a cooperative work education program in college or you took a seminar course in problem solving that involved sales-oriented cases. Just as new dentists refer to the knowledge they gained in dental school and as interns, new salespeople can refer to the experience they received in college research, job-training programs, or working with a top expert in the field.

> There is more credit and satisfaction in being a first-rate truck driver than a tenth-rate executive.
>
> B. C. Forbes

If you have no extensive experience to speak of, you should neither claim you do nor refer to the subject. Should your prospects ask you about your background, describe your training. If they seem skeptical of your abilities, ask to be given the opportunity to prove that you understand their situation and have the ability to solve their problem.

Demonstrating Your Product Knowledge . . .

Although there are ways to translate a checkered background into relevant experience, there is never a substitute for product knowledge. Likewise, there is no excuse for not having it. Inexperience can be overlooked, but ignorance of your product is unforgiveable. Not only is product knowledge essential to building the prospect's confidence in you, but lack of it is the surest, swiftest way to destroy all chance of gaining a sale.

You must be prepared to give your prospects a thorough education in the product or service you are selling. They may need one, and even if they don't, they will expect you to be better informed than they are. The person shopping for a computer printer for the first time will be impressed by the salesperson who takes the time to explain the differences among daisy wheel, dot matrix, inkjet, and laserjet types. The potential buyer gains an understanding of the available products and develops confidence in the knowledgeable salesperson. Figure 7-4 lists aspects of product knowledge you should possess.

Product knowledge can be acquired in many ways. You can attend a manufacturer's training school or seek out and talk to recognized experts in the industry. Learn all you can from the prospects on whom you call, and read whatever information is available on the product. Whether you sell chemicals, cameras, or cars, you can never know enough about the product or service you handle. Finally, your product knowledge should be acquired before and between sales calls, never on the prospect's time.

Aspects of Product Knowledge

1. Features and physical attributes

2. Uses and applications

3. Construction

4. Capabilities and results

5. Terminology

6. Intangible attributes (e.g., brand image and "personality")

7. Differences between brands, models, and types

8. Compatibility with other products

9. Warranty requirements

10. Servicing and care

Figure 7-4

Establishing Your Sales Success . . .

Prospects quite naturally link successful salesperson performance with quality products and suppliers. They associate sales volume with product quality and salesperson talent. For this reason, references to your sales success are good confidence builders. If your prospects happen to get a quick glance at your order book, they will probably be encouraged to find themselves in plenty of company. Everyone wants to be aligned with a winner, and your impressive sales figures show that both you and your product fit the bill.

Take every opportunity to refer discreetly to your performance as a salesperson. You might mention how many units of the product you have sold to date or on a weekly or monthly basis. However, be sure not to overdo it. Referring to your "closing ratio" (the orders you have received as a percentage of the sales you have attempted) may be seen by some prospects as high-pressure selling.

Give your prospects the impression that you are busy, but not harried. Most prospects will consider a busy person a successful person. Never say that your calendar is wide open next week or tell your prospects to select any time they want for an appointment. Instead, let them choose among several times that are good for you.

Proving Claims . . .

Don't expect a prospect to take your words at face value. Anyone can make claims about product performance or superiority, and sometimes they will be accepted as absolute truth. But regardless of how much a potential buyer seems to believe you, always give evidence to back up whatever you say.

Any proof that can be verified by the prospect will do. It might be the written results of a scientific test or survey, or pictures or videotapes of the product in use. When you provide this evidence, you are no longer just making claims, you are stating facts. By proving your statements, you portray yourself as an honest and informed salesperson. This builds confidence in you.

Mentioning Others You Have Helped . . .

Another excellent way of establishing trust is to let the prospect know that you have been of service to others. This is especially true if the people you have helped are known to your prospects or could easily be put in touch with them.

Confidence built on the basis of having helped others is sometimes established before the prospect actually meets you. If you are recommended by someone who told the potential buyer what a great service you offer, chances are the prospect will already have some confidence in you. These future customers look to the experiences of friends as an indicator of what's in store for them when they do business with you.

> If you don't know where you are going, every road will get you nowhere.
> Henry Kissinger

Referring to Your Long-standing Background in the Commmunity . . .

If you have a long-standing background in your community, this is an excellent way to establish confidence. One way to get across your background is to mention in small talk that you grew up in the prospect's neighborhood or that someone in your family knows a relative of the prospect. Perhaps you are acquainted with many people mutually or can swap memories about local events or schools. Your long standing in the community builds confidence in you because it shows your attachment and stability as well as shared knowledge.

During your preapproach, you are likely to uncover something that you and the prospect have in common. It may be your education, a hobby or business interest, or a similar family situation. Much like your long standing in the community, a common bond makes prospects feel as though they are dealing with someone like them, someone who shares the same interests or activities.

Sometimes in territory assignments, the background of the salesperson is matched up with the type of prospects in that area. If most potential buyers are small businesses, a salesperson with a strong entrepreneurial background might be successful. Reference to this small-business experience will help assure future customers that the salesperson understands their situations and needs. Prospects prefer salespeople who can personally relate to their circumstances because they feel more confident that their needs can be met.

Confirming the Qualification of Your Prospect . . .

Many prospects believe salespeople are determined to sell whether or not the buyer should buy. They see selling, or making the sale, as the foremost task, and salespeople as trying to sell to anyone regardless of whether there is a need for the product. Certainly not everyone feels this way. Many prospects will recognize you as someone with a job to do, namely, to sell your product. Of course, it's fine for your calls to think you have a job to do, as long as they also know you have principles. If you go into your presentation without first having properly qualified your prospect, you will only reinforce the image of salespeople as concerned simply with themselves.

Make it clear at the outset of your presentation that you are not interested in selling to someone who doesn't have a genuine need for the product or the ability to pay for it. This is what qualifying is all about. If you have any doubts, take immediate steps to confirm the firm's or person's qualification. This measure will go a long way toward establishing confidence in you by contradicting the presumption that salespeople don't care about anyone but themselves.

> If you keep saying things are going bad, you have a good chance of being a prophet.
>
> Isaac Bashevis Singer

Showing Concern for the Prospect . . .

Early on, establish your desire to meet the prospect's needs. Ask questions that show your interest in the potential buyer's situation and your concern over his or her problems. Remember, as the final step in the marketing process, the major obligation of selling is to assure that needs are satisfied. An attitude of sincere caring for the welfare of prospects and customers is a definite asset for any salesperson.

This attitude goes hand in hand with your short-run and long-run objectives. In the short run, your primary concern is satisfying needs with the purchase of your goods or services. In the long run, the objective is to maintain a healthy relationship with your customers so that they want to do business with you again.

Telling the Truth . . .

In selling, honesty is paramount. Under no circumstances should you ever tell the prospect something you know to be untrue, or guess at the answer to a query. There will be times when potential buyers will ask questions whose answers you do not know with complete certainty. Although you want to be honest with the prospect, you also want to maintain your image as an informed source of knowledge. Understandably, you fear that you may lose the prospect's confidence if you do not have an answer. There are only two choices: give the prospect the correct answer, or admit that you don't know it but will find out.

Even though lack of knowledge might weaken your image, honesty will strengthen the prospect's trust in you. Compensate for the weakness by telling the future customer that you are unable to answer the question at the present time but will research the matter. Potential buyers will have far greater respect for you if you admit that you don't know the answer than if you guess and are later proved wrong. Besides, your fear of losing the sale on the basis of one unanswered question may be unfounded. Prospects might be perfectly willing to give you the time to locate the solutions they need.

The temptation to guess at an answer is greatest when chances are that the prospect will never know better. For example, if potential buyers ask how much fuel they can expect to save each year once they have installed your home insulation, you know they will probably never determine the answer independently. Your temptation to guess may be quite strong. However, the prospect may have more experience or education than you thought and can tell your answer is wrong. In the moment that it takes you to make up the answer, the prospect's confidence in you will be shattered. You have been caught lying, and you may never again be believed.

Being Prepared is the Best Answer . . .

As long as your knowledge of your product and industry is fundamentally strong, there is nothing wrong with not having every detail on the tip of your tongue. However, it is important that you have quick access to information you don't happen to remember. Try to minimize the time gap between the question and the answer. In fact, you should expect certain queries to come up and have most of the answers at your fingertips. Your briefcase should be a kind of traveling file cabinet. You should not fumble through it in search of papers thrown in haphazardly. Keep your materials well organized, and develop a handy reference system that will enable you to retrieve anything with ease. Your ability to locate information quickly will show that you are prepared for your sales calls. Carrying a lap top computer is an excellent way to keep track of information and impress your prospects.

Only if you are frequently unable to handle questions will you lose your credibility. You should be without an answer only occasionally, and once you have learned the answer to a new question, you should never be unprepared for it again. If you often fail to know the answers, prospects may lose confidence because of your obvious lack of preparation. Eventually, promising to find out the answers will not be good enough.

Whereas an outright guess is unacceptable, an intelligent estimation might be appropriate. For example, suppose you are selling a product whose fuel consumption depends on a number of variables, and you have not had the opportunity to research each prospect's unique situation beforehand. If a potential buyer asks how much fuel they will use, you may be able to call upon related information to make a conservative estimate. Perhaps the biggest machine in your line uses a maximum of 100 gallons of fuel a week, and the model you are presenting is smaller and more energy efficient. You can safely tell your prospects, "Less than 100 gallons a week." Of course, they may be unimpressed by both your 100-gallon estimate and your inability to give them an exact figure, so your best bet is to frankly tell them it's a conservative estimate. Follow-up by calling your office or factory for more precise data.

Making Realistic and Relevant Claims . . .

When describing your product's performance, make only the most realistic claims. If you sell high-performance radial tires that are good for an average of 45,000 miles, tell your prospect to expect "at least 40,000 miles." If you sell a product that will be resold by retailers, and you know they will easily sell thirty-five units a week, say that stores will have no trouble selling twenty-five units a week.

Sometimes you may be tempted to make exaggerated statements or promises about your product or its performance. Perhaps you've had a bad sales period and your volume is down, or worse, you're not meeting quota. If you fear a sale will be difficult to make, you may try to rationalize to yourself that an outlandish claim has some basis. For example, suppose you represent an exterminating service, and your prospect emphatically states the desire to never see a bug in the house again. You might want to tell the prospect to expect ten years of freedom from pests after using your service. You rationalize that this is a fair claim because several of your past customers have enjoyed ten pest-free years. But the truth is, those lucky customers were exceptional since the average treatment lasts about six years. The latter is the period you should promise. Don't tell the prospect for radial tires to expect 50,000 miles just because several past customers have beat the guarantee. Don't tell the retailer to expect a sales volume of fifty units a week just because a handful of other retailers had booming business last month. Your exaggerated promises will backfire, later if not immediately.

Generally speaking, if your relationship with the prospect is new or you are in the beginning stages of the presentation, your claims should be more conservative. If potential buyers don't know you or doubt your abilities, you cannot afford to say anything that weakens your developing credibility. You must not give any reason for future customers to disbelieve what you say. If you fail to establish their confidence before making dubious claims, they may never trust you enough to purchase. Even if your statements are true, think about how they sound to a prospect who doesn't yet believe in you. A seemingly exaggerated claim made before you have had the opportunity to establish credibility can mean a quick end to your presentation.

Not only should your claims be realistic and conservative, they should also be relevant. Saying your product performs when the outdoor temperature exceeds 110 degrees will mean nothing to the prospect who lives in a mild climate. Similarly, the fact that your industrial-strength epoxy can be used on heavy equipment is irrelevant to the homemaker who wants to repair furniture and toys. Such immaterial comments undermine your attempts to gain confidence because prospects will think you are silly or inexcusably ignorant of their needs.

Here are a few other guidelines for establishing the prospect's confidence in you:

1. Pay the competition its due. When appropriate, admit the competing product has good points or admit your own product is not perfect.
2. Divulge all the necessary information that you can about yourself, your product, and your company. If there is anything that you can't state, tell the prospect why.
3. Present the model that generates the greatest interest if you have determined it to be appropriate.
4. Answer all questions immediately, or request permission to defer the answer until later.
5. Follow industry standards for dress and appearance.

> When one door closes, another opens. But we often look so long and so regretfully upon the closed door that we fail to see the one that has opened for us.
>
> Alexander Graham Bell

How To Lose The Prospect's Confidence . . .

If the techniques and guidelines just covered are ways to gain the confidence of potential buyers, the following are surefire ways to lose it:

1. You make no attempt to qualify the person as a prospect.
2. You do not determine need or isolate a problem.
3. You fail to determine which of the models you sell is best suited for the prospect.
4. You say something the prospect knows to be untrue.
5. You cannot find any good points about the prospect's present product or a competitor's product (keep in mind, someone decided to buy it in the first place).
6. You appear to be withholding information from the prospect.
7. You are determined to sell the prospect a certain model.
8. You avoid answering the prospect's questions.

Fortunately, avoiding these mistakes will help you gain the prospect's confidence.

SELF-CONFIDENCE IN SELLING . . .

In selling, as in anything else, you must have confidence in yourself if you are to instill it in others. This self-awareness of your selling abilities shows in your words, your conduct, and your mannerisms.

To strengthen self-confidence, think frequently about your experience selling the product or working in the industry, the college degrees you hold or the sales records you have set. Remember all the people whose situations you have helped improve, and recall the events or accomplishments that have established you as an expert in your product or industry. You will discover that whenever you think along these lines, you feel good about yourself and your confidence grows. Should you ever find yourself feeling discouraged, deliberately remind yourself of all that you have done. You might even update your resume at such a time.

Do not hesitate to refer to your experiences and achievements during casual conversation with the prospect. A potential customer's acknowledgment of their importance will help strengthen your belief in yourself.

BUILDING CONFIDENCE IN YOUR PRODUCT . . .

Whether you sell an established product or a relatively unknown one, you have the responsibility of building the prospect's confidence in it, in yourself, and in your firm. Potential buyers will be justifiably concerned about the product's

> **Product-related Factors that Improve Your Chances of Making the Sale**
>
> 1. The product is superior to competing brands in ways that matter most to the prospect.
> 2. The product is not complex when it comes to use or service.
> 3. The prospect can try the product before buying it.
> 4. The product's results are immediately or quickly observable.
> 5. The product is compatible with or can be used in conjunction with the prospect's present equipment or system.

Figure 7-5

performance. The importance of reassuring them is especially strong when security, health, or well-being is at issue.

Even if you are selling a long-established product, you should expect the prospect to be unfamiliar with it. Be prepared to introduce it and build the prospect's confidence in it at the same time. Here are some techniques to accomplish this end:

1. Conduct a product test.
2. Mention favorable publicity about your product.
3. Refer to the experiences of present and past users.
4. Refer to your own experiences with the product.
5. Discuss the product's performance record.
6. Show the product in its various stages of construction.
7. Promote your guarantee.

See Figure 7-5 for a list of product-related factors that improve your chances of making the sale.

Product Tests and Promotional Pieces . . .

Probably the most common and effective method of building the prospect's confidence is in the product test. Although testing is not possible with all items or in all instances, nothing establishes a prospect's confidence more than seeing what the product can do. We discuss product tests in detail in Chapter 10.

Another way of building the prospect's confidence in your product is to call attention to favorable publicity. Printed literature or broadcast coverage is always a confidence builder because it proves performance. Show potential buyers articles written about the product, advertising reprints, or reports from independent testing agencies.

Satisfied Users, Including the Salesperson . . .

The experiences of other customers builds confidence in several ways. Perhaps you know of present users who freely mention how pleased they are with your product. If so, consider asking them to write a brief testimonial letter. To make it even more convenient, offer to write down their comments and ask them to sign it. Your prospects will be able to read about firsthand experiences and develop confidence knowing others are satisfied with the product.

Even more effective than happy customers is a happy salesperson who believes in the product enough to use it personally. If you can display your own use of the product, do so. Describe your own experiences with it, and invite the prospect to take a look at the model you own.

Product Performance and Construction Details . . .

Yet another confidence builder is discussion of the product's operating or sales performance. Operating performance can mean any number of things. How well your product compares to others in technical tests, how well it stands up to wear and tear by the user, or its cost efficiency are important. Combining operating performance with sales performance can be quite simple. When you say that of the 200,000 television sets your company has sold in the past 15 years, 150,000 or 75 percent are still in use, you are stating something positive. Performance, both as a marketable commodity and as a satisfying product, carries a lot of weight.

Products that are complicated or take a long time to produce can be shown in their various stages of manufacture. For example, if you sell in-ground swimming pools, you can build prospect confidence by taking potential customers on a tour of pools that are under construction. Pick them up at their house and take them first to a poolsite that has just been prepared, then to one that is about half done, and ultimately to a pool that is almost completed. By conducting this tour, you will be able to point out all that goes into the construction of a high-quality product. The prospect will be able to see workmanship and materials that are invisible in the finished product. Finally, you should take the prospect to a finished pool, preferably one that is in use. Your prospect's conversations with satisfied homeowners, along with witnessing a swimming party, are excellent confidence builders.

This **building-block approach** has many applications. For example, a tour of your manufacturing plant or office facility can be very effective as a confidence builder, and prospects are usually quite receptive to the idea. Such a visit enables potential buyers to meet the key people in your organization, observe the production process, and develop a feeling for the operation of your company. You, your product, and your company cease to be strangers. Seeing how your product is built might be as important to the prospect as seeing it in operation when it's finished.

Guarantees and Warranties . . .

Another way to build confidence in your product is to promote its guarantee. This is especially important if potential buyers show initial lack of confidence in what you are selling. Whatever doubts your prospect may have about the

Presentation Checklist

____ 1. I have arranged for private, uninterrupted time.

____ 2. I have timed my presentation so that it will not exceed the other's span of concentration.

____ 3. I have cleansed the presentation of any possibly unfamiliar words.

____ 4. I use short sentences.

____ 5. I emphasize and repeat key words that promise benefits.

____ 6. I start my presentation with a key benefit so as to attract the other's attention.

____ 7. Immediately I establish a primary need.

____ 8. Early on in my presentation, I present a unique point.

____ 9. I follow up with dominant points.

____ 10. I demonstrate how my proposal is cost-effective or will result in benefits that outweigh the effort or costs to adopt.

____ 11. I have built-in questions that will elicit information and involve the other person.

____ 12. I have kept the presentation short enough to allow for questions from the other person.

____ 13. I have prepared visuals that will truly enhance the impact of my words.

____ 14. I am very clear as to what I want from the transaction.

____ 15. I have attempted to anticipate what the other person will want.

____ 16. Early in the presentation I will satisfy myself through questions that what I am saying is interesting.

____ 17. Everything in my presentation is designed to be valuable and interesting to the other.

____ 18. I show how adoption of or agreement with my idea can be easy for the other.

Figure 7-6   Source: *The Power of Persuasion,* **Thomas L. Quick. Executive Enterprises Publications, Inc., 22 West 21st Street, NY 10010.**

quality of your products may be alleviated by guarantees that prove the manufacturer's confidence and promise satisfaction. A written copy of your product's guarantee serves as an important reference during your sales presentation. If it is significantly superior to those of the competition, spend ample time explaining it. Confidence building is further enhanced by following a detailed presentation checklist such as the one presented in Figure 7-6.

BUILDING CONFIDENCE IN YOUR FIRM . . .

Confidence in you and your product will not be enough to solidify your relationship with potential buyers. If you neglect your firm, your prospect's overall assurance will be incomplete. Here are some ways of building trust in the company you represent: (1) provide a brief company history, (2) supply a profile of key company personnel, (3) give a nonconfidential list of present company customers, (4) furnish literature on your company.

Company History . . .

Providing the prospect with a brief summary of your firm's history is always a good idea. If your company has been operating for many years, the prospect who knows this will be assured that it is well established, here to stay. Future customers want to know that the organization you represent will be around long after the purchase is made. With newer businesses, it is wise to refer to the background of the owners or unique product position to overcome any concerns.

Businesses often advertise their longevity with slogans like "In business since 1919," or "Serving this community for 50 years." If a written history of your firm is not available, consider compiling one on your own. Even if you do present your prospect something in writing, it might be a good idea to give an oral history as well. Not only will telling the story add a personal touch, but it will also reinforce your relationship with the company.

Company Personnel . . .

A profile of key company personnel goes a long way to assure the prospect that your firm is both a team of experts and a group of people with broad social concerns. Equally important, it gives you an opportunity to describe any special talents or reputations for excellence that key employees possess. Profiles would summarize the aspects of each person's education, personal achievements, business experience, social contributions, and noteworthy recognition by the industry. You might say to the prospect: "Perhaps you have heard of Gloria Dasher, the head of our research department. Mrs. Dasher served on the committee that wrote the present industry guidelines on product testing."

Additionally, it is important to point out those key individuals with whom the future customer might have dealings. In most firms, employees other than yourself are likely to have contact with buyers. Credit and finance, shipping, manufacturing, and order desk personnel are regularly involved with purchasers, and potential buyers should know who to contact about what.

Present Customers . . .

A nonconfidential list of present customers can be very effective in building the prospect's trust in your company. Promotional pieces sent by college textbook publishers to professors frequently contain lists of the colleges that have already adopted the publisher's books. The reasoning is simple. By showing potential adopters a list of present customers, you inform them of others much like themselves who felt that their decision to purchase from your firm was the right one.

If the company that you represent sells more than one product, you should list all of its present customers, regardless of which product they buy. Be sure to mention your own largest, most successful purchasers first, or put their names at the top of the list. This is a subtle way of reminding potential buyers that you are a capable, successful salesperson.

Literature and Brochures . . .

You will recall the value of sending literature to the prospect in advance of your sales call first mentioned in Chapter 6. This practice not only serves as an introduction, it enables prospects to answer many of their own questions before your call. Sending out written information also builds confidence in your firm. Companies show the pride they take in themselves and their products by spending the time and money to produce high-quality promotional literature.

Salespeople should also carry promotional and informational literature with them when making calls. Some prospects or customers might misplace premailed brochures or simply not have them on hand. Generally, no amount of literature is too much. Many firms supply the sales force with reprints of advertising pieces. For example, the seller can begin the presentation or answer questions by saying, "Perhaps you have seen our advertisement in *Chemical Week*."

You Decide!

Lester has just landed a selling position with a vinyl siding company. Being Lester Spencer, Jr., the son of a well-known local builder, was a big help in landing the job. Both the company that hired him and many of the customers he called on knew his father. Lester's job was to call on local framing and building contractors to convince them to use vinyl siding, versus the typical wood, on new construction. Although he knew the business to a degree, he quickly found out that he was not too well prepared to try to convince builders to use his product. In fact, he often was not even given a chance to make his pitch.

At the end of a particularly discouraging day, Lester makes one last call on a builder who recognized the name Lester Spencer. Finally getting an opportunity, he responds to the prospect's question by saying yes, he was the son of Lester Spencer the builder, and then embellished it a bit by saying that he was a partner, at one time, with his dad. After all, he had put in a couple of summers working in the family business, even though it was mainly as a gofer. The prospect immediately welcomed the young man, and not only listened to the presentation but indicated interest. Lester said to himself, "Aha…now I have the answer. I'll just tell everyone that I was a partner in Dad's business. Really, what harm could come of that." **You decide!**

THE VALUE OF A GOOD REPUTATION . . .

Once you have built the confidence of many prospects, you are in an enviable position. In fact, your most important objective in selling is not to make the sale but to establish and maintain customers. An unblemished reputation goes a long way toward achieving this goal.

Reputation of Salesperson . . .

You should never put your short-term needs ahead of your concern for the prospect's well-being. Establishing a good reputation sometimes means sacrificing immediate sales and income. Such actions might include not attempting to close if your product isn't suited for the potential buyer, or selling a model that is less expensive than another. Even if using pressure or exaggerated claims would help you make a sale or meet your quota, such tactics damage your reputation in the long run.

Only with a good reputation will you achieve continued success. Such acclaim will precede you, and many sales will seem to automatically come your way. Customers have been known to switch brands to follow a respected salesperson who changed employers. Buyers want to continue receiving honest, expert service, and typically believe that such a salesperson wouldn't be selling the new brand if it wasn't among the best to be found.

Reputation of Product and Company . . .

Just as confidence in the salesperson may be preestablished, so may goodwill for the product or company. Long-time customers will naturally have confidence in your firm and its new products. Nonusers may be sold in advance by your product's famous name, its wide exposure in the marketplace, or your company's many years in business.

The salesperson who sells a well-advertised product and who represents an established firm has an advantage over unknowns. Prospects who have not previously purchased the company's merchandise are likely to be more receptive to the salesperson's message if the brand or firm is well known. Sellers representing lesser known companies or unknown products have an uphill road to climb.

ASKING FOR THE TRUST OF THE UNTRUSTING PROSPECT . . .

Some prospects will, for one reason or another, be unable to trust you despite all you do to win them over. If traditional confidence-building techniques have proved unsuccessful, you might try some variation of this approach:

Mr. Hundley, we must all rely on other people whether we want to or not. When you have your car's brakes repaired, your safety depends on the quality of the work. When you board an airplane, you put your life in the pilot's hands. Trusting others is something we must learn to do if we're to get on with our lives. I'm not a mechanic or a pilot, but I am worthy of your trust, and I wouldn't be asking for it if I weren't. If you will give me the opportunity to prove to you that I'm concerned with your interests, you will come to realize, through the benefits you receive from my product and the support you receive from my firm, that you were correct in giving me your trust.

Summing It Up . . .

Selling is best viewed as a problem-solving process. The presentation concentrates on the two steps in the middle of that process. The objectives of the presentation are to make prospects aware of the problem or need and to persuade them that your product will resolve the problem or need. To accomplish these objectives, you must make potential buyers aware of the shortcomings of their present situation, then present the relevant, problem-solving advantages of your product.

Most prospects pass through six buying stages, or states of decision, before making a purchase. As the salesperson, you are responsible for guiding potential buyers through any stages remaining at the time of the presentation. Otherwise, future customers might experience postpurchase dissonance. The design, emphasis, and length of the presentation will be determined by the prospect's buying stage. Sellers maintain control over the presentation by navigating prospects smoothly through the buying stages. You lose control by destroying potential buyers' interest or desire to buy.

Prospects must have confidence in you, your product, and your firm. They must believe without a doubt that you have the ability to properly assess their situation and recommend the most appropriate solution, and that you will put their needs before your own. It is during the early stages of your sales presentation that you must devote the greatest effort to establishing the prospect's trust. Gaining confidence can be accomplished in many ways, such as references to your experience, product performance, and your firm's history. Remember that the objective of selling is not to make the sale but to establish customers. Your reputation is your biggest asset.

Key Concepts and Terms . . .

building-block approach
postpurchase dissonance
problem recognition

problem solving
problem-solving approach

Building Skills . . .

1. Explain the two objectives of the sales presentation.
2. Describe what it means when we say that every prospect has a "problem" to be solved.
3. Examine why you should assume that your prospects see nothing wrong with their present situation.
4. Analyze the purpose of not covering buying stages through which the prospect has already passed.
5. Explore the reasons a prospect might make a buying decision without having passed through all six stages of the buying process.
6. Explain five techniques for building a prospect's confidence in the salesperson.
7. Evaluate the causes of prospect mistrust.
8. Explain why it is important to admit that you don't know the answer to your prospect's question, why you shouldn't guess, and why you shouldn't give an approximate answer.
9. Describe the ways that confidence in a salesperson can be established before meeting the prospect.
10. Examine the benefits of letting your prospect know about your sales performance.
11. Analyze what it means to be in control of the sales presentation, including how you might be in control even when the prospect is dominating the conversation.
12. Explore the loss of control of the sales presentation, the reasons it might happen, and the consequences.

Making Decisions 7-1:

Melvin Rock has recently become a sales associate with Linn Grove Distributors, an Iowa-based supplier of agricultural chemicals and fertilizer. He has little practical farming experience, but Melvin majored in farm economics and minored in dairy management in college. One afternoon Melvin drives out to Storm Lake, where he calls on a farmer named Norman Anderson. The farmer and his foreman are walking toward a pickup truck when Melvin pulls in.

Melvin:	(Walking toward the two men) Excuse me. Would either of you be Mr. Anderson?
Norman:	I am. What can I do for you?
Melvin:	(Extending his hand) I'm Melvin Rock from Linn Grove Distributors. I'd like to talk to you about your fertilizer and chemical needs for the coming season.
Norman:	Are you any relation to Bill Rock over in Sioux Rapids?

Melvin:	Why, yes, he's my uncle.
Norman:	Is he still farming? I heard he was in bad health.
Melvin:	He's still farming. In fact, he just bought sixty head of dairy cattle. That should almost double his milk production.
Norman:	You look pretty young to be selling plant food. Do you know what you're talking about?
Melvin:	Yes! Linn Grove has trained me thoroughly. They taught me about primary and secondary fertilizers, trace minerals....
Norman:	They're businesspeople, not farmers. I want to talk to someone who knows how to grow corn! Don't you have any farming experience?
Melvin:	Not really, but...
Norman:	I'm sorry, young man, but you need to learn a thing or two. Stop back again in a few years. Meanwhile (glancing at his foreman), I'll rely on Tom here to tell me what chemicals to use.

Describe the measures that Melvin should take to establish Norman's confidence. Point out the major confidence-building opportunity that Melvin missed.

Making Decisions: 7-2:

Margie Heimbach is an account executive for Royal Cellular, a firm marketing cellular telephones. One day she pays an unannounced visit to Jane Solomon, sales manager for Hickory Hill Distributors, a food wholesaler. Solomon heads a forty-three-member sales force responsible for a three-state region.

Margie:	Good morning, Ms. Solomon, I'm Margie Heimbach from Royal Cellular.
Jane:	Please, call me Jane. How can I help you?
Margie:	I understand your company cars aren't equipped with telephones, so I'd like to tell you the advantages of a mobile phone system.
Jane:	That's very nice of you, Margie, but our salespeople get along fine without car phones.
Margie:	(Removing a model phone from her briefcase) This is our newest mobile telephone. It's lightweight, uses only 3 watts of power, and accesses 832 cellular channels. It has a lighted keypad, last-number redial, and a muting button.
Jane:	I've been a sales supervisor for five years, and I can recall very few situations where having a car phone would have mattered.

Margie:	I can understand your feelings, Jane. You obviously run a successful operation. But I'd still like to explain the most recent advancements in cellular technology and review some cost data. I think it proves what a good investment a mobile telephone really is.
Jane:	I don't think so, Margie. I'm really not in the market.
Margie:	Okay, but let me give you some product literature. If you change your mind, here's my business card.

Describe the critical step in the selling process that Margie neglected. Rewrite Margie's dialogue as you would have presented it.

Making Decisions 7-3:

Describe the problems to be solved when selling (1) microfilm equipment to a business archive service, (2) an intercom system to a company with a large office complex, (3) a closed-circuit TV system to an expanding discount department store.

Practice Makes Perfect 7-1:

As a former hairdresser, you have just begun selling beauty salon equipment. Write out three things you would say to a prospect who seems to doubt your product knowledge.

☐
☐
☐
☐

Enhancing Understanding and Establishing Believability

THE JOB TO BE DONE . . .

Making an effective sales presentation is more than just sitting down and talking with someone. Success in selling comes from being able to communicate intelligently. As in any communication process, the message sent must be received, understood, and believed or it is worthless. Chapter 8 contains many helpful tips and suggestions to help you:

...understand the persuasive power of autosuggestion.

...develop the techniques of subtle persuasion.

...recognize the need for action as well as words.

...understand the concepts of direct and indirect suggestion, and positive and negative suggestion.

...appreciate the use of impartial sources of suggestion.

...recognize the superiority of specifics over generalities.

...focus on pleasant wording, and know the circumstances in which unpleasant wording is appropriate.

...recognize the importance of emotional wording.

...see the need for strong conviction in your product.

...see the need to show enthusiasm in your sales presentation.

...learn how to help the prospect imagine your product's benefits.

...recognize the problem of sounding "too good to be true."

ENHANCING UNDERSTANDING . . .

The purpose of this chapter is to explain techniques that will help you establish credibility and suggest in a nonthreatening way that the prospect purchase your product. Here you will find principles and methods that will prove valuable in your effort to persuade the prospect to adopt your way of thinking.

The ideas discussed in the following pages relate to broader topics that are found throughout the textbook. They will all help you in your effort to make the sale by enhancing the likelihood of the prospect's believing your message. Many of these concepts are extensions of discussions from previous chapters or to be covered later. Some subjects explained only briefly in other areas are covered in more detail here. Although there may be an overlap of information, this chapter is intended to offer a different perspective on the repeated subjects by introducing new points.

THE ART OF GENTLE PERSUASION . . .

Persuasion is the essence of selling. It permeates the selling process. The most successful salespeople are those who enjoy the challenge of persuasion. They seize every opportunity to win someone over to their way of thinking. This does not mean that selling efforts should be pushy. Selling should be an interactive, nonmanipulative process. To be successful in selling, you need to practice the **art of gentle persuasion**.

Although persuasion is the primary task of a salesperson, it is not limited to the selling profession. We learn many of the basic principles of persuasion in the course of everyday life. In reality, life sometimes appears to be one exercise in persuasion after another. Long before you decided to become a salesperson, you probably learned how to persuade someone to accept your ideas. Whether it be with instructors, friends, family members, children, or bosses, you practice the art of gentle persuasion continually.

In selling you discovered that the quickest way to win your prospects over was to show them how your suggestions would benefit them. You may have noticed that your own personal satisfaction was best realized as a byproduct of your efforts to satisfy another person, that putting others' happiness before your own is surprisingly persuasive. Salespeople sometimes say that the question most asked of them by their prospects is, "What's in it for me?" If your prospects ask you this question, be ready to tell them.

Some of our efforts to persuade are easier than others. This is as true in selling as it is in life. We usually recognize fairly quickly the occasions in which persuasion will be easy and those in which it will be difficult. A teenager may easily persuade a schoolmate to go out on a date Friday night, yet find difficulty in convincing parents to permit the use of the family car for the date. The salesperson presenting to a potential buyer whose budget has been cut drastically will have a difficult time selling a seemingly unnecessary item. Selling to a prospect whose funds have been increased will be much easier. The most successful salespeople enjoy the big challenges, those in which persuading the prospect to purchase is especially difficult.

> The difference between the impossible and the possible lies in a person's imagination.
>
> Tommy Lasorda

Autosuggestion . . .

Autosuggestion is the act of persuading oneself. The beauty of autosuggestion in selling is that your prospects do the persuading. They sell themselves by telling you what they want, rather than you telling them what they should have. As you might imagine, autosuggestion is an ideal worth striving for, a process that you should try to incorporate into your presentation strategy whenever possible.

The reasoning behind the use of autosuggestion is that people are more likely to follow a gentle suggestion than a command, and even more likely to follow advice if it is of their own making. We all dislike being told what to do. Prospects don't want to think they're being sold something, but rather that they're buying it. And they *really* want to think that buying is *their* idea.

To create a climate for autosuggestion, you need to present information and ideas rather than commands or direct advice. Instead of telling prospects what they need, ask for their ideas and respond with information that allows them to draw their own conclusions.

The subtlety of autosuggestion is especially desirable with strong-willed prospects. The more direct you are in telling such a personality what to do, the more likely he or she will refuse. Suppose you were presenting to a proudly independent retailer. You would not do well at all to tell your prospect that every retailer in town is buying your product and that four other stores in the same chain are stocking the product. Much better to allow this manager to use self-generated reasoning. "Mr. James," you might say, "sales of this product are up 400 percent in the past year, and our model is the best-selling one on the market." Let the retailer conclude that carrying the product will mean riding the tide of a growth market. There will be no need to spell it out.

Using Subtle Persuasion . . .

When prospects are wrong in their contentions or seem unwilling to alter their viewpoint, use **subtle persuasion** to change their way of thinking. Don't be forthright, and never damage your prospects' pride by openly proving them wrong or telling them how naive, backward, or uninformed they are. You must gently bring them around.

Suppose you sell computerized cash registers to retail stores, and your prospect's store is twenty years behind the times. No matter how amazed you are that this retailer can stay in business, subtlety dictates that you find a tactful way to update this potential buyer. You might start with a tour of a store where your cash registers are used. The prospect will learn firsthand how much more efficiently a retailer can operate using your state-of-the-art equipment. Or show the merchant a film in which different retailers are using your cash registers. Perhaps the potential buyer is aware of the shortcomings of the present equipment, and needs only a gentle nudge before deciding to modernize.

Subtle persuasion also implies modesty and discretion. Although you should seize every opportunity to point out your product's strong suits or your own relevant achievements, you should never appear boastful. Whenever you try to convince your prospect that your product is the best, your company is reputable, and you are competent, you must use conversational methods instead of "announcements." You would be none too subtle if you stated point blank that your product just won an award for excellence. The preferable way to make this point is to tack the information onto another statement: "I'm sorry to keep you waiting, Ms. Owens, but ever since we won the Industry Excellence Award, the office has been a madhouse."

Actions Speak Louder . . .

Although speech is an indispensable part of selling, remember that actions speak louder than words. For maximum effect, you might follow this general rule: Never just say what you can do, and never just promise what you can prove. Words alone cannot describe how cleanly a saw cuts or how quietly a machine runs.

Actions can reinforce words or even replace them. For example, you could succeed by merely saying to your prospect, "You are throwing away 20 cents for each minute your copier is out of service." But putting two dimes on the prospect's desk as you say it will give your words much more power. Each time your prospect glances at the coins on the desk during the remaining minutes of your presentation, that 20-cent savings will become more ingrained in the prospect's mind.

Actions that support your words will help you persuade your prospect, whereas those that contradict defeat you. When you tell prospects your dishes are indestructible but you handle them with excessive care, they will believe your dishes are breakable, even delicate. Of course, this does not mean you should treat your goods abusively since respectful handling conveys value.

Even though action can prove a point, it is to be used advisedly. Some actions are clearly inappropriate. For instance, no matter how sturdy those dishes are, you should not whack them against your prospect's coffee table. Likewise, if you want to demonstrate how effectively your cleanser removes stains, put a stain on a sample of fabric, not on your potential buyer's carpet or furniture.

> If you play it safe in life, you've decided you don't want to grow anymore.
> Shirley Hufstedler

Direct and Indirect Suggestion . . .

Both direct and indirect suggestion are useful tools in selling although they are not equally appropriate in every situation. **Direct suggestion** is open and straightforward advice. **Indirect suggestion** is an idea planted in the prospect's mind.

Direct suggestion is best when a prospect is looking for advice, would appreciate an authoritative opinion, and is not likely to feel pressured by the suggestion. The following are examples of direct suggestion:

"You'll need the larger model for an office of this size."

"I suggest a light countertop with that shade of wood."

"Why not try on a matching jacket while you're here? They're marked down 40 percent."

"If I were driving this truck across the country, I'd change those shocks now."

Many salespeople dislike direct suggestion for the same reasons customers dislike it. They think it is pushy. Granted, it can be, but direct suggestion is also highly credible. The more direct you are in making a suggestion, the more convincingly you convey your own belief in the suggestion. If a small-office manager expresses an interest in a large mainframe computer and the salesperson says, "I don't think you should order the mainframe for your office," the manager will read credibility into the salesperson's firm statement. Curious, the prospect will ask, "Why shouldn't I?" and the prospect will be especially receptive to the salesperson's explanation. The salesperson will have the manager's complete confidence when replying: "These mainframes are made for offices with tremendous data-storage needs. The PCs and a networking system should serve you more economically, even if your company doubles in size." The salesperson's directness implies complete sincerity.

Direct suggestion is usually not a good way to convince the prospect against purchasing a competitor's product. Suggesting that the prospect not buy from the competition can easily be construed as defensive selling. Directly criticizing the competition is unprofessional, and most prospects disapprove of salespeople who belittle their rivals.

Dealing with the competition should be left to indirect suggestion. This is especially true in cases of friendly competition, where there are two or more firms that make no direct attempt to win over the others' customers. For example, suppose a community college admissions counselor wants to persuade a high school senior to enroll in the college. The counselor knows the student is an athlete and the competing college's sports program is weak. The counselor also knows better than to say directly, "You won't like their athletic department." Instead, the counselor uses indirect suggestion: "What kind of sports program do they have there? Ours offers women's varsity golf as well as volleyball and basketball."

If, in this example, the counselor is aware that the student also wants vocational schooling, it would be appropriate to ask, "Do you know what percentage of their graduates find related employment upon graduation? You should find out." By asking questions like these, the counselor is in a position to supply favorable information about the school without detailing unfavorable facts about the competing school. Although the college is superior to its competition in areas of importance to the student, the power of persuasion in this instance lies in indirect suggestion.

If your potential buyer mentions a competing brand that offers little or no service backup, you would not want to be so obvious as to say, "They don't have much of a warranty." Instead, you should try indirect suggestion: "You'll want to be sure they service their product" or "You might want to compare their warranty to ours before making your decision." Although your indirect suggestion certainly implies the idea that the competition's warranty is weak, you maintain professionalism by avoiding direct criticism.

Competitive matters are not the only matters that can be handled with indirect suggestion. Indirect suggestion is especially desirable when direct suggestion would be inappropriate or in bad taste, as when you want to make a proud or boastful claim. Perhaps you feel uncomfortable bragging directly that your product is considered the best on the market. Indirect suggestion comes to the rescue: "When you're the top seller in the market for twelve years running, you must have something going for you" or "We've been selling this for 130 years, and people still beat down our door for it."

Indirect suggestion can also take the form of a **third-party question**. For example, you might say to a store manager: "More and more retailers are telling me that their customers are willing to pay more for a top-quality product? Do you find this to be true?" This is an indirect way of suggesting that carrying your brand will attract quality-conscious customers.

Positive and Negative Suggestion . . .

Suggestions can be either positive or negative depending on how they are phrased and what kind of response is expected. A **positive suggestion** invites an affirmative response, and a **negative suggestion** invites an opposing response. The question "Would you like to hear about the sale we're running?" is a positive suggestion because it is phrased to prompt the prospect to say yes. On the other hand, a comment such as "The list price is $400; you didn't want to pay that much, did you?" is a negative suggestion.

Whenever you make a suggestion, you will select positive or negative wording to encourage the answer you would prefer. Positive suggestions are important at the beginning of your presentation to put the prospect in an affirmative state of mind, and again at the close, since the ultimate answer you hope for is yes. Asking the prospect at the conclusion of your presentation, "I assume you will require delivery?" is an effective way of checking for interest or closing the sale.

Because affirmative responses are preferred in selling, you will most likely use positive suggestion more often than negative. But negative suggestion does have a place in selling. After discussing the prospect's present situation, you might find it very useful to say, "I get the impression that you aren't completely satisfied with your present service arrangement." You are looking for a no answer, and your wording encourages a no answer. The negative nature of the prospect's answer will be focused on the prospect's present situation rather than on the situation you are offering.

USING OUTSIDE SOURCES OF SUGGESTION . . .

Outside sources of suggestion are sources that add credibility to a salesperson's presentation because they are not connected to the salesperson, the company, or the product. To serve its purpose, a good outside source must be impartial, authoritative, and believable.

Printed sources of suggestion tend to be more useful than others because people are more inclined to believe what they read than what they hear. They usually consider the printed word more reliable than oral statements. If a new teacher says something that contradicts the textbook, the students tend to trust the book.

Outside sources of suggestion enhance your credibility by agreeing with your claims. You might show your prospect a magazine or newspaper article in which your product's benefits are praised by an editor or reporter. Credibility is further enhanced if the writer or someone quoted in the article is known to the prospect as a respected authority on the subject. The reputation of the publisher also adds to the credibility of an article. An item in *Forbes* or *Business Week* that deals with economic forecasts will have greater impact than does an article on the same subject appearing in a magazine that is not known for its business coverage.

Should you wish to call on more personal outside sources, look for someone (1) in a situation similar to the prospect's; (2) who cares about the prospect, such as a relative or close friend; (3) whom the prospect knows has nothing to gain if the sale is made.

Describing the Experiences of Others . . .

Describing the experiences of others is an excellent way of building the prospect's confidence in your product and illustrating your product's benefits. You can certainly describe the unfortunate experiences of people who do not use your product, but better yet, describe the pleasant experiences of those who do use it.

Prospects enjoy hearing about experiences of others. They find comfort in knowing that their situation is not unique. So when you tell prospects how you can satisfy their needs, explain how you helped someone else with similar problems. If possible, quote the happy purchaser. When preparing to describe the experiences of others to your prospect, remember to choose a situation that is similar and one that the potential buyer can relate to. Futhermore, tell your story in a "before-and-after" format.

Everybody gets their rough day. No one gets a free ride. So far today I had a good day. I got a dial tone.

Rodney Dangerfield

Keep in mind a number of situations suitable for description, and match them as closely as possible to your prospect's special circumstances. A small businessperson with several employees cannot easily relate to the predicament of a multinational corporation. A young, single man does not have the same circumstances as an older, married woman. A country dweller cannot connect with a city resident's experience. Avoid straying too far from the prospect's realm of relevance.

Although your stories should be similar to your prospect's experience, they can't always be identical. You might find it advantageous to describe situations that represent your potential buyer's goals and objectives, if not the present circumstances. For instance, suppose you sell group insurance to employers, and your prospect has ten employees and a burning desire to expand the business. Using a larger company as your example, you can explain how your insurance plan works just as well for a firm with forty employees as it does for a firm with ten. Businesspeople who plan to hire more employees will be glad to know how your coverage can continue to serve them as their firm expands.

As for the before-and-after format, telling your stories in this manner emphasizes how the person or firm you describe realized a completely different and improved situation by purchasing your product. Your prospects will imagine themselves progressing along the same path as the people whose situations you describe. Most of all, they should be able to see themselves obtaining the same fortunate results.

A final word: Avoid mentioning names or hinting at the identities of the people in your descriptions. This is often unnecessary or impolite. Nonetheless, make sure that your description is clear and complete, not vague or apparently missing information.

Describing Your Own Experiences . . .

The time may come when a prospect asks you about your own experiences with the product you sell. Needless to say, you should be able to describe many positive ones. Think of how it would look if you preferred a competitor's brand. What if your Chevrolet dealer drove a Ford, or your Ford service manager drove a Toyota? How could you discuss the great performance of Lawn-Boy lawnmowers if the one in your garage is made by John Deere?

Suppose your prospect asked about your experience with the multiple vitamins you sell and all you could say was, "Well, I really don't have any firsthand experience with it, but my friends tell me it's great." What if you were selling a product in which prospects would entrust their very lives, like an airplane? If you fly a different kind of plane, the statement you make with your personal preference negates all the glowing praise you heap on the brand you sell.

Personal experience with the product is almost always necessary, except perhaps in industrial sales or other unusual situations. Cosmetics salespeople who wear the makeup and cologne they are selling will be far more successful. Not only do they prove their belief in the product, they are living demonstrations of the product's use and benefits. If you are wearing an article of clothing that your store sells and the prospect asks you if it's easy to clean, you can answer with the authority of personal experience.

If the prospect doesn't ask you about your experience with the product, bring it up yourself. Describing your own feelings is even better than recounting a third party's experience because you can relate to the minor details of your situation as no one else can. Your prospects' confidence is enhanced because they know they're talking directly to a satisfied user.

Why Be Specific? . . .

Imagine you are a prospect, and a salesperson makes the following statement: "This product has saved many of our customers a lot of time and a great deal of money in only a few months." Now imagine trying to figure out what the salesperson has told you. How many customers is "many"? How much time is "a lot"? How much money is "a great deal"? How many months is "a few"? What you think those words mean may differ considerably from what the salesperson thinks they mean. By speaking in generalities, the salesperson has told you next to nothing. Only by using specific terms will the seller tell you what you need to know.

If the tables were turned and you were the salesperson, you might say this instead: "This product saved each of sixty customers more than $200 and four hours a week in operating time during the first three months of use." By using specifics, you enable your prospects to determine for themselves whether your product's benefits are significant.

Whether describing your product's qualities or the experiences of third parties, specifics are almost always superior to generalities, for several reasons:

1. Specific facts can be proved. Dates, locations, and quantities lend themselves to verification. If the facts relate to product performance, prospects can examine your records, conduct their own research, or use the product to prove the truth of your claims.

2. Specific claims carry more credibility. The prospect is less inclined to doubt you or to suspect you're making something up if you use specifics.

3. Specific information is useful to the prospect, something the prospect can relate to. If you say, "We're selling this at a tremendous rate," the prospect will wonder what you mean by "tremendous." Say instead, "On average, we're selling forty-five models a week."

4. Specifics enhance understanding. Generalities create the opposite effect. This is because different people have different perspectives. A forty-year-old person is young to a septuagenarian, but old to a teenager. A person who stands 5 feet, 10 inches is tall in the eyes of someone who stands four feet, but short to the average professional basketball player. If you are a real estate agent showing a condo, do not create confusion by claiming that the average electric bill is small. Such an adjective is a matter of opinion, which is shaped by personal experience. Instead of using an opinionated adjective, opt for specific, objective facts. Tell prospects that the monthly electric bill averages about $40, and let them decide how "small" that is.

The Appearance of Spontaneity . . .

Spontaneity, or impulsive behavior, adds life to the sales presentation. Although you may not always *feel* spontaneous (in fact, the planning that is so necessary to an effective presentation discourages spontaneity), you should always try to *appear* spontaneous. This means you will have to find new ways to present your much-repeated information. You can rejuvenate a tired statement by rephrasing it with each new presentation. As your understanding of the ideas behind your words increases, so will your ability to state them in a variety of terms.

One of the best techniques for creating the effect of spontaneity is responding to your prospects rather than delivering your whole speech unprompted. You should give your prospects the impression that you are following their lead. Like an improvisational acting troupe, you must be constantly alert to the "cues" supplied by your prospect and your surroundings. Seize upon your prospects' questions as lead-ins to your actions, making them appear tailor-made for each.

You enhance the appearance of spontaneity whenever you are able to deviate smoothly from your planned course of action. For example, when the prospect asks you how the product is put together, you should be able to take it apart and reassemble it immediately rather than waiting until the usual time in your routine. If prospects think disassembling the product is a part of your normal presentation, they won't attach as much importance to it as they will if they think you have taken it apart for their benefit only.

Take advantage of every opportunity to make your prospects feel that you are doing something special for them. Anything that seems unplanned will have greater persuasive ability than something that seems routine.

Spontaneity is desirable not only in your actions but in your product knowledge. When prospects ask questions that you aren't expecting, they will be that much more impressed when you know the answer. College students are impressed by their professor's knowledge of the subject not just because of her or his lectures, but because of the ability to field unanticipated questions about material that was not reviewed before class.

THE POWER OF PLEASANT WORDS . . .

Much of what we say can be said in at least two ways, with pleasant words or with unpleasant ones. Whenever you describe your product or the prospect's situation after the purchase, use pleasant wording. Keep the prospect's mind focused on happy thoughts. The sales interview should be a cheerful, contented experience. Consider the contrasting effects of these words or phrases:

economy/expense	relief/pain
durable/flimsy	safe/dangerous
win/lose	peace of mind/worry
burden/freedom	fail/succeed
sickness/health	trust/deceit
quality/cheap	

As a salesperson, you will need to develop your ability to choose pleasant words rather than unpleasant ones. Saying your product is safe is far more pleasant than saying it is free from danger. Describing your prospect's purchase as an investment is infinitely superior to saying it is an expense. Although it is pleasant to say your merchandise will bring in more customers, it is even more pleasant to state that profits will increase.

Words like *profit*, *savings*, and *luxury* are pleasant. Business prospects enjoy phrases like *cash flow* and *market share*. Words like *loss*, *fear*, and *trouble* are unpleasant, and even more so are *bankruptcy*, *fire*, *strike*, and *losses*.

Simply put, the use of unpleasant words or phrases will remind the prospect of bad things. Consider the negative impact of the unpleasantly worded statements illustrated in Figure 8-1. Even though you may intend to say something positive with such phrases, you will in reality cause your prospect to think negative thoughts. Saying, "You'll never suffer downtime with this equipment," will make your prospect think about the loss incurred during production lags instead of the profit enjoyed with constant output. Don't allow the concept of downtime or loss to enter the picture. Say, instead, "This equipment will operate around the clock." Rather than saying, "You'll never have to worry about late shipments from us," you should say, "You are guaranteed to receive all of your shipments on time."

Even modifiers like *no*, *little*, or *not many* will not erase the thoughts that unpleasant words provoke. "You won't pay as much in taxes" may seem like a great promise to you, but unfortunately the promise contains several very unpleasant words. "Competition will take less of your business" prompts unpleasant thoughts despite the use of the word *less*.

Although you cannot always avoid the use of unpleasant words, you should try to minimize the effects of the ones you must use. Try to offset any unpleasant statements with strong ones. This balancing act is not as easy as you might think. When you say, "This product is maintenance-free," you are saying a pleasant and an unpleasant word. The question is will the pleasant word *free* offset the unpleasant word *maintenance* in the prospect's mind?

Consider the negative impact of the unpleasant words in the following sentences:

"This won't wear out soon."

"It takes alot to break this."

"You won't get sick nearly as often."

"Your costs will be cut in half."

"You won't be in any danger with this model."

"You will have no worry."

"Your expenses will be minimal."

Figure 8-1

Sensitive	Discreet
Cheap	Inexpensive
Sign	O.K., authorize, endorse
Down payment	Initial amount required
Buy	Purchase, invest
Deal	Transaction
Monthly payment	Monthly installment
Bid	Offer
Salesperson	Agent, representative
Total cost	Overall investment
Commission	Fee
Contract	Agreement
Sell	Offer
Customer	Guest

Figure 8-2 Avoid sensitive words.

Of course, even this rule has its exceptions. Despite your objective to focus your prospects' thoughts on their life as it will be when they use your product, you might occasionally find the all-pleasant approach ineffective. Sometimes, you have to wake up potential buyers to the harsh reality of their present situation, and the use of unpleasant words is in order. There is nothing wrong with focusing on the shortcomings of the present situations if the prospect is otherwise unable to see them. If the future customer fails to appreciate the economy, safety, and comfort of your product, you may well have to talk about the expense, risk, and inconvenience being endured without it. When a prospect tells you that the purchase will be deferred for a year, explain how unpleasant the coming year will be as the present product deteriorates further. Take care to associate unpleasant words only with your prospect's present situation, not with your proposal.

Further, if you must use unpleasant words, choose them as carefully as you would choose pleasant ones. Avoid extremely intense words. Don't say, "You're going to kill yourself if you don't change those tires." Instead, use milder words, like *problem* or *trouble*. Even these words should be avoided if possible. Instead of using the word *problem*, say *barrier*, *difficulty*, or *concern*. Figure 8-2 provides a list of sensitive words to avoid, along with an acceptable synonym or substitute.

Emotional Words . . .

Certain words convey strong feelings. For instance, *love* is an emotional word, and *sin*, to people with strong religious convictions, is very emotional. Former president Ronald Reagan found the words *freedom* and *dignity* highly emotional, and used them often in speeches.

> Whether it's the best of times or the worst of times, it's the only time we've got.
>
> Art Buchwald

The emotional content of words is very subjective. Business prospects tend to be moved by expressions like *profit* and *tax* although obviously in different directions. Carefree teenagers think nothing of such words. The word *loneliness* may be extremely emotional to a senior citizen, yet almost meaningless to a popular student.

Many selling situations require the use of words that play on the prospect's emotions. In life insurance, for instance, provoking emotion with the word *death* may be unavoidable. Heads of households who see no need for life insurance don't want to think about their death. These potential buyers should be made to realize the dire circumstances their family would face if they carried no coverage. Less-intense euphemisms may also serve the purpose: "What will happen to your family after you're *gone*?" you might ask.

Persuasive Words . . .

An essential ingredient in any successful selling effort is the use of persuasive words. Salespeople with a mediocre product often outsell those with a much better product because they use the words that their prospects like to hear.

The advertising world recognizes the persuasiveness of words like *powerful* and *scented*. The power of these terms seems endless. We like to hear them, and we recognize their importance. The word *natural*, however, has lost much of its impact through overuse. With so many products being advertised as natural, how meaningful can the word continue to be? Figure 8-3 shows a few more examples of words considered strong or persuasive.

Persuasive Words		
New	Free	Save
Sale	Guarantee	You
Now	Money	Easy
Value	Tested	Health
Exciting	Security	Success
Results	Safe	Proven
Discovery	Benefit	Quality
Relax	Win	Natural
Power	Strong	
Love	Home	

Figure 8-3

Sherri Haibeck

Many students are attracted to advertising. It is surely one of the more glamorous aspects of marketing. Advertisers and advertising agencies are always looking for talented writers and artists, and many students opt for this creative end of the business. Others seem more interested in the business end of the business, helping clients to get the most bang for their buck. Sherri Haibeck chose this latter route after gaining her diploma in marketing from British Columbia Institute of Technology. She still credits the number of oral presentations at BCIT in helping her to succeed in the world of marketing.

Upon graduation, Sherri went to work for McKim Advertising, which was later purchased by BBDO. Her initial positions were a real learning experience, allowing her the opportunity to examine every aspect of the advertising industry. Western Canada's largest agency, Palmer, Jarvis Advertising, lured her away to become Director of Media Services for this firm. As a member of the management team, she was able to coordinate the efforts of the entire organization toward satisfying client and consumer needs. Sherri recently served as President of ABCOM, the Association of Broadcast Communicators.

She obviously did an outstanding job for Palmer, Jarvis, because this energetic young woman was hired away by Moffatt Communications, the parent company for Vancouver radio stations CKLG/CFOX. As Regional Sales Manager, Sherri is now on the other end of the business, selling her firm's media outlets to advertising agencies and advertisers in her area. She is now working every bit as hard promoting radio as she previously did boosting the agency. As an added measure of her success, British Columbia Institute of Technology has hired her as an adjunct instructor in its continuing education program. Sherri has also co-authored the textbook *Introduction To Media*, which is used in courses throughout Western Canada.

The Importance Of Conviction . . .

"You can't sell anything you wouldn't buy yourself," states Victor Kiam, author of *Going For It!* Ask successful salespeople if they personally believe in their product, and they will undoubtedly say yes. Conviction is the key to your success. Before you can convince someone else that your product is worth owning, you must believe it yourself. If you don't have such trust, you cannot persuade your prospects.

If you lose enthusiasm for your product, don't think you can rely on great acting to continue selling it. Your true feelings will show through. Most prospects can quickly tell the difference between heartfelt persuasion and insincere sales pitch. You need not be a topnotch salesperson if your convictions are sincere. Nor will you have to tell your prospects directly that you think your product is the best because they'll see it in your eyes and hear it in your voice. People transmit their real feelings without realizing it.

Legend has it that Emile Blondin, the first person to cross Niagara Falls on a tightrope, once exposed the true feelings of an onlooker during one of his stunts. According to the story, Blondin pushed a wheelbarrow across the Falls and asked a man in the cheering crowd, "Do you think I can make it back." "Yes! Yes!" the man exclaimed. "Are you sure?" Blondin asked. "Yes, I'm sure," the man replied. "Then get in the wheelbarrow!" Blondin dared. The man turned and ran.

Lack of conviction will show in your sales figures. Although it is possible for someone to sell a product that they don't believe in, success will be much harder to attain. Without belief in your product, you can never realize your full potential in sales. Only with the support of sincere conviction can you satisfy your customers and deliver top sales income to your company.

Understanding the Prospect . . .

Suppose you represent a dealer selling rare coins certified by the American Numismatic Association. You are likely to encounter prospects who say they are not interested in investing in rare coins because of the fluctuations in the precious-metals market over the years. Don't just plunge into persuading them that rare-coin investors have realized significant gains despite the volatility of the metals market. Instead, ask them questions, such as: "What do you know about the relationship between precious metals and rare coins? Do you have any experience in such investing? What market forecasts have you heard?" Your prospects' answers will tell you the basis of their feelings, and you will be able to use your insights to address the issues that are important to them.

If you want your prospects to adopt your way of thinking, you must begin by understanding their way of thinking. Dominating the conversation will only interfere with what you need. Ask plenty of questions, and listen patiently to the answers. Encourage prospects to express their opinions and ask their own questions. Everything that is said will tell you something about their situation. As you learn more about your prospects, begin to put yourself in their shoes. Imagine what it's like being in their situation.

Making Use of Your Enthusiasm . . .

You enhance both your believability and the prospect's reception of your message by making expert use of your enthusiasm. Since your excitement communicates as effectively as words, you should learn to control the intensity of your presentation to fit your various messages. Throughout the presentation, change your tone and mannerisms to indicate the mood of the moment. For instance, you might convey your excitement over your product's benefits by speaking a little more rapidly and emphatically, or by punctuating major points with expressive hand movements. You need not be loud to put emotion into your presentation.

Enthusiasm, or the lack of it, is contagious. If you have any doubt about that, think about the fire drills you have experienced in school. Each semester the teachers are notified in advance that the drill is planned, and the students are given routine instructions about evacuating the building. Right on schedule, the expected alarms sound and hundreds of students stroll casually out of their classrooms, savoring the short break. Imagine the day in midsemester, however, when no drill is planned and a security guard hurries into your classroom to deliver an ominous whispered message to your instructor. The frowning instructor quickly announces to the class that there is a bomb threat and everyone must leave the building immediately. No one strolls. Everyone knows, from the intensity of the message, that this is no drill.

Envisioning Your Product's Benefits . . .

No matter how persuasive you are, you will never convince prospects to buy a product they don't want. You may, however, be able to convince them that they want the product. This you do by helping them envision the product's benefits. Your task is to show how their life will improve when they own the product, to help them imagine themselves in a situation of need-satisfaction.

Not everyone can see the benefits of your product without your help. A sculptor envisions the horse to be carved out of a block of marble. Less-artistic onlookers see only a piece of marble. Like the sculptor, you will need to carve out the benefits of your product so that the prospect will see them as you do.

Use your descriptive powers to transport prospects to a pleasant setting, one in which they are using the product and enjoying its advantages. Potential buyers will feel good when you use such a description, and they will associate your product with enjoyable emotions. Call on the prospect's physical senses to heighten the effects of the imaginary experience. For instance, if you sell time-shares for a resort condominium, say, "Imagine the tickle of warm sand between your toes and the crash of the waves against the shore."

Improving the Prospect's Situation . . .

Whatever the prospect's present situation is, your purpose is not to correct it but to improve it. Potential buyers do not appreciate hearing that they sorely need help because they're in a terrible situation, even if you do offer a solution.

If you sell office management programs, your prospects want to hear that you know how important a well-organized office is to them, not that their office is in chaos. When selling exercise machines, a potential buyer wants to hear that he or she seems like the kind of person who wants to stay in shape, not that he or she is out of shape. Kitchen appliance sellers should stress that a microwave oven will help prepare the best of dishes more efficiently, not that it's ideal for heating frozen dinners. In short, tell people they're good at something, and your product will help them enjoy their talents all the more by adding efficiency, economy, or ease to their situation.

Translating Product Benefits . . .

Even the most appealing product benefits can remain vague in a prospect's mind—attractive but abstract. Savings of time or money may be abstract until it is "translated" into something concrete. Turning product features into buyer benefits means spelling out exactly how potential buyers will gain from the use of the good or service. Table 8-1 shows some products, along with several of their features, and a benefit the corresponds with each feature.

TABLE 8-1

TRANSLATING PRODUCT FEATURES INTO CUSTOMER BENEFITS

Product	Feature	Benefit
Automated telephone system	Voice mail	No missed messages
	Call holding	Improved customer service
	Call forwarding	You can be reached anywhere
Athletic club membership	State-of-the-art exercise equipment	The best for your individual needs
	One-on-one instruction	Learning to do it the right way
	Tennis, racquetball, basketball	Activities for anyone
Redi-mix concrete	Multiple formulas	You get what is needed for the job
	Cell-phone equipped trucks	On-time delivery
	NET 30 day terms	You can collect before the bill is due
Golf clubs	Graphite shafts	Greater accuracy
	Titanium heads	More length
	Three year warranty	Peace of mind
Landscaping service	Free delivery	No over-exertion
	Designer on staff	Expert layout and selection
	One year warranty	Hedge against potential loss

To make this translation, you will need to know and capitalize on your prospect's goals and priorities. Tell the family man and entrepreneur, "This accounting program will give you back your Saturdays, to spend with your family." To the stock-market dabbler comment, "Now you'll have $50 more every month to invest." To the hobbyist try, "Our courier service will save you ten hours of errand-running every week, time you can spend designing more of this beautiful pottery."

Whenever prospects make comments that reveal their desires, think of a way to translate your product's benefits into the fulfillment of those cravings. If prospects say they haven't been out to a nice restaurant lately because their expenses cut too deeply into their budget, remember their words when you talk about the economy of your product: "Every month, you'll save enough money to enjoy a lobster dinner for two at Trés Chic."

Arguing with Prospects . . .

A sales presentation should be a friendly conversation between two people who like each other. Under no circumstances should a conversation with a prospect turn into an argument. The temptation to argue with a prospect is sometimes surprisingly great. When you have delivered what you thought was an excellent presentation and your prospect still refuses to buy, or suddenly has a change of heart and says no, you might understandably feel frustrated. Nonetheless, your wisest course is to find the resiliency to go back over any missed points or even to begin again if that is called for.

If you scold or challenge the prospect or in any other way vent your frustrations, the meeting will turn into an unpleasant experience that neither you nor the prospect will forget. Remain dignified and professional even if the prospect is unpleasant. Arguments can create long-lasting or even permanent ill will.

Unpleasant prospects and those who refuse to buy are not the only frustrations you will encounter. Sometimes you are tempted to argue with a potential buyer who persists in disagreeing with you when you know you are correct. But remember the saying, "You may win the argument, but you'll lose the sale." In fact, there is no such thing as winning an argument with a prospect. Proving potential buyers wrong or arguing them down serves to assault their ego and make them angry. They will only hold their opinion more firmly. Even if you prove yourself right and the prospect wrong, the damage you will have done to the relationship between the two of you will destroy your chances of making the sale. The probability of the prospect's ever liking you is virtually eliminated.

Arguing with prospects damages your chances for success in several ways:

1. Arguing causes you to lose your composure. You will not be able to deliver an effective sales presentation after an argument.
2. Arguing makes prospects all the more certain that they don't want to buy your product.
3. Repeated arguing endangers your job. Although at first your manager wants to believe your side of the story, he or she will eventually lose confidence in you as more and more reports of arguments come in.

What is the alternative to arguing? Be philosophical. Accept the fact that you won't make every sale. Remember that the prospect's situation can change, which might cause the decision to reverse itself. You might even get another chance to make the sale after you've reformulated your selling strategy. Be professional enough to know how to take no for an answer, and smart enough to rework your presentation for future success.

Too Good to Be True? . . .

Although your product may be truly fantastic, you will need to think about how your claims are going to sound to new prospects. If you don't know them well, or they happen to be skeptical or unaware of your product's benefits, you run the risk of sounding too good to be true. Take care not to overwhelm your prospects with fabulous promises, even if you know them to be true. Potential buyers who have not developed confidence in you will be turned off by your seemingly exaggerated claims. They may decide that your judgment cannot be trusted. They may even ask sarcastically why they haven't heard of such a miraculous product before, or how many millions of dollars you've made selling it.

The best way to avoid sounding too good to be true is to prove yourself as a reliable source before making questionable promises. If a prospect is convinced that a good personal computer cannot be purchased for less than $1,000, you won't do well insisting from the start that all functions the prospect wants to perform can be handled by a $700 model. Instead, you should find out what the person knows about computers and prove yourself to be an expert in the field. Only gradually should you try to change the prospect's perspective.

Honest John and Other Myths . . .

Most people instinctively become suspicious of those who point out their own honesty. What is *your* first thought when you see a billboard for a used-car dealer named **Honest John**?

Avoid the use of expressions that stress your sincerity because they will only make the listener wonder why you are bringing up the issue. "I sincerely believe you're making the right move." Such a statement introduces the question of sincerity instead of assuming it exists. The same is true for these statements:

> "Honestly, I can't think of a better product on the market."
> "Trust me ..."
> "Would I lie to you?"
> "I would never play games with you."

You Decide!

While in college, Virginia produced a videotape for a sociology class portraying the horrors of Asian sweatshops. She received a top grade for this five-minute project and was quite proud of her work. After graduating, she was hired by a manufacturers' representative agency, handling a variety of American-made clothing and accessories from several different principles. She called on major department stores and boutiques introducing these lines in a medium-sized California city.

Although she did reasonably well in her first year, Virginia felt herself under pressure to produce a greater volume of sales. Competition is fierce in the "rag business," and her company was under the gun from its manufacturers to sell more goods. Since many of the firms she competed against sold imported goods, Virginia hit upon the idea of showing prospects clips from the video she produced in college. By seeing firsthand some of the conditions under which many of the competitive garments were made, she hoped to appeal to the patriotic nature of her audience, convincing them to "buy American." Should Virginia take this tack? **You decide!**

Summing It Up . . .

Just as communication is the essence of selling, so is persuasion. Successful salespeople are enthusiastic about their product, and they use their vocabulary and carefully selected examples to help prospects envision its benefits. Their words and emotion make them effective persuaders. They aren't pushy or oversuggestive. Their efforts to persuade are well planned, not haphazard. They adapt to both the prospect and the situation.

Although they sometimes use direct suggestion, they know that in most instances indirect suggestion is called for. And, though they rely mostly on positive suggestion, they can identify those instances where negative suggestion is required. They generate autosuggestion, use physical action, and employ the Ben Franklin balance sheet technique. They refer to the advice of respected authorities and the pleasant experiences that they and others have had with the product. Their remarks appear spontaneous, and they present specific facts rather than generalities. Their sales presentations have a pleasant tone, and they use words that have strong emotional impact. They don't flaunt their honesty, they avoid arguments, and they don't sound too good to be true.

Key Concepts and Terms . . .

art of gentle persuasion

autosuggestion

direct suggestion

Honest John

indirect suggestion

negative suggestion

outside sources of suggestion

positive suggestion

spontaneity

subtle persuasion

third-party question

Building Skills . . .

1. Name several principles of persuasion you have learned in the course of everyday life.

2. Explore the beauty of autosuggestion. Describe how you would introduce this concept to a real-estate prospect.

3. Using examples, describe the power of persuasive words.

4. If your actions contradict your words, explain which are likely to have a greater impact. Give your own example of how this might happen.

5. Compare the difference between direct suggestion and indirect suggestion. List the advantages of direct suggestion. Describe situations in which you would use indirect suggestion to remain professional in competitive selling.

6. Explain the difference between positive and negative suggestion. Give examples of each.

7. Describe the advantages of printed sources of suggestion.

8. Explain why prospects enjoy hearing about the experiences of others, including the purpose of using a before-and-after format.

9. Explain the ways in which specifics are better than generalities.

10. List some techniques for building spontaneity into your sales presentation.

11. "This product will save you a fortune in maintenance costs." Describe what is wrong with this statement, and create a more pleasant way to word this claim.

12. Explain the importance of believing in your product.

13. List the circumstances in which you would describe an unpleasant situation or choose unpleasant words.

14. Give some examples of translating product features into concrete benefits.

15. Describe how arguing with prospects damages your chances for success.

16. Explain how you can avoid sounding too good to be true.

17. Explain why you shouldn't point out your own honesty.

Making Decisions 8-1:

Grace Davis works behind the cosmetics counter in Harmon's department store. One day she sees Terri Bolton, an old friend from high school.

Grace: Terri! How are you?

Terri: Hi, Grace. I didn't know you worked here.

Grace: I've been here for three months now. It's great. I get to see so many people I know. Plus, I get to tell them all about our fantastic cosmetics.

Terri: Well, I don't buy much makeup these days. With two children to support, I sometimes wonder where I'm going to find the money to buy food.

Grace: You should leave that part up to your husband.

Terri: Bill and I are separated. But let's not get into that.

Grace: Even so, you've got to live it up once in a while! Besides, these cosmetics are very affordable.

Terri: No, I don't think so. Maybe I'll stop back around Christmas. I could buy my sister some perfume.

Grace: I'm telling you, Terri, you've got to try these products. You'll feel like a new woman!

Terri: Thanks, Grace, but I'll have to pass. Hey, it was good seeing you. I hope to see you again real soon.

Describe the effectiveness of Grace's technique of persuasion. Reread the dialogue and evaluate Grace's choice of words.

Making Decisions 8-2:

Malcolm Laws works for VanHorn Sporting Goods, a large golf equipment and supplies dealer. Years ago, Malcolm played golf a few times with Neil Lohman, manager of the pro shop at the Kenilwood Country Club. Neil once played professionally, and the country club's members often seek his advice before buying golf equipment. Malcolm decides to call on Neil and show him a couple of new items from VanHorn.

Neil:	How's the golf game coming, Malcolm?
Malcolm:	I'm still collecting divots. (He laughs and holds up a nine iron and a putter.) Take a look at these.
Neil:	(Gripping the putter) Pretty nice. How do they perform?
Malcolm:	From everything I've heard, just great. Several friends of mine own these clubs and say they wouldn't use anything else.
Neil:	Anyone I know?
Malcolm:	I don't think so. They usually play over at Green Arrows. Why don't you give these clubs a try? You're certainly under no obligation to purchase.
Neil:	It's a nice offer, Malcolm, but I don't need clubs right now. Besides, I haven't been playing that much lately. New equipment would be a bad investment.

Explain the shortcomings of Malcolm's presentation. Describe the persuasive technique that Malcolm failed to use.

You sell for a large automobile dealer, and your prospect lives twenty-five miles away. Even after you quote a price that is $600 less than the price quoted by a small dealer located three miles from the prospect's home, the potential buyer still intends to purchase locally. Using the Ben Franklin balance sheet, list three pros and cons of the prospect's decision.

Making Decisions 8-4:

List all of the ways that you could enhance believability when selling over the Internet.

Chapter 9

The Setting of Your Sales Presentation

THE JOB TO BE DONE . . .

Presenting your goods or services to potential buyers is the most exciting portion of the selling process. The presentation, as important as it is, should not be entered into lightly. Just as in the staging of a theatrical event, the setting of the sales presentation casts the tone for what follows. Read Chapter 9 and learn how to:

...properly assess the competitive setting.

...understand how to deal with the factor of competition.

...realize the importance of possessing competitive intelligence.

...examine the dangers of defensive selling.

...discover how to resume your presentation after it has been interrupted.

...appreciate the importance of the physical setting for your presentation.

...recognize a physical setting that is inappropriate for your presentation.

...recognize situations in which a sales presentation should not be attempted.

...know how to deal with difficult prospects or situations.

ASSESSING THE COMPETITIVE SETTING . . .

As early as possible in the sales process, preferably while you are preparing for your sales presentation, you will need to determine the **competitive setting**, that is, the extent to which competition will be a factor in the sale. The competitive setting will vary from one prospect to the next. The potential buyer you are about to call on might never have heard of your competition, be shopping around for other sources, or be a loyal user of a competing brand.

When your prospects say they have not considered buying from other sources, you can assume that competition is not a serious factor. If the potential buyer makes no mention of the competition, nor gives other indication that this is a serious threat, by all means, don't make it one. Prospects who know little about your competition, or are not even aware of its existence, are true finds. Don't sell a rival brand by giving it unnecessary attention. Prospects who hear the competition mentioned unnecessarily will leave the presentation with the opposition's name firmly planted in their mind. Your job is to familiarize the prospect with your product, not with your competitor's.

Don't be disappointed to learn that your prospect has checked out a competitor or intends to do so. Shopping around is a common practice. Customers want to familiarize themselves with everything and everyone related to the product before they make their purchase decision. Just remember that the shopper initially has no preference, so you and your competition will be on equal footing at least temporarily. Reputation, price, features, and convenience are all likely to be factors in the shopper's buying decision.

Industrial buyers shopping for the best buy often take pains not to let salespeople know who the competition is. When salespeople bid for their business, the buyers schedule presentations so that competing salespeople don't see each other. This helps ensure that the presentations focus on the benefits of the product rather than on the shortcomings of the competing brand or the disadvantages of dealing with another firm.

The Highly Competitive Setting . . .

As Figure 9-1 indicates, competitive settings can vary dramatically. You might discover that your prospect strongly favors a certain supplier. If so, you will be working in a highly competitive setting. The closer your prospects are to buying from a competitor, the more quickly you will need to get their attention. Because visual aids attract attention fast, you might prepare some charts or graphs that prove your product's superiority over that of the competition, and be ready to present them on a moment's notice. Although you should be armed for the competitive setting with reasons why the prospect is better off buying from you, remember that your objective here is to get the potential buyer's attention, not to "de-sell" the competition. De-selling will be discussed later in the chapter.

The prospect who is a loyal user of a competing brand presents a rare challenge. You may be fortunate even to gain access to this prospect, and the setting will certainly be combative from the start. You will have to field questions regarding how your product compares to its rival and will constantly have to respond to the prospect's reasons for not wanting to switch.

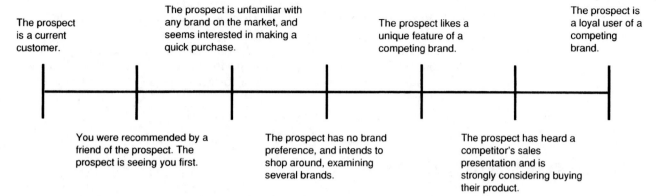

The prospect is a current customer.

The prospect is unfamiliar with any brand on the market, and seems interested in making a quick purchase.

The prospect likes a unique feature of a competing brand.

The prospect is a loyal user of a competing brand.

You were recommended by a friend of the prospect. The prospect is seeing you first.

The prospect has no brand preference, and intends to shop around, examining several brands.

The prospect has heard a competitor's sales presentation and is strongly considering buying their product.

Figure 9-1 Competitive settings.

Some prospects may be so loyal to the competition that you may wonder, during your preapproach or in the early stages of your presentation, whether you should be calling on them at all. Ask yourself if you have a superior product and can communicate this to them. If the answer is yes, make the call. If your competitor's product is identical to your product, and you are unable to offer faster delivery or more favorable terms of sale, your only recourse may be to become a second source of supply. Suppose you sell oil to industrial customers. You might say, "Ms. Crafts, you know how serious an oil shortage can be. Our policy in the event of a shortage is to see that our preferred customers always receive immediate shipment." Explain that if just 10,000 gallons of oil are purchased from you each month, the prospect will be put on your preferred customer list.

If competition turns out to be a very serious factor, you might have to make an extensive comparison between your product and the rival brand. This may be the only way to make the sale. Perhaps you can perform a side-by-side comparison test, showing that your product is superior in the ways that are most important. The only way of getting a toe hold with such a customer may be your ability to make these comparisons. Ask to make a comparative analysis. When prospects request a direct comparison, cover only the points they ask about. Address their concerns but nothing more. If there are no differences between your product and that of your competition, don't say that there are.

When the Prospect Mentions the Competition . . .

Sometimes during a presentation, a prospect will mention the competition, and you should be prepared to answer appropriately. The more serious a factor the opposition is, the more specific your responses to the prospect's questions and concerns must be. Have information handy so that you are always prepared, but discuss the competition only if absolutely necessary. Say no more about the competing product or company than you must.

You might, however, make use of the opportunity to plant questions about your rival in the prospect's mind. For instance, if you know that the competitor is very weak in service, say: "Service is very important with a product like this. Be sure you carefully examine their service arrangement. You might be in for a surprise." Or you might say: "They've been around for a long time, but their prices have doubled in the past year." These responses are litigation-proof. You are not defaming your competitor, and, by opening with pleasant remarks and avoiding direct criticism, you can keep the conversation on a professional level.

COMPETITIVE INTELLIGENCE . . .

Just as you must stay up to date with your own product, you must stay up to date with the competition. **Competitive intelligence**, that is, knowledge of the competition, is one of your job requirements.

You cannot isolate yourself from the competition. Don't pretend that it doesn't exist or won't be a factor in your sales. You should know almost as much about the competitor's product as you know about yours, and you should know it better than the prospect who buys from a rival regularly. There is no predicting how much competitive intelligence you will need in a given situation. In a highly combative marketplace, you must be aware of all the benefits your competitors have to offer. Your prospects are their prospects too.

With the help of competitive intelligence, you can develop a presentation that dwells on areas where your product is strong and the opposition is weak. This is especially true in making presentations to the loyal user. When prospects mention the latest feature of a competitor's product, you should know what they're talking about and how to respond.

Like preapproach data, competitive intelligence can be accumulated in various ways. One of the simplest ways to gather information is to acquire your competitors' sales literature or product information and read it. You can examine the product in the store or showroom, attend the rival's open house, or visit their booth at a trade show or convention. Don't forget to gather as much information as possible from prospects who are customers of the competition. Most important of all, you should try the competitor's product.

As you set out to gather competitive intelligence for your upcoming presentation, ask yourself the following questions:

1. Do I have any competitors in this sale?
2. Who are they?
3. How serious is the competitive factor in this sale?
4. Am I knowledgeable about the competitor's product?
5. Have I kept up with the latest developments in their product?
6. In what ways is their product weak and my product strong?
7. In what ways is their product strong and my product weak?

You should be able to answer all these questions with certainty. If you are uncertain about anything, you will know which areas to concentrate on in your search for competitive intelligence.

Defensive Selling . . .

Sometimes, particularly in a highly competitive setting, you might think you have to de-sell the competition in order to sell your own product. **De-selling**, or building a presentation around the competitor's weak points, is also called **defensive selling**. Usually, this type of selling is too oriented toward the competition, and should be avoided whenever possible. Although you may need to present a side-by-side comparison, you should do so only when the competitive setting calls for such measures. Do not build your entire presentation around the competition. This would appear defensive and might also be unethical.

The urge to sell defensively occurs for any number of reasons. Perhaps you fear your product is inferior, and you want to downplay its faults by showing how the competition's is even worse. Perhaps you run out of good things to say about your product, and you consider using the rival brand's weak points to lengthen your presentation. Or perhaps you heard that a competitor's salesperson said unkind things about you or your product, and you want to get even.

Defensive selling is also tempting to the salesperson from a new, small, or unknown company that is trying to penetrate a market dominated by strong competitors. A presentation slanted against the established companies may seem to be the only way to attract the interest of the competitors' loyal customers. The temptation is even stronger for the salesperson who hears time after time from prospect after prospect that there's no replacing their favorite brand.

Unfortunately, the use of defensive selling indicates that you have nothing different or better to offer. Defensive selling presents countless dangers. Here are a few:

1. Defensive selling is demeaning. You lower your professional image by purposely looking for faults in other people or products.

2. Defensive selling damages your rapport with customers. If prospects are using or considering the competitor's product, you insult them by criticizing it. When you say the rival product is junk, you imply that the prospect is foolish for using it.

3. Defensive selling diminishes your ability to gain the prospect's confidence. Prospects are inclined to dislike and disbelieve a salesperson who runs down the competition. A claim that your product is the only good one and that the others are worthless is considered inherently dishonest. The prospect thinks that the defensive salesperson says such things only to make the sale, not because they are true. If prospects don't believe you in this regard, they won't believe you in any other.

4. Defensive selling leaves the salesperson and the firm open to possible retaliation. There have been instances where friendly competitors turned into hostile rivals thanks to the introduction of defensive selling tactics. One firm's salesperson unfairly criticized the other firm or its product, the competing salesperson responded in kind, and the tit-for-tat selling accelerated until a once friendly marketplace turned into a battleground.

5. Defensive selling unnecessarily makes the competition a selling factor. Your criticism of the rival inspires the prospect to take a look at the other product: "Why is this salesperson so intent on running down the

competition?" the prospect wonders. "If there is such a fear that I will buy it, it must be pretty good. I'd better go check it out."

6. You may be breaking the law. You risk committing slander, libel, and product disparagement. We explain these terms in Chapter 19.

There are alternatives to defensive selling. You can compensate for your company's smallness or unknown name, for example, by reminding the customer that your firm can offer a better price and more personal service. This is not to say that your presentation can never include subtle references to competitors' shortcomings. Accounts are always being taken away from companies whose lesser-known competitors are able to find weaknesses and capitalize on them. Undoubtedly, these competitors capitalize without defensive tactics.

The best preventive measure for defensive selling is a strong conviction in your product and its strength in the marketplace, along with thorough product knowledge. The more you can say about the unique strengths and advantages of what you are selling, the less inclined you will be to talk about the weaknesses of your competition.

PLANNING FOR THE COMPETITIVE SETTING . . .

Your knowledge of the competitive setting can help you plan or change plans for your presentation. You need to know how important a factor the competition is and what other brands the prospect is considering. Familiarity with these issues will help you anticipate questions and objections, and plan your answers.

If you can assess the competitive setting before your sales calls, you will have time to research and make plans. If you know that the potential buyer has used or is using a rival product, you may have to ask what is liked or disliked about the competition. This will give you an idea of what to focus on during your presentation. For example, if your prospect tells you none of the competing brands of chain saws come with proper safety features, you know you should dwell on your saw's superiority in this area. Asking prospects what they like and dislike about rival brands is also a good way to determine their buying motives. In fact, sometimes the brand name alone tells you their buying motive.

The Physical Setting of the Presentation . . .

The physical setting of the presentation is the place where you conduct your sales call. In Chapter 6, we discussed several things a salesperson can do to make a comfortable setting at the outset of the presentation. Additional aspects of an ideal setting are covered in this section, as well as circumstances that make for a bad setting. Although a good setting may not "make" the sale, a bad setting may indeed "break" it. A bad setting that cannot be improved is no place to conduct a presentation.

Several attributes characterize the ideal physical setting:

1. The salesperson (or salespeople in team selling) is alone with the prospect or prospects, to the exclusion of uninvolved parties.

2. All parties are seated, unless the product or presentation requires otherwise (a walking tour, for example).

3. The lighting is suitable. It is bright enough for reading or dark enough for a film or slide presentation.

4. Outside or inside noises are shut out or minimized.

5. The climate is comfortable.

6. The chance for interruptions or distractions is low.

7. The salesperson is seated the proper distance from the prospect and at the proper angle.

Figure 9-2 summarizes the characteristics of the ideal physical setting for the sales presentation.

The Ideal Physical Setting For the Presentation

1. Private.

2. All parties are seated.

3. Salesperson and prospect are seated a comfortable distance apart, and at an angle, not side-by-side or directly facing one another.

4. A table or work desk is handy.

5. No distractions (loud noises, other people talking, sunblindness).

6. No personal or telephone interruptions.

7. Comfortable temperature.

8. No unpleasant smells or odors.

9. Outerwear can be removed and placed aside.

10. If all or part of the presentation is to take place out of doors—suitable weather conditions (no gusty winds, rain, etc.).

Figure 9-2

> I think we should follow one simple rule; If we can take the worst, then take the risk.
>
> Dr. Joyce Brothers

Positioning Yourself . . .

Your position in relation to the prospect should be comfortable for both of you in every way; physically, psychologically, and functionally. You should be close enough to go over papers, samples, and visual aids together, but far enough to respect each other's personal space. Remember that seeing unfamiliar items will be more important to the prospect than to you. When prospects back away from you or push their chair away from yours, you are too close to them.

When you visit prospects in their office, they will probably indicate a chair in which you can sit. If you have a choice of sitting either in front of the desk or beside it, sit beside it. This eliminates the psychological barrier that the desk places between you and your prospects, and puts you on more equal terms with them. If there is a choice between the chair on the left side of the desk and the chair on the right, sit in the chair on the prospect's left. Many salespeople think prospects pay more attention to them if they are on the prospect's left.

If you are in your own office, you should come out from behind your desk, especially if it is a large one, and take another chair, or sit next to the prospect at a small table. The position behind the desk is a "power" position, and by removing this difference between you and the prospect, you will make the potential buyer feel more equal and comfortable. Although sitting side by side with the prospect is not the ideal position, it allows you more easily to use your pen to direct attention to the important parts of the sales agreement. The same can be said of sitting near the prospect at an angle.

As we mentioned in Chapter 6, if the prospect doesn't offer you a seat, you should ask if you may sit down. Delivering your presentation in a standing position will make you appear nervous or anxious. Furthermore, people prefer making direct eye contact, which is difficult when there is a great height difference between them. When both people are seated, any height difference diminishes, and their eye contact is level. By being on an equal footing physically, the prospect and salesperson will feel equal psychologically as well.

Prospects who don't want their visitors to stay will sometimes place something on the chair by their desk. A stack of folders or a hat on the seat of a chair will definitely ward off a timid salesperson. If something is on the chair, ask if you may have a seat, but don't remove the object without first asking permission. Wise salespeople never take the liberty of rearranging the prospect's furniture to achieve a desired setting. Similarly, you should not select a location where visitors do not belong, at least not without first asking the prospect if you may do so.

The Poor Setting . . .

The physical setting is unsuitable for a presentation if some aspect of it hampers your efforts to present effectively. A wholesaler's representative can't expect to keep a retailer's attention in the middle of a busy store. An industrial equipment salesperson can't make an effective presentation in a noisy factory. If you encounter a poor physical setting and cannot improve upon it, you should not make the presentation.

Some elements that make for a poor physical setting are (1) inadequate lighting, (2) an uncomfortable climate, (3) limited seating, (4) no desk or worktable, (5) distractions or interruptions, (6) lack of privacy.

Poor lighting can interfere with your prospect's ability to read your printed material. It may also hamper your efforts because it doesn't do justice to a product that needs to be seen in bright light, such as a diamond ring. Bright lighting that cannot be dimmed sufficiently interferes with film or slide shows. An uncomfortable temperature, as in a hot kitchen or chilly warehouse, will interfere with your perspiring or shivering prospect's ability to concentrate. The same goes for a stuffy room, which induces sleepiness.

Wind and humidity can hamper a presentation that is being delivered out of doors. Seating limitations that require you or the prospect to stand will cause your presentation to lose effect because it forces one of you to "look down" on the other. If both of you have to stand, the presentation will feel rushed. When the presentation is lengthy, both you and your prospect will lose the ability to concentrate as your feet and legs grow tired.

If there is no desk or worktable on which to open your briefcase or assemble your product, you will be faced with the awkward and unattractive possibility of using a chair or the floor as your work surface. You may not even be able to get your presentation started. If the prospect's children are running through the house, buzz saws are screaming away next door, a radio is playing in the next office, or the telephone is constantly ringing, the noises, distractions, and interruptions will take their toll on your presentation. Neither you nor the prospect will be able to concentrate. A room full of occupied desks is not a good setting if privacy is an important factor. Find a different setting, or postpone your presentation until the setting is improved.

Just as you communicate the importance you place on a prospect's visit by the setting you create in your office, so do prospects in their places of business. If you are taken to a quiet conference room, or the office door is closed and all calls are put on hold, your visit is given greater importance.

All mankind is divided into three classes: those who are immovable; those who are movable; and those who move.

Benjamin Franklin

When a Poor Setting Can Be Changed . . .

An unsuitable setting is not necessarily a lost cause. Some aspects of the setting may be changeable, and you should seize the opportunity to make improvements. Ideally, the prospect will suggest relocating to another spot, but sometimes he or she isn't always aware of your need to change settings.

If proper lighting, good acoustics, and privacy are lacking, you should promote an improvement immediately but tactfully. Never bluntly declare, "Your office is too noisy, and the lighting is bad." The best way to suggest a change of settings is without any reference to your presentation needs. For instance, you could ask the prospect for a company tour. Then, should you come across a quiet spot while on the tour, take advantage of it. If you anticipate a poor setting before your sales call, phone ahead and ask the prospect what nearby restaurant do businesspeople meet at for lunch. Away from the office, prospects will be free from the interruptions that compete for their attention.

Many salespeople believe in getting the prospect out of doors for a refreshing change of scene. Weather permitting, you can try sitting on the homeowner's patio or taking a short walk on company grounds. If you visit a prospect located in the center of a city, buy a hot dog or ice cream cone from a street vendor and eat on a park bench.

Presenting on Neutral Territory . . .

Conducting a sales presentation on neutral territory has definite advantages. One major benefit is the neutrality itself. Not being in a setting that belongs to you or the prospect relieves you of dealing with any psychological power imbalance. Another plus is the ability to control your setting completely without rearranging your own territory or inconveniencing prospects. A conference room, small auditorium, or hotel suite functions as neutral territory.

In a neutral setting, you should be able to eliminate the possibility of distractions or interruptions and can use as much space as you need. You have complete control over the furnishings and the placement of your materials. In addition, you can take the most advantageous selling position in the seating arrangement. You should be able to arrange everything before the prospect arrives, and if there is more than one prospect, you can decide ahead of time where you would like each person to sit.

Presenting in Your Own Office . . .

Your own office might be even better for a presentation than neutral territory. Since you are thoroughly familiar with the setting, you will be in a perfect position to make best use of it and to know what adjustments will be necessary.

To create the best setting possible, pay special attention to details that you might have learned to ignore: noise, room temperature, lighting. Since you might not occupy your office often, chances are you have overlooked many shortcomings that will be noticeable to a visitor. If you don't have a receptionist, ask a co-worker to take your telephone calls and intercept other interruptions. Draw the curtains or position a chair so that the prospect will not be facing the glare from the window beside your desk; close the window to shut out the outside noises. Adjust the heating or air conditioning for your prospect's comfort.

Remember that you want to avoid distractions not only for your prospect but for yourself. Regardless of whose territory you are using, your attention must remain locked on your presentation. Don't let minor distractions destroy the flow. If you allow yourself to be distracted, the prospect will be distracted too, and the chain of thought will be broken.

WHEN A PRESENTATION SHOULD NOT BE MADE . . .

From time to time, you will encounter situations in which a sales presentation should not be made. Aside from problems with the setting, there may be circumstances relating to the prospect's frame of mind that conflict with the effectiveness of a presentation. Often, the problem is simply a matter of timing. If your telephone call interrupts a friend's dinner, your friend will not be very attentive to you. If you visit a football fan who is watching the Super Bowl, the prospect will be interested only in the game at hand. You could not expect a discussion about the stock market.

There will be some situations in which making a presentation would do more harm than good. You need to recognize those times when you are better off postponing your presentation.

Postponing your sales presentation takes discipline. It can be difficult accepting the fact that conditions aren't right, and the temptation to deliver it under any circumstances is great. You appointment may have been set weeks in advance, you may have spent hours preparing, you may have traveled many miles to see the prospect, and you can foresee no time in the immediate future that is convenient for your return. Nevertheless, you may get only one chance to present to this prospect, and you might waste it if conditions are less than ideal.

Here are some situations in which you should not attempt a presentation:

1. A third party is present, and you can see no way of providing for privacy.
2. The prospect is unusually busy.
3. The prospect is angry about something, or in an otherwise unfavorable mood.
4. The prospect is rushed and can give you only a small amount of time.
5. The prospect is mentally preoccupied with something else.

Flaming enthusiasm, backed by horsesense and persistence, is the quality that most makes for success.

Dale Carnegie

> In business, competition will bite you if you keep running; if you stand still, they will swallow you up.
>
> William Knudson, Jr.

The Third Party . . .

If a **third party** is present when you wish to make a presentation, you will need to excuse this person, otherwise, you should not attempt a continue. To put it bluntly, a third party can ruin your sales presentation in two ways:

1. The third party may insist on getting involved and may voice an unfavorable opinion of your product. Such uninvolved people may have no experience with your product and no understanding of the prospect's situation, yet they see themselves as experts on the matter and can sway the prospect to their way of thinking. You will find yourself not only trying to sell the prospect, but also trying to sell this third party.

2. The presence of a third party can and often does prevent the prospect from revealing personal information that you need to know. In private, prospects might be willing to give you pertinent details about their financial situation, health, or personal concerns. But the third party may be a friend, relative, or business associate in front of whom the prospect would rather not discuss these matters.

The Busy Prospect . . .

Occasionally, you will call on a **busy prospect** who is in the middle of a very hectic day. Maybe the dressmaker you're calling on has to alter six wedding gowns by tomorrow, or the homeowner's plumbing has just backed up. Salespeople in industry commonly enter office settings that are unusually busy. An important machine may have broken down or top management may be about to pay a visit. There are many demands on a prospect's time, and you must be flexible enough to rearrange your schedule to accommodate the unexpected.

Very rarely will you be able to present to a prospect who is busy handling a pressing matter. Any attempt to capture her or his attention will be at least ineffective and at worst destructive to your sales effort. You cannot expect prospects who are busier than usual to stop what they are doing for your presentation. Perhaps they will, but it is their place, not yours, to call time for a break.

When prospects are too busy to see you, they may tell you so directly, or they may reveal it by their reaction to your arrival or their conduct during the opening seconds of your presentation. You may quickly determine that gaining the prospect's complete attention will be all but impossible, and the best course of action is to postpone your selling efforts. If you are confident that you can both physically and mentally take the prospect away from the business at hand with a few words, go ahead and say them. However, if you fail in this initial attempt, and you realize you cannot eliminate the elements that are competing for the potential buyer's attention, you should forget about the presentation until another time. When prospects are overwhelmed with demands for their energies, you should not add to the pressure on them.

If you plow ahead and make a presentation to a busy prospect, you will surely be ineffective. You will be talking, but the prospect won't be listening. Your scenic drive will be a lonely trip, with you driving the car and the prospect asleep in the back seat. Further, your attempt to proceed with the presentation may make the customer feel uncomfortable. Prospects who don't have time to stop everything for you may nevertheless think it is impolite to ask you to leave.

Should you have to postpone your presentation, take comfort in the fact that tomorrow is another day. Your ability to capture the prospect's undivided attention for the time you require is crucial for a successful sales presentation.

The Moody Prospect . . .

A prospect who is angry or unhappy about business or personal matters is in no mood to listen to you. If the prospect just got a disturbing telephone call, or was in an automobile accident earlier in the day, you can't expect a receptive audience. Don't make the mistake of trying to present to **moody prospects**. However these angry or unhappy prospects show their unfavorable feelings, it won't be good. Making you the scapegoat, they will inexplicably find trivial faults in you or your product. You are not the reason for their anger, so why open yourself up to an unwarranted attack?

Perhaps the angry or upset prospect will turn inward, changing from a normally warm and open person to an irritable, resentful one who won't tell you frankly that you came at a bad time or that the product you have chosen to present isn't suitable. In some situations, all the prospect may require is a chance to blow off steam. We all have reasons for being in a bad mood from time to time, and many of us feel we need to unload our personal problems on someone else occasionally. Allow your prospects to blow off steam by complaining to you, and they may then be ready to listen to your sales presentation. But don't expect this technique to work with everyone and in all instances.

You must accept the negative moods of your prospects as a fact of life and realize that you can't always change their moods. If you can tell that a person's state of mind isn't going to change, don't make a presentation. An attempt to present to a moody prospect will not only fail to make the sale, but will also damage your future sales effort. The moody prospect will receive you unfavorably and remember you in a negative light the next time you come around. Subtly withdraw from the scene of a bad mood, and make your presentation at another time.

> An idea that is not dangerous is unworthy of being called an idea at all.
> Oscar Wilde

The Hurried Prospect . . .

A **hurried prospect** will not be able to give you the time you need for your presentation. Make sure that you don't create such a situation unnecessarily. When you make an appointment, specify the amount of time your presentation will require.

If the prospect sets a limit on the time you have to make your presentation, and there is the slightest chance that it will not be sufficient, explain that you will need more time to do a good job. Tell the prospect that the half hour being allotted you is insufficient, but that an hour is plenty of time. If the prospect sees no way of giving you an hour, defer your efforts until another time.

Some prospects never know when they can block out the amount of time you need for your presentation, or they may be unable to avoid untimely interruptions. For these prospects, suggest lunch, dinner, a game of golf, or a morning of fishing to get them away from their busy settings.

You can usually tell when prospects are rushed for time. They may seem restless or fidgety, or they frequently look at their watch or clock. When prospects tell you openly that they don't have much time, take their word for it. It is not your place to "slow them down." Don't assume that they are making excuses to avoid you. Just ask when would be a better time.

As a rule, you should respect the value of your prospects' schedule and assume that they do not have unlimited time for you. But don't go overboard: Never open your visit with "I know you're busy, but...." Such a statement makes it too easy for prospects to jump in and tell you that they are indeed busy, too busy to hear your presentation. You make yourself seem like an intruder and ruin your chances of starting the conversation with a small amount of socializing.

Salespeople who encounter hurried prospects often try either to speed up their presentation or to condense it. Both of these are mistakes. As we mentioned earlier, you may have only one opportunity to make your pitch, and if you speed it up or condense it, you might take the one chance you get and ruin it.

In a hurried presentation, you will give hurried answers to questions and provide inadequate responses to objections. The visit won't be the relaxed, free-flowing, friendly conversation it should be. Worse, you may rush for a close before the prospect is ready to make that decision. If, at the completion of your hurried presentation, the prospect indicates a lack of interest, that will be the end of the matter. You might ask to come back another time, knowing that you covered your selling points too fast and didn't allow ample time for the prospect's involvement, but the prospect will say, "No, that won't be necessary. I've heard all I need to hear."

The condensed presentation will be as disastrous as the hurried presentation. Cutting corners to squeeze a twenty-minute presentation into a ten-minute meeting will cost you the sale. You may like to think that certain points can be skipped because they won't be important to this prospect, or that hitting the highlights is all that really matters, but a condensed presentation is too short on substance. Regardless of the circumstances under which it is delivered, a speeded up version reflects a weak product and a lack of selling ability.

If circumstances are such that you know this will be your only chance *ever* to make a presentation to your prospect, and you are allowed only ten minutes,

Norm Frain

Many people in the selling profession credit their college education as being helpful in attaining their career goals, and Norm Frain is one of them. After obtaining an Associate of Applied Science degree from Villa Maria College, Norm went on for a Bachelors of Science degree in Organizational Management from Houghton College. Although many courses were of benefit, he feels that the Dale Carnegie sales training sessions were the most significant. Helping others as a group leader in these discussions really improved his skills.

Presently, Norm works as a Zone Manager for USA Today. He is in charge of supervision and development of two district sales managers and their field salespeople. Through regular training, coaching and seminar activities, he is instrumental in delivering the customer service that USA Today is noted for. Norm also supervises the delivery operations for this timely newspaper within his zone.

Norm Frain is not afraid of hard work. He advises anyone in sales to start the day with a tenacious attitude and not to shrink from the long hours that often are necessary in the selling profession. His own personal mission statement, adopted from President Harry S. Truman, is "Never quit, speak the truth, and work hard," and he reviews this purposeful message daily. He also strongly recommends to people in this business that keeping a good sense of humor comes in handy when keeping the sharks from the door or when facing rejection.

respond by saying, "Well, I doubt I can do it in ten minutes, but let me try." Then do your best, hoping that when the time has passed, you will have generated the prospect's interest to the point where prior commitments can be canceled or arrangements made to see you again at another time.

The Preoccupied Prospect . . .

The **preoccupied prospect** will be just as unreceptive as the moody prospect. As long as this potential buyer's mind is on other things, there will be no desire to talk business with you. Any number of thoughts could be running through this person's mind, and they need not be unpleasant in order to interfere with your ability to communicate. You might call on an office the day of the company Christmas party, or your prospect is getting married in a few days, or your contact at an auto shop has just won a service award.

Forget about trying to sell to preoccupied prospects. When you arrive on the scene, assess the situation realistically, and plan to come back when the excitement or preoccupation has subsided.

HANDLING INTERRUPTIONS . . .

Sometimes interruptions in the sales presentation cannot be avoided. Such a break might abruptly end the presentation, as when the prospect is called to the company warehouse to assist an injured worker. Otherwise, it may stop your presentation only temporarily, as when a momentary power failure causes a short period of havoc in the prospect's office.

Because interruptions are inevitable, you will need to know how to handle them without damaging your sales effort. A deterrent need not literally end a sales call to destroy its effectiveness. You should assess the effect of an interruption before proceeding. A brief but serious interruption can completely capture the prospect's thoughts, in which case resuming your presentation would be futile. However, if you determine that the potential buyer isn't preoccupied with what just happened, you may continue.

Before you cover new material after an interruption, however, you should draw the prospect back into the presentation. Since the flow of thought is interrupted, repeat the highlights of what took place before the interruption occurred. Ask the prospect several **confirmation questions** before continuing.

Repeating the highlights establishes a sense of continuity, connecting what occurred before the interruption to the events that begin when the presentation is resumed. Teachers often establish this continuity by spending the first five minutes of each class period summarizing what took place during the previous meeting. Similarly, television programs often begin with scenes from previous episodes to remind viewers of what happened last. You, too, should summarize the most important points already covered.

Confirmation questions will ensure that the prospect understood everything that occurred before the interruption, and refocus the thoughts on the presentation. Ask questions like these: "Did I finish explaining the operations manual?" "Exactly where were we?" "Do you understand the terms of the warranty?" "Do we agree that a portable model best suits your needs?" Of course, if you find that the prospect's full attention is impossible to recapture, you should end the call and return at another time.

DEALING WITH DIFFICULT PERSONALITIES . . .

As a salesperson, you will meet many different people, and not everyone will be easy to deal with. People often have personality traits that can pose a true challenge to the salesperson; you might be puzzled about how to communicate constructively with someone whose behavior is less than ideal. Some of the more difficult personalities you will run across are illustrated in Figure 9-3. What follows is a discussion of the ways to deal with each one.

The Complainer. Complainers are not necessarily unhappy people. They just find satisfaction in sharing their troubles with anyone who will listen. The complainer will protest to everyone, and about everything. Your strategy is to expect complaints from this prospect, but not allow yourself to become

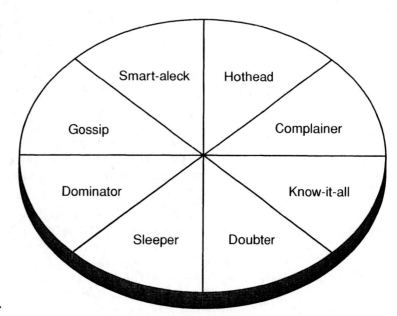

Figure 9-3 Thorny prospects.

upset or alarmed. If the complaint is not about your product, let the prospect carp away, and forget about it afterwards.

The Know-it-all. Know-it-alls think they possess superior knowledge about everything and want to have the last word in any debate. Again, as long as the subject is not your product or company, allow these people to have fun asserting their wisdom and intelligence. When you wish to correct the know-it-all, or give additional information, you will need to downplay any threat to your prospect's sense of authority.

The Doubter. The doubter is suspicious of your motives. By nature, this personality type is suspicious of everyone, be they salespeople or Sunday drivers. Making headway with doubters means convincing them that your intentions are honorable. Don't take it personally when they let you know that they consider you dishonest until you are proven honest. Just rely on the confidence-building techniques discussed in Chapter 7.

The Sleeper. The sleeper is an unresponsive prospect. Being naturally reserved, this person is not interested in participating in the friendly conversations you attempt. When a response is required, the prospect's comments will be brief. Getting this person talking is not impossible, but it is difficult and requires a great deal of tact. Take care in selecting topics and in creating a comfortable role for unresponsive prospects to play in the conversation. When you finally get them to talk, your job is not over, for you will need to keep them talking. Compliment them on their well-considered observations, and take their opinions seriously. The gratification you offer for their initial comments will give them incentive to keep participating.

The Gossip. The gossip is a person who engages in trivial talk about others or speculation about rumors of a personal nature. Although rumor mongering can sometimes be entertaining, it is not at all constructive to the sales effort.

In fact, if you participate in gossip, you will only demean yourself, reduce your image as a professional, and possibly damage your reputation. If your prospect likes to gossip, you can avoid participating by simply ignoring any gossipy remarks. Redirect attention to the subject at hand by saying something like, "Oh, before I forget, let me show you this performance chart we just published."

The Smart Aleck. The smart aleck, or "wise guy," is an offensively self-assured person who makes obnoxious jokes or flippant remarks. This is the prospect who makes wisecracks about your manner of dress or gives you a silly nickname. Although you recognize the smart aleck's behavior as inappropriate, ignore it. Remain professional by responding only with a quick smile, and get on with your business.

The Hothead. Hotheads are people who have a quick temper; they get angry easily and can be very argumentative. These prospects are often the most difficult of the challenging personalities you will meet, for their behavior is likely to be unpredictable. On one sales call, the prospect may be as pleasant as can be. On the next, she or he becomes furious over a minor and unintentionally inappropriate remark. Be extra careful with the hothead. Take no liberties in terms of joking or introducing what might be a touchy subject.

The Dominator. Dominators insist on doing all of the talking. Try as you might, you just cannot get a word in edgewise with these personalities. You understand the need for salespeople to be good listeners, but with a prospect who controls the conversation, listening becomes an art form. Politeness dictates that you should not interrupt, yet you must move the sales presentation forward. Look and listen for even the tiniest crack, and slip in a question that completely changes the subject. Dominators have more trouble controlling the conversation if it moves from subject to subject. Once slowed, this type of personality usually allows more openings for you to steer the presentation on the course you desire.

THORNY SITUATIONS . . .

Thorny situations, like difficult personalities, are an inevitable part of the salesperson's life. Sometimes the worst occur after the sale has been made. Listed here are six types of problematic situations you may encounter, and a discussion of how to handle each one.

1. The order is missing.
2. The product has been misused by the buyer.
3. The (retail) product isn't selling.
4. The prospect makes an untrue remark.
5. An unfortunate truth comes out.
6. The prospect is much older than the salesperson.

Figure 9-4 provides a short example of the first four types.

The Poor-Selling Product

"You sold me something that nobody wants. My customers just pass it by."

The Missing Order

"I only deal with suppliers who deliver when promised. Obviously that's not you."

The Untrue Remark

"Your price is totally out of line with your competitors. How do you stay in business?"

The Misused Product

"I tell you I did exactly what you said. It's not my fault the dumb thing broke."

Figure 9-4 Thorny situations.

The Missing Order.   When your customer tells you that a past order was never received, you must act immediately to resolve the problem. In this, the thorniest of situations, there is no time to relax. To say casually that you will "look into" the problem is to convey the impression that your customer's business is not important enough to bother with now that the sale has been made. This will surely cause ill will. You must let your customer know that you are equally concerned about the missing order and that you are acting on it now.

Even if someone else in your company is to blame for the customer's misfortune, you should still take responsibility for rectifying the situation and assure the buyer that the problem won't occur again. Blaming someone else does not reassure the customer, who will have reason to fear that the problem will occur again since you have said that you have no control over it.

The Misused Product.   Sometimes a customer has a problem with your product, and you discover that the dilemma was caused by misuse. Perhaps the customer installed the item incorrectly despite your careful instructions or used it for a purpose other than that for which it was intended. Perhaps the wrong fuel mixture was used or the product was not serviced at the recommended intervals.

The misused product can pose a sticky situation for you because you will have to enlighten the customer without causing embarrassment, defensiveness, or anger. Without taking blame for something that was no fault of your own, you must take responsibility for helping the customer correctly use the product. Admit that installation or maintenance of the product can be complicated for a person not used to doing it, and take time to review the proper procedures. Make absolutely certain that the prospect understands your instructions and suggestions.

The Product Isn't Selling. If you sell to retailers, you will occasionally deal with customers who tell you the product isn't selling. They may simply say they're overstocked, and you happen to know you sold an appropriate quantity to them. This is another situation that requires tact. You certainly can't say that you may have sold your customer an unrealistic quantity, but by the same token, you can't blame the retailer for a lack of sales effort either.

Find out if these retailers have adopted all the selling techniques you recommended, and correct any errors in their methods. Explain again the procedures that other retailers have found successful, and offer to demonstrate these for them with store customers. Redo the display or shelf area, or assist in relocating the merchandise to a more suitable section of the store. Review your recommended advertising and pricing strategies, and offer to assist them in developing special promotions designed to build customer traffic in their store.

An Untrue Remark. Every now and then prospects will say something that is absolutely wrong, and you cannot allow them to get away with it. They might say that your product could never withstand rigorous use or that it is greatly overpriced. They might even say something so untrue that it makes you angry, perhaps that they heard that you offer no warranty, when in truth you offer the best in the business.

Whatever they say, if it's not true, you must refute it immediately. Your silence would imply that there is truth in their remarks. Set these customers straight politely but firmly. Don't tell them they are uninformed or unintelligent, but by all means, prove them incorrect. This is easiest when you can back yourself up with verifiable data. For example, if the prospect says, "I understand that your product will cost $1,000 altogether," you can reach for your detailed price information and say, "That's just not so, Mrs. Stinson. Your investment will be no more than $600. Let me show you." Refuting a prospect's untrue remarks is further addressed in Chapter 12, where we discuss the direct denial method of responding to a prospect's objection.

An Unfortunate Truth. What if the prospect says something unfavorable about your product or company, and you know it is true? Simply put, you should agree and compensate. If the prospect says, "I hear your delivery takes four weeks," and it does, you cannot deny it. Offer an equally truthful compensating point: "That's true, but our delivery cost is only one-third that of our competitors." If the prospect says, "I understand you don't stock your own parts, and I'll have to wait three days to get them," you should agree and compensate this way: "Yes, but we offer a low price that makes it worth the wait."

Compensating for the unfortunate but true remark comes naturally when quality and price are at issue. A high price is compensated for by exceptional quality, and below-average quality is compensated for by a lower price. The only question is will the compensating factor be enough, in your prospect's mind, to offset the weak point? You may need to make a persuasive case for the compensating factor, but at least you will be doing so honestly. This subject is further addressed in Chapter 12, when we discuss the compensation method of responding to a prospect's objection.

The Older Prospect. Younger salespeople frequently find themselves dealing with much older prospects who underestimate their abilities. Older prospects might feel that they should control the discussion because of their wisdom and experience. This is fine as long as the ultimate objective of the presentation is accomplished. However, you cannot allow differences in age to determine authority or to influence the prospect's perception of your knowledge or ability. Young salespeople who put themselves at the mercy of older people will never gain the reputation they need as a true expert and authority in their industry. The only reason older potential buyers should be more difficult to persuade is that they may be more set in their ways and less likely to want to change a lifestyle or habits that have become comfortable.

You Decide!

Jamal's work for a major hardware manufacturer requires him to attend trade shows where he mans the company booth. His supervisor specifically instructed him not to attempt to make presentations during these noisy, often frantic, exhibitions, but rather to merely gather leads. Jamal's experience, however, shows that when he calls on many of the prospects generated through trade show leads, he is disappointed because they are usually small firms who rarely can meet his company's required minimum orders. Besides, Jamal sort of hates to hand out the firm's very expensive, full-color glossy literature packs to people who may never buy.

At a recent hardware show at Chicago's McCormack place, Jamal decides that rather than continue to collect leads and hand out literature, he will dig a little deeper, probing for needs and buying interest. He quickly learns that many of those visiting his booth are not in the position to buy, so he sends them on their way with a smile and a nice handshake…but no literature! Is Jamal out of line in refusing to follow his bosses request, or is he saving his company money? **You decide!**

Summing It Up . . .

When you set out to make a presentation, you need to assess the competitive setting. If your setting is highly competitive, as when a prospect strongly favors another brand or is a loyal user of another product, you should be ready to attract the prospect's attention or perform a product comparison. However, attention-getting and comparison techniques are best restricted to urgently competitive situations and should not become the focus of the presentation. Competitive intelligence, or knowledge of the competition, is as important to the sales effort as product knowledge. Defensive selling, or de-selling, is a selling effort built around the negative aspects of the competition and should be avoided.

The physical setting of the presentation is the place where it is conducted, along with the attributes that contribute to personal comfort. As you prepare for a presentation, you should see to it that both you and the prospect are physically, psychologically, and functionally comfortable. Such factors as lighting, climate, and seating must be taken into consideration. A poor setting may ruin a presentation.

Some situations can call for the postponement of your presentation. You should not try to sell if a third party is present, or if your prospect is busy, moody, rushed, or preoccupied. Interruptions are a fact of the salesperson's life, and you need to know how to resume a presentation after an interruption, as well as how to determine if a presentation should be resumed. Frequently, the salesperson encounters difficult personalities, such as the complainer, the smart aleck, or the sleeper, and such people must be dealt with tactfully. Tact is the byword for dealing with thorny situations too, as when an order is missing or a customer has misused the product.

Key Concepts and Terms . . .

busy prospect	gossip
competitive intelligence	hothead
competitive setting	hurried prospect
complainer	know-it-all
confirmation question	moody prospect
defensive selling	preoccupied prospect
de-selling	sleeper
dominator	smart aleck
doubter	third party

Building Skills . . .

1. Explain how you should deal with competition when you have determined that it is not a serious factor in the sale.

2. Explain the ways a salesperson might make a factor of competition when it wasn't one originally.

3. Describe competitive intelligence and some of the methods of gathering competitive intelligence.

4. Explore how you might use competitive intelligence to sell.

5. Define defensive selling. Explore the reasons that a salesperson should not use it. Describe the consequences of defensive selling.

6. Describe how a third party can destroy a presentation.

7. Define the dangers of presenting to a prospect who is angry about something.

8. List the disadvantages of attempting to fit an hour-long sales presentation into a half hour.

9. Describe the advantages of conducting a sales presentation in your own office or on neutral territory such as a conference room.

10. Explain the ways you would resume your presentation after it has been interrupted.

11. Describe your strategies when dealing with the know-it-all, the complainer, and the sleeper.

12. Describe your response when a prospect says that a previous order never arrived.

13. Under what circumstances should you directly challenge what the prospect says?

14. Explain why sitting alongside the prospect's desk is better than sitting across from it.

15. Explain the aspects of the physical setting that may make it inappropriate for your sales presentation.

Making Decisions 9-1:

Lucy Burns is a salesperson for Thorpe Water Systems, a firm that installs residential water softeners. One evening she receives a telephone call from Andrea DiMichael, a woman who is renovating a century-old farmhouse in the area. Lucy makes an appointment to visit Andrea the next evening.

Andrea: I'm glad you could come so soon. You're the first dealer I called.

Lucy: It's my pleasure. Thank you for thinking of us.

Andrea: Well, it wasn't hard. My father always dealt with Thorpe. Your name is very well implanted in my mind.

Lucy: We carry the best water softener on the market. Columbia may be the leading brand, but ours offers a better warranty. And from what I gather, it does a better job.

Andrea: Columbia makes water softeners?

Lucy: Yes, but our brand has made deep inroads into Columbia's market over the past few years.

Andrea: I'm really not familiar with brands. I just knew you were a local dealer with a long history.

Lucy:	You're right about that. You might pay a little more for our brand, but we're right here to stand behind it. You won't have to call someone fifteen miles away if it breaks down.

Evaluate Lucy's presentation line by line.

Making Decisions 9-2:

Pete Sassaman sells Apple Nutritional Supplements. One day, while driving by his health and fitness club, Pete notices Keith Donovan's car outside. Keith, an old high school buddy, has recently become serious about weight training, and Pete realizes he may be a true prospect for the Apple line. Pete pulls in, leaves his membership card at the front desk, and still wearing his street clothes, heads for the weight room. The room is about 10 by 30 feet, and three other athletes, all in much better shape than Keith, are present when Pete approaches.

Pete:	How goes it, Keith? Long time no see.
Keith:	(Grunting as he curls a 50-pound dumbbell with his right arm) Yeah. How's it going?
Pete:	Not bad. Say, I've been meaning to talk to you about my new sideline.
Keith:	(Completes his set, with visible strain, and lets the dumbbell drop on the rubber mat) Sideline?
Pete:	I'm selling Apple Nutritional Supplements. They can help you achieve your training goals. Say, how much are you bench pressing now?
Keith:	(Glancing at the other athletes and lowering his voice) About 300. But I'm getting there.
Pete:	That's great. How about your squats?
Keith:	(Whispering) They're not too good, but I'm working my lower body hard. (He looks around, not making eye contact.)
Pete:	Are you looking for someone?
Keith:	No.

Evaluate the setting for Pete's call on Keith. Explain Keith's nonverbal behavior.

Making Decisions 9-3:

You sell excavating equipment (front-end loaders, backhoes, bulldozers, excavators, trenchers, and so on). List four methods you would use to gather competitive intelligence.

Making Decisions 9-4:

You and your assistant sales manager are planning to take two people from a prospective customer to lunch, hoping to nail down a sizable order. One is the purchasing agent who physically signs the orders; the other is a young design engineer who is in charge of specifying the materials for a particular job that you are working on. Arriving at the restaurant, should you suggest where each person should sit? If so, what seating arrangement would you suggest? If not, who should? Which would be more preferable—a table, or a booth? Who should be closest to the server? Draw up several seating arrangements, analyzing the strengths and weaknesses of each.

Practice Makes Perfect 9-1:

You are a salesperson for archery equipment and supplies, and your prospect claims to be an expert archer. Your brand is the most durable on the market, but your prospect says it is poorly made. Role-play your response and the continuation.

Your Sales Presentation

THE JOB TO BE DONE . . .

At some point, the salesperson must make a presentation. Having learned the needs or problems of your prospects, now is the time to blend your products into satisfying their needs or solving their problems. Chapter 10 deals with the sales presentation, enabling you to:

...discover how a beginning salesperson can develop an effective sales presentation.

...know the advantages and disadvantages of a canned sales presentation.

...understand how to make a presentation clear and convincing.

...examine the techniques of creating attachment.

...appreciate the benefits of appealing to a combination of the physical senses.

...know which product features to present.

...understand pacing in a presentation, how to set it and when to change it.

...appreciate the importance of asking plenty of questions and encouraging the prospect's questions.

...understand how to deliver a group sales presentation.

> Every morning I get up and look at the Forbe's list of the richest people in America. If I am not there, I go to work.
>
> Richard Orben

A PRESENTATION FOR THE NEW SALESPERSON . . .

Beginning salespeople have the special challenge of developing a professional yet comfortable sales presentation from scratch. Whereas veterans can rely on the lessons of experience, a new seller has to start from scratch. You will recall from Chapter 1 that although some firms give their new salespeople several months or even a year or more of training, many other firms offer little or no guidance.

New salespeople, whether formally trained or not, should never hesitate to rely on the help of others in building the foundation of their sales presentations. If possible, you should go out on sales calls with senior members of the staff to observe their style, or ask them to accompany you on your customer visits. Although those you observe will have highly personalized styles, you might find certain aspects of their presentations useful or inspiring. Observe the seasoned salesperson's methods, and then use them as they are, modify them, or piece them together with other salespeople's methods to form your own presentation.

This is the presentation you should use on your first sales calls. If you feel uncomfortable adopting a technique you observed from a colleague, it may be out of tune with your own personality. You may not want to use it, but you can allow it to trigger ideas for new techniques that will be yours alone. As time passes, you will develop your own unique presentation, one that may have no resemblance to those after which you modeled your first one.

In the process of developing your presentation, you should test your evolving technique on your prospects, changing certain aspects of it from one prospect to the next as you learn better ways of doing things. You can also learn from competition. Observing the selling efforts made for a competing brand not only enables you to gain competitive intelligence, it provides you with yet another expert example. You may acquire something that can be incorporated into your presentation.

The Canned Presentation . . .

The **canned presentation** is a standardized pitch. The selling firm develops one selling script that is to be used without variation. It doesn't change from prospect to prospect or from salesperson to salesperson. The canned presentation was first developed by the National Cash Register Corporation (NCR) and is still heavily used, especially in telephone selling.

Canned presentations have both advantages and disadvantages. On the positive side, this type of pitch is guaranteed to be complete because the selling firm has built completeness into it. The canned presentation has been tested for effectiveness, and there is the possibility that the firm has discovered the one "best way" to make a point. It follows a logical sequence, reflects the experience of others, demands less preparation by the salesperson, and is most effective when selling time is short, as in telephone sales.

On the negative side, the canned presentation lacks freshness and vitality. It can sound rehearsed, mechanical, monotonous, unnatural, or even boring. Because it is identical from one sales situation to the next, it does not appeal to an individual prospect's unique circumstances and needs. The canned presentation does not accommodate untimely questions, interruptions, or a change of sequence. It cannot be deviated from, so it discourages creativity. This type of pitch also discourages dialogue since it consists mainly of monologue by the salesperson.

THE STIMULUS–RESPONSE THEORY . . .

The stimulus–response theory of selling is based on the assumption that given stimuli prompt a predictable reaction. Based on Pavlovian psychology, the stimulus–response theory assumes that the prospect will react favorably to the proper stimulus. Another assumption of this method is that all potential buyers will react the same way to the same incentives. The seller's primary task is to introduce a series of stimuli that will lead to favorable responses by the prospect.

The **stimulus–response theory** is the basis of most canned sales presentations. Canned presentations are salesperson dominated, consisting of a structured set of questions and expected answers. The salesperson does as much as 80 percent of the talking, with the prospect responding only as the presentation allows. The product's key selling points serve as the basic stimuli. The salesperson attempts to generate the prospect's interest by making reference to product features and benefits.

This method is most appropriate when the salesperson is not skilled, when a great deal of sales effort is not required, or when selling time is brief and calls for a short presentation. The method may be suitable when the prospect's need has already been stimulated, as when the prospect seeks out the salesperson, or when the need can be quickly stimulated. It is most common in the sale of low-priced products, where buying motives are simple and don't vary from prospect to prospect, or in telephone selling, where scripts are used.

There are several disadvantages to the stimulus–response system. First, this type of selling is neither flexible nor customer oriented. All potential buyers are treated the same, and there is no attempt to determine individual needs. The method is not particularly popular with prospects either because they often see it as a high-pressure selling tactic. Second, selling cannot always be reduced to a stimulus–response process. Many situations are too complex to fit into the narrow confines of this method. Finally, salespeople who use this method rely on their company to provide them with the right things to say. The firm has complete control of the sales presentation. Since creativity is not stimulated or encouraged, salespeople do not improve their selling performance over time.

THE SELLING FORMULA THEORY . . .

The **selling formula theory** is similar to stimulus–response in that it follows a strict method espoused by company management. The presentation method in formula selling is canned, and the salespeople are relatively untrained.

Managers are completely familiar with the selling situation, and they know what they want the salespeople to say.

The selling formula theory assumes that in order to make the sale, the salesperson must lead the customer through what is known as the **AIDA framework**. The AIDA framework is as follows:

1. Capture the prospect's ATTENTION.
2. Stimulate the prospect's INTEREST in the product.
3. Create the DESIRE to own the product.
4. Lead the prospect to ACTION (the act of purchasing).

Throughout the course of the presentation, the salesperson's work follows the AIDA framework. Questions and statements designed to capture attention are followed by those intended to stimulate interest, and so on. Of course, prospects will differ according to their present stage in the AIDA framework. The salesperson's task is to lead a given prospect through the stages that remain.

The reasoning behind this formula is that once you uncover a prospect's needs, you will know exactly how to proceed with your presentation. The salesperson dominates the presentation in the beginning by introducing the product's key features and benefits. As the presentation proceeds, prospect participation increases as the salesperson's questions uncover needs. Once these are out in the open, the salesperson explains how the product will satisfy them. The seller then regains control of the presentation at the time of the close.

This method of selling is most effective when a great deal is known about the prospect. Like stimulus–response, it assumes that prospects in similar situations can be convinced with the same basic sales presentation. However, it is more flexible than stimulus–response in that it follows a less structured outline and requires less direction by the salesperson. There is also more customer interaction. The logical sequence of the presentation ensures that all points are covered, and the salesperson can easily remember everything because it never really changes.

Formula selling is commonly used to sell consumer durables and real estate. Its fundamental weakness is that prospects don't always move smoothly from one step in the AIDA framework to the next, and determining the prospect's movement through the framework can be difficult. The need to follow the steps in the AIDA framework also has the effect of restricting the salesperson's flexibility and creativity.

THE NEED–SATISFACTION THEORY . . .

The **need–satisfaction theory** of selling is the most challenging and creative method, and its style is comparatively low pressure. Here, the sales process is seen in three stages: (1) need development, (2) need awareness, (3) need fulfillment.

Using this method, the salesperson offers a series of carefully planned questions to get the prospect involved in the sales presentation from the very beginning. The seller's immediate goal is to determine what will motivate the prospect to purchase. This selling style relies on a flexible, interactive sales presentation, and assumes that the most effective way to build customer awareness and interest is to have them discuss their needs. This is done even in instances where the salesperson already understands the prospect's needs.

You determine what questions to ask based on your analysis of the prospect's situation, which you may learn through observation. The prospect dominates the first 70 percent of the presentation explaining needs, while your participation increases as you explain how your product will satisfy those demands. In this respect, your presentation is customized, and by getting the prospect's immediate involvement, you can account for differences in potential buyers. Your presentation can focus on the model or style best suited for each individual.

Need-satisfaction selling is recommended when the selling effort is intense, as in the sale of industrial equipment or high-priced consumer goods. It is the most recommended method for selling real estate. In contrast, the method is not justified when the unit selling price or total order size is low.

One disadvantage to the method is that, although it is the most flexible and customer oriented of the three theories, it takes more time than the other methods and requires a highly skilled salesperson. Because the presentation is built around early customer involvement through questioning, a possible disadvantage is that the prospect may dislike excessive questioning. Another possible disadvantage is that to a certain degree the salesperson has less control of the presentation, and some salespeople are uncomfortable when they are not in control.

Canned or Custom: A Compromise . . .

Although the disadvantages of canned presentations in personal selling usually outweigh the advantages, you might see some benefit in incorporating a few "canned" segments into a custom presentation. For example, you may indeed discover that there is one best way to cover a given aspect of your offering, one best example to use, or one best question to ask. If this is the case, there is no reason that this portion of your presentation need change from prospect to prospect. You should certainly include proven selling techniques in each sales call. If there is one best way of saying something, say it that way. Just be sure that your overall presentation is tailored to the present prospect.

A less attractive compromise is the basically canned presentation that has custom touches. Although a memorized presentation is not as desirable as a completely customized presentation, you are at least personalizing it somewhat when you make unplanned remarks or personalize certain details on the basis of your preapproach findings. Your participation varies depending upon the type of presentation used, as shown in Figure 10-1.

Canned Presentation (Stimulus-Response)

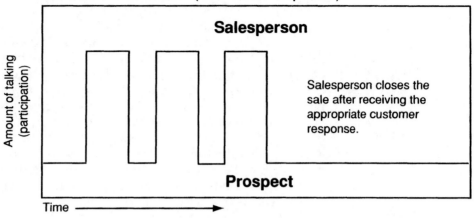

Salesperson

Amount of talking (participation)

Salesperson closes the sale after receiving the appropriate customer response.

Prospect

Time ➝

Selling Formula (AIDA Method)

Salesperson

Amount of talking (participation)

Salesperson dominates the conversation to stimulate AIDA.

Salesperson regains control of conversation once AIDA is established.

Customer involvement increases as the salesperson's efforts have a positive effect.

Prospect

Time ➝

Need Satisfaction

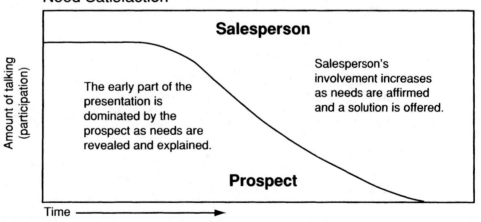

Salesperson

Amount of talking (participation)

The early part of the presentation is dominated by the prospect as needs are revealed and explained.

Salesperson's involvement increases as needs are affirmed and a solution is offered.

Prospect

Time ➝

Figure 10-1 Three sales presentation models.

Be Prepared . . .

The most important determinant of a salesperson's success is preparation. Only through careful preparation will you develop the most suitable way to make your presentation, and only when you are thoroughly prepared will you enjoy the self-confidence you need for success. There is never an excuse for a lack of readiness. Under no circumstances should you ever try to "wing" a sales presentation because you have made similar presentations many times before.

Preparation means much more than gathering preapproach data. For each presentation, you must decide ahead of time what to say and how to say it. You must arrange the sequence in which you will cover your selling points, and remember to be flexible enough to deviate from your plan if the prospect requests it or leads you into another sequence. Any use of math in the presentation, such as in price quotations, should be carefully double-checked. Be prepared in advance so that the numbers are accurate.

To be thoroughly prepared for every presentation, you should rehearse. A single mental rehearsal is the very least you can do. You might also hold a practice session with a friend posing as your prospect; put them on videotape and watch yourself in action. You will be amazed at how many minor flaws you will find when observing yourself on film.

Although planning and rehearsing are necessary to your sales effort, your presentation should appear fresh and unique rather than planned. It should seem natural and spontaneous, not rehearsed or repeated. It should flow like a friendly, casual conversation. You want your prospects to feel as though they are the first person to hear your presentation.

MAKING THE PRESENTATION CLEAR AND CONVINCING . . .

Your sales presentation will be effective in direct proportion to how clear and convincing it is. Here are some techniques for gaining effectiveness:

1. Use mental imagery.
2. Use sales aids and visuals.
3. Create attachment.
4. Show the product in context.
5. Appeal to a combination of the prospect's physical senses.
6. Use repetition.

Using Mental Imagery . . .

Using **mental imagery** means asking prospects to imagine themselves in a certain setting. Help your prospects do this by describing the setting in emotional terms. The setting you portray can relate to your prospects' present situation, the position once they own your product, or the circumstances they will face if they decide to defer the purchase. Describing a situation of ownership is ideal because the setting will be pleasant instead of unpleasant. An unpleasant setting may be more effective when the prospect seems determined not to buy or is close-minded to your proposal.

To use mental imagery most effectively, you will need a good vocabulary, which enables you to choose descriptive words for their emotional impact. Both you and the prospect should be able to relate to the situation. If you have not experienced anything that helps you relate to the setting you describe, your words will lack feeling, and you will not be able to convey a sense of drama to your prospect. Your prospect must also connect if your story is to be effective. If you want to say, "Susan, imagine yourself on a warm, sunny beach with a cool ocean breeze and the call of seagulls in the air," you must first be sure that Susan has been to a beach. The setting you describe cannot appeal to the emotions unless it is relevant to the prospect's experience.

The effective use of mental imagery enables you to appeal to the prospect's emotions even when you sell a product that is usually purchased for rational reasons. For example, suppose you sell cellular telephones. You might use mental imagery in a presentation to a prospect who frequently works late by saying:

John, imagine working late one cold winter's night. You don't get out of the office until after ten. The wind snaps in your face the minute you leave the building. You slip on the ice in the parking lot. You crawl inside your freezing car and sit there shivering. You turn the car key, and a soft, slow grinding noise is all you get. Your battery is dead. You're locked out of the building, so *you can't call home*. You know your wife is worrying about you, but there's no one around who can help you. What do you do?

You have described a scene that would be quite uncomfortable to those who have been in a similar situation or who can easily imagine themselves in it. Of course, if the prospect never works late, or has never experienced car troubles or freezing temperatures, your listener won't be able to feel the emotions that you are appealing to. Your story becomes even more dramatic if the situation you describe is one you have actually experienced. You can describe it just as it happened, and your memory puts emotion into your words.

Ideally, your prospects should have no difficulty imagining themselves in the setting you describe. If you are good at using mental imagery, you might want to use it even if your prospects have never been in the exact setting you describe. You would do so by drawing on things they have experienced. Susan may never have been to a tropical island, but she has been to the lakeshore. Capitalize on the things your prospects know and feed their imagination with the rest.

> Once the toothpaste is out of the tube, it's hard to get it back in.
> H. R. Haldeman

> The difference between the rut and the grave is the depth.
> Gerald Burrill

Using Sales Aids and Visuals . . .

A **sales aid** is any physical item that supports a selling effort by reinforcing your spoken words. Using sales aids and visuals is a very effective way of making your presentation clear and convincing. These tools reinforce your presentation by clarifying, simplifying, and expanding your message. Further, sales aids let you have a stronger impact on the prospect by developing a greater degree of involvement. These tools also provide entertainment and create a more receptive audience.

Research indicates that we retain far more of what we see than what we hear. In fact, the use of visuals in sales presentations leads to as much as a fivefold increase in the retention of the material presented. It also shortens the time you need to deliver the presentation, and increases your chances of making the sale by as much as 50 percent. Unlike **barehanded selling**, in which you rely solely on your words to sell the product, selling with visuals helps you tell your story quickly through the eye.

Several of the sales aids listed require the use of audiovisual equipment. Some of the more common types of AV equipment used by salespeople today are 35-mm slide projectors with synchronous tape decks, cassette tape recorders, video cameras, half-inch color videocassette recorder-players, overhead projectors, and portable videocassette recorders (VCRs). Video projectors are becoming a common alternative to the old 16-mm film projectors. They offer the same benefit, the projection of a motion picture onto a large screen, without the disadvantages of cumbersome equipment and disintegrating film.

With access to a personal computer, you can create professional graphics, such as multicolored bar charts and pie charts, for use as sales aids. Used with a desktop presentation system, this selling tool aids in the production of visuals in the form of overhead transparencies, audience handouts, or 35-mm slides.

The computer itself can also be a valuable presentation tool. For example, the image on the monitor can be projected onto a larger screen by way of a computer projection panel. You can make use of the client's personal computer as well as your own, by bringing all of your visual aids to his or her office on a floppy disk.

In the course of developing your own sales presentation, you will have to come up with sales aids and visuals that are both imaginative and effective. If you sell water softeners, your sales aids could include a cross section of an old pipe full of built-up mineral deposits, sample bottles of softened water, and a kit for testing the prospect's supply. If you sell mutual funds, your sales aids could include charts, graphs, and tables comparing the performance of your funds to others on the market or the stock market in general.

Different situations call for different types of sales aids. Some of the most common sales aids, scale models, videotapes and slide sets, and pictures, are better for some products than for others. A few ideas for making the best use of these popular items are as follows:

Scale Models

Use a scale model when presenting a product that cannot be brought to the prospect, or when the product's construction or interior is of interest. The model may take the form of a working miniature, a same-size cross section, or an enlargement. Cutaway models can be displayed along with the product to permit a detailed view of the product's inside. If the revenue from the sale justifies it and the model is easy enough to replace, let your prospects keep the model as a token of your appreciation for their meeting with you. Mechanics and engineers enjoy tinkering with working models, and the item may sell the product for you after your presentation is over.

Videotapes and Slide Sets

Videotapes and slide sets enable you to demonstrate an effect that would otherwise be impossible to illustrate, such as a long-term process. Time-lapse photography or slides shown in sequence allow the prospect to see an accelerated version of a process that in real life might take days, weeks, or months. People believe what they can see. If sound is used, they also enjoy a break from normal conversation. Slides can be just as effective as films, and black-and-white photography can be just as effective as color.

Pictures

Simply put, "One picture is worth a thousand words." A collection of pictures can be used to show the effects of your product over time, or how it looks in its different stages of construction or operation. Pictures are useful for any product that is photogenic, complicated to explain, or highly visual.

SELECTING SALES AIDS FOR A GROUP SALES PRESENTATION . . .

A group presentation is made in front of two or more people, all of whom have some influence over the buying decision. The group might be a company's buying committee, or it could be a one-time assembly of people from different departments. Group presentations commonly use flip charts, overhead transparencies, poster boards, and slides as sales aids. Each tool has distinct advantages and disadvantages, which you should consider when selecting from among them.

A flip chart is a large multisheet tablet displayed on an easel. This is an effective presentation tool if it is neatly illustrated, ideally with liquid ink markers of different colors. Its pages should not be scribbled up, and they should be replaced if they tear or start to yellow.

An overhead transparency is an image on a transparent sheet that is projected onto a large screen. The transparency should contain half-inch or larger lettering. If you project an ordinary typewritten page onto the screen, no one will be able to read it. A disadvantage of this presentation tool is that the presenter is beside the projector instead of next to the visual, and is usually facing the screen or looking down at the transparency instead of facing the audience.

A poster board is a heavy-duty piece of cardboard available at art supply houses. I comes in different colors, weights, and sizes. Poster boards are effective visuals for several reasons. They are easy to carry, hold their shape, and can be used virtually anywhere, making them a wise choice if you are not sure what physical setting to expect. If you have your poster boards laminated, you can wipe them clean, and they will last indefinitely.

Slide presentations (a set of slides and a slide projector) offer the advantage of allowing the presenter to stand next to the screen, perhaps with a pointer. In addition, there is no need for the sometimes awkward flipping or changing of pages that must be dome when using a flip chart or overhead transparencies. Because slides are inexpensively produced, you may want to assemble a different set for each presentation you make. If you do, the group will know it, and will respect you for the time and effort you have put into developing a custom presentation. It is one more way of showing your desire for their business.

Developing Sales Aids When Selling a Service . . .

If you are selling a service, your prospects can't see the "product," but you can help them visualize its benefits. For example, a management consultant can present a video of recently conducted workshops, a favorable magazine article, or increased productivity realized by companies that have used the consultant's services. A business writer can show published writing samples and awards. Advertising people can display a portfolio of print ads or a reel of television ads produced by their agency, or they could display a colorful booklet or short film explaining the interviews, research, creative development, and successful results the client will enjoy after signing on with the agency.

Many sellers of intangibles show pictures of their modern company headquarters or their latest technology. This can be very effective for businesses that must maintain a modern image. Others show photos of company officers and the people with whom the prospect will be doing business so as to promote personal service.

Using Sales Aids . . .

A word of caution about using sales aids and visuals: Don't overdo it. Just because you have them doesn't mean you should use them in all presentations. Sales aids are not always necessary. If you save your sales aids as long as they seem unnecessary during a presentation, you can always use them later if the need arises.

The temptation to use sales aids after you have gone to the trouble of creating them can be great. If a prospect buys your product before you have had a chance to use all of your audiovisual aids, you may feel frustrated. But coming out with your props after you have made the sale would be inappropriate in real-world selling.

Creating Attachment . . .

Creating attachment means building desire to own your product by allowing the prospect to possess and use it temporarily. Attachment leads to clarity and conviction by allowing the prospect to experience firsthand the benefits of the product. And, since your product is its own best salesperson, creating attachment is a good way to increase your chances of making a sale.

Here are five techniques for creating attachment: (1) product tests and demonstrations, (2) try-ons, (3) samples, (4) test drives, (5) trial periods.

Product Tests and Demonstrations . . .

Product tests and demonstrations create attachment by generating interest in the product and making the prospect want to try it out. Creating attachment this way will in turn help make the presentation clear and convincing because it engages the prospect in a personal experience. You need not always operate the product since a routine cleaning or maintenance procedure may serve the purpose. The most effective product test follows three criteria: relevance, simplicity, and involvement.

Relevance

A relevant test is one that demonstrates the product as it will be used by prospects when they own it. If different potential buyers have different uses for your product, you should be prepared to perform any test that will be relevant to any one of them. Prospects should be able to recognize that the trial relates to something they will do when they own the product. When parents are buying a computer for their children, you should demonstrate its ease of use and show them how to operate educational programs or games. When a small business owner is buying a computer for the business, you should demonstrate its practicality and speed, and explain how to operate appropriate business programs. Attachment and conviction can be established only if the test or demonstration relates to the prospect's needs.

Simplicity

A product test should be simple for three reasons: A simple test can be understood, will help make the prospect eager to use the product, and is more likely to go as planned.

If you were to perform a complicated test and your prospect didn't understand what you did or how the results came about, your test would be meaningless, even harmful, to your selling efforts. Potential buyers might think that only skilled users can enjoy the outcome you have demonstrated and that they are not qualified. Further, they might be too embarrassed to admit they couldn't follow your test. They will decline your invitation to try the product out, claiming they are not interested in owning it. Instead of creating attachment, you will have driven the prospect away from the product.

If your demonstration is unavoidably complicated, periodically check to make sure your prospect is with you. Ask, "Am I making this clear?" or "Am I going too fast?" The more difficult the test, the more often you should check with your prospect. If using your product requires special training or skill, the objective of your demonstration is to get the prospect to want to acquire that training or develop that skill. Avoid any test that immediately proves how difficult the product is to use. Introduce complications gently and gradually.

Finally, your product test must be simple because it must work. A failed demonstration contradicts everything you have said and done, and causes the loss of confidence in you as well as your product. A ruined test translates into a ruined presentation. In the unlikely case that your prospect buys the product after all, it will be in spite of you rather than because of you. For this reason above all else, you must plan and practice a simple presentation, and be certain that it works before ever trying it in the presence of a prospect.

If the prospect asks you to take the product apart and you have never done so, don't do it. If you cannot reassemble it, what choice will you have but to keep trying, demonstrating only that reassembly is a real problem? Or to let it sit in pieces, demonstrating that reassembly is impossible? The prospect will not want anything to do with such a troublesome product. Furthermore, as long as you are fumbling with the product, your presentation will be at a standstill.

Involvement

A Chinese proverb states, "Tell me, I'll forget; show me, I may remember; but involve me, and I'll understand." If prospects are personally involved with your product, their mind won't wander; they will be absorbed in its operation, and their concentration will enhance their ability to become attached. If you intend to ask your prospects to handle the product after you are finished demonstrating it, tell them so at the start so that they can pay more careful attention.

Enough cannot be said about creating attachment through involvement. To achieve prospect association, you must simply bring the potential buyer and the product together. Without this union, there can be no attachment. Early on, you should hand the product over to your prospects and invite them to enjoy it. Once you have them using the product, they may become so enthralled with it that it sells itself, or they sell themselves. As we mentioned in Chapter 6, prospect attachment to your product may be so great that you will need to regain possession of it in order to continue your presentation.

A product test that includes strong involvement can achieve multiple effects. It can promote concentration, enhance understanding, help establish credibility, and make the product's benefits readily apparent. Prospect involvement is so effective because it appeals to human nature. Potential buyers are much more inclined to believe what they see if they personally make it happen. This is especially true with tests of strength. Suppose you were to hit the product with a hammer with all of your might to prove that it will not crack. Some prospects will believe that they are stronger than you, and that you don't look strong enough to prove anything. Give them the hammer so that they can see for themselves that even they can't crack the plastic.

Although prospect involvement has many advantages, it is not always smart. You may be better off just allowing the prospect to watch if the demonstration is extremely complicated or could damage the product if performed improperly. The same is true of any trial that could be dangerous to the prospect. If chemicals are involved, for example, handle them yourself. If your demonstration requires special training or skill, explain to the prospect that using the product without this training would be imprudent, dangerous, or even illegal. Then perform a product test that will build the prospect's confidence in you by demonstrating your expertise.

Product tests that cannot involve your prospects should at least be performed in their presence. If that is impossible, record the entire test on videotape. Finally, when you conduct a harsh test, use a display model rather than the one the prospect will receive upon purchase. Give the buyer a brand-new model.

To be certain that you are prepared for your product tests and demonstrations, have a list of things to check on before each sales presentation and review it. Figure 10-2 presents a list of things you should do prior to each product test or demonstration you conduct.

Before a Product Demonstration

1. Check to be sure the product is working properly.

2. Determine which functions are most important to perform, and which you are likely to be asked to demonstrate. Practice these functions.

3. Replenish your supply of replacement parts, batteries, and accessories.

4. Ascertain that adequate electrical power exists at the planned site of the demonstration.

5. Be sure that physical conditions are favorable (proper lighting, enough seats, a comfortable seating arrangement where everyone can see the demonstration, etc.).

6. Determine who in the group (assuming it will be a group sales presentation) you might ask to assist you with the demonstration.

7. Arrive in time to check the physical setting and give the product a chance to warm up.

Figure 10-2

> The power of your ambition depends wholly on the vigor of the determination behind it. What you accomplish will depend on the amount of live energy, enthusiasm, and will power you put into your efforts to achieve.
>
> Randy D. Marsh

Try-Ons . . .

The **try-on** is heavily used as an attachment technique in retail selling and is indispensable in apparel sales. Clothing simply does not sell itself on the rack. Try-ons enable prospects to see and enjoy the clothing as it is meant to be enjoyed. Only by wearing the item will they see how the color complements their hair and eyes, how the cut flatters their figure.

The importance of timing cannot be stressed enough. Too much delay will allow customers to form an unfavorable opinion of the garment on the rack, where its best qualities are not very obvious. With an immediate try-on, customers don't form their opinion of the item until they wear it.

The try-on concept can be applied to nonapparel sales, too. Let the baseball player feel the grip and weight of a bat. Leave a few toys on display and available to playful children. Merchants often consider the breakage of a few display models an investment toward hefty sales.

Samples . . .

Product **sampling** is another selling technique that is heavily used in retailing, and is equally effective in creating attachment. Describing how rich, creamy, and smooth an ice cream tastes or how masculine a cologne smells is weak compared to giving samples away. When the prospect tastes the ice cream or dabs on the cologne, the product will sell itself. If you believe your product is worth buying, let the prospect sample it. Only those salespeople who are afraid the prospect will regret the purchase will deny their prospects a sample.

Test Drives . . .

One important objective of a **test drive** is to reveal the shortcomings of the prospect's present vehicle. Automobiles, trucks, and tractors, like many other products, tend to deteriorate slowly over time, so prospects don't notice a loss of benefits until they use a newer model. If you sell automobiles, you will frequently find your dealership's service customers browsing through the showroom while their cars are being serviced. Chances are, browsers don't believe they need a new car; they don't realize how much their car has deteriorated in comfort and performance over the past five years, even though those factors were important to them when the car was new. Driving a new car will be a striking difference to them and may be the only way to reveal the shortcomings of their present car. And by allowing them the pleasure of driving a new car, you can create attachment for the conveniences they miss.

Trial Periods . . .

Trial periods are recommended for any product that has a way of "growing on" the user. As prospects come to like the product, they are less inclined to give it up when the trial period ends. This is the reasoning behind those offers to use a camera for fifteen days or wear a ring for ten days.

Even children know the value of a trial period. Imagine a young child with a puppy to give away. When a friend is offered the puppy, the friend says, "I don't think my parents would let me keep it." The child replies, "Take the puppy home and ask them. I'll be home later, so if you're not allowed to keep the puppy, just bring it back." Of course the puppy never returns. By the time evening comes, the friend's entire family has grown to love the puppy.

SHOWING THE PRODUCT IN CONTEXT . . .

Many products are best appreciated when seen **in context**, that is, in the setting and use for which they were intended. Showing the product in this way makes your presentation clear and convincing because it helps the prospect better imagine using it. Whether your prospects are retail buyers visiting a manufacturer's showroom or at-home shoppers browsing through a catalog, they will comprehend your product better if it is shown in a setting appropriate to its use.

Retailers employ fashion coordinators and decorating consultants specifically to show their merchandise in context. Clothing and furniture are displayed in relation to other pieces that go well together. Notice how apparel stores dress mannequins in coordinated outfits and use props for extra effect. Even the clothes on racks are arranged so that complementary colors, fabrics, and styles are near one another. Shoppers who are uncomfortable choosing colors may be unable to imagine a red necktie going with a gray suit until they see them on display together. Similarly, furniture stores often display their wares in roomlike arrangements with everything from rugs to wallpaper in harmony.

If prospects visit you in your store or showroom, they shouldn't find your products sitting in isolation. In an office supply store, place the electric typewriter on a desk with plenty of paper and plug it in. If you visit the prospect, bring the product along with its accessories and attachments so that you can quickly arrange a display in the proper context.

Appealing to the Physical Senses . . .

One of the most effective ways of building clarity and conviction into your presentation is to appeal to the prospect's physical senses of sight, hearing, taste, touch, and smell. Automobile salespeople who slam a car door to show how solidly it is built appeal to the prospect's sense of hearing. A sensory message will have more profound impact than a purely verbal one. Retention is enhanced when a simultaneous appeal is made to the prospect's sense of sight and sound.

Even better, create **synergy** by appealing to a combination of the senses. Synergy is a total effect produced by the combination of sensory stimuli that no stimulus could achieve individually. People enjoy relaxing in front of a fireplace because of the synergetic effect it has on them. They are enchanted by the gentle agitation of multicolored flames, the warmth, the crackle of burning logs, and the exotic scent. No picture, not even a motion picture, could achieve the synergy of the real thing.

The synergetic effect of appealing to multiple senses is one of the greatest advantages of personal selling over advertising. Print advertising must rely on the sense of sight, radio on hearing alone. Television can combine the two and stir things up with action. But only personal selling can appeal to all five senses at the same time.

Using Repetition . . .

Repetition helps make your presentation clear and convincing in several ways. This process gives prospects another chance to hear and comprehend any points they didn't catch the first time. Repetition also helps the prospect retain your message and creates a synergetic effect.

The synergetic effects of repetition are well known to those in the advertising industry. Advertisers often see more benefit in reaching one person five times than in reaching five people once. If someone receives three different messages before deciding to buy, how can the advertiser know which commercial sold the customer? Although the purchase was made after the third message, it cannot be assumed that that one alone was completely responsible. It was the combination of all three that did it, and without each the purchase would not have been made.

Synergy of this sort can also be used in personal selling, by simply repeating your message to your prospect, just as advertisers do. Your "message" in this case will be the important points of your presentation, the ones that will be the most persuasive to your prospect. The continual referral to your key point does the trick. A word of advice: Rephrase an idea each time you repeat it. This way, you get the benefit of repetition without sounding redundant. Furthermore, each new way of wording your point adds to the prospect's depth of understanding and ability to remember.

> In the long run, the pessimist may be proved to be right, but the optimist has a better time on the trip.
>
> Daniel L. Reardon

DECIDING WHICH PRODUCT FEATURES TO PRESENT . . .

As you plan your first presentations, you will soon realize that you cannot always present every feature to every prospect. Although there is no such thing as knowing too much about your product, it is possible to say too much. The urge to tell everything must be avoided. Potential buyers could not possibly comprehend it all. You must choose only a small part of your total knowledge to relay to the prospect. Recognize that the future customer does not need to know all that you know, and limit your presentation to fit the prospect's needs.

You will need to choose from among your product's many features in order to develop the right presentation for the right prospect. When deciding on which features to present, make sure they fall under one of the following categories:

1. differentiating features
2. relevant and important features
3. new features

Differentiating features are those that make your product unique, ones that the prospect will not find anywhere else. There is no need to present features that your product has in common with others on the market. Talk only about the things that make your commodity distinctive. If prospects find these features desirable, they will have no choice but to purchase.

Relevant features are those that relate to the needs of the prospect, and that the potential buyer wants or finds most interesting. For example, if you are selling housepaint to homeowners who don't enjoy painting, they will be interested primarily in the fact that you offer a long-lasting, one-coat product. The information that your paint is compatible with many different surfaces will be irrelevant and unimportant. Be sure to talk first and foremost about your product's practical, everyday uses. Only discuss exotic, rare, or unusual functions if the prospect asks about them.

Remember, too, that what is relevant to one prospect may not be to another. Never assume that you know what product features are important to everyone simply because they seem to be of interest to one. Listen to each new prospect to discover individual tastes. If a potential buyer tells you that a certain feature is not important, do not dwell on it.

Always be sure to present your product's **new features**, those that have been added since the last time your prospect saw it. The potential buyer may be unaware of the ways in which your merchandise has been improved. New features may be enough to make prospects buy a product that they wouldn't buy before.

Further, when you have new features, use the word *new* a lot. "New" is one of the most powerful words in selling. If prospects consider themselves to be informed, up-to-date buyers, they will recognize the importance of keeping abreast of the latest developments.

Beginning with the Best . . .

Always begin your sales presentation with your product's best features, the ones that are most desirable to your prospect. Work your way down from the strongest to the weakest selling points. Again, you will determine which selling points are strongest by conducting a thorough preapproach and by observing reactions during a presentation.

There are several reasons for beginning with the best:

1. Beginning with the best allows you to appeal to the prospect's strongest buying motive first.
2. A good beginning helps you capture the interest of an indifferent prospect.
3. A strong start helps you if the prospect has a short attention span.
4. Beginning with the best saves time; the sooner you mention the true selling points, the sooner you might make the sale.

Most products appeal to multiple buying motives, and most prospects have more than one. However, different potential buyers have different priorities. Some may be attracted to your product's ease of cleaning, but may be even more drawn to its multiple uses. Beginning with the best for these prospects means demonstrating the product's multiple uses. Thus you will appeal to their strongest buying motive first.

The need to capture an indifferent prospect's interest is a major reason to begin with the best. As we mentioned in Chapter 6, your potential buyers may see you as an intruder trying to sell them something they don't want. You need to give them a reason for listening to you, and you need it fast. The weakness of saving your best selling points until the end is that you may never get to use them. If you fail to stimulate interest at the start, they will not allow you to go on.

A third reason to begin with your strongest selling points is to overcome a prospect's short attention span. Potential buyers who know little about you and your product are not inclined to pay attention. If your opener is too dull, prospects will stop listening before they ever really start listening.

A final reason to start with the best is to sell your product as quickly as possible. Wouldn't it be nice to make the sale early in the presentation, without ever having to get around to the minor details?

Saving a Key Selling Point . . .

During the sales presentation, you may be tempted to mention all of your product's benefits and features, but you will be better off if you don't. Keep at least one key selling point in reserve. This way, you can take advantage of an opportune moment to persuade the undecided prospect. Saving a key selling point until the conclusion of your presentation will give you one last chance to "sell" the prospect who could still go either way.

By keeping some ammunition in reserve, you increase the ability to influence the prospect favorably. For instance, if at the end of the presentation the potential buyer is undecided, you can add a remark like this: "Oh, by the way, with this purchase you will receive one year's worth of supplies free" or "Did I tell you that each of these models comes with a twenty-year guarantee?" The assumption behind this reserve strategy is that the prospect will have gotten so close to buying already that all that is needed is one last nudge.

Of course, it can be difficult deciding which selling point to save, since you do not want to withhold something that is necessary to the smooth flow of your presentation. When you are preparing your sales visit, list your product's selling points, and choose one or two that are important but not critical. These are the ones you will reserve for the end. You must not use a key "persuader" before it is actually needed, for if you do, you will have nothing exciting to tell your prospects in their moment of decision.

In the event you don't use your reserved selling point during your presentation, such as when the prospect decides to buy before you have the need to mention it, you can bring it up after the sale. Such belated mention makes for excellent postpurchase confirmation, reassuring buyers that they have made the right decision. Your persuasive remark will simply add another pleasing aspect to an already satisfying transaction.

Brian Shawver

One of the most helpful things that Brian Shawver gained from his college career was his involvement with Delta Epsilon Chi. While at Central Oregon Community College, where he earned his Associate degree in Marketing, Brian was an active member of DEC, ultimately becoming its president. He participated in local, regional, and national competition with this national student marketing group, winning numerous awards along the way. Although many courses were of benefit, Brian feels that his work in this organization truly honed his appetite for and skills in selling.

After college, Brian joined Centro Information Systems in sales, and after ten years with the firm currently holds the title of Vice President Marketing/Sales. He is responsible for the strategic and tactical marketing direction of his company, including supervision of an eight salesperson sales force. In addition, he is a Certified Forms Consultant, an honor held by only a little over 1,000 people worldwide. His reputation as an expert in the printed forms business has spread throughout the Pacific Northwest, helping his firm to grow to over $3 million per year.

Brian firmly believes in the marvelous opportunities afforded by America, where he says anyone can have anything they desire if they are willing to work for it. He advises young sellers always to think like a student rather than an expert, citing an ancient Chinese proverb that says, "When the student is ready, the teacher will appear." If we get to the point that we think we know it all, he suggests, we miss the opportunities that surround us daily. If we think like a student, Brian advises, then we are always looking for new things to learn, and new ways to expand our horizons.

THE PACE OF YOUR PRESENTATION . . .

The pace of your presentation is the rate of speed at which you deliver it. For each presentation, you must determine what your overall rate should be and when to change the tempo.

Overall Pace

As we said in Chapter 4, setting the correct pace for your sales presentation is an important objective of the preapproach. Your tempo must be set with respect to the prospect's desire for the product, experience with the product, and ability to comprehend the information you present. Your overall pace, the tempo of the presentation as a whole, should be fast enough to hold the prospect's undivided attention, yet slow enough for the prospect to understand you. Maintaining a proper pace is quite a challenge, but improper pacing has many pitfalls you will want to avoid.

Consider the disadvantages of adopting too fast a pace:

1. You appear to be in a hurry. The prospect might suspect you have another, more important engagement on your mind. Relaxing your speech, mannerisms, and actions will communicate the importance you attach to prospects and their business.

2. You are more likely to stray off course, and less able to keep your thoughts focused. You are also more likely to slur or skip words.

3. You might "lose" the prospect. If you know much more about your product than your prospects do (and you should), you run the risk of overwhelming them with too much information delivered too soon. Never try to force a potential buyer to rise to your preferred pace. Prospects will be more receptive to your message if they receive it at a comfortable rate. Cover one point at a time, and get confirmation that each point is understood before you move on. Prospects who become hopelessly lost have no other way of taking themselves "off the hook" than by refusing your proposal.

Now consider the disadvantages of presenting too slowly:

1. The prospect gets bored. Being ahead of you, prospects allow their mind to wander. You lose their attention.

2. You waste the prospect's time and yours. A potential buyer who feels that the interview is dragging on may put an end to it. Do not expect a busy person to be patient while you take your time.

3. You will insult some prospects. They think you should know they have more knowledge than you give them credit for. You seem to have assumed they lack the education and experience to keep up with you. Since you appear to be unaware of their intelligence and achievements, you reveal your own failure to preapproach.

When you don't know what pace to assume, start by going slower rather than a little too fast. If you detect that you are presenting too slowly, speed up. Experiment with your pace until you determine it to be appropriate.

Changing the Pace

Setting the overall pace of your presentation is only half the job. The other part is adjusting your tempo during the presentation. You may occasionally wish to slow down or speed up in order to achieve certain effects. A change of pace will keep your presentation lively and fresh, whereas a monotonous rate will become boring and tiresome. A change of pace also helps keep the prospect alert and attentive.

Finally, a change of pace helps you communicate the importance of the ideas you are presenting. Students can usually tell when their professor is covering material that will appear on an upcoming exam because the rate of delivery is slower and extra attention is given to it. They can also tell when less important material is being presented since it is tossed off quickly and casually. Of course, you would not want to change pace arbitrarily or strictly for the sake of variety. Any difference in tempo should be made purposeful and reasonable. Here are the times you should slow down your presentation:

1. When you are covering something that is difficult or easily misunderstood.
2. When you are at a critical point in the presentation, discussing something on which the sale depends.
3. When you are covering an important idea, and you want the prospect to appreciate its importance.

Here are the times you should speed up your presentation:

1. When you are covering elementary points or points familiar to and well understood by the prospect.
2. When you are mentioning things that are not of great importance to the prospect.

The prospect's education, experience, and interests should play a role in determining changes in your pace, just as it should the overall rate. Slow down or speed up according to your prospect's ability to comprehend the various parts of your presentation.

Pulse Taking . . .

Pulse taking means checking the progress of your presentation and the prospect's state of mind. Because comprehension is so important to your success, pulse taking is a necessary part of the presentation. Prospects rarely volunteer that they have become confused or lost, so you cannot assume by silence that what you do or say is understood. Pulse taking is your responsibility. If your perception check reveals that the prospect has missed a point, you must cover it again. If you discover that many of your prospects have difficulty with the same points, you must devise a different way of presenting them.

One of the more common pulse-taking methods is getting prospects physically involved with the product. For example, you can invite them to perform a function you have just demonstrated. Not only does this allow them to participate actively in the presentation, it will reveal whether they understood your demonstration. The most common pulse-taking method, however, is asking questions, which is a good all-around presentation technique.

Asking Questions . . .

Questions serve many purposes in the sales presentation. As a salesperson, you will come to appreciate the value of good inquiries and develop a healthy habit of using this technique. Some of the benefits of asking questions throughout the course of your sales presentation are:

1. Questions replace monologue with dialogue.
2. Questions help you determine how interested the prospect is in purchasing your product.
3. Questions enable you to determine if you are making progress in your presentation, appealing to the right buying motive, or overcoming the prospect's objections to purchasing.
4. Questions reveal whether the prospect comprehends your presentation.
5. Questions get the prospect's attention.
6. Questions phrased for a yes answer will condition the prospect to think affirmatively.
7. A question can be a good opener. For example, "Is increasing productivity important to you?"
8. A question can be a good closer. For example, "Where should we make delivery?"

As you know already, the most important task early in your presentation is to build a quick dialogue. Asking questions is the most effective way to do this. To serve as dialogue builders, your inquiries should encourage participation and progress. You might start out with questions like, "How many employees do you have?" But you cannot stop there; you will need to follow up with more questions in order to develop a free-flowing dialogue.

Be sure to ask plenty of questions that require more than a yes or no answer. Ask questions that require a detailed response. These questions are known as **open-ended** questions. These are generally superior to the opposite, or **closed-ended** questions, which require only a very short or even a one-word answer. "Have you ever used this type of product before?" is a closed-ended question. This type may give you the information you need, but it does nothing to encourage dialogue. How would you follow up such a question once you have your answer? You will find follow-up questions much easier if your initial questions are designed to get more information.

Open-ended questions are intended to elicit information about needs or problems that the prospect might be having. Closed-ended questions often lead to a dead end. Here are some examples that might help you better understand the importance of open-ended questions to the consultative salesperson:

Closed-ended	Open-ended
Do you use silicone lubricants on your equipment?	What types of lubricants are used on your equipment?
Who is your present supplier?	Are you experiencing any problems with your present sources of supply?
How many machines do you presently operate?	Could you give me a description of your present equipment?
Do you need non-petroleum based lubricants?	What are your requirements for equipment lubricants?

Bear in mind that when you first meet prospects, they probably will not be interested in talking to you, since they are not yet tuned in to purchasing your product. You will need to develop their interest. Use the **Lantern Technique**, as described in Figure 10-3, by beginning with questions that require short answers. This way you avoid rushing prospects into a conversation for which they may not be ready. Gradually move to open-ended questions that call for more prospect involvement, and return to closed-ended questions at the end of your presentation to check for understanding.

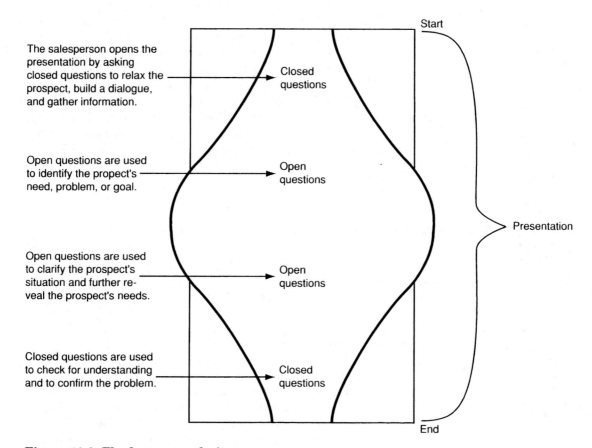

Figure 10-3 The lantern technique.

In this respect, being a good salesperson is like being a good interviewer. You draw your prospects out by questioning them, and stimulate their desire to make comments on their own. Some salespeople use the **two–one ratio**, asking two questions for every statement they make.

Asking questions is an excellent way to get the prospect's agreement on key issues. Unlike the information-gathering questions and dialogue-building questions, **affirmation questions** do not avoid yes answers; they require them. You might say, "Mrs. Walford, do we agree that this washer is big enough for your needs?" An affirmative reply indicates that you can move on. Further, by conditioning prospects to say yes, you put them in an affirmative state of mind.

Some salespeople like to save their affirmation questions for the end, when they are ready to close the sale. But why wait until the end? Better to condition your prospect to say yes from the very beginning. This is especially important if there is a likelihood of conflict over some aspect of the sale. For example, if some prospects think that the product is too small for their needs, ask at the outset, "Is size an important consideration to you?" You will receive your first yes answer, as well as your signal that you must convince them your product is big enough to meet their needs. Continually phrase your questions to get yes answers, conditioning them to answer affirmatively, and you will be more likely to get their agreement when you finally tell them that your product is the right size.

When you meet prospects who have difficulty pinpointing their needs or explaining their situation, ask them **probing questions**. For example, you might start out by asking about your prospect's biggest production problem only to learn that he or she cannot seem to focus on anything in particular. You will need to probe by asking questions focused on specific production considerations: "Do you think cost control is a factor?" or "Is your equipment in need of frequent repair?" If you ask prospects for the names of colleagues who will be using your product and they can think of only one or two, again ask them probing questions: "Who's involved in manufacturing research here?" or "What other departments use microcomputers?" Figure 10-4 provides examples of seventeen categories of questions that are useful throughout the course of your sales presentation.

Encouraging the Prospect's Questions . . .

Encouraging the prospect to ask questions is almost impossible with canned presentations, which would be disrupted by inquiries. Getting the potential buyer to ask questions is more than advisable in customized approaches specifically designed to uncover needs and wants. With few exceptions, you should encourage questions and answer them immediately. Here are some of the reasons for doing so:

1. Prospects whose questions are encouraged and answered will remain happily attentive. If they are forced to "bottle up," their questions will remain on their mind as you speak. Instead of listening to you, they will be thinking their own thoughts, looking for a chance to speak, and entirely missing your message. They will lose interest in your product.

Questions	Examples
Opening: states the purpose of your call.	Have you seen our latest model?
Qualifying: confirms prospect status.	Are your children under age 21?
Rapport-building: relaxes the prospect with casual conversation.	How long have you worked here?
Diagnostic: helps the prospect uncover needs and gathers information required for the sales presentation.	Which aspects of your operation take the most time and money?
Directional: guides the presentation in a certain direction or switches subjects.	Do others in your firm use this product?
Clarifying: asks the prospect to clarify something.	Would you explain that to me again?
Extension: asks the prospect to elaborate on something.	Can you explain that a little further?
Substantiating: asks for the logic behind the prospect's viewpoint.	How did you arrive at that conclusion?
Challenging: asks the prospect to validate his position.	Why do you think this one is better?
Comprehension: checks for the prospect's understanding of your message.	Are you able to relate the circumstances I've described to your own situation?
Confirmation: verifies that you understand the prospect and informs him or her of this.	So you consider the neighborhood to be one of your top purchase considerations?
Hypothetical: describes a set of circumstances that doesn't exist at the present time.	What would you do if your present product broke down today?
Progress: determines if you are ready to go on to the next part of the presentation, or are changing the prospect's mind concerning your product.	So do we agree that this product's safety features meet or exceed your company's standards?
Summary: requests a synopsis of your conversation with the prospect thus far.	What can we conclude from our discussion?
Action: asks the prospect to do something.	Why don't you try it for a week?
Trial Close: determines if you are ready to consummate the sale.	How does that sound to you?
Closing: finalizes the transaction.	Do you prefer the early American or the contemporary pattern?

Figure 10-4 Types of questions.

2. Your prospects' questions may reveal what competitors have told them. You will then have an opportunity to dispel misconceptions or build upon their knowledge.

3. Answers to the prospect's questions reveal your knowledge, thus building confidence in you. If you don't allow questions, the prospect may lose trust in you, thinking that you are afraid you won't be able to answer.

4. The prospect's questions may give you the opportunity to say something complimentary when you reply: "I'm glad you asked" or "Good question; not many people ask me that."

5. The prospect's questions may give more effect to your words. If the prospect asks, "Do you think the product will work for me?" and you reply, "As a matter of fact, I can think of six ways it will work for you," you are making a more powerful statement than if you listed the ways it will work without prompting.

6. The prospect's questions aid you in your pulse-taking efforts. If a question indicates that the prospect didn't understand a point you made earlier, you know that you need to cover it again. If the prospect understands more than you assumed, you will discover that, too.

7. The prospect's question can sometimes become the focal point of your presentation. It may even be the point on which the sale is made. Perhaps a question reveals the prospect's only reason for not buying, and your answer is all that is needed to conclude the presentation successfully.

8. The prospect's question may signal the time to close the sale. If your prospect can think of no more questions, and seems completely satisfied with all you have done and said, you should attempt a close.

Usually, questions should be answered immediately, but there are exceptions to this rule. You could delay if you know the question will be answered later in the natural course of the presentation or when a premature answer would defeat your selling efforts. For example, you should not answer a question about price until you have had the opportunity to build your product's value in the prospect's mind. If you are halfway through a lengthy presentation and the prospect suddenly asks what the product costs, request permission to defer the answer.

Occasionally, the prospect will interrupt you with a question or comment when you are trying to make an important point. Try not to allow an interruption to interfere with the matter at hand. It is perfectly acceptable to request permission to finish your point and promise to address the prospect's concern later. In fact, if you don't do this, your point could be forever lost. As long as prospects are assured that their concerns will be met as soon as possible, they will most likely allow you to finish what you are doing.

THE GROUP PRESENTATION . . .

Group presentations require a number of considerations that might not be necessary for a one-on-one presentation. For example, most typically call for the use of visuals that can be seen from a distance. You will need to make sure the setting of your presentation allows for this. You will also want to see that there is sufficient space for your equipment, and that electrical outlets, acoustics, and lighting are adequate.

You should arrive early, not only to set up your equipment, but also to adjust the curtains or blinds, and to rearrange the furniture or seating. If the room is equipped with a pull-down screen, or other audiovisual equipment, check beforehand to be sure that everything is clean, in usable condition, and working properly. Design the seating arrangement so that people can come and go from the back of the room so as not to disturb you and the other attendees. If possible, distribute your reading materials to the group in advance. Do not begin or continue your presentation immediately after distributing reading materials because people will be reading what they have just received instead of listening to you.

Understanding Group Dynamics . . .

Like synergy, **group dynamics** is a kind of combination effect produced by the mixture of personalities. You will not be the only person influencing a group member. The others present provide influence, too. The overall group personality will be a force to contend with.

Here are some guidelines for handling group presentations:

1. Make sure that you are communicating with each member of the group. Cover your material in terms that everyone can understand. Take extra steps to ensure that your message is received. Select your words carefully, and ask periodic questions of everyone present. Remember that each person has a different level of interest, knowledge, and education. Some members of the group may be less knowledgeable than others, requiring individual attention throughout your presentation.

2. Pay careful attention to everyone in your audience. Recognize how people react to you and to one another. Remember that in a group presentation, you need to present to more than one person. Maintain an equal amount of eye contact with each member, including those sitting to your extreme right and left. Don't overlook some or favor others. Each group member must feel as important as the rest. This seemingly simple advice can be difficult to follow, especially when high-ranking personnel are present or when you have identified the true decision makers.

3. Strive for equal participation from all attendees. Try not to allow one person to dominate the discussion. Show that you respect the input of everyone present. Attendees will be more likely to contribute if they know their input is welcome. Ask unresponsive attendees to share their opinions. Encourage those sitting in the back to move up into the middle of the room. If there is a loner in the group, socialize with this person during the break or after the presentation. Although some attendees may be reluctant to speak in front of the group, they might have an important say in the final decision.

4. Treat each group member as an individual. When you respond to one person's question or comment, address your remarks to that person, not to the whole group.

5. Avoid getting into a lengthy conversation with any one person. If you must talk to certain group members individually, refocus your discussion on the entire group as soon as possible.

6. Keep an eye on those who seem to be mentally drifting. Ask for their involvement and solicit their opinions. As long as all members think that they may be the next one called upon to comment, they are more apt to give you their attention.

7. As early as possible, try to identify those who favor your proposal and those who oppose it. Then when you make a point, ask those who agree with you for their opinion. Although the people who oppose may not be swayed by your words, they may have great respect for the opinions of their colleagues.

8. If you expect a difficult time from one particular member of the group, request that the person sit next to you, not across from you. Sitting side by side makes confrontation more difficult than does sitting face to face. Futher, breaking down the physical distance will help break down the emotional distance.

9. Provide frequent summaries throughout your presentation, and ask the group for its agreement on each point before you move on. If there is disagreement or misunderstanding on something, it should be resolved before you continue. This affirmation enables you to keep the group moving as a single unit, in the same direction.

10. If you are delivering to a quiet or unresponsive group, increase your requests for feedback. Do they need further clarification on certain points? Could the presentation be moving faster? Are they ready for a break?

11. Keep your presentation positive, and end it on an upbeat note. The attendees should come away from it smiling and cheerful.

Occasionally, group presentations take all day, or even several days. If a delivery is going to last several hours, take "stretch breaks" every hour or so. You should also consider the use of **team selling** when making a group presentation. In team selling, you make your presentation with the help of someone else, perhaps a fellow salesperson or someone from another division in your firm.

People with experience in specific fields often use language or references familiar only to those with similar backgrounds. Since, in group settings, many different individuals from different functional areas may be present, it is important to address each sub-group. The technical staff from your company should address their counterparts at the prospective business, your financial people should talk to their financial people, and so on. Not only do your specialists handle their own areas of expertise, but the introduction of different speakers tends to liven the presentation. In preparing such group selling efforts, make extra sure that your players are well-versed on the prospect's needs and concerns and how each member is going to address these issues. Team selling requires teamwork.

You Decide!

Carla was hired fresh out of college to work as a sales representative for a newly-developed ski resort in Utah. She is an avid skier and her job calling on travel agents throughout the West seems like an ideal situation for her. After a three-week training session, the marketing manager of the ski area proudly presents her with a brand new selling kit, containing brochures, photos, and even a short video showing off the resort's facilities. Carla is excited as she packs her car and heads out on her first swing through the Northwest.

On her first evening on the road, she settles down in her motel room to review the materials. While she marvels at the beautifully printed materials, Carla notices that most of the photographs are of the ski mountain's professional instructors posing as customers. She plugs in the video and again is alarmed at the presentation, as the snow appears deeper, the sky bluer and the lines much shorter than in reality. Although she is certain that the travel agents with whom she has contact will be very impressed, she is concerned that first-time visitors might be disillusioned by the differences. Should she make her presentations anyway, or should she discuss her disappointment with the marketing director? **You decide!**

Although team selling is usually inadvisable when presenting to one prospect, since he or she is likely to feel overwhelmed or intimidated, it works well when presenting to a group. Sharing the floor with other presenters breaks the monotony of hearing just one speaker. Also when one presenter adds to or reinforces something the other has just said, credibility is greatly enhanced.

If you have previously been unable to identify the true decision makers in an organization, a group presentation should make the power structure known. The group setting is ideal for revealing the key participants. Simply observe the reaction of the group members to others in their presence and the nature of their comments.

FOLLOWING UP ON AN UNSUCCESSFUL PRESENTATION . . .

Not every presentation you make will be successful, but a bad call does not have to mean the end of your sales efforts. Any number of factors may have caused your presentation to fail, and you should consider calling on your prospect again for a follow-up interview. When a presentation has not succeeded, examine the events and influences that shaped its outcome. Here are some things that might prompt you to call on your prospect again:

1. You realize that you appealed to the wrong buying motive, or that you improperly assessed the prospect's situation or needs.
2. You realize that you failed to give the prospect some relevant or important information.
3. You were unable to answer a question or overcome an objection that you are now able to handle.
4. You feel that bad timing or an improper setting was responsible for your not making the sale.

If you believe that a second call would prove worthwhile, you should make one. Granted, in some instances, it might be too late. Some prospects have a limited time frame in which to see all salespeople competing for their business, and they may have already made their decision. If this is not the case, and the prospect is willing to give you a second hearing, be certain that the presentation has everything going for it. The setting must be right, you must appeal to the correct buying motive, you must offer new and relevant information, and you must slant your presentation in the appropriate direction.

Summing It Up . . .

An effective sales presentation involves the prospect. In some situations, sales presentations that do not vary from prospect to prospect are appropriate, but in most instances, they should be custom-designed with the potential buyer in mind. If there is a best way of treating a topic or making a point, then do it that way each time; just be sure that the rest of your presentation is tailored to the prospect.

You build clarity into your presentation by using sales aids and visuals. Perhaps you can make use of computer technology in the design and presentation of your visuals. If possible, show your product in context, and build your prospect's involvement with attachment-creating techniques such as product tests and demonstrations, try-ons, test drives, samples, and trial periods. Determine which product features to present by analyzing the prospect's needs, interests, and characteristics. Begin with your strongest selling points, and appeal to as many physical senses as you can. Adjust the pace of your presentation to suit the prospect, and vary your pace to emphasize key points and avoid monotony. To be sure that your prospect understands your message, ask carefully worded questions, encourage the prospect's questions, and answer them as soon and completely as you can.

If you are making a group sales presentation, learn the dynamics of the situation. Determine which group members seem to favor your proposal and which seem opposed to it. Then, use this knowledge to your advantage.

Key Concepts and Terms . . .

affirmation question
AIDA framework
barehanded selling
canned presentation
closed-ended question
differentiating features
group dynamics
in context
Lantern Technique
mental imagery
need satisfaction theory
new features
open-ended question
probing questions

pulse taking
relevant features
repetition
sales aid
sampling
selling formula theory
stimulus–response theory
synergy
team selling
test drive
tests and demonstrations
trail period
try-on
two–one ratio

Building Skills . . .

1. Explore the ways that a new salesperson can develop a personal sales presentation.

2. Describe a canned presentation and the reasons is it used.

3. Explain the use of mental imagery in selling.

4. List the criteria mental imagery must meet to be effective.

5. Name some possible sales aids for magazine advertising, hot tubs, or a self-improvement course.

6. Explain the requirements of a good product test.

7. Describe showing a product in context. Give an example.

8. Explore why you should begin your presentation with the strongest selling features, including the dangers of saving the best until last.

9. Briefly explain the two aspects of pacing the presentation.

10. Describe the benefits of repetition.

11. List some of the benefits derived from asking plenty of questions.

12. Describe the advantages of encouraging and immediately answering prospects' questions, as well as the disadvantages of discouraging them.

13. Explain the effect of appealing to a combination of the physical senses. Give an example.

14. Establish guidelines to be followed when making a group presentation.

Making Decisions 10-1:

Courtney Haas is the showroom manager for Playtime Toys and Dolls. One morning she is visited by Linda Pasciullo, a retail buyer for Boyer and Sons department stores.

Courtney: Hi. Thanks for coming to our showroom. I don't think we've met. I'm Courtney Haas.

Linda: I'm Linda Pasciullo from Boyer and Sons.

Courtney: I know Boyer and Sons. You're one of the biggest retailers in the western part of the state.

Linda: Yes, and we're getting bigger all the time, which is why I'm here. We're expanding the toy departments in all of our stores, and I'd like to take a look at Playtime's line for the coming season.

Courtney: Great! Where do you want to begin? (She leads Linda through the showroom, where they spend fifteen minutes browsing.)

Linda: What kind of discounts do you offer?

Courtney: (Looking past Linda) We offer quite a few. I'll get my price book in just a minute, but first I'd like you to meet Ruth Lambour. That's her coming in. Ruth is our market research specialist, and she can tell you which toys and dolls are going to be popular this season.

Linda: OK, but I'm not sure I'm interested until I know the price.

Explain the pros and cons of Courtney deflecting Linda's price question.

Making Decisions 10-2:

Myna Elias is an account executive for *Today's Computer*, a national magazine for personal computer enthusiasts. She has made an appointment with Carl Lebeau, the marketing and advertising manager for Wordwrite, a regional computer software firm. Myna hopes to convince Carl to advertise in *Today's Computer*.

Myna: Good morning, Mr. Lebeau. Thank you for seeing me.

Carl: It's my pleasure.

Myna: Have you considered the benefits of advertising your software in a magazine aimed specifically at PC users?

Carl: The idea has come up at several staff meetings, but we're a small company. I think we would be wasting our money.

Myna: What forms of promotion do you normally use?

Carl:	We rely on our customer mailing list. We send product updates and new-product information to past purchasers and to people who request information from us.
Myna:	(Removing the latest issue of *Today's Computer* from her briefcase) Have you seen our magazine?
Carl:	Oh, yes. Its editorial content is excellent.
Myna:	(Turning to the table of contents and pointing to it) We think so. The computer experts who contribute articles every month are nationally recognized. I'm sure you've heard of most of them.
Carl:	Yes, I have.
Myna:	(Flipping through the magazine) You'll also notice the excellent production. Doesn't the color just jump off the page?
Carl:	It's quite nice, but...
Myna:	And, as you may know, we've been cited by the National Association of PC Users as a leading authority in the field.
Carl:	I really don't think I'm interested, Myna. Thank you anyway.

Evaluate Myna's choice of product features. Describe the product features you would you have presented. Explore the good points of Myna's presentation.

Making Decisions 10-3:

List the sales aids you might select in selling the following products:

Product	Sales Aids
Video surveillance system	_____
Resort convention facility	_____
Industrial cleaning solvents	_____
Fleet automobiles	_____
Workmen's comp insurance	_____
Business computers	_____
Web page design	_____
Lumber package for housing tract	_____

Making Decisions 10-4:

You represent a conference center located in the heart of a rapidly growing commercial area with a large number of new high-technology firms. You are planning a visit to the director of the local chamber of commerce, in hopes of convincing him or her to hold the chamber's annual fair at your center. Describe the sales aids you would take with you.

Making Decisions 10-5:

You are selling Hawaiian vacation packages using the Internet. Describe how you would demonstrate your product. Explain the mechanisms you might use to create attachment.

Practice Makes Perfect 10-1:

Try making a sales presentation for a high-tech product, such as a computer, cell phone, or fax machine, without using any sales aids. Remake your presentation with as many sales aids that you can muster. Ask for comments on the effectiveness of each.

Chapter 11

The Nature of Sales Resistance

☐
☐
☐
☐

THE JOB TO BE DONE . . .

Handling sales resistance is the essence of the selling game. Professional sellers welcome objections as the avenue to closing the sale. In Chapter 11 you will learn how to:

...understand each of the six categories of customer objections.

...identify the type of objection being raised.

...understand the reasons these objections are raised.

...develop strategies for dealing with each category of customer objection.

...appreciate the use of negotiation when dealing with customer objections.

THE WORD "NO" . . .

What was the first word your parents taught you as a child? Chances are, it was "no." People are used to saying no. It's easy. Saying yes to a purchase requires commitment and possibly action, but saying no requires neither. "No" is the essence of sales resistance, or buyer objections. It is an obstacle the prospect places between the salesperson and the sale, a reason the prospect gives for not buying.

Selling is a relatively easy job until the potential buyer says no. The sales presentation can progress smoothly until the prospect finds something about the proposition that is unsuitable and objects to it. Only when the prospect says no does the true selling ability of the salesperson become apparent.

Objections make the salesperson's work a constant challenge. Salespeople who sell products that are unfamiliar to the prospect, complex, expensive, or seemingly overpriced are especially likely to encounter frequent objections to buying. All of a salesperson's persistence, resilience, and determination are called upon to deal with prospect objections.

OBJECTIONS AND THE BUYING PROCESS . . .

You will recall from Chapters 4 and 7 that the buying process consists of six stages. Prospects who purchase have gone through these stages of decision:

1. They see the need for the product.
2. They are satisfied with the brand or model.
3. They recognize the ability to afford the product and are satisfied with the price.
4. They like the salesperson and believe the salesperson to be trustworthy and capable of satisfying their needs.
5. They are satisfied with the salesperson's company, believe in its claims, and consider it capable of standing behind its product.
6. They believe "now" is the right time to buy.

All objections that you will encounter as a salesperson are associated with the six stages of the buying process. The six categories of objections, therefore, are (1) need, (2) product, (3) price, (4) salesperson, (5) source, (6) time.

A prospect's objection indicates that she or he has not yet passed through the buying stage associated with that objection.

If the objection is raised early in the presentation, you can build a large part or even all of your presentation around it. This stage may be the only one through which the prospect has yet to pass, and once the obstacle is removed, a customer is created. If you have already covered the information relating to an objection, you may have to go over it again using a different technique.

THE NEED OBJECTION . . .

In the buying process, the first thing the prospect must do is see the need. All other aspects of your proposition will mean nothing if the potential buyer sees no need for your product. True prospects have a true requirement for your product. Their objection on the basis of lack of need means that they are unaware of either its necessity or the problem your product can solve. Your task is to help them see the need for your product, to help them realize their situation could be improved.

The **need objection** is not only the most common objection, it is one of the most difficult to overcome. This is because the prospect's attitude toward owning the product is negative from the very beginning. Unlike other obstacles, which may arise later in the presentation, the prospect with this type of reluctance poses it at the outset.

Of course, in order to make prospects realize the disadvantages of their present situation, you must first have the opportunity to make your presentation, an opportunity they may have no desire to give you. If you find yourself in such a predicament, you might offer to discuss the reason for your visit, and ask that the prospect suspend judgment until all of your ideas have been presented.

When you set out to overcome the need objection, you face two hurdles:

1. You must make prospects aware of shortcomings in their present situation.
2. You must make them aware of the improvements your product will bring.

The need objection must be handled with care and tact. Prospects can be offended by suggestions that their present situation is inadequate. A poorly chosen word or excessively strong suggestion can ruin your attempt to change the prospect's way of thinking.

Ideally, prospects who come to recognize the shortcomings of their situation will be happy to learn how they can improve it. This might involve long-term personal or financial goals or a minor aspect of their life. If prospects say they do not need a telephone answering service because someone is always available to answer the phone, they may be right. However, if they say they have no need because they have always managed without it, you can explain the many ways in which their business or personal life would improve if they subscribed to yours. Your presentation may prove to be an eye-opening experience for the prospect.

Change and the Need Objection . . .

Creating the need for your product means creating the desire for change. However, people are by nature opposed to change, especially when it is not their own idea. Two aspects of human nature are at the heart of prospects' objections: First, people don't readily change thought or action patterns. Second, prospects tend to resist ideas presented by salespeople. Indeed, if people didn't resist change, there would be no need for skilled salespeople, just order takers.

> Managers must have the discipline not to keep pulling up the flowers to see if their roots are healthy.
>
> Robert Townsend

Some people are completely close-minded toward change, be it in their consumption patterns, their lifestyle, or their way of doing business. They have no desire to make the change in method, habit, or routine that buying your product requires. They may be so opposed to the thought of change that, upon hearing your offer to explain the benefits of your product, they reply in effect, "My mind is made up. Don't confuse me with the facts." Prospects can be so resistant to change that even the potential of higher profits will not persuade them to try something new.

The more accustomed people are to doing things a certain way, the more likely they are to resist change. This inertia is not related to age. Older people can be very progressive, and younger people can be firmly set in their ways.

Salespeople facing the need objection not only have the task of telling prospects that an aspect of their life could be made better, they often have the difficult job of helping prospects overcome their fear of the new and unknown. Convincing the prospect to change from a familiar product or service to an untried one isn't easy.

If you represent an investment service and visit prospects with established investment habits, you must convince them not just that their returns will be greater but that the investments you propose are safe. Because they are satisfied with their present method of investing and know nothing about yours, they will require substantial convincing before they will consider your program. Fortunately, not everyone is opposed to change. Many prospects welcome the opportunity to hear a salesperson suggest ways to improve their lives.

If the Prospect Already Owns the Product . . .

The need objection is sometimes raised by prospects who already own the product you sell. You will recall from Chapter 10 that many customers are often unaware that their present product has deteriorated over time. Just as people who see themselves in the mirror every morning don't notice themselves aging, so the owner of a frequently used product doesn't notice its gradually deteriorating performance. Prospects who drive a ten-year-old automobile pose a need objection because they think the old bucket has plenty of life left in it. Only when they drive a new one will they come to see the weaknesses of their old car and recognize the need for a change.

The owner who sees no need to replace an aging product might never have seriously considered the costs associated with keeping it. **Out-of-pocket costs**, such as those incurred in maintaining or repairing a car, are not always readily apparent. They extend into seemingly minor expenses that add up, such as bus, cab, or other transportation fares. Then there are the nonmonetary expenses, which come in the form of foregone benefits. Owners who hang onto their old car are doing without many of the benefits of new-car ownership, such as safety, comfort, convenience, pleasure, and prestige.

Obviously, prospects who keep their old car pay dearly for their inertia, in both monetary and nonmonetary terms. Once prospects consider the true costs of keeping their old product, including the **nonmonetary costs**, they may be quite eager to change. By making prospects aware of all the costs they are paying, you instill in them a greater need to replace their present product. There are several questions you can ask to ensure that prospects consider the costs associated with keeping their present product. Here are some, applied to the car example:

1. "How many times has your car broken down in the past year?"
2. "What do your yearly car-maintenance expenses amount to?"
3. "How often is your schedule disrupted by car problems?"

If you have done your homework, you will know before asking that your prospect's car has broken down frequently, maintenance expenses are high and the individual's schedule is quite often disrupted by car problems.

THE PRODUCT OBJECTION

Prospects who raise the product objection have already passed through the need stage. They recognize the need for the good or service in general, but have not chosen your particular brand or the model you recommend. Unlike owners who think their ten-year-old car is satisfactory, prospects with a product objection know they need a new one, but are not convinced that your make or model is the one to buy. Brand objections and model objections are product objections; however, each objection has unique considerations to keep in mind.

The Product Brand Objection . . .

The **product brand objection** is particularly challenging because it usually means the prospect has some strongly held beliefs. Common reasons for the brand objection are:

1. The prospect prefers another brand.
2. The prospect perceives your brand as low in quality.
3. The prospect is not familiar with your brand.
4. The prospect has had problems with your brand.
5. The prospect knows someone who has had problems with your brand.

> Training is everything. The peach was once a bitter almond; cauliflower is nothing but a cabbage with a college education.
>
> Mark Twain

The Prospect Prefers Another Brand . . .

Competition is usually a factor whenever the brand-preference objection comes up. The prospect who raises it may be shopping around or may already be leaning heavily toward a rival. Remember that a potential buyer who is a customer of the competition or is seriously considering the competitor's product most likely will be well informed. You in turn must know enough about your competition to convince your prospects that your product is superior in the ways that matter most to them.

Of course, the brand-preference objection is not all bad news. An important fact of market life is on your side: Every firm that survives in the marketplace has qualities that are superior to those of its competitors. If this were not so, the product would have nothing in its favor and would be impossible to sell. So if your prospect is attracted to a prestigious competitor's product, you can point out that your lesser-known firm must offer a superior product in order to prosper.

If the prospect is a loyal user of a competitor's product, you must determine the basis and extent of that allegiance before attempting to change it. Brand loyalty is often founded on the customer's sincere belief that a given product is the best one on the market. However, this devotion could also be strictly emotional. Perhaps loyal prospects have a friend or relative who works for the competition, or perhaps their parents always bought the other brand, and they are simply following in their footsteps. Sometimes loyalty isn't loyalty at all, but habit. Prospects may simply be buying from the competition because they have always done so and don't know of any other way. Blind loyalty might be a matter of never having thought about changing brands.

If the prospect's loyalty is unrelated to rational considerations such as price, performance, or quality, you face a special challenge. Irrationally loyal prospects are not concerned with the selling factors that are important to the uncommitted or brand-neutral shopper. You face the task of making them realize that the emotional satisfaction they get in exchange for their loyalty is not worth the price they are paying. Perhaps if you use a pen and paper to add up the costs of their loyalty, they will come to see that the tangible benefits of your product outweigh the intangible satisfaction they get from dealing with the competition. In addition, you should let the prospect know that your firm, too, is worthy of loyalty.

The Prospect Perceives Your Brand as Low in Quality . . .

When prospects think your brand is of low quality, your first objective is to determine why they have this opinion. Their belief may be based on hearsay or on a widely held misconception. They might be associating low quality with your brand's seemingly low price or your firm's humble beginnings. Perhaps they know your company started out fifty years ago as a producer of substandard products, and they assume it is doing the same thing today.

Whatever your prospects' reasons for questioning your brand's quality, you can either convince them that they are wrong or prove to them that a higher-quality product is not required for their purposes. To overcome the perception of low quality, you can rely on product tests and demonstrations, written performance records, and the verifiable firsthand experiences of others. If the prospect is correct in saying that your brand is of lower quality than the other brand, all is not lost. In many instances, particularly in business or manufacturing, the client firm actually prefers to use lower-grade products as raw material.

The Prospect Is Not Familiar with Your Brand . . .

The prospect who has heard nothing or very little about your brand is not likely to want to buy it. People are most comfortable with familiar products and are often hesitant to try new brands on the market. If you are selling a new item, remind your prospects that the newest brands on the market are often the most advanced. They must be advanced in order to gain entry into a market dominated by solidly established firms. If not, they must have other clear advantages.

When presenting to prospects who know nothing about your brand, act on the assumption that no one has ever attempted to familiarize them with it. This complaint is usually easier to overcome than the loyalty or the bad-experience objection. Here, the problem is not that prospects have a reason *not* to want the product, it is that they simply have no reason *to* want it. Begin to educate your prospects early by sending them information in advance of your visits, and continue to familiarize them with your brand during the early stages of your visits.

The Prospect Has Had Problems with Your Brand

If prospects have had problems with your brand, your task is to assure them that unpleasant experiences will not happen again. Update them on improvements that have been made since they last used it. If the model they used has been discontinued, let them know that the problems associated with it no longer exist.

Prospects who have experienced problems with your product are likely to be very much concerned with service. Explain your guarantee and extended service contract in detail. Most important, assure the prospect that support and assistance are but a phone call away, that you will be available whenever you are needed, and that you do not disappear once the sale has been made.

> Those who enjoy responsibility usually get it; those who merely like exercising authority usually lose it.
>
> Malcolm Forbes

The Prospect Knows Someone Who Has Had Problems with Your Brand . . .

When prospects say they know someone who has had problems with your product or who is displeased with it, you should insist on meeting with this person to help resolve the problem. Not only does this show prospects that you are concerned about all of your company's past and present customers, it also helps you determine the true source of their objection. If they refuse to give you the friend's name, chances are they have another objection. If the prospect gives you the friend's name, then you have two opportunities: one is to satisfy the disappointed customer; the other is to build your prospect's confidence in you.

Rebecca Smith

Actually, Rebecca Smith had no intention of going into sales when she started her college career at Shasta Community College. She was originally a psychology major, but happened to take a sales course as an elective, and admits she was ready to drop the class after she learned the first day that she had to give a live presentation. She conquered her early fears of being "on camera" and impressed her professor with her well-thought-out, well-delivered selling effort. Rebecca quickly learned that she liked people better than psychology, and although she regrets leaving college, began her career in sales.

This active Californian first joined Holiday Inn, and after a stint at the front desk was recognized by the sales manager for her winning ways with people. She excelled when put in charge of promoting the firm's Priority Club memberships, earning plaudits from the company and bonuses for herself. Rebecca's good work for this hospitality giant was soon noticed by the Red Lion motel chain and she was lured away. Now in her seventh year with this local establishment, she herself is in charge of training others as Sales Manager.

Rebecca stresses product knowledge above all else in preparing sales people for the hospitality business. Whether talking to a prospective bride or a major corporation, you must know what your facility can and cannot do to satisfy the needs of the customer. Knowing what the customer needs then allows the seller to adapt the product features to maximize the benefit to the buyer. Although she is happy in her present position and plans to remain with Red Lion, Rebecca still entertains the continuation of her education by taking evening courses at Shasta.

The Product Model Objection . . .

Even when prospects are receptive to your brand, they may offer another kind of product objection, the **product model objection**. They might object to the unit or style you are recommending because they prefer another or because they aren't sure it will meet their needs. In some cases, this may mean you will have to convince them that the model they want isn't suitable for them. For example, a single prospect of modest means has fallen in love with a large sedan. Even if the prospect seems determined to buy the full-sized car, you must point out the disadvantages of owning it, such as the unnecessary interior room, the higher fueling expenses, and the larger monthly payments. If you don't create the desire for a smaller, more economical car, the prospect will eventually blame you for an unwise purchase.

Sometimes prospects seem to want the least expensive, lowest-quality model even though they can and should purchase a better one. In this case, you should point out the sacrifices they will make if they choose the smaller purchase: "Mr. Peck, are you prepared to sacrifice the superior performance and multiple uses that come with the better model, considering how many years you will own this product? The higher-priced model is the better buy for your needs, and it will actually prove to be less expensive in the long run." This approach is especially effective when the dominant buying motive is performance even though the prospect is also very cost conscious.

THE PRICE OBJECTION . . .

The **price objection** is one raised against any financial aspect of the sale. In addition to the list price of the product, this resistance may relate to terms of the sale, delivery costs, finance charges, or payment plans. When comparable products are available at lower prices, this type of objection can be extremely difficult to combat.

As a successful salesperson, you should be able to stand behind your product's price. Always remember the mutuality of your business transactions. You benefit by making the sale, and the prospect benefits by making the purchase. Because of this mutual benefit, there should be no need for a shy or apologetic price quote. After you state your price, remain silent and wait for the prospect's reply. Do not attempt to explain or compensate for your price. Let the prospect decide whether it is fair.

If customers frequently comment that your price is high, you might lessen the impact (again, without apology) by stating it in terms of the "package." For example, say that your stated total includes free installation, a three-year warranty, and the prospect's choice of two product options. By telling prospects what they are getting in addition to the product itself, you minimize the likelihood that your price will be challenged.

A good response to prospects who object to your price is to ask them why they think it is too high. Their reply will help you by telling you the true nature of their objection. If they can't give a clear reason for thinking the price is too high, they may have a hidden objection, or their reply may reveal that they are unaware of market trends or your product's benefits. Many first-time buyers of major products have no idea what the items cost. If you sell a sophisticated home-security system that sells at a competitive price and your prospect objects, you might be dealing with a first-time buyer. The potential buyer may never have considered the price in relation to the benefits to be derived from such a system. If the prospect's house has never been burglarized, thought may never have been given to what a home-security system would be worth.

Prospects have two basic reasons for raising the price objection: (1) they think they can't afford the product, or (2) they think the product isn't worth the price.

The Prospect "Can't Afford" the Product . . .

By definition, true prospects *can* afford the product. The problem is they may not realize they can afford it. They may want your product very much, but for some reason may think they don't have the ability to pay for it. The "can't afford it" objection often comes as a response to the list price of your product, which as a lump sum may sound quite large. But there are several ways to overcome this resistance. You can break the price down into smaller units, describe how the product will save or make money for the prospect, or explore financing alternatives.

Breaking the Price Down

When the selling price makes your product seem unaffordable, break it down into smaller units to show its economy. There is no limit to the number of ways a price can be broken down. Units can be days, trips, ounces, persons, miles, gallons, yards, square feet, and so on. Breaking the price down makes a high absolute price seem more acceptable. For example, instead of quoting $140,000 as the price of a new 2,000-square-foot home, say construction will cost $70 per square foot.

This technique is especially handy when your total price is greater than the competition's price but your unit price is smaller. By breaking your price down into units, you can prove to the prospect that your brand is actually cheaper. For instance, suppose customers object to paying $1,000 for your product when they can buy a competitor's product for $500. You should point out to them that the competitor delivers only 100 units, which means their product costs $5 per unit, whereas you deliver 500 units, which means your product costs only $2 per unit.

Another way to break the price down is in terms of the product's life. Suppose your product costs $300 and is guaranteed to serve the customer for three years, or 1,095 days. That amounts to an investment of less than 28 cents a day, less than the cost of a candy bar. Your prospects may think they can't afford $300, but will realize they can certainly afford 28 cents a day.

The price breakdown is also useful when prospects think they will be unable to meet large monthly payments. If the payment is $90 a month, ask them if they think they can trim their current expenditures by $3 a day. When they say yes, assure them that they will be able to make the payments because they amount to only $3 a day.

Describing the Product as a Money-Maker or Money-Saver

Often when prospects say they can't afford the product, they are not thinking of what the product gives back. You might effectively wonder out loud how they can afford *not* to own it. When they ask what you mean, go on to explain the many ways in which your product will pay for itself. Calculate the savings they will realize by way of reduced personnel hours, utility bills, fuel costs, or maintenance. Add up the increased productivity that will be theirs thanks to a more efficient system. Figure out how quickly the product will pay for itself. In specific ways, you can prove that your product will save money and even make money for your prospect, thus more than offsetting the purchase price.

Financing Alternatives

Sometimes, reassuring customers about your product's affordability means coming up with a payment arrangement with which they can be comfortable. Your first recourse is to discuss your firm's usual payment plans. Perhaps you have a flexible monthly system, a low down payment, or an extended payment program. Another alternative is to personalize the arrangements: Ask prospects what they think they can afford, and, to the extent that you know their financial situation, suggest ways to fit the additional amount into their budget. Yet another alternative is to arrange special financing.

Other alternatives might be guiding the prospect to a less expensive model or suggesting a lease or lease-purchase agreement. If you suggest leasing, be sure to mention the advantages of the accompanying maintenance agreement. If you discover that the person is correct in saying that your product is unaffordable, you were incorrect in qualifying this person as a prospect, and you should cease your selling effort.

The Product Is "Not Worth" the Price . . .

Sometimes prospects object to the price of your product not because they literally can't afford it but because they don't think it is worth the price. They mean that they are unwilling to sacrifice other items in their budget in order to buy it. They fail to see the **value** of your product, so they refuse to make room in their plans for it.

To overcome the "not worth it" objection, you have to convince prospects that your product will be valuable to them. Here are some ways to convince reluctant buyers:

1. Increase the product's perceived value.
2. Point out hidden qualities.
3. Point out savings or profits.
4. Justify the price difference between your product and a competitor's product.
5. Make a direct price comparison between your product and higher-priced competitors.
6. Make the prospect aware of current market conditions.

Increase the Product's Perceived Value

Prospects who know a product's price often perform a value assessment in their mind. They divide usefulness by price to obtain a **perceived value**. The greater a product's usefulness, the greater its value. Of course, this computation is entirely subjective. Usefulness is not a quality that can be measured numerically.

You can increaase your product's value by either decreasing its price or increasing its usefulness. The following formula illustrates this point:

$$\text{Value} = \frac{\text{usefulness}}{\text{price}}$$

To heighten your product's perceived value, you should either lower the price or increase its usefulness. For many salespeople, increasing usefulness is the only alternative since they have little authority over the prices of their products. To increase your product's usefulness, you can explain its many purposes and applications, including those your prospect may not have considered. Explain the ways it will save time, money, and frustration, and make issue of the product's dependability.

Point Out Hidden Qualities

Some or even most of your product's qualities may not be apparent to the prospect. For example, a $300 jacket might seem to be no better than a jacket that costs $150, but you happen to know that the materials and workmanship more than justify the price. Your task is to point out these unnoticed attributes.

Regardless of how well established your product's unseen qualities are, you should never assume the prospect knows about them. Potential buyers should never be embarrassed because they didn't recognize what you believe is an obvious fact. One way to inform them tactfully is to say that the qualities you are pointing out are the result of recent improvements.

Point Out Savings or Profits

There is no better response to the money-conscious customer than one that promises savings or profits. If the prospect's main concern is the money needed to purchase the product, you should talk about the amount to be saved or earned by using it. Many times the best-selling products on the market are the highest priced. This is because they save or earn more money for their users than do their lower-priced competitors. Saving and making money are major motives for purchasing such products.

The most difficult aspect of this tactic is persuading the prospect to take the long view. Prospects may objectively understand your reasoning, but short-term thinking might still prevail. They may allow the high purchase price of your product to outweigh the savings or profits you promise. You might have to help them realize how short a year or even a five-year period actually is. Even a seemingly modest savings or profit can add up to significant figures over time. For example, a new oil burner might save prospects only a few dollars a week in fuel costs, but over a period of months or years it will save them

Increase revenues by:

1. adding quality

2. improving efficiency

3. reducing defects

4. building volume

5. being more flexible to customer needs

6. improving image

Decrease costs by:

1. reducing equipment needed

2. eliminating downtime

3. minimizing maintenance or service

4. reducing labor

5. creating less overhead

6. using space more efficiently

7. demonstrating more effective and cost-efficient use of marketing

Figure 11-1 Improving Value.

more than they paid for it. See Figure 11-1 for ways in which a product may increase the prospect's revenues or decrease costs.

A curiosity tactic may be in order: Start by telling prospects that your product costs nothing. Then show them how it gradually recovers its initial price through greater profits and reduced expenses, until finally the product is free.

Justify the Price Difference

Sometimes prospects make a price objection that sounds like a product objection: They say they can buy a competing product for $200 less than yours. Although they are comparing your product unfavorably with the competition, their objection is not to your product but to paying more for it than they think they have to. Your job is to justify the higher price by proving your product is superior.

When prospects seem to be sold on the competitor's product, you need not justify your entire selling price, just the difference. They have already accepted most of the price, and they are ready to pay it to the competitor. You must make them see that your product, even at its higher price, is a better buy than your rival's. When your product is the most expensive on the market, stress the advantages that are exclusive to it. Justify its greater cost by making the amount above its next-highest competitor seem small in relation to the difference in quality.

Whenever you are called upon to justify price, base your justification on the quality of your product, not on the costs associated with producing and selling it. There are several reasons not to discuss your costs with the prospect:

1. The product may have qualities that cannot be measured in terms of costs; they may not even require monetary costs to create. These qualities are real and must be reflected in the price of your product, yet you may have no way of justifying them to your prospect.

2. Prospects are concerned only with the value of the product to them, not with the costs your firm incurs in producing and marketing it. The prospect's own perception of the product's want-satisfying ability is what counts.

3. The costs may seem too small to justify your price. If you arrive at a figure far short of the product's selling price, you will only open yourself up to a debate with the prospect over reasonable profit margins.

Remember, too, that when prospects mention a competitor's price quote, you should ask them for the particulars. Make sure that the same basic product or package is being compared to yours. Often, firms quote seemingly low prices that do not account for items you have included in your price. Perhaps your quote includes charges for features, accessories, or labor hours that are not in the competitor's price. Your charges may include delivery and a lifetime warranty, whereas the rival's does not. The competitor's price may be based on a certain volume to be purchased, and thus includes a quantity discount, whereas the price you quote may be based on a quantity too small to call for a discount.

Make a Price Comparison

Although initiating a direct comparison with a competitor's price is usually inadvisable, there are times when such a contrast may be called for. If you sell the least expensive product on the market but your prospect thinks it is very expensive, you should have documentation to prove your price is low. You might also consider comparing the product's price with that of the other sizes or models you sell. This will help the prospect put the price into clearer perspective.

Make the Prospect Aware of Market Conditions

Sometimes when prospects object to your price, they reveal their ignorance of current market conditions. You need to apprise them of present-day reality without making them feel foolish or outdated. A tactful way to educate them would be to make them feel that they are not alone: "A lot of people are surprised to hear of the recent escalations in the market," or "It's easy to understand why you might think that."

Adjust the Price

Some salespeople have the authority to adjust the product's selling price. If your company grants you this freedom, use it carefully. Do not lower your price without having good reason or receiving a concession in return. If you fail to justify your price concessions, not only will your asking price seem artificial, you will lose your bargaining position with future prospects. Your asking price will be considered fully negotiable. In addition, you open the door to complaints from customers who were not offered the same consideration. By asking for something in return for your lower price, you show that you do not make price reductions automatically or for everyone.

You might offer a special discount if the prospect is willing to purchase a certain quantity or agrees to close the sale by the end of the month. When potential buyers say they can get the product cheaper elsewhere, they will probably want you to beat the other price, not just meet it. "By how much do you expect me to adjust my price?" you might ask. If the prospect's figure is acceptable, ask, "If I meet that figure, will you give me a five-year contract on all of your service business?"

Sometimes price reductions are necessary, especially in highly competitive situations. Lowering your price need not be a distasteful experience. Some legitimate reasons for cuts include minor defects or soiled condition, new model due out, no delivery, or financing needed. For more information on this topic see "Price Negotiations" toward the end of this chapter.

When the Price Objection Is Hidden

If you suspect that price is a problem but your prospects won't tell you, ask them if they know the details of your fabulous credit plan. You might mention leasing or show them a low-frills model, suggesting that it might better suit their needs. Or you can say, "I have a few good used pieces that have features you may prefer," or "I still have last year's model in stock. Let's compare the two." This relieves prospects of the need to make up excuses on why they aren't interested in the better model and might save them the embarrassment of admitting their finances are strained.

THE SALESPERSON OBJECTION . . .

The **salesperson objection** is a reluctance to doing business with you, the salesperson. Of the six types of objections found in Figure 11-2, the salesperson objection is the most likely to be kept hidden. Prospects are usually willing to tell you that they don't need the product, don't like the price, or don't think now is the time to buy, but are very reluctant to say they don't like you or doubt your abilities. Many times, only your own intuition tells you a salesperson objection exists. If your prospect has such reluctance, you need to decide on its most likely reason and choose the appropriate strategy to overcome it. Prospects can object to you for several reasons:

1. They dislike you or sense a personality clash.
2. They consider you incapable of determining and meeting their needs or of handling their account.
3. They distrust salespeople in general.

Need objection

"We're satisfied with the way things are now."

"This model might be old, but there's still plenty of life left in it."

"I don't buy products I know nothing about."

Product objection

"No offense, but you sell the worst quality brand on the market."

"I bought a push-button model just like yours several years ago. I'll never do it again."

"I'll stick with the Woodlawn brand. As far as I'm concerned, it's tried and true."

Price objection

"At that price, you must think I'm made of money."

"This year's budget is so tight it squeaks. There's simply no room for another piece of capital equipment."

"Why should I buy your product when the Franklin brand is priced $200 less?"

Source objection

"After the way your firm treated my friend Mary, you're lucky I'm even talking to you."

"A firm located 40 miles away can't possibly meet our service needs. Sorry, but I'll buy locally."

"Come back once your company has made a name for itself."

Salesperson objection

"Aren't you a little young to be leasing commercial real estate?"

"Salespeople like you have ripped me off one time too many in the past."

"Now I've seen it all — a woman selling farm equipment."

Time objection

"Every market indicator points to falling prices. I'll wait until prices drop."

"Let me sleep on it."

"It's only March. Aren't you rushing the season a little?"

Figure 11-2 Types of objections.

The Personality Clash . . .

Prospects who sense a personality clash are not likely to want you handling their account, even if they consider you capable of doing so. One fact of selling never changes—prospects buy from salespeople they like and can get along with.

Personality clashes should not be a problem for you. You should be able to get along with all of your prospects, giving them no reason to dislike you. The seller who has recurring personality clashes with prospects does not belong in selling. A good salesperson is modest, compassionate, friendly, and courteous, and is capable of adjusting to the personality of the prospect. Most important, a good seller must like people. If you like people, they will like you.

If you do have a rare personality clash with a prospect, you should ask another salesperson in your company to switch accounts with you. For the sake of future dealings, you should also try to determine the reason for the conflict. Perhaps you said something tactless or took something too lightly. Your mannerisms might have been inappropriate or your behavior overbearing. Regardless of the reason, a conflict with a prospect should be a learning experience. By determining the reason for the hostility, you may be able to prevent such a conflict from happening again.

The Prospect Considers You Incapable . . .

Prospects may consider you incapable of determining their needs, and their reasons for this objection may be hard for you to accept. Commonly, this rejection is raised on the basis of something you can't change, such as your age or gender.

Recall from Chapter 1 that women are filling selling positions that have been traditionally occupied by men. Women might encounter the salesperson objection when selling products that have been stereotyped as masculine products, such as automobiles or machinery. These salespeople may have to prove their abilities to skeptical prospects. If you are a woman selling a product traditionally sold by or to men, expect and be ready to encounter a problem with some prospects. Do not have reservations about overcoming skepticism regarding your abilities and knowledge.

The age issue might arise when your prospects are noticeably older than you, especially if they have many years of experience in their industry. Such veterans may think that you are so young you couldn't possibly have the expertise needed to serve their account. They might assume a young salesperson lacks the wisdom to properly assess their needs and to exercise sound judgment. The objection can be even stronger when prospects are not certain what is best for them. This will make them especially uncomfortable about trusting a young salesperson's knowledge or expertise.

> You always pass failure on the way to success.
>
> Mickey Rooney

There are several ways to deal with a suggestion that you are incapable of meeting the prospect's needs:

1. Provide the prospect with the names of others who at first thought you were inexperienced and then found you to be capable.
2. Explain your schooling or training, which may be more up to date than that of your older counterparts.
3. Refer to your record of sales successes during your admittedly short career.

The optimism and enthusiasm of young people, or those new to a profession, are great personal assets. You must make the prospect realize that your youth, gender, or comparative inexperience is not a problem, and that you are every bit as qualified as your older, opposite-sex, or more experienced counterparts.

You should never apologize for your age, whether you are younger or older than the prospect. All salespeople have unique characteristics associated with their age. Older salespeople have the experience gained over a long career and a sense of worldly wisdom. Younger salespeople have the zeal of youth, the compelling need to establish themselves, and training in the latest technology. Neither should try to be something they are not.

The Prospect Distrusts Salespeople . . .

You will recall from Chapter 1 that salespeople are sometimes haunted by the poor image that has been associated with their occupation. Some prospects simply don't trust anyone in sales. In fact, general doubt of salespeople is the most common and most basic reason for the salesperson objection. This suspicion prevents the seller from meeting the prospect's needs. How can you meet a need you cannot identify? And how can you identify the prospect's needs if they will not open up to you because of their distrust of salespeople?

When you encounter distrustful prospects, you should remind them that the majority of salespeople are honest and want to satisfy their customers' needs to the best of their abilities. If they tell you they distrust salespeople because of a few bad experiences, you can point out that every profession is harmed by a small minority of people who, luckily, don't represent the whole group.

THE SOURCE OBJECTION . . .

The **source objection** is a disapproval toward the salesperson's company. A negative attitude toward your firm will affect the prospect's reaction to you and your presentation from the start. If the prospect objects to your company for any reason, these negative feelings create skepticism toward you and your intentions.

Prospects who have the source objection will rarely keep their feelings hidden. In fact, they may be quite vocal.

The source objection usually occurs for one of the following reasons:

1. The prospect or someone known by the prospect has had unpleasant past dealings with your company.
2. The prospect dislikes your company's image or reputation.
3. The prospect has not heard of your company.
4. The prospect feels your company is too new, too small, or located too far away.

Past Dealings . . .

When the prospect objects to your firm on the basis of bad past dealings, you will be responsible for amending events you may not have been involved in. But amend you must because bad past dealings, whether they involved the prospect or someone the prospect knows, will stand in the way of your relationship as long as they are left unresolved.

Prospects may bear ill will toward your company because they feel the firm never made good on a promise to correct a problem with a purchase they made. Perhaps a delivery was two months late or the product proved to be faulty and the company did not repair or replace it.

To assure that your prospects will not continue to feel mistreated by your company, you must convince them that what happened before will not happen again. You should place your personal guarantee behind any future dealings the prospect has with your firm. For example, if the past problem involved a late delivery, you should personally monitor any new shipment to make sure delivery is on time. If prospects have had an unpleasant experience with someone else in your firm, assure them that they will be dealing with you and no one else. If they felt their complaint was dismissed by uncaring employees or got tied up in red tape, prove to them that they will be communicating with an individual who cares about them and who is only a phone call away. If the past problem was one the prospect didn't report, make sure that your firm will stand behind its products even after a delay.

Image or Reputation . . .

An objection to your firm's image is a formidable challenge. If you work for a known firm, its reputation will precede you, and new prospects will know, or think they know, all about your company before you can even say hello to them. The salesperson whose firm is suffering image problems is likely to meet frequently with prospects whose minds are strongly unsympathetic.

Of course, since reputation is such a public thing, you should not be taken by surprise when the image objection comes up. If your firm has been the subject of unpleasant news reports or has received irate letters or phone calls because of its practices, you should be prepared to deal with negative reactions from prospects. Don't be caught speechless when your prospect says your company is destroying an agricultural district or exploiting laborers in undeveloped countries. Don't let your prospect be the first to tell you that your company is involved in a patent fight or that your board is paralyzed by in-fighting. You have the responsibility of keeping abreast of the news relating to your business so that you can answer objections and get on with your business.

Arguing with the prospect about challenges to your company's image is not advisable, nor is reacting defensively. Your best recourse is first to discover exactly what the prospect thinks. Often, people make vague or emotional remarks on the basis of limited knowledge. Ask prospects what they have heard and where they heard it. If they have heard only casual conversation, you will have the opportunity to fill them in on details they don't have. If they have followed the news, they may be better informed, but they still may have a distorted picture of the reality.

If what the prospect has heard is true, explain the steps your firm is taking to correct its past mistakes or problems. Inform the prospect of the positive contributions your firm has made for the benefit of consumers and society.

The Unknown Company . . .

The objection "I've never heard of your company" will be especially frequent if you sell for a new firm or one that keeps a low profile. People prefer to do business with familiar sources, so you should acquaint prospects with your firm before calling on them. Chapters 6 and 7 covered the need to send out information in advance of your sales call and to build the prospect's confidence in your firm. The techniques of advance information and confidence building should be combined to help overcome the unknown-source objection before the prospect has a chance to raise it.

If you frequently hear the unknown-source objection, ask yourself these two questions:

1. Why haven't prospects heard of my firm?
2. What do prospects want to know about my firm?

If your company purposely maintains a low profile, you will not be able to rely on advertising or other source-generated publicity. Instead, you should introduce yourself and your firm to prospects with a series of mailings before your first visit. By mailing information before calling, you will be almost certain to avoid the unknown-source objection.

Several small mailings are better than one large mailing for two reasons. First, several mailings give prospects multiple exposures to your firm's name; second, prospects may not read a single mailing, either because they missed it or because it appeared too long and time consuming.

> Life is now in session. Are you present?
>
> B. Copeland

The Company Is New, Small, or Far Away . . .

Sometimes prospects have no problem with your firm's dealings, image, or lack of exposure, but still object because they think it is too new, small, or far away to meet their needs. If prospects think your firm is too new to have established itself or accumulated sufficient experience, you must convince them that your company is made up of people who are established and experienced. Describe the knowledge and expertise of those who operate your company in terms that get the message across.

Your firm may be only two years old, but the six founders bring more than one hundred years of experience to the enterprise. Mention the phenomenal growth your firm has enjoyed. And, of course, point out that as a new company, your efforts to gain a foothold in the market are reflected in your prices, your service, and the quality of your products.

If the prospect says your company is too small, point out the advantages of smallness: Your firm is able to provide friendly, personal, and prompt service as no larger firm can. Because it has a select group of clients, it can develop a rapport with customers. You can prove your point by naming a few of your clients (assuming your client list is not confidential and the clients don't mind being named) who are in businesses about the size of your prospect's business.

If prospects say your firm is based too far away, you must assure them that you have daily contact with headquarters and will act as liaison to see that their needs are attended to without delay.

THE TIME OBJECTION . . .

The **time objection** is a reluctance to buying now rather than later. There are many different words a prospect might use to pose the time objection. Figure 11-3 gives examples of procrastinating statements, commonly referred to as stalls.

> "Give me some time to think about it."
>
> "See me again in the spring."
>
> "Stop by the next time you're in town."
>
> "Let me ask my husband what he thinks."
>
> "I want to look around some more first."
>
> "I'll see what my partner thinks of the idea."
>
> "Call me back in several days."
>
> "I'll discuss your proposal at our department meeting Monday morning."
>
> "This rainy weather has me behind in my work. I'll call you when I get things straightened out."

Figure 11-3 Stalls.

Although some time objections are legitimate, many are excuses used to cover up the prospect's dissatisfaction with some other aspect of the sale. For many potential buyers, procrastinating is the easiest way to say no. But if you have been sought out by the prospect, you can assume that she or he would act today if the right opportunity came along. Even if the time objection is sincere, you may be able to overcome it with the right technique.

The time objection can be very frustrating, especially if your prospect listens to an entire sales presentation before deciding to procrastinate. If you don't know how to overcome the time objection, you will lose many a sale to competitors who might be skilled in dealing with procrastinating prospects. Here are some ways to overcome the time objection:

1. Put a hook in the close.
2. Describe the disadvantages of waiting.
3. Report impending changes.
4. Give "standing room only" notice.

A Hook in the Close . . .

A **hook** is an incentive. To overcome the time objection with a hook, you offer prospects something special in exchange for acting swiftly. Let them know that the incentive will not be available if they wait until later. Give them a specific cutoff date.

Of course, your incentive must be truly enticing in order to work. Justifying the hook in some way also adds to its credibility. For example, you might tell the prospect that a 10 percent discount is in effect for the next ten days. Go on to explain that your company is grouping orders so that it can produce a larger quantity at less expense than a smaller quantity.

Another effective hook is the premium or gift. This, too, is a justifiable incentive. Since an early close eliminates the need for future sales calls, the time and travel expense you save will compensate for the cost of the premium. Remember that the time limit you place on your hook must be firm. If prospects think your discount or premium is always in effect or is sure to return, they will see no need to act quickly.

The Disadvantages of Waiting . . .

The disadvantages of waiting are not unlike those of failing to replace an older product. In general, they fall into two categories: (1) the sacrifice of benefits and (2) the costs, both monetary and nonmonetary. As a well-versed salesperson, you know the benefits of your product and should have no trouble describing the sacrifice your prospects make in deferring their purchase.

There are many ways to present the monetary costs of waiting. For example, if your product is a money-maker or money-saver, you can point out how much your prospect loses by not owning it. This also works for the product whose price is constantly rising. Suppose you sell condominiums. Your prospect wants to defer buying a $90,000 unit in a complex where prices climb 15 percent a year. In one year, you can say, the condo will cost $103,500; this means the cost of waiting has amounted to $13,500 in twelve months, or $260 a week!

Like monetary costs, the nonmonetary costs of waiting are real, and can be made clear to the prospect. For example, if the owner of an office building plans to wait a year before replacing a leaky roof, you should be able to think of several nonmonetary costs associated with this procrastination. Water damage poses the threat of more than mere frustration. There is also the chance that someone could slip and fall on a floor exposed to the roof or create an electrical fire that could be disastrous. Just as there are disadvantages to waiting, there are benefits to acting immediately—in this case, peace of mind.

Impending Events . . .

Sometimes the prospect's time objection is based on conditions that can change, such as the economy or your company's business practices. If this is the case, you may be able to overcome the objection by reporting **impending events**. Changes that relate directly to your product, such as price hikes or model modifications, are especially effective.

Price Increases

Because it has become a way of life, inflation is an ally of the salesperson. Prospects expect price increases, and they will not be surprised when you report any that are planned. A higher price next month is a strong incentive to buy today. The same goes for predicted or announced increases in carrying charges or other financial aspects of the sales transaction. For many prospects, the thought of a price increase will be more than enough to move them out of procrastination and into a purchase.

Model Changes

Like inflation, model changes are an expected reality of consumer life. If your prospects like the design or features of the present model, the mention of an impending model change may be enough to make them act immediately. They will also want to act if they expect any legal changes relating to purchases made by a certain date.

Standing Room Only

Standing room only means your product is in limited or dwindling supply, and that before long there will be nothing left to buy. Whenever you use this technique, you should describe not only the number of sales you are making but also the interest shown by people who are seriously considering the purchase. The standing-room-only approach appeals to a person's need to avoid being left out of something in which others are included. Of course, you must use it in complete truth.

A housing development is an excellent candidate for the standing-room-only approach. You might tell your prospect that two weeks ago you had twenty lots to sell, and now you have only five lots remaining. You sold eight lots in the past three days, and you expect calls tomorrow from several interested parties. If the prospect has even the slightest interest in owning one of these lots, there is a need to act quickly or forget about living in the development.

This method is also effective for seasonal products. As an air-conditioning salesperson, you might mention that winter is the best time to get immediate installation. If your prospects delay their purchase until spring, they may wind up on a waiting list throughout a long, hot summer. A representative for a certified public accounting firm can tell procrastinating clients that five people have attempted to contract with the firm in two days, and it's not even tax time. The firm can take on only so many new accounts, and will not take any after the new year begins. The person selling an alumni directory can tell grads that the publisher will print only as many directories as are ordered. It's a one-time offer, and there won't be extra copies to wait for.

The Sincere Time Objection . . .

Not all time objections are excuses to be overcome. Many are sincere and cannot be conquered by the techniques described in this section. Often, prospects pose the time objection because of real factors that influence or limit their purchase decisions. For example, an office manager may not want to make a purchase without first discussing the product with the office employees since they will be the ones using it. You can quickly determine if this reason is sincere by offering to demonstrate the product to the employees and answer their questions. If the manager quickly gives you another reason for deferring the purchase, you need to discover the prospect's hidden objection.

Another sincere objection may be raised by a retailer who doesn't want to stock your product because of the time of year. Perhaps you can describe the experiences of other retailers who felt the same way but decided to try stocking the product and were rewarded with surprisingly healthy sales.

Never push a prospect who has a sincere time objection. The business prospect may have to discuss all purchase decisions with someone else in the organization. Married couples usually discuss major purchases with each other before deciding to buy, and newlyweds may consult each other over even minor purchases.

If the decision to defer the purchase is handed down to the prospect from someone higher up in the organization, you must accept the fact that you are unable to make the sale at the present time. When prospects tell you their firm intends to postpone its purchase for a year, make sure they don't forget you. Make periodic visits or telephone calls to keep your name in their mind and to keep yourself informed on where the company stands regarding your product.

PRICE NEGOTIATIONS . . .

Price flexibility prevails in many industries, and the prices of many products such as raw materials are openly and competitively bargained. Some firms have the policy of meeting any verifiable quoted price that is lower than theirs. Although salespeople generally have no control over their product's price, some are authorized to meet a competitor's quote. A large prospect who exerts considerable influence in the market is likely to expect salespeople to negotiate their terms. Because selling in such an atmosphere tends to involve sophisticated **price negotiations**, a good salesperson must be a good negotiator.

Your negotiating skills will have a direct impact on your firm's profits. The stronger your skills, the healthier the firm's immediate profits will be. But the need for immediate profits must be balanced against the need for healthy relationships with your customers. As a negotiator, you must find ways to develop relationships that are both long term and profitable.

Price negotiations will come into play whenever your prospect wishes to haggle over the list price, delivery fees, service contracts, credit terms, deposits, or finance charges. Further, price negotiations will be affected by nonfinancial aspects of the prospect's order. For example, if potential buyers have to wait longer than they might like for delivery, they may want you to remove the delivery charge or lower their deposit. If they wanted the plain model and you have only the fancy model in stock, they will not want to pay the higher price.

Working with the Prospect . . .

The first step in negotiation is preparation. As Victor Kiam said, "Information is a negotiator's greatest weapon." To negotiate successfully, therefore, you should prepare yourself with information. Strong product knowledge and familiarity with your prospect are indispensable. You must be able to judge what concessions prospects will make and what their limits are.

Next, you and the prospect should agree on the matters to be resolved. Listen carefully and express yourself clearly from the outset to make sure you understand each other and avoid confusion. Then the two of you should discuss multiple options for resolving the sales transaction. Since the goal is for both parties to agree on a solution, you should work together. Don't just suggest options, solicit them from the prospect. If competition is an influential factor, try to develop solutions that are better than the competitors' terms.

Any number of solutions may come to mind, depending on the situation. If you can't lower your selling price, you might be able to offer longer credit terms. In another situation, the prospect might offer you a five-year contract in exchange for a 10 percent price reduction. You in turn might say that you can offer the discount only if the order size is increased. In yet another situation, you might want to ask the prospect what a fair price would be. "Would it be fair for me to earn 10 percent over cost?" you could ask. By using a percentage rather than a dollar figure, you help the prospect focus on the fairness of your markup.

When you finally quote a price, be firm. Don't reveal how anxious you are to make the sale. If the price is lower than you would normally quote, try to close then and there. For example, say, "If I can shave 4 percent off of the list price, can we sign the contract today?"

If you fail to close upon making a price adjustment, you leave the door open for the prospect to "nibble." **Nibbling** is when a buyer plays on the momentary euphoria you feel over making the sale by asking for an additional and sometimes costly concession. Skilled buyers are usually excellent nibblers and can make their gain your significant loss. Suppose you sell for a tree nursery and have just negotiated the sale of 150 *Pyramidal Arborvida*. Your excitement over this big sale is obvious, and suddenly the buyer says, "Now that we've gone this far, how about throwing in ten Canadian hemlock trees?" Think first! A buyer's nibble can take a big bite out of your profits.

Trade-Ins . . .

Trade-ins pose their own unique considerations when it comes time to negotiate. Before quoting an allowance for your prospect's trade-in, you should lay the groundwork for discussion. First, during the presentation, you must build the prospect's desire for the model you are selling. Second, you must quote the product's base price.

Some prospects will want you to tell them at the outset what their trade-in allowance will be. But if the figure isn't to their liking, they will end the dis-

You Decide!

After working for several years for an office machinery marketer, Suzanne was offered a selling position with a computer manufacturer, which she quickly accepted. Although relatively small in size, her firm was noted for being an industry leader in developing innovative technology. The company has found a niche market in selling its computers to the medical industry, mostly to hospitals and large clinics. Suzanne enjoys calling on doctors and is proud of the fact that she has quickly picked up the medical jargon common to her industry.

At a recent sales meeting, Suzanne learns that the company is about to make a breakthrough. This new technology will enable medical laboratories to process blood samples four times faster than presently possible. Although the advanced equipment is fully tested and proven, it will not be available for another six months. In the meantime, Suzanne has a major facility, on which she has been working for almost a year, on the verge of committing to the old, soon to be outdated, computer system. Should she tell her prospect of the pending breakthrough, or take the order for the present equipment in hopes of switching the client later? **You decide!**

Chapter 11 • The Nature of Resistance

cussion. This puts you in an awkward position: If you quote a trade-in allowance before building your prospect's desire for the new product, your presentation may end before it starts. You should tell prospects that an allowance can't be quoted until you know which model they will be purchasing or which options they will be selecting. By building desire for the product first, you have a chance to overcome the prospect's disappointment in the trade-in allowance.

When you finally quote a trade-in allowance, remember that more than money is involved. Suppose you sell motorcycles. To you, the prospect's used bike is worth only the price at which you can resell it although he or she may have spent countless hours maintaining it. To the prospect, it is exceptionally valuable. Out of respect for these feelings, you should compliment the owner on the care that he or she has taken to keep the motorcycle in excellent condition. Rather than bluntly state its worth on the market, you should resort to objective measures. Show the prospect a standard valuation book or recent newspaper ads listing the selling price of similar motorcycles. You may be able to point out a used model on your lot and mention that your selling price is only slightly more than the allowance you are offering for the trade-in.

GIVING PROSPECTS WHAT THEY WANT . . .

There are times when the only way to overcome your prospects' objections or conclude negotiations is to give them what they want. Perhaps there's a product feature the prospect dislikes or an aspect of the transaction that must be changed. It might be a matter of getting the product in a different color, having its design modified, or altering the payment plan.

You should be as flexible as possible in these instances. The salesperson who insists on following the standard course, perhaps thinking, "If I do something special for this prospect, I'll have to do it for everybody," simply doesn't want to make the sale badly enough. If you are unable to give prospects exactly what they want, emphasize what you *p* do for them. For example, if you can't arrange the payment plan the prospect prefers, offer some other concession. Arrange for a faster method of shipment or move up the delivery date. Making the sale will be easier when prospects know their special needs are important to you.

Whatever the points of contention, successful negotiation entails treating your prospects with respect. Never think of your prospect as an opponent; the object of negotiation is to agree, not to "win" by depriving the other party of something. Be fair, and ask for fairness in return.

Summing It Up . . .

Prospect objections fall into six general categories, each one relating to a specific stage in the buying process. The categories are need, product, price, salesperson, source, and time. To overcome the need objection, point out the disadvantages of the prospect's present situation, perhaps by totaling the costs the prospect incurs by keeping the present product or by reminding the prospect of the problems being experienced with it.

There are two types of product objections, the product brand objection and the product model objection. Prospects who raise the product brand objection believe your brand is low quality. They may have owned or used it once and had difficulties with it. Prospects who raise the product model objection want a lower-priced product or believe that another model would better suit their needs.

Prospects who raise a price objection consider themselves unable to afford the product or believe it is overpriced. You remove the first objection by proving the product's affordability, and you disarm the second by increasing the product's usefulness. You can do this by pointing out the savings the prospect will realize by using it.

No objection is more likely to be kept hidden than the salesperson objection. It is raised by prospects who sense a personality clash or who consider you incapable of meeting their needs, perhaps because of your age or lack of experience. It is also held by prospects who dislike salespeople in general.

The source objection, relating to your firm, is raised by prospects who think they have been treated unfairly or who are unfamiliar with your company. It also arises when the prospect is concerned with your firm's reputation or considers your company to be too new, too small, or located too far away.

To overcome the time objection, which is the prospect's desire to defer the purchase, you pinpoint the disadvantages of waiting. You can do this by totaling the costs the prospect incurs by keeping the present product or by mentioning the likelihood of product shortages or other impending events.

Key Concepts and Terms . . .

hook	price objection
impending events	product brand objection
need objection	product model objection
nibbling	salesperson objection
nonmonetary costs	source objection
out-of-pocket cost	standing room only
perceived value	time objection
price negotiations	value

Building Skills . . .

1. Describe some of the out-of-pocket costs and foregone benefits the prospect incurs by keeping an old computer instead of buying a new, state-of-the-art model.

2. List the reasons a prospect might raise the product objection.

3. Analyze your actions when your prospect refuses to try your skin-care products because a friend developed a rash from them.

4. Compare the methods of overcoming the price objection.

5. Explain the relationship between a product's usefulness and its value.

6. The prospect says your product is too expensive when, in fact, it is the lowest-priced product on the market. Describe your response.

7. Indicate why you should provide justification when you adjust your product's price.

8. List some of the reasons a prospect might object to doing business with your company.

9. The prospects you intend to visit should never be able to say that they haven't heard of your firm. Explain.

10. Explore some of the common reasons for the salesperson objection.

11. Analyze why the salesperson objection is often kept hidden.

12. Describe your response to prospects who say you are too young to be handling their account.

13. Explain four ways to overcome the time objection.

14. Indicate those occasions when time objections are legitimate excuses.

15. Discuss why inflation is your ally in your attempt to overcome procrastination.

Making Decisions 11-1:

Neil Ha is a market representative for Davis Gravity and Power Conveyors. He is calling on Rich Shervais, the plant manager of Lohr Manufacturing.

Neil:	Thank you for seeing me, Mr. Shervais.
Rich:	(Shuffling the papers on his desk) What can I do for you?
Neil:	I've learned of your company's plans to double the size of its warehouse. Are you familiar with Davis Gravity?
Rich:	Yes, I've heard of you.
Neil:	We manufacture equipment designed especially for your type of operation. (Reaching into his carrying case) I have some literature with me.
Rich:	I'm really not interested.
Neil:	May I ask why not?
Rich:	I was at a seminar last week in Manchester, and one of the fellows at our lunch table told us he was having a lot of problems with a conveyor system he bought from you just two years ago. Besides, I'm sold on Kline conveyors. They've been around for a long time, and I've always had good experience with them.

| Neil: | Well, thank you for seeing me. Perhaps we can talk again. |
| Rich: | Perhaps. |

Categorize Rich's objection. Describe how you would have addressed it.

Making Decisions 11-2:

Mary Ware is the owner of Oceanview Marine, an outboard motor dealership. One day in August she is visited by a man who says he is shopping for an outboard motor for a used boat he has just purchased. Mary asks him the size of the boat and his intended uses for it, and then takes him to the shop area of her building. She spends fifteen minutes showing him a 150-horsepower motor.

Shopper:	Cost is important. How much is this?
Mary:	Normally it retails for $12,000, but since we're near the end of the season, I can knock it down a thousand.
Shopper:	That's still more than I wanted to pay. I priced a motor this size at Shoreline Equipment, and it was only $9,500.
Mary:	Yes, but considering the $50,000 investment you've just made in a boat that will give you years of fishing and cruising pleasure, another $11,000 isn't much more. I'll be happy to tell you about our financing plan. It carries no...
Shopper:	That won't be necessary. Whether I pay for it now or pay for it later, I'll still be paying for it.
Mary:	Yes, I suppose that's true.
Shopper:	Let me think it over. I've heard good things about your brand, and I do like the features you've shown me. I'll make my decision and stop back if I'm interested.

Describe how Mary addressed the shopper's price objection. Rewrite the dialogue.

Making Decisions 11-3:

You represent a firm that installs pavement in driveways. What might you say to homeowners who are content with their present gravel driveway?

Making Decisions 11-4:

You are in charge of the Grand Hotel's banquet facility and are visiting a

When you quote your price, she tells you she can arrange a catered banquet in their company cafeteria for $1,500 less. Describe your response.

Making Decisions 11-5:

Comment on how you would handle the following objections.

1. The prospect does not see a need for your product or service, and is happy with the present supplier.
2. The prospect sees no advantage to buying now instead of later.
3. The prospect thinks your firm is too new or too small.

Practice Makes Perfect 11-1:

Plan a sales presentation with another student using a high-tech product. Ask the buyer to create as many objections as possible. Categorize and describe the nature of each obstacle raised.

Chapter 12

Responding to Sales Resistance

THE JOB TO BE DONE . . .

Sales resistance is standard in the field of selling. Learning to recognize the reluctance to buy and being able to successfully counteract it is the mark of a true professional. In Chapter 12 you will gain the skills needed to:

...develop the proper attitude toward prospect objections.

...distinguish between valid and invalid objections.

...distinguish between honest and dishonest objections.

...know how to deal with trivial objections.

...learn how to uncover and handle hidden objections.

...know when to respond to a prospect's objection.

...know how to handle a premature objection.

...know how to forestall a prospect's objection.

...learn five basic methods of removing customer objections.

THE PROPER ATTITUDE . . .

Prospect objections are a fact of the selling life. Almost every prospect you meet, including the ones who call on you, will offer some resistance to buying. The work of overcoming such objections is as common to selling as are prospecting, preapproaching, and presenting. The salesperson who becomes upset or frustrated by objections will never be happy in sales. For the sake of your success and peace of mind, you need to develop a philosophical attitude toward sales resistance. Here are some aspects of the ideal attitude:

1. You accept prospect objections as a normal part of the selling life.
2. You do not fear prospect objections; you see them as a challenge.
3. You are not upset or frustrated when a prospect poses an objection; you look upon the objection as communication.
4. You think of overcoming prospect objections not as an inconvenience or interruption but as a part of your job.

As we mentioned in Chapter 11, the word *no* is convenient. People say it without a thought, and it relieves them of the responsibility of acting. When a future customer says no, remember that you, too, are often a prospect who resists. Potential buyers rarely if ever intentionally offend a salesperson by saying no. An objection simply proves that the prospect fails to recognize a problem or a need for improvement. Resistance to buying is nothing more than an objection to your help.

Seen in this light, an objection is not at all threatening, nor is it a prospect's final decision. Objections raised by true prospects always contain qualifiers. That is, when potential buyers say no, they are really saying, "No, not until I can trust your judgment," or "No, not unless I know that I need the product." The prospect is not saying, "No, never."

Most objections can rightly be attributed to flawed selling techniques, particularly in the areas of information or communication. Either something isn't covered thoroughly or the salesperson fails to clarify a point and the potential buyer misunderstands. For this reason, you should not withdraw your selling effort just because your prospect has objected. Instead, you should assume that you need to improve your selling techniques.

The benefit in making this assumption is that you maintain control of the situation. You take responsibility for your role in creating the misunderstanding rather than shrugging off the objection as caused by some external factor. Since you have the power to control your own behavior, you have the chance to overcome the resistance. Further, by examining your own behavior each time an objection is posed, you continue to work on and improve your selling technique.

FORESTALLING: THE PREPARED SALESPERSON . . .

An excellent technique for dealing with commonly raised objections is **forestalling**. To forestall an objection is to address it before the prospect has a chance to raise it. You become the first to mention the problem by building it into the body of your presentation, along with your response. The prospect never has the need or the chance to raise a forestalled objection.

Of course, to forestall objections, you must know what kinds your prospects are likely to raise. You can anticipate many of them by studying the preapproach information you gather on your prospects. If you can predict objections during your preapproach, you will have ample time to prepare your strategy for overcoming them during your presentation. A forestalled objection can become a part of your custom-designed presentation.

Another way to discover predictable objections is through role-playing your presentation with fellow salespeople or friends who pose as prospects. It should not take long for you to determine what type of resistance to expect in real situations.

The sooner you forestall an objection, the better your chances of making the sale. This is not to say that you should try to nullify every reluctance you think will come up. Forestalling should be used only against the most common and significant objections you hear.

Many objections are fairly common, and they are often raised at predictable times during the sales presentation. If your product is the smallest on the market, for example, you can expect many prospects to object to its size, probably early in the presentation. You should accept this predictable fact and prepare to forestall the size objection.

Some objections can be forestalled even before the actual presentation begins. For example, you can forestall the "unknown firm" objection by sending information on your firm to the prospect in advance of the sales call. If you constantly hear that your product is too small, you can provide at least a temporary forestalling response by carrying a briefcase on which the words "Too small for what?" are stenciled.

The reason you can predict resistance during preapproach is that many objections are linked to demographics and other details you gather at that stage. These include age, income, family size, lifestyle, geographic location, or experience with a similar product. After hearing the same objections on call after call, you will begin to associate certain objections with certain categories of prospect. You might as well learn to expect this reluctance to buy and forestall it.

Suppose you frequently deal with prospects over the age of sixty, prospects who have large families, and prospects who live in heavily populated areas. These three categories of potential buyers might account for a large enough percentage of your sales to justify some careful forestalling efforts. If every prospect over sixty is concerned about the cost of your product, you should forestall the cost objection when you call on prospects over sixty. If every potential buyer who heads a large family seems concerned with your product's capacity, then this objection is the one to nullify. And you should anticipate the safety objection if that issue comes up with every prospect who lives in a heavily populated area.

How to Forestall Objections . . .

When you forestall an objection, inform the prospect that you are aware of its importance. Rather than appear to have stumbled across the reluctance by accident, you want prospects to know that you are covering the subject deliberately because you knew they wanted to discuss it. This shows your concern for prospects and your experience in dealing with the problems they face.

Consider these two examples of forestalling:

1. You know the prospect is concerned with capacity. You are selling a water heater that appears to be too small to suit the prospect's big family. Here is one way to forestall: "Mr. Dawson, this heater looks small. It appears to be incapable of handling your family's daily needs. I want to prove to you that the capacity of this unit exceeds that of most of the larger ones on the market today. And I want to show you why it's today's number-one choice among building contractors for installation in the homes they build."

2. You know the prospect is concerned with safety. You are selling a door that appears to be made of weak material, with a lock that seems small. Here is one way to forestall: "Mrs. Utley, I know that safety is an important concern of yours. You want the safest product you can buy, and when you examine this door, it appears incapable of keeping out intruders. Nevertheless, despite its appearance, safety research associations have determined it to be the safest door on the market. Here, let me show you their findings."

Dishonest objections are no less eligible for forestalling than are honest ones. Consider forestalling the time objection, which is frequently used to hide another concern. Before you begin the presentation, ask the prospect, "If the right opportunity came along today, would you be prepared to act?" If the prospect answers yes to the question, you will have successfully forestalled the time objection. Later in the presentation, the prospect will not be able to use "bad timing" as an objection. Figure 12-1 provides five examples of forestalling.

---

1. "This model's appearance conceals its most unique and significant benefit."

2. "Let me explain why our brand is high-tech plastic instead of wood."

3. "I understand that your present supplier carries this product. Let me explain how ours is different."

4. "Congratulations. I was happy to learn that you now have buying authority for the office products division."

5. (You and the prospect are driving out to see a house that you have listed for sale.) "The location is closer to schools, shopping, and recreation than other new homes in the area."

Figure 12-1 Examples of forestalling.

During the Presentation . . .

Throughout your presentation, ask the prospect if there is a disagreement or something you should clarify. Some salespeople shy away from asking for objections, but prospect reluctance must be dealt with openly. If an objection is not uncovered and addressed early in the presentation, it can have a negative influence on your entire selling effort. By checking with prospects often to determine resistance as you move along, you ensure coverage and clarification of every issue.

EXAMINING OBJECTIONS . . .

In Chapter 11, we discussed how objections are categorized according to the stage in the buying process to which they relate. There is another way to look at these hesitations as well: Not only can objections be categorized, they can also be characterized. When you try to interpret a concern, you should go beyond just determining what type it is. You should examine it more deeply to discover its other revealing traits. Figure 12-2 illustrates eight types of objections that are explained in this chapter.

Valid vs Invalid Objections . . .

Objections can be either valid or invalid. A **valid objection** is one based on an undeniable truth. If the prospect protests your inferior warranty, and your warranty is short, the objection is valid. Valid objections are often raised by people who are not true prospects. For example, if someone you classified as a prospect claims to be unable to afford the product, and indeed this is true, the objection is valid. You should cease your efforts to sell to this individual.

An **invalid objection** is one that lacks substance or basis in reality. If a prospect says a friend was unable to find servicing for your product, and a service center is located nearby, the objection is invalid. Even if the prospect and the friend are telling the truth, it is still groundless because it is based on a false belief.

Never imply agreement with an invalid objection. Your task in dealing with the objection is to overcome it, and you cannot do this if you suggest that it is valid. However, you can soften your response by showing understanding. For instance, you might say, "I can easily understand your feelings. It's hard for a lot of people to believe that a model so small can perform so many functions."

Trivial Objections . . .

A **trivial objection** is an insignificant or irrelevant reason the prospect gives for not wanting to buy. For example, the potential buyer may criticize the product's color even though it will be installed completely out of sight. A trivial

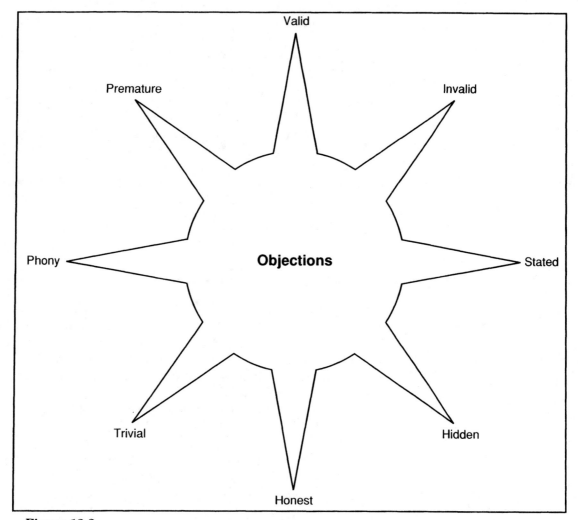

Objections

Valid

Premature

Invalid

Phony

Stated

Trivial

Hidden

Honest

Figure 12-2

objection plays no role in determining the outcome of the sale. Such reluctance may be raised for several reasons:

1. The prospect wants to throw the salesperson off track. In this case, the person has no interest in listening to the salesperson, so a trivial objection is raised in an effort to end the presentation.
2. The prospect wants to make conversation. Here, the potential buyer takes advantage of the conversational possibilities found in observations and impressions. The prospect might make fun of your product's name, for example.
3. The prospect is concealing a more significant objection. In this case, the future customer does not want to reveal the true objection, so it is concealed behind trivial comments.

Suppose a prospect criticizes the flimsiness of your product's package. However, the product doesn't require the protection of a stronger package, and you know the packaging will not influence the prospect's actual buying decision. How should you treat the objection? You should treat it as a trivial one.

Trivial objections, like the packaging one, are usually not well thought out. Nor are they worthy of serious replies. Purely out of courtesy, you may want to respond, but avoid dignifying a silly objection with a thoughtful answer. Pass over it with a very brief response—just enough to acknowledge the prospect's comment.

If the trivial objection is intended to poke fun, you may decide not to answer verbally at all. Move on with your presentation either by ignoring the remarks or by giving a short laugh. Do not waste your time responding carefully to meaningless remarks.

Honest and Dishonest Objections . . .

A prospect's honest or sincere objection is a real reason for not wanting to buy. **Honest objections** should be welcomed by the salesperson. Although you might be unhappy to learn that the prospect has a reluctance to buy, you should be happy to know exactly what the reason is. Armed with the knowledge of a sincere objection, you can formulate a plan to overcome it and make the sale.

You may be able to respond to an honest objection with a question whose answer will tell you exactly where you stand:

"Is that all that's bothering you?"
"Does your order depend on my providing those terms?"
"If I can get you the color you want, will you buy?"
"Is the delivery date holding you back?"

If the prospect answers yes to such questions, you will know what to do. An honest objection can and usually should be made the focal point of your presentation from then on. It is the shortest route to making the sale. If you cannot overcome it, at least you will know the reason you didn't succeed.

A **dishonest objection** is an excuse. It is a coverup used to camouflage the prospect's real reason for not buying. A dishonest objection differs from a trivial one in that it seems relevant or important to the sale. With a trivial concern, you know the complaint is minor and will not influence the prospect's

Do you know the hallmark of the second-rater? It's resentment of another man's achievement.

Ayn Rand

buying decision. A dishonest objection, on the other hand, is more significant, and you may not know at first whether it plays a role in the outcome of the sale. For instance, suppose your product is something delicate that requires protective packaging. In this case, packaging is relevant, and an objection to your packaging will be significant to you. But the objection still may be dishonest; prospects might use the packaging excuse to hide an objection they feel more strongly about.

Hidden Objections . . .

A **hidden objection** is a real concern that prospects keep to themselves. They conceal it by offering an excuse (an insincere or dishonest objection) or by keeping silent.

Prospects conceal their true objections for several reasons:

1. They are embarrassed to reveal their true objection.
2. They believe the salesperson will be embarrassed by the true objection.
3. They do not want to give the salesperson a chance to overcome their real objection.

The kinds of objections that might embarrass the prospect are the kinds that expose the potential buyer's weaknesses or reveal unflattering news. For example, prospects who are known as successful and well-to-do wouldn't want others to hear that they are experiencing financial difficulty. Customers who hold an engineering degree wouldn't want to admit that they don't understand the technical aspects of your product. Both of these prospects might try to conceal the truth from you. One might remain silent, whereas the other might claim dishonestly that there is no need for the product.

The kinds of objections that might embarrass the salesperson are the kinds that are personally critical, could cause a conflict, or create an awkward moment. For example, prospects might be afraid to offend you with their objection that you seem too inexperienced to handle their account or that you don't have the ability to advise them. Other buyers might sense a personality clash, and wouldn't want to be in contact with you repeatedly. These prospects feel much more comfortable saying nothing or making up excuses rather than reveal their true objections.

If the objection is not embarrassing to anyone, why wouldn't the prospect want to reveal it? Frankly, potential buyers know that by divulging their real objection they open the door to the salesperson's attempts to overcome it. Once prospects make up their mind not to buy, they will do whatever they can to avoid your efforts to change their mind. They remain silent or give an objection that they believe will stop you cold.

Suppose you sell personal computers. Perhaps some prospects secretly think your computer is too complicated for their children, and they no longer want to consider buying it. They don't want you to show them how simple the computer is, so they invent another objection: They tell you they can't afford it, expecting you to give up your selling effort then and there.

Paths to the True Objection . . .

When prospects conceal a concern, their dishonesty will reveal itself in sometimes bewildering ways. Detecting their true objection will require great sensitivity. You should be especially observant of the prospect's nonverbal behavior, which may reveal what words conceal. Chances are, if a potential buyer continually frustrates you, a hidden objection is the culprit. Here are two typical clues that your prospect is hiding an objection:

1. You overcome each **stated objection** to the prospect's apparent satisfaction, yet new ones continue to surface.
2. The prospect seemed very interested in your product at first, but suddenly and inexplicably cools to you.

Similarly, there are several ways to determine if the prospect's stated objection is real:

1. Ask if this is the prospect's only reason for not buying.
2. Ask the prospect for the reasoning behind the objection.
3. Ask for the prospect's complete honesty.

Consider the benefits of asking that most direct question, "Is this your only reason for not buying?" The prospect who answers yes is in effect telling you that if you can overcome the objection, he or she will buy. The prospect who answers no is in effect divulging that the stated objection is not real.

More tactful and no less effective is some variation of the question, "What brought you to that conclusion?" For example, suppose certain prospects say your price is too high. You might ask them how they would come up with a better price, or which aspects of the itemized price they disagree with and why. Once they are forced to think about their concern in concrete terms, they might withdraw the criticism. If they harbor a hidden objection, they might even decide to reveal it at this point.

Sometimes a direct appeal for the prospect's complete honesty does the trick. If prospects raise an objection that you are convinced is false, tell them that they deserve and always receive your complete honesty and that you deserve the same in return. Make them aware that you think there is something they aren't telling you, and that you only want to know what their real objection is. Salespeople often discover that this open, respectful approach works wonders.

When the Prospect Stays in Hiding . . .

Sometimes, despite all of your efforts and appeals, prospects refuse to tell you their real reason for not buying. This can be a very disheartening experience. If only they would tell you the truth, you could offer a confident response. But instead, they stay in hiding.

This does not necessarily mean the sale is lost. One approach you might take is to follow your hunches. Based on your experiences with prospects like this one, make an educated guess about the prospect's true objection. Mentally review your interactions with the prospect and the revelations the prospect has made. Then set out to overcome the objection that seems likely. For example, suppose you sell an expensive business item that the person you call on should be able to afford, yet your prospect keeps raising trivial or dishonest objections. Suddenly, you remember that this potential buyer recently reduced company personnel by half. This reveals a need to cut expenses, yet the prospect may not want you to think the business is suffering. The hidden objection could very well be price. Your approach: "Mr. McCurdy, would you like to take a look at our new 800 series?" Of course, the 800 series happens to be priced significantly lower than the series you originally presented.

When you discover the true objection, do not confront the prospect with it. Remember, there are personal reasons that it is kept hidden. The prospect will be no more willing to admit it after you discover it than before. In fact, your insistent "openness" might make the individual that much more determined *not* to buy.

Unfortunately, there will be times when you won't be able to guess the prospect's true objection. Sometimes you can gain insight into an unsuccessful sales attempt after some reflection or consultation with colleagues. If you are lucky enough to arrange a second interview, your new presentation should address what you believe to be the prospect's real concern.

RESPONDING TO OBJECTIONS . . .

You should be able to respond in some way to every objection stated by the prospect. This doesn't mean you must give precise and correct answers to each question as soon as it arises. It simply means you must have the poise to handle all objections gracefully. You should not appear stunned or confused when the prospect raises a concern you weren't expecting.

If in spite of your planning, a prospect catches you by surprise, you should offer a response like this: "That's an interesting point. Let me think about it for a moment." Not only does this compliment potential buyers for having raised a good point, it also shows that you are giving their objection serious consideration. Most important, it gives you a few seconds to formulate your reply.

Every reluctance deserves a professional response. Unless you are certain that the prospect's objection is trivial, you should treat it with importance. Respond politely and professionally, and let customers know that their concern is worthy of a careful answer. Salespeople sometimes make the mistake of belittling the prospect or treating an objection lightly or humorously. But remember, a curt, disrespectful, or sarcastic response to an honest objection can quickly cost you the sale.

If you're never scared or embarrassed or hurt, it means you never take any chances.

Julia Sorel

Even when you are almost certain that the prospect is joking, it never hurts to be serious. Salespeople who have no sense of humor are one step ahead of those who seem to enjoy making fun of their prospects.

Response Behavior . . .

How you respond to an objection is more than a matter of deciding what words to choose. Your behavior in responding should be careful, thoughtful, and receptive. Avoid magnifying an objection by overresponding to it. Once you have given an answer that you think is adequate, ask if the prospect is satisfied before saying more. Overdoing your response is just as bad as dismissing the objection as insignificant. The prospect might see you as insecure or suspect that the concern cannot be truly overcome.

Here are some response techniques to develop.

Pause First

Even if the prospect raises a familiar objection that you can easily overcome, don't swing immediately into a response. Pause for a moment to let the prospect think the objection is original and thought provoking. "That's a very good point," you might say, or, "Not many people consider that." Responding in this way maximizes the impact of your answer, possibly even allowing you to use the objection as the point on which to close the sale.

Although you should contemplate your response to any serious objection, you must avoid giving the impression that you are stumped. If you pause too long, the prospect might think you cannot completely overcome the objection.

Restate the Objection

The purpose of restating the objection is to establish true communication with your prospect. For this reason, you should paraphrase the objection rather than repeat it word for word, and pose it as a question. Prospects will know that you want to grasp their meaning, and they will be willing to explain themselves. They have the chance to say, "Yes, that's what I mean," or "No, that's not what I mean."

By restating the prospect's objection, you ensure that you understand it before addressing it. In addition, you give yourself a few extra seconds in which to compose your reply. Figure 12-3 lists five benefits of restating an objection.

Echo the Objection

The purpose of **echoing** is to prompt prospects to elaborate on their objection or explain it more clearly. If the prospect states a concern vaguely or too simply, you can echo it by choosing the key word or words and stating them in question form. For example, the prospect might say, "The problem here is capacity." You should echo: "Capacity?" This lets prospects know you don't understand what they mean, and they will realize they have to explain further.

The Benefits of Restating an Objection

1. You confirm that you understand it.

2. You give yourself time to formulate a reply.

3. You gather additional information about it by restating it and remaining silent, giving the prospect the opportunity to explain.

4. You prompt the prospect to rethink its validity.

5. You will be seen as confident in your ability to remove it.

Figure 12-3

METHODS OF RESPONSE . . .

There are five tried-and-true methods of response to consider when preparing to face prospect objections. These are illustrated in Figure 12-4. The boomerang method is surprisingly effective and can be used with almost any objection. The compensation method is useful, and may be your only alternative when a true prospect raises a valid objection. Invalid objections can be handled with the question, the direct denial, or the indirect denial method. Here are descriptions of the response methods and the situations in which they may be applied.

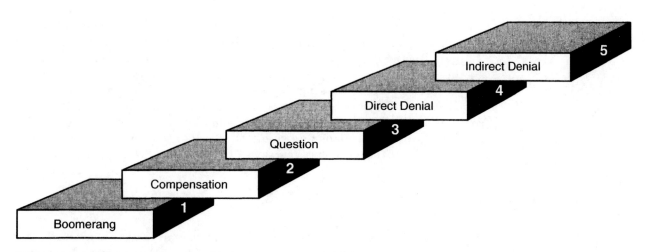

Figure 12-4 Methods of responding to a prospect's objection.

Boomerang . . .

In the **boomerang technique**, you simply take the prospect's objection and return it as the very reason the prospect should buy. The number of ways in which this method can be used is astonishing. Almost any objection the prospect raises can be boomeranged.

Consider the story of the parents and the encyclopedia salesperson. The parents tell the salesperson that encyclopedias would be a waste of money because their children do poorly in school and have no interest in their lessons. They would never use the books, the mother declares. Using the boomerang, the salesperson responds, "Your children will enjoy these books because they can browse through them at their leisure and look up things that interest them. They'll be able to complete their homework more easily because the encyclopedias will be a ready reference for them. And, most important, as their interest in lessons increases, their performance will improve, and their grades will show it." The beauty of the boomerang is that the parents' reason for not buying becomes exactly the reason they should buy.

What if prospects in their twenties object to buying life insurance because they are "too young" to worry about such matters? Try this boomerang: "Actually, this is the ideal age at which you should buy life insurance. Your rates will increase dramatically as you grow older. You need to buy now, while this insurance is still a bargain."

What if a company's owner tells you the firm is too small to need a computer? Boomerang: "If you want your business to grow, Ms. Brozeno, this computer will be essential. Not only will it manage more information after your company has grown, it will carry you through the busy growth period."

Here is a story told by a computer salesperson who uses the boomerang when prospects claim to be too busy to learn how to use a computer:

> I knew ahead of time that the prospect was a busy person who would object to taking the time to learn the computer. I also knew that he was an avid golfer. I decided to make the point that the purpose of buying the computer was to save time, not consume it. When I entered the prospect's office, I had my sales materials in my left hand and a three-pack of golf balls in my right hand. The prospect noticed the golf balls right away, but much to his surprise, I didn't offer them as a gift. I didn't even mention them. Instead, I put them down on the edge of his desk and got on with the presentation as if they weren't there. Deep into the presentation, the prospect objected to taking time out to learn the computer. I said, "You're right, it will take some time to learn. But once you learn it, you'll save at least ten hours a week on tasks that you're doing now manually." Then I picked up the golf balls and said, "And I'd like to give you these to enjoy during the first ten hours you save." The prospect got the point.

Compensation . . .

In the **compensation technique**, the salesperson uses the product's strong points to make up for the weak points objected to by the prospect. For instance, a product of very high quality usually has a very high price. But compensation comes to the rescue when a price objection is raised. One sports car salesperson had a showroom visitor who stated, "That's a lot of money." The car dealer replied, "That's a lot of car."

The compensation method calls for you to admit the validity of the objection and then to convince the prospect that your product's strong points outweigh its weak points. More than just explaining the product's advantages, you must show how they offset its high price. Compensate by telling buyers that your product's quality ensures a durability and dependability that will save years of service and replacement costs. Backed by an unsurpassed warranty and your firm's background in the industry, the product is a better buy than its lower-priced competition. Prospects appreciate the openness of the compensation method. When they raise an objection known to be valid, they respect the salesperson who admits it.

Salespeople who are unable to compensate for their product's shortcomings will fail in their selling efforts. Never underestimate the value of your product's off-setting features. The fact that so many products find a niche in the market is testament to the power of compensating features. A low-quality product comes with a low ticket, and a high-priced product offers superior features. By pointing out the compensating aspects of your product, you establish a tradeoff in the prospect's mind.

Jeffrey Ching

The haunting call of a career in sales beckoned Jeffrey Ching while he was still a student at the University of Hawaii. As much as he enjoyed his courses, especially in marketing, human relations, advertising, and selling, he became intrigued with the power of the media. Taking what he learned in the classroom, Jeffrey went out into the broadcast world of Honolulu to make his mark in selling.

Joining KSSK, Jeffrey quickly acclimated to the "real world" of marketing. His first position was as promotions assistant, where he was placed in charge of a number of the radio station's ventures. One of the promotional stints, involving an Easter extravaganza that benefited local charities. His planning, execution, and promotion of the event earned him praise at the station and throughout the community.

One thing that Jeffrey learned, both in college and at the radio station, was the importance of networking. Becoming active in local organizations and business groups expands the base for any salesperson in any field. Everyone has a circle of individuals with whom they communicate on a regular basis, and by expanding that circle you pull in others to your realm. One can never know or be acquainted with too many people. Jeffrey is also a firm believer that from the first meeting to the closing of the sale, image is everything!

> One machine can do the work of 50 ordinary men. No machine can do the work of one extraordinary man.
>
> > Elbert Hubbard

Question . . .

The **question technique** is an excellent choice when you suspect that the objection is dishonest or that the prospect has not given much thought to it. To use this method, you simply ask the prospect the basis of his objection: "What makes you think that?" or "How did you come to this conclusion?"

The question method can be very effective in eliminating insincere or trivial objections. Prospects who have not thought out their concerns will be forced to think about their statement. If they discover it was trivial, they will withdraw it. If they have raised an invalid objection, the reality will become apparent thanks to your question. For example, suppose you are told your price is too high and you reply, "Too high compared to what?" If the prospect isn't sure why the price seems high, then a weak response will be offered or he or she move on to another objection. If a dishonest objection has been raised, the prospect will probably withdraw it rather than try to argue in its favor.

When you use the question method, you challenge prospects to respond to their own objection. Once aware that you use this technique, they will be unlikely to raise careless objections.

Direct Denial . . .

Direct denial, coming right out and telling prospects they are wrong, is the most forceful and forthright response to an objection. As you might imagine, it is unsuitable for many concerns and can be dangerous when used improperly. Before using the direct denial make sure that you can verify your statements and that the subject is not up for debate. Even when you know that your denial is above question, be sure to word it in a manner that won't offend the prospect. Getting into an argument may win you some satisfaction, but will ultimately cost you the sale, and perhaps a customer.

This method should be used only when you have objective means of proving your point. Rely only on verifiable statistics, facts, or other data that you have on hand, or on a test that you can perform in front of the prospect. Using such means of proof is important because a personal direct denial can deeply offend your prospect. Even if you don't say the words "you are wrong," you are telling your prospect that he or she is. With objective facts, at least you can remain on pleasant terms because personal opinions and feelings are not at issue.

Suppose your prospect says, "Doesn't this type of fence turn a horrible color in the weather and require yearly painting?" You should use objective means to directly deny the claim: "No, it doesn't. Let me show you these photographs...." All the while, you explain that your fence is made of superior material designed to withstand harsh weather and still maintain its original finish.

If the prospect says, "I understand the temperature here often exceeds 100 degrees," you might reply, "No, Mr. DeWolf, the temperature here has not been over 85 degrees once in the past fifteen years. I'll be happy to obtain statistics from the weather bureau if you'd like to check." Even though you don't have statistics with you, the prospect knows you are willing to get them. And if your relationship with the prospect is a trusting one, odds are you will not be requested to go so far.

Used with the wrong objection or the wrong prospect, direct denial is undesirable even when done politely. What makes this method often inappropriate is that prospects do not like being flatly contradicted. Even when objective means are available, direct denial must be handled with care. You want to avoid starting an argument or personality clash, which can erupt easily if the prospect has a strong personality. Further, you should not allow your superior knowledge to inflate your ego. Don't give the impression that you enjoy proving the prospect wrong. Use direct denial only if you can keep the relationship a friendly one.

Indirect Denial . . .

Indirect denial is sometimes called the "agree and counter" or **yes, but technique**. This is because, without actually agreeing with the objection, you convey an attitude of understanding and respect for the prospect's point of view. Then you proceed to delete the objection. More diplomatic than the direct denial method, indirect denial allows you to correct prospects without telling them they are wrong. Indirect denial is the most common and most recommended method of dealing with objections. Whenever you are unsure whether to use direct or indirect denial, use the latter, because it's more tactful and safer.

The key to indirect denial is that you open your reply with a softener. Be advised that many prospects will consider your "yes, but" response a thinly disguised "no, you're wrong." Others, immediately recognizing your response as a rebuttal, will not begin listening until *after* you have said "but." You would be wise to avoid using the actual phrase "yes, but." "However," "and yet," "except," "still," "nevertheless," and "the only thing" are useful substitutes.

Here are some possible opening lines for an indirect denial:

1. "I can understand why you feel that way, yet this product is as versatile as any brand you will find."
2. "Your point is not uncommon. We find many customers who are suprised to learn just how versatile this product is."
3. "I used to feel that way myself, until I tried it out. The product has proved itself to me, and it's as valuable as we claim it to be."

The **feel-felt-found technique** is another common form of indirect denial. Saying that you understand how the prospect **feels**, or that others have **felt** this way, puts the prospect into a comfortable group rather than standing alone. You can then swing the conversation around to how some who originally questioned, have **found** that there was no objection. This technique is especially useful with prospects who are inclined to be argumentative or hostile.

Responding to an Objection with *Feel-Felt-Found*

Feel: "I know how you feel." "Many other people feel the way you do."

Felt: "I felt that way myself." "Some of my most satisfied customers felt the exact same way."

Found: "What I found was pleasantly surprising." "Every one of them has found this product to be maintenance-free."

To remain tactful, indirect denial usually requires a longer reply than does direct denial. Suppose your prospect for residential real estate says, "These houses are too high in price." Whereas direct denial would eliminate this objection just as fast as you can produce written data, indirect denial must be more leisurely and subtle: "I can understand why you think so. They do cost twice as much as a comparable home cost ten years ago. However, we compared them with every other development within twenty miles of here, and we found them to be the most reasonably priced houses on the market. Nowhere in the area will you get as much for your money as you are getting here."

DEFERRING PREMATURE OBJECTIONS . . .

As a general rule, you should respond to all objections as soon as they are raised. The quick resolution of an honest concern can often be made the basis of a sale. Delaying your response would be foolish. Further, there are several disadvantages to deferring objections: By refusing to deviate from your course to answer an unexpected objection, you give the impression that your presentation is canned. Prospects might lose confidence in you because they suspect you don't know how to overcome their objection, casting doubt over everything you say.

Failure to respond to objections immediately might leave the impression that your presentation is canned or overly rehearsed. If you can respond, do so and eliminate any doubt in the prospect's mind. If you need to find answers, say so and set a specific time to return with the information. When you know that a quick telephone call from the prospect's desk will get an immediate response, ask permission to make that call. Such a tactical move can be very impressive and is especially helpful if you need to continue the presentation. Carrying on the call could be difficult, at best, if the potential customer has lingering doubts.

Sometimes it is appropriate to defer objections, especially when the objection is premature. A **premature objection** is one that is raised out of context, before the subject can be adequately addressed. If you have not covered the subject and plan to do so later, you should defer your response. This is not inconsistent with the principle of responding immediately to objections. That rule refers to concerns that are raised at the "right" time, after the subject comes up in the presentation or during its discussion.

Responding immediately to a premature objection can be fatal to your sales effort. You might need to spend considerable time explaining ideas that your prospect thinks can be dispensed with quickly. Whenever deferring your response will allow you to make a more effective presentation, you should do so, but only with the prospect's permission. Ask if you can wait on that answer, and promise that you will address all concerns completely when the time is right.

The most common premature objection is the early price objection. There are many products whose price seems high to prospects who don't recognize their value or versatility. Potential buyers who know your price before they discover the value of your product will certainly object strongly. This is why the tariffs of many upscale products are unmarked. If your product's list price is published or otherwise known and prospects object to it prematurely, you will need to defer the objection. Request their permission to address the price aspect after you have fully explained your product's benefits.

The Early Price Question . . .

If your product's price is something the prospect must ask you in order to learn, deferring the premature price objection means deferring the early price question. Do not make the mistake of divulging your product's price before you have had the chance to build its value in the prospect's mind. Potential buyers cannot object to a price that they don't know.

Give a justifiable reason why you can't quote the price just now. If you simply refuse to discuss price, people will suspect that it is high, and their suspicion and curiosity will impede their ability to listen to your presentation. There are several ways to defer the early price question, depending on your situation:

1. Tell your prospects that your presentation takes a building-block approach, and that revealing the price at this time in the presentation would be taking the matter out of context. Explain that you are in the middle of another topic, and cannot satisfactorily address the price aspect until later, but that you do intend to address it to their satisfaction.

2. Tell your prospects that price is not a set figure, but rather a variable that depends on their needs. You need to know more about their situation before determining what size or model is best for them and therefore what the price will be.

3. Tell your prospects that a price is impossible to quote without first explaining the many options available and determining which options are most suitable. Make the point that you are creating a custom product for them, so you have no price to quote.

4. Tell your prospects that because your prices are constantly changing, you will first need to consult with your store manager or someone at company headquarters. This method is suitable only when the prospect makes an unannounced phone call or visit to you. If you are making the call, you should be prepared to discuss price without consulting others.

By deferring a premature price question, you give yourself the opportunity to build your product's value and the prospect's interest in it. Once you have done this, prospects who might have dismissed a seemingly unjustified price will instead come to desire the product before hearing the price. Then if the price is higher than they would have liked, they will think of ways to fit the purchase into their budget plans.

You Decide!

Kevin has been selling for a manufacturer of industrial pumps for five years. His company's products are purchased by contractors, public utilities, municipal authorities, and large corporations. In the past six months, a new centrifugal unit has shown a tendency to fail under high-pressure conditions when it is not properly maintained. Although the resultant loss of pumping pressure is temporary, and normal performance returns after a brief shutdown, the inconvenience caused to customers has been a major stumbling block in moving this item.

A recent edict from company management directs the sales force to use a firm denial when faced with this objection. The firm's logic is that when properly maintained, this type of failure rarely occurs. Kevin and other salespeople are encouraged to promote the proper maintenance procedures and under no circumstances are they to allow for return of faulty valves that have not been serviced correctly. Although he understands the company's position, Kevin is inclined to feel that he ought to forewarn prospects of this potential defect, and perhaps even refer potential customers to competitors. What tactic should he use? **You decide!**

Summing It Up . . .

Objections can be characterized as valid, invalid, honest, phony, trivial, stated, hidden, or premature. A valid objection contains truth, and when raised by true prospects, must be compensated for. An honest objection is the prospect's actual reason for not buying. Prospects will not reveal their honest objection if doing so would prove embarrassing to them or the salesperson, or if they wish to deny the salesperson the opportunity to overcome it. Instead, their objection remains hidden, and a phony objection is offered instead. Trivial objections concern matters that have no impact on the sale. They are raised to impede the salesperson's efforts. Premature objections concern aspects of the purchase that have not yet been addressed and must be deferred. It is often possible to forestall an objection. This is done by removing the objection before the prospect introduces it.

Five ways to respond to a prospect's objection are boomerang, compensation, question, direct denial, and indirect denial. To boomerang an objection is to return it to the prospect as the very reason the prospect should buy. To compensate for an objection is to admit its validity, and then show how your product's advantages more than offset it. Questioning a prospect's objection is recommended if you suspect the objection is invalid or not well thought out. It requires the prospect to rethink the objection's validity. To directly deny an objection is to bluntly declare it invalid. This is recommended only when you can refer to verifiable statistics. Direct denial is risky since you may offend the prospect. Indirect denial is a safer course of action. Here, you deny the objection only after telling the prospect that you fully understand why the objection was raised.

Key Concepts and Terms . . .

boomerang technique	indirect denial
compensation technique	invalid objection
direct denial	premature objection
dishonest objection	question technique
echoing	stated objection
feel-felt-found technique	trivial objection
forestalling	valid objection
hidden objection	yes, but technique
honest objection	

Building Skills . . .

1. Describe the proper attitude toward customer objections.
2. List some ways you can predict objections.
3. All objections have qualifiers. Explain.
4. Contrast the difference between a trivial objection and an invalid objection. Give examples of each.
5. Explain why the salesperson should be glad to know the prospect's honest objection.
6. Describe the reasons prospects might keep their true objection hidden.
7. Define two clues that the prospect is hiding the true objection.
8. List the questions you can ask to eliminate trivial or dishonest objections.
9. Describe your actions if your prospect refuses to divulge the real reason for not buying.
10. Explain why most objections should be addressed immediately.
11. Explain when it is appropriate to defer an objection.
12. List the methods used to defer an objection.
13. Describe the difference between restating and echoing an objection. Give examples of how these techniques are used.
14. Explain forestalling, including the ways it is used in planning a presentation.
15. Describe the dangers of magnifying an objection.
16. Compose the most diplomatic way to make a direct denial. Give an example.
17. Contrast indirect denial to direct denial.
18. Explain the types of objections for which compensation is your only logical alternative.

Making Decisions 12-1:

Frank Armstrong, a sales associate for Quickfreeze refrigerators and freezers, sells his product to industrial users such as restaurants and banquet facilities. One day he calls on Racquel Olivia, the owner of Stonecastle, whose catering service appeals to a wide range of clients. Stonecastle handles everything from small, private dinners to wedding receptions to corporate Christmas parties. Although Frank's visit is unannounced, Racquel seems glad to see him. Frank starts by asking Racquel a few questions about Stonecastle's operating methods and volume of business. He then opens his catalog to show her Quickfreeze Model 3160.

Frank:	This is the model I recommend for you.
Racquel:	(Studying the picture and reading the specifications) No, it's too small.
Frank:	I don't think so. This is the same model they use at Iron Bridge, which is the biggest banquet facility in this area. If it's big enough for them, I'm sure it's big enough for you.
Racquel:	I'm sorry, but I disagree. I see my four o'clock appointment is here, and I really must see you out. Perhaps we can talk again some other time.

Describe the method that Frank used to overcome Racquel's objection. Was it appropriate. Create your own method of handling the situation.

Making Decisions 12-2:

Russell Darby is a salesperson for Cocci Equipment, a maker of residential and industrial dehumidifiers. He also happens to be househunting. One afternoon his real estate agent takes Russell to see the home of Earl and Virginia Thompson, and while in the basement he notices some moisture at the base of the rear wall. Later that evening, Russell phones the Thompsons.

Russell:	Hello, Mrs. Thompson. I'm Russel Darby, the one who looked at your house this afternoon.
Mrs. Thompson:	Yes. How are you?
Russell:	Fine. Let me explain why I'm calling. I noticed some dampness at the base of your rear cellar wall, and I can help you do something about it.
Mrs. Thompson:	What do you mean?
Russell:	I'm a salesperson for Cocci Equipment. We have a dehumidifier designed especially for a house like yours.
Mrs. Thompson:	What will it do?
Russell:	It will dry out that cement block wall.

Mrs. Thompson:	Perhaps it will, but we want to sell the house. We're not interested in putting any more money into it. In fact, we called our real estate agent after you left and told him to tell your agent that we're willing to accept a lower price. If you're at all interested in making an offer, we're ready to talk.
Russell:	I'll think about that, Mrs. Thompson. In the meantime, if you change your mind about the dehumidifier, give me a call.

Explore how Russell could have addressed Mrs. Thompson's objection to a dehumidifier. Describe your response when Mrs. Thompson invited him to make an offer on the house.

Making Decisions 12-3:

You sell vitamins and are talking to a prospect who claims to be in excellent health and has no need for your product. How will you respond?

Making Decisions 12-4:

You are a sales representative for a condominium complex located in the Florida Keys. You are planning to call a retired Vermont couple who reportedly are moving to Florida and are looking for a small house near Miami. What objections will you want to forestall? How will you forestall them?

Practice Makes Perfect 12-1:

Plan a sales presentation using a fellow student as the buyer. Ask that person to create as many objections as possible without telling you in advance. Using your knowledge and skill, see how many of these hurdles you can overcome.

Closing and Servicing the Sale

THE JOB TO BE DONE . . .

Even professional salespeople sometimes have trouble closing, or "getting the order." Remember, nothing happens until something is sold, and there is no sale until the prospect becomes a customer. Since the goal of all sellers is to develop not just sales but customers, servicing the account is an important part of the selling job. Chapter 13 investigates these areas, allowing you to:

...adopt the "closing attitude."

...overcome closing difficulties such as the fear of closing.

...know when to close.

...consider the benefits of the trial close.

...recognize closing signals.

...explore various closing methods.

...understand the importance of getting the agreement in writing.

...develop ego-resilience in selling.

...recognize the dangers in underselling and overselling.

...appreciate the importance of reassuring the buyer that his or her decision to purchase was the right one.

...explore various customer service responsibilities.

...appreciate the need for postsale follow-up.

...know how to handle customer complaints.

CLOSING AND SERVICING THE SALE . . .

Closing the sale is not the last step in the selling process. Closing, along with reassuring the new purchaser, puts an end to the presentation only. Remember that the selling process continues beyond the purchase itself and includes a postsale period during which you must service the sale.

In this chapter, we will discuss both closing and servicing the sale. Closing, in its simplest terms, means asking the prospect to purchase. Servicing the sale includes all postpurchase follow-up activities that fall under the heading "customer service."

The Challenge of Closing . . .

Closing is the most challenging part of selling. It is the point at which you will encounter the greatest resistance, where your true persuasive ability is most important, where the sale is either won or lost. In looking back over unsuccessful sales efforts, salespeople trace their disappointments more to a poor close than to any other part of their presentation.

A good salesperson is a good closer, and a successful salesperson never ends a presentation without trying to close the sale, usually more than once. You will find that if you are a good closer, this process will be your favorite part of selling. If you can't close, you don't sell.

Face the facts. You won't find many people throwing themselves at you, begging you to let them buy your product. It is up to you to close your sales. The proper attitude for you to have is to accept responsibility for initiating the close. In many cases, the prospect is as anxious for the close as you. By asking a number of non-threatening questions along the way, you will find that the potential customer's affirmation sets a positive scene. The prospect feels part of the process; that rather than being sold something, he or she is buying benefit.

A good salesperson looks forward to closing the sale, and imagines a positive outcome. Some people believe that thoughts reproduce themselves in reality, and that the salesperson who imagines a positive outcome is likely to realize a positive outcome. Imagine the prospect saying yes to your suggestion to buy. Remember, potential buyers know you are a salesperson and expect you to attempt a close. Most prospects who allow a presentation to go on for any length of time assume you will try to close the sale.

Some salespeople, those unlikely to remain in selling, find closing the sale extremely uncomfortable. Many actually leave the selling profession because they have problems with closing. Their sales presentations progress smoothly until they must ask the prospect to purchase the product, and then their efforts come to naught. Either they close poorly or they fail to attempt a close at all.

> For every disciplined effort there is a multiple reward.
>
> Jim Rohn

Why Salespeople Fail to Close . . .

Many sellers, especially new ones, find closing to be difficult. Even with veterans, the process of turning prospects into customers can be a formidable task. Commonly, salespeople fail to attempt a close for one of three reasons, fear, guilt, or failure to perceive the need to close.

Fear

Understandably, salespeople hate to hear the word *no*. But sometimes the fear of being turned down can get out of hand. Some salespeople would rather leave a presentation without having made the sale than risk being told no. This means that if the prospect doesn't offer to buy, the sale won't be made. Obviously, salespeople who wait for prospects to make the first move cannot last long in selling.

Success is difficult to reach if you are leary of setbacks. If your fear of rejection interferes with your ability to close, find a way to downplay the importance of the word *no* in your mind. Condition yourself not to take it personally, learn to allow the sound of the word to roll off you like water off a duck's back.

Guilt

Some salespeople feel guilty for attempting to close, as if they are asking for a favor that will not be returned. They feel uncomfortable taking the prospect's money. They feel it is impolite.

To overcome such guilt feelings, ask yourself this question: Should you feel guilty about helping someone? Remember that any good sales transaction is an exchange, not a one-sided favor. You are providing prospects with a solution to a problem or an improvement of their situation in exchange for their money. If the transaction is one-way, then you are dealing with someone who is not a true prospect.

Failure to Perceive the Need to Close

Sometimes salespeople will fail to close not because of fear or guilt but because they see no need to finish. In this case, the salesperson thinks that if the prospect wants to buy, he or she will say so. If the prospect doesn't buy without prompting, the purchase wasn't meant to be. In effect, the salesperson leaves responsibility for closing in the hands of the prospect.

This common problem makes itself evident even in classroom situations. Often, students giving mock sales presentations in their selling classes leave the close to those who pose as prospects. The student salesperson goes through an elaborate demonstration, complete with visual aids, and then becomes silent, expecting the prospect to offer to buy. Of course, in a classroom setting, most of the prospects do offer to buy. But in the real world of selling, buyers have difficulty weighing the pros and cons of their decisions, for which they will pay with real, hard-earned money.

Indecision rules the transaction, and your close is the only way you have of influencing the prospect's decision in your favor. If you see no need to get the sale at this sensitive moment, you will lose most. An attempt to close is necessary because it provides a small, much-needed nudge. Remember your problem-solving role as a salesperson, and use the close as a way to help your prospects improve their lot.

THE TIME TO CLOSE . . .

When should you close the sale? Most veteran salespeople, if asked such a question, would answer "now." Many common sayings in selling relate to the goal of making the sale:

"You can never close too early or too soon."
"When you don't know what else to do, close!"
"Always be closing."

Although these sayings have merit, they don't tell the new salesperson how to develop the instinct for good timing. Experienced salespeople may claim they are always closing, but in reality they are sensitive to the circumstances of each selling situation. They know that "when" to close is not a question of how long the presentation has gone on, but of what has happened to make the situation favorable to a close.

Here are several times that are right for an attempt to close:

1. After making a successful trial close.
2. After overcoming an important objection.
3. When the prospect seems satisfied with your presentation.
4. Upon receiving a voluntary or involuntary closing signal.
5. After the prospect acknowledges a major product benefit.

THE TRIAL CLOSE . . .

The **trial close** is a prelude to a closing attempt. It is an indirect way of determining if prospects are ready to buy, or how far from buying they are. You can use this step when you need to assess the impact of your selling effort but are not ready to put the potential buyer on the spot. The usual time for the trial close is at the conclusion of your presentation, with the prospect silent and no information left for you to provide.

A trial close can take the form of a guiding question, such as "Is there anything else I can explain to you?" or "Where do we go from here?" It can also

"Have we resolved the price issue?"

"Does this all make sense to you?"

"What do you think of this product?"

"Have I answered all of your questions?"

"Is that what you needed to know?"

"How else can I be of help?"

"Shall we continue?"

Figure 13-1 Trial closes.

take the form of a request for an opinion, "How do you feel about this?" The trial close may be in the form of an open-ended statement, like "The rest is up to you," or "We stand prepared to serve your needs." Figure 13-1 provides additional examples of trial closes.

The prospect's response to your trial close will either give you the go-ahead for a close or indicate the need to continue with your presentation. Some salespeople use a trial close early in their presentation as a prelude to discussing their product's benefits. For example, once the prospect acknowledges a problem, the seller might ask: "Do you think it would be worthwhile to resolve this matter?" In this instance, a yes answer would be followed by an explanation of benefits. Using a trial close early in the interview is helpful in providing direction for your selling effort. If prospects indicate a lack of interest in ownership, they may even tell you why. This in turn will show you which buying stages they have yet to pass through, and you will then know how to proceed.

Overcoming an Important Objection . . .

After you have overcome an important objection, particularly the prospect's only remaining one, the sensible thing to do is attempt a close. You can also use it to make sure this objection is the only one left. For instance, suppose the prospect says the only bothersome aspect of the transaction is the payment terms, and you offer to extend them as the prospect prefers. You can close this way: "Can I use your telephone to verify these new terms with my office?" If your request is refused, you will know there are more objections.

The Prospect Seems Satisfied . . .

There is a saying in selling, "When the prospect is ready to buy, you should be ready to sell." Regardless of where you are in your presentation, you should close the sale as soon as the prospect seems satisfied and can think of no more questions or comments. Your objective is not to deliver a complete presentation. If the prospect's interest in your product has peaked, you should be happy to stop and close the sale. Delaying so that you can make one more point can actually move the prospect back into a state of indecision.

A close attempted after a short presentation is no less appropriate than one tried following a long one. All that matters is that the prospect has passed through every buying stage. In some rare cases, sales can actually be closed during your opening remarks. Imagine approaching a prospect in a retail store, opening with a remark, "Can I wrap it up for you?" and hearing the prospect say yes. Of course, even closing on an opening remark must be handled tactfully so that the prospect does not feel pressured.

BUYING SIGNALS . . .

In most effective sales presentations, the prospect will develop a rising tide of interest. When the prospect's interest peaks, you are sent a message, a buying signal. These signs may be voluntary or involuntary, verbal or nonverbal. It tells you the prospect is interested in your product or becoming more interested in it.

As soon as you recognize a buying signal, you should attempt to close the sale. Failing to notice or respond to this message is tantamount to ignoring a request to buy.

Verbal Buying Signals . . .

These prospect questions are examples of **verbal buying signals**:

1. "How soon could you ship it?"
2. "I receive a 20 percent discount, right?"
3. "Can I get this in blue?"
4. "I don't pay sales tax on this, do I?"

If these are not fact-gathering questions posed early in the presentation, they should signal the time to close the sale. Certainly, the prospect isn't coming out and asking "Where do I sign?" but the message is the same. The potential buyer wants to be a customer. Often your best response to such a question is a question of your own. You ask a closing question. See Figure 13-2, next page, for buying signals followed by closing questions.

> To fear is one thing. To let fear grab you and swing you around by the tail is another.
>
> Katherine Paterson

1.	Prospect—	"What's your best price?"
	Salesperson—	"With how much money down?"
2.	Prospect—	"Which model do you recommend?"
	Salesperson—	"Which model do you prefer?"
3.	Prospect—	"Does this come in green?"
	Salesperson—	"Do you want it in green?"
4.	Prospect—	"How long will you stock this?"
	Salesperson—	"When will you need it?"
5.	Prospect—	"What's the smallest order you will accept?"
	Salesperson—	"How small a quantity do you want?"
6.	Prospect—	"Do you have anything larger?"
	Salesperson—	"Do you want a larger product?"
7.	Prospect—	"What are your terms?"
	Salesperson—	"What terms are best for you?"
8.	Prospect—	"How much does this cost?"
	Salesperson—	"In what quantity?"
9.	Prospect—	"When can you deliver it?"
	Salesperson—	"When do you want it?"
10.	Prospect—	"When will the newest model be out?"
	Salesperson—	"Do you want the latest model?"

Figure13-2 Buying signals and closing questions.

Statements like "It's much nicer than my present model," or "This will fit nicely into my living room" are also definite indications of interest. Even something as simple as repeating the terms of sale as you state them indicates genuine interest and thus qualifies as a sign. Prospects react to these important points because they want your affirmation that they are hearing them right and because they know that by repeating them they commit them to memory. When the potential buyer starts repeating after you, it is a good time to close the sale.

Another verbal buying signal is when future customers start adding their own benefits to the list you have provided, as when they say, "Plus it can be used in my office, too." Similarly, prospects send a sign when they overcome their own objection to the purchase, as when they say out loud to themselves, "Two hundred fifty dollars is a lot of money, but it *is* what we need." This customer is giving a strong buying signal

A prospect's verbal buying signals are usually easy to detect and interpret. But some are offered involuntarily and are not always so obvious. An **involuntary buying signal** is one that prospects aren't aware that they are sending. These clues are subtle, and often missed by the inexperienced salesperson. One of these is when, through actions or words, the prospect "takes possession" of the product. If a real estate agent is showing a house to a young couple, and the wife says to an agreeing husband, "Tom, we could put the washer here and the workbench over there," the couple is taking possession of the basement. The smart agent will know it is time to close.

Nonverbal Buying Signals . . .

Nonverbal buying signals are those contained in the prospect's actions or relayed through body language. These are usually involuntary, like hesitation between words or sentences, voice inflections, or changes in tone of voice. When customers take the initiative to try on one of the wristwatches you sell and seem not to want to take it off, they have subconsciously "taken possession" of the product. When prospects indulge in a long stare at the product while tapping their fingers on the counter, or gaze off into space as they think about it, they are indicating serious interest.

Perhaps the new car shopper interrupts your demonstration to jump behind the wheel a second time, just for one more feel. When prospects tap their feet, rest their chin on their hand as they try to concentrate, or when their pupils dilate, they are sending involuntary buying signals. Perhaps the potential buyer reaches for a pencil and performs some calculations or rereads important sales literature. When two prospects share in the buying decision, a moment's eye contact between them suggests that at least one is interested and wants to know what the other one thinks.

The Prospect Acknowledges a Benefit . . .

You will recall from earlier chapters that it is important to introduce relevant benefits early in your sales presentation. When the prospect acknowledges an important product value, you should attempt a close. For example, if you appeal to the product's affordability, and the prospect replies, "I agree that this product is very affordable," attempt a close. If your emphasis is durability, and the prospect replies, "It's as strong as any model I've seen," try to close the sale.

> Work is the basis of living. I'll never retire. A man'll rust out quicker than he'll wear out.
>
> Colonel Harland Sanders

The Setting: Closing Has Its Place . . .

One of the most important considerations when choosing a setting for your close is the potential for interruptions. Do everything in your power to prevent them. An interruption can ruin your selling effort. If you decide to close in your office, ask the receptionist to hold all calls and drop-in visits until your meeting with the prospect is over. One of the most hazardous interruptions is the latecomer, a person who shows up just as you are about to close and wreaks havoc on your sales effort. When you plan the setting of your close, make sure to avoid any possibility of third-party interference. Such an interloper might know nothing about you or your product, yet suddenly enter the scene and talk your prospect out of the sale. All of your persuasive work will go down the drain in an instant.

The latecomer could be a friend or relative of the prospect, but he or she could also be a total stranger. Imagine this scene: A new car salesperson and prospect are standing near a minivan in a showroom, and the dealer is about to initiate a close. Suddenly, two strangers stroll up to the van, and one says to the other, "That thing can't be worth what they're asking for it." Even such an unqualified opinion could destroy the sale. Salespeople often invite prospects to an office or booth where the final details of the transaction can be worked out, just to avoid being defeated by such remarks.

A Poor Setting . . .

The rental agent for a small apartment building located on a busy city street arranges to meet prospective tenants. Although the vacancy includes a garage, a yard, and a basement, the tenants want to see the apartment itself first. It is located on the first floor, next to the front entrance of the building. The agent obliges, then shows the prospective tenants where they can park the car, place a barbecue grill, and do their laundry. But once the prospects have seen everything, they wind up at the front door again, facing that busy street. This is no place to try and close the transaction. The traffic outside is noisy, the agent and tenant can feel a draft from the front entrance, and there isn't even a place to sit down and review the terms of the lease.

Although the agent correctly arranged the tour in order of importance to the prospect, the setting for the close was improperly planned. A better option might have been to return to the apartment and work at a table next to a sunny window with a view of the yard; the agent might also have taken the tenant to the apartment management office, where coffee would be served and the tenant could sit on a sofa to look over papers.

> A little knowledge that acts is worth infinitely more than much knowledge that is idle.
>
> Kahlil Gibran

Methods of Close . . .

Several closing methods are commonly employed, and experienced salespeople know how to close naturally no matter which method they use. You might find some methods more effective than others, depending on your selling situation and your personal selling style. You might also find that a combination of closing methods works best in certain situations. The seven methods we will describe are asking for the order, continued affirmation, the assumptive close, the minor point close, narrowing the choice, standing room only, and closing on an objection.

Asking for the Order . . .

The most direct, and perhaps most overlooked, method of closing the sale is that of simply **asking for the order**, the most straightforward method. Regardless of what words you choose, when you ask for the order, you are simply inquiring, "Do you want to buy?" This method is appropriate when you are almost certain that you have made the sale and want only to confirm it. Here are some examples of asking for the order:

"Would you like to place an order?"

"Can I arrange for shipment?"

"As you see it, do we have an agreement?"

Salespeople sometimes avoid asking for the order because it leaves them open to a direct no answer. Purchasing agents often remark about how salespeople will do anything to avoid coming right out and asking for the order because they fear the possible negative consequences of the question.

You should not be timid or show any reservations about asking for the order. Granted, no other closing method draws so clear a line between success and failure as does this one, but it's an excellent way to immediately confirm that you have made the sale.

Continued Affirmation . . .

You will recall from Chapter 10 the benefits of asking a series of questions that call for affirmative answers during the presentation. The closing method called **continued affirmation** makes use of this positive psychology. By simply using a sequence of yes questions to lead up to the sales transaction, you elicit positive answers, encourage a receptive attitude toward your product, and condition the prospect to say yes to your closing question. The theory behind the use of this method is that if you get prospects into the habit of affirmation, they will have to fight their own inertia to say no to the purchase.

Here is an example of the continued affirmation method:

Salesperson:	"Mrs. Stranahan, are you satisfied with our terms of delivery?" (The prospect has already implied that the answer is yes.)
Mrs. Stranahan:	"Yes."
Salesperson:	"Have I explained clearly and exactly how we will provide you with after-the-sale service?"
Mrs. Stranahan:	"Yes."
Salesperson:	"Can we finalize the transaction today?"
Mrs. Stranahan:	"Yes!"

Read the dialogue aloud, imagining yourself as the prospect. Notice how easy it is to say yes to the last question. Now try the dialogue again, responding negatively to the close. See how saying no seems to break your stride.

Of course, you must be careful to phrase your questions to elicit positive answers. As long as prospects answer affirmatively as you expect, you will be able to move on to your next question. Suppose you were to ask this question: "Having a large, spacious office is important to you, isn't it, Mrs. Finnegan?" And Mrs. Finnegan replied, "No, it isn't. I prefer a small, cozy office." Your affirmation couldn't even begin, much less continue. All the momentum you would like to build is undone by this unexpected negative answer. Your chain of affirmative responses is broken from the start, and a conversation must ensue about why Mrs. Finnegan said no.

The Assumptive Close . . .

The **assumptive close** is the favorite of many salespeople because it dispenses with the awkwardness of asking for the order. The salesperson simply assumes the sale has been made. If prospects give no indication to the contrary, then they are going to buy. The salesperson assumes that if there were a problem, the prospect would have said so.

With the assumptive close, you do not ask prospects if they plan to purchase. Instead, you ask a "what," "when," "where," or "how" question. You discuss the agreement as a "done deal," asking only for whatever information is necessary to complete the sales transaction. Here are things you might say in an assumptive close:

"How's Tuesday for delivery?"

"What quantity can I put you down for?"

"How do you want this to be shipped?"

"What I'll need now is your check for the deposit."

"When would you like to pick it up?"

"Where would you like us to install it?"

If the salesperson, with pen in hand, glances at the contract and says, "Your address is 354 West Main Street, right?" or "Today is the eighteenth, isn't it?" or "I just need you to sign here," an assumptive close is being used. Here is one that does double duty: "I can install it either Monday or Thursday. Which is better for you?" Not only do you assume the close, you suggest to the prospect that you are a busy salesperson.

The assumptive method is similar to continued affirmation in that both types of close make it difficult for the prospect to break the rhythm you establish. If you take out an order form and ask for the prospect's mailing address, the prospect finds it much easier to dictate the address than to say, "Wait a minute. I never said I was going to buy!"

The assumptive close often involves physical action by the salesperson. You might reach for your pen, open your briefcase, and take out a contract or order form, or clear a space on your desk to write up the order. Retail salespeople can use the physical-action assumptive close when they wrap and bag a product placed on the counter. Without a word, they make the assumption that the customer is buying.

The Minor Point Close . . .

In the **minor point close**, the salesperson asks the prospect to decide on a relatively insignificant aspect rather than on the actual purchase itself. This method is somewhat similar to the assumptive close in that it allows you to treat the acquisition as a foregone conclusion. The minor point close lets you confirm the sale by prompting the prospect to voice a minor decision.

Using the minor point close, you do not ask if the prospect intends to buy, but rather whether it will be cash or charge, the white or the gray. This method is based on the principle that a minor decision is easier to make than a major one. Most sales agreements entail minor points that lend themselves to this closing method. Whether your product is a $10 t-shirt or a $200,000 townhouse, the customer must make certain decisions that are incidental to the purchase. The size of the shirt or the floorplan of the townhouse are incidental. Even a hamburger platter comes with seemingly countless options. Would you like it medium or well done, served with onions, pickles, mustard, mayonnaise, cheese, lettuce, or tomatoes? Do you want French fries or baked potato? Salad or soup?

The sales representative for a fitness center asks if prospects prefer the aerobics option or the racquetball option. The newspaper advertising representative asks retailers if they want the weekly or the semiweekly package. When the buyer makes the choice, the salesperson begins to write the order.

> When a thing is done, it's done. Don't look back. Look forward to your next objective.
>
> George C. Marshall

Narrowing the Choice . . .

The **narrowing the choice** method allows the salesperson to help the prospect decide among product options. This method, also known as the alternative or limited choice close, is based on the idea that people decide, often subconsciously, to purchase by choosing among the products available. Your role is to lead prospects to buy your product by narrowing their choices.

Narrowing the choice differs from the minor point method in that it deals with decisions among products rather than with options. You offer the prospect different products, and you reduce the decision to a question of which variety the prospect prefers. Suppose you sell shoes. In the minor point close, you would show your customer one pump and ask whether the black or the bone is preferred. When using the narrowing the choice close, you would show the customer a pump, a sandal, and a moccasin.

This method of close is most appropriate when the prospect is considering a large number of product alternatives and needs help narrowing them down to a few favorites. To use it effectively, you must observe carefully to determine preferences and eliminate excess choices as soon as you know they are unsuitable. If the prospect is considering eight different products, you might try to narrow the choices down to three before attempting a close. You should be able to make a recommendation at this point. "I think your best choice is the Thirty-Six model," you might say. "It's the same capacity as the Thirty-Two and the Thirty-Four, which you need, but it also comes with the extra parts and longer warranty."

Standing Room Only . . .

The notion of **standing room only** (SRO) was introduced in Chapter 11 as a way to overcome the time objection. SRO can also be used to close the sale, and the driving principle is exactly the same. You are capitalizing on the human tendency to want things that are available only to a select few, or to be among an exclusive group of people. This method is appropriate whenever you can truthfully tell the prospect that your product is one of a kind, in dwindling supply, or soon to be discontinued.

Closing with the SRO method is the same as overcoming the time objection in that you impress upon the prospect that time is of the essence. Using this close, you let prospects know how urgently they must make a decision if they want to avoid disappointment. Here are examples of SRO closing remarks:

"If I can still find one for you, can we come to terms today?"

"Blue is a popular color. Do you want me to see if we have any left in blue?"

Of course, the SRO method should only be used in complete honesty. You should not use it to scare the prospect into buying, but rather to stress the need to arrive at a decision that she or he can feel good about. For example, suppose you are trying to lease an office, and you have two undecided prospects. Approach one prospect and say: "If you can sign the lease and pay the deposit today, I'll tell the other party that the office has been rented." With this remark you not only stress the urgency of the decision, you make the prospect feel good with your assurance that you will reserve the office space as soon as you are told to do so.

Closing on an Objection . . .

Closing on an objection means firming the sale in exchange for a solution to an objection. In other words, when the prospect has only one remaining concern to the purchase, and you can overcome it, you should try to close on that basis: "If I can make the adjustment you want, will you place your order today?"

This method, which is also known as the concession close, is useful with any objection, but is most commonly built around the price objection. The prospect might say, "I'm sorry, but your price is too high. I can buy this product for $200 less at Bradley Equipment." Assuming you are willing and able to meet the competitor's price, you can close this way: "If I can meet Bradley's price, can we do business?"

CLOSING TECHNIQUE . . .

Closing is a routine part of selling. It is a natural response to your intuition that the time is right to consummate the sale. Quite literally, a sale could not be made without a close of some kind. Yet, even though closing is normal, salespeople sometimes treat it as something special. The close becomes a formal event that makes both the salesperson and the prospect uncomfortable.

To make sure your close feels as natural as it is, you should take pains to avoid calling attention to it. Some salespeople unwisely, and perhaps unconsciously, build up to the close. They change their behavior in some way that lets the prospect know the close is coming. You might even think that by signaling the close you are helping the prospect get ready to contemplate the decision. But instead of helping the prospect when you make a big issue of closing, you only create tension. "The close is coming," the prospect will think. "I can tell."

Not only should you avoid noticeable changes in your mannerisms, you should also shun any outward display of a closing "ceremony." Don't suddenly unload your briefcase or pull pens, contracts, and calculators out of your desk drawer. Make the mechanics of the transaction an almost invisible part of your conversation. Give the prospect the impression that closing is all in a day's work, not a big event. This is especially important when you are closing on a large order. You want the prospect to think: "This is nothing unusual. This salesperson is obviously making a lot of sales. That means it must be a good product, and I'm glad I'm buying it." Figure 13-3, next page, points out some common mistakes that salespeople make in closing sales.

Good Closing Advice

1. **Don't wait.** If you are overly enthralled with your presentation you might overlook buying signals.

2. **Keep the faith.** Self-doubts often become prospect doubts.

3. **Be fresh.** Avoid overuse of the same old close.

4. **Don't quit.** Customers are created, not found. Many prospects need many calls and repeated attempts to close. Treat each "no" as an invitation to look for the "yes."

5. **Be prepared.** Every sales call has room for a close, so practice in advance where and when the time is proper.

6. **Don't tarry.** Once you turn a prospect into a customer, you need not sit around and rehash your victory. Thank your new customer, give assurance that the decision was a good one, and get out!

Figure 13-3

Silence Is Golden . . .

Whenever you attempt a close, remain silent until the prospect responds. Do not interpret a momentary silence as a no answer because the prospect may only be contemplating the decision. If you speak before the potential buyer, you eliminate the need for a response. Worse, you will be forced to begin another close.

Some salespeople trust in the motto, "The person who speaks first loses." Although the concept of winning and losing is inconsistent with the principles of consultative selling, the saying has some merit. Your ability to outlast the prospect's silence at the time of the close does play a large role in determining the outcome of your selling efforts.

CLOSING PROCEDURE . . .

As soon as you have reached an agreement with the prospect, you should put it in writing. None of the terms or conditions of the sales transaction should be assumed or taken for granted. Although an oral contract can be legal, it can also be a source of problems. Disagreements arise when memories must be relied on. By putting everything in writing, you assure the prospect of the sincerity of the agreement.

If possible, use a sales contract that is short and nontechnical. Long legal documents may look impressive, but their language can put prospects off. The customer will feel more comfortable with a contract that is brief and clearly stated. If your sales transactions must be put into extended contracts with technical and legal terminology, you should help the customer interpret the agreement. Go over the contract and paraphrase its terms, translating the jargon into plain language. This way you save buyers the trouble of having to read every word at the signing and free them to concentrate on the aspects of greatest interest to them.

When it is time to sign the contract, sit next to the buyer with pen in hand, and point out the most important aspects as you go through the document. Remind customers that the purchase agreement is binding on you as well as on them. If the contract contains blanks for optional terms, you might want to fill them in ahead of time so that only the fine points and the signatures are needed. You should sign the contract first, then request the customer's signature.

The way you write up an order or complete a contract reflects your self-confidence. By writing the agreement carefully and without hurry, you show poise and self-control. If you use an order form that includes your product's guarantee, use that opportunity to show the prospect your order form early in the presentation. Recall from Chapter 7 that customers who get a glance at a well-used order book will be impressed by the volume of your business.

Suggestion Selling . . .

There are many selling situations in which the sale of related products or services increases the buyer's satisfaction with the original purchase. **Suggestion selling** means recommending these other items, usually at the time of the first purchase.

Suggestion selling might relate to the use of the main product, as when a real estate agent suggests that prospects choose the double fireplace for their new townhouse. Extended warranties and service contracts are other examples. This process is also known as multiple selling, which is covered in more detail in Chapter 18.

Underselling . . .

Underselling means selling a quantity that is too small to meet the prospect's needs. The salesperson can actually do more harm than good by selling buyers less than they should buy. If prospects succeed in purchasing too small a quantity for their needs, they will later blame you for any disappointment they experience. They will either accuse you of poor guidance or condemn the quality of your product.

Prospects frequently are reluctant to place a large first order. They prefer to "try out" the product with a small order, not wanting to invest too heavily until they've built up their confidence in the product. Retailers, for example, commonly reject the purchase quantities recommended by salespeople in favor of smaller orders. They want to test the product's sales potential. But if you allow a retail customer to buy too small an order, the experiment may backfire on both of you. Not only will buyers learn nothing about your product's true sales potential, but they will have little incentive to promote the small quantity they bought, thus almost guaranteeing small sales.

Whenever a product's usage or sales results take time to be seen, you should require a minimum purchase. This is true for sales both to middlemen and to end users. If you sell to retailers, set a minimum order quantity that is large enough to ensure that your product's resale potential can be accurately measured. If you sell to end users, make sure that the order size allows for enjoyment of your product's benefits.

Overselling . . .

Overselling means selling a larger quantity than the prospect needs. As with underselling, the customer who has been oversold has a good reason to dislike and distrust the salesperson.

If your buyers are retailers, the oversold product will become stale and soiled in their store before they can sell all units. Their regular customers will see it week after week, and they will be forced to engage in money-losing special clearance sales, or the merchandise becomes a waste of space. More and more retailers, supermarkets in particular, are protecting themselves from the dangers of overbuying with contract clauses that call for a buyback or stipulate a "failure fee." A **failure fee** is a dollar amount that the supplier (seller) agrees to pay if sales volume does not reach a certain amount within a stated period.

If your buyers are end users, similar problems will ensue after an overbuy. Your customers might have spent more money than they should have to buy more product than they needed. The remainder deteriorates with age or becomes outmoded. It takes up valuable space in their home, garage, or office, reminding them daily of their mistake.

The dangers of overselling cannot be stressed enough. Think of the ill will it creates: The only reason oversold customers want to see you again is to give you a piece of their mind!

Explaining Your Return Policy . . .

There will be times when prospects refuse to buy unless they know they can return the product within a certain period if they are not satisfied. Statements like "You must be completely satisfied or your money back" are commonplace in today's business world. Many customers expect the salesperson to offer this type of assurance.

If your product is what you say it is, very few of your customers will want to return it. The fear of returns should not be a problem for you, and your money-back guarantee should not be a threat to your business. Consider the option offered by magazines of allowing the subscriber to cancel the subscription at any time. In spite of this option, not many subscribers cancel.

Providing Postsale Reassurance . . .

There is a saying in selling, "A good deal is a state of mind." In fact, *any* deal is a state of mind. A buyer's emotions following a purchase can be wide-ranging, as shown in Figure 13-4, and customer satisfaction is your responsibility.

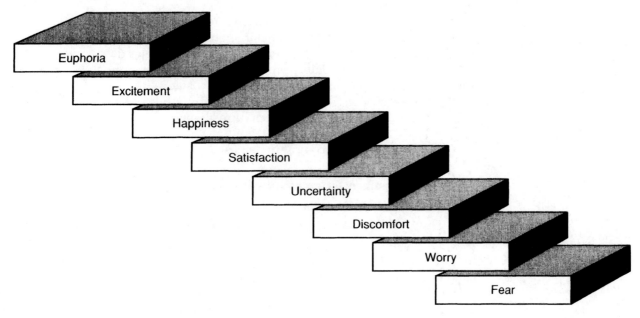

Figure 13-4 Range of post-purchase emotions.

Once you have secured the order, you should reassure the buyer that the decision was the right one.

You will recall from Chapter 7 that sometimes customers experience emotional discomfort known technically as **postpurchase dissonance**, or "buyer's remorse." "Did I do the right thing? Did I make the right choice?" they wonder. The more difficult the decision was, and the more important or expensive the purchase was, the greater the likelihood of postpurchase dissonance.

Although you may be unable to eliminate buyer's remorse, you should try to minimize your customers' negative feelings by reminding them of your product's many benefits. You should also congratulate them on their purchase. Tell them that you are confident that their purchase decision was the right one, and remind them that you look forward to serving them in the future. Send them a follow-up letter several days after the sale thanking them for the order and reminding them of your firm's excellent service capabilities.

The Need for Ego-Resilience . . .

A salesperson needs **ego-resilience**, the ability to rebound undaunted after a failed attempt to close. A prospect's negative answer separates the good salespeople from the poor: Good sellers, the ego-resilient ones, treat the word *no* as part of the selling senario. They have the strength to continue their presentation and try to close again. A poor salesperson views the failed attempt to close as the end of the sales effort.

In many industries, the salespeople couldn't possibly earn a living if they allowed the prospect's first refusal to end their interviews. If your prospective client has established relationships with other vendors, you can expect to make at least three to five visits before getting even a token order. According to some estimates, up to 80 percent of all industrial sales do not close until at least the fifth contact. Salespeople in these industries must be extremely resilient to keep going back until they make a sale.

The University of Notre Dame conducted a study of salespeople's closing practices and found a dismaying lack of resilience:

1. A whopping 46 percent of the salespeople interviewed attempted one close and quit.
2. Only 24 percent attempted two closes.
3. Only 14 percent attempted three closes.
4. Only 12 percent attempted four closes before giving up on a prospect.

The study also revealed that resilience pays: Some 60 percent of the sales made were not closed until the *fifth* attempt.

Ego-resilience means viewing the prospect's negative response as only a temporary setback. If you don't give up on the presentation, the prospect won't either. Your task upon rebounding from a failed close is to discover why the prospect remains uninterested in your proposition. There must be some information you didn't gather, benefits you didn't explain, or product features you didn't describe.

CUSTOMER SERVICE . . .

After the closing of the sale, the selling process continues indefinitely. For this reason, selling can be viewed as a two-step process. The first step is making the sale, and the second is serving the customer who has purchased or intends to buy. Surprisingly, making the sale is often the easier step. This is because established clients usually account for most of your business, and postsale service becomes a major part of your job.

Customer service is all those activities that enhance or facilitate the sale and use of one's product or service. In a broad sense, customer service entails all after-the-sale dealings, including securing credit, suggestion selling, delivery, installation, warranty work, and product servicing.

Customer service is often the most time-consuming part of the salesperson's job. Major purchases require a tremendous amount of postpurchase work, which goes on long after the customer says yes. Reviewing the owner's manual, explaining service and warranty stipulations, arriving at a payment schedule, demonstrating the product's operation—all these tasks are only the beginning of customer service. You will also have to plan periodic follow-up calls and visits to make sure your customer is satisfied, well supplied, and highly informed. If you deal with retailers, your customer service efforts might focus on helping them set up appropriate displays or control inventory. With other customers, you might spend much time training the users of your product.

Good customer service is the key to developing and maintaining a satisfied customer base. The most successful and profitable firms all seem to have customer-oriented values. Relying on customer service even more than on the strengths of their product, they often list goodwill (the value of a positive reputation) as an asset on their balance sheets. Goodwill is not the only way to profit through customer service. Many firms discover that servicing an established account is often a major source of sales volume and income.

Figure 13-5 provides some of the more common reasons for postpurchase dissatisfaction. Good customer service builds loyalty, whereas the opposite destroys it. Lack of postsale follow-up and salesperson indifference are disappointing to customers, and they respond by finding new firms to buy from. Further, buyers are quick to spread the news of their experiences, good or bad. Surveys prove that dissatisfied customers tell as many as ten to twenty people of their poor treatment, and a third of them stop purchasing the product altogether. Fortunately, most complaints are resolved to the customer's satisfaction, and they usually tell up to five people of the satisfactory resolution.

Delivery-related Causes

1. Delivery is late.

2. Product or package substitution was made.

3. Delivery charges are different or questionable.

4. The product was damaged.

Repair and Service-related Causes

1. Repairs fail to solve the problem.

2. Servicing was late or repair work delayed.

3. Service personnel are unfriendly or insincere.

4. The cost of servicing or repairs was more than anticipated.

5. Substitute or inferior parts were used to repair the product.

6. Product needs additional repairs and customer is billed for this work.

7. Customer is shuffled from person to person.

8. The conditions of the warranty are unclear.

9. The warranty doesn't cover what the prospect expected.

10. Unauthorized servicing or repair work takes place.

Figure 13-5 Causes of post-purchase dissatisfaction.

Happy customers are usually a salesperson's number-one source of referrals and testimonials. They are like an extension of the company's sales force, a group of people who will recommend the firm's salespeople and their product to their friends and associates. By personally adopting customer-service values, you will profit along with your firm. Customers remember salespeople who are "there" when they are needed. Loyalty to service-oriented salespeople can be so strong that customers follow them when they switch brands or firms.

Not only is customer service profitable because it generates sales and goodwill, it is also less expensive than creating new business. Firms often invest in costly advertising and promotional campaigns to attract new buyers, only to find that the sales generated by the effort are not great enough to recoup the expense. Established customers, on the other hand, know about your firm, so expensive advertising won't be necessary. Furthermore, established customers already have the habit of buying from your firm. New customers who are not acknowledged after their first purchase may never come back again.

Relationships with Colleagues . . .

There are many people on whom you must rely for providing excellent customer service. It is wise to be on good terms with your colleagues both in and outside your firm because often they handle details that will directly affect your rapport with buyers. For example, you may have to depend on your marketing department to send product literature to clientele whose names you submit. For the sake of your business, therefore, you will have to maintain an active, up-to-date, and friendly relationship with people in the marketing department. The same goes for your dealings with departments or outside contractors that deliver and install the product, supply parts, provide warranty servicing, handle complaints, or send invoices.

Securing Credit . . .

Depending on your industry, you may be responsible for arranging or securing credit for your customers. This is true in real estate and in the selling of farm machinery, for instance. Sometimes the financing arrangement makes the sale, as when a real estate agent closes on a property by way of a lease-purchase agreement after unsuccessful attempts to sell the property outright.

Many salespeople become involved with credit to some degree, whether it be providing information to customers, securing it for a buyer, or collecting on delinquent accounts. Even if you are not actually involved in arranging credit or making collections, you should be able to explain the financing and credit details to your customers. It is not uncommon for commissions that have already been paid to be deducted later from a salesperson's income if a financed purchaser defaults.

Sometimes the responsibility for collection will rest entirely with the salesperson. In other cases, the seller will only be involved in communicating initially with a late payer before the firm's credit department or a collection agency takes over. Customers expect salespeople to play an active role in the correction of any postsale credit problems. Customers who suffer billing errors are likely to ask the salesperson rather than the accounting department to have the error corrected.

Delivery and Installation . . .

Customer satisfaction often hinges on timely delivery and proper installation of the product. When selling to distributors such as wholesalers and retailers, on-time arrival of goods is critical. A late delivery can ruin an intermediary's resale plans. Often these purchasers will cancel orders that are too late to serve their purposes. Delivery also applies to services, such as when a newspaper "delivers" advertising by publishing it.

Proper installation is imperative with consumer durables, such as household appliances, and industrial goods, such as machinery or office equipment. Products installed incorrectly may not work properly. Many manufacturers have special staffs that are responsible for such postsale activities.

Salespeople do not usually handle delivery or installation, yet they must take responsibility for it in order to ensure customer satisfaction. Not only must you maintain good relationships with those who deliver and install your product, you must oversee the delivery and installation process on behalf of your customers. Make sure that the shipping department has your order, that a delivery date is set, and that you are notified when orders are shipped to your customers. And stay in touch with customers so that you will know when they have received their orders.

Complaints . . .

Dealing with customer complaints is probably the most unpleasant aspect of customer service. Not only must you listen to hostile remarks from disgruntled people, but you must endure them without responding in kind. If you handle complaints tactfully, they should not end in ill will or lost business. Remember that most dissatisfied customers simply stop buying, without a word. Only a small percentage actually take the trouble to protest. You should view a complaint as an opportunity to prove how much you value and wish to keep the customer's business.

Because an ethical salesperson with a good product will hear very few complaints, the cost of attending to disgruntled buyers should be negligible. Even if complaining customers receive more than they deserve for their trouble, you will be more than compensated in terms of lasting goodwill.

Often, after you have let customers air their dissatisfaction, you will feel compelled to suggest a solution. The better way, however, is to ask them to suggest an acceptable solution of their own. Most will be very reasonable in their requests. By giving customers the remedy they want, you ensure that you aren't just continuing the dissatisfaction by providing a solution as bad as the original. Try to keep the complaint between you and the customer, leaving appeals to management as a last resort.

Keeping Track of Customers . . .

Keeping track of customers is vital to your postsale effort. Your normal routine should include periodic phone calls, letters, and visits to people who have purchased from you before. As soon as a sale is made, put the buyer's name on your calendar as a reminder to make contact at specific later dates, but remember to always plan the purpose of your calls. Early on you will want to find out if customers have had new-owner problems with the product. Later, you might need to ask them if they are running out of supplies or if billing practices are satisfactory.

All purchasers like to feel appreciated. People enjoy shopping at stores where the clerks recognize them and take time to chat with them. The same goes for people who buy from nonretail sellers. A salesperson who sends a handwritten note or pays a personal visit to thank buyers for their order is far ahead of one who "takes the money and runs." Firms that make no effort to keep in touch with their customers not only deliver poor service, they are missing out on the chance to build healthy relationships or save deteriorating ones.

Before you get into the habit of neglecting customers, remember that the act of buying changes buyers psychologically: They feel they have done the seller a favor and the seller should remember the favor and return it. "Expectations are what people buy, not things," says Ted Levitt, author of *The Marketing Imagination*. Customers expect benefits from both the product and the salesperson, and once they buy, their expectations increase. If you don't keep track of your customers, you are failing to deliver on a major expectation, and the resulting dissatisfaction will be proportionate.

You Decide!

Ramon sells industrial spray washing equipment in Southern California. In almost all cases, this type of machinery is sold to businesses that use it in outdoor applications. Because of its size, and the overspray that occurs, the company has rarely come upon a suitable indoor application. Because the equipment is sensitive to dust and corroding agents, the firm insists that customers purchase an extended three year warranty for $500. The salesperson receives half of that fee as commission. With this program, the company provides periodic check-ups and maintenance to protect against contamination.

Ramon is contacted by a company that services large construction equipment. Due to the size of the rigs that this prospect handles, it has built a huge indoor complex. In addition, the equipment cleaned by the potential customer first passes through a shower tunnel that removes most of the dirt and grime. In talking with the prospect, Ramon discovers firm resistance to purchasing an extended warranty that the customer does not think is needed. On the other hand, the $250 would sure come in handy. What should Ramon do? **You decide!**

Summing It Up . . .

The final steps in selling are closing the sale and providing effective customer service. Good salespeople look forward to closing. To professionals, this step comes naturally, without guilt or fear, and their ego-resilience enables them to rebound unscathed from a failed attempt to sell. They plan a proper physical setting for the close and use an appropriate closing technique.

Skilled salespeople recognize those times during the presentation when a close should be attempted, as when the prospect offers a voluntary or involuntary buying signal, seems satisfied with the presentation, or has responded favorably to a trial close.

Methods of close include asking for the order, building the prospect's continued affirmation with a series of agreements, or simply assuming that the sale has been made, perhaps by wrapping the product, completing the order form, or asking where delivery is to be made. Other closing methods include asking the prospect to decide on a minor point of the transaction, such as color or option package, narrowing the prospect's choice by asking which model or variety is preferred, and closing on an objection. Skilled salespeople practice suggestion selling, understand the potential dangers of underselling and overselling, and provide postsale reassurance in order to eliminate buyer's remorse.

Once the sale has been made, customer service begins. This includes all postsale activities, such as scheduling or performing periodic maintenance and servicing, arranging for delivery and installation, handling customer complaints, and tracking former customers. These activities often take more time than selling. Even when others perform these duties, it is the salesperson's responsibility to oversee and coordinate them. This calls for a good working relationship between the salesperson and those in the firm who are responsible for customer service.

Key Concepts and Terms . . .

ask for the order close	nonverbal buying signal
assumptive close	overselling
closing on an objection	postpurchase dissonance
continued affirmation close	standing-room-only close
customer service	suggestion selling
ego-resilience	trial close
failure fee	underselling
involuntary buying signal	verbal buying signal
minor point close	voluntary buying signal
narrowing the choice close	

Building Skills . . .

1. Explain the common reasons for failing to close the sale.
2. Outline when you should attempt a close, naming at least four times.

3. Define a trial close, giving some examples.

4. Describe the difference between a voluntary and an involuntary buying signal.

5. Explain why the continued affirmation method of close demands that you be very careful in selecting your questions.

6. Explain the minor point close and the reasoning behind it.

7. List the kinds of products and circumstances under which the standing room only method of close is appropriate.

8. If you handle the rentals for your hotel's banquet facilities, describe how you might use the standing-room-only method of close.

9. Describe postpurchase dissonance.

10. Explain why making the sale is often the easiest part of the selling process.

11. Explain why maintaining good relationships with people in your company's shipping department is important.

12. Describe how customer service operations contribute to company profits.

13. Explain the proper way of handling a customer complaint about a product that malfunctions.

14. List the problems that sometimes arise out of product delivery and installation.

15. Comment on the conditions that might make you responsible for credit arrangements even if you don't actually handle them.

Making Decisions 13-1:

Ann Lundquist is a sales associate for Seaside Mobile Homes. Last week, Jim and Patty Greenwood paid her a visit after having purchased a vacant lot in a nearby mobile home park. As Ann arrives at her office this morning, she finds the Greenwoods waiting for her.

Ann: Hi! What brings you here so early in the morning?

Patty: Well, we wanted to take another look at that mobile home you showed us last Thursday.

Ann: Fine. I'll put my briefcase down and we'll go have a look.... Better still, why don't I just give you the key? You can take all the time you want in there.

Jim: That would be great. The price hasn't changed, has it?

Ann: No, it's the same price. Here's the key. Take your time.

The Greenwoods return to Ann's office after twenty minutes in the mobile home.

Ann: Well, what do you think?

Patty: Do you think we can get financing?

Ann:	Yes. It's part of my job to help you secure financing.
Jim:	How would we get the trailer moved over to our lot?
Ann:	That's easy. We do it free of charge. As a matter of fact (looking out the window), I see where they're getting ready to move one right now. Let's walk over to the other end of the yard and watch them.
Patty:	We're a little rushed for time right now. We have an appointment at the bank to finalize our loan for the lot. We'll call you back.

Describe the closing signal that Ann missed. Rewrite Ann's remarks from the time the Greenwoods returned to her office. Develop your own method of closing.

Making Decisions 13-2:

Lillian Randolph is the rental agent for the newly completed Chestershire Corporate Center. Allan Kraft, the owner of a successful marketing and consulting service, has spent more than an hour looking at a suite with Lillian. He has asked dozens of questions, and checked and double-checked every detail he can think of. Kraft is obviously very interested in leasing space at Chestershire.

Allan:	Is this suite available for immediate occupancy?
Lillian:	Yes. Would you like to draw up the lease? The painters will be in the building tomorrow. We can have them painting these walls with the colors of your choice by the end of the week.
Allan:	Wall color. That's something I haven't thought of. What colors do you think would look good in here?
Lillian:	Many colors would go nicely in these offices. I have a color book in my car. Would you like to take a look at it?
Allan:	Yes, I would.

Evaluate how the timing was for Lillian's attempted close. Evaluate her close, including any fundamental weaknesses.

Making Decisions 13-3:

Kathy Pechin, a sales consultant for New Image hair care products, makes an unannounced call on Lisa Phuong, the owner of High Point Salon and Beauty School.

Kathy:	Hello, Lisa. I'm Kathy Pechin, with New Image hair care products. You may have heard of us.

Lisa:	No, I haven't. And before you go any further, I should tell you I'm reluctant to buy anything I'm not familiar with.
Kathy:	(Handing Lisa a product brochure) I'm the same way, but this is a great line of products. We can supply you with everything you need, and your customers and students will love our hair care line.
Lisa:	Do you have any samples with you?
Kathy:	No, but I have several cases of shampoo and conditioner in the car.
Lisa:	OK. I'll try one case of shampoo. The shipment from my supplier won't arrive for several days, and this will tide me over. How much do I owe you?
Kathy:	A case is only twelve bottles. That won't go very far. With a business as large as yours, I'd recommend that you start with five cases.
Lisa:	No. One case is all I need. Besides, if my customers don't like it, I wouldn't want to be stuck with the extra supplies.

Explain whether Kathy undersold or oversold her product. Describe how Lisa might have been persuaded to buy more shampoo or try other products.

Making Decisions 13-4:

Describe various methods of closing that might be used in selling a product via the Internet. Include examples using both ordering from a standard web page, and creating dialogue between prospect and seller.

Making Decisions 13-5:

As a fitness consultant for a health club, you are told by a member who joined three months ago that despite his exercise regimen he hasn't lost weight. Describe your response.

Practice Makes Perfect 13-1:

In the process of making a sales presentation to another student posing as a buyer, see how often you can affect a trial close, noting the results.

Practice Makes Perfect 13-2:

Select a product and make a sales presentation to several of your fellow students using a different type of close on each.

The Selling Personality

THE JOB TO BE DONE . . .

Each of us is different; our personalities are not identical. Yet despite these individual differences, some specific traits, important to selling, are learnable. Chapter 14 teaches you to:

...appreciate the importance of personality in selling.

...understand the role of friendship in selling.

...identify and develop desirable personality traits.

...know the value of a good sense of humor.

...appreciate the importance of keeping relationships positive.

...develop good conversational skills.

...appreciate the value of small talk.

...understand the importance of active listening.

...take an interest in the prospect.

...respect the prospect as a unique individual.

...know how to handle personality differences.

THE SELLING PERSONALITY . . .

The desire to build friendships and get along with others is common among most humans. People want to be liked, and they want to develop positive relationships with those they encounter in their personal and business lives.

In selling, the ability to make friends is a vital part of the salesperson's success. Successful salespeople work to improve their personalities so that their relationships with customers will be pleasant and fruitful.

People who like and care about each other want to meet each other's needs. Suppose your best friend invites you to go to a movie that doesn't interest you. You might seriously consider accepting the invitation because you know your companion doesn't want to ask anyone else. Your desire to meet this need is the same as that which motivates the selling effort. When you behave as a friend to your prospects, they want to return your friendship and meet your needs.

A prospect is much more likely to grant a special request that comes from a salesperson who acts like a friend than a salesperson who appears a stranger. Remember, however, that friendship with a prospect is a byproduct of a good business relationship, not the other way around. You need not fear that exchanging favors with a prospect will be "trading on a friendship."

This chapter is devoted to the importance of personality in selling. It offers specific techniques for improving your selling personality and for developing positive relationships with prospects and customers.

THE SALES BICYCLE . . .

Because sales is an occupation that involves continual interaction with others, a pleasing personality is an absolute necessity to the salesperson's success. The prospects and customers you deal with want more than just a good product. They want a salesperson who cares about them. There are many industries in which the competing products and prices are the same, or have such minor differences that prospects don't notice or care much about them. In such markets, selling yourself becomes a prerequisite to selling your product.

Traditionally, a pleasing personality was thought to be something you either had or didn't have, something that could never change. But actually, anyone can develop a good personality. Success in selling requires two broad categories of expertise: **technical skills** and people skills. These two abilities must work together, like the wheels of a bicycle, or **sales bicycle**. Technical skills include all those abilities related to product knowledge. People skills (often called human relations or **soft skills**) include the expertise related to getting along with others. Not only are both "wheels" important to the bicycle, but also the individual spokes are an integral part of each wheel.

Some salespeople spend too much time working on the spokes of one wheel and not enough on the other. Historically, the emphasis in sales training has been on technical skills. Yet most successful salespeople today would agree that human relations skills are more important. Instead of being primarily product oriented, salespeople want to be more people oriented. Rather than be task oriented, professional sellers prefer to be thought of as being relationship oriented.

This is not to say that a pleasing personality is enough by itself. One's nature is in no way a substitute for technical knowledge. But without a pleasing personality, technical skills will do little to move the salesperson forward.

THE SALESPERSON'S PERSONALITY . . .

Personality is the combination of traits that make up an individual. It includes traits of character, behavior, temperament, emotion, and mind. A salesperson's personality should include the qualities we find attractive and desirable in most others. However, because your work will include so much exposure to prospects, you might want to pay extra attention to the traits that relate to meeting prospects' needs and doing business with them.

First, remember that salespeople with "good" personalities are friendly. They're genuinely happy to see both prospects and long-time customers. Because they enjoy people, they sometimes find their friendships with certain customers becoming even more important than their business relationships with them. Friendly salespeople also set themselves apart from others by being cordial to assistants and receptionists.

Salespeople with good personalities have an extra measure of sensitivity and concern for others. They respect the prospect's sense of dignity as well as the prospect's feelings. Salespeople with good personalities are noticeably professional and mature. Their eagerness to make the sale does not overpower their ability to be patient. Salespeople with good personalities are outgoing but not brash. They have a good sense of humor but are not silly. They are capable of showing assertiveness rather than aggressiveness or passivity.

Some adjectives that should apply to a salesperson with a good personality include cooperative, open-minded, thoughtful, understanding, sincere, caring, responsible, ethical, adaptable, energetic, industrious, tactful, punctual, courteous, sympathetic, empathetic, and knowledgeable. Sometimes personality traits can be imagined more easily when compared to contrasting traits. Consider the following pairs of contrasting adjectives, and think about how each trait would contribute something positive or negative to a salesperson's personality:

concerned/indifferent	cooperative/stubborn
respectful/irreverent	sympathetic/uncaring
empathetic/cold	conscientious/careless
sensitive/tactless	relaxed/tense
sensible/silly	outgoing/shy
generous/stingy	assertive/aggressive

> Drag your thoughts away from your troubles—-by the ear, by the heels, or any other way you can manage.
>
> Mark Twain

A Sense of Humor . . .

Most people appreciate a good sense of humor. Some salespeople contend that this trait helps increase the prospect's retention of their message. However, not everyone appreciates the same kind of humor, and not everyone is good at creating it. Even though a sense of humor is an indispensable personality trait (in selling and in life), it is also one that needs to be turned off and on.

In selling, your sense of humor can be turned on when you want to relieve tension, set a positive mood, avoid potential unpleasantness, or lighten up a conversation that has become too serious. If you disagree with a client and reach an impasse, make a joke about yourself. This will remove any suspicion that your ego or stubbornness is preventing an agreement. Be careful to observe your prospects' taste in humor. When prospects are noticeably humorless, avoid joking with them. Sometimes prospects will dislike your sense of humor. Or they might not be in the mood for jokes or light-hearted chatter about certain subjects.

The Salesperson as Friend . . .

As we mentioned earlier, people who consider themselves friends want to meet each other's needs. They care about each other and take an interest in each other's lives, values, and feelings. Salespeople cannot be successful for very long without being a friend to their prospects, without taking a sincere interest in their prospects' happiness. As you can see from Dale Carnegie's "Six Ways to Make People Like You" presented in Figure 14-1, your interest in others will determine their interest in you.

Because the ability to be a friend is such an important part of the salesperson's personality, sympathy and empathy are among the most important traits a salesperson could have. The words **sympathy** and **empathy** are sometimes used interchangeably, but their meanings are slightly different. Sympathy is an understanding of the other person's feelings. Empathy goes further: It is an identification with the other person, a heartfelt sharing of the other person's feelings. A well-developed personality will include both sympathy and empathy. If you lack sympathy, you will be seen as uncaring. Lacking empathy makes you seem cold and distant. Salespeople who can be compassionate are at a tremendous advantage over those who cannot.

Even when your experience is not identical to the prospect's, you may be capable of feeling true empathy. This is because the identification you feel is with the other person's feelings, not a concrete experience. Some experience of your own, one very different from the prospects', might have brought out the same emotions in you that your prospect is experiencing now.

Suppose, as a real estate agent, you meet prospects who are very sentimental about leaving their lifelong home. First, you sympathize. You understand how these prospects must feel because you realize they have ten, twenty, perhaps even forty years of memories attached to the house. Then, you empathize. You know they have put a great deal of hard work into renovating the house, just as you once put a great deal of work into restoring a 1965 Mustang. Your empathy need not come from an experience even as similar as

In a Nutshell

SIX WAYS TO MAKE PEOPLE LIKE YOU

PRINCIPLE 1

Become genuinely interested in other people.

PRINCIPLE 2

Smile.

PRINCIPLE 3

Remember that a person's name is to that person the sweetest and most important sound in any language.

PRINCIPLE 4

Be a good listener. Encourage others to talk about themselves.

PRINCIPLE 5

Talk in terms of the other person's interests.

PRINCIPLE 6

Make the other person feel important—and do it sincerely.

Figure 14-1 How to win friends and influence people.

the experience of restoring a car. You might be an artist in your spare time, and you know how hard it is to let go of a painting you have put yourself into.

The Role of Trust in Friendship . . .

As anyone who enjoys a good friendship will attest, trust is an indispensable part of our relationships with others. An honest connection will be impossible to establish if one party is unwilling or unable to open up to the other in some way. Even business friendships require a measure of mutual trust. This means that both parties should be willing to reveal a certain amount of personal information to each other.

Trust creates an environment in which friends can exchange confidences. The depth of mutual trust within a given relationship is reflected in the importance of what each friend reveals to the other. The greater the disclosures, the stronger the trust; the stronger the trust, the more rewarding the relationship. If one friend reveals profound confidences while the other shares only minor bits of information, an imbalance develops. Eventually, the bond of trust will be broken because it is not mutual.

STARTING ON THE RIGHT FOOT . . .

Of course, before a deeper friendship can develop between you and your prospects, you should be able to handle the more light-hearted aspects of making new friends. The moment you meet a prospect, you begin to make lasting impressions about you and your personality. Interest in the prospect's life is not a trait you can put on and take off like a mask. It reveals itself in many ways. If you greet new acquaintances with a distracted glance and forget their name quickly, you will not make a convincing show of interest.

The most important message to be conveyed when you greet prospects is your happiness to see them. This applies whether the individual is a new acquaintance or a past customer. Showing enthusiasm when you meet someone new is usually easier than when you meet a familiar face. If you fear that your greeting to a familiar person is going to fall flat, pretend that the two of you haven't seen each other for a long time. Then when you offer your greeting, your excitement about meeting the person again will shine through.

Remembering Names . . .

Although you probably would not forget the name of an important prospect, you might occasionally overlook the names of people you don't expect to meet again, or those you meet at large gatherings. If this is so, you might want to improve your memory for names. The ability to recall is a very likable personality trait. People are always pleased to find that they are remembered, and this simple act strongly conveys the impression that you have an interest in them.

Most people "forget" names less than five seconds after they hear them. Part of the problem is that they don't really hear new names at the time of introduction. You can overcome this problem simply by improving your listening technique. When you meet someone for the first time, concentrate your attention on the person's name, and maintain eye contact throughout the introduction. Then address the person by name when you shake hands: "It's nice to meet you, Mrs. Taylor."

Mentally spell out the name, and visualize it in print. If it is difficult to spell, you might even ask the person to help you. Request a business card and read the name carefully. You might also try concentrating on the person's initials, which will help you with future recall. Most important, use the name frequently during conversation. Not only does this help implant it in your mind, it pleases the person you are addressing.

When you are being introduced to several people at a time, repeat each person's name aloud as the host or hostess announces it to you. Then, whenever you look at one of the people, repeat that person's name to yourself.

Memory experts often recommend association techniques. For instance, you could associate a name or initials with the person's occupation. When you meet a banker named Carl Deakins, think "CD." The next time you meet Mr. Deakins, you'll remember CD, and you'll be only one step away from Carl Deakins. Another helpful technique is to associate the name with some real or imagined characteristic of the person. For instance, when you meet Judy Hacker, envision your prospect as a "hacker," a computer whiz. When you meet Laurie Graham, picture your prospect eating graham crackers. Sometimes the sound of the person's name will call an image to mind. When you meet Mr. Eisenberger, look into this prospect's eyes. The next time you see those eyes, you will recall the eyes of Eisenberger. Don't be concerned if the association you make isn't kind or flattering; it's only a memory technique to be used privately.

If you have to ask someone to repeat his or her name, don't make an issue of your memory problem. The reason you need to hear the name again is you want to remember it, so there is no call for embarrassment. Asking for the name a second time is much better than trying to carry on a conversation without it. Eventually, you will be found out. Remember also that the delightful effect of remembering a name will be lost if you mispronounce it or misspell it. Most people feel insulted when their monikers are misused, especially when the person who addresses them makes no effort to correct a noticed error.

Making Conversation . . .

Conversation is our primary vehicle for establishing and maintaining relationships. The ability to converse is the foundation of a pleasing personality. Unlike talk, which is one-sided speech, conversation is two-way communication, complete with active listening. Many people who are good talkers are not so good at making conversation. They like to hear their own voices and fail to take an interest in others. Others are forced to play the role of the audience.

Real conversation is an art, and it takes plenty of practice. As a salesperson, you should strive to be a good conversationalist. Take the initiative in making conversation with prospects, and never refuse an opportunity to communicate offered by another. Your primary goal in conversing with prospects is to get them to open up. You want to make them feel comfortable with and have confidence in you. Remember, too, that conversation should be enjoyable, for both you and your prospects. By sharing pleasantries with others, you help elevate their mood and make them more receptive to you and your product.

It is not the mountain we conquer but ourselves.

Edmund Hillary

Maintaining a Positive Tone . . .

Maintaining a positive tone in your conversation is a tremendous challenge, but a necessary part of selling. You must be careful to choose subjects that can only be discussed pleasantly, and know when to drop a topic that is leading to confusion. You must be careful not to communicate a bad mood to your prospects or cause their mood to turn bad. You must know how to choose words that create good feelings.

Figure 14-2 contains some characteristics of a good conversationalist. Here are some guidelines for making conversation with prospects and maintaining a positive tone:

1. Start by putting prospects in the "telling" position rather than the "listening" position. Prompt potential buyers to tell you about things they are interested in. Ask them about themselves, their company, or their family.

2. Try to work in harmony with your prospects' personalities. If a potential buyer wants to get down to business, forget about making small talk. When they seem serious-minded, don't try to force humor into the situation.

3. Stay away from controversial topics. In general, avoid politics and religion. In particular, stay away from subjects like abortion, nuclear power, and gun control.

4. Keep the conversation focused on pleasant subjects. Don't bring up things that remind people of unhappiness or prompts them to complain or pass judgment. Don't discuss your health or your prospects' health.

5. Abandon immediately any topic that seems sensitive to prospects.

6. Choose topics that interest prospects, and drop topics that seem to bore prospects.

7. Say only good things about people whose names come up in the conversation. If this isn't possible, change the subject. Don't ask prospects what they think of other people.

8. Propel the conversation forward with your comments. Ask open-ended questions. Whenever you respond, weave a portion of your prospects' comments into your own and build on it. Recall earlier comments, and share any new observations you develop as the conversation progresses.

9. Make sure your prospects participate as much as they like. Give them plenty of time to talk without interruption. Especially when the conversation is focused on personal topics, allow the potential buyers to dominate it.

10. Let prospects be the experts. Even if you know more than they about a given subject, allow them the pleasure of thinking otherwise. Proving prospects wrong will only cause negative feelings to develop, and it will stop the conversation as well.

11. Once you have begun a conversation, enjoy it for a while. Don't hurry to finish it before your conversationalists are ready.

12. Let prospects have the last word.

Tips for Being a Good Conversationalist

1. Be informed.

2. Show interest and warmth.

3. Avoid bias or stereotyping.

4. Adjust to others.

5. Tell the truth.

6. Minimize your own opinions.

7. Accept opinions of others.

8. Do not interrupt or make corrections.

9. Watch for signs of discomfort or boredom.

10. Be diplomatic.

Figure 14-2

Recall from Chapter 4 the discussion of keeping up-to-date files on each customer. Although the main purpose of keeping these is to support your direct selling effort, they also come in handy as conversational aids. A customer file kept on index cards or in a rotary file is a great memory aid for the salesperson who sees many buyers. This inventory should include notes about prospects' hobbies, activities, family life and so forth; anything that you would want to know the next time you review the file in advance of a visit. With the help of your customer file, you can meet someone after a long interval and ask questions like "How's your golf game coming?" or "Are you still taking night courses in accounting?" Customers will be flattered to think you remembered personal details about them, and your interest will set you apart from other salespeople.

Making Small Talk . . .

Small talk, or casual conversation about unimportant things, is a very important part of conversation. Most prospects enjoy idle chit-chat and expect salespeople to enjoy it too. Small talk is the preferred mode of conversation in any informal setting. Even in a serious business setting, such as a sales presentation, this innocent banter has its place. The salesperson who never engages in casual conversation is considered unfriendly. If you see your customers regularly, you will want to socialize informally with them. As you get to know your buyers, you will gradually come to learn what they like to chat about.

Probably the easiest way to make small talk with a new prospect is to start with a subject that relates to the product you sell. For instance, if you handle clothing, you might comment about a fashion designer's new line of evening wear. Whatever your product, be it insurance, industrial equipment, real estate, or management services, you will have many small observations and bits of news that can be used for small talk.

As you get to know your prospects, you will be able to generate small talk based on their current interests or topics of fascination. These people might clue you in with direct comments, such as "Have you heard that new compact disc by Whitney Houston?" Or you might find the prospect playing certain music when you arrive for your appointment. Some people display unusual items in their offices that make their interests obvious. Anyone who keeps an aquarium or a collection of exotic plants is undoubtedly open to casual conversation.

Bear in mind, however, that interests come and go, and casual conversation follows. Don't expect the same prospect to be playing Whitney Houston's CD on your next visit. Instead, remember that person's taste in music, and keep it in mind for the next time you chat.

Having a common interest, situation, or friend is another strong basis for small talk. If you and your prospect have similar musical tastes, for example, you can mention how you're looking forward to an upcoming concert. If a mutual friend just got a promotion, you can pass on the new telephone number. One major advantage to talking about common interests is that the prospect will take an interest in you and become a more attentive listener.

The prospect's setting, though a good source of ideas for small talk, has its limits. To make sure that you are always ready to make conversation, casual or otherwise, you should keep up with current events. Read the local newspaper every day, and watch the news on TV. If you sell in a territory away from your home, find ways to keep abreast of passing local interests. Pick up the newspaper that serves your territory. Chat with restaurant servers and hotelkeepers to learn about the local heat wave or the highway construction project across town. Another way to generate conversation with prospects is to think of the letters "P-R-O-S-P-E-C-T" (see Figure 14-3).

No matter what your location, you should cultivate a little knowledge about a variety of subjects. Use the Internet as a source of information about locales that you are visiting. Even if you are not a sports fan, for example, you should at least have some awareness of the popular teams in your area and how they are performing. Undoubtedly someone you meet will comment about a championship game, and you would not want to be caught speechless.

P –	People
R –	Recreational activities
O –	Occupation
S –	Sports
P –	Pastimes
E –	Educational background
C –	Current events
T –	Traveling done and travel plans

Figure 14-3 Converstion topics. Use the letters of the word "prospect" as reminders of possible conversation topics.

Follow the prospect's lead when engaging in small talk. Most people like to chat for a few minutes at the start of a meeting. When you come to a pause in the conversation, the time for small talk is over. If the prospect continues the pleasantries beyond a reasonable time, subtly change the subject. Another person might prefer to talk business first and wait until the end of your meeting to chat. This, too, is perfectly acceptable.

THE FINE ART OF LISTENING . . .

A good listener is a fascinating individual. Usually this is because the listener communicates a sense of appeal with the talker. The talker finishes a conversation, often one-sided, thinking the listener is a delightful person. Good listeners are delightful because they know how to make the talker feel great.

Every salesperson should practice the fine art of good listening. This creates a setting in which the prospect feels comfortable talking. It tells potential buyers that you are interested in whatever they have to say. Not only will good listening make prospects willing to talk, but it will also make them a more receptive listener when you are talking. Further, it helps you gather information that will contribute to the ongoing conversation.

Just as there are advantages in careful listening, there are disadvantages in failing to listen. When you don't pay attention to what others are saying, you miss out on the chance to know their thoughts. Worse, people will feel insulted by your lack of interest. They will give up trying to talk to you, and your inattention will make a poor impression on your prospects.

Unlike mere hearing, listening takes effort. It involves trying to comprehend what we are hearing. Learning to listen is difficult for most of us because we were not trained to listen, but rather to speak. We also tend to think of conversation as primarily speaking. If we are about to meet someone we don't know, we wonder, "What am I going to *say* to this person?" But as Diogenes wrote more than two thousand years ago, "We have two ears and only one tongue in order that we may hear more and speak less."

Lack of interest is a common reason for failing to listen well. If we feel that the information we're hearing will not affect us, we tune it out. Unfortunately, if the prospect asks a question related to an earlier comment and we can't answer properly, we reveal our failure to listen. Another reason for poor listening is that we are often more concerned with our own comments than with those of others. The prospect might say something that we want to respond to, yet we have to keep silent until it is our turn to speak. Our answer preoccupies us, and we don't hear the last few statements.

> Our self-image and our habits tend to go together. Change one and you will automatically change the other.
>
> Dr. Maxwell Maltz

With respect to disagreements, conversation with a prospect is different from that with a friend. In talks with friends, points of view are merely exchanged. With prospects, the element of persuasion enters the picture. If potential buyers say something that is out of harmony with your selling effort, you want to change their minds. This is where good listening comes in. Although your first impulse might be to interrupt and dispute their opinion, you must hear them out. Hold your tongue until prospects have their say, and resist judging them.

Active Listening . . .

Listening may be active or passive. **Passive listening** is silent but unresponsive attention. It allows the speaker an uninterrupted comment, but does nothing to support or encourage her or him to go on. In selling, passive listening is not much better than mere hearing. On the other hand, **active listening** is a form of conversational activity aimed at responding and soliciting responses. It is most effective in selling situations. Active listening involves asking prospects questions that encourage them to explain, and then responding to their explanations with comments that build upon what has been said.

Asking questions, smiling, making eye contact, and nodding the head are common characteristics of active listening. Another effective technique is called **linking**. This involves mentioning prospects' earlier comments in your own responses and pairing their ideas with yours. Whenever you link, use different phrasing than your prospect used. This will confirm that you got the message and show your comprehension.

Asking Questions . . .

Asking questions is both a listening and a general conversation technique. It is an ideal way to begin a discussion and keep one going. Questions serve the conversationalist. They do so by informing the questioner and drawing out the responder.

When talking with a prospect, you should try to ask open-ended questions. Closed-ended questions call for short, uninformative answers that contribute little to the conversation. A closed-ended question is any question that calls for a response like "yes," "no," "fine," "not much" or "the usual." As described in Chapter 10, open-ended questions call for complete answers that move the conversation forward. Instead of saying, "This is great weather, isn't it?" (a closed-ended question), ask, "How are you spending your time in this marvelous weather?"

In keeping with the notion that a conversation should be positive, ask only questions that the prospect will enjoy answering. Never ask to discuss personal tragedy or failure, and avoid private questions. If the situation calls for it, begin by saying, "Pardon my asking..." or "If you don't mind my asking..." Be sensitive to short, unenthusiastic responses. They indicate that the prospect doesn't want to discuss the subject. Ask questions that prompt answers that prompt more questions.

Dick DeKleyn

From the beginning, Dick DeKleyn knew that he wanted a career in real estate. He entered Fox Valley Technical College and earned an associates degree in this field. Although much of his coursework was specific to his career choice, his obvious love was in selling and Fox Valley provided excellent instruction in this area. After college he has actively continued his education in marketing and sales, earning the respected Certified Residential Specialist (CRS) and Graduate, Realtors Institute (GRI) designations.

Dick first joined the real estate firm of Temmer-Bytof, an affiliate of the Caldwell Banker organization. He has been with this company for fifteen plus years, and loves every minute of this fast moving field. He has established himself as a relocation expert, assisting corporate transferees to find suitable housing. He has been a corporate accounts director for the firm and is a member of the Employee Relocation Council. Never being satisfied with the status quo, Dick constantly updates his skills through seminars on real estate law and development.

Dick firmly believes that success in the real estate business depends upon quality customer service. Using his knowledge, coupled with hard work, he continually gives clients more than is expected. His colleagues often cite his attention to detail as paying big dividends for his customers. This commitment to professionalism has paid off well for Dick DeKleyn, who has sold over $45 million in real estate during his career with Caldwell Banker.

TAKING AN INTEREST . . .

When you look at a group photograph, who is the first person you look for? Chances are, if you are in the group, you look for yourself. Taking a primary interest in oneself is human nature, and it is something you should expect of others. Prospects are interested in themselves and whatever is relevant to their lives. The only way to gain the interest of prospects is to take an interest in them. If you do, they will be more inclined to return the favor because they will be complimented by your attention. Moreover, your sincere interest in prospects will lead you to learn more about them and how best to meet their needs.

A genuine interest in other people, along with the desire to meet their needs, is the only lasting basis for friendship. Friendship develops out of mutual interests. Although some of your customers may become friends, you cannot expect them all to. One way to develop an interest in prospects is to observe how they spend their time and money. These are strong indicators of values and

Taking an Interest

interests. For example, one who travels a great deal will usually display pictures and souvenirs. These clues will tell you where your prospects have gone and what their favorite activities are. They are natural conversation pieces.

Demonstrate your interest in the prospect by pointing out conversation pieces and asking open-ended questions. As you learn more, your involvement will continue to grow. If there is something you don't know or understand, that is so much the better because it gives you an opportunity to ask the prospect to inform or teach you.

The Prospect as a Person . . .

One of the most important things to remember when doing business in the selling field is that prospects are people, not numbers or accounts or companies. As businesses become bigger and more technological, they can become more impersonal. The distance between customers and firms becomes greater as human contact decreases and the personal touch is forgotten. Customers whose lives are filled with impersonalization in business will appreciate the salesperson who remembers "the little things."

Here are some guidelines for keeping the personal touch in business:

1. Recognize your customers. If you work in a retail selling environment, always acknowledge repeat buyers. Don't pretend you've never seen them before. Offer a friendly greeting, and if you know the shopper's name, say it. People stop going to stores whose salespeople treat them as invisible strangers time and time again.

2. Remember your customers during the holidays. Send them greeting cards with a personal, handwritten message.

3. Remember your customers on their birthdays. Put a birthday card in each customer's file at the beginning of the year so that you will be reminded to send it on time.

The personal touches are appreciated by people. Customers tend to remain loyal to a thoughtful salesperson rather than do business with a potentially less attentive stranger. The personal touch contributes to the prospect's feeling of importance, something all of us desire. There are several other ways to make potential buyers feel good, chiefly by showing recognition and appreciation for them. Here are some guidelines for showing prospects how important they are to you:

1. Recognize your prospects' accomplishments. Invite them to tell you about their work and business. Everyone excels in something, be it occupation, community activities, or personal life, and most take joy in personal success. Encourage prospects to talk about their successes, and offer ample praise.

2. Acknowledge the prospect's expertise by asking for advice or information. Most are an authority on something, and people delight in being acknowledged as such.

3. Show an extra measure of respect by following up on your prospects' suggestions. Go to the restaurants they recommend, and later tell them how you enjoyed it. Prove that you value their ideas and advice.

A Word About Compliments . . .

In Chapter 6, we described the use of compliments as a selling technique, but actually it is much more. Such an endorsement is an exercise in human relations. Unlike flattery, which is used to gain favor, a compliment is sincere praise intended only to make the receiving person feel good. Keep an eye out for opportunities to congratulate or praise the prospect. The only criterion is that you should be unquestionably honest.

Although a compliment can focus on any subject from decor to business success to personal strengths, not all subjects are suitable between salespeople and prospects. For example, praising the prospect's appearance would be inappropriate because this is too personal. People commonly enjoy hearing from friends and loved ones about how nice they look, but prospects would rather not hear the same kind of compliment from a salesperson.

Personality Differences . . .

Most prospects are easy to get along with, but occasionally you will encounter a prospect whose personality doesn't mesh with yours. Even when there's no "chemistry," though, you should be able to work around most personality differences by making use of your strengths as a salesperson.

Should the prospect become unfriendly or unpleasant, you need to be the opposite. One of the primary things to remember when dealing with a difficult personality is to maintain a positive attitude independent of the prospect's behavior. Prudential Insurance salesperson Ken Arnt says, "The more unreceptive prospects are to me, the harder I try to be friendly with them. When they see that I'm sincere, their attitude usually changes."

Frequently, you will be faced with the challenge of overcoming disagreements between you and the prospect. This common selling situation calls for tremendous tact. Obviously, you should not say anything that might ridicule the buyer or imply that he or she is wrong, but you must also avoid getting into a debate. Even a friendly confrontation is inappropriate because it pits the salesperson and potential buyer on opposite sides. The pressure to maintain one's opinion in a debate is strong, and the prospect may erect a psychological barrier against you and your ideas.

> You can't win races without working harder than the other guys.
> Ted Turner

State ideas as observations or suggestions, not as steadfast assertions. Preface your statements with phrases that imply nothing but open-mindedness. "Have you ever considered this?" you might say, or "What do you think of this idea?" Here are a few more possible ways to introduce your idea:

"It has been my experience ..."

"Well, it seems to me ..."

"As I see it ..."

"My opinion is ..."

"The impression I get is ..."

All these opening phrases help establish the fact that you see things differently without claiming to be more correct.

When prospects are convinced that your product is inferior to the competition's, their opinion must be disarmed, but in a way that preserves their self-esteem. Approach the matter as though you need to reconvince yourself, as though you may be wrong and need to examine things one more time. As you go over the facts, show flexibility and cooperation by expressing a willingness to look at the issue from the prospect's perspective. Say, "Well, I might be wrong. Let's see," or "Perhaps I should reexamine the facts." By presenting your opinions without openly condemning opposing points of view, you will find that prospects are more willing to listen to your ideas.

Tact must also be used when you need to correct the prospect in any way. A correction that suggests disapproval or criticism will likely cause resentment. The most tactful way to correct people is to call attention to their error in an indirect way. For example, if a customer has damaged your product by misusing it, you might say, "That's a novel way to do it, but my other customers haven't had much success trying it that way. They've enjoyed the product more by handling it like this."

If you discover that you made a mistake or said something incorrect, always admit it. Admitting your mistake to the prospect will reassure the prospect that you don't intend to repeat your mistakes. It will also prove you are being honest with yourself and that you do not let ego interfere with your relationships.

Tense Situations . . .

Sometimes tension arises between the salesperson and prospect over an unresolved issue or disagreement. The first thing to remember in these situations is not to become angry. If the prospect says something that upsets you, pause and take a deep, relaxing breath, and think about how to answer as diplomatically as possible. An irate response will only generate more animosity in return, and an angry prospect will never buy from you.

Recall from Chapter 9 that prospects will sometimes take out their frustrations on salespeople. Learn to recognize when your prospects are blowing off steam, and don't take their attacks personally.

Here are some guidelines for working through a tense situation:

1. Try to locate points that you and the prospect have in common, and concentrate on them first. By first talking about the things you agree on, you lessen the tension and provide the basis for keeping your conversation friendly.
2. Never be the aggressor. Say nothing that might be interpreted as antagonistic or insulting.
3. If the prospect says something unkind or sarcastic, let it bounce off you. Do not become defensive. Remember that the prospect is voicing an opinion influenced by anger, not a fact or observation.

Generally, you should be able to avoid extremely unpleasant personality clashes with prospects. With the help of a selling personality, you can learn to adapt to any situation with any prospect. Salespeople who have repeated clashes with prospects must either improve their personality or seek an occupation that involves less contact with others.

You Decide!

Michelle sells stocks and bonds for a major brokerage company. She has been in the securities business for a number of years, and has put together a package that is particularly attractive to retired prospects. One of her best sources of leads is her church, where she is very active. Besides being a lay reader and a founder of the young couples group, she is a member of the building committee, which is busily preparing for a major expansion. One of the hold-ups to the expansion is one neighbor who refuses to sell a needed piece of land because of a long standing dispute with another building committee member.

While calling on an elderly church member regarding a securities package, her prospect inquires about the delay in the expansion plans. Although Michelle knows full well the problem is due to the stubbornness of one churchgoer, she is reluctant to spread gossip. On the other hand, she worries that her prospect may see through her excuses if she, as a member of the building committee, does not answer this direct question. Making a quick decision, she decides to evade the inquiry by focusing attention on the securities package. Did she respond correctly? **You decide!**

Summing It Up . . .

Selling requires constant interaction with others, and you need a friendly, outgoing personality to succeed. Remember the sales bicycle. Although technical skills are necessary, they are insufficient to ensure your success. Traditionally, the emphasis in selling has been on technical skills, and too little importance has been placed on people skills. Salespeople, sales managers, and sales trainers have come to realize that a warm, sociable salesperson is at a strong advantage over one who relies solely on product knowledge.

Personable salespeople are friendly, outgoing, cooperative, open-minded, thoughtful, understanding, sincere, caring, responsible, adaptable, ethical, energetic, industrious, tactful, courteous, sympathetic, and empathetic. They have a sense of humor, and they learn names easily. Their conversations have a positive tone. They know the rules of conversation, and are never at a loss for it. They appreciate small talk, are attentive listeners, and direct conversations toward their prospects' needs and interests. They offer sincere compliments and are able to quickly adjust to their prospect's personality. When they find themselves in a tense situation, they remove the tension with respectful, courteous behavior.

Key Concepts and Terms . . .

active listening
empathy
linking
passive listening
sales bicycle

small talk
soft skills
sympathy
technical skills

Building Skills . . .

1. With reference to the sales bicycle, explain the two basic skills needed for success in selling.
2. Describe sympathy, empathy.
3. Explain how the salesperson–prospect relationship is like a friendship.
4. List some techniques for remembering the names of new prospects.
5. Compare the differences between small talk and conversation.
6. Describe some of the guidelines for making conversation and maintaining a positive tone.
7. Elaborate on the role and importance of small talk in conversation.
8. Explore how you might use an inventory of prospect information to help you make conversation.
9. Define active listening.
10. List some of the reasons we fail to listen.
11. Explore why open-ended questions are preferable to closed-ended questions.
12. Describe some ways to add the personal touch in business.
13. Compare the difference between a compliment and flattery.

14. Explain how trust is related to shared confidences in a relationship.

15. Give some examples showing how suggestions can be presented tactfully.

Making Decisions 14-1:

Gary Holskin, an account representative for Winslow Investment Services, has a number of conservative clients who buy and sell only infrequently. One such customer is Leland Lewis, an investor with a substantial portfolio of low-risk stocks. Out of the blue, Leland calls Gary.

Gary:	Leland! We haven't talked in over a year. What have you been up to?
Leland:	I'm not up to anything, Gary, and that's just how I like it. I retired last August.
Gary:	That's great.
Leland:	What's new in the financial world?
Gary:	Well, quite a bit. I'm sure you've kept up with the news.
Leland:	Not much. I've been traveling a lot lately.
Gary:	Well, the big news for us is the failure of Creative Money Management. Did you hear about that?
Leland:	A little. I recall seeing the name in the newspaper.
Gary:	Well, it's meant a lot more business for us. When a big brokerage house like that goes belly up, everyone in the industry feels it.
Leland:	I guess you're right. Winslow is still in good financial shape, isn't it?
Gary:	We couldn't be better.

Describe how Gary failed to introduce a suitable conversation topic. Based on Leland's cues, select topics that might be more suitable. If Leland was the one to mention the failure of Creative Money Management, describe how Gary should respond.

Making Decisions 14-2:

Lana Bryant is a sales agent for Aladdin Carnival Supplies. One day she calls on Jill Neary, the coordinator of Tyler City's annual summer fair.

Jill:	What do you think of the closing of the Elkview Amusement Park at the end of this season?
Lana:	I really don't know much about it. Between my job and night school, I don't get much time to read the newspaper. Doesn't it have something to do with a real estate developer?
Jill:	Lana, I thought Elkview was in your territory. Haven't you heard?
Lana:	Heard what?

Jill:	Everybody in town is up in arms about it. A big developer filed for a zoning variance and won. They're going to put more than two hundred townhouses on the site. They're even going to fill in the lake if the state permits them.
Lana:	I guess there's a big flap about it.
Jill:	You've got that right. Every day there are three or four letters to the editor in the newspaper complaining about it. There's even talk of a class action suit against the city council for granting the variance.
Lana:	I was just over at Elkview in April; sold them several popcorn and cotton candy machines. I guess that was my last visit ever....

Explain why Lana has no excuse for not knowing the details of the Elkview closing. Give Lana some advice regarding what to do now that she knows about Elkview.

Making Decisions 14-3:

List the five biggest conversation topics of the day. Describe which are suitable or unsatisfactory subjects for small talk by a salesperson.

Making Decisions 14-4:

Investigate the Internet for information about any three cities, worldwide. Briefly list the type of data that are available, making note of how such information could be of value to salespeople.

Practice Makes Perfect 14-1:

Select six different students from your class, using cultural diversity. Begin your sales presentation to each, varying your opening remarks to fit their gender, personality, or cultural background.

Practice Makes Perfect 14-2:

Ask several students to dream up different scenarios for your initial sales visit. Design your opening remarks to fit those specific scenarios. Describe how you will create communication that will enhance your presentation.

A Professional Image

THE JOB TO BE DONE . . .

Like personality, image is all important in the selling profession. How one looks and acts is just as meaningful as what one says. Chapter 15 deals with the role of image, enabling you to:

...appreciate the importance of a professional image in selling.

...appreciate the significance of a favorable first impression.

...understand the role of visual appearance in the professional image.

...examine the business wardrobe.

...analyze the role of color in the business wardrobe.

...know how to dress for the industry and for the prospect.

...appreciate the need for uncompromised professional standards.

THE PROFESSIONAL IMAGE . . .

One of the basic tasks of selling is impression building. The imprint you make on your prospects should reflect both your personal standards and those of your firm. As an extension of your company, you are in a position to make the business's strongest positive statement. **Visual image** is an integral part of professionalism because of its role in creating the all-important first impression.

The effort you put into building impressions is just as important as the effort you exert in developing product knowledge and selling skills. Your appearance, behavior, and ethical standards tell the prospect whether you are competent, honest, experienced, intelligent, and successful. Your prospects will respond to you on the basis of the image you project.

A professional appearance and behavior are the minimal requirements for success in selling. A salesperson who looks or acts unprofessionally will be thought incapable of meeting customer needs. Buyers may try to keep an open mind and overlook flaws in a salesperson's image, but a poor representation speaks strongly against all other parts of the selling effort. Figure 15-1 illustrates eight factors that contribute to a salesperson's "presenting image."

First Impressions . . .

Relationships are won or lost at the very beginning of an encounter. Experienced salespeople and sales consultants agree that the first thirty seconds are the most critical time the seller spends in the prospect's presence. It is at this first moment of contact that potential buyers begin to form a lasting image and impression of the salesperson. This all-important half-minute can make or break the sale. It is why the approach is known as "the most important thirty seconds in selling."

As the adage goes, first impressions last. If the first impression you make is negative, even wrongly so, you may never get a chance to make another. A prospect who observes you in a bad light and forms a negative image of you will be turned off to you. On the other hand, one who sees you in a favorable light will at least be willing to hear you out.

The first impression is expressed primarily through visual appearance. Many prospects, especially buyers in fast-paced businesses, use visual references to judge quickly and efficiently which salespeople they want to see. Receptionists and administrative assistants also use these allusions. This is why personal appearance is such an important part of the salesperson's professional image. It communicates messages about your individual qualities to people who don't know you.

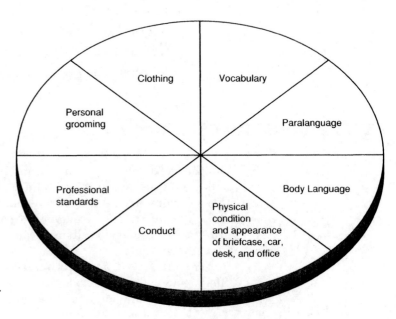

Figure 15-1 Aspects of your "presenting image."

Name:		Date:			

Name: _____ Date: _____
Sex: _____ Company: _____
Age: _____ Position: _____

Directions:
Circle your perceived level of development
for each item on the Profile.

Scoring and Interpretation:
Make sure each item is circled. Add all 10 circled
numbers to obtain a % score.

IMAGE FACTORS	LEVEL OF DEVELOPMENT				
	Very Low	Low	Moderate	High	Very High
Proportion Height and weight are proportional	2	4	6	8	10
Carriage Posture and gait exhibit refinement	2	4	6	8	10
Grooming Hair, skin, nails, and body are clean and attractive	2	4	6	8	10
Dress Clothing, shoes, accessories are role-appropriate	2	4	6	8	10
Speech Vocalizations are distinct and modulated	2	4	6	8	10
Diction Words, phrases, and sentences are well-chosen	2	4	6	8	10
Gestures Expressive movements are used skillfully	2	4	6	8	10
Etiquette Proper manners and protocol are adhered to	2	4	6	8	10
Habits Personal idiosyncrasies are non-offensive	2	4	6	8	10
Style Projected image matches identity and purpose	2	4	6	8	10

Results: **Comments:**
• Excellent Development   80–100%
• Good Development   60–79%
• Fair Development   40–59%
• Need Work   20–39%

Score _____%

©1989, 1997 Karen Kaufman & Don Kaufman, All Rights Reserved.

Figure 15-2

The Primacy Effect . . .

The **primacy effect** is the image you create in someone's mind at the point of introduction. It is the combined effect of these eight factors:

Appearance	Eye contact
Conduct	Gestures and mannerisms
Smile and other facial expressions	Posture
Handshake	Opening remarks

Notice how many of the factors that make up the primacy effect are visual. This initial impact on the prospect determines whether you get "your foot in the door" or "the door in your face."

A Professional Appearance . . .

Creating a professional appearance requires a relatively small investment of time and money compared to the return it provides. Maintaining this image is possible for anyone who wants to put some effort into it. Although no salesperson wants to project a poor image, some do exactly that by neglecting their visual side. They erroneously assume that product knowledge and selling skills outweigh image in selling. But appearance is extremely powerful. A good image may help boost a poor selling effort, and a poor one will definitely harm even the best presentation. On the basis of your appearance, the prospect decides whether to let you use your product knowledge and selling skills.

HOW IMAGE COMMUNICATES . . .

A professional image communicates many messages. It proclaims self-esteem, competence, self-confidence, success, status, and respect. All these messages are important to the selling effort. Here are some of the ways in which image transmits these messages:

Self-Esteem. By looking professional, you reinforce your own feeling of self-esteem and communicate your attitude to others.

Competence. When your appearance is appropriate to your professional situation, it proves you are aware of and comfortable with the realities of your business. A professional appearance tells the prospect that you know what you are doing.

Self-Confidence. Knowing you are maintaining a professional image makes you feel good about yourself. And if you feel good about your appearance, you will behave in a way that projects your belief in yourself and your abilities.

Success. A professional appearance signals an attitude of accomplishment. A poor appearance suggests a lack of care for one's image, which in turn signals unhappiness over failure or a lack of ability to succeed.

Status. Dress and personal appearance communicate one's position in society and business. People rely on appearances to determine the status of strangers. Have you ever noticed how the attire of employees improves as they advance in their firm, or how you assume that an employee wearing a t-shirt is a laborer and an employee wearing a suit is a manager or executive? Receptionists and assistants are more willing to summon the boss if the salesperson "looks important."

Respect. When you look professional, you show respect for prospects because you prove that you care enough to look your best in front of them. Imagine calling on a businessperson in your jeans: What does this casual attire say to the prospect who dresses in a suit and works downtown in a sophisticated environment?

Your ability to succeed in selling yourself doesn't depend on what happened in the past, but on how you see your future. Convince yourself that you will be successful and you'll convince others as well.

Dorothy Leeds

IMAGE FIRST . . .

All salespeople, particularly new salespeople, should concern themselves with their image. Those seeking their first selling position should take pains to look professional at all times. Employers, whether they say so or not, are very concerned with an applicant's ability to project the proper image. They need not worry about a beginning salesperson's image if the new hire already has the right one. An inexperienced applicant who looks and acts professionally will require less training and will be more likely to succeed in selling. The employer can devote more time to training the newcomer in product information, company procedures, and selling techniques. Prospective employers also infer that a person with a professional appearance and image will be more devoted to the job.

This same chain of thought holds in salesperson–prospect relationships. A salesperson who is new to the prospect but looks professional will require less "training"; that is, customers will be more confident that the seller has the ability to understand and address their needs. By looking professional, the new salesperson communicates commitment to prospects and their business.

WARDROBE AND IMAGE . . .

The so-called **IBM image**, an appearance cultivated by the giant computer company for many years, was a symbol of professionalism throughout the business world. This corporate image is still conveyed today largely through conservative business attire. In this section, we offer some guidelines for developing a wardrobe that will contribute to such an appearance, followed by separate notes for women and men.

Buy Quality . . .

If you have a limited budget, your wardrobe money should be devoted to quality rather than quantity. A few well-chosen pieces will serve your business needs far better than a closet full of cheap, inappropriate items. Look for good materials and fine workmanship, and balance cost against utility when choosing from among alternatives. For example, if jacket A costs twice as much as jacket B, ask yourself if jacket A will deliver twice as much value as jacket B. Will you wear it more often? Can its color, lines, and fabric be coordinated better with other items already in your wardrobe? Will it keep its shape, style, and neat appearance longer?

Choose Classic Styles . . .

Classic styles are styles that look good year after year. Because this clothing agrees with perennial sensibilities rather than changeable fashion trends, it can also be the most economical wardrobe alternative in the long run. More tailored than high-fashion apparel, timeless clothing relies on basic, versatile pieces that can be mixed and matched at will. A good, classically styled blazer can last many years more than a markedly fashionable one, which could go out of style before the garment wears out. Classic styles can be counted on to be appropriate in almost any selling situation, and they lend themselves to personal statements with small, fashionable accessories.

Use Basic Colors . . .

The business wardrobe is predominantly made of basic colors, which appear more "businesslike." The basic colors for a woman's business wardrobe (suits, dresses, skirts, and blazers) are black, blue, navy, burgundy, brown, beige, and gray. The basic colors for a man's wardrobe (suits, jackets, and trousers) are navy, medium blue, beige, and gray. Smaller pieces such as ties or blouses can be lighter colors. Here, too, basic colors are the rule. Loud or flashy shades should be avoided in most business situations.

Power colors include black, dark blue, dark gray, and brown. A dark blue pinstripe suit is considered the ultimate power suit, and is useful when presenting to top corporate executives. Because dark colors make the wearer appear taller and more commanding, large men may want to avoid wearing power colors in certain situations. A salesperson who transmits too much power could intimidate prospects. By the same token, a person who is small in stature could use power colors to great advantage. For women making their place in a male-dominated industry, effective power colors are navy, charcoal gray, and black.

When a less powerful message is desired, wear medium shades. Lighter colors like beige or blue are also good when you want to appear friendly and approachable. Remember, too, that choices will vary somewhat with the season and the weather.

Here are some considerations to keep in mind when choosing colors for your wardrobe:

> *Black* is the ultimate power color, but it is too overpowering as a men's suit color. Salesmen should reserve black for formal wear and accessories such as the belt, wallet, briefcase, and shoes. Saleswomen may wear black suits, skirts, and dresses as well as black accessories.

Blue is the most preferred color for men and women; it is universally flattering. Navy blue is a true power color, especially for men. It suggests sincerity and money. Medium blue is ideal for communicating that you are open and approachable. Blue transmits messages of harmony and consistency.

Gray conveys stability and strength. Gray in almost any shade or pattern is an excellent choice for the major pieces in men's and women's wardrobes. Charcoal gray is a power color for both sexes. Lighter gray is more relaxed and friendly.

Brown, great for suits, is better in herringbones and tweeds than in solid brown. A good choice for the briefcase, belt, and shoes. Your hair color should determine which shade of brown is best for you. Brown is a better color choice for women and older men than for younger men.

Beige is a very versatile color for men and women. Ideal as a summer wardrobe color, beige is friendly and businesslike, but not overpowering. A beige suit is excellent for presentations to blue-collar prospects or those who won't be wearing suits. For men, a beige suit looks great with a powder blue shirt.

Burgundy conveys authority and is both flattering and very versatile. For men, burgundy should be restricted to the tie, belt, wallet, and briefcase. Women may wear burgundy suits as well as burgundy accessories.

Red may or may not be appropriate, depending on the wearer's sex, the exact shade, the garment, and whether it is the major color or an accent color. Yellow should be used with similar caution. Purple, long associated with royalty, is extremely noticeable. Because it is a fashion color, it may be inappropriate in many industries for the major pieces of a woman's wardrobe. Men should definitely avoid it. Green is also inadvisable.

Dress for Your Industry, Prospect, and Region . . .

Standards of dress will differ according to the industry, prospect, and region. You might notice, for example, that businessmen in the Southwest sometimes wear cowboy boots with their suits, or that New Englanders seem to prefer the classic look. Be careful to observe whether the styles you see are chosen by your prospects and by the successful people in your industry.

Conservative industries like insurance and finance tend to favor a traditional look because it conveys a sense of stability and dependability. By contrast, a more contemporary appearance is appropriate for industries such as home furnishings, communications, and computers. Creative industries like cosmetics, apparel, music, and theater will favor a more flamboyant style. Extremely fashionable clothing will be common only in fashion and related fields. Advertising, because it is a creative industry that serves businesspeople, accepts a look that includes both conservative and flamboyant elements. As you become more familiar with your industry, you will develop a feel for the appropriate wardrobe.

Like industries, individual prospects vary in the wardrobe standards they find acceptable. To dress for potential buyers means to vary your dress according to personal preferences. Recognize that no two people are exactly alike, and that taste in clothing will be influenced largely by age, occupation, financial status, and so on.

Remember that your business wardrobe should be a tool for attracting prospects to you. Although the business suit is the standard "uniform" for men and women in selling, it has its limitations with respect to certain industries, prospects, or regions. In some situations, the suit can have exactly the effect you don't want, such as when it distances you from your prospects.

Underdressing is not the only danger of inappropriate attire; you could overdress as well. How would you dress to call on a prospect during a workday when he or she is a farmer? A potential buyer in overalls will not be comfortable or receptive to a salesperson wearing a suit. Worse, you will look silly, all dressed up in the middle of a cornfield. When calling on casually dressed prospects in rural areas, you may find it appropriate to choose a sporty look that would never be right for the city.

Some salespeople call in manufacturing arenas where prospects are likely to be up to their elbows in raw materials or grease. A seller who is all decked out in coat and tie may be thought of as being unlikely to know how to get his hands dirty. In those selling jobs that require the salesperson to "get amongst the customers," overdressing can create a negative image. If you are selling fiberglass or plastic resins, you might have to meet your customers in the work area, and you should dress prepared to get dirty.

Choose Versatility . . .

Just as quality will serve you better than quantity, versatility is preferred over variety. A small wardrobe can be sufficient as long as it contains versatile pieces, such as basic colors and fabrics that can be mixed in a variety of ways to achieve many different effects. You should be able to combine your clothing and accessories to vary in their degree of power and formality. By changing your appearance, you will be able to meet any occasion with the appropriate look.

You must also learn how to assess and respond to each new selling situation quickly. For instance, if you are dressed up for a setting that turns out to be casual, be prepared to remove your jacket and roll up your sleeves. If you plan to call on one prospect several times in a row, make a note of the outfit you wear on each visit. You can thus be certain not to wear the same clothing too often in front of the same person.

> Any man can be in good spirits and good temper when he's well dressed.
> Charles Dickens

Cheri Mason Naudin

Professional selling is not the career for everyone. To achieve any degree of success, one has to have a genuine care for and interest in others, but being a "people person" is usually not enough. Salespeople need to be self-starters and achievers. The long hours and constant pressure often take a toll on those who need constant direction and want to work a regular nine-to-five day. Similarly, sales management requires a special type of person. Although some field representatives rise through the ranks to leadership positions, many filling these seats are from other disciplines.

Sales managers must control the activities of the sales force to assure maximum company benefit. This process starts with the hiring of the proper individuals. Since not everyone has what it takes to produce in this arena, the initial selection is the key to establishing an efficient and workable team. Training recruits in territory control and time management are necessary tasks for anyone in sales management. Above all, sales managers need to motivate. Often this position is described as being a combination of mother hen, scout leader, and fiscal wizard. Cheri Mason Naudin fits that mold to a tee.

Cheri is Manager, Inside Sales for Air Touch Cellular, a group with an annual budget in excess of $10 million. She rides herd over some eighty telemarketers who produce sales of between 3,000 and 11,000 cellular units per month. Prior to accepting her present position, she spent almost five years in the business-to-business cellular division and Direct Sales Manager. Cheri captured the Sales Manager of the Year awards for her company in both 1992 and 1994. She became interested in this lucrative business through marketing and selling courses at Rancho Santiago College, and is presently pursuing a Bachelors degree through the University of Phoenix. Cheri fills up her "spare" time looking after her three small children.

The Business Wardrobe for Women . . .

We do not portend to be experts in the art of dressing for success. However, there are a few basic tips that could project the professional image of the female seller that are worth mentioning. Rather than taking these suggestions as being gospel, use them to adapt to your own tastes and those of the industry in which you work.

Suits and skirts. A tailored suit for a saleswoman is a solid invest-ment in the future. The best choice is a classically styled business suit that will look right year after year and is very versatile. Ideally, the pieces of a classic suit should combine easily with jackets or skirts from other suits. The suit should have a slightly loose fit, and some shoulder padding is acceptable for a more authoritative appearance. Accessories can provide sufficient variety.

Select a few classic skirts to wear with your suit jackets. Skirts can be straight, A-line, or pleated. They should have a back or side zipper opening. Avoid skirts with a button front. Of course, a suit is not necessary in every situation. A classically designed dress may be appropriate, and one with a matching jacket has more formality and authority. Pantsuits are too infor-mal for most selling situations.

Dresses and blouses. A one- or two-piece dress can be worn with a suit jacket, as long as the colors, styles, and fabrics harmonize. Dress colors can be brighter than suit colors.

The blouse to be worn with a suit can be collared or collarless, and it may be worn with a scarf or modest necklace. A flat shoulder is a wiser choice than a gathered shoulder, although a gathered shoulder works well without a jacket and has fashion appeal. Sleeveless blouses are inappropri-ate. However, a short sleeve or three-quarter-length sleeve is acceptable in most situations.

Sweaters. Though inappropriate for men in conservative selling situa-tions, sweaters are acceptable for women. A collarless, solid-colored sweater is best, and it should not be bulky. Bear in mind that a sweater always looks more casual than a blouse.

Shoes. Shoes should be in basic colors, like black, navy, taupe, or dark brown, depending on the predominant colors in your wardrobe of suits. Your shoe color should be the same shade or darker than the rest of your outfit. Genuine leather will provide comfort and quality, both necessary in an occu-pation that requires the wearer to spend a great deal of time standing or walking. Avoid white, pastel, and fashion colors. They draw attention to your feet and may be considered too casual. The preferred type of shoe is a pump with a moderate heel (1 -1/2 inches high; 2 inches for a very short woman). Sandals are too casual. Wear neutral-colored hosiery.

Talent and merit alone will rarely get you past the smiling receptionist, the protective secretary, the wary agent. A personal introduction to someone on the inside will.

Barbara Sher

Jewelry. Tasteful earrings, lapel pins, and watches help complete the woman's business wardrobe. These accessories should be understated. Wear a simple, functional watch, preferably with a metal or leather band. Real gold and silver are highly desirable, but good costume jewelry is acceptable. A string of pearls, whether real or a fine imitation, adds elegance to a business suit or dress. Single bracelets are acceptable; ankle bracelets are not.

Jewelry should be seen and not heard: Avoid anything that jingles or clanks. Avoid dangling earrings and hoops, and avoid jewelry that glitters. Earrings should be of classic design, such as round, knot, or geometric. Limit rings to one on each hand, except for matched wedding and engagement sets. Avoid plastic rings, pinky rings, and dinner rings.

Purses and briefcases. A briefcase is preferable to a purse for carrying a large volume of items such as papers. There may be times when a leather notepad will suffice along with a purse. If a briefcase is called for, never substitute a purse for one, and *never carry both*. It is easy enough to store your necessary cosmetic items in your briefcase. The briefcase should be sturdy, and either soft- or hard-sided. An advantage of a soft one is your ability to access its contents without having to open it on a desk or your lap. It should be made of leather or a good imitation leather. Choose a dark, basic color like burgundy, brown, or black.

Your purse is your most important accessory, so buy the best you can afford. It should be leather, and also in a dark, basic color like brown, black, burgundy, or navy. It should never appear bulky or stuffed, and should harmonize in style and formality with the rest of your outfit, particularly your shoes. Both purses and briefcases should be scaled to your size and height. Remember, if you use a briefcase, avoid looking clumsy by carrying a purse as well.

Other accessories. A silk scarf is a good choice. Be sure your raincoat completely covers your dress. Your wallet should be a dark shade, like burgundy, and should contain only what is required for the sales call. Choose a wallet that matches your purse. Hats generally make too much of a "statement," but if you wear one for warmth, be sure its style and color blends with the rest of your outfit. Belts are also a high-fashion item, so select a classic style. Wear gloves only in winter, and be sure they match or blend with your coat. Avoid wearing designer eyeglasses. Test your Image Index using Figure 15-3, next page.

Change and growth takes place when a person has risked himself and dares to become involved with experimenting with his own life.

Herbert Otto

The ImageIndex© For Women

Test Your Potential for Getting Ahead.

The following test is based on the probability of making the best first impression on the greatest number of people in business and professional situations. To take the test, simply circle the number opposite the entry that *best* describes you. Then, total up your score according to the directions below, and gauge your Image Index.

BLOUSES
1. Long-sleeved, silk or cotton, solid or small print, with conservative necklines.
2. Oxford cloth shirts with bows.
3. Lace and ruffles, sheer fabrics, or plunging necklines.

SUITS
1. Classic cut, navy, grey, or black, made of quality fabric and well-fitted.
2. Coordinating jacket and skirt in complimentary colors.
3. Never wear suits.

DRESSES
1. One- or two-piece, natural fabric, classic styling, long sleeves, in navy, grey, or black with a jacket.
2. Same as above, without a jacket.
3. Ruffled, sheer or minidresses.

SHOES
1. Dress shoes, always freshly shined.
2. Casual or dress shoes, rarely shined.
3. Don't think about shining shoes.

MAKE-UP
1. Lightly applied to enhance features and coloring.
2. Don't always wear make-up.
3. Applied heavier so that everybody notices it.

HAIR
1. Classic style, well-groomed, shoulder length or shorter.
2. Generally groomed, no particular style.
3. Wear latest style to stand out.

NAILS
1. Manicure at least weekly.
2. Occasionally file and groom.
3. Wait until nails are chipped before polishing.

JEWELRY
1. Regularly wear one or two important pieces.
2. Wear small, barely noticeable jewelry.
3. Wear as much as possible.

PURSES/BRIEFCASES
1. Carry one well-shined classic leather bag for everything.
2. Carry a well-organized briefcase and a purse.
3. Briefcase and/or purse is always overstuffed.

HANDSHAKE
1. Firm with men and women.
2. Only shake when a hand is offered.
3. Don't shake hands.

EYE CONTACT
1. Make frequent eye contact.
2. Not comfortable looking at someone often.
3. Normally look around the room or at feet.

POSTURE
1. Usually stand and sit erectly.
2. Don't pay attention.
3. Tend to slouch.

How to Score Your Image Index: Give yourself 6 points for every #1 answer, 3 points for every #2 answer, and 0 points for every #3 answer. If your total score is:

54–72	Congratulations, you're on your way.
36–53	You're on the right track, but have some work to do.
18–35	Careful, you may be sabotaging your chances of getting ahead. There's still hope, though.
0–17	You've got a real problem. Without immediate action, your chances of making a good first impression are virtually nil.

Figure 15-3   (*Source*: Kiwi Brands)

The Business Wardrobe for Men . . .

Similar to the remarks made regarding attiure for women, you should accept these suggestions on the male wardrobe as being just that—suggestions. Certainly the seller of resins and fiberglass, who must visit his prospects in the production areas of surfboard or boat manufascturers, might be out of place in a coat and tie. You ought to adapt these wardrobe guidelines to your own circumstances.

Suits and jackets. As with women, a quality men's suit is a dependable investment. A classically styled suit is ideal. It should have a two- or three-button jacket and the lapels should be 3 or 3-1/2 inches wide. Men's suits can be solid, herringbone, pinstripe, chalk stripe, or a subdued plaid. A pinstripe conveys the most authority. Natural fibers like wool or wool-polyester blends are preferred.

A blazer can be combined with different pairs of trousers for a variety of suited looks. Most men's two- or three-piece suits do not have this versatility. Avoid jackets with elbow patches.If you wear a suit, keep the jacket buttoned unless you are sitting down. Heavier men should avoid double-breasted suits, as should shorter, stockier men, unless there is shoulder padding to add a "tapered" look. A suit tends to make a man look taller and slimmer than does a blazer with contrasting trousers. Proportion, along with what hides and what flatters, should be the main considerations

Shirts. Shirts should be lighter than the suit and necktie. Solid colors like white and pale blue are the basic conservative colors for men's shirts, and white creates more credibility. A subtle red or blue pinstripe is also acceptable. Salesmen in the less conservative industries can wear ecru or pale pink shirts, as well as pale, solid-color shirts with white collar and cuffs. Short-sleeve shirts are inappropriate as a rule.

Neckties. Neckties, being small accessories, may be the only wardrobe item that allows men in business to indulge in fashion and express their individuality. Keeping considerations of taste and conservatism in mind, salesmen can choose ties in colors and patterns that could not be worn on bigger pieces such as suits. Top-quality, silk ties are ideal. This is one wardrobe item on which you should not try too hard to economize. Compared to the larger pieces, the necktie is an inexpensive vehicle for color and variety. Bowties should be avoided, and the same goes for gaudy or joke neckties.

Shoes. Leather, lace-up shoes are ideal and should be in black or dark brown. Slip-on, loafer-style shoes are often too casual for conservative industries. For more casual businesses, they are acceptable with blazer–trouser combinations. Avoid two-tone shoes, boots in most situations, white shoes, and colors that are lighter than your suits. Socks should cover the calves of your legs. Avoid socks with designs; they should be dark, solid colors.

Briefcase. Your briefcase or attaché case must be large enough to hold your materials without appearing to be overstuffed. Either a soft- or hard-sided briefcase is acceptable. An advantage of a soft briefcase is the ability to keep it at your feet and access its contents from there, keeping things inside it neat. Your briefcase should be sized in proportion to your body, and it should be a dark color. Burgundy goes well with any suit color and can be more versatile than black or brown.

Other accessories. Your wallet should be burgundy, black, or brown, and in a high-quality leather. Limit rings to one on each hand. A wedding band or a signet ring is appropriate, whereas large stones and glittering gold are not. Wear a simple wristwatch, but do not don a bracelet, pin, or earring. Religious medals and neck chains should not be visible. Cufflinks and belt buckle should be small and plain. Your raincoat or overcoat should reach below the knees, and the umbrella should be either black or brown. Don't wear sunglasses when you are inside with a prospect. See how your Image Index shapes up using Figure 15-4.

Comfort, Fit, and Care Guidelines . . .

1. Natural fibers, or blends that look and feel like natural fibers, are the best for both men and women. Not only do they look better, they feel better. Because natural fibers breathe, they are more comfortable in temperature extremes.

2. Always use a three-way mirror to try on clothing. Know what you look like from all sides before buying a new garment. More people see you from the side and back than from the front.

3. Make sure that your clothes fit perfectly. Have your clothing tailored if necessary. A garment that is too small will look cheap. A garment that is too big will look sloppy.

4. Remember to consider comfort in your wardrobe choices. Regardless of how good you think you look in a favorite outfit, any discomfort you experience while wearing it will take away from your appearance. Ill-fitting shoes will make your feet hurt, and your face will show it. They will also make you walk awkwardly. Tight clothing can be very uncomfortable. Avoid heavy clothes in the summer and lightweight clothes in the winter.

5. Shirts should be laundered after each wearing to prevent body oils from becoming embedded in the collar and cuffs. Suits and blouses should be dry-cleaned regularly.

6. If you travel, buy clothes that resist wrinkles. Wool-blend suits and cotton-blend shirts travel very well. Wool garments hold their shape and stand up to the rigors of a suitcase or garment bag. When traveling, you can remove the wrinkles from your shirts by hanging them in the bathroom while you take a hot shower.

7. Shoes should be shined and kept in good condition at all times. Don't allow the heels of your shoes to become worn down. Repair or replace your shoes before they get shabby.

The ImageIndex©
For Men

Test Your Potential for Getting Ahead.

The following test is based on the probability of making the best first impression on the greatest number of people in business and professional situations. To take the test, simply circle the number opposite the entry that *best* describes you. Then, total up your score according to the directions below, and gauge your Image Index.

SHIRTS
1. Long-sleeved, all-cotton, white, striped, or pastel.
2. Button-down oxford, any color.
3. Short-sleeved, or anything that is wash-and-wear.

TIES
1. All silk with a subtle pattern or stripe.
2. Knit ties.
3. Clip-ons.

SUITS
1. Traditional single-breasted, navy or grey pinstriped, expertly tailored and well-pressed.
2. Designer double-breasted, with bold patterns or weave, molded to body.
3. Prefer sports jacket and slacks.

SHOES
1. Classic dress shoes that tie, always freshly shined.
2. Usually casual, rarely shined.
3. Don't think about shining shoes.

SOCKS
1. Mid- or over-the-calf, brown, navy, or black.
2. Mid- or over-the-calf, textured or patterned.
3. Ankle length, dress or casual.

FACE
1. Always clean-shaven.
2. Have a well-groomed mustache or beard.
3. Not always clean-shaven.

HAIR
1. Regularly cut in a conservative style.
2. Sometimes need a haircut.
3. Always worn in the latest avant-garde style.

NAILS
1. Groom at least once a week.
2. Clip and clean nails occasionally.
3. Bite regularly.

JEWELRY
1. Classic tyle watch, leather or metal band.
2. Wear a sporty watch.
3. Don't usually wear a watch.

HANDSHAKE
1. Firm with both men and women.
2. Firm with men and limp with women.
3. Squeeze hard to show superiority.

EYE CONTACT
1. Make frequent eye contact.
2. Not comfortable looking at someone often.
3. Normally look around the room or at feet.

POSTURE
1. Usually stand and sit erectly.
2. Don't pay much attention.
3. Tend to slouch.

How to Score Your Image Index: Give yourself 6 points for every #1 answer, 3 points for every #2 answer, and 0 points for every #3 answer. If your total score is:

54–72	Congratulations, you're on your way.
36–53	You're on the right track, but have some work to do.
18–35	Careful, you may be sabotaging your chances of getting ahead. There's still hope, though.
0–17	You've got a real problem. Without immediate action, your chances of making a good first impression are virtually nil.

Figure 15-4   (*Source*: Kiwi Brands)

Wardrobe and image

Casual Day Attire

In many organizations today, "casual" or "dress down" days are a common practice. Sometimes occurring as often as once a week, as a rule on Fridays, these designated times allow employees to wear more comfortable, less formal attire. Karen and Don Kaufman of the Kaufman Partnership, a professional image consulting firm, describe dress on casual days as attire which expands the range of styles, colors, fabrics, and accessories typically worn in the business setting. While such dress down days are helpful in promoting high company morale, most firms still require attire that maintains the dignity of the individual and the image of the business.

If you decide to dress informally on these designated days, you should follow the previously-listed comfort, fit, and care guidelines. Casual does not mean sloppy, wrinkled, or dirty. Normal personal grooming standards and habits should still be followed. If you are uncertain about how you will be perceived by others, or simply feel uncomfortable dressing down in a business environment, you are better off sticking to your standard business wardrobe. Keep in mind, however, that you can feel just as uncoomfortable overdressed as you can being casual.

In some industries and in some parts of the country, casual dress is the norm rather than an occasional practice. It is important that you dress appropriately for your job or position. Simply because the owner of the company feels comfortable in a golf shirt and slacks does not mean that you are expected to make sales calls in the same attire. You should dress so that you feel comfortable and acceptable.

PREPARING FOR AN IMPORTANT SALES CALL . . .

The first sales call you make on a new prospect is most important in terms of establishing visual presence. Not only will you want to look your best, but you will want to be relatively formal. On later calls you might be less formal, but until you know the prospect, a certain amount of decorum is necessary. A nice touch is to carry a gold or silver pen (gold is preferred), and hand it to the prospect when it is time to sign the sales contract.

You should include considerations of personal appearance when scheduling sales calls. Ideally, your most important visits should be scheduled around mid-morning. You should look and feel energetic, and your clothes should still be fresh at this time. A woman's makeup will not have faded, and a man's beard will not have started to show after a morning shave.

There is room for debate about whether to wear new clothes on an important sales call. A new outfit can make you feel good about yourself when you need an extra boost of self-confidence. On the other hand, you may not be sure how your new outfit makes you look, and your misgivings may detract from your performance. With familiar clothes, you can count on being comfortable and good-looking. Unless you are completely sure of your new clothing, there is something to be said for relying on the tried and true, and saving the new outfit for a less important occasion.

Remember that maintaining a perfect appearance at all times is impossible. Wear your clothes, don't let them wear you: Don't let concern over your personal appearance dictate or restrict your behavior. If you have to visit the restroom to fix your hair every time you move your head, you will succeed only in looking silly, not well-groomed. Salespeople who refuse to help a prospect carry something because it will wrinkle their suit or soil their shirt allow vanity to interfere with their selling effort. Instead of appearing to be in command of their appearance, they seem to be too self-conscious to be concerned with the prospect's needs.

Personal Grooming . . .

Wardrobe is a major aspect of the professional appearance, but it is not the only image concern. The other major part of image is **personal grooming**. Any neglect of these details will take away from your overall appearance. Salespeople, whose occupation involves constant contact with other people, should have impeccable personal grooming.

Hair. Hairstyles that require constant attention and upkeep are problematic for the salesperson, male or female. If your hair in unmanageable, it will be a burden and a source of constant interruptions. For maximum convenience, saleswomen should select a style that requires as little setting as possible, and keep their hair short to medium. Hair that is longer than shoulder-length is best worn up or back, secured by clasps or barrettes. Long hair that is not worn up tends to be unruly. Salesmen should keep a simple, neat haircut. According to barbers, a man's hair looks best about four days after a haircut, so remember this when scheduling important sales calls. Both sexes should avoid trendy hairstyles, which are usually unacceptable in conservative industries. Split ends should be cut often.

Because your hairstyle is affected by the shape of your face, choose a style appropriate for your features. And consider the length of your neck when you select a hairstyle. If your neck is short, your hair should be short, creating an appearance of distance between your head and shoulders. If your neck is long, your hair should be long. Short hair will only make your neck appear longer.

Oral hygiene. People are extremely conscious of teeth. Most prospects will notice your dentistry within the first minute of your visit. Consider capping or straightening your teeth if they are not an asset to your appearance. Brush your teeth after lunch, even if it means doing so in a public restroom. Avoid eating pungent foods before or during sales calls, and use a mouthwash to keep your breath fresh.

Hands Like the teeth, hands are noticed more than you might realize. Any selling situation that requires you to demonstrate the use of your product or fill out papers with your prospect, and most selling situations do, will call attention to your hands. If you have the habit of biting your fingernails, break it. Clip and file your nails regularly. One manicure every other week should be sufficient, with occasional repairs made in between. Men's nails should be short and blunt, and can be buffed.

Women who wear nail polish should be extremely conscientious. No polish at all is better than chipped nail color. If your hands aren't your best asset, don't wear polish since color calls attention to your hands. Subdued colors are a good alternative to red. Women's fingernails can be longer than men's, but should not be extreme. Buffing is a good alternative to polishing. Your nail polish can be darker or lighter than your lipstick, but it must blend.

Salespeople who have hobbies that take a toll on their hands should take extra steps to pamper them. For instance, if you enjoy gardening or carpentry in your spare time, be especially careful to clean and soften your skin and manicure your nails. Before you take to hammer or hoe, wear gloves or push soap underneath your fingernails to keep them from getting too soiled. Men and women should apply lotion to their hands to soften dry skin and cuticles. Calluses should be removed.

Fragrances. Fragrances are not as appropriate in business as they are in off-hours. The prospect may dislike certain scents or be allergic to them. A light cologne may be used sparingly if you know the customer. Heavier scents should be avoided altogether. You can never go wrong by wearing no fragrance at all.

Makeup. Makeup should be used to enhance your better features and downplay your lesser features. It is a finishing touch, without which a woman's grooming seems incomplete. Makeup for men, although available, is unacceptable in most selling situations. Makeup should not be noticeable, but cosmetic sales might arguably be an exception to this rule. The lips are second only to eyes in attracting attention; many people watch the lips instead of the eyes of a person who is talking. Women should keep this in mind when coordinating lipstick and eye makeup.

Beards. A clean-shaven look is always the safest in sales since it offends no one. Older men tend to look younger without facial hair. Younger men who use facial hair to look more mature should stick to a well-trimmed mustache. In many selling situations, a beard reduces credibility. When one is worn, it should be very neatly trimmed. If your beard starts to show as the day progresses, keep a small electric razor in your desk or car so that you can give yourself a quick shave before an afternoon sales call.

Physical Conditioning . . .

Selling is an occupation that requires a lot of physical energy. Men and women need to maintain vigor and vitality by staying in good physical condition through frequent exercise. The choices are endless. Jogging, swimming, bicycling, and playing tennis or racquetball are only a few of the many ways to stay physically active. Regular exercise keeps your weight under control and your stamina high, and your good conditioning will reflect on your appearance.

EXTENSIONS OF YOUR PERSONAL APPEARANCE . . .

Your personal appearance extends beyond wardrobe and grooming to include your briefcase, car, desk, and office. For this reason, you should apply the wardrobe and grooming guidelines to these extensions as well. They are all symbols of your image as a salesperson, and they communicate messages in the same way that your clothes and grooming do.

Habits of neatness, cleanliness, and organization are the grooming customs that apply to your car, desk, and briefcase. Keep your vehicle washed and waxed, empty the ashtrays, and clear out clutter. A dirty car is a source of embarrassment when you have to give your prospect a ride. Apologizing for the mess will be a meaningless gesture.

As for your desk or office, keep papers filed away when you are not working on them, wash out your coffee cup, and polish your desktop regularly. If prospects visit you at home, the interior must be clean and orderly, and the exterior well maintained. As a kind of mini-office, your briefcase should be extremely organized. Go through it before a sales call, and put away everything that isn't necessary to that visit. Keep papers and brochures in sequence according to need so that you won't have to sift through papers during the sales call.

Professional Standards . . .

Although image is strongly influenced by visual appearance, it is nothing without high **professional standards**. The term *professional* has many different meanings, but here the term refers to dignity, ethics, self-respect, and respect for others. In establishing and conveying your professional standards, do not allow yourself to be compromised. Whatever you say and do should be acceptable in all professional circles.

Here are some guidelines for maintaining high professional standards:

1. Don't use profanity. It degrades your image and may offend the prospect. Rather than add emphasis to your comments, it shocks and distracts the prospect. It reveals coarseness and lack of vocabulary.

2. Don't tell tasteless jokes, even when the prospect tells one.

3. Don't use slang. It reveals ignorance and lack of imagination.

4. Don't say anything prefaced by "Don't let this get around" or "You didn't hear this from me." Such opening remarks are a sure sign that you are saying something you should be ashamed of, and you demean your professional image.

5. Don't say things that indicate lack of control over your emotions: "That really upset me" or "What burned me up was ..." or "What frightens me is ...." Become known as a person with an even temperament.

6. Don't belittle public figures, your competitors, or your superiors. Never take sides against your company. If you're having a problem with a superior, it's not professional to talk about it. The prospect will respect you for your loyalty to your firm and for your refusal to criticize others.

7. Don't drink excessively at business lunches, social functions, and informal get-togethers. In fact, your safest course of action is not to drink at all. Socializing in a club or tavern at the end of the business day may be an excellent way to pick up sales leads, but if you're seen there night after night, you may be labeled someone with a drinking problem.

8. Don't take off your suit jacket unless it is necessary, and never enter a prospect's office not wearing it. Men who show an unbuttoned top shirt button or loosened necktie are conveying a lack of respect for their prospects. Psychologists say that an opened shirt on a man indicates aggressiveness. It is acceptable to unbutton your suit jacket as you sit down.

9. Don't wear fur. Some prospects may object to the thought of killing animals to make wearing apparel. Others might be envious of you because of your apparent wealth. No matter how you look at it, fur is a bad choice.

Through your behavior, you tell on yourself. Professional standards, whether high or low, are difficult to disguise. High professional standards consistently held can overcome a prospect's negative image of salespeople and impress those around the prospect. Business associates, friends, and relatives of the prospect should all see you as a professional.

Summing It Up . . .

Your visual presence and professional standards are important contributors to your image. They will work either for or against you in your selling efforts. Like personality, a professional appearance and behavior are basic requirements for sales success.

Prospects will see you before they hear you, and will look for immediate indicators of your ability to satisfy their needs. Through observation, they evaluate you even before you speak. By mastering the art of visual projection and presenting a professional image, you increase your chances of both making the sale and advancing in your career.

Your vocabulary, paralanguage, body language, and conduct all contribute to your image. They were discussed in Chapter 2 as channels of communication. The focus of this chapter was on wardrobe, personal grooming, and professional standards. Wardrobe components for men and women were examined, and aspects of personal grooming, such as hands, teeth, and hair care were discussed. Rules of professional behavior were also presented.

Looking and acting professional improves self-esteem and enhances self-confidence, and it doesn't require a large investment of time or money.

You Decide!

Sean and Willie work together in the men's clothing department of a major department store. Sean, the older and more experienced of the two, has taken on a mentor's role for his younger coworker. Willie really looks up to his colleague and appreciates Sean's knowledge and selling capability. These two personable young men have become an outstanding team, with each backing up the other in their selling efforts. One often becomes the closer for the other, even though they work under a commission system. They have truly become good friends, from a business standpoint.

One day Willie is surprised to find Sean telling an off-color racial joke to an acquaintance who has stopped by the department. Although convinced that the slur was unintentional, Willie nonetheless is concerned that it was told loud enough for he, and perhaps others, to hear. Deeply hurt, Willie is torn between confronting his friend or writing an anonymous note to the manager, pretending to be an outraged customer. He is concerned that Sean might be able to identify him as the author of such a note, and yet wonders if he can meet face-to-face with his buddy without becoming angry and offensive. **You decide!**

Key Concepts and Terms . . .

classic styles   power color
conduct   primacy effect
IBM image   professional standards
personal grooming   visual image

Building Skills . . .

1. Discuss why the approach is considered "the most important thirty seconds in selling."
2. Compare visual image in importance to product knowledge and selling skills.
3. Describe how a professional appearance enhances self-confidence and communicates respect for the prospect.
4. Explain the significance of appearance for the job applicant or new salesperson. Explain the interviewer's or new prospect's concerns.
5. Explain why classic clothing is preferable to fashion clothing.
6. Examine why a quality wardrobe is more economical than a large wardrobe.
7. Describe how versatility serves better than variety in the business wardrobe.
8. Discuss the wardrobe color that is universally flattering and the one that can be used in almost any shade or pattern by men and women.
9. Define power colors.
10. Describe when a salesperson might wear a light or medium-colored suit.
11. Describe what it means to dress for the industry and prospect, giving examples.
12. List the pros and cons of wearing a new outfit to an important sales call.
13. Describe the hairstyling guidelines that apply to both men and women.
14. Describe special hand-grooming techniques that apply to someone who has a hobby such as gardening.
15. Examine the guidelines for wearing fragrances.
16. Explain how your car, desk, and briefcase are extensions of your personal appearance, including some of the grooming guidelines that apply to these items.
17. Explain the guidelines for high professional standards.

Making Decisions 15-1:

Joe Roberts owns a small business that sells and services lawnmowers, chain saws, and other motorized lawn and garden equipment. One morning he is in front of his shop unloading several pieces of broken-down equipment from his van when a salesperson pulls up into the driveway. Although Joe has never seen Herb Baker before, he knows he is a salesperson: Who else would be strolling up to a lawnmower business in a dark blue suit and black wingtips and carrying a briefcase?

Herb: (Extending his hand) Mr. Roberts, I'm Herb Baker from the *Herald Times*.

Joe: (Wiping his greasy hands on his overalls) Hello. Shaking hands isn't such a good idea. What can I do for you?

Herb: (Placing his briefcase on a clear spot in the driveway) Have you ever considered purchasing newspaper advertising space?

Joe: Nope. I have all the customers I can handle as it is. I get my business from word of mouth. (He pulls a heavy, dirty lawnmower from his van.)

Herb: (Stepping out of Joe's way) Newspaper advertising will help your business grow.

Joe: Don't want to grow. I'm a one-person operation, and I like it that way.

Herb: Thank you for your time, Mr. Roberts. Here's my business card. Please call me if I can be of service.

Explain why Herb's attire worked for him or against him, or why it didn't matter. Describe a better way for Herb to approach Joe.

Making Decisions 15-2:

Ken Jackson has just been appointed regional marketing representative for Photo Right photographic equipment and supplies. He's very excited as he tells his friend Tara Parks about his new position. Tara, however, questions his appearance.

Tara: I'm so happy for you, Ken. When do you start?

Ken: Next week. I can't wait.

Tara: Will you be selling to consumers?

Ken: No, I'll be calling on dealers and professional photographers.

Tara: What about your beard?

Ken: What about it? Lots of guys have beards. My cousin Hal is a successful salesperson, and he's had a beard for years.

Tara: Yes, but Hal sells wilderness outfitting.

Ken: That kind of thing doesn't matter any more, Tara. Lots of photographers have beards.

Tara: True, but maybe you should think about this. Aren't your customers mostly businesspeople and corporate photographers?

Examine whether Ken should take Tara's advice.

Making Decisions 15-3:

Pay attention to the grooming and attire of three successful salespeople. Describe whether their visual image is symbolic of their achievement, looking for any room for improvement.

Making Decisions 15-4:

List three ways you could increase the versatility of your major wardrobe items for less than $100 total.

Practice Makes Perfect 15-1:

Conduct a brief sales presentation with a classmate dressed in standard business attire, and again while dressed casually. Ask for input from the class regarding your presentations, including your own personal feelings regarding your performance.

Chapter 16

Attitude, the Key to Success

THE JOB TO BE DONE . . .

Attitude, like image, quickly separates the successful from the failures. There is no quicker way to alienate others than through a "bad attitude." Chapter 16 helps you:

...appreciate the importance of a positive attitude in selling.

...maintain a positive self-image, develop self-esteem, and increase self-confidence.

...develop a healthy attitude toward the prospect, your product, your firm, and your career.

...adopt the proper attitude toward successes and setbacks in selling.

...assume an attitude of responsibility for one's selling performance.

...appreciate the value of goal setting in selling and its relation to attitude.

...use goals as tools for self-motivation.

...follow the steps of the goal-setting process for career success.

...learn to use visualization to create success,

...appreciate the elements of a positive attitude, including open-mindedness, optimism, resiliency, and adaptability.

...recognize the importance of a positive outlook on life.

Success has a thousand fathers, but failure is an orphan.

Old proverb

396

ATTITUDE, THE KEY TO SUCCESS . . .

Most chapters in this text focus on prospects: how to find them, learn about them, approach them, present to them, persuade them, overcome their objections, and establish meaningful communication with them. Others, such as Chapters 14 and 15, focus primarily on the salesperson, but always with respect to the prospect. Only this chapter and Chapter 17 are devoted entirely to you.

Chapter 16 examines ways of helping you maintain a healthy attitude toward yourself, selling, prospects, your product, your firm, and your career. Taking responsibility for your selling performance is discussed. The relationship between goal setting and motivation is described, as are the techniques of developing and achieving career goals. The elements of the positive attitude, including optimism, resiliency, adaptability, and open-mindedness, are also discussed.

Attitude is an aspect of personality. It is your outlook, disposition, frame of mind, or point of view. People with an "attitude problem" have a difficulty because their outlook, not their real situation, is poor. Attitude is influenced by many factors, among them the quality of one's health, upbringing, family life, and friendships.

A positive attitude is a characteristic of all top salespeople. The products of this behavior are achievement, self-fulfillment, and the continuing desire to meet your fullest potential. A positive attitude is the foundation of happiness and success in selling. Salespeople who possess equal talent, intelligence, and skills will be set apart by their differing demeanor; the one with the positive outlook will likely be more successful than others.

An unhealthy attitude is a major reason for poor job performance. Negative feelings have bad effects on others. Those around you are likely to be distracted by your behavior, wanting to distance themselves from you. A number of attitude-related causes of poor job performance are found in Figure 16-1, next page.

Selling is a demanding occupation. It requires tremendous discipline. Only people who can maintain a positive disposition are cut out for selling. Attitude permeates every part of life. To be a successful salesperson, you must feel positive about yourself, your product, your prospects, your firm, and your career. Some people love to sell. Others hate the very thought of selling. Those with a strong opposition to selling would be better off looking for other career options.

YOUR ATTITUDE TOWARD YOURSELF . . .

In selling, only the most favorable attitudes toward yourself will do. You must have a strong personality to stand up to the many challenges to your ego that selling presents. The most important elements of your attitude toward yourself are self-image, self-esteem, and self-confidence.

> No one can make you feel inferior without your permission.
> Eleanor Roosevelt

Attitude Affects Job Performance

Attitude and job performance are directly related. Attitude-related factors that hamper job performance include:

1. Low self-image.

2. Low self-esteem.

3. Low self-efficacy.

4. Pessimism.

5. Lack of initiative.

6. Lack of enthusiasm.

7. Lack of self-discipline.

8. Fear of failure.

9. Inability to adapt to change.

10. Unwillingness to consider or accept new procedures, techniques, or ideas.

11. Unwillingness to accept responsibility.

12. Lack of goals.

13. Poor motivation.

14. Inability to see a relationship between personal and company goals.

Figure 16-1

Self-Image . . .

Self-image is the way you see yourself, the person you see in the mirror. You behave in a way that goes along with your self-image. Your demeanor toward others is influenced by your feelings about yourself. You are only the salesperson you make yourself out to be.

Most of our limits are self-imposed. Based on our feelings for ourselves, we decide what we can or cannot achieve and then behave accordingly. Self-doubt serves to counteract even the highest degree of talent, whereas a strong self-image serves to encourage us to achieve more and more.

Just as self-image determines performance, performance modifies self-image. Salespeople who do not think highly of themselves or their profession perform worse and worse as time passes. Their repeated poor performance drives their self-image lower and lower. On the other hand, sellers with a strong self-image get better and better as time passes, and their successes enhance their feelings about themselves. Salespeople should adopt the image of caring individuals who succeed only by providing benefits to their customers and firm. By seeing yourself as this concerned person, you set the stage for the personality and behavior modifications that will help you realize your ultimate goals.

Sometimes we have a negative self-image and don't realize it. For instance, you might jokingly say, "I'm a born loser," but are you really joking? Achievers and happy people have a strong self-image. Underachievers and unhappy people have negative feelings about themselves. If you think you are a loser, others will agree. If you like and respect yourself, you will be liked and respected by others.

Self-Esteem . . .

Whereas self-image is the overall picture you have of yourself, **self-esteem** is the *opinion* you have of yourself, a sense of self-worth and self-respect. High self-esteem is a characteristic of all successful people. Even while recognizing that there is always room for improvement, salespeople with high self-esteem view themselves as worthy people with a contribution to make. Their gift to the world includes the many benefits they provide for customers, the advancement of their firm, and the achievement of personal goals. Salespeople with high self-esteem see themselves as necessary members of their firm's sales team. They know that the team is better off because of their presence and that it would suffer in their absence.

Self-esteem is enhanced by the support of those around us. We feel more worthy when others acknowledge our accomplishments and reward us for jobs well done. **Positive reinforcement** is important to receive and to give. Success helps us develop our self-esteem, but recognition and praise confirm and solidify it. The opposite feeling occurs when others ignore us or punish us. Salespeople who are not encouraged and reinforced by others rarely achieve their full potential or learn what it might be.

A sales manager would be wise to build the self-esteem of new salespeople by making them feel as if the team couldn't function without them. Sometimes upper management sends new sellers out on calls that are almost guaranteed to end in a sale, just to start them out on a positive note.

Self-esteem varies according to how well you live up to your self-image. For instance, if you say, "I know I should apply for that promotion at work, and I'll be mad at myself if I don't," you are saying that your self-esteem will be lower if you don't make the effort. Your self-image, in this case, is that of a confident, ambitious salesperson.

Self-Confidence . . .

Self-confidence is belief in yourself and your abilities. In selling, this means knowing that you are a good salesperson and believing you have the ability to succeed. This attitude is essential to success in selling.

Like self-esteem, self-confidence is a state of mind. A reliant salesperson expects to sell and envisions nothing less. As the salesperson's greatest source of courage, self-confidence precludes thoughts of failure. These types of people think "success." The thought of not succeeding doesn't occur to them.

The foundation of self-confidence in selling is preparation. The reason such salespeople do not fear failure is that they protect themselves against it by preparing for success. They research their prospects, plan their presentations, and maintain current product knowledge. Any source of anxiety is eliminated by preparation. The self-confident salesperson makes sure that failure is impossible.

Self-Efficacy . . .

Self-efficacy is your belief in your own ability to perform a specific task. Although you may have high self-esteem, you might question your competence in a specific area. For example, even though you might be an excellent golfer, you might not be able to reach the green on a long par five hole in two strokes. As a salesperson, it is important that you do not lose faith in your ability to perform your primary task. You need to address the issues if you have had difficulty in dealing with a certain individual or account. Past performance and encouragement from others help to overcome any doubts that you might have regarding your selling capability.

Locus of Control . . .

Locus of control can be either external or internal. People feel either that their circumstances and destiny are controlled by outside forces, or that they themselves have some determination over the outcome of events. Extremes of these conflicting viewpoints are undesirable. If your locus of control is strongly external, you may fail to exert your influence over everyday happenings. On the other hand, if you strongly believe in being the captain of your own destiny, you may accept too much blame or self-condemnation for things beyond your power. But generally salespeople with an internal locus of control are better performers..

The Pygmalion Effect . . .

This philosophy generally refers to expectations determining outcomes. Similar to an internal locus of control, if you strongly believe you have the ability to command your own destiny, it becomes like a self-fulfilling prophecy. When you feel that you will make the sale, you physically and mentally prepare for the call. Since so much of a salesperson's success depends upon preparation, having the right attitude beforehand does impact the results.

The Performance Equation . . .

Various factors contribute to a salesperson's overall performance. Controllable individual factors include natural abilities, acquired skills, and motivation. External situations, which may be largely uncontrollable, would be your company's policies, the sales manager's style and personality, and the attitudes of your co-workers. Luck and circumstances also play a part in your success. Since many of the parts of this formula are not under you control, you might do better to concentrate on those that are. Certainly self-motivation and acquired skills, along with your physical and emotional well-being, are the portions of the performance equation over which you have a direct effect.

YOUR ATTITUDE TOWARD SELLING . . .

What is your attitude toward this course? Are you taking it because you hope to use the material you're learning, or only because it's a required subject or a convenient elective? A poor attitude toward selling might even affect people who are seemingly committed to sales and sales education. But selling is selling, and any pretense that it is otherwise only betrays a poor attitude toward the profession.

Now, what is your attitude toward selling? Which of the two attitudes below fits you better?

> "Selling is an occupation that will require me to ask people for their money, which they don't want to give me. I must somehow persuade them, though, because that's the nature of the job."

> "Selling is an occupation that will allow me to make life better for my prospects by helping them satisfy their needs."

In a proper selling transaction, both parties benefit. The prospect and the salesperson equally feel they are receiving more than they are giving up. To succeed in selling, you must adopt the attitude that you are helping the buyer as much as the customer is helping you. Never think that you are subservient to the prospect or that you are asking for a handout. As a salesperson, you are an equal to whomever you are facing, and you provide benefits in exchange for the customer's money. Your aim in selling is to achieve the highest standard of living you can, but only by benefiting those who purchase.

Eugene Mayberry, a successful suburban Philadelphia real estate agent, has the right attitude toward selling:

> "Selling houses is the greatest job in the world," Gene says. "Oh, sure, it takes time to sell a house, but when I see the glow in the eyes of a young couple as I'm taking them through their dream house, it's a greater feeling for me than when I pick up my commission check. I know I've helped improve their life. I've sold them more than a house. I've sold them a future."

Each time you enter a new selling situation, ask yourself, "How can I be of service to this prospect?" Realizing that you are a solution and not a problem to the prospect will boost your attitude toward selling.

> Experience is a hard teacher because it gives the test first, the lesson afterward.
>
> Vernon Law

YOUR ATTITUDE TOWARD THE PROSPECT . . .

Any prospect should be viewed as someone whose situation could be improved with your help. This person is not an opponent to be conquered or won over, but an ally in your search for solutions. Some salespeople see prospects as holders of power in the selling situation, but this attitude creates failure. You are not at the mercy of the prospect. You have the power to influence the outcome of all selling situations. You should see prospects as equals, according them all the respect they deserve.

The proper attitude when negotiating a sale with your prospect is a **win–win attitude**. This means that both of you must gain. If the prospect loses, so do you. You cannot claim victory if you make a sale to a customer who will soon be disappointed. Only when the purchaser wins by receiving the benefits of your product are you a winner as well. See Figure 16-2 for a synopsis of what your attitude toward customers should be.

YOUR ATTITUDE TOWARD YOUR PRODUCT . . .

Your attitude toward your product is a major influence over the prospect's attitude toward it. Potential buyers are sensitive to a salesperson's feelings toward what he or she is selling. Customers notice the way you introduce your product; they notice the tone of your voice and the level of respect you show for

---

Our Customers

1. They are the most important people ever to come into our business in person, by mail, or by telephone.

2. They are not outsiders to our business, but a part of it.

3. They are not dependent on us. We are dependent on them.

4. They aren't someone to argue or match wits with, they are someone to be served with courtesy and dignity.

5. They aren't merely a number or a name. They are flesh-and-blood human beings with feeling and emotions like our own.

6. They are people whose continual goodwill we must hold so they will return again and again.

7. They are never an interruption to our work, but the purpose of it.

8. We are not doing them a favor by serving them, they are doing us a favor by giving us an opportunity to do so.

Anonymous

Figure 16-2

> The pride you take in your product or service will give you the strength to deal with rejection in a positive manner.
>
> Victor Kiam

your product. These signals will tell them whether you are sharing the product or just selling it. If you believe in your product, you'll deliver your sales presentation with enthusiasm and vigor. If you question your product's merits, your doubt will show the moment you introduce it.

It is vital to your success that you believe in the product you sell, and that you sell a product you believe in. If the product disappoints you and you cannot improve your attitude toward it, you must look for something else to sell.

YOUR ATTITUDE TOWARD YOUR FIRM . . .

What is your attitude toward your firm? Does it owe you a living, or do you have the obligation to make a positive contribution to your company? The latter attitude is the only acceptable one for a person in sales. A salesperson must have a feeling of commitment to the firm's advancement and take a role of responsibility for its success. You have a fiduciary responsibility to serve your company's aims, and knowing this will contribute to your drive for success.

The idea that your company depends on you will enhance the perception of your power and position in selling. You assume more initiative because you feel that you are responsible for your firm's sales and profits. This attitude is a far cry from the failure-driven attitude of those who feel like powerless, grateful recipients of a paycheck.

Ideally, you should identify completely with your firm. Remember that you are often the only representative that your prospects ever meet, so in their eyes you *are* the company. Embrace this identity, both privately and publicly. See the home office as part of your family, and represent the family when you call on prospects.

YOUR ATTITUDE TOWARD YOUR CAREER . . .

There is a saying, "Find pleasure in your work or you will not find pleasure." Your selling career must be more than a source of income, it must be a source of personal satisfaction and accomplishment. Successful salespeople find pleasure in their work that goes beyond the financial gains. They derive satisfaction from the knowledge that they are helping others. They grow personally by making constant progress toward achieving their fullest potential. They need never daydream about doing other work because their careers in selling bring them all the professional satisfaction they want.

A sales career offers both short- and long-term self-fulfillment. In the short run, the pleasure of meeting people, solving their problems, satisfying their needs, and earning a healthy income bring reward. Long-term fulfillment comes from the knowledge that you are a positive force shaping the advancement of your company, your customers, your family, and yourself.

Because career growth and personal growth are often inseparable, career advancement is a motivator and a reward. Earning a promotion is an important source of personal satisfaction. Companies often award promotions and titles in place of substantial salary increases, knowing that an improvement in position boosts the salesperson's self-esteem and motivation. Your attitude toward your career will remain high as long as you believe there is the potential to grow in some way. If the possibility of promotion exists for you, work for it. Being promoted from account executive to senior account executive may be just what you need to boost your attitude toward your career.

Your ability to meet personal objectives through your work will influence your attitude toward your career. If your selling position requires you to do something that conflicts with your personal aims, your demeanor will become negative. For example, constant travel may conflict with your desire to be home and available to the family. This will cause you to resent your career as an interference with your personal life instead of looking to it as the means by which you provide for your family.

SUCCESSES AND SETBACKS . . .

In the words of Calvin Coolidge, "nothing can take the place of persistence." Successful salespeople understand a simple fact of the selling life: You won't make every sale you attempt. In most situations, the unsuccessful selling attempts greatly outnumber the successful ones. Salespeople must rely on strong egos and positive attitudes to overcome discouraging statistics. They are not alone. The professional baseball player who gets only three hits for every ten times at bat is considered a good hitter; the batter who gets four hits for every ten times at bat is looked upon as *exceptional*.

As a salesperson, you should keep a "batting average," too. Regularly count your sales in relation to your attempts, and celebrate your successes instead of bemoaning your setbacks. If you make six sales out of eight attempts, be proud of your commendable success rate. If you make only two sales out of the next eight attempts, remind yourself of your previous, more successful count.

Describe your unsuccessful sales attempts as setbacks, not failures. The terminology you choose has a surprisingly great influence over your attitude. If you view your unsuccessful tries as mere setbacks, you set the stage for future success. A failure is final, but a setback is temporary, something that can be corrected.

A success-driven salesperson looks for the value in every setback. In this context, a misfortune can be viewed as a minor crisis that conceals an opportunity to learn. No failed attempt to sell should ever be written off as inexplicable. Review your presentation and all of your actions leading up to the prospect's refusal to buy. Try to find the reason or reasons for the unsuccessful outcome. Ask yourself, "What can I learn from this?" and "What should I have done differently?"

Once you discover the causes of your disappointment, you can correct your selling technique and resolve never to make the same mistakes again. Because each sales call is a learning experience, even unsuccessful visits are worthwhile. We often learn more from unpleasant experiences than we do from pleasant ones. View the lesson you learn as the benefit of the experience.

An unsuccessful sales attempt may also yield indirect benefits, which you won't recognize without the proper attitude. Perhaps the prospect mentioned the name of someone who is likely to buy, or gave you valuable information about the industry.

Responsibility as an Attitude . . .

"The prospect was unreasonable."

"My company provided no follow-up."

"The competition lied about us."

These are the kinds of comments made by salespeople who blame their setbacks and misfortunes on other people or on outside factors. Countless excuses are available to those who deny responsibility for their performance. But assigning blame for a missed sale does nothing to improve the selling effort. It relieves the blamer of responsibility and the courage of action. It allows the blamer to indulge in self-pity. It does not increase sales or generate income.

Only an attitude of responsibility has a positive effect on selling performance. Responsibility is not the same as fault. Accepting accountability for your sales performance does not mean taking the blame, but rather understanding your role in a given situation and recognizing how your actions influenced the outcome. The salesperson cannot control everything about a situation. Customers' preconceived notions, mood, and attitudes are not in your control.

Taking responsibility for your performance may be a matter of degree. Suppose you are a baseball outfielder, the opposing team has two outs, and it's the ninth inning. You drop a flyball, and the rivals score a run that wins the game. What should your attitude be? Should you think, "I had nothing to do with the other five runs that were scored against us, so don't blame me?" Should you think, "I dropped the ball that scored the winning run. I lost the game for my team?" Neither attitude is appropriate. The first takes no responsibility, and the second takes too much. The proper attitude should be, "I made a mistake that helped contribute to the loss of the game." Accept your partial responsibility while recognizing the other influences over the outcome. Figure 16-3, next page, explains how to distinguish a winner from a loser. Winners willingly accept their share of the responsibility when the outcome is less than desirable, but they do not blame themselves for things beyond their control.

GOALS, MOTIVATION, AND ATTITUDE . . .

You will recall from Chapter 5 that motivation is the inner drive that transforms desire into action. **Goals** are the basis of **motivation**. The desire to reach a worthy goal will provide you with the drive to work toward it. The more important the goal, the stronger the motivation. If you lack worthy goals, you will not be turned on, nor will you be well directed if your objectives are not clearly defined. Instead of saying, "I want to make a lot of money," give yourself true motivation by saying, "I want to earn $40,000 in commissions over the next twelve months."

Goals provide a scale against which you can measure your accomplishments. They lend motivation and purpose to your actions, and once achieved, they become a source of satisfaction and pride. Success in reaching goals generates the motivation to strive for more goals. It provides the link between goals, motivation, and attitude. To maintain a healthy attitude, you must enjoy success through the achievement of your goals. Knowing that you are accomplishing what you set out to do helps create a positive attitude. Each time you reach a goal, the feeling of success enhances your motivation and your attitude.

Those who find satisfaction in their work are motivated to outdo themselves, knowing that their improved performance will lead to still more reward. Success-driven salespeople are motivated by reward, not punishment. They are driven by the desire to achieve, not the fear of failure, embarrassment, or losing their job.

There was a husband and wife sales team who hated to get out of bed in the morning because they made only one sale in twenty calls. One day, feeling depressed about their sales ratio, they computed the money they made per call by dividing their pay by the number of calls they made. They discovered that they made $25 per call. This was cheering news: They made money on every call, even when they didn't make a sale. The thought of earning $25 per call motivated them to get up early and make more calls than usual. Not surprisingly, their spirited presentations brought them an increase in sales. Soon they were making more calls, and making one sale every ten calls instead of one sale every twenty. Each call they made now was worth $50. As their success ratio increased, they became more and more motivated to make calls, and their calls became more and more valuable to them.

Although it is important to set goals in all aspects of your life, the ones that we focus on are sales-related objectives.

Goal setting is a six-stage process:

1. Define your goal or goals specifically. Instead of saying, "I want to increase sales," say, "I want to increase sales by 10 percent within one year."
2. Set a timetable for achieving your goals.
3. Develop a strategy (plan of action).
4. Plan your tactics, the specific elements of your strategy.
5. At planned intervals, evaluate your progress. Analyze the feasibility of the goal, timeframe, strategy, and tactics.
6. Adjust your goals to make them more realistic or more ambitious.

> Efficiency is doing things right. Effectiveness is doing the right things.
> Stephen Covey

Suppose your goal is to increase sales to existing customers by 10 percent over the next year. Your strategy is to improve communication with them, and your main tactic is to send them a monthly newsletter about your firm. Every quarter, calculate your increase in sales. If you are gaining by only 8 percent, examine your efforts to determine if your goal, timetable, strategy, and tactics were realistic. Make any necessary adjustments when planning your next sales goal.

SETTING AND WORKING TOWARD GOALS . . .

Goal setting is a practice that focuses on the future. If you are not in the habit of setting goals for yourself, you may encounter difficulties. Goal setting must also be done carefully. Figure 16-4, next page, describes some of the barriers to (and problems with) goal setting, along with barriers to goal achievement.

When you set out to define your goals, be sure to choose ones that vary in magnitude and time frame. Successes with smaller, short-term objectives will help motivate you to continue working toward more important, long-term goals.

Suppose you set the following goals:

1. Opening twelve new accounts each month.
2. Selling 400 units a month.
3. Being the top regional salesperson every month.
4. Being a member of the firm's Summit Club, the top 5 percent of the sales force in terms of earnings.
5. Earning enough bonus points to qualify for an all-expense-paid trip to Tahiti.
6. Becoming sales manager within two years.

The goal of selling 400 units a month is short term, whereas becoming sales manager is long term. As you spend longer hours at work and increase your unit sales, the success of achieving tactical objectives will encourage you to continue taking management courses at night to achieve your ultimate goal of becoming sales manager.

Setting a variety of goals not only adds to your motivation but also increases your chances of success. With only one goal, your chances of success are 50-50, and failure could be devastating. With several goals, any disappointment in one area will be offset by success in another.

Barriers to Goal Setting

1. Lack of a goal orientation.
2. Inability to adopt a long-term perspective.
3. Imperception of need.
4. Inability to prioritize objectives.
5. Inability to achieve past goals.
6. Fear of failure.
7. Fear of success.

Problems with Goal Setting

1. Inability to define a goal in meaningful, quantifiable terms.
2. Setting unrealistic goals.
3. Setting goals that aren't challenging enough.
4. Setting too many goals.
5. Failure to set multiple goals.
6. Setting wrong or improper goals.
7. Setting conflicting goals.
8. Setting goals with too long of a time frame.

Barriers to Goal Achievement

1. Inability to focus one's efforts.
2. Lack of commitment.
3. Failure to benchmark progress toward a goal.
4. Early setbacks and frustrations.
5. Burnout.
6. Failure to appropriate the necessary time.
7. Conflicting demands on your time.
8. Lack of financial resources.
9. Abandonment in favor of newer goals.

Figure 16-4

Be sure to divide your long-term goals into shorter time frames. A sales goal of 1,200 units a year should be divided into 100 units a month. The segmented goals will be much more manageable. Further, monthly progress checks will help you make adjustments early in the year if your objective proves unrealistic or unambitious. A yearly sales goal broken down into a monthly figure is possible even if your business is seasonal. If 50 percent of your yearly sales volume comes during the last four months of the year, simply assign a lower monthly goal to the first eight months and a higher one to the remaining part of the year. Breaking a long-term goal down into shorter time frames is sometimes called **chunking**. You work on the goal one "chunk" at a time.

PRIORITIZING AND SETTING NEW GOALS . . .

Even though you might be enthusiastic about all of your goals, you should prioritize them. Rank your objectives according to which successes are more important to you. Prioritizing your goals will come in handy as you evaluate your progress and set new ones. For example, suppose you discover yourself overworked by taking night courses and putting in extra hours toward your sales goal. If you have prioritized, perhaps you already know that selling 400 units a month is more important to you than becoming sales manager within two years. Knowing your priorities, you abandon the night courses to concentrate on your sales goal for now. You may still want to become sales manager, but you decide to set a longer time frame for that objective.

Goal setting is not something that stops with the achievement of the end. Achievement motivates the successful goal setter to go further. You will always be simultaneously working toward, achieving, and resetting objectives. Salespeople who achieve their goal of becoming salesperson of the year will not stop there. They will set the new goal of becoming the first salesperson in the firm to be named salesperson of the year two years in a row. This practice of continually setting new goals is common to all success-driven salespeople.

THE POSITIVE ATTITUDE IN PRACTICE . . .

Many philosophers and psychologitsts suggest that you are what you think you are. If you can't imagine yourself doing something, then you can't do it. Your ability to envision an experience will translate into the ability to realize the experience. The practice of forming a mental picture of success is what sets successful salespeople apart from the unsuccessful. Those who are underachievers lack the ability to envision success. Failure is the result of many factors, as Figure 16-5 suggests.

> You will be liked or disliked more on your mannerisms and your attitude than on the way you dress.
>
> John T. Molloy

> **Why Salespeople Fail**
>
> 1. **Poor Planning** — Driving halfway across town to visit a poorly-qualified prospect while passing dozens of well-qualified prospects on the way.
>
> 2. **Poor Attitude** — The inability to separate each rejection and think of it in separate terms.
>
> 3. **Lack of Continuous Training** — Thinking that there's nothing new left to learn.
>
> 4. **Poor Use of Time** — The common denominator we all share is a 24 hour day. The key to success, therefore, isn't how much time you have, but how you use it.
>
> 5. **Lack of Specific Goals** — Not knowing where you're going.
>
> 6. **Lack of Self-discipline** — Self-discipline is the quality which enables a person to finish a task long after the initial enthusiasm and commitment to do it has passed.
>
> 7. **Procrastination** — This often results from a fear of the unknown. Not making or acting on a decision leads to a predictable outcome — nothing will change. Because making a decision often means taking an unknown direction, fear develops.
>
> 8. **Lack of Concentration** — The inability to focus 100% of your attention on the prospect. Personal matters and other concerns must be set aside when you are trying to sell.
>
> 9. **Lack of Self-Evaluation and Appraisal** — The fear of asking customers or associates "What could I do to improve?"
>
> 10. **Inability to Cope with Rejection** — Selling is a failing business. Success is determined by your ability to fail and still keep trying, learning and improving.
>
> 11. **Lack of Creative Imagination** — Selling the same way today as you did last year, or attempting to sell each customer the same way.

Figure 16-5 (*Source*: Tim Connor, *The Soft Sell*, Training Associates International, Ann Arbor, MI 48106. ©1988)

Forming a mental picture of an upcoming sales call helps you prepare for success. If you are apprehensive about entering a selling situation, chances are you are poorly prepared for it. Use this technique to take control of your anxiety: Try to imagine the worst possible situation you could encounter and how you would successfully handle it. Then, even if the worst possibility comes true, you will be prepared for it and be able to cope. Preparation through **mental simulation** is a very effective technique for building the courage to make a difficult sales call.

Since selling is a self-fulfilling prophecy, you should envision only positive outcomes. Before entering a selling situation, imagine what it will be like in its entirety. Imagine greeting the prospect, making your presentation, successfully answering questions and overcoming objections, and finally closing the sale.

Open-Mindedness and Optimism . . .

Salespeople with positive attitudes have several characteristics in common. Among them are **open-mindedness** and optimism. Open-mindedness is extremely important in selling. The salesperson needs to encourage prospects to maintain an open mind so that they will consider the proposal. **Close-mindedness** will only generate the same feeling in the prospect. Further, since salespeople encounter many people of different points of view, having an open mind is the only guarantee for success in such an environment.

Optimism, the tendency to expect a good outcome or to see hope in any situation, is equally important in selling. The optimistic salesperson expects nothing less than success. The thought of failure does not cross the optimist's mind.

Pessimism, the tendency to expect a bad outcome or to see hopelessness in any situation, fosters defeat. Murphy's law, the maxim that if something can go wrong it will, is based on pessimism. No salesperson can succeed for long with an attitude burdened by cynicism. Furthermore, a pessimistic attitude in life will spill over into your work. There is no line drawn between your attitude at home and your attitude at work.

Judi Eppihimer

Not all successful salespeople have college backgrounds. While what is learned in the classroom might be helpful in pursuing a career in selling, nothing beats the learning experiences of the real world. Judi Eppihimer is a shining example of this truism. As an Independent Sales Director for Dallas, TX based Mary Kay, Inc., she has learned that selling is 90% attitude, 10% skill. She describes her most likely customer as a professional, career-oriented woman who cares about her personal appearance, and says that her task isn't about getting them to buy, buy, buy but rather, about building their self-esteem.

Having begun her working life in banking, Judi began work with Mary Kay on a part-time basis. "Before Mary Kay," she says, "I had always thought that in sales you had to be pushy and aggressive. Mary Kay's philosophy is to build a customer base, not just to see how much you can sell." The firm has developed an excellent reputation in the direct selling arena, and Judi reaps the benefits of that esteem. Her base of over 450 customers extends through several states, and her customers remain loyal because of the service she provides.

As far as advice for new salespeople, Judi stresses the importance of people skills, of listening to what people want, determining their needs, and reacting to them. She states that you must be able to relate to people and convey a positive attitude. It is important that salespeople understand that not everyone will be receptive to your products and that you should strive not to become discouraged. This kind of attitude has been instrumental in earning Judi two new cars as well as numerous awards. Her positive attitude is contagious!

You Decide!

Being employed by an office equipment marketer, Yvonne calls on businesses of all sizes, selling copiers, FAX machines, computers, paper shredders, and recording equipment. Although she has been moderately successful, she has fought hard to overcome severe depression when she loses a sale. Through some encouraging help from her manager, and some strong self-therapy, she has gradually begun to accept rejection without falling apart.

One of the little tricks that she plays on herself is to always check the "Maybe" box on her sales report forms where it asks for future possibilities, rather than the more truthful "No chance" area. This little deception seems to give her a lift, making her feel that there is always hope, although in her heart she knows that there is none. One morning she finds a voice mail message on her answering machine from her boss. He has requested a conference to discuss her call reports, and she is certain it is in regard to how she has fudged. While on the one hand she feels that she has been deceptive, Yvonne still believes that this small hoax has been a big morale booster, which her manager should appreciate. **You decide!**

Resiliency and Adaptability . . .

Salespeople with positive attitudes are also noted for their resiliency and adaptability, two qualities that are indispensable in the world of selling. You will recall from Chapter 13 the importance of ego-resilience. This is the ability to rebound from a setback. In selling, the frequency of setbacks is a constant challenge to salespeople, and salespeople must rely on their **resiliency** to meet the challenge and move forward. Resiliency is what enables the salesperson to try to sell again, to return to a customer who said no, to approach new customers. It is what helps put unsuccessful sales attempts in perspective and move on to new challenges.

One technique for boosting your resiliency in the face of setbacks is to remind yourself of past successes. Take pride in your accomplishments by displaying awards, trophies, diplomas, and other honors. This is for your benefit as much as for the benefit of others. A quick glance at a certificate on the wall or a file of thank-you notes from past customers will lift your spirits and boost your motivation. Any diminishment of self-esteem caused by a setback will disappear and be replaced by feelings of pride.

Like resiliency, **adaptability** is an essential element of the salesperson's positive attitude. The only thing that is certain in life is change, so adaptability, the ability to accept and adjust to change, is of paramount importance in life and in selling. Salespeople must be able to handle changes in all aspects of their situation: changes in the firm, the product, the territory, the very nature of business.

To develop your adaptability, look for the positive aspects of each change that comes along. Adapting will then be simply a matter of taking advantage of the new situation. Dwelling on the negative aspects of a change will do only harm to your efforts to adapt. It will cause you to resent the change and the people responsible for it, and you will not have the energy or ability to participate in the positive aspects of the change.

THE POSITIVE ATTITUDE . . .

The ideal attitude in selling is the positive attitude. This demeanor enables you to create happiness by seeing the good in everything. Happiness in your work, your home, your health and your personal life will translate into success in sales.

A positive attitude will generate all the other qualities you will need as a salesperson. Through the eyes of happiness, you will see the positive qualities of your firm, your job, your product, and yourself. You will take responsibility for your successes and setbacks, and embrace your world with a spirit of optimism. You will know that you are there to help your prospects and to serve your company. You will be resilient in the face of setbacks, and adaptable to change. You will be motivated to set goals, and you will have a healthy, success-driven attitude toward your career.

As a salesperson with a positive attitude, you will focus on the opportunities that accompany crises, and you will find the learning experience contained in every unsuccessful sales attempt. Most of all, you will look to the future with anticipation and not to the past with regret.

Summing It Up . . .

As a salesperson, you are a professional problem solver. Your self-image and your attitude toward your product, prospect, firm, and career should focus on this fact. The way you see yourself influences how others see you. Is the purpose of your sales effort to perform a needed service for a prospect who will benefit from your visit, or are you asking the prospect to do you a favor by buying your product? The first outlook results in high performance, whereas the second undermines your chances of success and nullifies your product knowledge and selling skills. If you believe in yourself and your abilities, recognize your product's benefits, believe that you work for an ethical organization that is concerned with your well-being, and see your prospect as a friend to be served and not an enemy to be conquered, you will succeed in selling.

A sales career can provide short-term and long-term satisfaction. Immediate satisfaction comes from knowing that you are helping others; future contentment comes from knowing that you are a positive force shaping the direction of your family, firm, and customers.

Successful salespeople are optimistic and self-motivated. They are cheerful, open-minded, resilient, and adaptable, and they practice positive mental simulation. Their attitude remains strong in the face of temporary setbacks because they focus on the successes they have achieved, and they see their setbacks as learning experiences. They are goal-oriented individuals. They set goals that are energetic yet realistic, and though they do not blame themselves for things beyond their control, they willingly accept responsibility for the outcome of their efforts.

Key Concepts and Terms . . .

adaptability	performance equation
attitude	pessimism
chunking	positive reinforcement
close-mindedness	pygmalion effect
goal	resiliency
locus of control	self-confidence
mental simulation	self-efficacy
motivation	self-esteem
open-mindedness	self-image
optimism	win–win attitude

Building Skills . . .

1. Define self-image, self-esteem, and self-confidence.
2. Explain the proper attitude toward selling as a profession.
3. Describe a win–win situation, including how it is possible to "lose" when you make a sale.
4. Explain why your attitude toward your product influences the prospect's attitude.
5. Describe the attitude salespeople should have toward their firm.
6. Explain the relationship between goals, motivation, and success.
7. Describe how success influences attitude.
8. Explain what it means to take responsibility for your performance.
9. Contrast calling an unsuccessful sales attempt a setback to calling it a failure.
10. List the steps of the goal-setting process.
11. Describe some of the problems commonly associated with goal setting.
12. Explain why your goals should be of different magnitudes and time frames, along with the benefit of prioritizing your goals.
13. Define chunking, including how it is used in relation to long-term goals. Give an example.
14. Describe the benefit of forming a mental picture of a successful sales call, and describe how you can use visualization to overcome anxiety about a difficult sales call.

Making Decisions 16-1:

April Hollis attended an in-home demonstration of Holiday Kitchenware hosted by her sister-in-law, Judy. Judy asked April if she would like to become a Holiday sales representative, and April is talking things over with her friend Carol Fritchie.

Carol:	Why don't you give it try? It sounds like a great opportunity. From what I've heard, some of those Holiday reps earn fabulous incomes.
April:	I know. Judy made $45,000 last year. But something still bothers me....
Carol:	What's the problem?
April:	After each demonstration, you're supposed to ask the guests to make a purchase. I don't think I'd feel right asking people for their money.
Carol:	I know what you mean. I wouldn't either.
April:	Besides, with the economy the way it is, people just can't afford to buy something they don't really need.
Carol:	Look at it this way, April: Some people will probably volunteer to buy, so you won't always have to ask.
April:	It wasn't that way the other night. *No one* offered to buy! Judy came right out and asked us for our orders.
Carol:	Was she pushy?
April:	Well, no. But the whole thing still makes me uncomfortable.

Summarize April's perception of selling and her attitude toward Holiday products.

Making Decisions 16-2:

Alex Walsh was hired six months ago as a sales consultant for Bobcat Inc., a manufacturer of power tools. His six-month performance evaluation, written by regional sales manager Jose Mendez, arrives in the mail, and Alex opens it eagerly. Much to Alex's surprise, Mendez mentions several things that Alex doesn't find favorable.

Mendez begins the review by saying that Alex is hard-working, reliable, and enthusiastic, and that because of his pleasant personality, he has a nice rapport with clients. However, Mendez also reports that Alex lacks certain basic selling skills and needs to build on his product knowledge. He says Alex is well groomed, but that his presentations are occasionally marred by grammatical errors. Although Alex obviously wants to do a good job, says Mendez, he sometimes demonstrates a lack of self-confidence. Mendez also notes that Alex uses only a limited range of selling techniques, and that he needs to develop a better understanding of buyer behavior. He goes on to recommend that Alex take a course in consumer behavior at a local college and attend in-house seminars on selling techniques.

Alex is shocked that his review is anything less than perfect. He confides his hurt feelings to his wife: "He butchered me. I've opened many new accounts. My customers praise me for the advice I've given them. I've received thank-you letters from several of them, and some have specifically requested that I be the Bobcat rep who calls on them. Who does he think he is? He hasn't sold in years. He probably couldn't if he had to. When I meet with him next week, I'm going to tell him exactly what I think of this review!"

Do you think Alex received a bad evaluation? Help Alex in setting goals to maintain a healthy attitude toward his job.

Making Decisions 16-3:

Name an endeavor in which you would like to be successful, but in which you have a difficult time envisioning success. Why is success hard to imagine?

Making Decisions 16-4:

Break down your career goal into shorter, more manageable time frames. What are the steps along the way to your goal? How much time will each phase of the process involve?

Managing Your Time
and Territory

THE JOB TO BE DONE . . .

A salesperson's time is precious. Since closing can be achieved only when with prospects, the more time that one is involved in person-to-person communication with customers or potential buyers the better. Managing your day, week, and month becomes an important part of the job. Chapter 17 helps you:

. . .appreciate the value of time management in selling.

. . .learn the common techniques of time management and enjoy the benefits derived from their use.

. . .schedule time for quiet work, personal satisfaction, and long-term goals.

. . .know how to prioritize activities according to importance.

. . .learn how to conduct an efficient meeting.

. . .understand the function of territory management.

. . .know how to plan call patterns.

. . .know how to plan sales routes.

TIME AND TERRITORY MANAGEMENT . . .

A surprisingly small portion of the salesperson's busy schedule is devoted to profitable selling efforts such as prospecting and delivering sales presentations. According to Figure 17-1, face-to-face and telephone selling combined

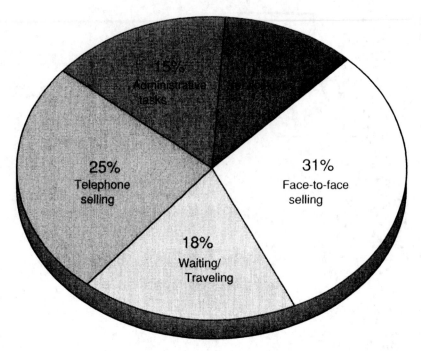

Figure 17-1 How salespeople spend their time. (*Source*: Dartnell Corporation: 29th Survey of Sales Force Compensation, 1997. Reprinted with permission.)

31%
Face-to-face selling

18%
Waiting/ Traveling

25%
Telephone selling

15%
Administrative tasks

account for only half of the average salesperson's schedule. Most of the time, sellers are engaged in other, nonselling activities. Servicing accounts, attending meetings, traveling to and from sales calls, waiting for appointments, doing paperwork, keeping abreast of product and industry developments are necessary parts of the salesperson's job. Unfortunately, they are also among the least profitable activities.

Salespeople can squeeze the most out of their work only by making good use of the techniques of time and territory management. Today's sellers are blessed with a variety of time-saving devices, such as cellular telephones, FAX, voice mail, e-mail, and portable computers. The purpose of this chapter is to introduce you to some of the principles of time and territory management. By using the techniques described here, you can increase your efficiency and thereby your profitability as a salesperson.

TIME MANAGEMENT . . .

Selling is independent work. Many salespeople operate from their homes and have little more than occasional telephone contact with their employers. Even those who go to an office every day are responsible for structuring their own schedule. Because selling requires so much self-motivation and self-discipline, salespeople have a tremendous need for time management skills. Figure 17-2 lists seven time-related problems that are common among salespeople.

The goal of **time management** is to make more productive use of available time. It does not "create" time; rather, it enables one to use what is available more productively. For the salesperson, this translates into profit. As an

Time Management-Related Problems

1. Devoting too much time to low-yield or low-probability prospects.

2. Starting a task without adequate preparation.

3. Beginning a new task before completing your present task.

4. Allowing telephone and face-to-face conversations to drift away from the subject at hand.

5. Failure to utilize the latest technology.

6. Being overly concerned with record-keeping. (Keeping too many records, or overly-detailed records.)

7. Gathering and recording information that has little or no bearing on the sale.

Figure 17-2

effective and efficient manager of your time, you will know how to minimize the periods you spend on low-profit, but necessary, work. The hours once spent unproductively can then be devoted to the most profitable selling activities.

For example, you might save two hours a week by delegating your paperwork to an assistant. But if all you did with this time was take a long lunch, the additional hours would not profit you. On the other hand, you might use the extra time to call on new prospects or plan a presentation. In this way, you have managed your time to lead directly to profit.

The time management principles and techniques described in this chapter are familiar to experts in this field as well as to many successful salespeople. If the ideas are completely new to you, you might want to try only a few at a time rather than completely change your work methods. Learning new techniques can take a significant amount of time in itself, but after you become comfortable with them they will make up for the loss in spades.

First Things First: Setting Priorities . . .

The core around which time management revolves is priority. To manage yourself effectively, you start by setting priorities, and continue by remembering where they lie. For the salesperson, top priority goes to any activity that helps increase productivity and job satisfaction by increasing sales. These activities deserve the greatest amount of the salesperson's time, whereas nonproductive tasks deserve the least. Many sellers fail to concentrate on prospects with the greatest profit potential. This is a common time management problem.

To identify your priorities, measure each of your present work activities in terms of its productivity. Productivity in this case means the income derived in relation to the amount of time devoted to the task. Suppose, for instance, you spend equal amounts of time each month on two different prospecting methods. If you measured your productivity, you might discover that one system yields ten sales per month, whereas the other yields only one. There should be no question which method deserves priority treatment. Knowing your priorities, you decide to double the amount of time you spend on the most productive prospecting method, and abandon the other entirely.

Suppose you know that one of your prospects might place an order so large it would surpass the total of several other orders combined. Yet you also know that that potential buyer isn't as likely to purchase as the other, low-volume customers. In this situation, you would do best to prioritize your prospects according to both their likelihood of buying and the size of their projected orders.

An excellent way to determine which activities are most productive is to keep a daily log. Record the time you spend on every activity, no matter how important or unimportant it seems, or how much or how little time the activity takes. If your schedule is quite variable, keep the log for several weeks. As time passes, you will come to see a relationship between your income and your activities. You will notice that certain actions seem to be very profitable, whereas others seem only to consume time.

If you have difficulty abandoning unproductive activities, ask yourself what would happen if you did. Imagine the worst possible thing happening. If the "worst possible thing" isn't bad, you might decide to deal with the result of dropping the task. If the activity is unprofitable but necessary, such as routine paperwork, consider delegating it. Eliminating all low-profit activities will be impossible. Low-volume customers cannot be ignored, and paperwork must be completed. The goal of time management is to make the best use of time, given the reality that some secondary activities will always be necessary.

Long-Term Goals . . .

One of the greatest challenges of time management is finding room in your schedule to work on long-term goals. This is because salespeople are often faced with a conflict between urgent and important activities. Activities are "important" if they are rewarding regardless of their urgency. They are "urgent" if they seem to demand immediate attention regardless of their importance. Pressing activities have a way of interrupting more important work even though they can usually be delayed with little or no harm. Because these situations are a constant threat to your schedule, you have to take special pains to set aside and protect time for long-term goals. Remember always to set your priorities on the basis of importance, not urgency.

Devoting time to long-term goals can seem inconvenient because the rewards are not immediate. Making sales presentations and servicing accounts, on the other hand, seem much more important because they are gratifying in the short term. Indeed, they are the source of your livelihood, but may not improve your long-term financial situation, advance your career, or meet your personal ambitions for the future. Even though the rewards of working toward future goals are not immediate, you must set aside several hours a week for them, or they will never be achieved.

Suppose your long-term goal is to buy a house, and you know you will never buy a house on your present salary. The only way you can achieve your plan, you realize, is to increase your salary by expanding into a new region.

> When I look to the future, it's so bright it burns my eyes.
>
> Oprah Winfrey

Because you can spare only a half-day each week to work toward expanding, though, you question the wisdom of taking time away from more immediately profitable activities. It might be more than a year before you will have penetrated the new region to your satisfaction. Should you bother? Yes. Just think of the reward you would realize if you didn't devote time to your aspirations. None. You would be in exactly the same position next year as you are in today because you will have devoted your extra time to routine work.

Admittedly, unforeseen crises are always pressing upon the busy salesperson, and protecting your long-term goals will be extremely difficult. But only you can make time to devote to your future plan. Until you do, they will seem unreal and unreachable. One way to begin is to apply the time management techniques found in this chapter until you carve out some free time for yourself.

Organizing Your Work Area . . .

An organized work area is not only an important part of your professional image, as described in Chapter 15. It is also key to effective time management. A clean, orderly work environment is conducive to clear thinking and efficient work. Its opposite—messy, haphazard surroundings—wastes time by creating confusion and interfering with concentration.

Keeping your work area organized is primarily a matter of handling mail and paperwork, which can pile up if neglected. Know which papers should be kept current, which should be filed for a later time, and which should be discarded. This is not to say that your desk or work area should be empty.

Ideally, your system should allow for quick retrieval of anything you file. A database is "right" if it works for you. Generally speaking, you should try to devise broad, memorable categories for your work, and avoid subcategories. Carefully-kept records provide you with important information relating to your selling efforts.

The necessity of an orderly desk and work area cannot be overemphasized. If your desk and files are not organized, you will waste time trying to find important papers when you could be making calls or prospecting. Worse, you might miss appointments and important events. The same need for an orderly work space applies to your automobile, attaché case, and price book.

TIME PLANNING TOOLS . . .

Failing to plan means planning to fail. Effective time management means effective planning. Several time planning tools are used by businesspeople and private individuals alike. Among them are the to-do list, the calendar or appointment book, and the tickler file.

The To-Do List . . .

The most basic tool for short-term planning is the daily **to-do list**. This is a list of small tasks that you plan to accomplish each day. Most people set aside a few minutes every morning or evening to write their list for the coming day. They make a new, updated schedule every day.

If you are working on a major project, you should divide it into smaller parts that could be accomplished little by little each day. Include the smaller parts rather than the whole on your to-do list. "Marketing report," for example, could be broken into small items such as "telephone research," "update mailing list," and "write outline." Each task would be a separate to-do item.

As you proceed through the day, try to do the items on your list in order of priority. This will ensure that you will complete the most important activities you had planned for the day; it will also give you a greater sense of accomplishment. Remember to prioritize your activities according to both their immediate reward and their contribution to your long-term goals. Some time management experts suggest assigning one of three priority levels to your tasks: Write a 1 or A next to top-priority tasks, things that *must* be done; 2 or B next to tasks that *should* be done; and 3 or C next to tasks that it would be *nice* to do.

Any task you don't accomplish one day should be carried over to the next day's to-do list. If you find yourself forwarding the same items day after day, consider the possibility that they are low priority and could be eliminated.

Your to-do list should be just long enough to challenge your abilities yet not so lengthy as to produce frustration. If you realize you are working at too leisurely a pace, your list may be too short. Try writing one that is a little longer to motivate yourself to keep a stiff pace in order to meet the day's objectives. You won't feel too frustrated if you don't get through the whole list because you knew it was going to be a challenge. You will feel better if you complete ten out of twelve items than if you complete ten out of twenty.

Calendars and Appointment Books . . .

Like the to-do list, the calendar or appointment book is an indispensable time planning tool for the salesperson. Most time management experts strongly suggest that you maintain only one calendar, a portable one that contains your entire schedule of appointments, dates, and time commitments. This would eliminate the possibility of scheduling a business date at the same time you have a personal commitment. It would also solve the problem of transferring (or forgetting to transfer) notes from one calendar to another, or remembering which calendar has which activities.

Since many salespeople must keep co-workers abreast of their whereabouts, a second appointment book that remains in the office is not inappropriate. If you do keep an office calendar for others, remember to record all of your activities, including the ones for which you personally need no reminder. For example, if you have a standing engagement every Friday at 3 p.m., mark it down in the office calendar. This way, your office will be able to locate you on Friday afternoons. A daily schedule planner, such as the one found in Figure 17-3 lets you plan your day and keep colleagues informed of your activities.

Name _____ Date _____

Time	Monday	Tuesday	Wednesday	Thursday	Friday	Saturday	Sunday	Time
06:00								06:00
07:00								07:00
08:00								08:00
09:00								09:00
10:00								10:00
11:00								11:00
12:00								12:00
01:00								01:00
02:00								02:00
03:00								03:00
04:00								04:00
05:00								05:00
06:00								06:00
07:00								07:00
08:00								08:00
09:00								09:00
10:00								10:00

Figure 17-3

Nothing can stop the man with the right mental attitude from achieving his goal; nothing on earth can help the man with the wrong mental attitude.

Thomas Jefferson

The Tickler File . . .

People who handle a great deal of paperwork, juggle a wide variety of tasks, or face a multitude of deadlines often find a **tickler file** very helpful. A tickler file, also called an everyday or daily file, stimulates your memory by helping you keep date-sensitive papers until they are needed, at which time they surface.

Tickler files are usually divided by month, day, or date, and can be tailored to the user's particular needs. For a monthly tickler, you might use either twelve file folders or an expanding file divided into twelve slots; for a daily tickler, you might use one folder for each weekday or an expanding file divided into thirty-one slots. There are also file books with dividers marked "1" through "31" and "January" through "December."

Whenever you have a time-sensitive piece of paper, file it in the appropriate tickler file for later action. Then regularly look through it to find the reminders you've put away. Ideally, you should review your current and upcoming tickler files daily, at the time you are preparing your to-do list. The following example shows how a tickler file works.

Suppose it is a morning in early February, and you find two date-sensitive items in your mail: a bill due April 1, and a notice about a conference you would like to attend. Although the conference is not until July, reservations begin May 15. Store the bill in your *March* tickler file because you must act on it before the due date. Store the conference notice in the *May* file so that you'll remember to make reservations on time.

Toward the end of February, you will review the March file, and transfer the month's papers into daily files. You store the bill in the file marked "20" because you plan to pay it on March 20, ten days before it is due. Then on the morning of March 20, you find the bill and either pay it immediately or mark it 1 or A on your to-do list. The conference notice, meanwhile, is safe and sound in the May folder. When late April comes around, you'll transfer it to the "15" folder, and on May 15 you'll make reservations for the conference.

STRUCTURING YOUR TIME . . .

Figure 17-4 lists twenty-four **productivity** blocks. At least half of these relate to poorly structured time. One of the greatest challenges of time management is that of structuring one's schedule in order to accomplish something in the face of countless projects, small emergencies, and interruptions. The constant variety that salespeople enjoy can also be a rigorous test of the salesperson's

Productivity Blocks

1. Failure to delegate.
2. Poor use of waiting time.
3. Poor use of travel time.
4. Perfectionism.
5. The inability to say no to requests for your time.
6. An absence of "quiet time."
7. A disorganized work area.
8. Interruptions.
9. Scattered thinking.
10. Oversocializing.
11. Keeping too tight of a schedule.
12. A carelessly-planned schedule.
13. A lack of goals.
14. Unclear goals.
15. Too many goals.
16. Conflicting goals.
17. Confused priorities.
18. Disrespect for outside deadlines.
19. Lack of personal deadlines.
20. Unnecessary correspondence.
21. Failure to group related activities.
22. Unnecessary meetings.
23. Unproductive meetings.
24. Failure to use peak energy hours wisely.

Figure 17-4

efficiency and organization. Many things compete for one's time and attention every day, making it hard for the salesperson to remain focused.

To keep your day from becoming scattered by surprises and interruptions, plan your schedule by grouping similar activities together and setting appointments for completing them. This is an especially good way to handle routine tasks like opening mail and unimportant interruptions like casual calls.

Almost any repetitive task in your workday can be grouped and scheduled along with similar tasks. You can set aside special times to check on customer orders, fill out sales reports, visit co-workers, run errands, read your mail, or return phone calls, all at times convenient to you. Other tasks that can be grouped include bill paying, typing, dictation, reviewing prospect profiles, designing visuals for sales presentations, and conducting new product research.

If you set aside an hour each morning to place phone calls, make this the time you receive calls as well. Leave messages saying you will be available during that period, and save until tomorrow morning the routine contacts that you couldn't get to today. If you decide to handle your mail during the last half hour of your business day, set all mail and interoffice correspondence aside until then. By reserving specific times for related tasks, you free your mind for other matters the rest of the time.

Take a moment each day to look several days ahead on your calendar and plan a more efficient schedule. If you have two sales calls in the same neighborhood on different days, try to reschedule them so that you can make just one trip to that area. If an appointment has been set more than a week in advance, call a day or two ahead to confirm it. This is especially important when the visit involves significant travel time. If the other party must cancel the date, your call will save you travel time and allow you to make other plans.

Remember to schedule time for the activities related to your long-term goals, and also for keeping abreast of your product and industry. Even though being informed doesn't seem to produce immediate income, your overall success depends on it. Several hours a week is not unreasonable for this important activity. Use this time to meet with other professionals in your industry, read trade journals, and watch TV reports related to your business. You might even consider using the services of a clipping bureau, a business that clips articles on specified subjects.

Quiet Time . . .

Every salesperson needs quiet time for planning, evaluation, and reflection, as well as for attending to work that requires concentration. Try to devote at least one hour a day to such work, whether it be planning the coming day, assessing past performance, making difficult calculations, or preparing contracts.

Quiet time may be difficult to find, but it is vital to your productivity. You may have to go to the office early, before the switchboard opens or your co-workers arrive. You may have to lock yourself in the bedroom at home for an hour at the end of each business day. Even your car may be a haven for quiet time.

Just remember, happiness is having a poor memory about what happened yesterday.

Lou Holtz

Using Peak Energy Hours . . .

When scheduling your many activities, keep in mind your **peak energy hours**. The work that is most important, most challenging, or meant to yield the greatest results should be scheduled for this period. Trying to do difficult work during a low-energy time can be very frustrating. Not only will your rate of success diminish, but also you will spend more time on the task than you would during high-energy periods. Make use of your elevated moods when you need them most by scheduling your most challenging sales calls during those hours.

Your peak energy hours are the times when you are at your best; your mind is clearest, energy level is highest, and interpersonal skills are sharpest. Different people have different peak hours. You probably have friends who claim to be "morning people" and others who claim to be "night people." If you don't know when your own peak hours occur, pay special attention to your energy level and mood throughout the day. Do you "rise and shine" early, only to crave a nap after lunch? Or do you fumble around in a fog each morning, not coming alive until the afternoon?

Another way to determine your peak hours is by attempting a difficult mental task several times throughout the day. When are your concentration and performance the best? This is your peak energy time. If your schedule is flexible, save your low-energy hours for less demanding tasks, such as reading the mail, completing routine reports, or returning phone calls.

How to Schedule Enough Time . . .

Delays and interruptions are a fact of business life. Even though specific difficulties are unexpected, the likelihood of some kind of obstacle is very much to be expected. Never make the mistake of squeezing a one-hour appointment into the same size opening in your calendar. Even though you cannot know exactly when a delay or interruption will occur, you must allow for it in your schedule.

A schedule that is too tight to allow for the unexpected will be impossible to keep. An urgent phone call from a client will make you fifteen minutes late for your next sales call. Then your sales call will drag on until rush hour, and then you'll get stuck in traffic and miss your plane. To avoid ruining your plans like this on a daily basis, you have to pad your schedule with extra time.

One way to pad your schedule is simply to overestimate the time each appointment, task, or errand will take. If you think a meeting will take about forty-five minutes, block off an hour in your appointment book. If you can drive from one sales call to the next in twenty minutes, plan for thirty. A generous cushion of time between appointments will absorb the delays you incur while sitting in traffic, waiting for a tardy prospect, or trying to start the car.

Salespeople who schedule themselves too tightly are likely to be very tense because nothing can be added to their day. They often discourage potential buyers from making casual conversation because they are too hurried and impatient. Worse, they seem to be too busy for the prospect. By working a sufficiently loose schedule, the salesperson can always be available to tend to needs or engage in small talk. Furthermore, a looser schedule is not easily disrupted by delays. Salespeople who allow for obstacles can keep a cool head and go about their business without frustration.

> Procrastination is opportunity's natural assassin.
>
> Victor Kiam

Fear of Deadlines . . .

Fear of deadlines is a major cause of stress in the working world. Not surprisingly, one of the chief objectives of time management is to help meet deadlines. As you become more and more the master of your own time, the knowledge that you can and will meet deadlines will increase, and your deadline-related stress will decrease.

Often the most profitable work, such as long-term personal goals, has no deadline associated with it. But without these time restrictions, a project will lose its sense of importance in your mind. Whenever you are working on something that has no outside constraints, set your own internal deadlines. This will help you focus on how to structure your time. If you decide to buy a house within a year, for example, you will need to complete a number of money-saving tasks, each with its own short-term deadline. As long as you respect your own restrictions as you would those set by others, you will accomplish much, and avoid the pressure and stress that come with procrastination. If you continually put off a task, set a deadline by which you will either complete it or forget it. If it is truly important to you, you will be motivated to meet your deadline.

Setting personal deadlines helps you prioritize your work. If you are not sure what the constraints are for a given task, ask yourself how it contributes to the achievement of your goals. Then you will know whether to begin work on it at once, defer it, or forget it altogether.

Using Unstructured Time . . .

No matter how efficient you become, there will always be stretches of potentially unproductive waiting time in your schedule. Waiting for sales appointments can take a huge bite out of a salesperson's day. If the time is not put to good use, the wait can be very frustrating, even if you padded your schedule to allow for it. Then there is all the nonwork time idled away at other chores and places. Because waiting time is such a significant part of the seller's schedule, the wise person knows how to make productive use of it.

You should develop an almost instinctive habit of filling in your waiting time with productive activities. Recall from Chapter 4 that this is an excellent opportunity to gather additional information on the prospect. Ask questions of the company receptionist or request reading material. You should also bring along your own reading material or a laptop computer to keep yourself busy during the time you spend in reception areas. Completing sales reports will give you a much greater sense of accomplishment than staring at the ceiling.

Plan on doing paperwork while waiting for personal chores. You not only get the work done, but you free up an hour or so each week for making sales calls. If tomorrow morning's car tune-up will keep you waiting for a while, plan to take along the sales reports that need reviewing. If you normally wait half an hour for your haircut or perm, bring along a notepad and jot down ideas for an upcoming presentation.

Surprisingly few salespeople make advance plans for their unproductive waiting time. An electrical parts salesperson shares this story:

I recall being on a sales call to a company where an unscheduled meeting of all buyers was going on. There were three of us in the waiting area, all salespeople. At first, none of us knew how long this meeting would take, and as is the case in most waiting rooms, we didn't talk. The other two each grabbed a magazine and paged through it. I took out my outdated phone book, which I had saved for just such an occasion, and started recopying it. Time went by.

Before long, the other two had gone through every magazine on the table. Having nothing else to do, they started to talk to each other, and after several minutes, one got up and left. The other stood up, started walking around, tried to make conversation with the receptionist, and began mumbling about the time being wasted.

I felt sorry for them. Surely this kind of situation had happened to them before. Why weren't they prepared for it? I don't know if the second salesperson made the sale when the meeting finally ended, but I could tell that this person's day had been ruined.

Like waiting, time spent on the road takes up a tremendous part of one's schedule. If you spend two hours a day driving to and from sales calls, you could benefit from the use of a tape machine or mobile cellular telephone. On the way to each call, review any preapproach data you have recorded about the prospect, and as you drive home, record the important points of the call while they are still fresh in your mind. You can play back the information before your next visit to the prospect.

Use your cellular telephone to confirm upcoming appointments or to notify a prospect if you will be late for your meeting. Many salespeople who once considered car phones a luxury have come to find them an absolute necessity.

By turning your road time into productive time, the tape recorder and cellular phone make something valuable out of the many hours you stand to lose while driving. Instead of becoming frustrated by fighting traffic, you will be able to maintain a healthy attitude and friendly disposition because you are not wasting time at all.

> It is the love of what you do that helps you move beyond the rejections to the next interview.
>
> Charlton Heston

Time Wasters . . .

As you can infer from reading the top items ranked by sales representatives in Figure 17-5, interruptions take up a great deal of a salesperson's time. Sellers commonly have problems dealing with distractions and disruptions. Lengthy casual conversations can severely interfere with your work if you let them, and it is up to you to exercise control over their influence. The same can be said of the unintentional distractions caused by the flow of people all around you.

One way to discourage time-wasting conversations with others is to cut them short by stating that you have to get back to work, and then doing just that. Chat with your co-workers freely during coffee breaks or lunch hour, and before long they will respect the clear distinction you make between work time and conversation time.

Whether you are meeting with others or they are visiting you, you should take responsibility for limiting conversations that can cut into your productive time. When you are with customers who have placed a large order, spend ample time with them but don't allow your conversation to wander too far from the reason for the visit. If you have a choice, wait until you complete all of your business before initiating small talk. You will then be in a position to end your visit at a tactful moment.

This is not to downgrade the importance of small talk in any sales presentation. You should use this tool wisely to develop relationships with buyers. But when this type of verbal communication becomes excessive, you should be aware of the need to cut it short. If you have to end a casual conversation that seems unfinished, suggest another place and time to continue it. "I have to go now," you might say, "but maybe we can pick up where we left off over lunch next Monday." Chances are, the prospect will decline the invitation.

Time Wasters

1. Telephone interruptions.

2. Drop-in visitors.

3. Lack of self-discipline.

4. Crises.

5. Meetings.

6. Lack of objectives, priorities, and deadlines.

7. Indecision and procrastination.

8. Attempting too much at once.

9. Leaving tasks unfinished.

10. Unclear communication.

Figure 17-5

When a customer or co-worker is visiting you, a good way to end a conversation is to say that you have to be somewhere else shortly, and leave your office along with the visitor. This seems more cordial than asking the visitor to leave while you remain. Another good idea is to instruct your secretary or assistant to interrupt you in person or by phone after a certain amount of time has passed. You will then be able to end the talk by saying you must tend to an urgent matter.

To limit unexpected visits, rise when visitors approach. They won't be inclined to take a seat while you are standing. If the meeting turns out to be important, invite the visitor to sit. Yet another technique is to keep chairs away from your desk or to put something on them to prevent sitting.

One effective way of escaping is to ask your host if you can use the telephone. Then call your office or your next client and tell him or her you might be a little late. Your chatty prospect will quickly end the meeting out of respect for your schedule. You can also plan ahead by telling someone else to phone you if you haven't returned by a certain time. When the call comes in, you can leave easily by saying you have urgent business to attend to.

If your problem is with unintentional distractions rather than conversations, you might consider rearranging your desk or work area. Unless you are supposed to be available to customers entering your building, you can turn your desk away from the entrance. The same can be done to avoid the traffic of co-workers. Perhaps you can have a partition placed around your desk, or between it and the busy corridor in front of you.

If you have an office of your own, you can close the door. Some businesses frown upon closed doors, but employees have gotten around that problem with humor: They close the door for limited times and put a note up saying, "Crazed salesperson at work; enter at your own risk!" Salespeople who work from an office at home often have the special problem of dealing with people who don't think they're really working. Tell your friends you cannot take personal calls during certain hours, and make sure the family doesn't interrupt you except in an emergency.

Traveling . . .

For many salespeople, travel is a way of life, and delays take up a huge portion of that activity. Salespeople who are on the road frequently will encounter traffic jams, automobile breakdowns, late flights, congested airports, missed connections, and jet lag. To avoid this constant frustration as much as possible, you should question any planned business trip. Ask yourself, "Is this really necessary?" If a conference call or series of letters will do the trick, or if someone else can make the trip for you, strongly consider these alternatives.

If you must travel, learn to do it as efficiently as possible. Save time preparing for frequent trips by keeping necessary personal items ready at all times so that you won't have to pack and unpack them repeatedly. Set up a portable office in your briefcase. Carry reading material and paperwork to keep you busy during lengthy waits. When you fly, limit your luggage to carry-on items so that you can avoid waiting for baggage upon arrival. When you drive, plan your trip to avoid rush-hour traffic snarls. Carry light snacks to keep your energy level high and to keep driving from becoming monotonous.

Meetings . . .

Many salespeople feel that nothing interferes with their income-earning activities more than meetings. Not only do such sessions detain salespeople during times they could be engaging in selling activities, but they are especially frustrating when unproductive. Salespeople estimate that fully half the time they spend in meetings is wasted because they don't start on time, the speakers are too long-winded, or the attendees get off the subject at hand.

Correcting these problems isn't easy, especially for the salesperson who is not in charge of meetings. However, some remedies may be available to you. For instance, you might be able to notify the leader that you can attend only for a specified time. This notice may motivate the chairperson to control the course of the meeting more tightly so that you will not miss anything important. If the get-together has a discussion period, you can use that opportunity to mention the problem of overlong sessions and offer ideas for shortening or eliminating them. Some of the information given in meetings can be shared in memos.

If you are in charge of the meeting, here are several suggestions you can employ to make sure it is efficient and productive:

1. Call ahead and remind attendees of the starting time.
2. Set a limit on the time for socializing, and start the meeting promptly. Don't wait for tardy attendees to show up.
3. Openly express your concern with meetings that are long or unproductive, and state your desire to move quickly through the present session.
4. Distribute a written agenda, complete with time limits for each item on the agenda.
5. Specify a time by which the meeting will end. You and the attendees will be more productive knowing how much time there is to accomplish the meeting's objectives.
6. Plan for the meeting to be shorter than usual, even if the agenda is typical. Remember **Parkinson's law**: Work expands to fill the time allotted.
7. Intercept conversations that go off on a tangent and bring them back on track. Promise to add new items to the next meeting's agenda or to cover them at the end of this one if time permits.
8. Don't allow telephone calls to be put through to the meeting unless they are urgent.
9. If some attendees need additional information after the meeting is over, allow others to leave.
10. Consider having stand-up meetings. People are more likely to participate actively when they are standing, and more quick to get to the point when their feet get tired.
11. Hold the meeting right before lunch or quitting time so that people will be motivated to get the meeting over with.

Delegating . . .

All too often, salespeople try to attend personally to every matter that confronts them, without ever considering the benefits of **delegating**, which is simply appointing someone else to perform certain tasks in your place. It is an excellent way to save time. By delegating your unprofitable tasks, you free yourself to devote more time to profitable tasks.

You may be able to create this additional hour by delegating. If your company makes secretaries or clerks available to you, use their assistance to the fullest. If needed, delegate any overflow to someone you have hired yourself. Over the long run, you will find that paying an assistant is the least expensive way to handle much of your work. If you would rather not delegate your nonselling tasks because you admittedly enjoy them, you need to reexamine your priorities. Perhaps you should sacrifice the minor enjoyment you gain from handling them yourself for the greater satisfaction of profit-making activity.

Your decision to hire an assistant should be based on whether you can justify the expense by making use of the time you gain from delegating. If your paperwork requires four hours work a week, consider the value of the sixteen hours a month you will gain. If the commission you could make in that time exceeds the amount you would pay an assistant, then you should certainly hire one. After all, the primary purpose of delegation is to increase your income by freeing up your time for selling. Carefully kept records provide a number of benefits, as illustrated in Figure 17-6.

Carefully-Kept Records Will Tell You:

1. The average number of new prospects your prospecting systems generate per month.

2. The ratio of new prospects to total sales.

3. The average number of phone calls it takes to secure a sales presentation.

4. Your closing ratio — i.e. the ratio of successful sales presentations to total presentations delivered.

5. The average number of visits it takes to close a sale.

6. Your average daily, weekly and monthly sales volume.

7. Your average income or commission per sale.

8. The average number of sales you make per day, per week or per month.

9. The percentage of sales that come from new customers, from repeat customers.

10. The percentage of former customers that buy again.

Figure 17-6

Of course, delegating will entail training someone, and this takes time. But teaching your assistant is a small price to pay compared to the return. Delegation also forces you to become more organized. You will want your assistant to be able to work independently and find materials without having to ask you where they are.

If you are a perfectionist, you will have to abandon this characteristic when you delegate. Remember the relative importance of the various tasks, and realistically assess their need to be perfect. Don't ask, "Can she or he do this as well as I can?" but "Can it be done satisfactorily?" You may need to teach someone how to perform the work to your comfort, but don't expect this person to do things exactly as you would. Stress the truly important things, those that will affect your success: Prospects' names must be spelled correctly, calculations must be accurate, and deadlines must be met.

Your assistant's character and personal abilities determine the extent to which you can delegate. The more competent the assistant, the more you can comfortably rest on his or her shoulders. The less competent the help, the more of a chore delegation will be. You won't want an assistant who causes you *more* work.

The ideal tasks to delegate fall under routine work, such as record keeping, bill paying, or filing. Most likely, these are chores that you recognize as a waste of your time even though they are necessary to your business. Each hour spent on paperwork is an hour you could devote to prospecting and selling. Even though not all nonselling activities need be delegated, most should. Make a list of necessary but repetitive activities when you are considering hiring an assistant. You might be surprised to discover how much work can be delegated.

Once you get the hang of delegation, you will see it as an important part of your success. You will come to depend on your assistant in the same way you depend on others in your organization. Nothing establishes a feeling of teamwork like delegation.

TERRITORY MANAGEMENT . . .

Territory management is one of a salesperson's most important duties, particularly those who are self-employed or who work without direct supervision. This task involves the geographic design of selling boundaries, the establishment of call patterns, and the planning of sales routes. The territory manager also must reevaluate and redesign territories when the need arises, accounting for a given territory's sales potential and the number of accounts that can be handled by one salesperson.

Of the various facets of territory management, the geographic design, that is, the subdivision of a region into individual selling areas, is the one most likely to be strictly a managerial function. Responsibility for call patterns and sales routes, on the other hand, is shared by the sales manager and salespeople. It is not uncommon for the sales manager to make the salesperson completely responsible for those functions.

If you have sole responsibility for management of your territory, you should handle it as if you were in business for yourself. You alone are responsible for your territory's contribution to your employer's profits. Managing your territory will increase your effectiveness, help you improve your planning and organizational skills, and foster a managerial attitude.

Territory Design . . .

A **sales territory** is a geographic area encompassing present and potential customers. It is assigned to a salesperson or sales office. Sales territories can range in size from entire nations to several city blocks. Although usually described in geographic terms ("Smith has the southeast region"), sales territories are actually measured in terms of customer buying power rather than physical area. A small geographic area may be a "large" territory in terms of profitability.

Rachel Turoscy

For Rachel Turoscy, education was an important part of her life and her career planning. Attending Lehigh University, she earned bachelor's, master's, and doctorate degrees in physical chemistry, and is presently pursuing an MBA. Her initial interest in science led her to a career path in research, which she worked at for six years. During that period she had numerous published articles and presentations to her credit, as well as a patent for Organofunctional Silane Paint Coagulants and Detackifiers.

In spite of her highly technical background, Rachel found that she was a people person. Switching careers, she was hired by Bio-Rad Laboratories in Hercules, CA as an Account Manager. She describes this position as running her own business without the financial risk of total autonomy. Rachel went into sales because it was an exciting new challenge that allowed her to couple her technical expertise with her native people skills. She also enjoys the financial rewards possible operating as an independent representative.

Rachel has always credited her listening skills for her success in both research and sales. Being an excellent organizer and problem solver were added bonuses. She suggests that people new to selling learn good time management, always follow up and don't forget to ask for the order. She also believes that overcoming the "no" and learning not to take rejection personally has been a tremendous help in her growth as a salesperson. Rachel is an excellent example of what one can do by blending technical abilities and knowledge with interacting skills.

Designing a sales territory entails determining the boundary lines to be drawn around groups of customers, preferably on the basis of sales potential. The number of key accounts in a proposed territory, customer concentration or dispersion, the degree of competition, and the market size that can be handled by one salesperson must also be considered. Sometimes the territory manager must subdivide small geographic areas that happen to contain high concentrations of key accounts. Territories might also have to be designed on the basis of which areas receive more promotional assistance and which require more travel.

If competitive or other economic factors change, sales areas should be redesigned. The territory manager may have to reduce large geographic regions that have seen an increase of population, or expand territories that are in an economic decline. A redesign might also be in order if the salesperson cannot realistically handle an overlarge territory or is failing to profit from a small territory.

Good territory design helps management evaluate its sales force accurately. Poor territory design has the opposite effect. A salesperson's performance is measured against the territory's potential. If one area has too great a sales potential, the salesperson can profit handsomely with little effort. Another with too low a sales potential may require the seller to work extremely hard toward minimal profit.

Call Patterns . . .

Establishing call patterns means determining how often and at what intervals you will call on prospects and customers. In most firms, salespeople and sales managers jointly determine how often each account will be visited over the coming year. **Call patterns** should be set according to your prospects' potential sales volume. To help you determine individual call patterns, try classifying your prospects by level of sales potential. For example, A accounts, those with the greatest potential for profit, should be visited most frequently, perhaps weekly. B accounts should be visited monthly, and C accounts quarterly. The Standard Industrial Classification code, which assorts firms according to their industry and function, is often used as an aid by salespeople who are trying to establish call patterns. You might also try ratings generated by your firm's computer.

Other factors that influence call patterns include the type of product sold, customer buying habits, competition, and the expenses incurred in making calls. If you sell a high-turnover product to retail stores, you will need to visit prospects more frequently than if you sell an industrial good with little possibility of repeat sales. If you launch a strongly competitive effort, you will need to establish a high frequency of calls as well as increase the length of your calls.

Once you establish your call pattern, write out a monthly or quarterly **itinerary**. Many employers insist that all accounts be visited at specified intervals regardless of their sales potential. They might even refuse to pay the salesperson's commission on accounts that have not been called upon as required. One purpose of call patterning is to improve customer relations by improving customer service. With well-planned call patterns, you can visit customers at predictable intervals and provide regular assistance and service to existing accounts.

> The bridges you cross before you come to them are over rivers that aren't there.
>
> Gene Brown

Sales Routes . . .

A **sales route** is the course or circuit you travel to cover your territory. Usually salespeople plan their sales route for a coming sales period and then submit the plan on a map or route sheet to the sales manager. If routing is one of your responsibilities, you should establish routes that minimize travel time and expense. To avoid backtracking and crisscrossing your territory, you may have to spend several nights on the road rather than try to be home every evening.

The first step in developing a routing pattern is to list all of your prospects and plot their locations on a map of your territory. You will arrange your sales route primarily on the basis of geography, clustering your visits to take advantage of the shortest travel routes. Other factors that will influence your sales route are the call patterns you have established, as well as customer buying habits and preferences. Your route sheet should be easy to complete and easy to understand, both by you and by others. It should be prepared far enough in advance for you to set appointments, and copies should be distributed to everyone in your firm who needs to know your whereabouts.

For computer users, software now exists to help salespeople and their managers establish sales routes. The programs are made to factor in such variables as travel time, waiting time, customer profit potential, and purchase probability. However, not everyone feels the need for this technological boost. The use of a complicated computer program often requires assistance from a technical consultant, which may not be worth the trouble and expense for many territory managers.

Summing It Up . . .

The purpose of time management for the salesperson is to increase sales income by minimizing time spent on nonselling activities and maximizing the time spent on profitable ones. Successful salespeople spend only half the time on administrative duties as unsuccessful people. They also spend more time prospecting and qualifying leads. Unsuccessful salespeople spend more time making sales presentations because they try to sell to unqualified leads.

The most important aspect of time management is assigning priorities to your work. Priority should be assigned on the basis of importance and profitability, not urgency. Set aside time to plan each coming day, and make sure to set aside special time for working toward long-term goals, quiet time, and keeping abreast of your industry.

Eliminate or decrease the time you spend on unprofitable activities by delegating them or assigning them low priority on your schedule. Group similar tasks, such as phone calls, paperwork, and errands, and work on one project at a time to avoid becoming scattered. Faithfully use a calendar or appointment book, a daily to-do list, and if necessary, a tickler file.

Arrange your work area to minimize distractions, and learn to avoid interruptions and time-wasting activities. Be prepared to make use of waiting time. Know how to conduct or make suggestions for an efficient meeting, and discover the advantages of delegation. Applying the techniques of time management will not guarantee an increase in sales income, but it will lay the groundwork for enhanced success.

Territory management is viewed as primarily a sales management function, but understanding territory management can also benefit the salesperson. Territory design, the determination of geographic boundaries for a proposed market, is the responsibility of the sales manager. The other aspects of territory management, establishing call patterns and planning sales routes, are either shared by managers and salespeople or given over completely to salespeople. A call pattern is the schedule of intervals for making sales calls, and should be determined on the basis of prospect purchase potential. A sales route is the course taken in covering a sales territory, and is determined primarily on the basis of travel and distance considerations.

You Decide!

After cultivating a large, new potential customer for months, Chuck is on the verge of a breakthrough. This prospect is big, with a mere trial order being a carload of product. In what he hopes is the big call, Chuck is asked by the purchasing agent if he can promise delivery in two weeks. Since he had just checked with the factory before calling on this potential customer and found that plenty of stock was available, Chuck happily replied "Yes. You can have that initial carload in ten days." After confirming the order number and briefly discussing future potentials, this happy peddler went out to celebrate.

The next day, Chuck faxed the order to the plant indicating the required shipping date. When he received his copy of the order acknowledgment by mail, he neglected to notice that shipment was not scheduled until after the date that he promised the buyer. It was not until he heard an angry call from this new customer on his voice mail that he realized the problem. A quick call to the plant confirmed Chuck's worst fears. A sudden spurt in business wiped out the inventory and it would be impossible to meet his customer's shipping date. As he dialed the buyer's number he pondered if he should just own up to the mistake and risk losing his toehold in this new lucrative account, or weasel his way out of the dilemma by fibbing a bit or blaming the factory. **You decide!**

Key Concepts and Terms . . .

A accounts	sales route
call pattern	sales territory
circular pattern	skip-stop pattern
cloverleaf pattern	straight line pattern
delegation	territory management
high spotting	tickler file
itinerary	time management
Parkinson's law	to-do list
productivity	peak energy hours

Building Skills . . .

1. Describe a to-do list, including its purpose in time management.
2. Explain why it is best to keep only one calendar or appointment book.
3. Discuss the use of a tickler file. Give examples.
4. Discuss the importance of long-term goals.
5. Describe methods of prioritizing activities on your to-do list.
6. Set up methods to allow for delays in your schedule.
7. Discuss the importance of peak energy hours in setting your schedule.
8. Discuss the importance of a neat and organized work area in saving time.
9. Describe the benefits of grouping similar activities together.
10. Explain the types of work that are best for delegation.
11. List some ways that you can increase your income by hiring an assistant.
12. Evaluate setting your own deadlines for work that has no outside deadline.
13. Describe some of the techniques for avoiding distractions and interruptions in your office.
14. Explain why it is better to meet someone in his or her home or office instead of yours.
15. Describe five techniques for running an efficient meeting.
16. List some ways you can make productive use of waiting time and driving time.
17. Explain how well-designed sales territories aid management in evaluating its salespeople.

Making Decisions 17-1:

Dawn Saltzer is a sales representative for Eagle Press, a publisher of college textbooks. Her territory, part of Eagle's Western States region, includes colleges located in and around Denver, Pueblo, and Colorado Springs. At the end of each sales period, Dawn meets with her sales manager, Florence Menyo.

Florence:	Dawn, something concerns me. College enrollments in your territory have increased, yet our sales in that region are off. Do you have any idea why?
Dawn:	I just don't understand it. I call faithfully on every four-year, community, and junior college in my territory. I make a point of seeing every professor, and you know how hard that can be. Some are almost impossible to get a hold of, but I wait for them in the halls between classes if I must.
Florence:	It's good to know you've been so conscientious, Dawn. Do you visit every college with the same frequency?
Dawn:	Yes, I try to.
Florence:	Do you think they all deserve the same frequency?
Dawn:	Yes, they're all important to me. You never know when a professor might decide to change textbooks. Besides, even a small school can make a difference: A teacher who adopts one of our books may use it for years to come. Also, some departments have a policy of switching course textbooks every two years.
Florence:	That's exactly what I'm getting at, Dawn: Perhaps you should change your pattern to call *more* frequently on the schools that seem to change textbooks regularly, and *less* frequently on those that don't. I also suggest that you maintain regular contact with professors who like to change books often or who send us response cards telling us they intend to change soon. And I recommend that you call less on the professors who have been using the same books for the past twenty years.
Dawn:	But we've got some exciting new titles on our list, Florence. I think I can convince even the professors who are the most loyal to their present books to give ours a try.

Describe your reaction to Dawn's philosophy, Florence's advice, and whether Dawn is making the most of her time.

Making Decisions 17-2:

Martin Logan is the floor manager of Green Hills Landscaping Equipment and Supplies. For several months, Martin has been confined to the Green Hills showroom; he has not made any personal calls on regular clients. One morning, he is visited by Brad Mendenhall, a local landscaper and steady customer.

Brad:	Where have you been keeping yourself, Martin?
Martin:	Right here, Brad. I never get out of the showroom anymore.
Brad:	I heard you have some new equipment in stock, so I thought I'd stop by and take a look.

Martin:	I'm glad you did. I've been meaning to stop by your shop and show you our latest catalog, but I couldn't get away.
Brad:	Why is that?
Martin:	Well, for one thing, we've been negotiating new contracts with all of our lessees, and that has me pretty tied up. Plus I'm training two new salespeople.
Brad:	Can't your assistant manager help you out?
Martin:	I suppose he could, but I'm the one who's paid to run things around here. Besides, he's been tied up making deliveries because we're short a driver.
Brad:	This can't be good for your business. How are you going to open up new accounts if you're stuck in the showroom?
Martin:	Beats me. I guess I'll have to rely on customers coming to me for a while. But I'll be back in action before long. Then I'll let people like you know I haven't forgotten about them.

Discuss some of the major ways Martin could improve his time and territory management. Describe exactly how he could use delegation.

Making Decisions 17-3:

Set a time by which you will complete a personal project that presently lacks a deadline. Explain why your time frame for completing the task is realistic.

Making Decisions 17-4:

For the coming week, list the activities you perform randomly throughout the day that could be grouped.

Practice Makes Perfect 17-1:

Ask a fellow student to design a tickler file and compare it with your own, asking the class for a critique.

Retail, Industrial Selling, and Telemarketing

THE JOB TO BE DONE ...

Selling jobs differ depending upon the industry, types of products, and potential customers. Two major areas are retail sales and industrial sales, yet the characteristics of these arenas are like night and day. Chapter 18 explores these fields in depth and tackles the relatively new area of telemarketing as well. Here you will learn to:

...appreciate the salesperson's role in the full-service retail store.

...understand how retail selling is unique among selling situations.

...understand the mechanics of the retail sales presentation.

...explore the industrial buying process and the scenario in which it takes place.

...examine the role of the industrial buyer's purchasing department.

...know the classifications of industrial purchases.

...become familiar with common practices in industrial selling.

...learn some of the terminology associated with industrial selling.

...recognize the economic advantages of telemarketing and the reason for its growth.

...compare the techniques of telemarketing to those of face-to-face selling.

...know how firms might employ telemarketing as a supplementary selling activity.

SPECIAL AREAS OF SELLING . . .

The purpose of this chapter is to examine three specific types of selling: retail, industrial, and telemarketing. The retailing area includes a discussion of the importance of the retail salesperson, and the qualities that make selling in this field unique. Emphasis will be on the responsibilities of the salesperson, the mechanics of the presentation, and compensation.

In the section on industrial selling, the setting is discussed, and an extensive description of the industrial buyer's job is included as well. This segment also includes the classifications purchases, some of the mechanics of this type of buying, the needs of buyers, and the terminology associated with industrial selling.

Telemarketing, or selling by telephone to consumers or industrial buyers, is growing in importance as a selling category. The reasons for this growth will be explored. There is also a discussion of the elements of the telephone presentation, compensation of telemarketers, the use of this tool as a supplementary selling activity, and finally, the disadvantages as well as economic advantages of telemarketing.

RETAIL SELLING . . .

No book about personal selling could be complete without a discussion of the retail arena. A retail sale is defined as any purchase made by the ultimate consumer. The selling efforts of department store and variety store salespeople, and the work of supermarket and convenience store cashiers, are perhaps the first things we think of when we hear the word *retailing*. However, this field also includes door-to-door selling, party-plan selling, vending machine operations, telemarketing, direct mail, and catalog sales. Our focus in this section is on the retail selling that goes on in stores, or "across-the-counter" selling.

Personal selling is an essential ingredient in the success of retail stores to varying degrees. Self-service stores, such as supermarkets, discount stores, and convenience stores, require their salespeople to do little more than direct shoppers to the merchandise and ring up sales. But service-oriented stores need personnel who are capable of assisting customers with buying decisions that will satisfy needs.

The role of personal selling in **full-service retailing** is not always given the credit it deserves. Retailers spend large sums of money on advertising, displays, and promotional events to attract customers to their stores, but the expenditure is useless if shoppers don't purchase. Once the shoppers are inside the store, personal selling becomes all-important.

Figure 18-1, next page, lists twenty reasons customers patronize retail stores. Customer patronage is important, because typically, shoppers must return many times before a store can break even on its promotion expenses. This is why the goal of most retailers is to build a large base of repeat

Figure 18-1

Reasons For Customer Patronage

1. Location is safe, convenient, and attractive.
2. Prices are reasonable.
3. Atmosphere is warm and friendly.
4. Merchandise is always fresh.
5. Repeat shoppers are recognized as valued customers.
6. Advertising is truthful and informative.
7. There is status associated with shopping there.
8. Friends shop there.
9. Other stores are nearby.
10. Ample parking.
11. There is a wide range of customer services; e.g. credit, lay-away, free alterations.
12. Merchandise is carried that is not found in other stores (unique assortment).
13. Fast, personal service.
14. Helpful, friendly, courteous, and knowledgeable salespeople.
15. There are incentives to visit often, such as frequent sales, sales promotions, and so on.
16. A wide variety of quality merchandise is carried.
17. The internal and external appearance is clean and fresh.
18. Good reputation.
19. In business for many years.
20. Habit.

shoppers. For service-oriented retailers, repeat business comes only from customers who trust and respect the store's salespeople. A salesperson's knowledge of merchandise, friendly personality, and honest advice contribute to an image that inspires customer loyalty. Salespeople are the store's key to a solid base of regular clientele.

Sales expertise also can provide a store with its strongest competitive advantage. Professional assistance offered by trained and knowledgeable salespeople attracts buyers. Shoppers like to frequent stores that have good salespeople. They are even willing to pay higher prices for merchandise found at these stores rather than shop at outlets where the sales effort is lacking.

Convenience, Shopping, and Specialty Goods . . .

Retail store merchandise can be placed in three broad categories, each with some bearing on the importance of retail selling. An item of store merchandise may be a convenience good, a shopping good, or a specialty good.

Convenience goods are low-priced products that are purchased frequently and often on impulse. Because they are presold through national advertising and available at many locations, the sale of convenience goods does not require personal selling skills. The only relevant consideration for the customer is that the item can be bought conveniently.

Shopping goods are products for which the consumer shops around, comparing selling points like price, quality, and selection. Shopping goods can vary widely in terms of cost and frequency of purchase, and the consumer is flexible with respect to brand or store. The consumer who is in the market for a shopping good may compare factors such as salesperson expertise and dealer reputation. Because the consumer relies on input from store personnel, salesmanship is a very important factor in purchasing shopping goods, especially for higher-priced items.

Specialty goods are products whose name, style, or type are very important to the consumer. Buyers take pains to locate the preferred item, and may be trying to satisfy an emotional buying motive. Specialty goods also tend to be higher-priced products. Because factors such as brand identification and customer preference are at issue, specialty goods require strong personal selling skills. Salespeople must know their product thoroughly and be capable of persuading consumers to reconsider a strongly held conviction.

How Retail Selling Is Unique . . .

Retail store selling is unique among categories of salesmanship. Here are some of the things that set retailing apart:

1. The retail store customer comes to you, an advantage over outside selling. In most other fields, the seller goes to the buyer. Whereas outside salespeople may visit prospects who are preoccupied with other matters, retail sellers typically meet prospects who are there to shop.

2. The retail store presentation is done without notice or advance preparation. Because you never know who might enter your store, you must observe the prospect and gather prospect information on the spot.

3. The retail store is a physical territory that must be maintained for optimum selling potential. You must see that customers are promptly assisted, displays are neat and attractive, merchandise is available, and the selling area is clean and safe.

4. Retail store customers cannot be expected to know the merchandise. Whereas industrial buyers are professionals who must research the products they purchase, retail customers tend to be consumers making a one-time purchase. In the retail setting, the salesperson must be an educator with patience, understanding, and the ability to communicate effectively.

5. The retail store salesperson sees many more customers in the course of an average day than do industrial or commercial sellers. In this arena, one must be comfortable working with a wide variety of personalities from all walks of life.

6. The retail store salesperson usually handles the customer's money, which is not true with industrial salespeople. It is common in retail for the salesperson to make change, verify checks, and conduct credit card transactions.

Other qualities make retail selling unique, for better or worse. Store salespeople work indoors, out of the weather, and their employment rarely, if ever, requires travel. Store selling usually requires standing all day, and salespeople usually are called on to work evenings, weekends, and even holidays. Long hours during peak seasons, such as the holidays, are also common.

Responsibilities and Challenges in Store Selling . . .

Strong product knowledge is essential in retail store selling. Service-oriented stores seek out salespeople who are well acquainted with the merchandise they sell. They also look to hire personable, outgoing individuals who will make a favorable impression on customers.

Further, retailers want their salespeople to "look the part." The salesperson's appearance indicates an understanding of the merchandise and the ability to relate to customers. Clothing shops and department stores may give their employees generous discounts on apparel and cosmetics to encourage them to look their best on the sales floor. The salesperson's use of store merchandise also enhances the selling effort.

Although the retail salesperson's responsibilities are many, the first and foremost is to the customer. Virtually every in-store activity, including paperwork and housekeeping, is driven by principles of customer satisfaction. Because the salesperson must be in constant contact with customers, personal appearance and telephone techniques are of utmost importance. Store salespeople are instructed to acknowledge incoming customers and, depending on the philosophy of the store, to offer help or immediately respond to requests for help. Stores often require their salespeople to promptly answer the telephone and instruct them on how to deal with callers.

Salespeople play an important part in the retailer's effort to judge customer buying trends. If sellers notice that a particular item is moving well, they should tell management about it so that appropriate buying decisions can be made. Some outlets encourage their salespeople to contact customers when new merchandise arrives or when a sale is in the offing. Retail salespeople in high-priced specialty stores often keep a **client book** that contains detailed information on the needs and preferences of their regular customers. With the help of this selling tool, the salesperson keeps an eye out for the customers' needs and calls them when particular items arrive.

Of course, any job that involves as much customer contact as retail selling will encounter a wide variety of challenges. Chief among them is the customer complaint. Dissatisfied customers frequently take their frustrations out on salespeople, who must learn not to take angry words personally. Store managers usually advise their staff to deal with complaints initially by explaining store policies. If the customer continues to be dissatisfied, the salesperson then is advised to refer to a manager.

Another typical retail occurrence is the return or exchange of merchandise. Most retail stores have policies allowing for returns and exchanges, usually stipulating the need for a receipt or a certain time limit to be observed. A customer who is not allowed to return or exchange an item may become irate. For this reason, store management might make an exception to its policy for the sake of smoother relations.

Retail salespeople have a number of responsibilities relating to the physical upkeep of their store or department. For example, they must keep the selling area well stocked. As New Jersey lawn and garden supplies retailer Al Gaudio puts it, "We don't sell shelves. Even in a store filled with merchandise, the first thing a shopper will notice is an empty shelf, and that creates a negative impression." To ensure a positive imprint on customers, the salesperson must do more than keep merchandise visible. Goods must be clean, in good condition, neatly displayed, and tagged. Clothing store salespeople are required to check fitting rooms periodically and rehang unsold items left behind by customers. Retail sellers are sometimes responsible for marking prices, and many are expected to participate in periodic inventories.

Frank McShan

After receiving his degree from Thomas College, Frank McShan went to work at Bell Industries in Andover, Massachusetts. Although he gives due credit to his college studies, including marketing and selling classes, the sales bug didn't really bite him until he began his work as a customer service representative with Bell. After six months, Frank requested his position in inside sales with the corporation.

Frank works primarily over the telephone in selling a variety of electronics components and other associated services, such as Electronic Data Interface (EDI). His goal from the beginning has been to be the number-one seller in the company nationwide, which he has achieved the past four years. From a base of $300,000 in the beginning, his account package has grown to $17 million today.

Frank realizes that selling is not an eight hour per day job. He strives to go the extra mile for his customers, and prides himself on keeping a detailed client database. Knowing the likes and dislikes, as well as the family and personal information of his customers keeps him one step ahead of the competition. In addition, he is an avid reader and recommends Tom Hopkins' bestseller, *How to Master the Art of Selling*. Frank is also quick to point out that a successful salesperson needs the strong support of a helpful spouse.

Although some **vendors** (manufacturers, wholesalers, and jobbers) build and restock their displays within the store (particularly in grocery operations), most display work is done by in-store personnel. In some instances, employees must follow sophisticated merchandising techniques required by store headquarters. In others cases, management decides how best to display merchandise.

Housekeeping duties are also among the retail salesperson's responsibilities. Store employees are often kept after hours to vacuum or mop the floor, dust shelves, and clean restrooms; these duties are sometimes designated to specific people on certain days or handled informally as needed.

Training and Knowledge in Retail . . .

Retail salespeople typically do not receive as much formal training as do outside salespeople. New employees are regularly expected to have gained knowledge of store merchandise on their own time, and will be specifically trained in this area only if the merchandise is unusual or technical, which may take place solely on the sales floor or include classroom instruction. Trainees are instructed in the use of their store's equipment, and also are briefed on policies and selling techniques. Salespeople may receive ongoing education by way of vendors' visits and manufacturers' seminars.

Store salespeople are responsible for all manner of knowledge relating to their store's activities and merchandise. As a retail salesperson, you should know the details of the goods handled thoroughly, as well as where various items are located in the store or department. You should know if your emporium carries a certain product and whether it can be special ordered. You should always be aware of when new merchandise comes in. Furthermore, whenever you don't know something with certainty, you should be able to find out.

Department store salespeople should acquaint themselves with their entire store. They should know the location of the other departments, and something about the merchandise found in them. They should be able to direct shoppers anywhere in the building.

Store salespeople should always be aware of unique activities such as sales, special events, and new displays. To keep abreast of your store, you should read the company newsletter, staff memos, and bulletins, as well as any other promotional materials the organization is dispensing. Study window displays, and follow print and broadcast advertisements so that you will know when a sale is going on and what image your store is projecting.

> A professional is someone who can do his best work when he doesn't feel like it.
>
> Alistair Cooke

A related responsibility is that of keeping abreast of the competition. You should become familiar with the activities of competing stores, including those in your shopping district, mall, or outlet center.

Dishonesty in the Retail Environment . . .

Dishonesty may occur in any selling situation, but certain forms are predominant in retail store selling. Because merchandise and money are handled all day, retailers are especially concerned with theft, by customers and store personnel alike. Retail stores also contend with constant exposure to the possibility of being paid with bad checks, revoked credit cards, or stolen travelers checks.

Employee theft is thought by some to be a greater threat than shoplifting. The reasoning is that employees know where large amounts of money are kept, and they know when cash or valuable merchandise is unattended. To minimize the potential for employee theft, many stores require staff members to enter and exit through special doors, or forbid egress through stock rooms. Security personnel might be authorized to inspect employees' incoming and outgoing packages, handbags, and shopping bags.

Some policies may call for personnel to keep their belongings in lockers that may be inspected at any time. Antitheft policies also preclude employees from ringing up their own sales or walking through the store before or after operating hours. Some operations have a **silent award program**, offering employees a reward for the return of information leading to the conviction of co-workers caught stealing.

In addition to the security measures relating to internal theft, store salespeople take steps to minimize external dishonesty. For example, register cashiers must observe customers signing travelers checks and gift certificates to make sure the signature and countersignature match. Stores often have policies requiring certain kinds of identification whenever customers pay by personal check or credit card, and others require that all such purchases be cleared by management. Computerized credit card verifying systems alert store personnel when a card should be confiscated. In this unusual and stressful case, the sales clerk is usually offered a reward.

Stock shortage due to shoplifting is one of the stickiest problems facing retailers today, and minimizing this loss is a concern of store management and, to a certain extent, salespeople. Some stores offer incentives to the sales staff to catch shoplifters, such as cash rewards based on the value of the shoplifted items. However, legal considerations limit the actions of retailers significantly, and managers must be careful in what they advise salespeople to do when they suspect shoplifting.

Figure 18-2, next page, provides six guidelines in preventing shoplifting. Generally, salespeople should never directly accuse a customer. An act is not technically shoplifting until the suspect is out the door. Even if you are certain someone is shoplifting, your best recourse is to say something like, "Excuse me, did you forget to pay for that?" This gives the person the opportunity to save face by paying for the item. It also protects you and the store from being sued for slander. Never try to physically stop or detain a suspected shoplifter. Most

Figure 18-2

Guidelines in Preventing Shoplifting

1. Greet all shoppers immediately. This lets customers know that you are aware of their presence and have seen them.

2. Beware of shoppers who spend a considerable amount of time in one area of the store or department, or who look suspicious.

3. Beware of group shoppers who ask an unusual amount of questions or occupy your time while others in the group wander away.

4. Be alert to shoppers who ignore you, or who try to work themselves away from you.

5. Periodically check on shoppers who are taking merchandise in and out of fitting rooms.

6. Limit the number of items a shopper may take into the fitting room at one time.

retailers admit that when a thief is particularly bold, there is little they can do to prevent the loss.

Retail managers follow a few general guidelines to help minimize shoplifting. For instance, they advise salespeople to greet all shoppers as soon as they enter the store to let them know the establishment is aware of their presence. Staff should be wary of buyers who spend a great deal of time in one area of the store or department. Group shoppers who ask an unusual number of questions as other members wander away may be suspect. Further, retailers are wary of shoppers who avoid sales personnel or take too many items into fitting rooms.

THE RETAIL SALES PRESENTATION . . .

The typical retail sales presentation can be broken down into three basic parts: First, the salesperson approaches (or greets) the customer; second, the merchandise is presented; and, finally, the salesperson overcomes objections and closes the sale.

Approaching the Customer . . .

There are several different ways to approach a customer in the retail store. In this area, common techniques are the social, the service, and the merchandise approach. The **social approach** is also known as the salutation or greeting approach. Saying "Hello" or "Good evening" is the essence of the social approach. This method offers a nonthreatening, low-pressure opening. It invites dialogue without obliging the shopper to discuss merchandise or make a purchase. It is recommended when you aren't sure of the prospect's intentions or degree of interest in buying. The social approach is flexible in that it leaves the noncommittal shopper freedom to browse while still remaining open to the merchandise approach if the shopper becomes more serious.

The **service approach** is both the most popular approach in retail selling and the weakest. It usually takes the form of a question, the most common one being, "May I help you?" This question is ineffective for several reasons. First, it has become trite with overuse. Second, many customers automatically respond by saying, "I'm just looking," even if they're shopping seriously. Customers often prefer to examine the merchandise before accepting a salesperson's help, feeling that accepting assistance obliges them to purchase. Third, the question invites the customer to close the door on further opportunity. If the shopper says, "I'm just looking," the dialogue ends.

A more effective service approach is "Have you been helped?" or "What can I show you?" The service approach is meant to let the shopper know that you are available to provide assistance at any time. It is suitable only when the shopper obviously needs assistance.

The **merchandise approach** is a variety of the product approach, discussed in Chapter 6. It is recommended when the shopper is carefully examining the merchandise at the time you come closer. The more carefully the customer examines the wares, the more serious she or he is about purchasing, and the more effective your merchandise approach will be.

To execute the merchandise approach, you simply open a conversation with the shopper by making a comment about the merchandise. Preferably, your remark should give the shopper more information. For example, if a potential buyer is looking closely at a gray suit, the merchandise approach might be, "This color is so versatile. Did you see our display of accessories that go with it?" Another good use of this technique is to tell the shopper where to find the product in other sizes, colors, and brands. The merchandise approach can also involve physical action, as when you tap a wind chime so the customer can enjoy the sound of it.

Presenting the Merchandise . . .

Gathering prospect information, making an appeal, encouraging closer examination, suggesting additional merchandise, encouraging a trade-up, and suggesting a substitution or special order are all elements of the presentation of store merchandise. They have all been discussed in previous chapters, so in this section, we will discuss them only in relation to retail store selling.

Your efforts to gather prospect information should take place in the opening moments of your retail store presentation. Ask questions, listen carefully, and observe your prospect's nonverbal behavior. You can usually determine fairly quickly whether the looker is a true prospect. However, since many people shop only casually, it is especially important to determine whether the shopper is serious about purchasing. Another concern is whether he or she is buying for personal use or for another party.

Making an appeal is the act of pointing out product benefits relevant to needs. Depending upon your store and the merchandise in question, your appeal may be based on price, quality, convenience, uniqueness, or style. Your store's reputation may be the appeal you use most often. A gift or specialty shop might be known for its unique merchandise, an appliance outlet for its brand-name products, a furniture emporium for the sophistication and style of its line of goods.

If your appeal succeeds in building the shopper's interest, encourage a closer examination. In clothing sales, this suggestion comes in the form of a try-on. With other merchandise, it may be a test of the product's benefits, as when a customer listens to a stereo system. Closer examination helps create attachment and builds dialogue between you and the customer.

This element of the presentation is especially important in clothing sales. Because a try-on ensures the customer that the garment fits and looks good, it reduces the incidence of returns and exchanges, thus increasing satisfaction. If the fitting room is located away from your selling area, escort the shopper to it, repeat your name, and encourage him or her to ask for you if assistance is needed. If several minutes go by, return to the fitting room area and offer again to help the customer.

Suggestion selling, defined in Chapter 13, is especially important in retailing. Also known as add-on selling or multiple selling, this technique lets you build on your original sale by recommending that the shopper make additional purchases. You might suggest items that relate to the original purchase, such as options, accessories, or attachments, or you might advise a larger quantity.

If the customer is purchasing a dress, you would employ suggestion selling by showing a scarf, belt, or jewelry. To the buyer of a tape recorder, suggest a package of cassettes. Suggestion selling allows you to increase the utility of the purchase, thereby increasing customer satisfaction; it also increases the total purchase amount.

Suggestion selling involves more than saying, "Is there something else I can show you today?" It calls for specific suggestions. If the product is one that requires frequent replacement, remind the shopper of the time and money saved by purchasing multiple units. When the merchandise requires supplies or replacement parts, remind the customer of the importance of having an adequate quantity of these items on hand.

People who purchase products that cannot meet their needs or expectations become unhappy customers. For this reason, you should encourage the customer to **trade up** whenever you know that the price range or brand selected by the shopper will not be satisfactory. To encourage a trade-up, you simply suggest a higher-quality product than the customer is planning to purchase. Of course, a trade-up should be suggested only to the prospect who can afford the increase in price.

Salespeople who are able to justify a trade-up usually find that customers go along with their recommendations. Further, after shoppers trade up on a given purchase, they often will return to upgrade future purchases as well.

Customers often want merchandise that is out of stock, not carried by your store, or unsuitable for their needs. In all such cases, you should freely suggest substitutions or **special orders**. If the desired item is simply out of stock, you might offer to place a rush order. Be careful not to promise quick arrival of an item over whose shipment you have no control. If the item is not carried by your store, you might be able to place a special order; this, too, is subject to store policies and shipment realities.

If the customer wants a brand that your store doesn't carry, recommend the brand you do carry without disparaging the other. When equal products are not available, suggest merchandise of higher quality, never lower. "Selling down" is poor selling.

Overcoming Objections and Closing the Sale . . .

Overcoming objections, a way of life in most situations, is considerably less common in retail store selling. Retail sellers are not prone to responding to customer objections unless their environment provides special motivation. For example, if salespeople are competing among themselves for commissions or must meet a sales quota, they will be more inclined to try to overcome customer objections than if the atmosphere is less competitive. Sometimes a retail store will have a policy against paying commissions because it wants to discourage high-pressure selling. However, there are many stores in which overcoming customer objections is necessary. Every technique found in Chapters 11 and 12 will work in retail selling.

Closing the sale is also a weak area in retail selling. Many people don't know how to close or feel uncomfortable closing. But in retail as in every other form of selling, no sale is made without some kind of close. The most common closes are questions like "Will that be all?" or "Is that cash or charge?" However, because such queries have become trite, they are less desirable than more imaginative questions such as "Would you like a necktie to go with that?" or "Should I gift-wrap that for you?"

Some retail salespeople use **physical-action closes**. These include folding, wrapping, or ringing up the merchandise that is placed on the counter, wordlessly assuming that the shopper intends to purchase. Because of the limited number of retail closes actually in use, there is much room for creativity in developing closing statements and questions.

When the sale is completed, say thank you, and invite the customer to come again. When shoppers use a charge card, you will also have the opportunity to personalize the transaction by addressing them by name.

> Wit has truth in it; wise-cracking is simply calisthenics with words.
> Dorothy Parker

MISTAKES IN RETAIL SELLING . . .

Because of the nature of retail selling, there is rarely an opportunity to qualify or gather background information on prospects before meeting them. In addition, retail sellers meet many shoppers who aren't prospects at all, but rather just browsers. Further complicating the situation is the availability of a wide selection of merchandise in the store. These realities help explain the mistakes commonly made by retail salespeople:

1. "Sizing up" shoppers to quickly
2. Talking down to prospects or making them feel that they lack product knowledge
3. Overwhelming shoppers with choices

COMPENSATION AND EVALUATION OF RETAIL SALESPEOPLE . . .

The retail salesperson's compensation may be straight salary, straight commission, or salary plus commission. Salaried positions are among the lowest-paying sales jobs to be found, with hourly rates often at or barely above the minimum wage. Retail salespeople who sell **durable goods** on commission have higher earnings. However, because durable goods are often financed and their purchase postponable, the salesperson's income is affected markedly by changes in economic variables such as interest rates and the level of unemployment.

A typical benefit in retail selling is the employee discount. Salespeople may enjoy discounts as high as 30 percent on store items purchased by them or their dependents. Sales contests are fairly common in retailing where commission sales are involved. Retailers find that these promotions generate friendly competition among salespeople, and those that involve groups foster teamwork as well.

Retail salespeople are usually subjected to regular performance evaluations, and merit raises are based on these evaluations. Commissioned staff may be assigned a monthly sales goal that figures into their performance evaluation. Many salespeople are expected to maintain a level of productivity that can be measured in terms of dollars sold per hour, revenue generated from multiple sales, contest results, or income received from the sale of selected items.

> No man ever became great except through many and great mistakes.
> Sophia Loren

INDUSTRIAL SELLING . . .

Salespeople sell to many different kinds of customers. These include consumers, service organizations, distributors, wholesalers, retailers, and government. This section will focus on industrial selling, that branch of salesmanship involving "producer" buyers. Industrial buyers are customers who use your product or service in their own firm's operations. The product might make manufacturing possible, as would a piece of machinery, an operating supply, a business service, or even an entire manufacturing facility. Or the product might become a part of the buyer's final product, such as a raw material or a component part. Some industrial sales representatives work out of company headquarters, but most work out of branch offices located in large metropolitan areas throughout the country.

Whereas retail salespeople sell to consumers who may know little about their product, industrial sellers call on trained professional buyers. These purchasers must know their suppliers and their products thoroughly. Industrial buyers purchase according to their firm's policies, which in the case of large firms, are usually in writing.

CLASSIFICATIONS OF INDUSTRIAL PURCHASES . . .

Industrial products and services can be categorized as follows:

Installations and capital equipment, including buildings, such as factories, warehouses, or office complexes; equipment that is fixed in place, such as turbines, pumps, boilers, air compressors, conveyor belts, or drill presses; and office furniture and equipment, such as paper shredders, desks, or computers

Accessory equipment, which is light equipment such as small tools, drafting room instruments, office furnishings, and safety gear

Raw materials, such as natural products, like minerals, crude oil, and coal, and farm products such as sugar, cotton, and livestock

Processed materials, including plastics, rubbers, iron, steel, nonferrous metals, chemicals, textiles, lumber, and cardboard

Manufactured component parts, such as subassemblies, semifinished goods, and prefabricated parts, like electric motors, castings, forgings, bearings, fasteners, pipe fittings, brass inserts, and wire

Maintenance, repair, and operating (MRO) items, which would be any routinely purchased item that is required for the normal operation of the company, such as brooms, floor cleaner, office stationery, printing supplies, paper bags, spare parts for machinery, paint, shipping supplies, lubricants, and adhesives

Facilitating services, including machine repair, advertising, consulting, janitorial services, and automated payroll services

The Purchasing Department . . .

Purchasing departments vary from one firm to the next. Purchasing departments in large firms have many levels and deal with extensive buying operations. Smaller firms may have only two levels, with a manager overseeing three or four buyers and reporting directly to the vice president of operations. The smallest firms don't have a separate purchasing department. Buying is done by the production manager, the department managers, or perhaps the company president.

Names for purchasing department personnel will also vary. Titles include buyer, assistant buyer, senior buyer, **purchasing agent**, assistant purchasing agent, purchasing manager, assistant purchasing manager, and vice president of purchasing. Some firms have adopted the more sophisticated title of vice president of material for the top-level purchaser.

If the purchasing department has more than one buyer, each may be assigned a specific buying responsibility. For example, if purchases are divided by product category, one buyer may handle only those items that fall under a particular classification. The larger the firm, the more specialized the buyers become. One may purchase only office supplies, another metal piping, and so on. A large, decentralized firm may have buyers from each division who are responsible for day-to-day purchasing and who report to a departmental manager. When major contracts are negotiated, the vice president in charge of purchasing may become involved.

Responsibilities of the Industrial Buyer . . .

Professional buyers have both functional and ethical responsibilities (see Figure 18-3 for a list of ethical obligations). The duties of industrial buyers and purchasing departments extend far beyond just placing orders. If you are an industrial salesperson, you should have some understanding of their job.

One of the primary responsibilities of the industrial purchaser is to see salespeople. The majority of buyers prefer to see visitors by appointment only. Others may establish scheduled hours where they meet salespeople on a first-come basis. This is how William E. Baker, purchasing agent for Triumph Controls, Inc., puts it: "We want to see anyone who may be of help to us either now or in the future, and we have a responsibility to see this person in an expeditious manner. If we don't, we're not doing our job."

Buyers are also responsible for keeping abreast of developments that could affect the purchasing decisions of the firm. Always willing to consider alternatives to their company's present products, processes, and procedures, and ever on the lookout for ways to save money, buyers welcome the opportunity to talk to salespeople who offer innovative or unfamiliar products. They keep files on sales presentations of products that their firm might be able to use in the future.

Another responsibility of the buyer or purchasing department is to locate suppliers of needed products. Says George McNally, purchasing agent for Crompton and Knowles Inc., "Purchasing's responsibility is to keep the plant going, to get the various departments what they want when they need it. In

Principles and Standards of Purchasing Practice

National Association of Purchasing Management

LOYALTY TO YOUR ORGANIZATION
JUSTICE TO THOSE WITH WHOM YOU DEAL
FAITH IN YOUR PROFESSION

From these principles are derived the NAPM standards of purchasing practice.
(Domestic ad International)

1. Avoid the intent and appearance of unethical or compromising practice in relationships, actions, and communications.

2. Demonstrate loyalty to the employer by diligently following the lawful instructions of the employer, using reasonable cars and only authority granted.

3. Refrain from any private business or professional activity that would create a conflict between personal interests and the interests of the employer.

4. Refrain from soliciting or accepting money, loans, credits, or prejudicial discounts, and the acceptance of gifts, entertainment, favors, or services from present or potential suppliers that might influence, or appear to influence, purchasing decisions.

5. Handle confidential or proprietary information belonging to employers or suppliers with due care and proper consideration of ethical and legal ramifications and governmental regulations.

6. Promote positive supplier relationships through courtesy and impartiality in all phases of the purchasing cycle.

7. Refrain from reciprocal agreements that restrain competition.

8. Know and obey the letter and spirit of laws governing the purchasing function and remain alert to the legal ramifications of purchasing decisions.

9. Encourage all segments of society to participate by demonstrating support for small, disadvantaged, and minority-owned businesses.

10. Discourage purchasing's involvement in employer-sponsored programs of personal purchases that are not business related.

11. Enhance the proficiency and stature of the purchasing profession by acquiring and maintaining current technical knowledge and the highest standards of ethical behavior.

12. Conduct international purchasing in accordance with the laws, customs, and practices of foreign countries, consistent with United States Laws, your organization policies, and these Ethical Standards and Guidelines.

Approved 1/92

Figure 18-3
Reprinted with permission from the publisher, the National Association of Purchasing Management, *NAPM Principles & Standards of Purchasing Practice,* **January 1992.**

this respect, we are a 'reaction department.' We go into action when another department needs something." Purchasing agents rely on the Thomas Register of Manufacturers and other industrial directories in addition to their own files, which may contain thousands of potential suppliers.

Along with locating supplies, evaluating vendors is a responsibility of the buyer or purchasing agent. Gathering information may be a simple task in industries served by a small number of well-known suppliers. In others, evaluation may be time consuming and complex. Some companies require their

How Purchasing Agents Rate Salespeople			
Quality	Good	Not So Good	Awful
Honesty	X		
Graciousness	X		
No follow-up		X	
Gets Personal			X
Bad-mouths competition		X	
Is well-prepared	X		
Smokes			X
Is pushy			X
Doesn't listen		X	
Lacks knowledge		X	
Professional	X		
Whines			X
Admits own mistakes	X		
Doesn't mention my mistakes	X		
Discredits me and my position			X
Wastes my time		X	
Solves my problems	X		
Is dependable	X		
Smart-aleck attitude			X

Figure 18-4

purchasing departments to evaluate suppliers personally at least once a year. It isn't unusual for a team of buyers and nonpurchasing personnel to travel thousands of miles to inspect the manufacturing facilities of present or potential suppliers. See Figure 18-4 for the ways that purchasing agents rate salesperson qualities.

THE ROLE OF THE BUYER IN INDUSTRIAL SELLING . . .

The industrial buyer or purchasing department plays an indispensable role in industrial selling. Salespeople in this arena must usually go through the purchasing department before seeing anyone else. Purchasing usually acts as a screen, arranging for sellers to meet with members of other departments in which products are used, such as engineering or manufacturing. If salespeople could bypass purchasing, these other offices or individuals would be barraged by vendors' telephone calls and visits.

A major role of the industrial buyer or purchasing department is to participate in buying negotiations. The extent of this group's power over a buying decision will vary according to the importance of the purchase or the internal practices of the buying firm. The same can be said for the influence exerted by the departments or plants actually using the products or services. In some instances, purchasing actively participates with using departments. In others, buyers operate autonomously.

Even when the key decision maker is from a using department, purchasing usually participates. For example, if a piece of capital equipment is being purchased, those people attending sales presentations along with the buyer or purchasing agent might be the manager of the using department, a plant engineer, the head of plant maintenance, and a representative from the firm's financial division. All of them have a say in the purchase decision. This is commonly known as **team buying**. If an engineering group is involved, as with large industrial projects, purchasing joins company engineers in the buying process.

Many buying decisions are made independently by purchasing, especially with raw materials and MRO items. In these cases, buyers are free to purchase without consulting managers or using departments about vendors or quantities. For example, a department manager may request 500 floppy disks, but the buyer may decide to purchase 5,000 if the cost is right, knowing the diskettes will be used by other departments. In such purchases, the salesperson might never meet anyone from the using departments.

In many companies, plant managers buy certain items from local suppliers without going through purchasing. Even so, the professional buyers are responsible for overseeing all purchases. Purchasing agents typically have the authority to buy items that plant managers could also purchase. If the same product is used at many company facilities, purchasing may negotiate a contract to supply all units.

An industrial buyer does not have unlimited purchasing power, however. When a purchase exceeds a certain dollar amount, the buyer may have to receive approval from the purchasing manager or other company executives. Very large purchases may require approval from the company comptroller.

INDUSTRIAL BUYING CLASSES . . .

Industrial purchases may be categorized according to buying classes, which is a term describing the nature of the buying situation. There are three buying classes: the straight rebuy, the modified rebuy, and the new task purchase.

A **straight rebuy** takes place when purchasing buys regularly used products from a regular supplier. Component parts and MRO items are frequently subject to straight rebuys. When a using department requisitions an item or when parts inventory falls below a certain level, purchasing asks the usual supplier to fill an order for the same product as before, at the same price as before. In this respect, the straight rebuy presents no formal purchasing process.

Long-term contracts, where price and quality are established for the duration of the agreement, open the door to straight rebuys. This type of purchase may appear to be nothing more than order taking, but actually the salesperson must serve the customer as diligently as ever. The buyer's relationship with suppliers in straight rebuys is often well established. Salespeople who are trying to win a buyer's business may be very frustrated if the buyer is involved in a straight rebuy arrangement with another supplier.

A **modified rebuy** takes place when the buyer wants to purchase the same item as before but requests changes in the product or terms of sale. This buying class also occurs when a purchasing agent decides to switch suppliers. For example, if the present vendor cannot meet the customer's demand for modified quality, features, or terms of sale, the buyer will seek out a new supplier.

A **new task purchase** occurs when the goods or services have not been previously bought. Some of these types of purchase are fairly simple, as when a buyer makes the initial purchase of raw materials that will go into the manufacture of a new product. However, other new tasks can be quite complicated, and selling in such an arena can be extremely time consuming and challenging.

The buying firm's engineering department may give purchasing specifications, asking the buyers to locate a vendor that can supply the product. The purchasing agent then contacts salespeople and reviews information obtained during past sales calls. When a new material is purchased, product samples are requested and tested. In a particularly extensive new task, as in construction decisions, the buying firm may assemble a team of purchasing, manufacturing, engineering, and financial personnel. Meanwhile potential suppliers assemble sales teams to go after what promises to be a major contract.

The Purchase Order . . .

A **purchase order** is a contract between a buying firm and a supplier that describes an agreement to buy products at a specified price. It is a legally binding document, and when signed by both parties, constitutes an offer and acceptance in compliance with Division 2 of the Uniform Commercial Code.

The purchase order specifies the name and description of the item, the part number, the quantity to be purchased, the unit price, and the total price. The supplier keeps the original copy and returns the acknowledgment copies to the buyer. Copies of the order are typically kept by the purchasing department, the accounting department, and any other department affected by the transaction. Terms and conditions of the sale often appear on the back of the original copy of the purchase order.

Competitive Bidding . . .

Industrial selling frequently entails **competitive bidding**. Soliciting bids from competing suppliers is a recurring function of a buying firm's purchasing department, especially when the firm buys in large volume, purchases capital equipment, or plans a construction project. The buying firm usually seeks a minimum of three bids.

The customer provides prospective suppliers with the information needed to calculate their bids. It also tells bidders what products it plans to purchase in connection with the contract, what delivery or production schedule it wants to follow, and so on. If the contract is for a construction project, blueprints and other engineering details are usually provided with the request for quote (RFQ). Potential suppliers then submit their bids, which are reviewed by purchasing personnel along with company executives and user departments.

Contract Buying . . .

Like competitive bidding, **contract buying** is common in industrial selling. Often the buying firm will solicit competitive bids before awarding what is known as a purchase contract. A **purchase contract** is an agreement between the buyer and seller that stipulates the conditions of a sale over a long term. Purchase contracts may run for six months, one year, or more. The contract may specify the products to be purchased, the quantity, the price, and the delivery schedule.

One variety of contract buying is **annual buying**. Once a year, the purchasing department invites suppliers to bid on the firm's high-volume purchases for the coming year. Many firms bid all of their "storeroom" items annually, awarding bids to three or four prime vendors. Suppliers prepare their bids with the help of a list of the buyer's storeroom stock, along with the buyer's yearly usage rates.

Another type of purchase contract is the **blanket purchase order** (BPO). Used primarily in the purchase of materials inventory and MRO items, the BPO creates a straight rebuy situation. The blanket purchase order is issued at the start of the contract, and each time the product is needed, the buyer requests shipment by sending the supplier a release form containing the purchase order number.

A blanket purchase order may be issued for a single product or for a range of products. The BPO may stipulate the quantity to be purchased, or it may be an open-end order. A steel buyer may negotiate such a purchase with a supplier to avoid stocking excessive quantities of metal. In this case, the buyer tells the vendor each month how much is needed, and when and how to deliver it. Product prices on a BPO may be fixed, or they may float. **Floating prices** are those that vary according to market conditions and are usually contained within a 10 percent range.

Many deliveries made under purchase contracts are timed by means of **electronic data interchange** (EDI) or computer linking. EDI involves a direct hookup between the buyer's and supplier's computers. Used mostly for straight rebuys, this ordering method makes for "paperless purchasing," enabling a supplier to stay informed of the buyer's current level of inventory. Another trend in contract selling is the establishment of computerized reorder systems, whereby a customer's new orders are automatically forwarded to the supplier when inventory drops below a certain level.

Systems Selling . . .

Systems selling, or package-plan selling, is another common industrial practice. This involves the sale of interrelated products or services as one package. For example, a customer may purchase every component of a data processing system from a single vendor.

Buying an entire system from the same supplier assures the purchaser that the various parts and components will be compatible. Furthermore, the buyer's bargaining power is strengthened because of the size of the purchase. Salespeople find systems selling a complex process. Much time is needed to analyze the buyer's needs, and once the sale is completed, a great deal of time must be spent overseeing the installation of the system and training the buyer's employees in its use.

Value Analysis . . .

Value analysis is the technique used by industrial buyers to determine whether a purchase is worthwhile. Wanting to reduce cost without sacrificing quality or performance, the buyer evaluates the benefits derived from a product in relation to its cost. Value analysis is often performed by a team comprising members from purchasing, engineering, and manufacturing. It is used for expensive and inexpensive products alike.

The typical value analysis involves probing questions like these:

1. Is the item really needed?
2. Does the item offer more than what is really required?
3. Is there a fair relationship between the item's cost and its usefulness?
4. Would the item be cheaper to make than to buy?
5. Would the item be cheaper to buy than to make?
6. Is the item available elsewhere at a lower cost?
7. Are we buying similar items that could be substituted?
8. Are there lower-cost products that could be substituted?
9. If it is not a standard item, can a standard item be used?
10. Have suppliers been consulted for cost-saving suggestions?

Industrial salespeople should conduct a value analysis of the products they sell and include their findings in their sales presentations. To conduct an appropriate value analysis, you should carefully study your prospect's operations and analyze the products the prospect firm is already using. Often the only way to compete with current suppliers is to prove through value analysis that your product can help the prospect realize a cost savings. Salespeople who sell products that cost more than competing brands should conduct a value analysis to justify their price.

BUYER–SUPPLIER RELATIONS . . .

As an industrial salesperson, you should be aware of buyer preferences that affect buyer–supplier relations. Typically, industrial buyers prefer to purchase from multiple suppliers. This is partly because they want to be assured of a ready supply of the products they need. Purchasing agents don't want to depend solely on one vendor for regularly needed products.

Further, buyers who work with multiple suppliers are careful to divide their business among only a few vendors. This ensures that each order is sizable enough to be meaningful to the supplying companies. If the buyer works with too many vendors, the orders are too small, and the buyer loses influence as a major customer. Industrial buyers frequently prefer to buy locally. Local suppliers help assure quick delivery, which is often considered more important than price. Local buying also contributes to the local economy, which is important to a community-conscious buyer.

Another reality of industrial buyer–seller relationships is that they tend to become solidified. Industrial buyers prefer strong relationships with their vendors, and rationalize against switching solely for the sake of a better price. Unless a purchasing agent wants to expand the firm's supplier base, competing vendors are not likely to woo the customer away. New suppliers must find a niche rather than offer the same services provided by existing sellers.

Vendors not presently used by the firm, commonly called **out suppliers**, should adopt a long-term attitude when trying to develop a strong relationship with the firm's buyer. Salespeople for new or unfamiliar firms should not expect to receive an order on their first visit, but instead must cultivate relationships with potential buyers through continued contact. Many contacts and sales calls may be required before a buyer places an order with a new salesperson.

TELEMARKETING . . .

Telemarketing, or telephone selling, is a form of marketing in which all or most of the selling and sales-related activities are conducted over the telephone. Using the telephone for selling is described as outbound or inbound. **Inbound telemarketing** occurs when the customer calls the salesperson, as when magazine ads or shop-at-home TV channels invite people to phone in an order. Retailers that publish merchandise catalogs typically have telecatalog call-response centers. Many firms that use the call-response method offer a network of toll-free telephone numbers for customers to call.

Outbound telemarketing is when the salesperson calls the customer. Outbound calls usually take longer than inbound ones and require better salespeople. This means, of course, that the outbound telemarketing salesperson is paid more, and the cost per call is significantly higher.

Although this method has traditionally been associated with consumer products and routine order taking, increasing numbers of industrial sales organizations are adopting telemarketing as an aggressive selling tool. Marketing and sales managers view this process as being extremely cost effective. Anything that can be sold in person, they reason, can be sold over the telephone, regardless of price, technical complexity, or type of customer. Industrial sellers use telemarketers as they use face-to-face selling, to build solid, ongoing relationships with buyers. This is in contrast to consumer telemarketing, which concentrates on the one-time sale.

Telemarketing

When you don't take no for an answer, you might end up with a yes.

Brett T. Snow

The largest telemarketers employ thousands of people. Their sales staffs contact customers and prospects from computerized workstations. These sellers use automatic dialing equipment and specialized software available from such firms as Telemagic. Telemarketers also employ the services of mailing list brokers such as Dun and Bradstreet for custom-designed data cards for prospecting and lead qualification.

The telemarketing industry is about thirty years old, and in recent years, has grown very rapidly. This phenomenon can be attributed to several factors, most notably long-distance calling rates, the cost of outside selling, and the sheer convenience of telephone marketing. Increased competition among long-distance telephone companies has reduced the cost of telephone selling considerably. Telemarketers have been able to shop around for the best rate package and increase their activities relatively inexpensively.

Although telephone rates have become competitive, the cost of outside selling has increased dramatically. Today it is common for an industrial sales call to cost in excess of $300. By comparison, the average cost per telephone call is as low as $1. A firm can reduce its cost per contact to less than 10 percent of the cost of personal visits by simply switching all or part of its selling effort to telemarketing.

Not only is telemarketing cheap, it is very convenient. Any firm can increase its selling base by leaps and bounds through the use of telemarketing. Whereas an outside salesperson might be able to make five personal visits a day, a telemarketer, selling the same product, might make up to fifty calls a day.

The Telescript . . .

The telemarketer's basic tool is the **telescript**. This is a written outline of the telephone conversation, and serves to guide the salesperson through the call. The well-written telescript should have the following qualities:

1. It should get the prospect's attention.

2. It should be short, simple, and to the point.

3. It should provide important facts.

4. It should encourage two-way conversation.

5. It should focus on relevant information.

6. It should be able to allow for differences in prospects.

7. It should prompt the prospect to action.

There are two basic types of telescript, verbatim scripts and conceptual scripts. The one to use depends on the product being sold and the complexity of the sales process.

Verbatim telescripts are those that employ the same words every call. A verbatim script may come in the form of an electronically recorded message, or it may be read by a live telemarketer. The electronically recorded message is used when all mechanical aspects of the selling process, including number selection and dialing, are computerized. Because it is a one-way form of communication, the recorded message is suitable only for calls meant solely to provide information. It is impersonal, and customers who are called this way feel no compunctions about hanging up as soon as they realize the caller is a computer. Another weakness of the recorded message is that it can't close a sale or confirm an order.

A verbatim script followed by a live telemarketer is somewhat more personal although not much more flexible. Here, the salesperson recites the presentation word for word, and there is no outlet for creativity. The script contains the telemarketer's planned responses to the prospect's most likely questions and objections; it also provides different ways to close the sale. The live verbatim script is best used when selling a product that is not complex and when the prospect's buying motives are easily understood.

The **conceptual telescript** is the most personal form. This script provides the salesperson with the foundation for a custom-designed sales presentation. Telemarketers can create a different presentation for each prospect, using the script only as an outline. The conceptual script is used for selling expensive products and those that contain many features or appeal to a variety of buying motives. A conceptual script contains six basic steps: the personal introduction, prospect qualification, presentation, overcoming objections, the close, and confirmation of terms.

In the first step of the conceptual script, the personal introduction, you identify yourself and your product. You state your name, your firm's name, and the reason for your call. Next, qualifying the prospect, you try to determine the prospect's needs by asking questions. Unlike the verbatim script, the conceptual script allows for ample participation by the prospect and creative, flexible thinking by the salesperson.

In the third step, the presentation, you explain how your product will solve the prospect's needs. Because the telephone presentation must move along more quickly than a personal visit, you must be able to focus immediately on the points that are relevant to the prospect. To overcome objections, you employ the same techniques as in a personal presentation. Welcome prospect objections, listen carefully, and choose the appropriate technique for overcoming them. This aspect of the conceptual script calls for considerably more selling skill than the verbatim script.

In the fifth step, the close, you may employ a number of methods, whichever is appropriate to the situation. Again, this aspect of the conceptual telescript is open to the salesperson's skill and instincts. Like face-to-face selling, the telemarketing presentation may call for more than one attempt to close. Finally, confirming the terms of the sale, you review and verify the details of the transaction before concluding the call. Ask prospects if they have further questions, and ascertain whether the terms and conditions of the sale are understood. Postpurchase dissonance is extremely common among telephone buyers, so you should call your new customers a day or two after the sale to reassure them that their decision to buy was the right one.

Telephone Guidelines

1. Be prepared for the conversation before you call. Have prospect information, product information, price lists, and pens and pencils handy.

2. Jot down notes during the conversation and re-copy them into meaningful form as soon as it ends, while things are still fresh in your mind.

3. Use short, easy-to-understand words and phrases. Don't use buzz-words or technical jargon unless you are certain that the prospect understands your terminology.

4. Use expressive and highly descriptive words, such as luxurious, fool-proof, velvety, detectable, and flawless.

5. Use dynamic words, such as breakthrough, power, and trust.

6. Use personal pronouns, such as you, your, I, me, my, we, us, and our.

7. Use colorful adjectives that arouse feelings of pleasure, such as cool, fragrant, and elegant.

8. Use phrases that paint word pictures, such as lush, velvety, crimson upholstery.

9. Have an optimistic attitude. Expect to be welcomed. The feeling that you are intruding on the prospect will hamper your attempt to sell.

Figure 18-5

Figure 18-5 provides guidelines for effective telephone conversation. Because telemarketers lack the benefit of face-to-face contact with prospects, proper diction and good vocal qualities are especially important.

Telemarketing Operations . . .

Companies that decide to use telemarketing can choose between two operating options. They may open their own center, or they may contract an independent agency. Both options have their advantages and disadvantages.

Operating an in-house telemarketing center offers the firm greater freedom, flexibility, and profit potential than is possible with an agency. However, the cost of opening and operating such an operation can be very high. The initial investment in capital equipment for even the smallest telemarketing center can easily exceed $50,000. Staffing the center is also a challenge.

A dream doesn't come any closer by itself. You have to run after it.

Anonymous

A telemarketing agency, on the other hand, offers assistance and expertise that may be well worth the price. These firms can handle all aspects of the telephone selling process. They compile prospect lists, ship the product, collect the bills, and provide after-the-sale service.

Companies accustomed to outside selling often try to assemble telephone sales teams comprised of former sales support personnel and salespeople who are tired of traveling. These individuals often make poor telemarketers. Someone who was successful in personal selling will not necessarily be effective in telephone sales. Working conditions are much different. The factors that often contribute to an outside salesperson's success, such as the flexible work schedule, the freedom to come and go at will, and the personal contact with customers, don't exist in telephone selling.

Compensation of Telemarketers . . .

Telemarketers' incomes vary in relation to the product they sell, the expertise required, and the complexity of the process. Some telephone salespeople have technical degrees or training, and their income is relatively high. Incomes for other telemarketers are low compared to their outside selling counterparts, despite significant salary increases in recent years. The low income potential is a prime reason that successful outside salespeople rarely go into telemarketing. A telemarketing compensation plan might be salary only, commission only, or base salary plus an incentive linked to sales volume. Some firms run sales contests or offer special incentives to telephone salespeople to gain maximum productivity.

A salary plus commission plan is more effective than a straight salary or straight commission plan. Straight salary offers little incentive for salespeople to expand their customer base or increase their call volume, and commission only seems to promote overaggressive selling. Some telephone selling companies have been criticized for penalizing top performers by decreasing their commission percentages as their sales volume increases or for placing a cap on the amount of sales eligible for commission.

Only those who risk going too far can possibly find out how far one has to go.

T. S. Eliot

Telemarketing as a Supplement . . .

Firms that rely on face-to-face selling sometimes employ telemarketers to perform supplementary functions, such as qualifying leads or performing after-the-sale follow-up. Because the cost of qualifying leads in person is high, the use of telemarketers for this task makes good economic sense.

Some firms reserve their outside sales force for their most profitable customers, delegating their low-volume accounts and low-probability prospects to telemarketers. In some businesses, when an account normally serviced by telephone reaches a certain sales volume, it is turned over to an outside salesperson. Many companies also use telemarketing to revive inactive accounts. Other applications include marketing research, technical support, lead qualifications, and customer service.

Although some firms that switch from outside selling to telemarketing find that their customers feel neglected, others find that they are just as happy hearing from a telemarketer as from an outside salesperson. Telemarketing methods are also used by outside salespeople for repeat contacts with their prospects or customers. Sellers often find that after a first contact is made with a potential customer, telephone calls are sufficient. Repeat orders from established customers can be readily taken over the phone after an initial order has been placed in person.

Disadvantages of Telemarketing . . .

Telemarketing is not without its shortcomings. Perhaps chief among its weaknesses is that it does not include personal contact in the selling effort. Outside selling, or face-to-face selling, allows salespeople to "read" the prospect's nonverbal behavior, something that is virtually impossible over the phone.

Many prospects prefer a personal visit to a telephone call. The feel very comfortable refusing to hear a presentation made over the phone. For this reason, telemarketing is less likely than face-to-face selling to gain an audience. Telemarketing also faces strong resistance from prospects. Businesses and consumers alike become annoyed when they receive too many sales calls, especially when calls come at inappropriate times.

A number of federal and state laws have been passed to restrict or ban all unsolicited outbound telemarketing. The proliferation of voice mail systems and services such as call block and caller ID have also had the effect of interfering with telemarketing efforts. Further, increased complaints of rudeness, harassment, and telephone fraud hurt the efforts of reputable telemarketers. The American Telemarketing Association's Code of Ethics (see Figure 18-6) was developed to help combat the abuses of unethical and inconsiderate telemarketers.

> A faceless voice coming in over the telephone is never hard to dismiss.
>
> Victor Kiam

Excerpts from ATA's Code of Ethics Brochure

Recommended standards for professional and ethical telemarketing conducted by members of the American Telemarketing Association.

- Telemarketers must be trained and aware of all applicable federal, state, and local laws.

- Telemarketers must receive adequate training in professional telemarketing skills and follow recognized procedures and practices for proper etiquette.

- All sales offers must be stated clearly and honestly. Claims which are untrue, misleading, deceptive, fraudulent or unjustly disparaging of competitors are deemed by the ATA to be unprofessional and dishonest.

- Calls to private residences will not be made during hours that might be considered unreasonable. No calls should be initiated on major national holidays, and callers should take into account any inconveniences caused by calls on other holidays, especially recognized religious holidays.

- Calls should always be targeted to people or companies likely to have a use for the particular product or service being offered.

- Telemarketers must comply with the terms of the specific offer, always informing consumers of their options should this commitment not be met. At a minimum, all offers should be in compliance with the FTC's Mail Order Merchandise 30-Day Rule.

The American Telemarketing Association, a not-for-profit trade association founded in 1983 to represent and serve the telemarketing profession, is committed to meeting the needs of its members while protecting the rights of consumers and businesses who have telephone contact with its members.

Figure 18-6 Adapted from the American Telemarketing Association's Code of Ethics. American Telemarketing Association, Inc., 1996.

Summing It Up . . .

The chapter explored three important selling scenarios: retail store selling, industrial selling, and telemarketing.

The retail salesperson contributes to the full-service retail store's image by enhancing customer satisfaction through sound product knowledge and courteous service. Retail selling is unique in that prospects visit the salesperson, there is a physical territory to maintain and a large amount of merchandise to care for, and more prospects are seen in the course of the day than are seen by outside salespeople. However, most of the selling techniques found throughout the text apply to retail.

The typical retail sales presentation involves approaching the customer, presenting the merchandise, overcoming the shopper's objections, and closing the sale. The most effective retail salespeople greet shoppers with the merchandise approach, suggest additional merchandise, and encourage shoppers to trade up to better-quality products.

The industrial section of the chapter dealt with the unique aspects of industrial selling and the specifics of industrial buying. Industrial salespeople sell to trained, professional buyers who adhere to rigid purchase guidelines, and whose role in the buying process varies depending on the product being purchased. Various categories of industrial purchases—installations and capital equipment, accessory equipment, raw materials, processed materials, manufactured component parts, MRO items, and facilitating services—were discussed. The three industrial buying classes, the straight rebuy, modified rebuy, and new task, were covered. Functions and responsibilities of the purchasing department were examined, and competitive bidding, contract buying, value analysis, and systems selling were explained.

Telemarketing is a growth area of selling. Here, all or part of the sales process takes place over the telephone. This includes inbound calls, where customers call salespeople to place orders from a catalog or in response to an advertising message containing a toll-free number, and outbound calls, where salespeople make the contact. Telemarketers use a verbatim or a conceptual telescript, depending on the product being sold and the complexity of the selling process. Reasons for the rapid growth of telemarketing were explained, and the characteristics of a well-written telescript were provided.

You Decide!

Howard is new to his sales job, which involves calling on buyers in the aerospace industry. After three disappointing months of getting nowhere with busy purchasing agents, he sought solace from a senior sales representative in his firm. "What you have to do," responded his mentor "is scare them a bit. Make them think that you really have an inside track with someone high up in the company. Hey, you're a golfer. Find out where any of the executives plays the game, and let the buyer know that you've had a round with so-and-so."

Howard mulled over this scenario during the weekend. He knew that he was being a bit timid in calling on prospects. The truth is, he was somewhat awed by the size and scope of most of his prospects. He also knew that the typical buyer would not be inclined to check up to see if his story was true, because the purchasing department personnel rarely spent time with the engineering and manufacturing people. By the same token, he was not used to telling stories and really wondered if the buyers would care one way or another. The senior salesperson was very successful, and Howard was anxious to get a good start with his company, but didn't know how to proceed. **You decide!**

Key Concepts and Terms . . .

accessory equipment
annual buying
blanket purchase order
client book
competitive bidding
conceptual telescript
contract buying
convenience good
durable good
electronic data interchange
facilitating services
floating prices
full-service retailing
inbound telemarketing
installations and capital equipment
manufactured component part
merchandise approach
modified rebuy
MRO item
new task purchase
outbound telemarketing
out supplier

physical-action close
processed materials
purchase contract
purchase order
purchasing agent
raw material
service approach
shopping good
silent award program
social approach
special order
specialty good
straight rebuy
suggestion selling
systems selling
team buying
telemarketing
telescript trade up
value analysis
vender
verbatim telescript

Building Skills . . .

1. Describe how skilled retail salespeople help a store build a solid customer base.
2. Explain the difference between convenience, shopping, and specialty goods.
3. Explain the qualities that make retail store selling unique.
4. List the housekeeping responsibilities of retail store salespeople.
5. Describe some of the customer-relations challenges faced by retail store salespeople.
6. Discuss the most predominant forms of dishonesty in retail store selling.
7. Describe why further examination of the product is advisable in clothing sales.
8. Discuss the compensation and evaluation systems for retail salespeople.
9. Compare industrial buyers with retail consumers.
10. Describe the responsibilities of industrial buyers or the purchasing department, including those factors that make the role indispensable.
11. Describe contract buying. Explain how the competitive bidding process works.

12. Define straight rebuy, modified rebuy, and new task. Explain why out suppliers are frustrated by straight rebuys.

13. Define purchase order and BPO.

14. Explain how the preferences of industrial buyers affect buyer–supplier relations.

15. Explain how the industrial buyer uses value analysis.

16. List the factors that account for telemarketing's rapid growth.

17. Compare the verbatim and conceptual scripts.

18. Explain the importance of telemarketers calling customers after the sale is confirmed.

19. List the advantages of using an agency over an in-house telemarketing center.

20. Describe how telemarketing is used to supplement outside selling.

Making Decisions 18-1:

Jim Walters is a twenty-five-year-old sales associate for Hatcher and Keck, a quality men's clothing store located in Pennwood Mall. One evening he notices a well-dressed young man browsing in the rear of the store. Jim approaches the shopper.

Jim:	Good evening. Is there anything I can show you?
Shopper:	(His eyes fixed on a dark brown suit in front of him) Yes. I've looked a long time for a dark brown suit like this. It's a size 39, which is usually what I wear. May I try it on?
Jim:	Certainly. (Jim hands the jacket to the young man and stands behind him as he tries it on before a mirror near the suit rack.)
Shopper:	(Buttoning the jacket) This is great.
Jim:	It's too small. Look at how it pulls at the shoulders. You could never wear it.
Shopper:	It looks fine to me. Besides, I like my clothing tight.
Jim:	No, it's definitely too small. You wouldn't be happy with it. Let's move up a size. (Jim helps the man remove the jacket, returns the suit to its hanger, and pulls a jacket from the rack of size 40s.)
Shopper:	There aren't any dark brown suits here.
Jim:	Do you see another color you like?
Shopper:	No. I don't want a pinstripe, and I already own three gray suits and two blue suits.
Jim:	(Removing a light gray pinstripe suit from the rack) Try this on, just to get an idea of the fit. I want to be sure we're looking at the right size.

Shopper:	It feels good. I see what you mean about the fit, but I still don't care for these pinstripes.
Jim:	If you don't mind my asking, why don't you like pinstripes?
Shopper:	Pinstripes are for older men. I don't want to look old-fashioned.
Jim:	Well, I'm sorry we can't help you this evening. But we receive new shipments every week. Why don't you stop back in a week or so?
Shopper:	Maybe I will. I haven't been to the other stores here in the mall yet. Who knows? Maybe I'll find something somewhere else.

Discuss Jim's actions in discouraging the shopper from buying the dark brown suit. Find the holes in Jim's handling of the objections, indicating how you would have acted.

Making Decisions 18-2:

Leslie Kramer, a representative for Strong Bond Industrial Adhesives, has been supplying Laurel Packaging, a maker of cardboard boxes, for the past year. Laurel has been a client of Strong Bond's for seven years, and when Leslie took over the account he learned that Laurel was also buying from two other suppliers. Leslie decides to call on buyer Sung Pyen in an attempt to get all of Laurel's adhesive business.

Leslie:	Sung, I would like to negotiate with you. My firm's marketing manager and I have discussed this, and we think we can offer you significant savings in return for all of your adhesive orders.
Sung:	Perhaps you can. But that's not the point.
Leslie:	We're already four cents a gallon less than both of our competitors, and we're willing to go even lower for your increased business. Don't you want to save money?
Sung:	Of course we do, but we don't want to limit our options in the bargain. We can't operate without this product, and we feel more comfortable with multiple sources of supply.
Leslie:	Sung, Strong Bond hasn't let a customer down yet. We're in great financial shape, and we're not going anywhere.
Sung:	I respect your reputation, Leslie, but we have sound reasons for working with several suppliers.

As Leslie drives back to his office, he decides to meet with his marketing manager again, determine the lowest possible price he could quote Sung, and visit Laurel with another offer next week.

Evaluate Leslie's plan. Discuss the likelihood that Leslie will gain all of Laurel's business.

Making Decisions 18-3:

You work in a clothing store that caters primarily to teenagers and young adults. Your customer is ready to purchase a pair of wildly patterned casual pants. Describe your opportunities for multiple selling.

Making Decisions 18-4:

You are a photographer who telephones new parents to explain your portrait subscription package for their baby's first year. Write out your opening remarks and your first four questions.

Practice Makes Perfect 18-1:

Design telescripts for prospecting and for making a presentation. Try these out on classmates to determine their effectiveness.

Legal and Ethical Issues in Selling

THE JOB TO BE DONE . . .

Perhaps no area of business is subject to a higher degree of scrutiny than selling. Because of the personal relationships existing between buyer and seller, there is more opportunity for unethical or illegal behavior than in most other commercial dealings. Chapter 19 directs your attention to:

...understand the need for high ethical standards in selling.

...appreciate the importance of adhering to a personal code of ethics.

...understand the ethical roles of companies and professional associations.

...explore the history of sales-related laws and regulations.

...know the purpose and impact of the Uniform Commercial Code.

...examine the federal, state, and local laws that relate to selling.

...examine the legal and ethical dilemmas that face people in selling.

THE IMPORTANCE OF BEING LEGAL AND ETHICAL . . .

Ethics in selling is a bigger concern today than at any time in the past. Reports of unethical and illegal business practices seem to be on the increase, and the opportunity to profit through such behavior seems to outweigh the rewards of honesty. The notion that nice guys finish last has taken hold with many businesspeople to the point that dishonest behavior is even defended in some circles as being necessary.

In such an atmosphere, salespeople who show integrity, honesty, and fairness are to be admired. Those who behave illegally or unethically, on the other hand, contribute to a host of problems that reflect on the entire profession. Illegal or unethical behavior destroys the prospect's confidence, causes ill will, makes the salesperson look foolish, tarnishes the firm's reputation, and incites retaliation by competitors. It can result in dismissal, loss of license, fines, or even jail terms. Salespeople must understand the laws that pertain to their profession, product, and industry. They also must adhere to a set of high personal ethical standards as well as to those guidelines set forth by their employer, industry, and professional association.

The purpose of this chapter is to examine the federal, state, and local laws that relate to salespeople and selling, and to explore the ethical responsibilities of salespeople toward their customers, their firm, their competitors, and themselves.

ETHICS AND THE LAW . . .

Ethics and the law are related concepts in that both are based upon our view of morality and rightness. However, they differ in that one is informal and the other formal. **Ethics** is a personal sense of morality and rightness. Each individual possesses her or his own code of ethics, which is often, but not always, shared by society at large. Law, on the other hand, is a formal statement of moral rules applied to everyone in a society. Unlike ethics, law is enforced by statute.

Whereas law is imposed upon us from outside, our own code of ethics is something we create privately. We adhere to these standards because we believe in them, not because we fear punishment or want social rewards. This does not mean, however, that we are not influenced by social considerations. Often our need for social acceptance plays a role in shaping our personal ethics. We tend to behave in ways that our supervisors, peers, and society in general will approve of. As you can see from Figure 19-1, ethical behavior is shaped by many forces. In addition to those illustrated, a salesperson's moral standards are molded by those of buyers, competitors, and fellow salespeople.

Our personal ethics may be more stringent than social norms in some instances, and more lax in others. Rarely are the two in total agreement. There are things we may consider unethical that society deems legal, and others that we find acceptable that society has declared illegal. Whether our individual standards are higher or lower than society's moral code, we believe we are acting ethically when we follow them.

A well-defined and closely followed set of personal ethics enables salespeople to fulfill their moral obligation to customers, competitors, and their firm. Salespeople with high standards are more successful in establishing long-term customer relationships than are those whose ethics are easily compromised. Trust and respect, the foundation of all lasting customer relationships, are established only when buyers believe that your moral code meets or exceeds their own.

Determinants of Ethical Behavior

1. Family.

2. Early home life, childhood experiences, school.

3. Religious beliefs and commitments.

4. Societal and community values.

5. Ego strength.

6. Consequences of past ethical behavior.

7. Company standards, policies, and practices (corporate culture).

8. Availability of a professional code of ethics.

9. Supervisor and peer behavior.

10. Organization-initiated consequences for unethical behavior.

11. Ethical climate in the industry.

12. The need to conform to organizational and reference group norms.

13. Legal constraints.

14. Behavior of past and present role models.

Figure 19-1

Formal Codes of Ethics . . .

As an increasing number of business organizations strive to be known for their moral conduct, formalized **codes of ethics** are becoming a standard part of company mission statements and philosophies. An estimated 90 percent of all major U.S. corporations have drawn up written codes of ethics to ensure consistent ethical behavior by their employees. These standards of conduct are typically higher than required by law, and employee behavior that fails to live up to a company code is considered unethical by that company.

Figure 19-2, next page, explains how to build ethical conduct. Commonly, firms post their code of ethics on company bulletin boards and distribute it to stockholders, customers, and suppliers. Some firms set up special hotlines for their employees to call when ethical questions arise. Usually the code of ethics is developed by a committee established by top management. A compliance committee, responsible for clarifying and interpreting the code, investigates possible code violations, renders judgment, and imposes sanctions.

To ensure that salespeople and sales trainees understand the company code of ethics and are prepared to deal with legal and ethical issues, most firms hold training and orientation sessions concentrating on ethics. These meetings may include case studies, role playing, analyses of the actual experiences of company salespeople, and discussions of the ethical dilemmas likely to confront salespeople.

```
┌─────────────────────────────────────────────────────────────────┐
│                                                                   │
│  How to Build High Ethical Standards                              │
│                                                                   │
│  Provide ethics training.                                         │
│                                                                   │
│  Publish a written code of ethics.                                │
│                                                                   │
│  Have employees sign the code of ethics and add it to their file. │
│                                                                   │
│  Use company leaders as role models.                              │
│                                                                   │
│  Punish unethical behavior.                                       │
│                                                                   │
│  Screen potential employees.                                      │
│                                                                   │
│  Develop a mechanism for reporting unethical behavior.            │
│                                                                   │
│  Create a booklet that contains ethical guidelines, signed by the │
│  organization's CEO.                                              │
│                                                                   │
│  Distribute the ethical guidelines of your industry or profession.│
│                                                                   │
│  Distribute a list of the organization's ethical standards to all │
│  of the organization's constituent groups.                        │
│                                                                   │
│  Provide introductory and ongoing ethics training.               │
│                                                                   │
└─────────────────────────────────────────────────────────────────┘
```

Figure 19-2

By addressing subjects such as gift giving, extortion, collusion, and conflict of interest, a company code of ethics helps educate employees in legal and moral issues and provides them with clear guidelines for their daily decisions and actions. It helps salespeople develop their own set of high moral standards and provides support for those dealing with customers or colleagues who invite unethical behavior. A company code of ethics that is known to the public is especially advantageous because it builds prospect confidence in both the salesperson and the firm. Salespeople should encourage their employers to include this in literature that can be distributed to prospects and customers.

Professional Associations . . .

Most professional marketing and sales associations have written ethical codes for their members to follow. The Code of Ethics of Sales and Marketing Executives International (Figure 19-3) provides salespeople with clear, specific guidelines. For example, the code reminds salespeople that customers must not be coerced into taking unwanted products. The SMEI code also covers the salesperson's relationship to her or his company, the competition, and the community. Individuals who attain the Certified Professional Salesperson status with this organization pledge to abide by these standards.

SMEI Certified Professional Salesperson Code of Ethics...

The **SMEI Certified Professional Salesperson (SCPS©) Code of Ethics** is a set of principles that outline minimum requirements for professional conduct. Those who attain SCPS© status should consider these principles as more than just rules to follow. They are guiding standards above which the salesperson should rise.

An **SMEI Certified Professional Salesperson (SCPS©)** shall support and preserve the highest standards of professional conduct in all areas of sales and in all relationships in the sales process. Toward this end an **SMEI Certified Professional Salesperson (SCPS©)** pledges and commits to these standards in all activities under this code.

I. **With respect to *The Customer*, I will:**

Maintain honesty and integrity in my relationships with all customers and prospective customers; accurately represent my product or service in order to place the customer or prospective customer in a position to make a decision consistent with the principle of mutuality of benefit and profit to the buyer and seller; and continually keep abreast and increase the knowledge of the product(s), services(s), and industry in which I work. This is necessary to better serve those who place their trust in me.

II. **With respect to *The Company* and other parties whom I represent, I will:**

Use their resources that are at my disposal and they will be utilized only for legitimate business purposes; respect and protect proprietary and confidential information entrusted to me by my company; and not engage in activities that will either jeopardize or conflict with the interests of my company. Activities that may be or which may appear to be illegal or unethical will be strictly avoided. To this effect I will not participate in activities that are illegal or unethical.

III. **With respect to *The Competition*, regarding those organizations that I compete with in the marketplace, I will:**

Only obtain competitive information through legal and ethical methods; and only portray my competitors and their products and services in a manner which is honest, truthful, and based on accurate information that can or has been substantiated.

IV. **With respect to *The Community and Society* which provides me with my livelihood, I will:**

Engage in business and selling practices which contribute to a positive relationship with the communities in which I and my company have presence; support public policy objectives consistent with maintaining and protecting the environment and community; participate in community activities and associations which provide for the betterment of the community and society.

I Am Committed to the letter and spirit of this code. The reputation of salespeople depends upon me as well as others who engage in the profession of selling. My adherence to these standards will strengthen the reputation and integrity for which we strive as professional salespeople.

I understand that failure to consistently act according to the above standards and principles could result in the forfeiture of the privileges of using the SCPS© designation.

Figure 19-3

> No matter how many calls you make, how great your product is, or how
> good you are at selling it, your customers aren't always going to buy.
>
> John Graham

Buyers' Codes of Ethics . . .

Industrial, commercial, and retail store buyers follow standards of ethical conduct just as salespeople do. Buyers are often required to sign an ethical statement that prohibits them from taking gifts or entering into questionable or unusual arrangements with vendors. Retail store buyers follow company guidelines as well as a set of voluntary vendor trade guidelines adopted in 1973 by the National Retail Merchants Association Vendor Relations Committee.

BUSINESS LAW . . .

We mentioned earlier that the law is a formal codification of ethical standards enforced by statute. Legislation relating to marketing and selling generally come under the categories of business law, contract law, or tort law, which have been enacted at all levels of government. Business law spells out society's expectations as to a salesperson's ethical obligations and the rights and responsibilities of buyers and sellers. Its overriding purpose is to ensure fair business practices while maintaining a competitive selling environment.

Of particular importance to salespeople is the branch of law called torts, or **tort law**. This is a collective term for all varieties of civil litigation involving injury to another's person, property, or reputation. Torts are generally classified as intentional, negligence, or strict liability. Those that relate specifically to selling include invasion of privacy, breach of warranty, embezzlement, fraud (lies and nondisclosure), defamation (slander and libel), disparagement of a competitor's product, and failure to meet product safety standards.

BUSINESS AND GOVERNMENT PRIOR TO 1890 . . .

Before 1890, the philosophy of government toward business was *laissez faire*, or "let it be." Government officials saw no reason to interfere with commerce, and they allowed companies to compete without regulation. The resultant growth of big business in the nineteenth century brought with it the philosophy that only the strongest businesses should survive. Charles Darwin's doctrine of survival of the fittest was twisted to justify practically any business activity, regardless of how unscrupulous it might be. Legal matters that needed to be resolved were settled by reliance on the precedent of previous court decisions, otherwise known as common law.

By 1890, it became apparent that common law could not curb the abuses of power taking place in business. Courts were no longer hearing cases that involved small, local firms. They were dealing with national companies that were trying to monopolize their industry. Government's hands-off philosophy changed, and it began evolving into an active overseer of business.

Government regulation of commercial activity started with the Sherman Antitrust Act of 1890, and continued with the Clayton amendment of 1914 and the Federal Trade Commission Act of 1914. Over the years, government has increasingly intervened to establish specific legal standards of business activity. Laws are enforced through criminal and civil actions brought by the Antitrust Division of the Department of Justice, civil actions brought by the Federal Trade Commission, and lawsuits brought by private parties asserting damage claims.

From Caveat Emptor to Caveat Venditor . . .

As laissez faire gave way to government intervention, the doctrine of caveat emptor gave way to caveat venditor. **Caveat emptor**, or "buyer beware," was the rule of the times until government and the courts took steps to regulate business. This principle exempted the seller from any liability associated with a sale. It was the buyer who was responsible for examining, judging, and testing merchandise independently. Buyers bought at their own risk, with no assurance as to product quality or performance. In such an atmosphere, sellers frequently sold unfit or unsafe merchandise and refused to accept returns.

As time passed, societal attitudes toward responsibility for product safety and quality began to change. The doctrine of **caveat venditor**, or "seller beware," started to take hold. Court decisions began to favor the buyer, with laws that guaranteed buyers' rights and held sellers liable for customer safety and satisfaction. The doctrine of caveat emptor still holds in certain situations, such as public auctions and sheriff's sales, but caveat venditor continues to be the trend.

The Sherman Act . . .

The **Sherman Antitrust Act** was a landmark piece of federal legislation aimed at regulating business activity. Its passing expressed Congress's commitment to a free market economy, a commitment so strong that there was only one dissenting vote to the act. The Sherman Act's primary purpose is to maintain a competitive environment by preventing big businesses from driving competitors out of the market. The act prohibits any unreasonable interference with the free pricing and distribution of goods in interstate trade.

Section 1 of the Sherman Act deals with competition. It prohibits contracts, combinations, or conspiracies that restrain trade in interstate and foreign commerce. Competitors are prohibited from making agreements on selling prices or conditions of sale, and cannot allocate markets or customers among themselves. **Price fixing** between competitors is illegal, as is price fixing among the members of a product's distribution channel. Firms are also prohibited from refusing to deal with current or former customers for other than good business reasons. Section 2 of the act deals with market control. It prohibits actual monopolies and all attempts to manipulate any part of trade or commerce.

Sherman Act violations are punished as criminal felonies. The U.S. Department of Justice alone is empowered to bring criminal prosecutions under the Sherman Act. Individual violators can be fined up to $250,000 and sentenced to up to three years in federal prison for each offense. Corporations can be fined up to $1 million for each offense. Under some circumstances, the fines can go even higher. The Sherman Act is supplemented by antitrust laws at the state level. Most states have their own legislation that is enforced through the state attorney general's office.

The Clayton Act . . .

The Sherman Act was amended by the **Clayton Act**. This civil statute (it carries no criminal penalties) clarifies and strengthens the Sherman Act by clearly spelling out actions that are illegal. Its key phrase is "where the effect…may be to substantially lessen competition or tend to create a monopoly in any line of commerce." Particularly important to salespeople are Sections 2 and 3.

Section 2 of the Clayton Act deals with price discrimination, and states generally that it is illegal for a seller to offer the same merchandise to different buyers at different prices. Sellers who charge different prices must prove that there are differences in the grade, quantity, or quality of the goods; that there are differences in manufacturing or selling costs; or that they are trying to meet a competitor's price.

Section 3 concerns itself with **exclusive dealing arrangements**. An exclusive dealing arrangement is an agreement between a manufacturer and a distributor prohibiting the distributor from carrying competitors' products. These are illegal in instances where competition is substantially lessened, as when a large sum of money or a large share of the market is involved. Section 3 also restricts **tie-in contracts**, agreements that require a customer to buy one product in order to purchase another. These are legal only if the proper use of one product requires the use of another, or when service is necessary to the proper functioning of a product.

The Clayton Act permits the government to challenge mergers that are likely to increase prices to consumers. A provision of the act permits private parties injured by an antitrust violation to sue in federal court. State attorneys general may bring civil suits under the Clayton Act on behalf of injured consumers, and groups of consumers often bring class action suits on their own. Under this law, the government no longer needs to prove conspiracy or actual monopoly as it did under the Sherman Act. However, it does need to prove that competition is substantially lessened.

The Clayton Act also restricts company mergers, interlocking boards of directors, and stock purchases in which a firm buys the stock of competitors. The original act was significantly amended in 1950.

> Salespeople who break the rules aren't likely to break records.
>
> Gerhard Gschwandtner

The Federal Trade Commission Act . . .

Like the Sherman Act, the **Federal Trade Commission Act** was passed to promote free and fair competition in interstate commerce. The FTC Act serves to supplement the Sherman Act by prohibiting or restricting unfair business dealings. Trade practices that injure competitors or consumers, such as price fixing, false advertising, fraud, misrepresentation, and illegal combinations of competitors are declared illegal under the FTC Act. Like the Clayton Act, the FTC Act carries no criminal penalties.

The Federal Trade Commission Act established the **Federal Trade Commission**, an agency of the federal government with a five-member board of commissioners. The FTC works with the Justice Department in enforcing the Sherman Act, the Clayton Act, the Federal Trade Commission Act, and all the related acts that have followed. The FTC has the power to investigate any competitive practice thought to be unfair and any sales practice thought to deceive or mislead customers.

The FTC investigates reports of deceptive advertising and allegations of collusion in pricing among competitors, and it monitors reciprocal buying arrangements that might restrain trade. The FTC has the power to issue cease and desist orders if it deems that an unfair act is being committed. If the violator refuses to accept the order, the commission can take the violator to federal court to have the order enforced.

Although the FTC Act stipulates that "unfair methods of competition in commerce are unlawful," it does not spell out specific examples of illegal methods. **The Wheeler–Lea Act** of 1938, which amended the FTC Act and censures "unfair or deceptive acts or practices," is similarly vague. Both acts left interpretation up to the FTC and the courts. The FTC Act also restricts reciprocal buying arrangements when they become highly systematized or if substantial sums of money are involved. Reciprocity is illegal if it hampers competition.

These business practices have been deemed illegal under the Federal Trade Commission Act:

1. Misrepresenting a product's delivery date
2. Substituting goods different from those purchased
3. Shipping unordered goods or a larger quantity than ordered
4. Failing to represent clearly the terms and conditions of the sale
5. Misrepresenting the way a product is made
6. Intimidating a customer by using scare tactics or threats of legal action
7. Bribing employees or customers to acquire an account

8. Using bribery or espionage to learn competitors' trade secrets

9. Misleading customers to think they are getting a reduced price or free product when they are not

Salespeople should keep abreast of FTC-related court cases and the commission's regulatory activities. Although the FTC Act has been considerably modified over the years, the basic premises of the law still hold.

The Robinson–Patman Act . . .

The **Robinson–Patman Act** of 1936 is considered the single most important federal law for marketers. It revised Section 2 of the Clayton Act, strengthening the Clayton Act's price discrimination provision significantly.

Enacted during the Depression, when large retail chains enjoyed a growth period, the Robinson–Patman Act was designed to protect small wholesalers and retailers from price discrimination by suppliers. Mass merchandisers were driving smaller stores from the market with their ability to buy in huge quantities and demand unjustifiably large quantity discounts. Suppliers were granting them discounts that were disproportionate to the quantities purchased, thus discriminating against smaller retailers. Under the provisions of the Robinson–Patman Act, it is illegal for anyone engaged in interstate commerce to discriminate between purchasers of goods of "like grade and quantity" if the price difference (1) substantially lessens competition; (2) tends to create a monopoly; (3) injures, destroys, or prevents competition with a seller, a buyer, or customers of either; (4) is not based on differences in cost of manufacture, sale, or delivery of the product.

A supplier is restricted from offering different prices or terms of sale unless the seller is meeting a competitor's low price or the seller can realize a savings because of the quantity ordered or the buying method.

The Robinson–Patman Act also disallows **promotional allowances** not offered on "proportionately equal terms" to all buyers. Because a **broker's fee** is considered a price reduction if an independent broker isn't used, **brokerage allowances** paid to anyone other than an independent broker are prohibited. Suppliers may not pay broker's fees to buyers that purchase directly from them or to brokerage houses owned by buyers.

The Robinson–Patman Act is interpreted and enforced by the Federal Trade Commission. Under this law, the FTC can establish limits on quantity discounts offered by sellers and declare illegal any discount not based on a confirmable difference in cost to the seller. A selling firm must be able to prove that a price lower than that offered to other buyers is quoted "in good faith to meet a competitor's equally low price." The burden of proof of innocence rests with the alleged violator, and buyers are equally guilty if they "knowingly" receive such discounts.

Although suppliers are permitted to charge competing buyers different prices if differences in grade, quality, or cost can be proved, history has shown that justifying price variances on this basis is extremely difficult. Most firms that have been called to defend their quantity discounts have been unsuccessful.

> In order to get ahead of your competition, you've got to get out of your comfort zone.
>
> Mary Lou Retton

The Wheeler–Lea Act . . .

The **Wheeler–Lea Act** was an amendment to the FTC Act, passed in response to a court decision relating to the power of the Federal Trade Commission. The court determined that the FTC had power only in cases involving injury to competitors, not to consumers. The Wheeler–Lea amendment expanded the FTC's power by giving it the authority to protect consumers as well as competitors from unfair business practices. Consumers now had federal protection from false, misleading, and deceptive advertising. The Wheeler–Lea Act also added clout to the FTC's cease and desist orders by making them automatically effective if not appealed by the alleged violator within sixty days.

THE UNIFORM COMMERCIAL CODE . . .

The **Uniform Commercial Code** is the primary legal guide for commercial transactions in the United States. It was written in Philadelphia by the American Law Institute, a scholarly group responsible for many of today's uniform state laws. Over the years, it has been expanded to its present size of more than 800 pages.

The UCC codified all the common law regulations relating to business, many of which had been interpreted differently from state to state, into one unchanging package. It also established a set of standards for interstate commerce, the sale of goods across state lines. Divisions of the UCC have been adopted by all fifty states, the District of Columbia, Guam, and the American Virgin Islands. Pennsylvania was the first state to adopt the code.

The UCC has achieved greater acceptance than many other uniform codes, perhaps because it encourages interstate trade. It covers all aspects of commerce, and is updated as ways of doing business change. Businesspeople feel comfortable with it and the many court decisions it has influenced.

Of primary interest to salespeople is the UCC's Division 2 (formerly called Article 2), which is entitled "Sales." This seven-chapter division (Chapters 21–27) deals primarily with contracts. It revised the Uniform Sales Act of 1906. Here is a brief chapter-by-chapter description of Division 2:

> Chapter 21 (Short Title, General Construction, and Subject Matter) includes an index and defines sales-related terms such as merchant, goods, contract, agreement, sale, and cancellation.

Chapter 22 (Form, Formation, and Readjustment of Contract) describes the formal requirements for a contract, firm offers to buy or sell, offer and acceptance in formation of contract; modification, recision, and waiver; delegation of performance and assignment of contract rights.

Chapter 23 (General Obligation and Construction of Contract) addresses the general obligations of contract parties; pricing terms, express and implied warranties, terms of shipment, obligations of the buyer and seller relating to shipment; letters of credit, sale on approval, consignment sales, and sale by auction.

Chapter 24 (Title, Creditors, and Good Faith Purchasers) covers the passing of title, the rights of the seller's creditors against sold goods, and good-faith purchases.

Chapter 25 (Performance) covers insurable interest in goods, manner of seller's tender of delivery, shipment by the seller, rights of financing agencies, payment for goods, and the buyer's right to inspect the goods.

Chapter 26 (Breach, Repudiation, and Excuse) addresses the rights of the buyer on improper delivery, rejection of goods by the buyer, duties of the buyer as to rejected goods, what constitutes acceptance of goods, the right to adequate assurance of performance, and breach of installment contract.

Chapter 27 (Remedies) covers seller's remedies on discovery of buyer's insolvency, seller's remedies in general, seller's stoppage of delivery of goods in transit, damages of seller for nonacceptance or repudiation, buyer's remedies, buyer's damages, and a statute of limitations for sales contracts.

Salespeople must understand their rights and obligations as well as the rights and obligations of buyers under the Uniform Commercial Code. The following section provides an amplification of topics discussed in the UCC's Division 2.

Sales Agreement . . .

A **sales agreement** is a legal contract that transfers merchandise from seller to buyer for a price or other consideration. The UCC states that a written contract is required for all sales of tangible property of $500 or more. The attempt to follow UCC regulations has led to the near-standardization of sales agreements.

Because sales agreements are subject to conflicting interpretations, the UCC addresses both buyers' and seller's rights and obligations relating to these contracts. The UCC stipulates that salespeople and their firm are legally responsible for fulfilling any oral or written agreement that qualifies as an offer and acceptance. The code also distinguishes between a genuine offer and an invitation to bid, the latter being not binding on either party. The UCC explains sale on approval, which is a conditional sale in which the buyer can return merchandise with no obligation to purchase. The code also deals with payment obligations, methods of contract termination, and the seller's recourse in the event that merchandise is not paid for.

Agency . . .

An **agent** is a party authorized to act on behalf of another party. As a salesperson, you are your firm's agent, authorized to make, modify, or terminate contracts with buyers or their agents. The legal relationship between salesperson and firm is an agency relationship, the firm being called the principal. An agency relationship requires no contract; it can be implied between the parties. Legally, a principal is responsible for the actions of its agents when it has knowledge of those actions and when the actions are performed in the normal course of the agent's duties.

Warranties and Guarantees . . .

It is a common practice for sellers to provide buyers with an oral promise of satisfaction or a written guarantee of product performance. These assurances reduce the risk associated with a purchase and are effective promotional tools.

A written warranty, the seller's pledge that its product is or will perform as promised, may be full or limited. A **full warranty** takes responsibility for all aspects of product performance for a stipulated period, relieving the buyer of the expense of repairs or replacement. A full warranty must be honored by the seller within a reasonable time. A **limited warranty** does not meet all the requirements of a full warranty. It may cover parts but not service, or some aspects of parts and service but not all. Sometimes products are under a full warranty for a time and then a limited warranty for some time beyond that.

Warranties may also be express or implied. Express and implied warranties are explained in Chapter 23 of the UCC. An **express warranty** is any statement or product representation made by the seller and relied upon by the buyer as a fact about the product. Any product description or affirmation of fact qualifies as an express warranty. The express warranty need not be in writing, nor does it have to include the word *warranty* or *guarantee*. Whether it is oral or written, the statement or representation in an express warranty convinces the buyer that the product is as described, shown, or demonstrated.

An **implied warranty** is an unstated assumption that the product will do the job it is supposed to do. For example, a hair dryer is expected to dry hair. Even if there is no express warranty stating that the hair dryer will dry hair, an implied warranty exists. The seller is responsible for selling a product that does its job, even if the seller never stated that it would. Even though certain aspects of product performance are not mentioned in product warranties, buyers have the right to expect their products to perform these functions. The two types of implied warranties, the **implied warranty of merchantability** and the **implied warranty of fitness** have long been recognized.

The Magnuson–Moss Warranty Act . . .

The regulations relating to warranties in the UCC were refined by the **Magnuson–Moss Warranty Act**. This law strengthens consumers' rights and increases sellers' responsibilities by requiring the use of clear language in warranties, refunds, and corrective advertising. Because it requires that written warranties fully and clearly state their terms and conditions, the Magnuson–Moss Act has had the effect of making warranties stronger and more understandable. It also has led to the decision by some manufacturers to replace their full warranties with limited warranties.

Breach of Warranty . . .

A **breach of warranty** occurs whenever a product fails to meet the standards promised or implied by the seller. Because all claims made by sellers are legal obligations of performance, any assertion that proves untrue constitutes a breach of warranty whether or not the seller made the false claim knowingly.

As a salesperson, you will constantly be in a position to say things that can be construed as warranty statements, so the danger of committing a breach of warranty is great. Be especially careful not to make claims about your product or company that you cannot substantiate. Know the difference between misrepresentation and **sales puff** or "seller's talk." When you say, "This is as good a product as you'll find anywhere," you are merely stating an enthusiastic opinion, and your remark will be considered harmless puffery. On the other hand, when you say, "This is the last such product you will ever need to buy," you are misrepresenting your product as one that will last forever.

Obligation and Performance . . .

Because the UCC defines the rights and obligations of both seller and buyer in commercial sales transactions, it is particularly useful when returns, cancellations, delays, and substitutions cause friction between the parties. Both buyers and sellers can turn to the code for guidance on their respective responsibilities.

The seller's obligations as outlined by the UCC include making goods available at reasonable times and allowing the buyer a fair amount of time to take possession of the goods. The buyer's obligations include accepting responsibility for the goods while they are in the buyer's possession. The ways a buyer may take possession of goods are defined, along with the buyer's options for rejecting unwanted goods.

The UCC stipulates who is responsible for insuring merchandise and at what point the liability for goods in transit shifts from seller to buyer. It also addresses terms of shipment, methods of payment, the buyer's right to inspect merchandise before paying for it, and legal remedies available when the other party fails to fulfill his or her contractual obligations.

> Selling should benefit both the customer and the salesperson. You're supposed to be having a good time and to be learning while you are doing it. You are supposed to be producing something of value in the world.
>
> Tim Gallwey

LAWS AFFECTING CUSTOMER FINANCING...

Financing is an important part of many sales transactions, particularly those involving large amounts of money. Although salespeople are not always involved with the credit aspects of sales, it is important that they understand the legal ramifications of credit. Customers frequently ask salespeople to explain their credit rights, and the better you understand the laws concerning credit, the less likely you will be to violate them.

Truth-in-Lending and Regulation Z...

The Consumer Credit Protection Act (also known as the **Truth-in-Lending Act**) and the Federal Reserve Board's **Regulation Z** both relate to the financial aspects of sales transactions.

Strengthening the terms of the Uniform Commercial Code, these acts require that lenders clearly and completely disclose all the terms of their lending agreements. Finance charges, including the **annual percentage rate (APR)**, the interest cost fixed in annual terms, must be stated. Lenders must also state the number of payments required, late payment fees, service fees, carrying charges, fees for credit investigations, charges for required insurance, and appraisal fees. In addition, escrows for future payments of taxes and insurance, the date by which payments must be made in order to avoid additional finance charges, minimum monthly payment terms, annual membership fees, placement fees, actions that may be taken by creditors to collect bad debts, the circumstances under which the interest rate can increase, and any limitations on the increase must be made clear.

Truth-in-Lending and Regulation Z give standardization to credit terms and spell out the rights of both borrower and lender. They prohibit the use of vague and evasive language, hidden costs and "fine print," and require that the annual percentage rate be included in all disclosure statements and advertising.

The Equal Credit Opportunity Act and Regulation B...

The initial version of the **Equal Credit Opportunity Act** outlawed discrimination on the basis of gender and marital status. The objective was for women to be treated in the same manner as men when requesting credit. The law came about in response to a policy discriminating against young, married females by some lending institutions.

Almost ten years after its inception, the act was amended to include other discrimination bases. The new law, **Regulation B**, banned bias against any prospective borrower based upon gender, marital status, race, color, national origin, religion, or age. The original proponents of this amendment were concerned that divorced women were being treated unfairly by lenders, hence the word *divorced* was removed from the marital status section of credit applications. Today, the permissible categories are married, unmarried, and separated, with divorced individuals classified as unmarried. The act also requires lenders to permit married women, or anyone else, to open credit accounts in their own name.

The Fair Credit Reporting Act . . .

The **Fair Credit Reporting Act** of 1970 deals primarily with credit reports and a person's rights with respect to his or her credit history. It is common practice for a seller to request a credit report on a prospective buyer before granting credit. These reports are usually compiled by one of the small number of credit reporting services that operate nationally. Credit repositories are tapped, and the applicant's complete credit history is assembled. If credit is denied, or if its terms are adversely affected by the report, the applicant must be informed in writing by the lender within thirty days. The Federal Reserve Board provides lenders with a standardized form for advising the applicant of the reason for the denial.

The FCRA also gives those who have been denied credit the right to inspect a summary of their credit history without charge. Although they aren't allowed to see the actual credit report or their file, they may obtain a condensed version showing its nature and substance as well as the sources of the information it contains. Those who feel their file contains inaccurate information have the right to challenge it by requesting a further investigation. If the report is found to be incorrect, the file must be updated and whoever received the incorrect information must be informed of the changes. If there is a dispute over information contained in the file that cannot be resolved, the person has the right to have his or her side of the story included in the file.

The FCRA also guarantees that a person's credit history remains well guarded by spelling out the acceptable reasons for requesting it. A credit history may be requested (1) in connection with a credit transaction involving the consumer or for the review or collection of an account, (2) for employment purposes, (3) in connection with the underwriting of insurance, or (4) in connection with a business transaction involving the consumer.

Those who knowingly and willfully obtain a credit history for the wrong reasons are subject to fines of up to $5,000 or imprisonment of up to one year.

Diplomacy is the art of saying, "Nice doggie," until you can find a rock.

Will Rogers

Chapter 19 • Legal and Ethical Issues in Selling

The Cooling-Off Period Rule . . .

The **Cooling-Off Period Rule** is a trade regulation issued by the Federal Trade Commission relating to sales of more than $25 made outside the seller's normal place of business. Enacted to protect consumers from high-pressure sales tactics, the Cooling-Off Period Rule gives in-home purchasers the right to cancel their purchase within three days without penalty. Under this rule, the salesperson is required to explain the buyer's right to cancel and provide the buyer with a cancellation form.

Most states and a number of cities have adopted their own cooling-off rules similar to the FTC's. State versions are usually included in the state's unfair and deceptive trade practices act and are administered by a consumer protection bureau overseen by the state attorney general. These regulations, which are fairly consistent from state to state, may be stricter than the FTC rule but not more lenient.

The cooling-off period regulation in the Pennsylvania Unfair Trade Practices and Consumer Protection Law reads as follows:

At the time of sale or contract the buyer shall be provided with:

1. A fully completed receipt or copy of any contract pertaining to such sale, which is in the same language (Spanish, English, etc.) as that principally used in the oral sales presentation, and also in English, and which shows the date of the transaction and contains the name and address of the seller, and in immediate proximity to the space reserved in the contract for the signature of the buyer or on the front page of the receipt if a contract is not used and in bold face type of a minimum size of ten points, a statement in substantially the following form:

"You, the buyer, may cancel this transaction at any time prior to midnight of the third business day after the date of this transaction. See the attached **notice of cancellation** form for an explanation of this right."

2. A completed form in duplicate, captioned "Notice of Cancellation," which shall be attached to the contract or receipt and easily detachable, and which shall contain in ten-point bold face type the following information and statements in the same language (Spanish, English, etc.) as that used in the contract.

The Consumer Goods Pricing Act . . .

The **Consumer Goods Pricing Act** makes it illegal for manufacturers engaged in interstate commerce to enter into resale price-maintenance agreements with resellers of their merchandise. This act repealed the Miller–Tydings Act of 1937, a law that exempted such agreements from antitrust prosecution. It also rendered obsolete all state-level resale price-maintenance laws that still existed.

Price-maintenance laws, which were enacted during the Depression as "fair trade laws," gave manufacturers the right to set a minimum resale price for their product. Their purpose was to protect small retailers from the penetration tactics of large chains, but they resulted in higher prices for consumers. Today, a manufacturer or distributor engaged in interstate commerce cannot legally stipulate the price at which a dealer must sell its product.

The Fair Debt Collection Practices Act . . .

Congress passed the Fair Debt Collection Act to end alleged harassment and abuse on the part of some debt collection agencies. The mistreatment of debtors, through chastisement, bullying, or real or veiled threats, was made illegal. Debt collectors must state clearly who they are and their intended purpose in all written and verbal communication.

The FTC Improvement Act . . .

The **FTC Improvement Act** reversed the trend toward governmental protection of businesses and consumers by restricting the Federal Trade Commission's activities. It added new limits to FTC powers and gave Congress the right to veto FTC regulations. Passed during a period of general deregulation, it reflected the feelings of the political leaders of the time that business should regulate itself. Critics of the act contend that it has changed the Federal Trade Commission from an active watchdog to a passive observer.

State Unfair Trade Practices Acts . . .

Most states have enacted their own version of the Federal Trade Commission Act. These **little FTC laws,** as they are known, prevent deceptive trade practices by giving the state attorney general's office the power to prosecute "false, misleading, or deceptive acts or practices in the conduct of trade or commerce."

Such laws generally apply to all salespeople, whether they sell to businesses or final consumers. A seller who causes confusion about delivery, transportation costs, or terms, or who makes false or misleading statements about profit margins, market share, sales territories, or markets may be violating his or her state's unfair trade practices law and is subject to prosecution. Little FTC laws should not be confused with the loss leader laws, which are also referred to as unfair trade practices acts. Loss leader laws, still on the books in some states, require middlemen to mark up their merchandise by a certain percentage over cost.

Green River Ordinances . . .

Green River ordinances are local ordinances regulating door-to-door selling. Named after the town of Green River, Wyoming, which became the first to regulate door-to-door selling, these regulations are designed to protect residents from unfair selling practices and high-pressure salespeople.

Rural communities are less likely than urban areas to have Green River ordinances, and those that do impose fewer restrictions. Contrary to popular belief, even the most affluent communities commonly permit door-to-door selling as long as it follows local regulations. Green River ordinances do not pertain to private property such as apartment buildings, condominium complexes, and shopping centers, where solicitations of any kind are usually prohibited by the owners. Salespeople who sell door-to-door should first check with local government officials about possible restrictions.

A community may display its Green River ordinance at city hall or in the township municipal building. Salespeople seeking a license or permit may be required to register with the township manager, the local police, or the department of licenses and inspections. The permit fee can range from several dollars to several hundred dollars. Some communities issue a photo license, and others require salespeople to post a bond. Most ordinances restrict selling to daylight hours, and some distinguish between resident and nonresident sellers. Salespeople found soliciting without a permit are subject to a fine.

Unduly vague or restrictive local ordinances have been challenged by sellers and struck down. It can also be argued that local selling ordinances violate the First Amendment and the U.S. Constitution's Commerce Clause, and place an undue restraint on trade. A local regulation that places an unreasonable burden on interstate commerce may well be declared invalid if challenged.

Laws Affecting Telemarketing . . .

Because of the potential for invasion of privacy, many legislative bodies have targeted telemarketing. While Congress has addressed issues concerning this selling tool in two pieces of legislation, a number of states have applied more stringent laws and rules. In addition, as was discussed in Chapter 18, the American Telemarketing Association has also adopted some strict guidelines and a code of ethics.

The Telephone Consumer Protection Act . . .

The Telephone Consumer Protection Act of 1991 is the first federal law regulating the actions of legitimate telemarketers. The purpose of this legislation is to protect the rights of consumers while allowing businesses to use telemarketing effectively. Regulated by the Federal Communications Commission, the law requires telemarketers to formalize their existing policies, or create new ones, to come into compliance.

Some of the issues covered by this legislation include the requirement that identification of the caller be established during the introductory phase of all "live operator" telemarketing calls. Calls to private residences are restricted to the hours between 8:00 a.m. and 9:00 p.m., and a list of those people who do not want to be contacted must be maintained by the telemarketer. The law also covers the use of automatic dialing recorded message players, it regulates messages sent to facsimile machines (FAX), and spells out the penalties of violations.

Telemarketing and Consumer Fraud and Abuse Protection Act . . .

The Telemarketing and Consumer Fraud and Abuse Protection Act of 1994 combats intrusive telemarketing by providing law enforcement agencies with powerful tools. Under this act, the Federal Trade Commission adopted the Telemarketing Sales Rule, requiring telemarketers to come under rigid compliance of the law. Besides reinforcing those regulations spelled out in the Telephone Consumers Protection Act, the FTC rule requires a consumer's rization" for use of bank account information. It also prohibits misrepresentation of any material aspect of the offer and bars obtaining access to the credit card system through another's merchandise account without authorization of the financial institution.

In addition, the FTC rule specifically prohibits the use of threats, intimidation, or the use of profane language to pressure consumers into accepting a sales offer. Repeated calls on a prospect who has refued the offer are considered abusive. The rule states that telemarketers are responsible for keeping a "do not call" list and may not telephone consumers who have requested to be removed from calling lists or who have asked to receive no more calls regarding specific goods or services.

LEGAL AND ETHICAL DILEMMAS FACING THE SALESPERSON . . .

In a world in which one category of law can take up 800 pages of documentation, there is no shortage of legal and ethical dilemmas facing the salesperson. Nine such tangles are illustrated in Figure 19-4 and explained in the pages that follow.

Opportunities for illegal sales-related activities seem endless. As a seller, you might add charges after the sale without first notifying the buyer, sign a contract without the proper authorization, sell unneeded products, or give wrong or incomplete use or care instructions. Likewise, you must be careful not to offer promotional allowances on unequal terms to buyers, violate the contractual delivery date, ship a brand, model, or size other than the one you sold, or grant price concessions to favored customers. Similarly, you may not act to limit competition among suppliers or buyers, make promises that can't

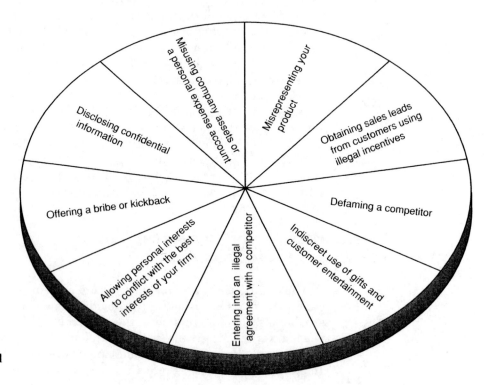

Figure 19-4 Legal/ethical tangles.

be kept, promise savings that don't exist, use the testimony of shills, or use confidential information without authorization.

Because you can never hope to know every letter of the law, you should at least develop a strong personal code of ethics in selling. Such conduct can help guide you toward legal behavior when you don't know the law. It is also the only way to succeed in selling with your reputation and conscience intact.

Fraud . . .

Fraud is any form of willful misrepresentation or any deliberate distortion of the truth, either by words, conduct, or failure to disclose certain information. Salespeople who deliberately misrepresent themselves, their product, or their company are committing fraud.

A product is fraudulently misrepresented when its side effects aren't disclosed, when it is said to have features or benefits it doesn't have, or when it is said to be imported when it is not. Fraudulent claims may also constitute a breach of express warranty. The product may not be of the standard or quality described, it may be used instead of new, or it may not be the brand, model, or style the customer ordered. Fraud is also committed when damaged or soiled merchandise is concealed by good merchandise.

Referral Schemes . . .

You will recall from Chapter 3 the practice of offering a reward as an incentive to customers for providing you with sales leads. When the reward is contingent on a purchase by the *new* leads, this **referral plan** is ordinarily legal. It becomes illegal if you reward the lead provider by reducing or eliminating the price on his or her present purchase. In other words, a salesperson cannot say, "Give me the names of ten other people and if they all purchase, the product you buy today is free."

Defamation . . .

Defamation is any statement intended to injure another party's reputation. A salesperson who insinuates that a competitor is selling inferior merchandise, engaging in illegal business practices, or experiencing financial difficulty defames the competitor. Defamatory acts violate the FTC Act and various states' unfair trade practices laws. Defamation is of three basic types: slander, libel, and product disparagement.

Slander is oral defamation. It is any spoken statement that causes harm to another's reputation or means of livelihood due to its false or malicious content. **Libel** is written, printed, or pictorial defamation. It includes any misleading or untrue words, pictures, or illustrations that harm another's reputation or expose another to ridicule.

Product disparagement includes any false or misleading statement about the quality or salability of a competitor's merchandise. Such statements are usually made in an attempt to stop the prospect from buying a competing brand. They may involve denouncing the competitor's performance claims or demeaning its product when discussing your brand's performance. Examples of product disparagement include manipulating research data to make your product look better than competing products, suggesting that competing brands have harmful side effects, or implying that a competitor is selling stolen merchandise.

You will recall from Chapter 9 that a presentation focused on a competitor's weak points lacks content and is in bad taste. You stand to lose the prospect's trust, and you do nothing to build the desire for your product. If you must compare your merchandise to competing brands, rely on statistical evidence gathered by independent testing agencies such as Underwriter's Laboratory. The prospect will recognize these sources as impartial, and competitors cannot accuse you of disparaging their product.

Gifts and Entertainment . . .

Gift giving, especially during the holidays, is a long-standing practice among salespeople. A carefully selected gift tells loyal customers that you appreciate their business and reminds infrequent purchasers of your willingness to serve them. There is nothing wrong with gift giving as long as the gift and the manner in which it is given are ethical. A present should be given as a token of appreciation, never as an incentive to purchase. It should not be presented near the time of a buying decision since the prospect may feel obliged by it. Relating a gift's value to the volume of the customer's business is also inappropriate. Very expensive presents and money are never appropriate. In fact, money is considered a bribe, not a gift.

Customer **entertainment** is another part of sales work, and a great deal of money is spent on it. Like gift giving, entertainment must be ethical. Offering entertainment will insult some prospects, and others will feel that accepting it obliges them to purchase. Before offering a gift or suggesting entertainment to a business prospect, learn the prospect firm's policies on gifts and entertainment. Many companies do not allow their employees to accept gifts or entertainment. Some state so in writing.

Some firms limit the monetary value of the gifts their employees may give or receive. Still others state in their purchasing guidelines that buyers may accept only a "business lunch," and that the sole purpose of the lunch is to talk business.

Although purchasing personnel were once thought to be in need of "freebies" from vendors to offset their relatively low salaries, better pay and tighter ethical guidelines have changed the minds of many in business. Product samples, premiums, free meals, and complimentary ballgame or theater tickets are a thing of the past for many buyers. Buyers are often required by their employers to take turns paying for lunch with salespeople. Others must always insist on separate checks.

Bribery . . .

A **bribe** is any incentive offered to a prospect for the purpose of influencing the prospect's buying decision. A salesperson convicted of bribery is subject to fines and imprisonment, and the principal firm is equally guilty if it knew of the salesperson's actions.

A bribe may be monetary or not, and it may be suggested by either the seller or the prospect. Bribes suggested by buyers often come as hints, with the salesperson left to determine what is being asked for. The buyer may subtly

> Under any and all circumstances tell yourself often and mean it, "I don't believe in defeat.
>
> Norman Vincent Peale

suggest that the order can be yours in return for a small favor. For example, prospects might say they would like to purchase, but before they do, they must find the money for a "special gift" for a friend. What they want in exchange for their order is a bribe.

Manufacturers' salespeople have been known to offer "spiffs" or **push money** to retail sales clerks. Spiffs are offered in return for the clerk's promoting the manufacturer's product. Some reputable manufacturers offer this incentive directly to the retailer in the form of a promotional allowance, which can be considered perfectly legal. If this practice is used without the retailers permission or as an "under the table" incentive, it can be considered a bribe. Many retailers attempt to prevent spiffs by requiring their salespeople to sign a statement prohibiting them from accepting gifts from the manufacturers or distributors who sell to them.

Salespeople working in overseas markets often deal with buyers and government officials who expect gifts or money and won't buy without them. If you sell to international customers, you should become familiar with the **Foreign Corrupt Practices Act**. This law, which was passed in response to widespread reports of international bribery in the 1970s, makes it illegal for a U.S. businessperson to bribe a foreign government official.

A **kickback** is a kind of commercial bribery. In a kickback, the salesperson pays a percentage of the sales commission to another party who has the power to control or influence a buying decision. For example, a building contractor might offer a kickback to a politician who can change zoning ordinances in the contractor's favor. Salespeople are most tempted to offer bribes when the sale is likely to result in further sales or repeat orders. Such bribery is often disguised as a gift. Both giver and receiver face fines or imprisonment if caught and convicted, regardless of who suggested the kickback.

Collusion . . .

Collusion comes in many forms, but in selling it usually entails an agreement among competitors to fix prices or divide markets. Collusive agreements have been made to eliminate price differences, allow for the rotation of bids among competitors, and drive unwanted rivals from the market. These agreements have been made among several large firms that dominate a national market and among smaller firms that sell in a given geographic area.

Collusion is illegal even if it takes place unintentionally. For example, if you discuss your selling prices with competing salespeople and your conversations result in competitors' charging a price the same as yours, you may be found guilty of collusion. This is why many firms state in their code of ethics that employees should have little or no contact with competitors.

Conflict of Interest . . .

Conflict of interest occurs when your personal interests or part-time activities contradict the best interests of your firm. The most common form of conflict of interest is moonlighting, or working on a second job. For example, you might try to sell other products during your off-hours as a way of supplementing your income. Selling something else in your free time is a conflict of interest if the product competes with or is similar to the product you sell in your primary job. It violates your employer's trust and damages the firm's competitive position. Furthermore, if your dalliance is discovered, you are likely to be dismissed or even fined and subjected to criminal charges.

Even when your part-time employment doesn't involve selling, the long hours you spend working two jobs can cause your energy level to slip and your sales figures to drop. If you find that your evening or weekend employment affects your ability to sell, you owe it to yourself and your firm to give it up.

Privacy and Confidentiality . . .

As a salesperson, you are in a position that allows you to know a great deal of private or confidential information. Generally, such information should remain private. Disclosure may be both unethical and illegal. Although noncompeting salespeople frequently share prospect names and other contact information, you should be careful not to disclose details the prospect would deem sensitive. Information shared in confidence by a customer should always remain private.

Salespeople frequently have knowledge of their company's engineering designs, research findings, patent applications, production plans, manufacturing practices, sales results, and competitive bidding activities—all information that competitors would like to know. Occasionally, competitors are even willing to pay for this knowledge. But to sell or exchange confidential information does more than impair the firm's ability to compete: It is illegal espionage.

Misuse of Company Assets or Personal Expense Account . . .

Many firms furnish their salespeople with automobiles and expense accounts, in addition to giving them access to various types of company equipment. It is not uncommon for firms to provide their salespeople with an advance against future expenses or reimburse them for costs already incurred. An expense account and a company car are important benefits to salespeople, and make sales positions all the more attractive.

However, such benefits can be abused on ethical and legal levels. Salespeople who inflate their expenses or employ company assets for personal reasons are breaking the law and violating company ethical codes, in addition to stealing from their employers. Although salespeople who use company assets for personal purposes probably don't think of themselves as embezzlers, their seemingly harmless use of the company telephone, copier, computer, or gasoline credit card proves costly to the firm over time.

Summing It Up . . .

The primary purpose of this chapter was to help you gain an appreciation of the rewards of high ethical standards in selling while exploring the consequences of unethical or illegal behavior. The roles of individual, company, and professional association codes of ethics were examined.

We examined the various laws and regulations that affect salespeople and their profession, including the Sherman Act, the Clayton Act, the Federal Trade Commission Act, the Robinson–Patman Act, the Wheeler–Lea Act, the Fair Credit Reporting Act, the state unfair trade practices acts, local selling ordinances, and the Federal Trade Commission's Cooling-Off Period Rule. We analyzed many of the practices declared illegal under these laws. In addition, we examined Division 2 of the Uniform Commercial Code and code-related topics such as sale on approval, agency relationship, warranties and guarantees, and obligations and performance.

We discussed the legal and ethical dilemmas that commonly face people in selling, including defamation, gift giving and entertainment, kickbacks, collusion, conflict of interest, privacy and confidentiality, moonlighting, and misuse of company assets or personal expense account. Although no one can ever know all the laws relating to selling, salespeople with a strong personal code of ethics can usually behave legally and succeed with their conscience intact.

You Decide!

Carolyn works for a major food wholesaler and has been working on getting a twelve-store Florida supermarket chain to switch suppliers. Although the competition has been selling this company for years, Carolyn feels that her firm can offer more than competitive prices, faster delivery and better customer service. She has not only been calling at the headquarters location for this chain but has made impressive independent presentations to the individual store managers. She has even dragged her company's CEO into the act, getting her to call with her on two occasions.

In spite of her effort, Carolyn has not been able to dislodge her competitor. Even a well-publicized recent incident involving a vice-president from her competing firm was unable to give her headway. In talking with one of the store managers, she learned that the president of the chain was an avid deep sea fisher. Checking with a friend of hers who ran a marina, she learned that the fishing was great and she could hire a boat and crew for $500 a day. Knowing that the prospect's contract with the competing wholesaler was up for renewal in a few weeks, Carolyn thought this was a great opportunity to get the prospect out for a little R&R, while cementing the relationship. Should she or shouldn't she? **You decide!**

Key Concepts and Terms . . .

agency
annual percentage rate (APR)
breach of warranty
bribery
brokerage allowance
broker's fee
caveat emptor
caveat venditor
Clayton Act
code of ethics
collusion
conflict of interest
Consumer Goods Pricing Act
Cooling-Off Period Rule
defamation
entertainment
Equal Credit Opportunity Act
ethics
exclusive dealing arrangement
express warranty
Fair Credit Reporting Act
Fair Debt Collection Practices Act
Federal Trade Commission
Federal Trade Commission Act
FTC Improvement Act
Foreign Corrupt Practices Act
fraud
full warranty

gift giving
Green River ordinance
implied warrenty
implied warranty of fitness
implied warranty of merchantability
kickback
libel
limited warranty
little FTC laws
Magnuson–Moss Warranty Act
notice of cancellation
obligation and performance
price fixing
product disparagement
promotional allowance
push money
referral plan
Regulation Z
Robinson–Patman Act
sales agreement
sales puff
Sherman Antitrust Act
slander
tie-in contract
tort law
Truth-in-Lending Act
Uniform Commercial Code
Wheeler–Lea Act

Building Skills . . .

1. Discuss the difference between ethics and law.
2. Explain how the various influences found in Figure 19-1 have helped you shape your own ethical standards.
3. Describe the role of businesses and professional associations in shaping ethical behavior, and how businesses help employees behave ethically.
4. Describe the philosophy of government toward business before 1890.
5. Compare the doctrines of caveat emptor and caveat venditor. Discuss how society's use of these doctrines has changed over the years.
6. Define the purpose of the Sherman Act of 1890.

7. List the subjects discussed in the Clayton Act that are particularly important to salespeople.

8. Explore how the Robinson–Patman Act is significant to retail sellers.

9. Analyze the conditions under the Robinson–Patman Act that permit sellers to charge different prices to different buyers.

10. Explore how the Wheeler–Lea Act changed the power of the FTC.

11. Explain why the Uniform Commercial Code (UCC) has been so widely accepted.

12. Define a sales agreement, including the rights and obligations described by the UCC with reference to contracts.

13. Describe agency and the occasions that an employer is responsible for a salesperson's actions.

14. Compare the differences between an express warranty and an implied warranty.

15. List what actions constitute a breach of warranty.

16. Describe the statements required of lenders under the Truth-in-Lending Act and Regulation Z.

17. Explain borrowers' rights under the Fair Credit Reporting Act.

18. Explain a seller's obligation under the FTC's Cooling-Off Period Rule.

19. Describe a Green River ordinance.

20. Explain the difference between fraud and sales puff.

21. List the three forms of defamation, explaining how each causes harm.

22. List the ethical considerations involved in gift giving and entertainment.

23. Explain how buying firms regulate their buyers' behavior with respect to gifts from vendors.

24. Explain how collusion can take place unintentionally.

25. Describe the conditions under which moonlighting is unethical.

26. List the ways that one's use of the company car might be unethical.

Making Decisions 19-1:

Joyce Lasky and Kevin Hale are salespeople for Lansing Safety Equipment. On the way back from an out-of-town conference, Joyce and Kevin are given a ride to the airport. Joyce is disturbed by a discovery she makes when she and Kevin get out of their friend's car.

Kevin: Do what I do: Put down $6 for cab fare on your expense form. That's what a taxi ride out here would have cost.

Joyce: But Bill wouldn't take anything. We got a free ride.

Kevin: Yeah, but suppose we wouldn't have run into Bill. We would have paid for a cab, right?

Joyce: Yes, but we didn't.

Kevin:	So what? For the small amount of money I make, I've got six bucks coming to me.
Joyce:	Aren't you afraid you'll get caught?
Kevin:	They'll never find out. I only do this for things I know they can't trace.
Joyce:	But why bother? It only amounts to nickels and dimes.
Kevin:	Hey, over the course of a year, a few dollars here and there can really add up. Besides, the guy who had my territory before me did this when he trained me. He's a company manager now.
Joyce:	No thanks, Kevin. You put down the $6. I'll say I walked.

Discuss whether or not Kevin is justified in adding unincurred cab fair to his conference expenses and whether or not Joyce should report Kevin to company management.

Making Decisions 19-2:

Scott Strubrilla, an account representative for Springdale modular buildings, has a four-state territory. Because he lives in the center of his territory, he is always home on weekends. One Friday evening, Scott runs into one of his accounts, Henry Schade, a dealer in modular buildings based in Scott's hometown.

Henry:	You know, Scott, I'm really glad I ran into you. I've been meaning to call you.
Scott:	About what?
Henry:	You're an excellent salesperson, Scott. You know your product better than anyone else I know.
Scott:	That's very flattering, Henry....
Henry:	I know that you and your wife just had a baby, and I also know you bought a house not long ago. Money must be a little tight for you.
Scott:	True.... Henry, what are you getting at?
Henry:	Well, my showroom gets very busy on Saturdays. I could really use a person like you to help out.
Scott:	I couldn't do that, Henry. That would be a conflict of interest for me.
Henry:	Why's that?
Scott:	Well, for one thing, you sell for other manufacturers besides Springdale. I'd be selling competitors' products. Springdale would fire me for sure.
Henry:	They're based in Chicago! And your nearest customer besides me is forty miles away. Nobody's going to know what you're doing.

Scott: I don't think so, Henry.

Henry: Do me a favor. Just think it over this weekend, while you're paying your bills. I guarantee I can make Saturday your most profitable day of the week.

If you were Scott, would you take the job? If you were Scott's manager at Springdale, what would you do if you found out Scott was selling for Henry on Saturdays?

Making Decisions 19-3:

Write a seven-point code of ethics for one of your college's clubs or organizations.

Making Decisions 19-4:

Visit or telephone your local government and request a copy of its door-to-door selling ordinance. Compare your ordinance with those of your fellow students.

Index

Brokerage allowances, 484
Broker's fee, 484
Brothers, Joyce, 220
Brown, Gene, 437
Brown, John Mason, 88
Buchwald, Art, 203
Building-block approach, 182
Burckhard, Kevin, 67
Bureau of Labor Statistics, 2, 23
Burrill, Gerald, 246
Business buying process, roles in, 99–100, 101
Business card, presentation of, 138–39
Business law, 480–88
    federal legislation, 481–85
    prior to 1890, 480–81
    Uniform Commercial Code (UCC), 485–88
Business prospect, preapproach for, 98–104
    knowing business of prospect, 101–2
    personal interests of prospect, knowing,
        102–3
    person to see, knowing, 99–100
Business purchases, motives for, 113. *See also*
    Buying behavior
Business television (BTV), 13
Busy prospect, 224–25
Butler, Samuel, 319
Buyer(s), 101
    codes of ethics, 480
    industrial, 456–59
    referrals from, 64–65
Buyer-seller relations, industrial, 462–63
Buying behavior, 109–34
    buying motives, 90, 111–22
        appealing to strongest, 256
        benefits approach addressing, 148–50
        defined, 111, 118
        determining strongest, 118–22
        relating product features to, 119–21
        variety of, 111–17
    factors shaping, 122–30
        frame of reference, 88, 128–29
        goals and objectives, 124
        personal values, 127–28
        physiological and psychological needs,
            123–24
        reference groups, 129–30
        self-concept, 124–27
    satisfaction of needs and wants, 110–11
Buying center, 19
Buying classes, industrial, 459–60

Buying signals, 331–33
Buying stages, 91–92, 165–68
    objections by, 274–96
        need objection, 274–77
        price objection, 281–87
        product objections, 277–81
        salesperson objection, 287–90
        source objection, 290–93
        time objection, 293–96
    presentation design and, 166–67
    timing of presentation and, 167–68

C

Calendar, 422–23
    customer files on daily, 105
Call patterns, 434, 436
Call report, 18
Canned presentation, 239–40, 242, 243
"Can't afford it" objection, 282–83
Capability, salesperson objection based on,
    289–90
Car, as extension of personal appearance, 390
Career, attitude toward, 403–4
Carnegie, Dale, 223, 356
Carriage, posture and, 39
Caveat emptor, 481
Caveat venditor, 481
Cellular phones, 16, 429
Center of influence method, 65–69, 72
Certification, professional, 17
Chamber of Commerce membership directory,
    78
Change, creating desire for, 275–76
Channels of communication, 32–33
Channels of distribution, 9
Charity, as buying motive, 117
Ching, Jeffrey, 317
Chunking, 409
Churchill, Winston, 124
Claims
    believability of, 208–9
    making realistic and relevant, 178–79
    proving, 175
Classic styles, 378
Clayton Act (1914), 481, 482
Client book, 446

Gallwey, Tim, 489
Gatekeeper, 99, 101
Gaudio, Al, 447
Gender, salesperson objection based on, 289.
    See also Women
Gender identity, as buying motive, 117
Geographic location, frame of reference and,
    128
Geographic profile, 58
Gerkhe, Rick, 171
Gestures, 40
Gibran, Kahlil, 334
Gift giving, 496
    to overcome time objection, 294
Goals
    attitude and, 406–9
    buying behavior and, 124
    long-term, 420–21
    prioritizing, 409
    setting and working toward, 406, 407–9
Goods, types of, 2, 4, 445, 453
Goodwill, 345
Gossip, 229–30
Government, business and, 480–88
Graham, John, 480
Green River ordinances, 492–93
Greetings, 139–42
    avoiding early dismissal, 141–42
    building immediate dialogue, 141
    creating comfortable setting, 140–41
Grizzard, Lewis, 22
Grooming, personal, 388–90
Group dynamics, 265–67
Group presentation, 264–67
    selecting sales aids for, 247–48
Growth stage of product, 8, 9
Gschwandtner, Gerhard, 115, 483
Guaranteed draw (nonrecoverable draw), 24
Guarantees, 182–83, 487
Guest register, signing and scanning, 97
Guilt, failure to close sale and, 328
Gum chewing, 45

H

Haibeck, Sherri, 204
Hair, 388–89

Haldeman, H.R., 245
Hands
    grooming, 389
    nonverbal communication with, 39–40
Handshake, 38–39
Hard-sell types, 11
Heston, Charlton, 429
Hidden buying motives, 114–15
Hidden objections, 287, 311
Hidden qualities, pointing out, 284
Hierarchy of needs, Maslow's, 123
High-volume purchasers, 59
Hillary, Edmund, 359
Holtz, Lou, 426
Home shows, 78
Honest objections, 310–11
Honesty, 177
    appeal for prospect's complete, 312
    with compliments, 367
Hook in the close, 294
Hopkins, Tom, 447
Hothead, 230
Housekeeping duties of retail salesperson, 448
Household life-cycle position, 58, 88–89
How to Master the Art of Selling (Hopkins),
    447
Hubbard, Elbert, 318
Hufstedler, Shirley, 194
Humor, sense of, 356, 391
Hurried presentation, avoiding, 226
Hurried prospect, 226–27

I

Iacoca, Lee, 104
Iapoce, Michael, 6
IBM image, 377
Ideal other, 126
Ideal self, 125
Identification influence of reference group,
    129
Image
    professional. See Professional image
    source objection based on, 291–92
Image Index, 387
Imagery, mental, 244–45
Immortality, as buying motive, 116

512

J

K

Q

defined, 418
delegating and, 433–34
long-term goals, 420–21
meetings and, 432
organizing work area, 421
problems related to, 419
setting priorities, 419–20
structuring your time, 424–28
  fear of deadlines and, 428
  peak energy hours, 427
  quiet time, 426
  scheduling enough time, 427
time-planning tools, 421–24
time wasters, 430–31
traveling and, 429, 431
unstructured time, using, 428–29
Time objection, 293–96
  forestalling, 307
Time wasters, 430–31
Timing
  of sales call, 94
  of sales presentation, 167–68
To-do list, 422
Tone, 35
Tort law, 480
Townsend, Robert, 275
Trade directories, 78, 97
Trade-ins, 298–99
Trade selling, 20, 21
Trade show, 78
Trade up, encouraging, 452
Training, sales, 12–13
  for retail selling, 448–49
Traits of salesperson, 11, 355–58
Traveling
  sales routes for, 437
  time management and, 429, 431
Trial close, 329–31
Trial periods, 253
Trivial objections, 308–10
  question method to eliminate, 318
True prospect profile, 58, 88
Trust. *See also* Confidence-building techniques
  role in friendship, 357–58
  of untrusting prospect, asking for, 186–87
Truth-in-Lending Act, 489
Try-ons, 252, 452

Tupperware, 21
Turner, Ted, 367
Turoscy, Rachel, 435
Twain, Mark, 277, 355
Two-one-ratio, 262

U

Underdressing, 380
Underselling, 341–42
Unfair business practices, 483–84, 485
Unfortunate truth, compensating for, 232–33
Uniform Commercial Code (UCC), 485–88
U.S. Department of Justice, 482
  Antitrust Division of, 481
U.S. Department of Labor, Bureau of Labor Statistics, 2, 23
Unit price, 282
Unknown-source objection, 292
  forestalling, 306
Unstructured time, using, 428–29
Untrue remark, refuting prospect's, 232
Usefulness/value formula, 63
User, 101

V

Valid objections, 308
Value(s)
  perceived, 284
  personal, 127–28
Value analysis, 462
Vendors, 448
  evaluation of, 457–58
Verbal buying signals, 331–33
Verbal communication, 32, 33–34
Verbal skills, 33–34
Verbatim telescripts, 465
Versatility in wardrobe, 380